BEDOUIN POETRY
from Sinai and the Negev

Rabīa' Abū Ḥarbī, reciter of the Ṣawālḥa 'Awārma tribe (playing the *rabāba*)

CLINTON BAILEY

BEDOUIN POETRY

From Sinai and the Negev

With a Foreword by
Wilfred Thesiger

Saqi Books

British Library Cataloguing-in-Publication Data
A catalogue record for this book is available from the British Library

ISBN 0 86356 330 9 (pb)

First published in hardback by Clarendon Press, Oxford, 1991
This paperback edition published by Saqi Books, 2002

Saqi Books
26 Westbourne Grove
London W2 5RH
www.saqibooks.com

To the memory of my parents
BENJAMIN and EDNA GLASER
of Buffalo, New York,
who endowed me with the temperament and the means
that made this study possible
and
to my spiritual father
NOAH JACOBS
for wise counsel, friendship,
and good company along the way.

Foreword

CLINTON BAILEY believes, as I do, that the disappearance from Arabia of the traditional Bedouin way of life, the result of the inevitable involvement of the Bedouin today with the materialistic civilization of the modern world, is a tragedy. He has spent much of his life trying to preserve for posterity something of their culture and traditions. In *Bedouin Poetry from Sinai and the Negev* he has succeeded magnificently. Ostensibly, this book, with its many selections of their poetry, its scholarly introduction, and the valuable notes that accompany these selections, deals with the Bedouin of Sinai and the Negev: in fact, it presents a picture of Bedouin life as it was throughout Arabia, portraying many aspects of Bedouin experience and aspirations. I would have profited greatly had this book been available when I went to southern Arabia in 1945, where I spent the next five years travelling with some of the Rashid tribe in and around the Empty Quarter.

The Rashid and other tribes whom I encountered had never experienced any contact with a world other than their own: all of them were illiterate. They lived a life of incredible hardship: hunger, often starvation; thirst that clogged throat and ears, quenched only with bitter-tasting water from occasional wells; incessant journeying and the anxiety that their camels, on which their lives depended, might collapse from lack of grazing; the constant watch for raiders, with their rifles always at hand; the burning heat of summer in a shadeless land and the bitter cold of winter nights, when they slept on the sand, often covered only with a loin-cloth. For them everything that was not a necessity was an encumbrance. Any of them could have abandoned this life and sought a livelihood among the villages and towns of the Hadhramaut or Oman. Their proud boast 'We are Bedu' was their answer to every hardship and challenge. Their reward was the freedom they valued above all else, a freedom which we, with our craving for possessions, can never really know.

All that is best in the Arabs has come to them from the desert, and there the harder the life the finer the type it has produced. Any Arab today, even a king, would be proud to claim Bedouin lineage. When I went among them I knew I must fall short in physical endurance: they, after all, were born to this life. I did, however, expect to equal, or even excel, them in civilized behaviour. I found it humiliating so often to fall short, when faced by the hardships of these journeys.

Bedouin are renowned for their hospitality, but frequently, with a long journey still ahead of us, I was exasperated when my companions fed chance-met strangers on our dwindling rations. We lived for the most part on lumps of dough, cooked in the sand under a small fire, on a few dates, and on such lizards, skinks, and small rodents as we could catch; all too seldom we ate the meat of a gazelle or a hare. On one occasion I remember how the five of us, all desperately hungry, had killed a hare. We had just finished cooking it when three Arabs appeared unexpectedly over a nearby sand-dune. My companions greeted them, made them welcome, and set the hare before them. They pressed us to eat with them: my companions refused, insisting that they were our guests, that God had brought them, and that for us this was a blessed day. I confess that I felt murderous.

There were other occasions when someone whose encampment we were passing would hail us and, brooking no refusal, would slaughter a young camel to feed us. He would set the meat before us with rice and liquid butter that would have sufficed his family for a week. Then in the morning he would see us off, having half convinced me that we had conferred a favour on him by accepting his hospitality.

Once an old man in rags joined us. My companions, some thirty of them (for we were travelling through hostile territory), greeted him with great respect. I asked the youngest why they paid him so much deference. 'Because he is famous,' he answered. 'For what?' I asked. 'For his generosity,' he replied. 'I should not have thought he had anything with which to be generous.' 'He hasn't now, but once he owned many camels; he killed them all to feed his guests, till at last he had none left.' I could hear the respect, even the envy, in the boy's voice. This old man's generosity made him a figure typical of Bedouin poetry.

I have never forgotten the open-handed generosity of my companions with any money they had acquired: their absolute honesty; their pride in themselves and their tribe; their loyalty to each other and to me, a stranger of another faith and of another race, on whose behalf they more than once risked their lives. Courage they rated high, and they often spoke of the bravery of individuals in the raids and counter-raids that played so important a part in their lives. The killings that resulted involved them in blood feuds, which honour demanded should be settled without mercy. But I remember many acts of kindness and thoughtfulness, their patience and their sense of humour.

The Rashid, like all Bedouin, could never have survived without their camels, whose welfare was their primary concern and on whose behalf they readily endured every hardship. They loved these great-hearted beasts, admired above all their patience and endurance. Often I watched one or other of my comrades fondling and caressing his mount while he murmured endearments.

In winter the men left the women and children at the wells with their flocks of goats, the only other animals they owned; none of them even possessed a dog. They then moved out into the desert to such grazing as had been previously located by their scouts, the hardest and most enduring among them. Rarely, and then only in years of exceptionally widespread and heavy rain, this grazing extended over a great area; more often it covered scattered patches, somewhere in the vast emptiness of the Empty Quarter. Wherever sufficient rain had fallen the desert came to life; the sands were covered with yellow-flowering tribulus, with heliotrope and other plants, and were alive with butterflies, larks, jerboas, and gerbils, even gazelle and occasional oryx. Here these herdsmen remained until the approaching heat of summer drove them back to the neighbourhood of the wells. The nearest water was often more than a hundred miles away. For food and drink they depended on the milk from their camels. Several times on my journeys I chanced on such small groups of men and camels. They had no tents; they had left them behind with their womenfolk. The camels being in fine condition, their humps large from the abundant grazing, their owners were utterly content, praising God for this bounty of the sands.

However many or few we might be, we were always crowded together, our mounts jostling each other on the march, while in camp we sat or slept within a few feet of one another. My companions talked unceasingly. 'What is the news?' all these Bedouin invariably asked of anyone they encountered. In consequence everything that had happened, and almost everything that had been said, even hundreds of miles away, was eventually known and discussed. The Rashid and the other tribes demanded high standards of their fellow men and were quick to condemn any who fell short. Public opinion thus ensured a general standard of acceptable behaviour. Living among these tribesmen and sharing the hardships of their lives, I encountered a nobility I have met among no other people except sometimes among individuals.

My Arabic was sufficiently fluent to understand without difficulty the everyday talk of these Bedouin, but it was never good enough properly to follow the poetry in which they delighted. As soon as someone began to recite, a hush fell over the assembly, however large.

Then as I watched their intent faces I realized what a store these illiterate herdsmen set by the beauty of their language.

In 1950 I heard a ballad recited by some Manahil near Abu Dhabi: in those days Abu Dhabi consisted only of a fort, a small market, and a few coral-built houses on the shore of the Arabian Gulf. The ballad told of the death of bin Duailan, better known as El-Bis (the cat), in a camel raid by the Manahil. Bin Duailan had accompanied me for a while in 1945 when I was travelling through his tribal territory to the north of the Hadhramaut. A small, lean man of about thirty-five, he was famous as a raider. He had joined us again the following year and had then tried to persuade us to take part in a retaliatory raid on the Dahm tribe of the Yemen: my Rashid companions had, however, refused since their tribe had recently concluded a truce with the Dahm.

The following year we encountered a party of Manahil returning from a raid on the Yam, a Saudi tribe in the desert east of Nejran. They had with them some thirty camels they had captured. They told us bin Duailan and four others had been killed. Ibn Saud, in retaliation for this and other raids, released the Yam and the Dawasir on the Mishqas, the collective name for the southern Bedouin tribes including the Rashid. I intended to cross the Empty Quarter to Sulayil in Saudi Arabia, and the ensuing tribal warfare greatly increased the hazards of the journey. My four Rashid comrades, however, agreed to come with me.

After we had eventually arrived at Sulayil two Yam were dining one night with the Amir. One of them described how he had killed bin Duailan. A party of Manahil had attacked his encampment, killed his nephew, and driven off the camels. He and others of his family went in pursuit; they shot four Manahil, but then bin Duailan remained behind to cover the escape of his companions with the captured camels. He took cover behind a small dune on an open plain. He had shot five of the pursuit party before his rifle jammed. 'We had reached the dune,' the narrator said, 'and I stabbed and killed him with this dagger.' Someone later identified the dead man as bin Duailan, the famous Bis. The man showed me the rifle and field-glasses he had taken from the corpse and asked me if I had given the rifle to bin Duailan. He had identified me as the 'Nasrani' who travelled with the Mishqas. I told him that I had given bin Duailan the glasses, but that he had captured the rifle during a raid on a police post in the Hadhramaut. 'By God,' he said, 'he was a man. I thought he would kill us all.' Two years later bin Duailan's exploit was being declaimed on the far side of Arabia.

WILFRED THESIGER

Preface

The bedouin of the Sinai and Negev deserts among whom I worked and often lived from 1967 to 1988 were the last generation whose lives were formed within the context of traditional bedouin culture. When I began to study their culture, most of them lived in tents, migrated with their flocks in search of pasture and water, rode camels as their main means of transportation, wore traditional bedouin dress, used traditional artefacts in their daily lives, and maintained a daily diet of grain-foods and the dairy products of their livestock. No longer were they the masters of the desert, raiding one another's camel-herds and waging intertribal wars. In many other respects, however, the lives of the older people had changed little from those of their grandparents and even comprised elements from the lives of their nomadic antecedents in these deserts stretching back to biblical, and often pre-biblical, times.

An unlettered nomadic culture tenacious enough to survive so intact for millennia is a rare phenomenon in the annals of human experience. A detailed study of contemporary bedouin life, therefore, sheds new light on ancient cultures that interest Western civilization, most notably that of the nomadic Israelites. As the options for survival in a desert are limited, a traditional bedouin's way of life in the recent past must be similar to that of a desert-dwelling nomad in the distant past.

A study of bedouin culture also deepens our understanding of contemporary Arab life, many of the attitudes and customs of sedentary rural and urban Arabs today having been set by the experience of their desert-dwelling ancestors many generations before. The origins of some notable Arab characteristics, such as hospitality, independence, clanishness, and vengefulness, are best understood when perceived as indispensable requisites for coping with the conditions of desert life.

My personal fascination with bedouin life was mainly with the bedouin's ability to survive in the inhospitable desert, not just economically, but socially, spiritually, psychologically, and aesthetically. I learned that virtually every facet of bedouin culture constitutes an adaptation to the arid environment, aspects as disparate as beliefs, social behaviour, law, poetry, diet, and dress having evolved as answers to challenges that the desert posed. The human qualities that survival in the desert requires—hardiness, independence, loyalty to friends and kin, hospitality, faith, courage, patience, and the ability to view daily events from a long-term perspective—were present in almost all the bedouin I met throughout the years of my work, rendering the personal–human side of the experience as rewarding as the scholarly interests that this subject aroused.

Bedouin have always enjoyed poetry, although most were illiterate until recently. They appreciated it as the pinnacle of their aesthetic, creative ability, as an aesthetic relief from the starkness of the desert, a comfort from the arduousness of their lives, and a practical vehicle for communication, expression, instruction, and entertainment. In 1968 I decided to collect and study their poems, not only fascinated by the wealth of bedouin culture that the poems comprise, but also aware that they would shortly disappear under the impact of imminent bedouin modernization and the growing indifference of young bedouin to their poetic heritage. It was through my effort to understand the terminology and cultural allusions of these poems with the help of many bedouin, all of whom appreciated the effort and displayed great patience to enlighten me, that I gained familiarity with the details and nuances of bedouin culture. I owe these people, especially Mūsā Ḥasan al-ʻAṭāwna and Muṣliḥ Sālim al-ʻAwāmra of the Tiyāhā confederation, Jumʻa ʻĪd al-Farārja and Sulēmān ʻĪd Ibn Jāzī of the Tarābīn, and Swēlim Sulēmān Abū Biliyya of the ʻAzāzma, a debt of lasting gratitude for their friendship, patience, and willingness to share their knowledge with me.

I am also indebted to many others for encouraging words and deeds that kept me at the project for so many years and enabled me to bring it to fruition. Lack of space permits me to mention only a few. I am grateful to Michael Levine, who became director of the educational institution, Midrashat Sde-Boker in the Negev in 1970 and urged me to go on living there, specifically to continue my collection and study of bedouin poetry; to Professor R. B. Serjeant of Cambridge University, whose interest in the progress of this study was of great moral support; to 'Chichko' Naveh, of the Field School at Sde-Boker, whose help and company on some early field trips are recalled with pleasure; to Sandy and Cecile MacTaggart on the island of Islay in Scotland, to Amos and Beth Elon in Buggiano, Tuscany, and to the Oxford Centre for Postgraduate Hebrew Studies for their hospitality amid quiet and pleasant surroundings conducive to translating the poems and preparing this manuscript; to my friend of many years, the philosopher and translator, Dr. Noah Jacobs, who always encouraged me to persevere and who contributed his great skills to editing this manuscript before I sent it to the publishers; to three poets, Shirley Kaufman and Robert Friend of Jerusalem and Richard Buchanan-Dunlop of Skiathos, who went over my translations and made many useful suggestions for improving their quality (and who are not responsible for what is deficient owing to my preferences); to the linguist, Dr Haseeb Shehadeh of the Hebrew University, Jerusalem, who insisted that I make a phonemic transliteration of the Arabic texts of the poems and instructed me on how to do it; to Sami Salman Elyahu of Keset, Ltd, Jerusalem, who set the Arabic script of the poems with much patience and skill; to Hilary Walford, of Cheltenham, who copy-edited this difficult manuscript for Oxford University Press with obvious dedication; to the Arabian explorer, Wilfred Thesiger, whose books are ever stimulating, for offering to write a foreword to this study; and last but not least to my devoted wife Maya and to my sons, who always made the bedouin welcome in our home and shared my bedouin experience of many years with goodwill and personal involvement. The preparation of this volume was made possible in part by a grant from the Division of Research Programs of the National Endowment for the Humanities, an independent federal agency. I am also grateful to the Ford Foundation (via the Israel Foundations Trustees) for some early support. Most of the twenty years of work that went into this project, however, were personally financed.

C.B.

Contents

Note on Plates xvii
List of Maps xvii
Notes on the Arabic Text xviii
Introduction 1
1. Poems of Expression 18
2. Poems of Communication 72
3. Poems of Instruction 120
4. Poems to Entertain 164
5. Episodes in Poetry I: Poems from the War of Zāri‘ al-Huzayyil (1875–1887) 253
6. Episodes in Poetry II: Poems Sent from and to the Sinai Smuggler–Poet ‘Anēz abū Sālim during a Prison Term (1962–1970) 288
7. Poems on the Margin of Historic Events (1882–1982) 341
8. Composing Bedouin Poetry: Art and Technique 381
9. Perspective on Bedouin Poetry: A Cultural Document for the Ages 406
Glossary of Bedouin Words and Usages 430
Bibliography 458
Index of Subjects 463
Index of Arabic Names and Tribal Groups 470

Note on Plates

Plates 1–20 depicting individual Bedouin poets can be found between pages 202 and 203.

List of Maps

1. The position of Bedouin Tribal Confederations in Sinai and the Negev, early twentieth century 4
2. Places in Sinai mentioned in the book 20–1
3. Places and the Nineteenth-century position of some Bedouin Tribal Confederations in Arabia and the Fertile Crescent 51
4. Places in the Negev mentioned in the book 111
5. The position of Bedouin Tribes in the Negev prior to the War of Zāriʿ al-Huzayyil 254

Notes on the Arabic Text

I. THE PRESENTATION OF THE POEMS

In addition to the English translations, all the poems in this book appear in an Arabic script that reflects aspects of the bedouin vernacular as transcribed by literate bedouin, and in a phonemic transliteration into Latin characters. The Arabic script is presented for the benefit of Arab readers and students of Classical Arabic; the phonemic transcription is for the benefit of Arabic linguists. As these poems are a product of the desert's specific culture, they contain allusions, idioms, and words unknown in the non-bedouin Arab world, in addition to unique meanings for some otherwise commonplace words. It is hoped that this material, gleaned from a live context and including a glossary of approximately one thousand new words and meanings, proves a contribution to the understanding of bedouin and general Arab culture and the Arabic language. The original texts of oral poems heard in Sinai and the Negev are also essential for the comparative study of Arabic dialects and contemporary bedouin poetry, such as Arab scholars have begun collecting in other deserts, and for further research into the Classical poetry of the pre-Islamic period.

In presenting these texts, accuracy was sought by having elderly, literate bedouin transcribe all the poems from recorded recitations, and by referring the transcribed texts to other bedouin for comment and correction. While the texts do not stand the test of Classic Arabic poetic scansion according to quantitative metres (which, as I maintain in Chapter 8, are inapplicable to illiterate composition), and although the rules of gender are occasionally violated, their correctness is indicated by the fact that the bedouin from whom the poems were recorded were reciting them for other bedouin, who, in turn, accepted the recitations as genuine and compatible with their expectations of a bedouin poetic text.

II. THE TRANSLITERATION OF ARABIC IN THE ENGLISH GENERAL TEXT AND FOOTNOTES

To facilitate the recognition of Arabic names and words by Arabists unfamiliar with bedouin Arabic and by non-Arabist readers, those appearing in the English general text and the footnotes are not transliterated phonemically, but in accordance with the system followed by the *Encyclopaedia of Islam*, with the following exceptions:

1. Differing letters.
   - (*a*) In keeping with the bedouin pronunciation, the Arabic 'ḳ' appears as 'g' and is pronounced as in 'give'. In words derived from the specific root *ḳ-t-l*, the 'ḳ' is represented by 'k' in keeping with bedouin pronunciation. The letter 'q' is used for 'ḳ' in the English text in words appearing outside the context of bedouin pronunciation (e.g. the names of persons and places (S͟huqayr, Iraq, Aqaba), and citations from, and titles of, Arabic literary sources).
   - (*b*) The EI digraph 'dj' appears as 'j'.
   - (*c*) In words in the bedouin vernacular, the diphthongs appear as 'ay' (for 'i' as in pile; e.g. *aḥaywāt*), 'ē' (for 'a' as in say; e.g. *s͟hēk͟h*), 'aw' (for 'ow' as in cow; e.g. *awṣīk*), and 'ō' (for 'o' as in go; e.g. *yōm*).
   - (*d*) The long vowel 'ī' with a *tas͟hdīd* will mostly appear as 'iyy'; e.g. *gaḍiyya*.
2. In words used in the context of bedouin pronunciation, the *hamza* is not added (e.g. *akal*, *jā*, *d͟hīb*), except after a long vowel in the middle of a word, when it appears as a 'y' (*nāyif*, not *nā'if*). In words derived from the roots *s-'-l* and *r-'-y*, the *hamza* often appears as an *ʿayn* (e.g *saʿal*, *raʿā*).
3. In Arabic words used in the context of bedouin pronunciation, the *tā' marbūṭa*, following a long *fatḥa*-vowel in a non-construct state, will appear as an 'h' (e.g. *s͟hāh*, not *s͟hāt*).
4. In words used in the context of bedouin pronunciation, the definite article of a word beginning with a sun-letter will carry that letter in place of the usual 'l'; e.g. at-Tarābīn, not al-Tarābīn.

III. THE TRANSLITERATION OF THE POEMS

To enable Arabic linguists to utilize the texts of the poems themselves, I transliterated them phonemically, as I heard them pronounced by bedouin reciters, into Latin characters, in a script with the following equivalents:

a	ء	x	خ	š	ش	f	ف	h	ه	ē	اي
b	ب	d	د	ṣ	ص	g	ق	w,u	و	ay	اي
t	ت	ḏ	ذ	ṭ	ط	k	ك	y,i	ي		
ṯ	ث	r	ر	ẓ	ظ ض	l	ل	o	او		
j	ج	z	ز	ʿ	ع	m	م	aw	او		
ḥ	ح	s	س	ġ	غ	n	ن				

The influence of emphatic letters on their environment are not marked.

A number of vernacular deviations from Classical Arabic appear in the phonemic transliteration and the English text. For explanations of the phenomena cited, the reader is referred to Haim Blanc, 'The Arabic Dialect of the Negev Bedouins'.

1. Elision. Elision is natural in any spoken language; but because the written Arabic and vernacular differ so greatly, the problem arises of how to present the elided forms. In the present texts,
   (*a*) Some elided words appear in elision (*yallī* ‹ *yā illī/allī*; *mānī* ‹ *mā ana*; *mint* ‹ *mā inti*; *miḥna* ‹ *mā iḥna*; *linkī* ‹ *law inkī*; *linna* ‹ *law inna*; *lin* ‹ *li-in*, *kanna* ‹ *ka-inna*);
   (*b*) some words appear with letters elided *šawš* ‹ *šawīš* as in *šawš al-ʿaskar*; *mink* ‹ *minnak*; *rākb* ‹ *rākib*; *lna* ‹ *lina*);
   (*c*) some elisions, enunciated as a single word, are hyphenated to avoid writing them as such (*rākb-illī* ‹ *rākib illī*; *jā-lna* ‹ *jā lina*; *mā-lna* ‹ *mā lina*; *fi-š-šīḥ* ‹ *fī iš-šīḥ*; *fi-l-lēl* ‹ *fī il-lēl*; *mi-l-lēl* ‹ *min il-lēl*; *gaẓẓa-l-lēl* ‹ *gaẓẓā al-lēl*; *limma-l-lel* ‹ *limma al-lēl*).
   (*d*) some elisions have become fixed words in their own right (*kiḏī* ‹ *ki-hāḏī*; *šinlāš* ‹ *šī-innah-lā-šī*).
2. Free variation between the short vowels i/a and i/u, as follows:
   (*a*) 'i' often replaces 'a' in the definite article (e.g. *al-bēt/il-bēt*), in certain verb forms (e.g. *tafraḥ/tifraḥ*, *amšī/imšī*, *yimšan/yimšin*), in nouns and adjectives (*afʿāl/ifʿāl*; *dalīl/dilīl*; *dalla/dalli*; *galīl/gilīl*; *raziyya/raziyyi*), and in other words (*man/min* (whoever, who); *allī/illī* (which, who); *hā/hī* (3rd pers. fem. pronominal suffix);

(*b*) 'a' often replaces 'i' in the prefix of the fifth conjugation past tense (*takaffēna/tikaffēna*), and in the prefixes of first conjugation future tense verbs that take 'a' as the vowel between the second and third radicals;

(*c*) 'i' often replaces 'u' in words such as *dunya/dinya*; *buyūt/biyūt*.

3. The frequent replacement of 'a' by 'e' in the words *al-beriḥa*, *tell*, *el-'arīš*, and 'i' by 'e' in the word *'end*.

4. The occasional deletion of the short vowel 'i' (*kasra*) between two long vowels (*yāklū* ‹ *yākilū*), and between an 'originally stressed consonant' (see para. 5 below) and a long vowel (*yiḥaṭṭmū* ‹ *yiḥaṭṭimū*).

5. The pronunciation of stressed (*mushaddad*) consonants as unstressed when, owing to elision, they carry a *sukūn* rather than a *kasra* vowel (*yi'ajjin* › *yi'ajn-al-'afig*; *daggit* › *dagt al-withr*).

6. The frequent occurrence of a non-vowelled consonant (*sukūn*) following a long vowel, particularly in the names of tribes, such as Ḥasāblah, ʿAṭāwna, ʿAzāzma, and Ṣawālḥa. In the poems, it may often be found in imperatives such as *gūl!* and *gūm!*.

7. The occasional inclusion of a short vowel ('a' or 'i') where a *sukūn* would be found in Classical Arabic (*ʿugib* ‹ *ʿugb*; *ʿendina* ‹ *ʿendna*; *saʿadana* ‹ *saʿadna*).

8. The occasional metathesis, or changing the order of a vowel and consonant, by which the vowel 'i' begins the word, especially in participles (*Imbārak* ‹ *Mubārak*), words with a short vowel/long vowel sequence (*islāh* ‹ *silāḥ*; *ibyūt* ‹ *biyūt*), and the prefixes of second person, future tense verbs (*itkawdib* ‹ *tikawdib*). Metathesis also takes place in the middle of some words (*aturk* ‹ *atruk*; *tidifg* ‹ *tidfig*.

9. The occasional deletion of the first vowel, a short 'u', from diminutive forms (such as the names Swēlim, Swēriḥ, and Frēḥ), and its retention in others (Ḥuwēṭāt, Huzayyil).

10. The occasional substitution of two characteristic bedouin forms: *mū*, *mī* for *mā* ('not') when preceding the personal pronouns *hū*, *hī*; and *lā* for *law*: 'if'.

11. The occasional pronunciation of the preposition *'alā* as *'a* and *'al*.

12. The occasional pronunciation of middle radical *hamza* as *'ayn* (*sa'al* ‹ *sa'al*; *ra'a* ‹ *ra'a*).

13. The occasional pronunciation of long vowels as short, especially in the words *yā* and *mā*.

14. The occasional substitution of an emphatic 'ṣ' for a non-emphatic 's' (*ṣurba* ‹ *surba*; *ṣarāya* ‹ *sarāya*; *garbūṣ* ‹ *garbūs*) and vice versa (*sār* ‹ *ṣār*; *sagīl* ‹ *ṣagīl*; *rūbās* ‹ *rūbāṣ*).

15. The occurrence of a *tanwīn* in both indefinite and definite nouns and adjectives, transliterated by being underlined (*dārin*, *šugrun*).

16. Instances of ungrammatical changes as poetic licence, usually to facilitate a rhyme: *xaḏēna* ‹ *axaḏna* ('we took'); and *tagayt* ‹ *tagyat* ('she hid'); *ġaẓāk* ‹ *ġāẓak* ('he angered you').

17. The pronunciation of 'e' or 'a' between a final *'ayn* preceded by a long vowel (*rabīe'*, *marbūa'*, *ijdēa'*).

18. The occasional replacement of the successive consonants 's' and 'j' by 'š' and 'z' (*šizin* ‹ *sijin*).

19. The occasional accentuation of the definite article of a noun rather than one of its syllables (*ál-bil* ‹ *al-bíl*; *ál-xaṭa* ‹ *al-xáṭa*; *aś-sama* ‹ *as-samá*). Such articles are marked with an acute accent mark.

IV. THE ARABIC SCRIPT

The Arabic script mainly reflects the structure of the words in the bedouin vernacular. Hence:

1. Some words frequently pronounced in a non-Classical Arabic form are written as pronounced (*'alā* as *'al* or *'a*; *gul!* as *gūl!*; *inti* as *intī*).

2. Some words pronounced in elision are written as pronounced (*yā illī* as *yillī*; *mā inti* as *mint*).

For the convenience of non-linguist Arabic readers, however, some words appear in their Classical Arabic form (*ṭayyabnākum*, *'arētum*, *ru'ūs*), their pronunciation in the dialect (*ṭayyabnākū*, *'arētū*, *rūs*) being shown in the phonemic transliteration opposite the Arabic script.

Introduction

THE BEDOUIN WORLD OF SINAI AND THE NEGEV

Most bedouin of Sinai and the Negev are the descendants of tribesmen that came from the Arabian peninsula at various times between the fourteenth and eighteenth centuries.[1] Until the mid-twentieth century they lived, like their Arabian ancestors, in tents in the desert, where they raised livestock and migrated in search of pasture and water. They were organized in tribal confederations, which assured them access to grazing grounds and wells; and, for security while migrating in remote stretches of the desert, they formed groups of close kin to avenge violations of person, property, and honour.

Bedouin values in Sinai and the Negev were like those we find in other bedouin areas, values essential for the survival of every desert society, such as hospitality to guests and travellers, and unfailing devotion to kinsmen. Women were treated as inferior and subordinated to the needs of the society as perceived by the men. To keep the peace, men were careful to treat each other with respect; when the peace was violated they were quick to seek revenge. Like bedouin everywhere, those in Sinai and the Negev practised an unorthodox Islam, replete with animistic practices designed to ward off the dangers of the desert. In settling disputes they referred to traditional bedouin law; when they were ill, they applied desert cures common to all bedouin.

The bedouin of Sinai and the Negev were only slightly less 'bedouin' than the great camel-raising tribes of the bedouin heartland. Whereas in Arabia, Iraq, Syria, and Jordan the yearly migrations of some tribes took place on a tribal scale extending at times over hundreds of kilometres, migrations in Sinai and the Negev rarely exceeded fifty kilometres from the summer waters, and comprised small groups of one or more families and occasionally a clan. These limited movements arose from the circumstance that, in addition to camels, the bedouin of Sinai and the Negev also raised flocks of fat-tailed sheep and black goats that could not traverse great distances and, whenever practicable, they

[1] Bailey, 'Dating', pp. 20–49.

sowed a few acres of winter wheat and barley, which had to be harvested after five months—activities that earned them the anthropological designation of semi-nomads and a certain contempt from the more easterly camel-breeders.

Although the Negev and Sinai bedouin raided and were raided by Transjordanian and Arabian tribes for camels, and occasionally participated in their wars,[2] the Red Sea and the great Syro-African Rift, called Wādī al-ʿAraba,[3] effectively cut them off from the bedouin of the east, making them a separate entity with their own wars, internal relations, and local concerns. Despite the border that was drawn between Sinai and the Negev in 1906, they remained a single social unit with five of the tribes found on both sides of the border. They took little interest in the affairs of the eastern bedouin, unless these were 'parent' tribes of the not too distant past, such as the Ḥuwēṭāt and Bilī of the northern Ḥijāz, or immediate neighbours, such as the ʿAdwān of the Jordan valley or the Saʿīdiyyīn of the ʿAraba. Of the more distant large tribal confederations they had only scant information brought into Sinai and the Negev by traders and travellers who came to the markets of Beersheba, Gaza, and el-ʿArīsh or who crossed from Arabia to Egypt over the northern coastal route in Sinai or by way of the southern route which brought them by boat to Sharm ash-Shēkh and then overland to Suez. Thus, many bedouin throughout Sinai and the Negev might know nothing but the names of such major tribes as the Ḥuwēṭāt, Banī Ṣakhr, ʿAdwān, and Banī ʿAṭiyya of Jordan; the Juhayna, Shammar, Imṭēr, and Sharārāt of Arabia; and the Rawala of Syria.

[2] For traditions on raids and wars between the Sinai and Negev bedouin and those of the more easterly tribes, see Shuqayr, pp. 574–8; al-ʿĀrif, *Taʾrīkh*, pp. 169–70, 182; Bailey, 'Nineteenth Century', pp. 55–8, 73.

[3] Note on pronunciation of the Arabic. Most of the transliterated letters are pronounced as in English. The following explanations should clarify any ambiguities for the non-Arabic reader:

(*a*) pronounce 'g' as in girl; 'th' as in think; 'ḍ', 'dh', 'ẓ' as 'th' in these; 's' and 'ṣ' as 's'; 't' and 'ṭ' as 't'; 'ḥ' as a slightly rasped 'h'; 'kh' as 'ch' in Scottish loch; 'gh' as 'r' in Parisian French;

(*b*) pronounce long vowels (marked with a line above): 'ā' as in (Southern Standard English) hart; 'ī' as in machine; 'ū' as in prune; 'ō' as in go; and 'ē' as in prey;

(*c*) pronounce short vowels (unmarked): 'a' variously as 'a' in at, and 'u' in sun; 'i' as in thin; 'u' as in put; and 'e' as in pet;

(*d*) pronounce diphthongs 'ay' as 'i' in pie, and 'aw' as 'ow' in cow;

(*e*) the mark 'ʿ' represents an Arabic letter (*ʿayn*) which is pronounced deep in the throat introducing or following vowels.

Henceforth (and in the maps), the names of wadis will be given without the definite article *al-*; i.e. Wādī ʿAraba instead of Wādī al-ʿAraba.

The bedouin of Sinai and the Negev also had little contact with the non-bedouin world, although some were aware of its existence from the Muslim pilgrims they conducted on camels over the Sinai stretch of the Cairo–Mecca route (until 1884), or from the Christians they brought from Jerusalem and Cairo to Mt Sinai. Some bedouin also frequented the markets of Gaza, Beersheba, Suez, and Cairo, where contact with settled Palestinians and Egyptians led them to adopt elements of their dialects and dress. Bedouin also knew about the outside world through the rulers of Sinai and the Negev—Turks, British, Egyptians, and latterly Israelis. The Turks, except in the north, were known from a distance, but had the reputation of being severe: 'government by bayonet' (*ḥukm bi-sanja*) is still a common bedouin phrase to describe the period of Ottoman rule. The British, by contrast, were considered gentlemanly and just, and were thus appreciated by the bedouin, who believed themselves endowed with the same qualities. Owing to improved communications, more bedouin had contact with the British than with the Turks, and countless legends circulated, especially in Sinai, relating the eccentricities of colourful British officials, such as 'Barkil Bey' (A. C. Parker), 'Bremley Bey' (W. E. Jennings-Bramley), and 'Mister Charfis' (C. S. Jarvis).[4]

Bedouin life in Sinai and the Negev was for the most part confined to this area, or only to parts of it, and this was the outer limit of bedouin experience. Their world was one of tribes, each tribe or, more correctly, confederation being a nation unto itself, constituting the individual bedouin's broadest identification and allegiance; and each such tribal confederation made its specific mark on the consciousness of the others.[5] The members of the largest confederation, the Tarābīn (numbering 35,000 in the 1970s and spread over several areas of Sinai and the Negev), were known for their superior military prowess; many

[4] Col. A. C. Parker, DSO, was Governor of Sinai, 1907–23; W. E. Jennings-Bramley was an intelligence officer in Sinai prior to the First World War, and the author of the series 'Bedouin of the Sinaitic Peninsula', which appeared in the *Palestine Exploration Fund Quarterly* (1905–14); Maj. C. S. Jarvis, OBE, was Governor of Sinai, 1923–36, and wrote *Yesterday and To-day in Sinai* and other works on his experiences.

[5] For the locations of these confederations, see map 1. A confederation (*g̦abīla*) is a territorial group, and comprises member-tribes (sing. *'as̲h̲īra*), each with a chief (*s̲h̲ēk̲h̲*) at its head. A tribe may be divided into sections; similarly, several tribes may form a division of the confederation. While the composition of the groups within a confederation may change with demographic or political developments, they will be cited here as they were at the time of the events described—the name of the confederation first, followed by the tribe (without the definite article *al-*): e.g. Tarābīn Ḥasāblah, Tiyāhā Ṣgērāt, Muzēna Darārma. For the most detailed descriptions of the Negev bedouin see al-'Ārif (*al-Qaḍā'*, pp. 7–34; *Ta'rīk̲h̲*, pp. 17–159; and Von Oppenheim, ii. 81–132); for Sinai, see Murray, pp. 243–70; Bailey and Peled, *passim*; and Von Oppenheim ii. 135–66.

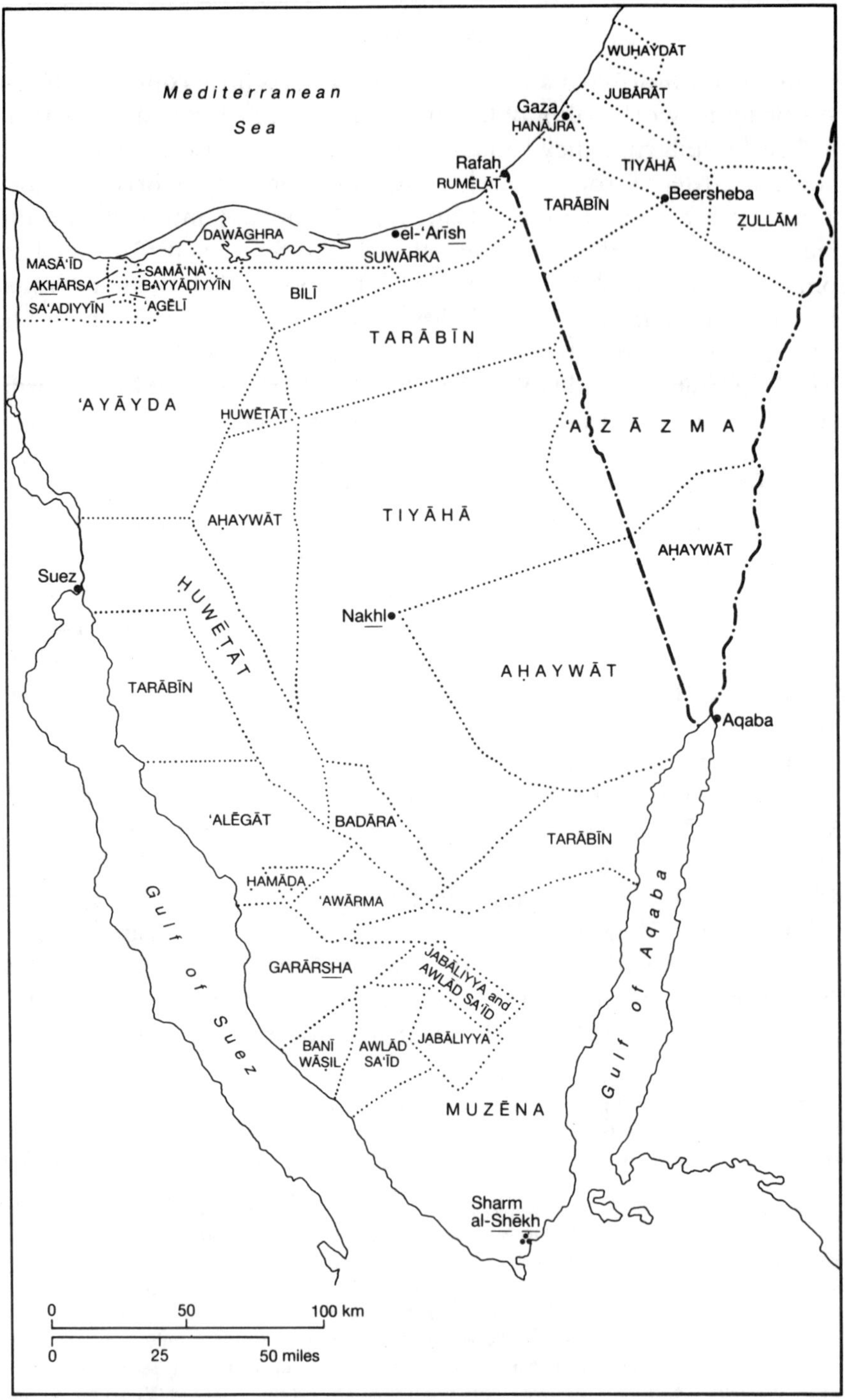

MAP I. The position of Bedouin Tribal Confederations in Sinai and the Negev, early twentieth century.

legends were told about how they had wrested their tribal areas from weaker tribes, and of the heroic exploits of their nineteenth-century heroes, like Ḥammād aṣ-Ṣūfī and Sulēmān Abū Sitta. Their traditional enemies, the Suwārka of north-eastern Sinai, were also known to be numerous, and were envied for their relatively rich, rain-fed lands. The Tiyāhā, of east-central Sinai and the Negev, were renowned for their ancient and noble ancestry. Some believed they were descended from the ancient Israelites who had wandered in their tribal territory (known in the Qur'ān as the Tīh, from which the name Tiyāhā derived); a more modest but equally august claim was that they were stragglers who had fallen behind the large Banī Hilāl tribe that emigrated from Arabia to North Africa in the tenth century and was well known to all from the bedouin epic based on the legendary exploits of its leader, Abū Zēd. The Ḥuwēṭāt, although few in Sinai, were known because of their powerful fellow tribesmen in Jordan, Arabia, and Egypt; and, latterly, because some had come to Sinai as refugees after a desperate rebellion against Arabia's ruler Ibn Sa'ūd in 1932.

Four tribes were famous for having produced judges who specialized in important categories of bedouin law. For serious violations of a woman's honour the bedouin resorted to judges from the small Masā'īd tribe in north-western Sinai; and for marital problems to the 'Ugbī section of the Negev Tiyāhā. Members of the 'Ayāyda were called upon when the ordeal by fire (licking a red-hot iron) was applicable in cases for which there were no witnesses, and cases involving bodily damage were referred to judges from the Bilī. The tribes inhabiting the oases of north-west Sinai, such as the 'Agēlī and Bayyāḍiyyīn, were known by their Egyptian accents, manners, and dress; the 'Azāzma and Aḥaywāt in the barren, stony deserts of the central sections of Sinai and the Negev were distinguished by their wild appearance; while the Dawāghra and Malālḥa tribes of northern Sinai were suspected of bearing ignoble blood for historic misdeeds buried deep in the remote past.

The bedouin tribes of southern Sinai were collectively known as the Ṭawara, People of the Mountain, because of the services they were entitled to provide to St Catherine's Monastery near Mt Sinai, especially the conveyance of monks, pilgrims, and provisions. In the seventeenth century these tribes fought a war among themselves over these rights, with the 'Alēgāt and Muzēna remaining allies down to the present day, as have their rivals, jointly called the Ṣawālḥa. Tribes respected for their alleged antiquity in Sinai and the Negev were the Badāra, Banī Wāṣil, Ḥamāḍa, Jubārāt, and Ḥanājra; but the most senior tribe in Sinai, the Jabāliyya, were looked down upon as not true bedouin, their ancestors from Wallachia and Egypt having been sent by a Byzantine emperor to serve the monks of St Catherine's Monastery.

Until the second half of the twentieth century modern civilization made little impact on the 125,000 bedouin of Sinai and the Negev who still resembled their desert ancestors of the biblical period more than they did their non-desert dwelling contemporaries.[6] The Arab–Israeli War of 1948 was a turning-point for the Negev bedouin, for it resulted not only in the flight of 80 per cent of them to the Gaza Strip, the West Bank, Transjordan, and Sinai, but also in the subsequent sedentarization and modernization of most of those who remained in Israel.[7] Sinai, after Egypt took control from Britain in 1946, underwent a more gradual modernization, which, however, was greatly accelerated under Israel's fifteen-year occupation between 1967 and 1982.

The highway that Israel built along the south-eastern coast of Sinai opened up that isolated area to outside influences. The highly fortified front that was erected between Egyptian and Israeli forces along the Suez Canal and the Gulf of Suez caused a decrease in smuggling activity (an important source of bedouin income), obliging many men to take wage-labour jobs in Israel and in Israeli enterprises in Sinai. Some sections of the population were also exposed to Western civilization through contact, sometimes friendships, with Israeli and European tourists—and this disinclined many, especially the youth, from ever returning to a traditional way of life. Egypt's resumption of authority in Sinai between 1979 and 1982, moreover, was accompanied by plans to settle the bedouin permanently, to develop Sinai economically as a base for absorbing excess population from Egypt proper, and to open up hitherto remote parts of Sinai with new highways. Owing to these developments the traditional bedouin world of Sinai and the Negev that had changed little over thousands of years was irrevocably modernized during the second half of the twentieth century.

When I began to study bedouin culture in 1967, while teaching at the fledgling educational centre, Midrashat Sde Boker, sixty kilometres south of Beersheba, the bedouin of Sinai and the central Negev were

[6] The figure of 125,000 for mid-century is approximate based on the most reliable estimate of 65,000–90,000 Negev bedouin in 1946 (Muhsim, p. 280), and an Israeli census figure of 70,000 Sinai bedouin, in 1975 (Bailey and Peled, pp. 109–115). The latter figure undoubtedly represents considerable growth since mid-century, judging from the easily observable number of young people, whose large proportion in the population was considered unprecedented by the older bedouin.

[7] For demographic and economic changes among the Negev bedouin after 1948, see Marx, chs. 1, 2.

still not sufficiently affected by the modern world to have significantly changed their basic way of life, and most of them remained the same for another six years; some of them down to the present. Consequently, I was able to observe traditional bedouin life and behaviour at first hand through daily contact, either near my home or further afield among the tribes in Sinai with whom I often spent weeks and on some occasions months. Thus, ethnographic studies were pursued and friendships made among all the thirty tribal confederations in Sinai and the Negev, studies and friendships which continued, if somewhat less intensively, even after I moved to Jerusalem in 1975.

POETRY AMONG THE BEDOUIN IN SINAI AND NEGEV

My first experience with bedouin poetry in Sinai and the Negev of the last generation before the advent of Western civilization was in November 1968 during a census of the bedouin population of south-west Sinai conducted by the Israeli military authorities at Wādī Gharandal, where I heard a young chief, ʿAwda Ṣāliḥ Imbārak[8] of the Muzēna Shaẓāẓna tribe, recite twenty poems, which I recorded. It was on this occasion that I discovered the bedouin love of poetry and witnessed a scene, often to be repeated, of men, women, and children spontaneously gathering around the reciter in a semi-circle on the ground, row upon row, listening intensely, repeating after him the monorhymes with which he unexpectedly ended the successive lines,[9] and laughing at ironical, poetic depictions from the otherwise humdrum events of desert life. They were also clearly proud to hear aspects of their culture elevated into verse. It was a seal of common approval that compensated them for their arduous lives. To find an illiterate people so enchanted by poetry moved me to undertake the present study.

On a subsequent visit to the town of el-ʿArīsh on the Mediterranean coast, I played the recording from Wādī Gharandal for an elderly chief of the Tarābīn, Sulēmān Ibn Sariaʿ. Pleased by an outsider's interest in

[8] A bedouin's full name will henceforth be given according to the bedouin tradition: i.e. his name (ʿAwda), followed by his father (Ṣāliḥ) and father's father (Imbārak). In the case of persons mentioned frequently only the first name may be cited, together with a clan-name (e.g. Muṣliḥ Ibn ʿĀmr, Mūsā al-ʿAṭāwna, Ḥusēn Abū Sitta), a nickname ('Abū Khubēza', 'Abū Furthēn'), or a patronym (e.g. ʿAnēz abū Sālim). The designations for 'father of' (*abū*) and 'son of' (*ibn*) will not be capitalized unless they have become part of a clan name (hence, Ḥamdān abū Salāma Abū Masʿūd, signifying Ḥamdān, the father of Salāma, of the Abū Masʿūd clan).

[9] Repeating monorhymes is common when bedouin listen to poetry, as was noted in northern Arabia by Doughty (i. 306) and south-eastern Arabia by Thesiger (p. 86).

bedouin poetry, Ibn Sarīaʿ introduced me to other bedouin reciters and poets of his acquaintance throughout Sinai and they, in turn, similarly pleased by this unexpected interest, introduced me to other poets and reciters, so that in the course of the following eighteen years I recorded some seven hundred individual poems, of which the latest was composed in May 1985.

In Sinai, poetry was a matter of lively and widespread interest. Many bedouin had committed to memory poems they had heard on various occasions for their personal enjoyment, and, when urgently requested or when personally moved to do so, would recite part of their stored-up repertoire. This repertoire consisted mainly of poems composed by Sinai poets of the last few generations (notably, Rabīaʿ az-Zmēlī of the ʿAlēgāt confederation, Faraj Sulēmān of the Rumēlāt, ʿAliyyān Imṭēr of the Aḥaywāt, and Ḥamd al-ʿArādī of the Tarābīn); poems composed in north-west Arabia and 'brought' to Sinai by bedouin passing on their way to Egypt; poems from long prose–poetry stories (like the epic of Abū Zēd al-Hilālī or the Romance of Jidēaʿ Ibn Ha<u>dhdh</u>āl and Irgayya); the bedouin-style poems attributed to a Syrian Druze, <u>Sh</u>iblī al-Aṭra<u>sh</u>, composed in a Turkish prison near the turn of the century; and poems composed by contemporary bedouin.

Poems recited by persons who had not composed them were called 'conveyed poems' (*nagl*); and it was said of such a reciter that he 'has *nagl*'. He was not called a poet (*<u>sh</u>āʿir*) nor accorded any other title, because recitation was a casual and non-professional activity. Yet, the capacity of these persons, mostly illiterate, to recite from memory large repertoires of poems was remarkable. On one memorable night in 1971 I heard forty poems recited by Ḥamdān abū Salāma Abū Masʿūd of the Muzēna Darārma tribe in Wādī aṭ-Ṭūr in south-west Sinai. I recall similar poetic experiences with Ṣāliḥ Imbārak ʿĪd and his son, ʿAwda, of the Muzēna <u>Sh</u>aẓāẓna tribe, Muṣliḥ Sālim Sulēmān Ibn ʿĀmr of the Tiyāhā Ṣgērāt, Lāfī Faraj Sulēmān of the Rumēlāt Busūm, and Muḥammad Luwēmī Ṣabāḥ Abū Nadā of the Tarābīn Nadāyāt—to mention but a few of many reciters with astounding memories for poetry.

Another aspect of poetic activity was the composition of 'impromptu poems' (*bidaʿ*), usually improvised on the spot during group-dances on a festive occasion. In the course of such a dance anyone could feel moved to compose light, rhyming verses, with simple diction and lines of six feet, generally of a suggestive, erotic nature, poems greatly enjoyed, especially by the youth. Such a poem, if well received by friends, might be repeated on other occasions. The subject-matter of these poems was usually amusing, although serious subjects might sometimes be dealt with in this form by those ill-equipped to compose the more intricate and generally 'serious' *gaṣīda*-poem (pl. *gaṣīd* or *gaṣāyid*). Nevertheless, those whose *bida'* were circulated came to be known as *baddā'īn*—creators of *bida'*—a title they may well have found flattering. Ḥamdān abū Salāma, mentioned above, was a noted *baddā'*, as were Ṭu'ēmī Mūsā ad-Dagūnī of the Jabāliyya Awlād-Jundī tribe, 'Aṭiyya Miẓ'ān 'Awwād of the 'Alēgāt Zmēliyyīn, and Sulēmān az-Zēt, of the Ṣawālḥa Garārsha.

The most exciting poetic event in Sinai, however, was the eight-year exchange of poems between 'Anēz abū Sālim al-'Urḍī[10] of the 'Arayḍa section of the Tarābīn Ḥasāblah tribe of south-east Sinai (who was then in prison in Egypt) and other bedouin from the peninsula who wished to comfort or reproach him, or simply to inform him of matters he would find of interest. 'Anēz was reputed to have been one of the biggest smuggling ringleaders in Sinai, and the operations he had organized were a source of income for hundreds of bedouin from many tribes; in addition, he had earned a reputation for being a gifted poet whose poems could both entertain and wound. To have a man of such unbridled spirit and a lover of freedom confined within the four walls of a prison cell for fifteen years (his original sentence) was felt as a grave injustice throughout Sinai. Consequently, when 'Anez sent his friends poems describing his despair and his pessimistic reflections on life as seen from prison, they were learned by heart and circulated throughout the peninsula, where bedouin who had only heard of him listened attentively to every word. Similarly, when I received a smuggled tape-recording of 'Anēz reading his own poems in 1971 and played them to the members of an encampment, people would gather around and listen with rapt attention.

'Anēz (born in 1920) was considered the finest living poet (*shā'ir*) in the peninsula—although he himself considered Silmī Dakhīlallāh al-Jibrī of the Ḥuwēṭāt and Jāzī Imsallam Ḥamd al-'Arādi of the Tarābīn Ḥasāblah (poets not in Sinai when this study was made) to be his equals. Another competent poet, ten years his junior, was Ṣabāḥ Ṣāliḥ al-Ghānim of the small 'Agēlī tribe of north-west Sinai, also a reputed smuggler who spent time in an Israeli jail in 1971 on suspicion of spying for Egypt. Although the serious and highly-regarded *gaṣīda*-poem was normally the genre to which a *shā'ir* such as 'Anēz would

[10] Properly, 'Anēz Sālim Swēlim (cf. n. 8 above). Al-'Urḍī means 'of the 'Arayḍa clan'. Depending on the context, he will be referred to in the text as 'Anēz, 'Anēz abū Sālim, or 'Anez abū Sālim al-'Urḍī.

apply his talent, it was not the *shāʿir*'s exclusive preserve. The composition of such poems, as of all the other genres, being casual and non-professional, many tried their hand at it when they wished to express themselves poetically or send a message. One of the finest *gaṣīda*-poems in the present collection (poem 6.13) was composed not by a *shāʿir* but by a *baddāʿ*, Ḥamdān abū Salāma, who chose the *gaṣīda* as the most suitable poetic form for sending his greetings to ʿAnēz in prison. Others who were considered neither *ashʿār* nor *baddāʿīn*—such as the humble fisherman, Jumʿa ʿĪd Dakhīlallāh, and the camel-shepherd, ʿĪd Imfarrij Imsāʿid, both of the Tarābīn Ḥasāblah of south-east Sinai, or the autodidact, Muṣliḥ Ibn ʿĀmr—proved capable on occasion of composing a commendable *gaṣīda*.

Compared to the Sinai, poetic activity in the Negev was feeble when I began this study. The dispersion of the bedouin population in 1948 and the modernization of the youth had eroded this aspect of traditional life. Only one living *shāʿir* was encountered (Sulēmān ʿAwwād Ibn ʿAdēsān of the ʿAzāzma Masʿūdiyyīn) and only one *baddāʿ* (Sālim 'Abū Furthēn' al-Wajj of the Ẓullām Janābīb). Yet, the Negev had a poetic heritage (in some respects greater than that of Sinai) which was still enjoyed by the older people when recited to them by those of their generation—such as Mūsā Ḥasan ʿAlī al-ʿAṭāwna, Sālim Muḥammad Sālim al-ʿUgbī, ʿAmr Muḥammad aṣ-Ṣāniʿ, ʿĪd Ḥimēdī al-Aʿsam, and ʿĪd Iṣbēḥ Sālim al-Imṭērāt, all of the largest post-1948 Negev confederations, the Tiyāhā and the Ẓullām. The poems they recited had been composed by revered figures of the previous two generations, such as Muṣṭafā Zabn al-ʿUgbī and 'Abū Khubēza' aṣ-Ṣāniʿ of the Tiyāhā; Swēlim 'Abū ʿArgūb' and ʿAyyād ʿAwwād Ibn ʿAdēsān of the ʿAzāzma; and Swēlim 'Abū Haddāf' of the Tarābīn. As in Sinai, their repertoires also contained poems that had been brought by travellers from the east.

After attempting to understand some of my own early recordings of poetry with the aid of a Western-educated Palestinian Arab from the Gaza Strip, I realized that the language and imagery of the poems could only be grasped by one who had grown up in a bedouin culture before it began to lose its traditional form. Fortunately, I found two persons highly qualified for this task and willing to assist: Mūsā al-ʿAṭāwna, the chief of the ʿAṭāwna section of the Tiyāhā in the Negev, and Muṣliḥ Ibn ʿĀmr of the Ṣgērāt section of the Tiyāhā in Sinai. As the sons of prominent chiefs during British rule in Sinai and the Negev, they had received a rudimentary education in Beersheba and el-ʿArīsh, respectively, and thus knew how to read and write. Even more important, both had been designated by their fathers to succeed them as chiefs. They thus had spent much time in their fathers' company, listening to the poems recited by travellers from the east (who naturally spent a night in the tents of these prominent chiefs) and to the many problems that tribesmen brought before their chiefs for solution. Consequently, they both were well-versed in poetry and familiar with the details of other aspects of bedouin life; and their ability to transcribe the poems from recordings proved an aid against error.[11]

Nevertheless, to assure the maximum accuracy of both text and content I always referred the transcribed poems to bedouin from the same tribe as that of the poet or reciter, if possible, double checking the meanings of words and clarifying local imagery and allusions to persons and places. The remote context of a poem, especially those from Arabia, might give rise to different opinions as to its meaning and origin among the various bedouin consulted. It was only through an increasing familiarity with bedouin poetry, gained by recording and studying hundreds of poems, and by constant questioning of several knowledgeable bedouin regarding each poem, that the proper meaning could be ascertained.

AIMS OF THE PRESENT STUDY

This book presents the bedouin poetic heritage in Sinai and the Negev as the author found it between 1968 and 1988. It contains 113 bedouin poems, most of which are not anonymous. The authors of seventy poems can be identified with certainty; those of fifty-five were known by me personally. Most of the poems are of relatively recent origin. Only ten poems can be said with certainty to antedate the nineteenth century: poem 4.16, composed during an invasion of the Negev in the seventeenth century; and the nine poems comprised in the Romance of Jidēaʿ Ibn Hadhdhāl (4.20 A–I), who lived in the second half of the

[11] Mūsā al-ʿAṭāwna's father, Ḥasan, was a member of the Governmental Tribal Court in Beersheba, during the British Mandate. Muṣliḥ Ibn ʿĀmr's father, Sālim, was called 'the most important sheikh in Sinai', by its governor, Jarvis (pp. 4, 80). His grandfather, Sulēmān, served as guide to several writer–explorers, such as Professor E. H. Palmer in 1869 (p. 268) and Jennings-Bramley in 1905 (*passim*). Two others who occasionally helped me in transcription were Imsallam Sālim Abū Nīfa of the Tarābīn Ḥasāblah and Rāḍī Swēlim ʿAtayyig of the Muzēna Darārma; and I more than once benefited from the help of the bedouin anthropologist, 'Ārif Abū Rubē'a, of Beersheba, in understanding some otherwise inscrutable text. In all cases, transcription was done with my participation; and it was in these sessions that the clarification of concepts and terms from the poetry provided an occasion to hear explanations of various aspects of bedouin life and culture that I have sought to convey in the textual notes accompanying each poem in this book.

eighteenth century. Poem 2.3 dates from 1830; and all the poems of Chapter 5, which deal with a war that took place between 1875 and 1887, were definitely composed during that war or shortly thereafter. One cannot date for certain most of the advice-poems of Chapter 3, especially those from Arabia; but, judging from various of the allusions that they contain and the attributions of authorship proffered by the reciters, it seems unlikely that they originated before the nineteenth century. Most of the poems in this book, therefore, are as recent as the twentieth century, suggesting that the life of a poem—as a single integral creation notwithstanding the changes that characteristically occur in oral transmission—seldom exceeds three generations.

Fifty-five poems originated in Sinai, thirty-two in Arabia, and twenty-six in the Negev—the poems from Arabia being included since they were part of the poetic heritage of Sinai and the Negev. All but five poems were recorded directly from bedouin; these five poems are known from earlier studies of bedouin life in Sinai and the Negev by the Czech explorer, Alois Musil, the British–Egyptian official, Naʿūm Shuqayr, and the British–Palestinian official, ʿĀrif al-ʿĀrif.[12] These published poems were read aloud and, where necessary, corrected by Mūsā al-ʿAṭāwna and Muṣliḥ Ibn ʿĀmr.

The 113 poems included here represent a gleaning from some seven hundred recorded compositions, and were chosen on the basis of their popularity among the bedouin, the extent to which they contain material important for understanding bedouin experience and poetry, and the fidelity and clarity of the text. The course of oral transmission may have left some poems, especially those from Arabia, in fragmentary form, but they were none the less included in this book because they met the criteria cited above.

In addition to presenting original bedouin poems in Arabic and translation, this book has two main purposes: first, to discover by means of numerous examples the motives that induce illiterate bedouin to compose poetry; second, to explore the functions of poetry in an illiterate bedouin society. An examination of the poems in this volume shows that bedouin have four basic reasons for composing a poem; namely, to express an emotion, to send a message, to impart instruction in the art of living, and to entertain. A single chapter is devoted to each of these motives for composition, consisting of an

[12] i.e. Musil, *Arabia Petraea* (1908), Shuqayr (1916), and al-ʿĀrif, *Taʾrīkh* (1934). Al-ʿĀrif was District Officer for the Negev from 1929 to 1939. The value of the contribution of all three men to our knowledge and understanding of the bedouin of Sinai and the Negev is inestimable.

introductory essay and a selection of poems, each poem with an introduction giving its specific background.

Chapter 1 contains fifteen poems of expression, composed against a background of varying emotions: longing, relief, anger, despair, grief, and love. These poems are more than an aesthetic mode of expression such as one finds in Western cultures; because of social constraints in his society against exposing emotional weaknesses, a poem is often the only way a bedouin can express himself.

The second chapter presents the poem as a message sent from one place to another, serving much as a letter does in other cultures. Being unwritten, however, the bedouin message is composed in rhyme to prompt the memory of the illiterate messenger. As reflected by the twelve poems in this chapter, poems-cum-missives may be sent for different reasons: to threaten, to placate, to share an emotional burden, to impart information, to complain, and to make a request—for things as different as mercy, intercession, or the gift of a camel. Existing in an almost constant state of migration and dispersion, bedouin could hardly have maintained communication without the aid of poems. The quasi-mystical aura of rhyme among bedouin also endowed their poetic messages with added import.

Chapter 3 is a study of the poem as a credo, consisting of a group of proverbs, maxims, and admonitions that instruct the person to whom the poem is addressed in matters of proper conduct. However, deliberate and ordered instruction being unknown in bedouin culture, these poems more likely served the poet as yet another channel of expression, prompted perhaps by the birth of a child and anxiety about its upbringing, by improper behaviour, or by personal failures and disappointments. In such circumstances this genre, which has come down from a long desert tradition older than the Bible itself, would naturally suggest itself to the poet. The motive for composition notwithstanding, these poems could still be used for instruction, since many lines might circulate among the bedouin as proverbs and be cited in support of one course of action or another.

The fourth chapter contains poems that are composed in order to entertain. The entertainment may consist of efforts to flatter someone, to evoke laughter, or to arouse interest in a story—usually one in which the norms and conventions of bedouin society are challenged. This chapter also examines the components of bedouin humour, indicating how it may serve as both a relief from convention and its affirmation. Chapter 4 also contains a long narrative story told in alternating passages of poetry and prose, the Romance of Jidēaʿ Ibn Ha<u>dh</u><u>dh</u>āl, in order to demonstrate a once-popular means of using poetry for entertainment. The variety of bedouin entertainment-poems deserving attention has made this chapter longer than the preceding three. It should not be inferred from this, however, that entertainment is the chief impetus to poetic creativity among bedouin.

After these discussions of the four reasons that impel an illiterate bedouin to compose a poem, the next two chapters demonstrate the extent to which poetry plays an active role in bedouin life: examples of 'poetry in action'. Chapter 5 presents thirteen poems composed during a bedouin war in the Negev, the War of Zāriʿ al-Huzayyil (1875–87). The poems were collected piecemeal from different reciters and from the books by Musil, Shuqayr, and al-ʿĀrif, and then integrated into the various accounts of the war as related by bedouin born a generation thereafter. At different stages of the war, poetry was used to intimidate the enemy, hearten allies, and express joy after victory or sorrow after rout.

Chapter 6 recounts, through poems, events of a more personal nature that took place ninety years later surrounding the imprisonment in Egypt of the smuggler–poet ʿAnēz abū Sālim al-ʿUrḍī of Sinai. For eight years poems written down by literate prison-mates and itinerant merchants passed between ʿAnēz and his family, friends, and acquaintances in Sinai dealing with his experience in prison, the unfaithfulness of his wives, and unsettled smuggling accounts. Eighteen of these poems are presented in this chapter.

If bedouin culture were to continue for another hundred years in Sinai and the Negev, the contents of Chapter 7 might eventually be told—with the help of historical perspective—as one continuous story, like the Romance of Jidēaʿ Ibn Hadhdhāl or the War of Zāriʿ al-Huzayyil. It would then be called 'The Loss of Bedouin Autonomy to Modern Government'. The twelve poems of this chapter relate to events that took place during the century between 1882 (when Great Britain gained control of Egypt and Sinai) and 1982 (when Israel returned Sinai to Egypt). This chapter may also be said to constitute a document of Fourth World History, since native poets recorded their attitudes towards the activities of Turks, British, Egyptians, and Israelis—activities which shaped the political and cultural destiny of the bedouin, but over which they had no control. Still, these poems were composed neither to record nor to instruct but, more in keeping with the genuine bedouin tradition, to express anger or relief, to warn of impending danger, or simply to entertain.

Chapters 8 and 9 are a critical discussion of the selection of poetry presented in the previous chapters. Chapter 8 departs from an investigation of the 'what' and 'why' of bedouin poetry and turns to the 'how'. How does an unlettered person compose a meaningful poem in metre and rhyme? We find, firstly, that bedouin are born into a culture of rhyme; and that, when wishing to channel their inborn talent at rhyming into creating poems, their task is facilitated by a licence to use unnatural stress in simple poems and irregular, accentual metre in more intricate ones. That does not mean, however, that a bedouin's poems are doggerel. To the contrary, his poems, as shown, excel in elevated diction and rich imagery. In bedouin as in other folk-poetry, the poet is aided by a certain fund of stock or formulaic expressions, from which he can choose when 'getting into' a composition. However, examples taken from the previous chapters show that the use of formulas in bedouin poetry is limited, and that the bedouin poet draws deeply, by association, upon his own memory for much of his resource. Chapter 8 establishes that a bedouin folk-poem has an original version and an original poet, both of which were encountered by this writer regarding nearly half the poems in this book.

The interest in bedouin poetry does not end with the light it sheds on folk-poetry, for bedouin poetry is not merely another instance of folk-poetry nor is it the poetry of one more tribal society. Bedouin poetry, like bedouin culture, is heir to a Middle Eastern desert tradition that goes back four thousand years and has had a profound effect on both Jewish and Arab civilizations. Moreover, contemporary bedouin poetry and culture are not offshoots of these civilizations, but spring independently from the same environmental conditions. Hence, desert poems, the circumstances of whose origins can be authenticated and studied, must shed light on ancient Hebrew and Arabic poems just as bedouin society and behaviour, as reflected in recent poetry, must illuminate social conditions of previous millennia. The final chapter of this book, Chapter 9, indicates the cultural and poetic continuity from the ancient to the recent, and presents a new perspective on poetic activity in the pre-Islamic period.

Just as the experience of the bedouin in Sinai and the Negev helps us to understand the Middle Eastern desert dwellers of past ages, it can also shed light on the lives, values, and attitudes of contemporary bedouin of the great eastern deserts from Syria to Arabia. The constraints of life in the desert call forth the same patterns of survival, whichever the desert. Until now our understanding of how a bedouin

[13] Monroe, pp. 1–53.

survives in the desert has been obscured by stereotypes that arose from insufficient knowledge of his daily life. Survival in such an environment, as individuals and as a society, demanded the qualities generally attributed to bedouin: bravery, generosity, dependability, and pride. This book indeed reveals the extent to which these attributes occupied the bedouin mind: in addition, however, it also stresses the human aspect of the bedouin personality as revealed not only in the excitement of war, but in the bedouin's personal tragedies and joys, and in his humour. It shows the things that move a bedouin to laughter, anger, and despair.

Bedouin poetry, being a reflection of bedouin life, must be more than one Saudi Arabian scholar claimed it to be: boastful and panegyric compositions about fighting and raiding expeditions.[14] While such compositions kindle pride—reflecting the best in bedouin character and the most exciting aspects of bedouin life—and are what the bedouin themselves would gladly present to an outsider as their poetry, they are but a small part of the bedouin poetic production, most of which is more immediate, relating to the events of every day. As a result of years of continuous contact with bedouin, often close involvement in their affairs and problems, and the recording of hundreds of their poetic compositions, it was possible for me to break through the stereotypes in the literature and find poems about subjects as unheroic as smuggling-debts, or humour meant to relieve bedouin of their society's strict bonds of convention. Life in the desert is difficult, and, unless the bedouin possessed qualities and observed customs not commonly found in settled areas, they would not have survived for so long. Therefore, the candid portrayal of their character as revealed in the poetry of this book cannot detract from their many virtues; if anything, it can only add to them by showing how the bedouin practised these virtues without being less 'human' than others.

Except when addressing customs that pre-dated even the traditional bedouin of the mid-twentieth century, the notes and essays of this book are set in the present tense. Although bedouin culture is approaching its end, there are bedouin in Sinai, the Negev, and elsewhere who are still faithful to their ancient desert culture, and one is therefore reluctant to anticipate their cultural demise, however inevitable, by referring to them prematurely in the past tense.

I have translated most of the poems in this volume into versified English, often into rhyming couplets. While aware that translating

[14] Sowayan, p. 2.

poetry into rhymed verse is controversial, I none the less decided on this course, not because I imagined that I could reproduce, or even approximate, the beauty of the original, but because I felt it was the only way to convey the exceptional aesthetic and practical importance that the bedouin themselves attach to rhyme in their poetry. In translating the lines of the poems—even the relatively few lines that I translated freely—I tried to maintain the original imagery, convey the author's intention and spirit, and avoid introducing allusions that are foreign to bedouin culture.[15] Wherever I encountered lines in which these goals could not be attained in the context of rhymed verse, I translated them into blank verse, trying to maintain the general rhythm of the poem. I generally chose iambic and anapaestic metres, which approximate the rhythm of most of the original poems, and tried, where possible, to keep the feet of a line commensurate with those used in the Arabic text.

Most bedouin poems are in monorhyme, which is an important aspect of the bedouin cultural ambience; two-thirds of the poems in this book contain two different rhymes in every line. The English language does not permit the translation of long (or even short) Arabic monorhyme poems into monorhyme; all the more so double-monorhyme poems. Thus I chose the couplet as the scheme with which to rhyme most of my translations. The couplet—usually rhyming the two hemistiches of a single line—has the advantage of expressing the single integral thought characteristically embodied in each individual line of the Arabic original as a single rhyming couplet. Moreover, although couplets unfortunately do not reflect the monorhyme characteristic of the original text, their use *does* reflect the bedouin concern with rhyme, an aspect of the bedouin cultural ambience that would be lost if I were to translate into free verse or prose. In any case, the proximity of the transliterated Arabic text to the English translation should enable the reader to note that the original poem was in monorhyme.

Finally, while the content of these compositions is clearly of anthropological value, they are none the less poems. As this attempt may be the last opportunity to present bedouin verse, the worthy heir to a long but dying tradition, to an English-reading public, I feel it a trust I owe the bedouin to show with rhyming translations that, although unlettered, they loved poetry.

[15] The relatively few lines that I translated freely should not prove an obstacle to scholars owing to the presence of the original Arabic text and to the glossary of bedouin words and meanings at the end of the book.

I

Poems of Expression

THE BEDOUIN, HIS EMOTIONS AND THE POEM

The entire gamut of the bedouin's emotional life lends itself to poetical expression; not as abstractions, however, but as concrete manifestations of daily life. Thus, all the poems in the present chapter arose from direct personal experience: a man in jail longing for home at holiday time; a woman longing for menfolk away at war; a murdered boy's father seeking vengeance; a traveller after a hearty meal and good cheer; a man incensed by a slur on the memory of a dead cousin; a bedouin snubbed at a state reception; another neglected during drought; a third denied welcome in a desert tent; others disconsolate at the loss of dear ones or of worldly possessions; a lad inspired by a shepherdess at the well.

The experiences that provided the settings for these poems may vary greatly, from the historical (the impact of a world war on a humble shepherdess) to the mundane (a meal given to travellers in a strange land); from grief occasioned by the death of a husband to the exuberance of youthful infatuation. Yet, all the poems have one thing in common: the expression of an emotional experience. Among bedouin, however, expressive poems are more than a way to put order into emotion; they also have a social role.

The present poems indicate the nature of that role, by revealing facets of emotional life that are characteristic of bedouin culture. In particular, some emotions expressed in a poem would be largely taboo in daily conversation or behaviour. A bedouin man, for example, rarely discusses his amorous-yearnings, exploits, or frustrations, even with an intimate friend, any more than he would cry or tear his clothes at a funeral—demonstrations of grief left to the domain of women, when they visit their burial-grounds alone. If bedouin men wish to express emotions such as longing, love, grief, or despair, it is mainly in the form of a poem.

These restraints on emotional expression are reflected in the opening line of the first poem in this section, composed by an imprisoned bedouin longing to be home at holiday time: 'Yesterday night I slept unsound / Yet how few to whom I'd complain of my pain.' Bedouin men are reluctant to display emotion, aware that their society deems 'an emotional person' weak and unfit to handle the serious business of life: survival in a dangerous social environment.

The subjects of the following poems and the impetus for their composition confirm the central place that security and a reputation for strength occupy in a bedouin's thoughts and actions. Anger, for example, is a common theme in bedouin poems; and, although the immediate circumstances that give rise to poems of anger may differ, all are composed in response to either an insult or an injury. To bedouin, an insult is more than a social slight; it is an expression of contempt for one's ability to retaliate. Ignoring an insult is thus an admission of impotence and renders life in the desert impossible. To acquire a reputation for weakness in desert society, where 'his hand is against every man's, and every man's hand's against him', makes a bedouin constantly vulnerable to violation. Insult, of course, may be less serious than actual injury (a violation of one's own person, kin, or possessions); yet, whenever a bedouin's strength is called into question, whether by insult (being rejected as a worthy guest, poem 1.8) or injury (being deprived of provisions during a drought, poem 1.7), he must react so as to dispel the impression of impotence.

Though ostensibly incommensurate, incidents of insult and slight injury occur, for which bedouin consider the composition of a poem an ample reaction. To a threatened bedouin, his poem with its 'hard words', is a weapon he can hurl at his foe with impunity; and being heard by others, it also serves to salvage his self-respect.

When ʿAwda Ijmēaʿ al-Ajrab was angered by the contempt shown by some people for his cousin's deceased son, Sulēmān Ibn Sarīaʿ, he ended his poem (1.5) with an implicit warning that the sons of Ibn Sarīaʿ would bring them to shame. When the Egyptian authorities prevented ʿAnēz abū Sālim from meeting King Ḥusēn at a reception for the Jordanian king, the poet concluded his angry poem (1.6) by asserting that when God wanted the two to meet they would not need anything as insignificant as Egyptian permission. Jāzī al-ʿArādī (poem 1.7), on being cheated by the chiefs who failed to deliver government provisions sent to him during a drought, declared that a (faithless) Egyptian peasant is more dependable than a bedouin chief—a devastating insult. On being poorly received, travellers near Beersheba cursed this city of buildings that had sprung up in the desert (poem 1.8), and Ṭuʿēmī ad-Dagūnī, whose seventeen goats were killed by a panther owing to the misbehaviour of his shepherdess-daughters, ended his poem (1.9) by ridiculing them for leading his goats to slaughter as one would bring wood 'for a carpenter's saw'.

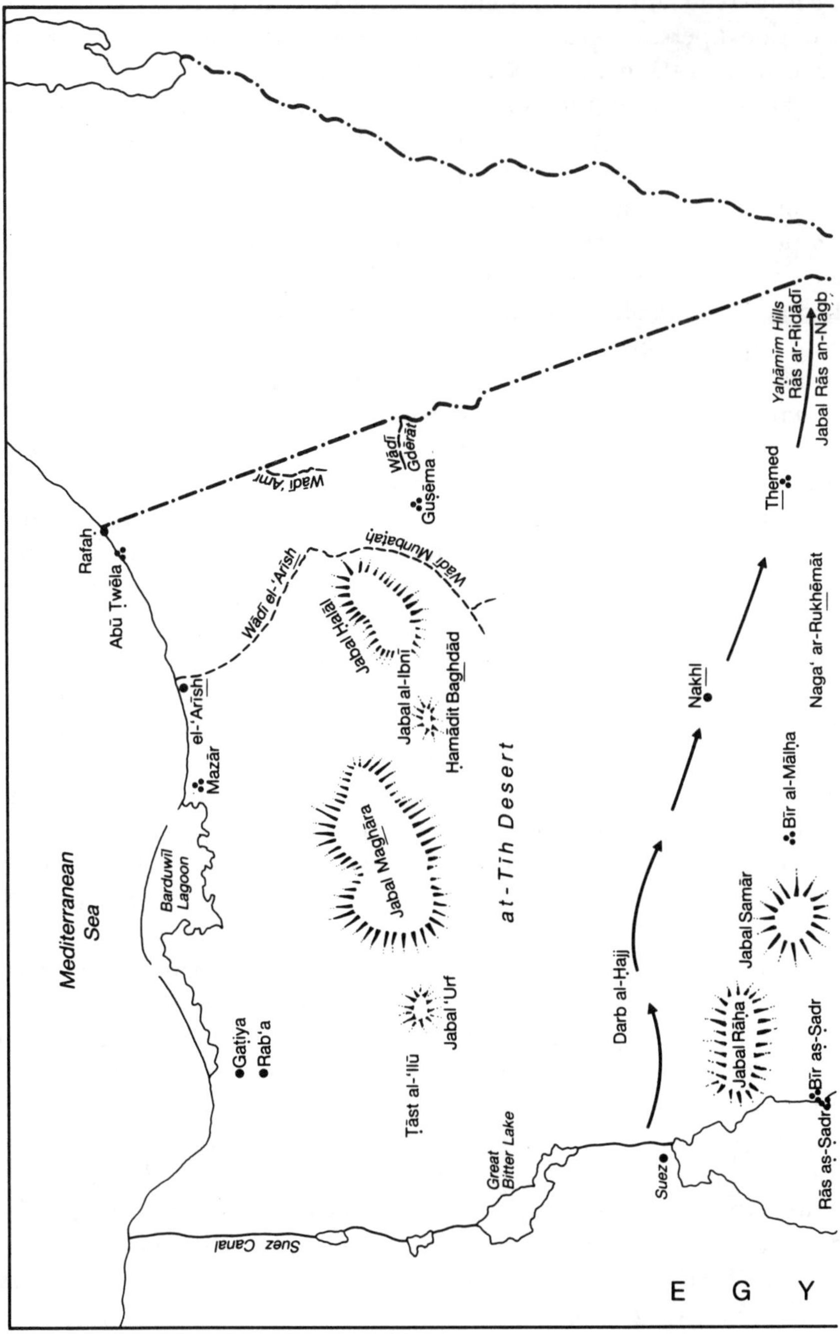
Mediterranean Sea
Barduwīl Lagoon
Rafah
Abū Ṭwēla
el-'Arīsh
Mazār
Gaṭiya
Rab'a
Wādī el-'Arīsh
Wādī 'Amr
Wādī Gdērāt
Guṣēma
Wādī Munbaṭaḥ
Jabal Halāl
Jabal al-Ibnī
Ḥamādit Baghdād
Jabal Maghāra
at-Tih Desert
Jabal 'Urf
Ṭāst al-'Ilū
Great Bitter Lake
Suez Canal
Suez
Darb al-Ḥajj
Nakhl
Naga' ar-Rukhēmāt
Themed
Yahāmīm Hills
Rās ar-Ridādī
Jabal Rās an-Nagb
Bīr al-Mālḥa
Jabal Samār
Jabal Rāḥa
Bīr as-Ṣadr
Rās as-Ṣadr
E G Y

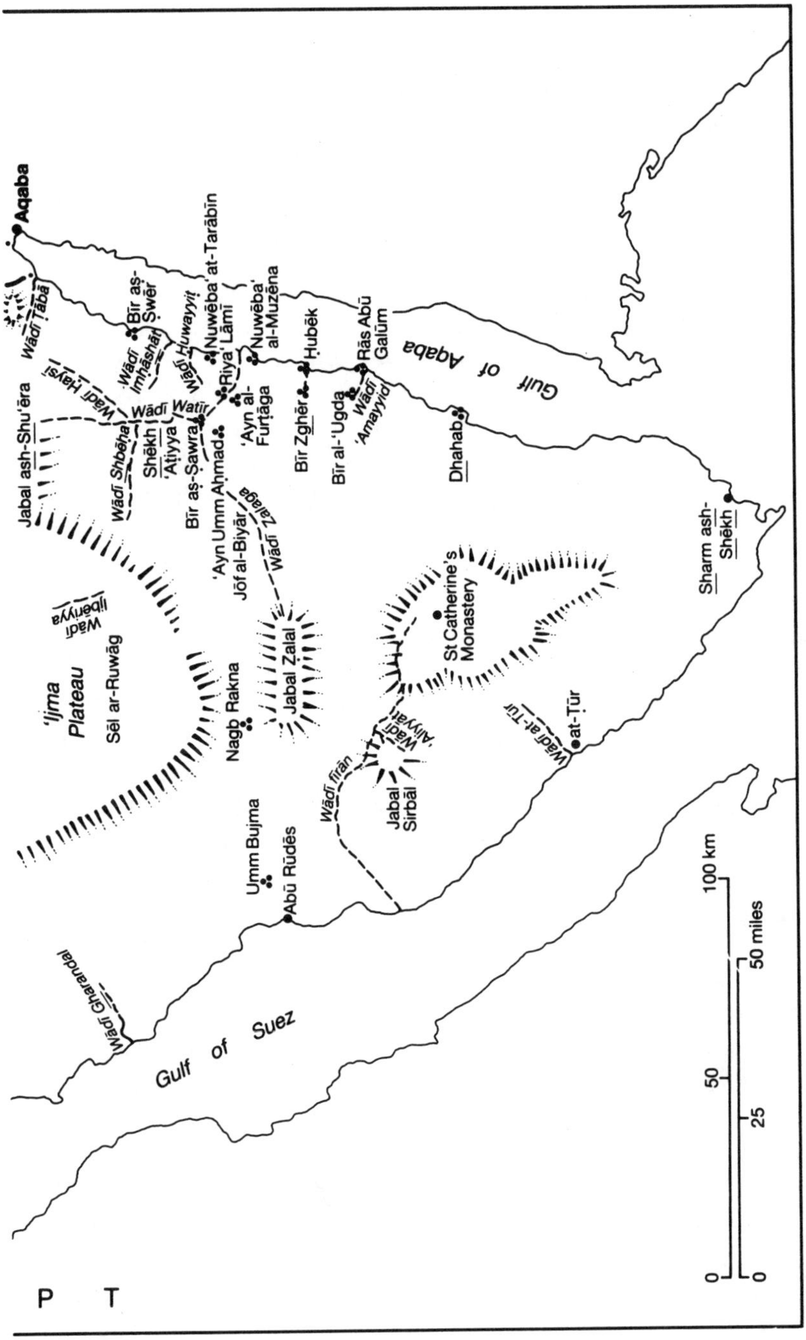

MAP 2. Places in Sinai mentioned in the book.

One explanation for a rhymed barb being a means of retaliation sufficiently potent to restore a bedouin's sense of self-respect in a society of contentious and violent men, is simply that it may be readily recalled and repeated in several tents where men gather, causing dreaded insult to its butt. On a more esoteric level, bedouin often attribute magic to rhyme—a type of sympathetic magic, according to which, objects neutralize the evil of similar objects having not only the same colour, texture, shape, and sound, but also the same nature.[1] Accordingly, an uttered harsh word may have the impact of a harsh blow. Not every bedouin that composes a poem need be conscious of trying to hex the object of his anger with a type of voodoo; a long tradition of striking an opponent with a degrading rhyme (*hijā'* in Classical Arabic poetry) is sufficiently inexorable.[2]

There are occasions, however, in which bedouin are violated and do not seek relief in a feisty poem of anger; it is when they clearly possess no means of redress. A poem composed against this backdrop of implicit weakness would be a poem of despair. In two such poems—one composed after a raid in which a bedouin lost all his worldly belongings (poem 1.10), the other after a bedouin visited his brother in prison (poem 1.11)—the poets' despair derives from their inability to cope against fellow men. In the first instance an enemy tribe is too distant and powerful to attack; in the second, the foe is government, the awesome image of whose power is reflected in the bedouin proverb 'There's no revenge for him whom government kills' (*katīl al-ḥukūma, mā lih ṭrād*). Even ʿAnēz abū Sālim's nostalgic poem from prison (1.1) ends on a note of despair, since his calamities, too, were caused by humans: kinsmen who seduced his wives while he was in jail, and the authorities that put him there. Despair in men's poems is characterized by unrelieved dejection.

When, by contrast, a person's calamities are caused by nature, fate, or God, rather than fellow men, a bedouin can be resigned to his impotence; it does not impair his social status. The poem he then composes will be 'a poem of grief', such as those composed by ʿĪd Imfarrij Imsāʿid (1.12 and 1.13) after the deaths of his daughter and his brother. Poems of grief end with resignation rather than despair—the poem on the daughter's death with a touch of morbid fatalism ('Well, what of it? We'll all meet with fate one night / When the worms eat us all, and with appetite').

[1] Bailey, 'Religious Practices', pp. 81–5.

[2] For the magical origins of *hijā'*, see Goldziher, pp. 24–6; for the *hijā'* heritage in bedouin poetry, see Chapter 9.

The centrality of honour and status is brought home in a curious aspect of the poem of despair by the bedouin who had lost everything in a raid (poem 1.10). According to the narration that accompanies the poem in the oral tradition, he had also lost his wife in the raid, as well as his slave whom he considered a friend.[3] However, there is no allusion to them in the poem. The poet only mentions his former social prominence and the loss of his material possessions primarily to inform his hosts and guardians that he is a person of power. The poem is introduced into the narrative as a composition that the poet sang to his hosts in a tent where he had been taking refuge for months without telling them the reason. Thus, when he finally 'opened up', it was not to express his grief at the loss of his wife and slave but to mention the things that had given him status—his large tent, his thoroughbred horse, his herd of fine camels, his hospitality, and his brave kinsmen—all in the hope that his hosts would treat him as an equal. Even if he had felt grief, he would have been reluctant to express it to others—to whom one does not 'complain of one's pain'.

Indeed, the poems of relief and of love in this section also contain the 'power' motif: there is, for example, the relief of the man who avenged his son and thereby retained his reputation for strength (poem 1.3). The poem of relief by travellers who were hospitably received (1.4) might at first seem to belong to a different category of feeling—until we recall that their rebuff at the first encampment they came to was a show of disdain and, hence, a threat to their safety in a strange land. Even in the poem of simple infatuation (1.15) the poet included a line about the readiness of his kinsmen to fight, if need be, to obtain his beloved for him.

Unlike their menfolk, bedouin women may be less restrained in expressing emotions, for they, unlike the men, are not responsible for the defence of themselves, their families, or their possessions, and have not the man's need to project an image of constancy. This difference is reflected in the two poems of this section composed by women: one in which a woman is longing for men who have gone off to war (poem 1.2); the other in which a woman is lamenting the death of her husband (poem 1.14). Both poems deal with helplessness in the face of circumstances beyond one's control; but, unlike their male counterpart who laments the death of a daughter (1.12) and a brother (1.13), the female poets need demonstrate no resignation to their fate. They may allow themselves to grieve without relief.

[3] For the complete Arabic narrative and a translation, see Bailey, 'Narrative', pp. 86–99.

Poems of expression mainly relate the experience that gave rise to the emotion, as in ten of the fifteen present poems; and some allusion is always made to that experience, if only in a single line. Dealing with emotion the poems are often introduced by a sentence, either lyrical ('I'm sad out herding goats today') or narrative ('I rose and climbed a mountain dry'); or, as oral poetry, they may contain some of the standard clichés that commonly introduce poems of this genre. Thus, a poet might begin by declaring that he has not been able to sleep, eat, or drink for three days;[4] or, he may state that he has 'climbed a mountain' to compose his poem—an allusion to the emotions that have removed him from the normal routine of life.

Poems of expression may vary according to the talents of the poet, the circumstances under which he composes, and the nature of his experience. In the present selection the poems range in length from four single-rhyme lines to twenty-two double-rhyme lines (one rhyme for each hemistich), half the poems having fewer than ten lines, and half more. Although these poems express an emotion, they have few lyric lines. When, however, such lines do appear they are of rare beauty. Animal imagery abounds together with allusions to the customs, attitudes, sayings, and artefacts of bedouin culture.

1.1

Longing for Home at Holiday Time

A Poem of Nostalgia

ʿAnēz abū Sālim al-ʿUrḍī, reputedly one of Sinai's leading smugglers, suffered a reversal of fortune in 1962 when he was arrested and sentenced to fifteen years' imprisonment. In addition, two of his wives ran off with men of his own clan and tribe. In the present poem, composed in prison at the time of the main Muslim holiday, the Feast

[4] This theme was common to Arabic folk-poetry in places as far away as South Yemen (Serjeant, p. 11).

Poem 1.1 was heard, recited by its author, from a recording made at Birshāg, Egypt, in 1971, and given to the present writer shortly thereafter. It was also heard recited by Ḥamd Sulēmān Salām Abū Nadā of the Tarābīn Nadāyāt tribe, in Wādī Munbaṭaḥ, 3 December 1970.

of the Sacrifice (*ʿīd al-aḍḥā*), the poet longs for the holiday festivities in his native Wādī Watīr (a narrow wadi that winds for some eighty kilometres between limestone and granite mountains from central Sinai down to where it pours into the Gulf of Aqaba) and laments his fate.

ʿAnēz first tells how he spent a sleepless night tormented with longing, a feeling he could not share with his prison-mates lest they think him weak. He then describes the sights and sounds of the holiday celebrations: the social drink of bitter coffee; shooting matches with Mauser rifles; lamb roasted on coals of the desert genista bush; the shrub booth erected to provide shade; and the women with their facial tattoos and collyrium-darkened eyes.

This backward look into the pleasant past, however, only aggravates the harsh realities of the present, as depicted in the following four lines, especially the shame that his wives' faithlessness and kinsmen's betrayal have brought upon him. To attenuate his own humiliation ʿAnēz (in line 9) blames the betrayal of his wives and kinsmen on their 'inherent defects': the women, being women, are weak and the men, being poor, are envious and insidious. His gibe at the deceitful men—'the poor take heart when calamities come'—is an adaptation of the popular, ancient proverb 'The misfortunes of fighters are the common man's gain' (*maṣāyib gōm ʿend al-akhirīn fawāyid*).

Yesterday night I slept unsound
  Yet how few to whom I'd complain of my pain. 1

O how pleasing's the cup one sips under palms
  And the Mauser's sound where the wadi bends[1] 2

And lamb's meat we've heaped on embers of broom[2]
  With friends in the shade of a booth,[3] reclining[4] 3

[1] In the mid-twentieth century Mauser rifles, which bedouin call 'the German', *al-almānī*, were populat among Middle Eastern smugglers. On festive occasions bedouin men enjoyed holding shooting competitions, and at Rīyaʿ Lāmī in winding Wādī Watīr they would shoot where 'the wadi bends'.

[2] Freshly slaughtered meat is customarily boiled in large pots, a process which softens it, often taking three hours. To appease the hunger of guests in the meantime, organs of the animal—the heart, lungs, liver, intestines, and colon—are roasted on the embers of an open fire, sliced, and passed among those present in a bowl. This hors-d'œuvre is called *shawāya*—'that which is roasted' (from *shawā*, to roast). The broom bush (genista) is often used for firewood.

[3] In the summer and autumn, when the bedouin of northern and southern Sinai are almost stationary near water sources, they construct shrub booths, called *ʿursh* (sing. *ʿarīsha*), which they

Near darkened-eyed lasses with fine even teeth,
Their tattoos as green as the pasture of spring.[5] 4

But today I'm trapped in the tangles of fate,[6]
Imbibing, by draughts, purest poison. 5

Others are covered but we are exposed,[7]
As jerboa-mice frolic within my abodes.[8] 6

Though I've whitened the withers of mares,[9] I'm despised;
Even those who wear the black shawl[10] shun me. 7

My clan's like hyenas at small stinking pools,
Crouched to the ground like hyenas drinking.[11] 8

use instead of tents for shelter and common sitting spaces. The booths are made of Artemisia monosperma (*ʿādhir*) in the north and palm fronds (*siʿāf*) in the south. This is the prototype for the Jewish Feast of the Tabernacles, based on the biblical command to construct booths (Heb. *sukkot*) each year in early autumn to commemorate the Israelite sojourn in Sinai.

[4] In bedouin terminology, reclining is literally 'to rest on one's elbow' (*kawwaʿ*, from elbow *kūaʿ*); hence, the Jewish Passover holiday—also held to commemorate the Israelite sojourn in Sinai—is observed by reclining at the table during the meal.

[5] Two forms of adornment among bedouin women are darkening the eyelids with collyrium (*kuḥl*) and tattooing (*washm*) the face.

[6] Bedouin envisage fate as ensnaring one with ropes (*aḥbāl al-manāya*) or snares (*asbāb al-manāya*) (cf. poems 1.14, 6.1, 6.5). For the antiquity of this concept, see Chapter 9.

[7] 'Exposed'—lit. 'naked' (*ʿarāya*)—means 'we have no good name to cover us; we live in shame'. From the poet's point of view, his kinsmen, in seducing his wives, committed an act for which there is no possible justification or 'cover'. The justification they offer, on the other hand, is that they had to provide for these women, as ʿAnēz had been sentenced to prison for fifteen years. (Oral communication from ʿĀyd ʿAbēd Muhammad of the Tarābīn Sarāyʿa, at Wādī Zaghara, 5 May 1978; cf. poem 6.6.)

[8] A house or tent in the Arabic text—the bedouin call their tents 'houses of goat-hair' (*buyūt shaʿr*)—is another image of honour deriving from the ability to keep one's womenfolk 'covered', i.e. unviolated. The violation of a woman is thus termed 'destruction of the house' (*kharāb al-bēt*). The poet here laments that his own personal honour has been utterly destroyed since, in his absence, his reputation failed to prevent the violation of his women. Not even men who were usually as timid as the jerboa (or kangaroo mouse) feared him! (Cf. poem 6.6, introduction.)

[9] This is a reference to the status that the poet once enjoyed as a leading smuggler, who packed hashish on the backs of camels. This is clearly understood in the Arabic text by the phrase 'after the white withers'—it being known that the hairs on a camel's withers turn white from continual saddling (Cf. Musil, *Manners*, p. 365; poem 4.20B, l.2.)

[10] i.e. the poet's wives. Unlike Arab peasant women, who cover their heads with white shawls (*shāsha*), bedouin women wear black head shawls, the *gunʿa* worn outdoors, and the shorter *magnaʿ*, indoors.

[11] Because of his cousins' ill-treatment, the poet compares his clan to hyenas, believed to eat one another from stupidity and to keep themselves hidden from the eyes of other animals because of this shameful behaviour.

As life must end, so women are lesser than men,[12]
And the poor take heart when calamities come. 9

And I, once a wolf that preys inside camps,[13]
Who charged upon non-bearing mares[14] like Jidēaʿ,[15] 10

Am now but a walker with shattered bones
Stumbling and fumbling midst boulders and stones. 11

1 al-beriḥa fi-l-lēl bitna gisāya
ū-gilīl min niškī ʿalē hal-mawajīeʿ

2 ya ma-ḥala-l-finjāl bēn il-widāya
ū-ḥiss alamaniyyāt fī ḥinwit ir-rīeʿ

3 ū-jamr ar-ratim nurẓum ʿalēh-aš-šawāya
war-rabaʿ fī ẓill al-ʿarīša makawīeʿ

4 ʿend akḥal al-ʿaynēn ū-zēn iṯ-ṯināya
allī-ūšāmhin miṯil ʿišb al-marabīeʿ

5 wil-yōm ṣirnā fī iḥbāl al-manāya
našrab min as-samm al-imkarrar garaṭīeʿ

6 wan-nās miktasyyīn wiḥna ʿarāya
wi-dyārna ṣārat malāʿib jarabīeʿ

7 sirna baʿd šīb al-ġawārib razāya
ū-sirna baʿd sumr il-magāniʿ magaṭīeʿ

1 البارحة في الليل بتنا قسايا
وقليل من نشكي عليه المواجيع

2 يا ما حلى الفنجال بين الودايا
وحسّ المانيّات في حنوة الريع

3 وجمر الرتم نرضم عليه الشوايا
والربع في ظل العريشة مكاويع

4 عند اكحل العينين و زين الثنايا
اللي اوشامهن مثل عشب المرابيع

5 واليوم صرنا في احبال المنايا
نشرب من السمّ المكرّر قراطيع

6 والناس مكتسيّين واحنا عرايا
وديارنا صارت ملاعب جرابيع

7 صرنا بعد شيب الغوارب رزايا
وصرنا بعد سمر المقانع مقاطيع

[12] In order to stress the inferiority of women, the poet compares it to a law of nature: the certainty of death. Bedouin men primarily attribute this imputed inferiority to a lax regard for social responsibility (cf. poem 3.9, n. 4). They are also wont to say, 'Women cannot keep a secret' (*an-niswān, mā ilhin sirr*). For more on the inferiority of women, see poems 3.11, n. 12; 6.2, l.4.

[13] i.e. a fearless wolf.

[14] Camel mares that are prevented from mating are considered the strongest and fastest runners—hence the frequent use of 'barren' to allude to swift camels in bedouin poems (cf. poem 2.9).

[15] A reference to the legendary bedouin hero, Jidēaʿ Ibn Hadhdhāl (see poem 4.20).

8 waṣ-ṣirba allī zē ẓbāʿ al-habāya
all-iykarʿū fī sākint ir-rīḥ takrīeʿ

8 وسربة اللي زي ضباع الهبايا
اللي يكرعو في ساكنة الريح تكريع

9 al-ʿumr fānī wan-nagīṣa walāya
wi-yifraḥ gilīl al-māl yawm iz-zaʿazīeʿ

9 العمر فاني والنقيصة ولايا
ويفرح قليل المال يوم الزعازيع

10 ū-min ʿugub mānī miṯil ḏīb al-garāya
wašidd fōg al-ḥīl ma-šaddha ijdēaʿ

10 ومن عقب ما انا مثل ذيب القرايا
واشدّ فوق الحيل ما شدّها جذيع

11 amšī ʿala rijlī ū-aẓmī šaẓāya
wagūm wagʿud fi-l-blād al-jarajīeʿ

11 امشي على رجلي وعظمي شظايا
واقوم واقعد في البلاد الجراجيع

1.2

Men away at War

A Poem of Longing

During the First World War, when the Hashimite Sharīf of Mecca, Ḥusēn ibn ʿAlī, in collusion with the British agent, T. E. Lawrence, organized a revolt against Ottoman rule in western Arabia, many bedouin joined his ranks, as related in Lawrence's *Seven Pillars of Wisdom*. The abrupt departure and long absence of the men left their womenfolk despondent, as expressed by one bedouin woman in this poem.

I'm sad out herding goats today,
Crying for those who're far away, 1

Who've pitched their tents where death goes by;
What luck if we see them again some day. 2

Poem 1.2 was heard recited by ʿAwda Sulēmān ʿAliyyān of the Aḥaywāt Ḥamādāt tribe, in Wādī Ṭābā, 10 December 1971. The authoress was reportedly from the ʿAwdāt section of the Ḥuwēṭāt Ibn Jāzī tribe of Transjordan, many of whom joined the Sharīf of Mecca, under their chief ʿAwda Abū Tāyah.

And woe to the walker or he who rides slow
When chargers veer, their sticks asway. 3

Looking out as far as anyone can,
I see only tattered dresses swaying. 4

All that remain are virgins and flocks
And asses, in the wormwood, braying.[1] 5

1 ana saraḥt il-yōm sarḥa ġabīna
dam'ī badār ya-mba''idīn il-masarīḥ

1 انـــا سرحت اليوم سرحـــة غبينـــة
دمعي بذار يـــا مبعّدين المساريـــح

2 banaw xyāmhum 'a sakkt al-mawt
la ya hanī min šāfhum 'ugub maṣabīḥ

2 بنو خيـامهم علـى سكّـة الموت
لا يـا هني مـن شافهم عقب مصـــابيح

3 wajdī 'al ar-rijlī ū-rā'i ar-radiyya
lin šawšaḥū bi-l-miš'āb wi-sakkū 'āl-fīḥ

3 وجدي علـى الرجلي وراعي الرديّـة
لِن شوشحو بالمشعاب وسكّو على الفيح

4 ra'ayt biš-šōf ḥadd ma-yjīb
war'a mṭawṭḥāt iš-šalatīḥ

4 رعيت بـــالشوف حدّ مـــا يجيب
وارعـــى مطوطحـــات الشلاتيـح

5 ẓallan ġēr al-ġanam wal-'adāra
wal-ḥamīr tināfir fi-š-šīḥ

5 ظلّـن غيـــر الغنـــم والـعذارى
والـحمير تنـافـــر فــــي الشيـــح

[1] This image arises from the attraction of asses to pungent plants, such as the various desert species of wormwood (cf. Bailey and Danin, 'Plant Utilization', p. 148).

1.3

Vengeance for a Murdered Son

A Poem of Relief

There was once a bedouin chief in Arabia whose son was killed in a raid by distant bedouin under their leader, Ṣāliḥ. It was difficult for the father of the murdered lad to avenge his son's blood, since his own tribe was too small to mount an attack against the enemy and the enemy lived too far for him to go alone without being detected along the way. The old chief thus resorted to a subterfuge and, disguised as a poor demented beggar in tattered clothes, begged his way from one encampment to another until he reached the camp of Ṣāliḥ.

There he lodged in the guest tent which belonged to Ṣāliḥ himself, living off alms and waiting for the day when his enemy would return from a raid. When that day came, however, Ṣāliḥ grew suspicious of the old man's intent look, and had him removed to the tent of a black slave at the edge of the camp. It was with this slave that the dead boy's father plotted his revenge; he entered Ṣāliḥ's tent at night, aroused him from sleep (in keeping with bedouin custom), and stabbed him. He then fled to a nearby mountain, while the slave, by prior agreement, led the camp's dogs off in the opposite direction. As he watched his son's murderer being borne to burial on the following morning, the man felt a sense of relief and composed the present poem, in which he taunts Ṣāliḥ's people, boasting of the cunning and courage his vengeance required.

This daring act of revenge caught the imagination of the bedouin. Although the poem was heard recited by only two different persons, it must once have been well known, since one reciter lived in southern Sinai and the other in the northern Negev. Its concluding hemistich—'My side-heavy saddlebag's now been put right'—the image of bedouin justice, was known to almost all the elderly bedouin with whom I spoke. The first eight lines of the poem are an 'epic' review of the poet's experience.

Poem 1.3 was heard recited by 'Īd Imfarrij Imsā'id of the Tarābīn Ḥasāblah tribe, at Sēl ar-Ruwēg on the 'Ijma plateau, 17 March 1971; and by 'Īd Iṣbēḥ Sālim al-Imṭērāt of the Ẓullām Abū Rubē'a tribe, at Ksēfa, 17 March 1973. The story behind the poem, as related by 'Īd Imfarrij, may be found verbatim with translation in Bailey, 'Narrative', pp. 76–81; the text of the poem has been corrected for the present rendition.

I was your guest before Ṣāliḥ came your way;
Ṣāliḥ alighted at your camp just today. 1

I sat without shame and ate unrestrained[1]
And though among dregs was myself disdained. 2

A reed of *ʿawarwar*[2] my arms against mongrels
With which I beat back every howling hound, 3

But a dagger of the Ijbāra lay at my waist;[3]
You could hear it scraping inside its case. 4

I plunged it in twice, perhaps even thrice
Quickly; I had no time. 5

I plunged it in twice, perhaps even thrice:
Jets from a rain cloud for a droughty land![4] 6

Thank God for the slave at the edge of the waste
Diverting the dogs in another direction. 7

It's morning and I'm in a steep mountain crag;
Wild animals only had been here before. 8

I retired encumbered, but rose feeling light:
My side-heavy saddlebag's now been put right.[5] 9

1 ana-llī ẓayfkū min gabl ṣāliḥ yiẓīfkū
wal-yōm ṣāliḥ ʿala ʿarabkū nizīl

1 انـــا اللي ضيفكم مـــن قبل صالح يضيفكم
واليوم صـــالح علـــى عربكـــم نزيـــل

2 bugʿud bila ḥišmi ū-bākil bila ḥaya
ū-sirt ila-hilbāj ir-rjāl hibīl

2 بـــاقعد بـــلا حشمـــة وباكـــل بـــلا حيـــا
وصرت لـــهلبـــاج الرجـــال هبيـــل

[1] Being outspoken and eating ravenously is unseemly conduct for a bedouin guest.
[2] A species of Verbascum.
[3] An unidentifiable kind of dagger.
[4] i.e. the spurting blood.
[5] The bedouin word for justice is *ʿadl* (lit. 'balance'), a concept borrowed from the image of a camel that can only keep going in the desert if the load in its saddlebags is balanced. Similarly, a person cannot go on living in the desert if he has been violated and not taken revenge, since his society will consider him weak and vulnerable. Justice is thus seen as a demonstration of strength and is compared to the balancing of a camel's load, because it enables a violated person 'to keep going' in the desert. (See Bailey, ''ADL', pp. 133–5.)

3 islāḥī ʿin il-ʿuklān ʿūd il-ʿawarwar
wuṭrud ibhā mi-l-ʿuklān kull ʿiwīl

3 سلاحي عن العكلان عود العُوَرْوَر
واطرد بها من العكلان كلّ عويل

4 fi ṣulbī xanjar min diggit ijbāra
fi-jwāha tismaḥḥa laha ṣagīl

4 في صلبي خنجر من دقّة اجبارة
في جواها تسمعها لها صقيل

5 bujtha bōjtēn walla ṯilāṯi
ʿala ʿwējlin mānī ʿalē timhīl

5 بجتها بوَجتين ولّا ثلاثة
على عويجلٍ ماني عليه تمهيل

6 bujtha bōjtēn wall̤a ṯilāṯi
ū-li nidd min šaxatīr mizni wil-blād maḥīl

6 بجتها بوجتين ولّا ثلاثة
وله نِدّ من شخاتير مزنة والبلاد محيل

7 uškur all̤a wil-ʿabd fī ṭart al-xala
yiharbis lil-ʿuklān ʿinnī nū ḥiwīl

7 اشكر اللّه والعبد في طرف الخلا
يهربس للعكلان عنّي نو حويل

8 aṣbaḥ ṣabāḥī fī ʿujra makšaxirri
waṯrāha l-ūlād il-wiḥūš giddāmī migīl

8 أُصبح صباحي في عجرة مكشخرّة
وثراها لاولاد الوحوش قدّامي مقيل

9 imsēt mahamūmin waṣbaḥt fāẓī
ū-sawwēt lil-xurj iṯ-ṯigīl ʿadīl

9 إمسيت مهموم واصبحت فاضي
وسوّيت للخرجٍ الثقيل عديل

1.4

Hospitality in the Desert

A Poem of Relief

Unlike the blood-revenge in the preceding poem, the event that inspired the present composition was only a meal eaten by hungry and tired travellers. A band of bedouin riders, journeying through an unfamiliar desert, suddenly came upon an encampment. Their hopes for a hospitable reception, however, were disappointed when, suspected

Poem 1.4 was heard recited by ʿAwda Ṣāliḥ Imbārak, of the Muzēna Shaẓāẓna tribe, in Wādī Gharandal, 11 November 1968.

of being on a scouting mission to plunder camels, they were not invited to stay and had to go on.[1]

Their fortune changed when they alighted at another camp where they were heartily welcomed. As they were hungry as 'hawks whose talons are lowered for prey' (line 3), a sheep was slaughtered to feed them, and, having eaten their fill, they set out again. One of the party, pleased with their good fortune, composed the present poem.

Judging from names mentioned in the text, the action must have taken place in north-western Arabia, near the Nabatean site of Madā'in Ṣāliḥ, for in its vicinity were the traditional camping grounds of the tribes called Fugarā (sing. al-Fagīr (line 1), perhaps a reference to the chief) and Shawāma (line 3).[2]

Fagīr said 'Move on', so we moved;
A guest goes by nought but his host's desire.[3] 1

Not he that deprived us, but rather our luck;[4]
And luck sometimes brings pain, then takes it away.[5] 2

For we stopped to alight at a camp of the Shawāma
Like hawks whose talons are lowered for prey. 3

[1] The reputation for wariness on the part of the small Arabian tribe, the Fugarā, whom the reciter of the poem in Sinai did not know, was apparently based on fact, for it was also related ninety years earlier (1877) to the British explorer, Charles Doughty, who recorded it in an eloquent passage in his *Travels* (i. 263).

[2] See, e.g., Doughty (i. 104, 270–1, 427, 502, *et passim*) for mention of the Fugarā, a tribe of the large 'Anēza Wild 'Alī confederation, and the Abū Shāma (i.e. ash-Shawāma), a tribe of the Bilī Mawāhīb (see Map 3). These tribes were again visited *in situ* in 1910 by Alois Musil, who mentioned them in *Northern Hegaz* (pp. 128, 221).

[3] This line refers to a bedouin custom which requires a guest to accept whatever his host offers without complaining or asking for more (cf. al-'Ārif, *al-Qaḍā'*, p. 192), a custom reflected in the proverb 'A guest is the prisoner of his host' (*aḍ-ḍayf asīr il-miḥillī*). (The use of *miḥillī* for host is more prevalent in Sinai and the Negev than *mu'azzib*, the term found in this poem in accordance with the usage of Arabia; both terms denote authority for a specific dwelling.)

[4] This line derives from the proverb 'Food and generosity are matters of fate and fortune' (*al-akl wa-l-jōd naṣīb w-inṣāb*).

[5] This line derives from the proverb 'It is luck that both pains and heals' (*al-bakht yōja' wi-yiṭīb*); *ḥaẓẓ* (the term for luck in the poem) and *bakht*, are interchangeable.

There, Muḥammad Sirḥān,[6] whom perfumed women long for,[7]
Swore he'd divorce his wife if we didn't stay.[8] 4

Then he poured out hot suet that hissed round our hands[9]
And stacked fattest sheep's meat high on the tray. 5

So we ate of this bounty until we were full;
Then, like well-watered camels, we went on our way.[10] 6

1 gāl al-fagīr imšūn wiḥna mašēna
waẓ-ẓayf mā lih ġēr rāy al-maʿazīb

2 mā hū rada fīna rada ḥaẓẓ fīna
wal-ḥaẓẓ yajaʿ al-ʿaṣr wi-yiṭīb

3 ʿa farīg aš-šawāma ḥana lafēna
lafēt aṣ-ṣgūr imdalliyyāt al-maxalīb

4 imḥammad as-sirḥān ṭallag ʿalēna
ya šōg min hī tidifg al-ʿaṭar fa-l-jēb

5 xalla-š-šaḥam la faḥfaḥa fī-yiddēna
ū-xallā jazūr aẓ-ẓān ʿendinā maṣalīb

1 قال الفقير إمشون واحنا مشينا
والضيف ما له غير راي المعازيب

2 ما هو ردّا فينا ردّا حظّ فينا
والحظّ يجع العصر ويطيب

3 ع فريق الشوامة حنا لفينا
لفية الصقور مدلّيّات المخاليب

4 محمّد السرحان طلّق علينا
يا شوق من هى تدفق العطر في الجيب

5 خلّى الشحم له فحفحة في يدينا
وخلّى جزور الضان عندنا مصاليب

[6] The Sirḥān (or Sarāḥīn) were the chief clan of the Shawāma in the late nineteenth century (Doughty, 1. 502).

[7] An image often used to compliment the male recipient of a poem (cf. poems 2.6, 5.7, 6.7).

[8] The verb *ṭallag*, 'to divorce one's wife', also means 'to swear that one will divorce one's wife unless certain conditions (bearing no relation to one's wife) are fulfilled'. An occasion on which a bedouin might use this oath would be to persuade visitors or passers-by to accept his hospitality. The actual expression is *ʿalayy aṭ-ṭalāg* ('divorce is incumbent upon me!') or *anā ṭallāg min marātī* ('I shall divorce my wife!'). Even when such persuasion is unnecessary, as in the circumstance of the present poem, a prospective host may still utter this oath to remove any doubt that his invitation is sincere. For a different use of the oath, see poem 5.1.

[9] Bedouin consider the boiled fat of a slaughtered animal (*wadak* from a camel; *shaḥam* from a sheep or goat) a great delicacy. The allusion to hands refers to the fact that bedouin eat with their hands directly from a large bowl or tray.

[10] To indicate the abundant food the guests had consumed, the poet in the Arabic text compares them to camels that were not only sated but large, using the expression 'those whose canine teeth are cut' (*shallakh an-nīb*). When a camel gets these teeth in its sixth year and hence is able to graze on even the thorniest plants in the desert, it is considered full-grown and proudly designated 'a possessor of canine teeth' (*minwab*, pl. *manāwib*).

6 wakalna minna limma tikaffēna
wi-ṣadirna kama ṣadarat šallax an-nīb

6 واكلنا منه لمّا تكفّينا
وصدرنا كما صدرت شلّخ النيب

1.5

Dishonour to the Dead

A Poem of Anger

When a bedouin, as any other Muslim, hears that someone he knew has died, he repeats, 'May God have mercy on him' (*allāh yarḥamuh*). To refrain from uttering this blessing is considered disrespectful to the dead. When the chief of the Tarābīn Sarāy'a tribe of south-eastern Sinai, Sulēmān Salīm Muḥaysin Ibn Sarīa', died in August 1973, some of his acquaintances, and even several of his fellow tribesmen, refused to ask mercy for his soul, perhaps because he had become contentious in his old age or, as some thought, had collaborated too closely with Israel, which then occupied Sinai. This undisguised disdain angered the chief's maternal cousin, 'Awda Ijmēa' 'Awda al-Ajrab of the Muzēna Sakhāna tribe,[1] who soon thereafter composed the present poem as a reprimand.

The composition, in the style of a light, improvised poem (*bida'*), begins on a note of sorrow over the passing of Sulēmān Ibn Sarīa' (lines 1–2), and then praises the chief for his generous hospitality and magnanimity (lines 3–6). The following two lines attempt to defend the dead man's reputation, and the last two threaten those who dishonour him.

Abū Muḥaysin; since he died, there's nothing round Ẓalal to find.[2] 1

His life was riches, but he died and left it all behind. 2

Poem 1.5 was heard recited by its author, at Nuwēba' al-Muzēna, 31 January 1974.

[1] The mother of Sulēmān Ibn Sarīa' was a paternal first cousin of the composer of this poem, 'Awda al-Ajrab. The chief's parents were thus of two different tribal confederations, the Tarābīn (his father) and the Muzēna (his mother).

[2] The mountain Jabal Ẓalal and its neighbouring wadis in south-east Sinai form the tribal area of the Tarābīn Sarāy'a. The portent of this line—that none of the Sarāy'a measures up to Sulēmān Ibn Sarīa'—is a deliberate insult aimed at those who did not honour his memory.

Now nothing's left when lions die, except what men recall,[3] 3

And in his guest tents velvet cushions welcomed one and all. 4

How many men he sprang from jail! How many worked in drought![4] 5

How many mounts he smeared with blood and trays of meat served out![5] 6

I, too, was here, when Israel came, and saw a chance for gain; 7

But then to sell a friend for nought, only a slouch[6] would deign! 8

A lion whelps but men of pride, whose smell none would defame.[7] 9

So ask God's mercy for my cousin's son,[8] or have your beards be shamed.[9] 10

مـن عقب ميتة ابو محيسن مـا باقبل لظلل شيفة 1

1 min ʿugib mētt abū-mḥaysin ma bagbal laẓ-ẓalal šīfi

[3] The importance of a good posthumous reputation is often stressed in bedouin poetry (cf. poems 5.1, l. 7; 5.10, l. 15).

[4] i.e. how many he employed in smuggling when there was no other source of income! In the Arabic text drought is expressed as 'the thin years' (*as-sinīn an-naḥīfa*).

[5] It is customary for a host to smear the blood of an animal he has slaughtered for a meal on the hinds of his guest's mount. This is a way of advertising the host's hospitality, for the guest will be questioned by those whom he meets about the origin of the blood (cf. poem 3.5, l. 3).

[6] A 'slouch' expressed by the word *hāmil* (lit. 'neglectful') in the Arabic text, is one that either does not understand or simply neglects bedouin conventions regarding social relationships and obligations, and is hence likely to betray friendships.

[7] Smell, here, refers to a reputation for good character (cf. poem 4.8, l. 5, for the same image). This line states 'a law of nature', namely, that qualities are hereditary, a belief often expressed in proverbial lines of poetry with animal imagery, such as

adh-dhīb mā khallaf ḥalālīf wi-ḍbāʿ
  adh-dhīb dhīb ū-yinsil adh-dhīb dhīb

A wolf never bore a hyena or boar
  A wolf is a wolf; and will whelp but a wolf.

[8] In the Arabic text the poet calls Ibn Sarīaʿ 'my brother's son' (*ibn akhī*) although he was his female cousin's son. A man's obligations to and dependence on his brother's son (as on his other paternal male kinsmen) for security renders his relation to him closer than to the child of a female cousin or a sister. To blunt the distinction, however, the latter is also called euphemistically 'my brother's son'.

[9] The beard is an object of veneration and honour; a supplicant might touch the beard of a potential benefactor, for example, when asking for a favour, forgiveness, or mercy.

وفات الدنيا وخلّاها ما اخذ معد تعريفة 2

2 ū-fāt id-dinya ū-xallāha ma-xad̲ ma'a ta'rīfi

والسبع يوم وانّد بيموت بيظلّن غير خراريفد 3

3 wis-sabi' yōm winni biymūt biyẓallin ġēr xararīfi

وامّا مقاعد ابو محيسن فوق اللحيفان والقطيفة 4

4 wamma magā'id abū-mḥaysin fōg il-lḥīfān wil-gaṭīfi

وياما فكّ عالرجاجيل وفي السنين النحيفة 5

5 ū-yāma fakk 'ar-rajajīl ū-fi-l-isnīn in-niḥīfi

وياما حنّى الركايب جاب اللحم عالشريفد 6

6 ū-yāma ḥanna-r-rikāyib jāb aĺ-laḥam 'a šarīfi

وانا في حكم اسرائيل وشايف في العالم شيفة 7

7 wana fī ḥukm isra'īl ū-šāyif fi-l-'ālam šīfi

والهامل بيبيع الرفيق يا عالم بتعريفة 8

8 wil-hāmil biybīc' ar-rafīg yā 'ālam ib-ta'rīfi

والسبع يعقّب رجاجيل ولا بيعقّب لد جيفة 9

9 wis-sabi' yi'aggib rajajīl wilā biy'aggib li jīfi

واللي ما يرحّم ابن اخي دقند تستاهل الكسيفة 10

10 willī mā-yraḥḥim ibn axī digni tistāhl-il-kisīfi

1.6

An Official Slight

A Poem of Anger

In May 1985 Egypt opened a ferry-boat link with Jordan, running between Nuwēba' on the eastern Sinai coast and the Jordanian port of Aqaba. To inaugurate the new port at Nuwēba', which the Egyptians had built on resuming authority in Sinai in 1982, President Ḥusnī Mubārak invited King Ḥusēn of Jordan and Sultan Qābūs of Oman (then on a state visit to Egypt) to attend the celebrations on 28 May. To lend the event local distinction, the bedouin chiefs and notables of the area were invited to meet the royal guests.

'Anēz abū Sālim al-'Urḍī, perhaps the most notable bedouin in all Sinai because of widespread and successful smuggling operations and unusual poetical skills, was omitted from the official guest list. Whether this slight was the result of local manipulation or of official disapproval of his record, which included prison terms for smuggling, 'Anēz was greatly vexed. He was angered not only by the affront but also by the missed opportunity to meet and perhaps impress King Ḥusēn by composing a poem or engaging in witty conversation. He also hoped to derive some benefits for his smuggling operations from a connection with the Jordanian monarch; he was aware that the king's late maternal uncle and close adviser, Sharīf Nāṣir Bin Jamīl, himself had been a noted smuggler.

Rejecting the alternative of attending the festivities with the common bedouin, 'Anēz betook himself to the 'Ayn Umm Aḥmad oasis some sixty kilometres up-wadi to distance himself from the insult. Once there, however, his anger at the Egyptians vented itself in a poem in which he engages Ḥusēn in an imaginary conversation, avowing that the bedouin's chief loyalty was to the Jordanian monarch, rather than the Egyptian president (lines 3, 4, 11) and stressing the special connection between the poet's own Tarābīn tribe and the Hashimite royal family (lines 8a, 9, 10), which he wished to strengthen through marriage (line 8b).

Late last night I woke and yearned
To meet the one who kindles pride. 1

Poem 1.6 was heard recited by its author, at Nuwēba' at-Tarābīn, 18 July 1985 (seven weeks after its composition).

We'd heard he was coming before he arrived
But 'our boys'[1] posted sentries to keep me outside. 2

Your deeds give us joy, O Abū Ṭalāl,[2]
When battles rage and men rise and fall.[3] 3

Though Ḥusnī Mubārak calls Sinai 'our land',[4]
It's we helped them in when they'd no hope at all.[5] 4

Had the luck of Ḥusēn and myself so conspired,
A meeting of worthies would have transpired. 5

Now all we have left is the hope he'll return;
We'd take in his words, our men sitting round, 6

Cheered by copper-red coffee-pots brewing,
People of shame, not faithless nor vain. 7

Your grandsire's mother, was bedouin, Ḥusēn,[6]
And if we married your girls, we could now gain.[7] 8

[1] i.e. the Egyptian authorities, stated ironically to highlight the estrangement between them and the bedouin.

[2] The sobriquet of King Ḥusēn, following the Arab tradition of referring to someone familiarly but respectfully by addressing him as 'the Father of . . .' (*Abū . . .*) his eldest son (or his father, after whom, it is assumed, he will name his future eldest son).

[3] Battles in the Arabic text are referred to as 'the watering' (*al-warīd*), because of their ups and downs, which allegorically resemble the descent and ascent to and from a large well (oral communication from ʿAnēz abū Sālim). Musil is of the opinion that a battle is likened to a well because warriors drink death there, quoting the line of a poem: 'He who waters at the trough of death fears it not' (*ḥawḍ al-manāyā wāridah mā yihābah* (*Manners*, pp. 304–6)).

[4] i.e. Egypt's land.

[5] This is an empty boast, as the bedouin of Sinai did little to help Egypt prepare or wage the war of 1973 which led to the restoration of its sovereignty there. Often heard among the bedouin, the boast reflects a reluctance to concede that others—in this case the Egyptians—might control their destiny.

[6] The reference is to King Ḥusēn of the Ḥijāz (d. 1931), whose mother belonged to the Banī Shahr tribe of western Arabia.

[7] Since 'honour comes from the woman's thighs, just as fire comes from tinder' (*al-ʿizz min awrāk an-nisā, wa-n-nār min migḥāshā*), Arabs believe that men derive their qualities from their maternal 'uncles' (*khwāl*, sing. *khāl*). When a bedouin weds a girl from an unrelated family, for example, he justifies it by saying 'I'm seeking a good maternal uncle for my child' (*anā badawwir lil-walad khāl*). Accordingly, the poet would remind King Ḥusēn that, as he apparently acquired his good qualities from the bedouin, the Tarābīn would like to have their own offspring acquire the good qualities of Ḥusēn and his family by marrying their girls. Another proverb has it that 'Two-thirds of a child are attributable to his maternal uncle' (*thilthēn al-walad lil-khāl*).

For we are Begūm,[8] and you know more than one
Who've served through the crises, reckoned true men.[9] 9

Many stallions we've chased, and from many we've run,[10]
Spirited stallions who charge when told: Turn![11] 10

We're all Ḥusēn's troops, for Ḥusēn's our chief man,
From the Gulf in the east to far Meknes Gate.[12] 11

An 'Abdallī[13] bounds back like a bent *shintiyān*[14]
And the foe he tramples won't rise again. 12

Those you pursue will never know joy;
Turmoil takes place when you seek revenge.[15] 13

To give the call 'Charge!' you never delay;
Your valour's not measured the usual way. 14

A lion rallies though bound thigh to shank,
Asking only God's shield from the spears of the rank.[16] 15

When, in friendship, we two at last will embrace,
By decree it won't be, but by Allah's good grace.[17] 16

[8] The Tarābīn claim descent from the Begūm tribe of the southern Ḥijāz, and explain their name as 'people from the Turaybā area' (which is in Begūm territory). For Begūm, see al-Kaḥḥāla, i. 89.

[9] In particular, the poet was referring to Jum'a Ḥammād Abū Jahāma of the Naba'āt division of the Tarābīn in the Negev that took up residence in Sinai after the Arab–Israeli War of 1948. Jum'a Ḥammād, as he was generally known, moved to Jordan in 1953 and became a staunch supporter of the Hashimite regime and eventually the editor of the main pro-government daily newspaper, *al-Ra'ī*. The crises referred to in this line are the various clashes that took place between the Palestine Liberation Organization (PLO) and the government in Jordan between 1968 and 1971.

[10] i.e. we've had our share of combat experience, and against good fighters.

[11] The command 'Turn!' (*inḥās*, also *ḥās*) is given to horses when the rider, feigning retreat, wishes to charge at the enemy.

[12] i.e. the large Bāb Manṣūr gate of Meknes, Morocco, which is a proverbial reference to the distant west among bedouin.

[13] 'Abdallī is the collective name borne by the descendants of King 'Abdallāh of Jordan.

[14] *Shintiyyān* was a highly regarded type of sword, the temper of whose steel was so fine that its thin blade reportedly could be bent double and spring back to its original form.

[15] According to the author of the poem, vengeance is serious when pursued ruthlessly and relentlessly, and completed within ten days.

[16] i.e. even intrepidity is no defence against treachery.

[17] i.e. we will not need Egyptian permission next time.

1 al-bāriḥa fi-l-lēl gumt atamanna
imgābil illī šōfta tarfaʿ ar-rās

1 البارحة في الليل قمت اتمنّى
مقابل اللي شوفتد ترفع الراس

2 ū-min gabl ma yilfī ʿulūmi lafanna
bass rabaʿna ḥaṭṭū ʿal al-bāb ḥarrās

2 ومن قبل ما يلفي علومد لفنّا
بسّ ربعنا حطّو على الباب حرّاس

3 ya-bū ṭalāl ifʿālkū yisʿidinna
yōm al-warīd yisīr ṭalʿa ū-minkās

3 يا ابو طلال افعالكم يسعدنّا
يوم الوريد يصير طلعة ومنكاس

4 ū-ḥisnī-mbārak gāl hāḏa waṭanna
jīna ḥuṭm gabl yigbal ʿala yās

4 وحسني مبارك قال هذا وطنّا
جينا حطم قبل يقبل على ياس

5 ḥaẓẓī ū-ḥaẓẓ iḥsēn law sāʿadanna
kān il-mugābal ʿaraf an-nās bin-nās

5 حظّي وحظّ حسين لو ساعدنّا
كان المقابل عرف الناس بالناس

6 wabġi-ḥsēn in la ʿalēna-mṯanna
wajna ḥadīṯ iḥsēn war-rabaʿ jallās

6 وابغي حسين ان لد علينا مثنّى
واجنى حديث حسين والربع جلّاس

7 ʿa dlāl šugr ilwānhin yifarḥinna
wa-nufūs ḥaya mā-bha ḥubiṯ wiġlās

7 ع دلال شقر الوانهن يفرّحنّا
ونفوس حيا ما بها حبث واغلاس

8 ya-ḥsēn jiddak kān li sās minna
warīd yōm al-bēt mabnī ʿal asās

8 يا حسين جدّك كان لد اساس منّا
واريد يوم البيت مبني عل اساس

9 ḥina ibgūm wi-ʿendikū nās minna
rabaʿ nahār al-azma tinḥisib nās

9 حنا بقوم وعندكم ناس منّا
ربع نهار الازمة تنحسب ناس

10 yāma ṭaradna-l-ḥuṣn ū-yāma-nṭaradna
ḥuṣnin tixūẓ ad-damm maʿ gōlit inḥās

10 ياما طردنا الحصن وياما انطردنا
حصنٍ تخوض الدم مع قولة انحاس

11 ḥina jinūd iḥsēn wiḥsēn minna
imn al-xalīj la wara bāb miknās

11 حنا جنود حسين وحسين منّا
من الخليج لورا باب مكناس

12 ya-l-ʿabdallī zē iš-šintiyān yitiṭanna
yidūs ʿa xiṣmi wihū xiṣim mindās

12 يا العبدلّي زي الشنتيان يتطنّى
يدوس ع خصمد وهو خصم منداس

13 maṭrūdkū fī ʿīšti mā tihanna
ū-ṭarādkū bēn il-maxalīg miḥtās

13 مطرودكم في عيشتد ما تهنّى
وطرادكم بين المخاليق محتاس

14 gōlit ʿalēhum ʿendakū mā tiwanna
ū-migyāskū nāyif ʿala kull migyās

15 as-sabaʿ yagẓī lāżmi law mitanna
ū-midxili ʿallā ʿend mazarīg al-injās

16 yōm il-mahabba jat minnak ū-minna
hāda karam mi-rabbna miš min-in-nās

14 قولة عليهم عندكم ما تونّى
ومقياسكم نايف على كلّ مقياس

15 السبع يقضي لازمه لو مثنّى
ومدخله عاللّه عند مزاريق الانجاس

16 يوم المحبّة جت منك ومنّا
هذا كرم من ربّنا مش من الناس

1.7

Drought

A Poem of Anger

Few things distress the bedouin more than drought. Despite frequent droughts, a natural desert phenomenon, the bedouin, whose livelihoods depend on pasture for their livestock, live in constant anticipation of a year of rainfall. When drought strikes, however, and the livestock dwindles for lack of fresh pasture, the bedouin demand aid from two sources they otherwise avoid—the government and the chiefs; yet, if that aid is not forthcoming, a bedouin feels deprived and cheated. Thus, when the Jabal Rāḥa area of south-west Sinai suffered from drought in the late 1950s and early 1960s, Jāzī Imsallam Ḥamd al-ʿArādī, of the Tarābīn Ḥasāblah, vented his anger in the following poem.

The land our tribe pastures in hit us with drought,
Leaving there nothing to gain; 1

With her stick she beat us till we up and got out,
Concerned lest the strength of our swift camels wane. 2

But now that we've left she won't let us back;
With drought every year she mounts her attack. 3

Poem 1.7 was heard recited by Sulēmān Ḥamd al-ʿArādī of the Tarābīn Ḥasāblah tribe, at el-ʿArīsh, 30 October 1972.

And our chiefs don't aid us despite all their 'ins',
While the flour gets dear and our livestock grows thin. 4

O Lord, O Compassionate, look at our luck;
What's a poor soul to do when misfortune has struck? 5

We appealed to the Sultan[1] for aid: no effect;
Our fodder got lost on the way through neglect. 6

Were we not down and out we'd surely rebel;
Asking aid from a peasant had served us as well.[2] 7

1 ad-dīri allī bal-maḥal ʿaḏḏabatna
walla nʿaggib minha ṣamīli

1 الديرة اللي بالمحل عذّبتنا
ولا نعقّب منها صميلة

2 šaddat ʿalēna bakūrha waḏhabatna
ḥawf aḏ-ḏalūl illī milīḥin dimīli

2 شدّت علينا باكورها واذهبتنا
حوف الذلول اللي مليحٍ ذميلة

3 bil-awwal jafēnāha ū-tālī jafatna
šaddat ʿalēna bas-snīn al-maḥīli

3 بالاوّل جفيناها وتالي جفتنا
شدّت علينا بالسنين المحيلة

4 walla-š-šuyūx ibi-rāyha dabbaratna
wal-ʿēš ġālī wal-mawāšī hizīli

4 ولّا الشيوخ برايها دبّرتنا
والعيش غالي والمواشي هزيلة

5 ya rabb ya raḥmān tunẓur baxatna
wēš ḥīlt il-miskīn yōmin tijī li

5 يا ربّ يا رحمان تنظر بختنا
وايش حيلة المسكين يومٍ تجي لة

6 maʿīnt as-silṭān fi maḥkamatna
nāmū ʿalēha jāyibīn an-nafīli

6 معينة السلطان في محكمتنا
نامو عليها جايبين النفيلة

7 waḷḷāhī law la-l-gill mā ṭawwaʿatna
inṭānb il-fallāḥ naṭlab jamīli

7 واللّهِ لو لا القلّ ما طوّعتنا
نطانب الفلّاح نطلب جميلة

[1] The bedouin poet refers here to government as 'the Sultan', although, when the poem was composed, Egypt had long ceased to be ruled by a sultan.

[2] As bedouin in Egypt despise the Egyptian peasant, or *fallāḥ* (commonly, fellah), they cannot conceive of any benefit deriving from peasants; nor would they deign to ask them for aid or protection. This line is thus an insulting reference to the helplessness of the chiefs and the government.

1.8

Disappointed Expectations

A Poem of Anger

Until the camel gave way to the motor vehicle in the inter-war period of the twentieth century, members of an Arabian tribe, the ʿAgēl, were the main camel merchants of the Middle Eastern deserts. They moved about the area buying camels from bedouin in Arabia and elsewhere and selling them in the markets of the chief cities, such as Cairo, Gaza, Damascus, and Baghdad.[1] The ʿAgēl depended for lodging and provisions in each place on the local bedouin, who were interested in their commercial transactions and welfare. When the ʿAgēl had finished their commerce each year and were returning to their native land, they expected to find odd jobs in their line of work among the various bedouin tribes, digging and cleaning cisterns and wells.[2] After the First World War, however, a group of ʿAgēl passing through Beersheba and its district found neither work nor hospitality in the bedouin tents, and, on leaving the area, one of their number composed a poem to express his anger and disappointment.

We came to Beersheba; may a drought strike the town
And a star-wrought quake bring her tall buildings down![3] 1

Their guest-tents are tiny and give no repose;
Their guest-tents seem burdened with worry and woes.[4] 2

Bin Sudēs and his friends found no work to do
And Bin Khalaf wished coffee that no one would brew. 3

Poem 1.8, which is anonymous, was heard recited by Muṣliḥ Ibn ʿÂmr of the Tiyāhā Ṣgērāt tribe, in Wādī Munbaṭaḥ, 15 June 1972.

[1] For more on the ʿAgēl, see Doughty, i. 49 ff.

[2] In the Negev, the term "Agēlī workmanship' (*shughl ʿAgēl*) became proverbial for good workmanship. Apparently their expert work at digging wells also prepared the ʿAgēl for the task of destroying them—a task delegated to them in the First World War by T. E. Lawrence (see *Seven Pillars*, p. 244).

[3] In the Arabic text only 'star' is mentioned, but, according to Swēlim Sulēmān Abū Biliyya, the reference was to an earthquake caused by a star. Although the buildings of Beersheba were rarely more than two storeys when this poem was composed, a tent-dwelling bedouin would have thought them tall.

[4] Hospitality is meant to enable a guest to relax, mentally and physically, and feel that he is no burden on the host. In the Beersheba area, according to the poet, such repose was impossible.

If your luck is outstanding, you might get one cup
But you'd better not blink or ever look up; 4

Even their barley-bread[5]—half bran and dry—
For the same loaf the children and ninety dogs vie. 5

We came to Beersheba; may a drought strike the town
And a star-wrought quake bring her tall buildings down! 6

1 jīna-s-saba' rayti bal-amḥāl ū-najmi̲n̲ iyḥaddir ma-'tala min mabanī	جينـــا السبع ريتـــد بالامحـــال ونجم„ يحدّر مـا اعتلى مـن مبانيـد 1
2 law jīt šigg ibwēthum mi-l-hamm taktāl talga šigg ibwēthum al-hamm walī	لو جيت شقّ بويتـهم من الـهمّ تكتال تلقـى شقّ بويتهم الـهـمّ واليـد 2
3 ibn sudēs ū-raba'ti ma ligi-šġāl wibn xalaf ma ligī min yigahwī	ابن سديس وربعتد ما لقي اشغال وابن خلف مـا لقي من يقهويد 3
4 win kān ḥaẓẓak jiydi̲n̲ jāk finjāl wila taḥwall 'awēntak wint tar'ī	وان كـان حظّـك جيّد„ جـاك فنجال ولا تحولّ عوينتـك وانت ترعيـد 4
5 win jābū lak riġīfi̲n̲ yābsi̲n̲ niṣfi inxāl tis'īn kalbi̲n̲ wiẓ-ẓa'afīn titlī	وان جابو لك رغيف„ يابس„ نصفد نخال تسعين كـلب„ والضعـافين تتليـد 5
6 ū-hāḏa as-saba' rayti bal-amḥāl ū-najmi̲n̲ iyḥaddir ma-'tala min mabanī	وهذا السبـع ريتـد بالامحال ونجم„ يحدّر مـا اعتلى مـن مبانيد 6

[5] The bedouin of the Negev were known to plant winter barley, which is more resistant to rainless months than wheat (see Bailey, 'Star-lore', p. 591). Hence, most of their bread was made from barley.

1.9

A Panther's Attack on the Flock

A Poem of Anger

Besides drought, occasional attacks on a flock by wolves or panthers (*Felix Pard*, found in southern Sinai) are the greatest hazard of raising livestock in the desert. These attacks are normally fatal and represent a great loss to the owner, livestock being his main source of sustenance. One such owner was Ṭu'ēmī Mūsā ad-Dagūnī of the Jabāliyya Awlād-Jundī tribe in the high mountains of southern Sinai. His usual grazing grounds having suffered from a lack of rain, he found alternative pasture in Jabal Ghadīr, where he and his family remained for thirty-seven days before they moved back to Wādī 'Aliyyāt in Jabal Sirbāl.[1] There a panther attacked the flock one night, killing seventeen goats.

Reflecting upon the events that led to his misfortune, Ṭu'ēmī recalled that it was the shepherdesses who had urged the men to return to Jabal Sirbāl to meet there some shepherds of their liking. He remembered, too, that the lasses who remained in Jabal Ghadīr had cried with envy as his people left, while his own girls laughed—unaware that their seemingly successful intrigue would also bring them to tears in the end. The anger this aroused in Ṭu'ēmī impelled him to compose the following lines.

I rose and climbed a mountain dry, the green'ry there had still not shown; 1

So putting shoes to both my feet, I sought a spot where pasture'd grown. 2

When I came to high Ghadīr, that mountain thick with shrubbery lay; 3

So we broke camp, got under way, and stopped at Aṣbaḥ's tomb to pray.[2] 4

Poem 1.9 was heard recited by its author, near St Catherine's Monastery, 5 November 1978.

---

[1] Massive Jabal Sirbāl is immediately south of the Fīrān Oasis in southern Sinai. Smaller Jabal Ghadīr is approximately thirty kilometres to the east.

[2] Aṣbaḥ is a by-name for any beneficent or saintly person, dead or alive, including those to whose tombs bedouin make pilgrimage. Hence, although the specific tomb herein referred to was that of the poet's ancestor, Shēkh 'Awwād, it is referred to as the tomb of Aṣbaḥ. Bedouin use

Then in ʿAgīda,[3] second day, a camp site we'd select, 5

When some said: those who're camped nearby treat neighbours with respect. 6

Full thirty-seven days we stayed, a fact none would deny, 7

Until one night—'Let's leave this place,' our girls said on the sly. 8

This thought, sprung straight from women's minds, caught us menfolk unaware: 9

"ʿAliyyāt is full of flowers,' they said. 'Ghadīr is almost bare.' 10

They got their way and we packed off after we had slept. 11

Descending wadi our girls laughed, passing neighbour girls who wept. 12

Their own tears tarried till the day our flock of black-haired goats fell prey. 13

They'd led them to the panther's lair, where he had but to choose and slay; 14

Felling this, ignoring that, choosing but the really fat.[4] 15

Our girls thus lost us seventeen, while all the other goats just scat. 16

See our virgins how they cry? Their tears in thick succession flow. 17

this by-name, derived from the image of 'morning' (*ṣubiḥ, ṣabāḥ*) for a beneficent person, because the early morning is thought of as moist, owing to the desert's dew. A beneficent person is also often depicted as 'having a moist face' (*wijhih aṣbaḥ*) or 'a green face' (*wijhih akhḍar*)—green alluding to succulent spring pasture—as moisture in the dry desert is seen as goodness. By contrast, a miser, or someone devoid of means, may be depicted as 'having a dry face' (*wijhih yābis*) or 'grey skin' (*ashhab al-jild*).

[3] A wadi in Jabal Ghadīr.

[4] The allusion to 'fat' goats derives from the term 'a raider's goat' (*shāt al-ghayyār*) in the Arabic text. The reference is to goats 'stolen' from another's flock in order to entertain a guest. In bedouin law, this type of theft is permitted if one's own flock is inaccessible at the time a guest appears. The bereft herdsman is entitled to compensation, but must give the 'thief' a reprieve of fourteen or forty days (depending on local custom) in which to pay it. For more on this custom, called 'aggression' (*ʿadāya*), see al-ʿĀrif, *al-Qaḍā*, pp. 109–12.

Ask them: 'Why this crying, girls? Life's full of ups and downs, you know. 18

Yes! Tell us why you're crying, girls. That butcher's skill inspires awe! 19

Accepting all the goats you brought, like wood for a carpenter's saw.' 20

قمت طلعت الجبل اليابس ما يطاد الخضار 1
1 gumt ṭala'ʿt al-jabal al-yābis ma yaṭā al-xaẓār

حطّيت نعالي في رجلي ماشي لرعي دوّار 2
2 ḥaṭṭēt inʿālī fī rijlī māšī lir-riʿī dawwār

نزلت على جبل غدير ولاد مطلّق بالاشجار 3
3 nizilt ʿala jabal ġadīr walā imṭallag bi-l-išjār

جينا شلنا عربنا عل اصبح حطّينا زوّار 4
4 jīna šilna ʿarabna ʿal aṣbaḥ ḥaṭṭēna zawwār

ثاني يوم في العقيدة وصرنا نتشاور في الدار 5
5 ṯānī yōm fi-l-ʿigīdi ū-sirna nitišāwar fa-d-dār

قالو ننزل عالعرب وعريبة زينة بالمقدار 6
6 gālū ninzil ʿāl-ʿarab wa-ʿaraybi zēni bil-migdār

قعدنا سبع وثلاثين في الحقيقة ما فيه انكار 7
7 gaʿadna sabʿ ū-ṯalaṯīn fil-ḥagīgi ma fi-nkār

ليلة قالن غير نشيل لزّهن الراي المكّار 8
8 lēli gālin ġēr inšīl lazzhin ar-rāy al-makkār

راي ينبع لحريم وكلّهم عدمين الاشوار 9
9 rāy yinbiʿ li-ḥarīm ū-kullhum ʿadmīn il-išwār

قالو كيف نقعد في غدير عليات مفقّعة النوّار 10
10 gālū kēf nugʿud fī ġadīr ʿaliyyāt imfagʿat an-nuwwār

حكّمو الراى وشالو الصبح مع طلوع النهار 11
11 ḥakkamu-r-rāy ū-šālū aṣ-ṣubḥ maʿ ṭulūʿ an-nahār

فاتن طنيباتهن يبكن وكتّن عليهن قرقار 12
12 fātin ṭanībāthin yibkin ū-kattin ʿalēhin girgār

إثراة بكاهن متأخّر يوم العزل في السمار 13
13 iṯrāt ibkāhin mitwaxxar yōm il-ʿazl fa-s-samār

للنمر ودّن معزاهن وصار في وسطهن مختار 14
14 lin-nimr waddan miʿzāhin wi-ṣār fī wasaṭhin muxtar

يزقح هذا ويقرط ذيك ينقّي غير شاة الغيّار 15
15 yizgaḥ hāḏa ū-yugruṭ ḏīk yinaggī ġēr šāt al-ġayyār

فقايدهن سبعة عشر ومخلّي بقيتهن فرار 16
16 fagāyidhin sabʿat ʿašr wi-mxallī bagiythin farār

ولا العذارى بتبكي بالدمع اللي ينزل حدّار 17
17 ū-lā al-ʿaḏāra ibtibkī bid-dimʿi-llī yinzil ḥaddār

قلت : عليش بتبكن يا بنات ما هذي الدنيا دوار دوار 18
18 gult ʿalēš ibtibkin yā banāt ma hāḏi-d-dinya-dwār idwār

عليش بتبكن يا بنات كود ما عجبكن دوس الجزّار 19
19 ʿalēš ibtibkin yā banāt kōd ma ʿajabkin dōs ij-jizzār

يوم تسلّم غنمكن خشب تسلّمه النجّار 20
20 yōm tisallam ġanamkin xašab tisallimi-n-najjār.

1.10

Tragedy and Misfortune

A Poem of Despair

This is the poem of a bedouin who accepted a challenge to his honour and lost everything. The man, newly wed and of good stock, had his reputation for courage challenged when a rival dared him to camp with all his herd and household alone in Ṣaʿāfīg, a no man's land between their tribe and its enemies. His pride did not permit him to ignore such a challenge, and he migrated to Ṣaʿāfīg, taking with him his large black tent, his herd of camels, his thoroughbred mare, his wife, a shepherd, and a black slave. After the bedouin had been camping in Ṣaʿāfīg for about ten days, the enemy raided while he was away hunting. Upon his return he found his camels, his mare, and his shepherd gone. He also found his wife dead, killed by his own slave, who, thinking his master had been murdered by the raiders, attempted to violate her. The bedouin thereupon shot his slave.

In utter despair he then left all his possessions behind, including his tent, and began travelling on foot until he came to a large bedouin camp, where he sought refuge in the main tent, the tent belonging to the chief. There he remained for thirty or forty days (i.e. longer than the three and a third days allowed by custom) without divulging his story; and, since he was obviously not a beggar, his hosts refrained from questioning him. Finally, however, his torment gave rise to the present poem, which he sang one night to the minor strains of a *rabāba*-violin that he had taken down from the centre pole of the tent where it customarily hung.

Judging from the name Ṣaʿāfīg, the events that led to the poem took place in north-central Arabia, near the mountains called Jabal Mismā, at a place passed in 1915 by the Czech explorer, Alois Musil, who called it Umm Ṣaʿāfīg.[1] As reported by Musil, the Mismā range was a no man's land between the traditionally hostile S͟hammar and ʿAnēza tribal confederations to the east and west.[2] It is also likely that the author of

Poem 1.10 was heard recited by Muṣliḥ Ibn ʿĀmr of the Tiyāhā Ṣgērāt tribe, in Wādī Munbaṭaḥ, 18 October 1971; Mūsā al-ʿAṭāwna of the Tiyāhā Nutūsh tribe, at Bīr as-Sgātī, 15 December 1971; and Maḥmūd Muḥammad Abū Badr of the Ṣāniʿ section of the Tiyāhā Gdērāt tribe, at Tell ʿArād, 20 February 1972. The present version is as related by Muṣliḥ Ibn ʿĀmr, with the addition of lines 7, 20, 22, which were part of the poem as recited by Mūsā al-ʿAṭāwna. The story behind the poem, as related by Muṣliḥ Ibn ʿĀmr, may be found verbatim with translation in Bailey, 'Narrative', pp. 86–101; the text of the poem has been corrected for the present rendition.

[1] Musil, *Negd*, pp. 138 ff.

[2] Ibid. 118.

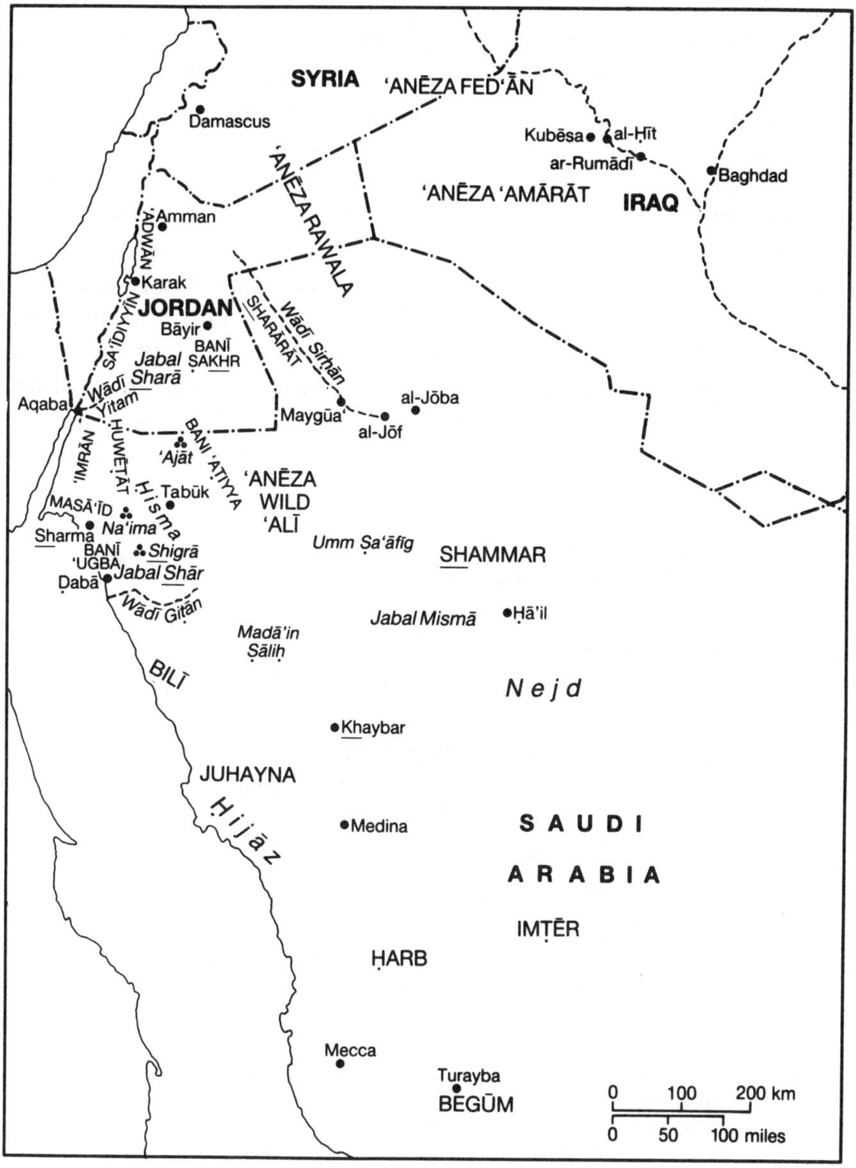

MAP 3. Places and the Nineteenth-century position of some Bedouin Tribal Confederations in Arabia and the Fertile Crescent.

the poem belonged to one of the Shammar tribes since Ṣaʿāfīg lies slightly to the north-west of the Mismā, closer to the lands of the ʿAnēza. When Charles Doughty, in the company of ʿAnēzī guides, crossed that same area in 1877 and found there a lone 'family of Shammar faring in the immense solitudes', he observed that 'doubtless, seeing us, they had felt a cold dread in their loins . . . They watched us ride by them with inquiet looks, for there is no amity between ʿAnēza and Shammar.'[3]

The poet begins with two lines of emotional experience followed by seven lines lamenting his lost tent and the hospitality it once afforded. The next six lines describe the highborn kinsmen from whom he is separated, and their admirable qualities: generosity, light-heartedness, geniality, love of adventure, and bravery. Two lines lament his lost camels and four his missing mare; the last line expresses his despair.

I crossed lofty and jaggy peaks,
  O heart rent with longing, 1

And tears that deluge me,
  For anguish and for what my soul yearns. 2

I sigh for my tent pitched in far Ṣaʿāfīg,
  For fine silken carpets in its sitting space;[4] 3

For four Qurēshī coffee-pots tall as cranes,[5]
  Holding drink pure as rain trapped in a jug, 4

With their spices from India out in the east
  From Ṣanʿa they come, from burning climes,[6] 5

[3] Doughty, i. 622.

[4] A bedouin tent is divided into two main sections separated by a woven curtain, called a *maʿnad* (lit. 'the side'). One section, where the men sit, is called *mag̣ʿad* ('sitting place'), *shig̣g̣* ('section'), or, as in the present text, *rubʿa* ('quarter'). The other section, where the women cook and receive female guests, is called the *maḥarama*—'the place of the women' (*ḥarīm*, sing. *ḥurma*).

[5] *Qurēshiyyāt* may have been a designation for a type of coffee-pot made either in Mecca (hence Qurēshī—the name of the Prophet Muḥammad's clan) or elsewhere in the Ḥijāz region. This type of coffee-pot was characterized by its height and its thin neck, and is compared to a crane, a coastal fowl probably unknown to inland, desert people; it must have found its way into their poetry as a stock phrase or formulaic word that originated in poems composed by people living near the sea. In the Yemen a fowl called *gharnūg̣* (as in the Arabic text) has been identified as a Cattle Egret (communication from Prof. R. B. Serjeant, Cambridge University).

[6] The main spice used by bedouin in their coffee is cardamom (Ar. *hēl*), which originated in the Malabar district of southern India (*Encyclopaedia Britannica*, 11th edn., 'Cardamom'). The

Conveyed under sail on the treacherous sea,
Pushed by the sweep of the wind on the deep. 6

What joy to the taste is that cup rightly spiced,
As the scent fills your nostrils the second you sip; 7

Or that broad wooden bowl[7] once flowing with ghee[8]
For desert travellers and the men of our camp.[9] 8

How delicious the meat of those fat-limbed lambs,
Where men get together and guests know no want. 9

If ninety chiefs had we, none would ask me to leave;
All to me are first cousins—full brothers, indeed.[10] 10

How fine these my brethren, who camp near the highway,[11]
Lovers of joy, ever cheering their friends.[12] 11

reference to Ṣanʿa may be an allusion to Yemen, in general, where spices coming from India were often trans-shipped or sent on with caravans. The poet, in alluding to the Yemen, may also have confused spices with coffee, for the coffee drunk in Arabia since the late fifteenth century came from Yemen (Lane, *Manners*, p. 339).

[7] Bedouin eat out of a common wooden bowl called a *bāṭya* usually made of the wood of a desert tree, such as Pistacia atlantica (*buṭum*) or Tamarix aphylla (*ithl*). In this case, the bowl, called *jōziyya* in the Arabic text, seems to have been made from walnut wood (*jōz*), probably obtained from a settlement.

[8] The ghee referred to here is *samn*, the clarified butter made from goat's milk. Although *samn* is produced during the spring when the goats lactate freely, even small quantities require considerable amounts of milk for production. Then, preserved in solid form in goatskin bags throughout the year, it is the family's only source of oil. Thus its use is always considered a minor extravagance, and, when poured freely by a host, an act of great hospitality. In poetry, accordingly, this liberal use of *samn* appears as a symbol of generosity (cf. poems 1.4, 1.13, 2.12, and 6.7).

[9] A bedouin that provides sustenance to the indigent members of his camping unit, as well as to travellers, is noted for his generosity (cf. poem 5.5, l. 7).

[10] Here the poet, using hyperbole, reassures his host of his reputation with his leaders, who would treat him, not just as a first cousin but as a full brother (*shagīg*, lit. 'from the same slit' (*shagg*)). Paternal cousins (*awlād ʿamm*) are more important to bedouin than to non-tribal societies since they are mutually responsible for each other's defence. According to the tribal rule of consanguinity, however, a brother takes precedence over a cousin. A bedouin proverb says 'I and my brother will close ranks against my paternal cousin, but I and my cousin will fight the outsider' (*anā w-akhuwī ʿal ibn ʿammī, w-anā w-ibn ʿammī ʿal al-gharīb*).

[11] Camping near main routes is considered meritorious, indicating a willingness to receive and provide for guests despite the expense and drain upon one's limited resources. In the poetry, therefore, this choice of camping ground is another sign of generosity.

[12] It is part of the bedouin chivalric code to be light-hearted (lit. 'green-hearted' (*akhḍar al-galb*)); that is, being unconcerned about mundane matters and desirous for adventure and danger,

They follow a chief desirous of danger;
  Like feed to a pure-bred, he cannot forego it. 12

They'd raid for camels at wide mountain trails,
  Aware one would gain while another would lose. 13

You could hear their blood-thirsty gunshot ejecting,
  Blazing a path for the tribe to pass through. 14

Horse chases horse in that hour of fray,
  Spurred on, even wide-open deserts seem tight. 15

Woe for a small herd of camels I've lost,
  Tawny and white ones, whose whiteness shone bright; 16

Returning at night, foals scrambled to meet them:
  How fine the soft moan of the foals while they milk. 17

And woe my Kaḥīla-horse,[13] lengthy of limb,
  Whose belly was slim like a wolf on the prey, 18

Whose tail was like girls' hair tossed to tempt lovers,
  Her chest a broad doorway, perfect in shape.[14] 19

Were she stacked high with packs, and with other things hung,
  Even purebreds, though barebacked, she'd take on the run. 20

Her drink was the milk of bud-nibbling camels;
  Her fodder from pure grains of barley was made.[15] 21

as evidenced in the following four lines, especially l. 13 (cf. poem 4.20H, l. 7). Another aspect of the code is to cheer up one's companions, giving them a sense of worth and acceptability.

[13] *Al-kaḥīla* is one of the main strains of thoroughbred bedouin horses (see Burckhardt, i. 204 ff; and Blunt, pp. 437 ff.).

[14] In choosing a horse, bedouin look for three *broad* features: the chest (*ṣadr*), to hold air; the nostrils (*manākhīr*), to breathe easily; and the hoofs (*ḥawāfir*), to run in the sand. Three essential *long* parts of the body are the legs (*gawāyim*) for speed; the neck (*ragaba*) for easy breathing; and the ears (*adhān*) for beauty. Three *short* parts necessary in a fine horse are the back (*ẓahr*) for strength in carrying a rider; the ankle (*gīn*) so that it does not stumble; and the root (*'aṣīb*) of the tail, which must 'hold the tail beautifully high' (*yishawwil*). (Oral communication from Mūsā al-'Aṭāwna.)

[15] Camels are noted for nibbling on the buds (*'ilif*) of the acacia trees, straight from the branch, and their milk is considered particularly salubrious for horses; as is barley, which can be grown in desert areas, requiring only 150 millimetres of rain.

I slap my cheeks and clap my hands[16]
In despair, O men, for all that's befallen. 16

1 ana ʿaddēt rūs imšamrixāt iš-šawahīg
allā min galbin tišagga bi-šīgī

2 ya dmūʿ ʿaynī ġawraganni ġawarīg
ʿala mirād an-nafs wa-yabs rīgī

3 ya-llā min bētin binī biṣ-ṣaʿafīg
bi-rubʿati firš al-ḥarīr ar-ritīgī

4 warbaʿ gurēšiyyāt mitl-al-ġaranīg
šarābhin ṣāfi-l-maṭar fi-l-birīgī

5 wi-bhārhin min dīrit al-hind tišrīg
yijīk min ṣanʿa al-yamm al-ḥarīgī

6 yijīk ib-sufun al-bḥūr al-ġawarīg
sawwāghin zajr al-hawa maʿ al-ġamīgī

7 ya ma-ḥala šurb il-imbahhar ʿala rīg
tukruf bi-xašmak rīḥti gabl ma dīgī

8 ū-jōziytin yiddifig ibha is-samn tadfīg
min šan haššāl al-xala wal-farīgī

9 ya ḥilū dabḥ imhazzaʿāt al-maʿalīg
bi-rubʿat-illī biẓ-ẓayf mā yiẓīgī

10 ū-tisʿīn šēxin ma daʿū bat-tafarīg
hāda walad ʿammī ū-hāda šagīgī

11 ya ḥilū xuwwa ẓarbīn aṭ-ṭawarīg
xuẓra-l-gulūb imdalhīn ar-rafīgī

1 انا عدّيت رؤوس مشمرخات الشواهيق
اللّد من قلبٍ تشقّى بشيق

2 يا دموع عيني غورقنّي غواريق
على مراد النفس ويبس ريقي

3 يا اللّد من بيتٍ بني بالصعافيق
بربعتد فرش الحرير الرتيق

4 واربع قريشيّات مثل الغرانيق
شرابهن صافي المطر في البريق

5 وبهارهن من ديرة الهند تشريق
يجيك من صنعة اليمّ الحريق

6 يجيك بسفن البحور الغواريق
سوّاقهن زجر الهوا مع الغميق

7 يا ما حلى شرب المبهّر على ريق
تكرف بخشمك ريحته قبل ما ذيق

8 وجوزيّةٍ يدّفق بها السمن تدفيق
من شان هشّال الخلا والفريق

9 يا حلو ذبح مهزّعات المعاليق
بربعة اللي بالضيف ما يضيق

10 وتسعين شيخٍ ما دعو بالتفاريق
هذا ولد عمّي وهذا شقيقي

11 يا حلو خوّة ضاربين الطواريق
خضرا القلوب مدلّهين الرفيق

[16] Gestures of grief and despair, repeated alternately.

12 yitlawn šēxin ẓaryin lal-hadalīg
wal-ḥurr lin ḏāg al-ʿalaf mā yilīgī

12 يتلون شيخٍ ضاريٍ للهداليق
والحرّ لن ذاق العلف ما يليقِ

13 ġārū ʿal al-bil maʿ fijūj aṭ-ṭawārīg
ḥadin kisib wi-ḥadin imni-n-nās ʿīgī

13 غارو عل البل مع فجوج الطواريق
احدٍ كسب واحدٍ من الناس عيقِ

14 tismaʿ al-ʿaṭšān aṯ-ṯalāṯī tarašīg
nabġi-nsawwī lal-ʿašāyir ṭarīgī

14 تسمع العطشان الثلاثي تراشيق
نبغي نسوّي للعشاير طريقِ

15 wil-xēl tanḥa-l-xēl fī saʿat aẓ-ẓīg
yōm lizzha wisʿ al-xala lal-maẓīgī

15 والخيل تنحى الخيل في ساعة الضيق
يوم لزّها وسع الخلا للمضيقِ

16 aḷḷa ʿala šaršūḥ ḏōdin mišafīg
šugrun ū-wuẓḥin min bayāẓhin lihīgī

16 اللّد على شرشوح ذودٍ مشافيق
شقرٌ ووضحٍ من بياضهن لهيقِ

17 win ʿaṭafan ḥīrānhin ʿal-malaḥīg
ma-ḥsan raṭīn al-xilf min ʿugib fīgī

17 وان عطفن حيرانهن عالملاحيق
ما احسن رطين الخلف من عقب فيقِ

18 il-wā ʿal-kiḥīla min ṭiwāl as-samaḥīg
gabbha ẓāmir itgūl ḏībin imwēygī

18 الواد عالكحيلة من طوال السماحيق
قبّها ضامر تقول ذيبٍ مويّقِ

19 aḏ-ḏēl rās imʿaḏbāt al-ʿašašīg
waṣ-ṣadr bāb ū-wāfyin bal-liḥīgī

19 الذيل راس معذّبات العشاشيق
والصدر باب ووافيٍ باللحيقِ

20 wilaw ṣammaṭū sumūṭha wit-taʿalīg
tumrug ʿala jurd al-aṣāyil marīgī

20 ولو سمّطو سموطها والتعاليق
تمرق على جرد الاصايل مريقِ

21 šurbha ḥalīb imgaṭfāt iz-zabanīg
ū-ḥabb iš-šaʿīr imṣaḥṣaḥin liha ʿalīgī

21 شربها حليب مقطّفات الزبانيق
وحبّ الشعير مصحصحٍ لها عليقِ

22 aẓrub ʿal al-xaddēn w-aṣaffig taṣafīg
mi-llī jarāy ya nās wi-yabs ar-rīgī

22 أضرب عل الخدّين واصفّق تصافيق
من اللي جراي يا ناس ويبس الريقِ

1.11

The Visit to a Brother in Jail

A Poem of Despair

The brother of Ṣabāḥ Ṣāliḥ al-G͟hānim of the ʿAgēlī tribe of north-west Sinai was imprisoned in Egypt in the 1960s for smuggling. Shortly after his internment, Ṣabāḥ visited him and fell into despair. Among bedouin, imprisonment is not a social stigma; yet it is an uncommon hardship since they are accustomed to more freedom than settled people. On his way back to the tribe, Ṣabāḥ's despair at his brother's condition gave rise to the present poem, in which he imagines himself taking the prison by force and freeing the inmates, before he reverts to the customary fatalism in the last two lines.

Last night how I moaned when the pain became tight
  And my eyes kept declining sleep's sweet delight;[1] 1

From the hour the evening sun slunk behind clouds,
  Sleeplessness stayed till the first morning light. 2

And for three days unable to swallow a bite,[2]
  My spit went salt and my gums turned white.[3] 3

Entering the gate of the jail when I came,
  He was there with his mates dressed in garments of shame.[4] 4

How I wished I had fighters, a million or more,
  All of them trained, with spears in their hands; 5

How I wished I had fighters, a million or more,
  Mounted on horseback with arms in their hands.[5] 6

Poem 1.11 was heard recited by its author, at Rabʿa oasis, 24 October 1970.

---

[1] Moaning and sleeplessness are two conventional themes often used to introduce a poem of emotion (cf. Serjeant, p. 11; Ingham, p. 66).

[2] Not eating for 'three' days is a standard image in poems of emotion (cf. poems 1.15 and 4.10).

[3] Bedouin believe that the drying of the spittle (*yabs ar-rīg*) accompanies anger and fear. White gums, though normally resulting from a dry mouth, are not alluded to in the Arabic text.

[4] Being both traditional and ethnocentric, bedouin consider any form of dress other than their own disgraceful, expecially prison garb.

[5] This repetition is similar to the ancient Semitic poetic device of repetitive parallelism. In the Arabic text, the final words of the successive lines—'spears' (*rimāḥ*) and 'arms' (*silāḥ*)—rhyme,

How good to have headed a raid on that jail
And with news they were free, the brave souls hail! 7

When I came through the gate, and my brother beheld,
My tears were so copious, they could have filled bowls. 8

Then sitting to talk, not a moment had passed,
When they said, 'That's all, guys! Your time's up. So let's go!' 9

The sigh I heaved when I rose was a blast
Breaking mountains to flintstones, just from the 'Woe!' 10

But that's life, O camelmen, heading for home;[6]
My clansmen, who breed a pure-white riding-mare.[7] 11

I'll just pray for 'the Beauty' and finish my poem:
That's Muḥammad, whose coming has taught us to fare.[8] 12

1 al-beriḥa min ẓīgit il-wajid wannēt
ū-'ayyit 'iyūnī l-ad̲ūg al-marāḥī

2 min yōm šams al-'aṣr fi-l-ġayn tagēt
ẓallat sahāra yōm lāḥ aṣ-ṣabāḥī

3 ū-layya t̲alāt̲ ayyām 'an iz-zād 'ayyēt
baḥiss rīgī fi jid̲ūmī malāḥī

1 البارحة من ضيقة الوجد ونّيت
وعيّت عيوني لاذوق المراحِ

2 من يوم شمس العصر في الغين تقيت
ظلّت سهارة يوم لاح الصباحِ

3 ولي ثلاث ايّام عن الزاد عيّيت
باحسّ ريقي في جذومي ملاحِ

thus lending themselves to the construction of a parallelism. For other examples, see poems 1.15, 3.7, 4.20B, 4.20C, 4.20H, 5.12.

[6] Here, the expression 'going home' (*'āmd al-bēt*) is an adaptation of the more regular 'going to Mecca'—that being 'the first house' (*awwal bēt*).

[7] Many bedouin prize a white camel, called *awḍaḥ* (fem. *waḍḥā*), over camels of other colours (see Musil, *Manners*, p. 334). Poem 2.12, l. 14, indicates that this preference is not unanimous.

[8] Ending a poem with a blessing for the Prophet, Muḥammad, is common in bedouin poetry (cf. Serjeant, p. 6, for the usage in southern Arabia). As part of this blessing, a particular quality of the Prophet is generally evoked, chosen either for its connection with the overall theme of the poem (e.g. poems 2.11, 4.4), or because it fits into the rhyme-scheme of the poem (as in the present case—*falāḥ*). 'The Beauty' mentioned in l. 12a (*az-zēn* in the Arabic text) is again Muḥammad, who is often referred to by this epithet in blessings, as a substitute for the word 'prophet' (*nabī*).

4 yōm jīt yamm is-sijn wi-ʿal-bāb laffēt šufti maʿ-ṭ-ṭābūr labsi afẓāḥī	4 يوم جيت يمّ السجن وعالباب لفّيت شفته مع الطابور لبسه فضاحِ
5 ū-malyūn fī malyūn ʿizwi taḥarrēt wi-mʿallamīn ū-māskīn ar-rmāḥī	5 ومليون في مليون عزوة تحرّيت ومعلّمين وماسكين الرماحِ
6 malyūn fī malyūn ʿizwi taḥarrēt ʿa-ẓuhūr xēl ū-māskīn is-slāḥī	6 مليون في مليون عزوة تحرّيت ع ظهور خيل وماسكين السلاحِ
7 ma kān ana bal-gōm ʿas-sijn haddēt waʿṭēt an-našāma yibišrū bar-rwāḥī	7 ما كان انا بالقوم عالسجن هدّيت واعطيت النشامة يبشرو بالرواحِ
8 ū-lamma daxalt al-bāb laxūwī lagēt min damaʿ ʿaynī tišrabū bil-gadāḥī	8 ولمّا دخلت الباب لاخوّي لقيت من دمع عيني تشربو بالقداحِ
9 gaʿadt anī wiyyā walla tiwannēt dirja ū-gālū yā našāma-r-rwāḥī	9 قعدت انا ويّاد ولّا تونّيت درجة وقالو يا نشامة الرواحِ
10 wannēt wanni yōm ana gumt wagfēt inhadd al-jabal ṣārat iḥjāra igdāḥī	10 ونّيت ونّة يوم انا قمت واقفيت انهدّ الجبل صارت حجاره قداحِ
11 ū-yā rākbīn al-fīḥ ya ʿāmd al-bēt rabʿī ya hēl ir-rkāb al-awẓāḥī	11 ويا راكبين الفيح يا عامد البيت ربعي يا هيل الركاب الاوضاحِ
12 waxtim kalāmī ib-ṣalātī ʿal az-zēn wi-mḥammad illī jā-lna bal-falāḥī	12 واختم كلامي بصلاتي عل الزين ومحمّد اللي جا لنا بالفلاحِ

1.12

The Death of a Daughter

A Poem of Grief

ʿĪd Imfarrij Imsāʿid of the Tarābīn Ḥasāblah, a camel-herder and grindstone maker in the interior of southern Sinai, composed this, his first poem, after his small daughter had been fatally bitten by a snake. The sad poem relates the girl's dying, but the concluding line departs abruptly from the preceding emotional narrative, being a touch of macabre humour that helps us understand how fatalism may give a bedouin comfort and relief in the face of nature's adversity.

Though I asked you, O God, who can grant each request,
To lift every harm from upon us, 1

The fates came along and our dear dispossessed,[1]
And after the sweet gave us bitter to taste. 2

The fire of this grief my heart cleaves in two,
Draining my kidneys and liver.[2] 3

I had sent off my girl with hardly a thought,
Then behold: there she came, burning with fright, 4

And, as camels' teeth here are clenched so tight,
So mine, that night, as I sucked at her bite.[3] 5

Two brave men passed by and stopped to alight,
But brave though they were they wept at this sight. 6

Poem 1.12 was heard recited by its author at Sēl ar-Ruwēg on the ʿIjma plateau, 17 March 1971. The text of the poem contains corrections of a version that appears in Bailey, 'Religious Practices', p. 72.

---

[1] The term for 'fate' (lit. 'fates') in this poem from twentieth-century Sinai is *manāyā* (sing. *maniyya*)—lit. 'portion' or 'lot' (cf. Hebrew *manah*)—the same term with which bedouin defined death-bearing fate in pre-Islamic Arabia. The *manāyā* are conceived of as women. (See Ringgren, pp. 9–29).

[2] Bedouin believe that a man's strength comes from the liver, which digests food. 'Kidneys' here is hyperbole: i.e. grief is so strong that it drains not only the poet's liver (which would be natural), but his kidneys as well.

[3] Sucking the poison out of scorpion stings and mild snake bites is a traditional cure performed by persons specially endowed (sing. *ḥāwī*; lit. 'someone who deals with a snake' (*ḥayya*)).

Nights like these swell our burden already not light,
Like a judge who delivers his sentence slowly. 7

Well, what of it? We'll all meet with fate one night,
When the worms eat us all, and with appetite. 8

1 ṭalabtak ya rabb ya wisīʿ al-maṭalīb
tirfaʿ ʿanna jimīʿ al-balāwī

1 طلبتك يا ربّ يا وسّيع المطاليب
ترفع عنّا جميع البلاوي

2 jatna-l-manāya wa-šālat ġawalīna
wa-d̲awwagatna-l-murr ʿugb al-ḥalāwī

2 جتنا المنايا وشالت غوالينا
وذوّقتنا المرّ عقب الحلاوي

3 ya nārhum tišʿab al-galb tišʿīb
wi-tmuṣṣ al-kibid wiyya-l-kilāwī

3 يا نارهم تشعب القلب تشعيب
وتمصّ الكبد وايّا الكَلاوي

4 šayyʿat bintī bi-lid̲t il-xāṭir
wa-jatnī bintī bi-nārin tikāwī

4 شيّعت بنتي بلذّة الخاطر
وجتني بنتي بنارٍ تكاوي

5 unẓur ijmaylī šābik an-nāb
linnī had̲īk al-lēli sirt ḥāwī

5 انظر جميْلي شابك الناب
لنّي هذيك الليلة صرت حاوي

6 jawnī it̲nīn irjālin ṣanadīd
wil-kull minhum ʿendaha bad-dimaʿ dāwī

6 جوني اثنين رجالٍ صناديد
والكلّ منهم عندها بالدمع داوي

7 hēd̲i-l-liyālī ʿābyāt iʿbāna
mit̲il il-gāẓi-llī bi-ḥagga tilāwī

7 هيذي الليالي عابياتٍ عبانا
مثل القاضي اللي بحقّد تلاوي

8 lā budd inmūt wi-nzūr al-manāya
ū-yākil minna-d-dūd wakl-iš-šihāwī

8 لا بدّ نموت ونزور المنايا
وياكل منّا الدود وكل الشهاوي

1.13

The Death of a Brother

A Poem of Grief

When Jumʻa Imfarrij Imsāʻid died in early manhood and left no children, his brother, ʻĪd Imfarrij, buried him in the tribal burial-ground at ʻIdwit al-ʻAyn, an elevated ridge opposite the oasis ʻAyn Umm Aḥmad in south-east Sinai. After the burial, ʻĪd, sitting with his son, Farrāj, composed a short poem which expresses deep grief, tempered only by a deep acceptance of fate.

How deeply I've sighed over all sorts of pain,
But the heaviest sigh was the sigh today.[1] 1

I laid brother Jumʻa at ʻIdwit al-ʻAyn:
I'll never meet any like him again! 2

We cried, O my son, and we cried once more;
But this crying, my boy, what good is it for?[2] 3

The Lord returned Jumʻa to the Lord's own domain;[3]
Just took him. That's that! Our sorrow's in vain. 4.

1 ya wentī wannētha ʻa kull il-mawajīaʻ
wal-yōm wannētha wanni tagīli

1 يا ونّتي ونّيتها ع كلّ المواجيع
واليوم ونّيتها ونّة ثقيلة

2 ḥaṭṭēt jimʻi ʻala ʻidwit al-ʻayn min fōg
wi-yiḥrim ʻalayy ʻad ma-lga badīla

2 حطّيت جمعة على عدوة العين من فوق
ويحرم عليّ عاد ما القى بديله

3 bakēna ya-būwī tamma bakēna
wi-bkāna ya-būwī ma ʻaggab ṣamīla

3 بكينا يا ابويّ تمّا بكينا
وبكانا يا ابويّ ما عقّب صميلة

Poem 1.13 was heard recited by its author in Wādī Shbēḥa, 25 September 1971

---

[1] Sighing is one of the conventional themes in introducing a poem of emotion.

[2] This sentiment is reflected in the bedouin proverbs 'If death's come by, it won't help to cry' (*in fāt al-fawt, mā yinfaʻ aṣ-ṣawt*), and 'The grief of a multitude won't revive a decaying man's bones' (*kuthrit al-ḥazīn mā yaḥyā ʻaẓām ar-ramīm*).

[3] This line reflects the Muslim concept of God reclaiming (*istirjāʻ*) the souls of the dead, and derives from the Qur'ān (2. 156), 'We are Allah's and unto him we return.'

4 haḏa jim'i axaḏa rabba wa-'āda
waxaḏa wala bal-yadd ḥīli

٤ هذا جمعـــة اخذد ربّـــــد واعـــادد

واخـــــذد ولا باليـــــد حيلـــــة

1.14

The Death of a Beloved Husband

A Poem of Grief

The present poem expresses the grief of a woman in north-west Arabia after being told that her newly-wed husband had been killed while on a camel raid. The couple had been denied permission to marry for eight years when their secret love was discovered.[1] After the girl's parents finally relented and the couple were married, the young husband was killed leading a party of eighty warriors on a raiding expedition to plunder camels. Before arriving home, however, the raiding party agreed to tell his wife that he had merely been wounded and was recovering in a distant camp.

For two years the young widow waited for her husband's return, ever questioning passers-by for news, until someone finally informed her of the sad truth saying 'Ask recompense from God!' (*uṭulbī al-'awaḍ min allāh*), whereupon she composed the present poem of seventeen lines. The metre, although irregular, has seven accentuated feet to a line, and is called a *hijēnī*, considered to be composed to the rhythm of a *hijn*, or riding camel. Poems of this scansion were popular among women poets, who are said to have composed their poems sitting in a camel-litter, while migrating.

The first line is an expression of a deep emotional experience (that has removed the girl, figuratively, out of her normal frame of mind) followed by four lines of confusion between bitter grief and guilt over

Poem 1.14 was heard recited by Muṣliḥ Ibn 'Āmr of the Ṭiyāhā Ṣgērāt tribe, in Wādī Munbaṭaḥ, 18 October 1971. The story behind this poem may be found verbatim with translation in Bailey, 'Narrative', pp. 80–5; the text of the poem has been corrected for the present rendition.

---

[1] While not unknown in bedouin society, pre-marital romantic alliances are discouraged as an obstacle to rational marriages that are contracted primarily in the interests of the respective families. Therefore, it is not unlikely that the parents punished the young couple (as related by the reciter of this poem) to retain their social respectability; nor that the girl remained unmarried for eight years, especially if her reputation had made her an undesirable match.

not being able to accept her fate. The next ten lines review the ordeal she has undergone, with the final two lines a lyric longing for death.

I peer from atop a look-out hill,
  I look out from upon a lofty peak, 1

I beweep my lover,[2] so long gone,
  My tears pour forth like a cloudburst! 2

My heart with my friend is somewhere suspended,
  Yearning like a maid taken far from her home;[3] 3

Two years, yet the wound of our love hasn't healed—[4]
  So forgive me, Receiver of penance,[5] 4

Who arranges the fate[6] of each one in a book,
  But can't you just bring my love back?[4] 5

I thought: Here's my brave one upon a swift camel,
  The commander of riders, eighty in all; 6

'Urge on the mounts! Welcome and greetings!
  I have a friend; what news of him have you?' 7

[2] For the sake of propriety, the designation 'loved one' appears in the Arabic text in the plural (*aḥbāb*), in order to avoid the direct expression of a woman loving a specific man. Similarly, l. 5b refers to the 'heart's love' rather than a more direct 'my love'. For the same reason, female lovers may be alluded to in the masculine, as in poems 1.15, 2.1, 2.6, and 4.10.

[3] Feelings of intimacy and security are so integral a part of belonging to a bedouin family that an abducted girl (as stated in the Arabic text), or even one who has been married off into a distant family and removed from her familiar environment, would suffer from nostalgia and insecurity.

[4] ll. 4 and 5 are a classic expression of the tension felt by a Muslim between the need to accept fate as predetermined by Allah and the individual's will to live life according to one's own desires. Thus, while God's omnipotence is acknowledged in this poem (l. 5a), the girl still expresses her desire to have her beloved back (l. 5b). Aware, however, that this desire in itself may be sinful, she asks merciful God, the 'Receiver of penance', for forgiveness in advance (l. 4b).

[5] God's reputation for mercy, as the 'Receiver of penance' (*g̣ābil at-tawba*), comes directly from the Qur'ān (9. 103, 41. 24).

[6] The term for fate in the Arabic text (*mag̣ādīr*, sing. *mig̣dār* ('measure'), while known to bedouin from the Qur'ān, dates back to their Arabian ancestors prior to Islam (see Ringgren, pp. 63–8).

They said: 'Ill is your friend, but well he will get;
Each thing takes exactly the time that is set.'[7] 8

O, if only my eyes could see my love,
And these other words were all untrue! 9

Then birds of the air passed by in formation,
Circling the peak over Jōba,[8] 10

A hawk out in front with the eagles behind,
I said: 'This time surely you'll bring me some word; 11

By God, O eagle, I would ask
About my friend. Where's he been?' 12

Replied the hawk: 'Your friend the snares of fate[9] have caught;
We do have news—that won't amuse you. 13

On your friend they've heaped the turf,
And o'er his gravestones[10] flung his cloak.' 14

I felt my heart pierced and hurt
As if stabbed in a broken breast. 15

My life just left, my time had come,[11]
My soul to God was beckoned home,[12] 16

[7] l. 8 is another expression of fatalism similar to the Classical Arabic proverb 'Events happen in their fixed time' (*al-'umūru marhūnatun bawqātihā*) (Lane, *Lexicon*, p. 1173).

[8] If we take the word al-Jōba as a place-name, it could either refer to al-Jōf (alternately al-Jōba), an oasis area in Wādī Sirḥān of north-central Arabia (mentioned as al-Ǧūba, by Musil, *Arabia Deserta, passim*), or to the Jōba depression along the Ḥijāz Railway line, north of Madā'in Ṣāliḥ (see Musil, *Northern Hegaz*, pp. 220 ff.). However, Jōba may also be taken as a common noun, a topographical term meaning 'deep basin' or 'valley', in which case, although the poem certainly originated in Arabia, we cannot determine its exact location.

[9] For more on 'the snares of fate' (*asbāb al-manāyā*) see Ch. 9; also cf. poems 1.1, n.6; 1.12, n.1.

[10] Gravestones appear here in the plural since bedouin mark their graves simply with two rough stones from the desert, one at the head of the grave and one at the foot. It is considered meritorious to leave the clothes of a deceased bedouin (who would be buried in a shroud) on his grave in anticipation that a poor person might find them.

[11] The concept that 'one's time has come' is expressed in the Arabic text as *bi-ajal wi-kitāb*, just as it was in pre-Islamic Arabia (see Ringgren, pp. 86–95).

[12] See poem 1.13, n.3.

So on to God I leave you, friends;
Take what's left of my life and enjoy it.[13] 17

1 ṭallēt ana ʿālī-l-mirgāb
ašraft min fōg mašḏūbi

1 طلّيت انا عالي المرقاب
اشرفت من فوق مشذوبة

2 abkī ṣaḥībī zimānin ġāb
damʿī šahalīl maṣbūba

2 ابكي صحيبي زمانٍ غاب
دمعي شهاليل مصبوبة

3 galbī tiʿallag maʿ al-aḥbāb
wajdī bihum wajd manhūbi

3 قلبي تعلّق مع الاحباب
وجدي بهم وجد منهوبة

4 ʿāmēn jaraḥ al-hawa mā ṭāb
ġufrāk yā gābil at-tawbi

4 عامين جرح الهوى ما طاب
غفرك يا قابل التوبة

5 yā man naẓẓamt al-magadīr bi-ktāb
rajjiʿ ʿal al-galb ḥabūbi

5 يا من نظّمت المقادير بكتاب
رجّع عل القلب حبوبه

6 linnī bi-nišmī ʿala mihḏāb
gāyid ṯamanīn manjūbi

6 لنّي بنشمي على مهذاب
قايد ثمانين منجوبة

7 kuzzu-l-maṭāya hala wi-tirḥāb
lē ṣāḥbin kēf tadrū bi

7 كزّو المطايا هلا وترحاب
لي صاحبٍ كيف تدرو به

8 gālū ṣaḥībak ʿalīl ū-ṭāb
kullin tabaʿ ar-rahin maktūbi

8 قالو صحيبك عليل وطاب
كلٍّ تبع الرهن مكتوبة

9 ū-yā lēt ʿaynī tara-l-aḥbāb
wat-tālya ʿilūm makḏūbi

9 ويا ليت عيني ترا الاحباب
والتالية علوم مكذوبة

10 marran iṭyūr il-hawa sirsāb
ḥāmin ʿala mirgib al-jōbi

10 مرّن طيور الهوا سرساب
حامن على مرقب الجوبة

[13] Alongside the popular belief that the period of one's life is predetermined, there exists a contrary concept that certain lives do not run their full course, and that the balance of that full course may be assigned to someone else. Thus, when condoling a bereaved person, one expresses the wish 'May what remains of the deceased's life be added to yours' (*al-bagiyya fī ʿumrak* or *ʿumrak al-bāgī*).

11 ṣagrin fi-l-awwal tilāh aʿgāb
gult al-xabar maʿak han-nōbi

11 صقرٍ في الاوّل تلاه عقاب
قلت الخبر معك هالنوبة

12 ballā ū-widd-asʿalak yā ʿagāb
ʿan ṣaḥbī wēn ġadō bi

12 باللّه وودّي اسألك يا عقاب
عن صاحبي وين غدو به

13 radd al-kibēdī ġada bi-sbāb
maʿina xabar mā tahannō bi

13 ردّ الكبيْدي غدى باسباب
معنا خبر ما تهنّو به

14 ṣaḥībak hālū ʿalē hit-trāb
ʿal an-nṣāyib ramaw ṯōba

14 صحيبك هالو عليه التراب
عل النصايب رمو ثوبه

15 ḥassayt galbī jiriḥ winṣāb
ṭaʿna ʿal al-jōf maʿṭūba

15 حسّيت قلبي جرح وانصاب
طعنة عل الجوف معطوبة

16 furiġit ḥayātī bajal wi-ktāb
wir-rūḥ li-llā maṭlūba

16 فرغت حياتي باجل وكتاب
والروح للّه مطلوبة

17 wan-awdaʿtkū li-llā ya-ḥbāb
wixḏūn ʿumrī tahannō bi.

17 وانا اودعتكم للّه يا احباب
وخذون عمري تهنّو به

1.15

A Girl Met at the Well

A Poem of Love

When the young Ḥamdān abū Salāma Abū Masʿūd of the Muzēna Darārma was herding camels near the well called Bīr aṣ-Ṣadr in south-west Sinai, some shepherdesses came to the well to water their flocks. As the pulley above the well was broken, Ḥamdān helped the girls draw water, during which he was smitten with love for one of them. Before he could make any advances, however, an Egyptian soldier posted nearby told them all to move on. The girls took their flocks

Poem 1.15 was heard recited by its author, at aṭ-Ṭūr, 31 March 1971 (when he was in his late fifties).

home and, perhaps frightened by the soldier, did not return to that well for some time. Ḥamdān's infatuation for the shepherdess in the meantime kept growing, nurtured daily by her absence. The result was the present poem, composed after a few days. Its desultory style and shifting views reflect the agitated excitement of one in love.

For three whole days I've not touched food,
  My liver's long been dry;[1] 1

My heart's been restless since she left,
  My soul just leaks away. 2

O tell the girl that herds the goats:[2]
  Bring back the trust you took; 3

O why'd she take my heart and go,
  This empty frame forsook? 4

Say: Even if the sergeant's vexed,
  I'll water all her flock, 5

I'll let the young kids drink up first,
  Till they take their fill. 6

And then I'll set a date with her—
  Late summer till it rains— 7

And I'll be patient, which is good;
  Her father's name not stain.[3] 8

[1] As bedouin consider the liver to be the organ that digests food (cf. poem 1.12, n.3), a person's well-being, gauged by his appetite, is thought, to be a function of the liver. Accordingly, when the liver has 'refused' (*ʿayyā*) to eat, one is 'sick' (*ʿayyān*, lit. 'refusing').

[2] As a matter of propriety, reference to the shepherdess in the Arabic text is in the masculine: *rāʿī al-amā'iz* ('the goatherd') (cf. poem 1.14, n.2). However, because the monorhyme at the end of each line of this poem is the Arabic suffix *hā*, which generally translates as 'her' or 'hers', the beloved is also referred to in the feminine.

[3] 'Patience is good' (*aṣ-ṣabr ṭayyib*) is a popular expression deriving from the Qur'ānic term 'beautiful patience' (*ṣabr jamīl*) (see poem 3.11, n. 26). The poet vows not to sully the reputation of his beloved's father by tempting her to dissolute behaviour.

Three sturdy camels has her dad,
That bear the load though far; 9

Her mother's like a Mauser shot,
Whose range is very far.[4] 10

My love is worth the mining men,
Their boss and what he owns; 11

She's even worth the station chief,
And all the land he's sown.[5] 12

She's worth the smugglers of hashish,
And soldiers running after:[6] 13

So if you like it, or you don't,
Though ugly, yet I'll have her, 14

Even if her tent's of rags,
Her dinner's filled with sand. 15

My clan are all Muzēna lads,
Who'd help me make a stand. 16

And I've a box that's stuffed with bills
And silver yet untold, 17

All guarded by a sergeant,
Wearing stripes that last, though old. 18

1 ṯalāṯt ayyām wana ṣāyim
wil-kibd imṭawwil ẓimāha

1 ثلاثة ايّام وانا صايم
والكبد مطوّل ظماها

2 ar-rūḥ fī jiṯṯatī tugṭur
galbī mā yuṣbur bilāha

2 الروح في جثّتي تقطر
قلبي ما يصبر بلاها

[4] Praise for the mother is intended to show that the girl comes of good stock (cf. poem 1.6, n. 7).

[5] The company referred to by the poet is the manganese mining company that operated at Umm Bujma in the mountains of south-west Sinai prior to 1967. The 'sown land' is the agricultural project undertaken in Wādī aṭ-Ṭūr in the early 1960s.

[6] For the prominence of hashish-smuggling as a subject in Sinai, see Ch. 6.

3 ma-tgūlū li-rāʿi-l-amāʿiz
yirudd al-amāna majrāha

3 ما تقولو لراعي الاماعز
يردّ الامانة مجراها

4 lē yāxiḏ galbī wiygōṭar
ū-ġēr il-jiṯṯa xallāha

4 ليد ياخذ قلبي ويقوطر
وغير الجثّة خلاّها

5 law yizʿal šōš al-ʿaskar
walla ġēr asgī maʿzāha

5 لو يزعل شوش العسكر
واللّه غير اسقي معزاها

6 waʿṭi-l-bahāyim tirawwī
lamma tāxiḏ hawāha

6 واعطي البهايم تروّي
لمّا تاخذ هواها

7 waʿṭīha wiʿda mafhūma
tāxiḏ gēẓiha wi-štāha

7 واعطيها وعدة مفهومة
تاخذ قيظها وشتاها

8 ū-buṣbur waṣ-ṣabr ṭayyib
karāma lillī rabbāha

8 وباصبر والصبر طيّب
كرامة للّي ربّاها

9 ṯalāṯa min zaml abūha
talḥag la ṭawwal mašḥāha

9 ثلاثة من زمل ابوها
تلحق لو طوّل مشحاها

10 amma zē dagg al-amānī
ṣāyib law yibʿid mirmāha

10 امّها زي دقّ الالماني
صايب لو يبعد مرماها

11 ibtiswī šuġlīn al-baṭīn
wiš-širka willī banāha

11 بتسوي شغلين البطين
والشركة واللي بناها

12 wibtiswi-mdīr al-maḥaṭṭa
ū-kull al-mazāriʿ tifdāha

12 وبتسوي مدير المحطّة
وكلّ المزارع تفداها

13 ū-tiswī naggalt il-ḥašīš
wal-ʿaskar illī warāha

13 وتسوي نقّالة الحشيش
والعسكر اللي وراها

14 ġaẓibtū walḷa riẓītū
law šēna galbī hawwāha

14 غضبتم ولاّ رضيتم
لو شينة قلبي هوّاها

15 law inha tiskin fī xayša
was-safī yamla ʿašāha

15 لو انّها تسكن في خيشة
والسفي يملا عشاها

16 wi-rabʿī ṣubyān imzēna
tafzaʿ yōm innī banxāha

17 ʿendī ṣandūg milyān warag
wil-fuẓẓa ma ḥasabnāha

18 lēha šawīš ʿa ktāfi rīš
dīma ma yanšaf ṯarāha

وربعـــــي صبيــــــان مزينــــــة 16
تفـــــزع يوم انّـــي بـــانخـــاهـــا

عـــندي صندوق مـــليــــــان ورق 17
والـــــفضّـــة مـــــا حسبنـــاهـــا

لـــهــــا شاويش ع كتافـــــه ريش 18
ديمـــا مـــا ينشف ثـــراهـــا

2
Poems of Communication

ELEGANCE BETWEEN UNLETTERED MEN

Illiterate cultures abound in rhymes which aid the memory in important specific areas of life, such as economics, law, and religion, as well as in everyday living. It is also not surprising to find rhymes in poems composed as missives, such as those in the present section, sent from one bedouin to another to threaten, complain, pacify, cajole, request, impart information, or share an emotion. Firstly, it is easy for an illiterate messenger from this society to remember the lines of a rhymed poem; he has heard rhymes all his life. Moreover, a bedouin message often contains more than bare information. It may convey certain subtleties and allusions (often the bulk of a composition) which can be more easily expressed in a poem than in a direct prose address.

Subtleties are introduced at the very outset of a poem. Most poems of communication begin with the poet hailing an imaginary rider and asking him to deliver a message. This standard opening is followed by a description of the (usually) thoroughbred camel that the messenger will be riding, and the trappings that adorn it. The recipient of the message is thus subtly informed that he is respected, being considered worthy to receive messages borne on such camels. Then, after a route is set out for the rider to guide him to his destination, the intended recipients of the poem and their kin are praised by recalling instances of their generosity, hospitality, honesty, bravery, prowess in battle, and the like. From poem 6.18, for example:

O Rider on one like an ostrich in flight,
  One whose forelegs require no fire to be right.

His mother's full udders three years went unbound,
  Nor has he been couched to lift loads off the ground.

Through the desert direct him o'er the peaks of Samār,
  Leaving Jebel Riḍāwī on the right not too far;

And the chalky white ridge circumvent on your left,
  Through badlands by hand lead him on, but with care.

You'll come to a camp where they greet with respect;
  No sheep-herder's flock do their fleshpots neglect.

Such sentiments may be applied to friend and foe alike in order to elicit the desired response. In either case, however, a bedouin's pride would restrain him from uttering such praises in a direct prose address or in conversation with the recipient.

Poetry is also of value to a bedouin, even in its mundane role as a missive, because hearing poetic diction elevates him; it introduces certain novelty into a largely monotonous and austere existence. Thus, we find messages conveyed in rhyme even in circumstances that require no subtleties. The first poem in this section, for example, was composed by a shepherd to thank his employer's son for not having killed him for kissing his sister. As both lads were sitting together over morning coffee, the shepherd could have conveyed his message in a few simple prose sentences. Yet he chose to express himself in verse, apparently to endow his words with worth.

The other poems in this chapter were actually sent as missives with a definite purpose; the variety of this selection of eleven poems indicates the important role of the poem-cum-missive in bedouin life. Poems 2.2 and 2.3 were composed as a warning and a threat. The first, from Sinai, was composed in 1983 in the wake of a murder in which the tribe of the victim warns the paramount chief of the other tribe of the consequences if the murderers are not brought to justice. To indicate the cultural continuity in this use of the poem, another poem of threat is included, this one composed more than 150 years earlier: it was sent by the leading Negev chief to the head of an Arabian tribe that had entered the Negev to graze their flocks without the permission of the local tribes, and had even begun to sow the land. The poem warned them to leave the Negev or be driven out—as they finally were in 1830.

These threats of blood and warfare are followed by two poems containing information about the arrival of a shipment of hashish. Both are poems by a fisherman in the Gulf of Aqaba, and were sent to two smuggler-employers to announce that the hashish he had brought them in his fishing boat from the port of Aqaba had arrived in Sinai. It might have sufficed to send a messenger with the report: 'Jum'a has brought the goods.' But, to inject some novelty into his bosses' lives and perhaps to 'celebrate' the arrival of a promising consignment of contraband, the illiterate fisherman chose to compose a poem which he anticipated would amuse his employers, both of whom were renowned for their own poetic skill. The two poems indicate that the custom of sending messages in verse need be no more than an illiterate poet's artistic delight, an occasion to try his hand at the poetic art—and his skill in rhyming.

In the next poem (2.6) a heartbroken lover informs a friend of his misery after his beloved's family has broken camp, and migrated to an unknown destination. This is followed by a masterly poem (2.7) sent in 1984 by one of the Tarābīn tribes to the chief of a Tiyāhā tribe in Sinai in an attempt to placate him; the chief had just lost a lawsuit against a young 'Turbānī' who had run off with a Tiyāhā girl, and it was feared that his tribe would seek to avenge their wounded honour. The next poem (2.8), which also revolves around a murder, was sent by the victim's family to their chief, who had supervised the terms of a truce between the two contending parties, complaining that their enemies were violating the truce. In the following poem the complaint was of less importance—nothing more than the failure to pay twenty-five Egyptian pounds owed to the poet for the purchase of a camel.

Finally, we have three compositions (2.10–2.12) in which the poets make requests—for mercy, intercession, and the gift of a camel. The poem asking for mercy was sent by the Bilī tribe to King Ibn Saʿūd after their rebellion against him was suppressed in 1932; the Bilī not only lost most of their men in the rebellion, but were being harshly treated and closely watched. In the following poem the influential Negev chief, Salmān al-Huzayyil, is requested to intercede with the Israeli authorities: a man of the Sinai Rumēlāt tribe had entered Israel illegally; and, assuming that he had been detained, his fellow tribesmen sent this poem to al-Huzayyil asking for his help. Finally, when ʿAnēz abū Sālim heard that King ʿAbdallāh of Jordan was generous to bedouin poets whose compositions he admired, he sent him a poem requesting a camel.

2.1

From a Hired Shepherd to his Master's Son

A Poem to Express Gratitude

One day the son of a herd-owner saw their hired shepherd kissing his sister at the well as the two were tugging the pail ropes, but said nothing and turned away. The next day, sitting with the brother over their morning coffee, the shepherd recited these six double-rhyme lines, telling his companion of the passionate love he felt for his sister, his frustration at not being of her kin so that he might marry her, and his gratitude to the brother for sparing his life (although bedouin custom would have justified his murder).

O long live the watering wells of Maygūaʿ,
My friend's noontime rest, then her[1] working anew; 1

The dress that, when raised, put her calf in full view,
And the sleeves rolled high when the pail-rope she drew.[2] 2

How I wished that rope two, even four, times as long,
For eighty more times I'd have pulled on it strongly; 3

How I wished that rope two, even four, times as long:
And if only our grandsires were kin I'd belong.[3] 4

The whole of last night I lay parched and pale,
But my liver's revived[4] and I no longer quail, 5

Poem 2.1 was heard recited by Muṣliḥ Mabrūk Imbārak, a black appended member of the Tiyāhā Sgērāt tribe of central Sinai, at Bīr al-Mālḥa, 4 April 1971. The poem originated in north-west Arabia, where Maygūaʿ (l. 1) is the southernmost watering-place in Wādī Sirḥān. In Alois Musil's *Manners* (pp. 360–1) we find a ten-line poem that includes some of the lines presented here, but with a slightly different narrative context. The six lines of the present rendition, however, are sufficient to constitute an integral poem. Discrepancies between the two texts were resolved according to the judgement of Muṣliḥ Ibn ʿĀmr.

[1] The girl is presented in the Arabic text in the masculine (see poem 1.15, n. 2).

[2] Women tuck the hems of their dresses under their belts when watering and tie the ends of their extra-long sleeves behind their necks.

[3] If he and his beloved were related through their paternal kin, the poet might have had the 'closest cousin's right' (*ḥagg ibn ʿamm*) to marry her (see Bailey, 'Weddings', pp. 111–12).

[4] For the role of the liver, see poems 1.12, n. 2; and 1.15, n. 1.

For Jaddūaʿ, it seems, won't uncover my tale;
We don't count our friend's faults, lest in friendship we fail.[5] 6

1 ya rabb tiḥyī maṣadīr maygūaʿ
wi-tiḥyī magīl iṣwēḥbī maʿ maraddi

1 يـــا ربّ تحيا مصـادير ميقـوع
وتحيا مقيـل صويحبي مـع مردّد

2 ū-tiḥyi-llī ṯawba ʿal as-sāg marfūaʿ
wi-mšalwaḥin li-d-dalū ḥabli yišiddi

2 وتحيا اللي ثوبد عـل الساق مرفوع
ومشلوحٍ للدلـو حبلـد يشدّد

3 ʿālyōm lin al-ḥabl maṯnī ū-marbūaʿ
wana-šidd al-ḥabl ṯamanīn šaddi

3 عـاليوم لـن الحبل مثني ومربوع
وانـــا اشدّ الحبـل ثمانين شدّة

4 ʿālyōm lin al-ḥabl maṯnī ū-marbūaʿ
walla jiddī garībin li-jiddi

4 عـاليوم لـــن الحبل مثني ومربوع
ولّا جـدّي قـــريب لــــــجدّد

5 wal-beriḥa bayyatt šanšūn wi-ẓilūaʿ
waṣbaḥt kibdī lil-ḥayā mistiriddi

5 والبـــارحة بيّتّ شنشون وضلـــوع
واصبحت كـبدي للحيـــاة مستـردّة

6 was-sirr ma yiṭlaʿ ʿal ġēr jaddūaʿ
min šāf ʿaybāt al-xuwī mā-yʿiddi

6 والسرّ مـــا يطلع عـــل غير جدّوع
مـــن شاف عيبات الخوي مـــا يعدّد

[5] Lit. 'He who sees his friend's faults won't count them'; bedouin consider it proper to overlook a friend's faults so as not to call attention to his weaknesses. A bedouin proverb has it, 'When one counts his friend's faults, he's already left him' (*man ʿadd zallāt ar-rafīg jafāh*).

2.2

From ʿAnēz abū Sālim of the Tarābīn to <u>Sh</u>ē<u>kh</u> Sulēmān al-Guṣayyir of the Aḥaywāt

A Poem to Warn of Revenge

In 1981 Fihayd Salīm Fihayd Ibn Jāzī, a young man of the Tarābīn Ḥasāblah tribe of south-eastern Sinai, was killed by men of the Aḥaywāt Karādma tribe, just west of the Israeli town of Eilat. The Aḥaywāt declared that they had caught Fihayd in *flagrante delicto* with a young woman of their tribe and that therefore neither the laws of blood-vengeance nor blood-money were relevant to them. The Tarābīn, however, asserted that the bullet wound in Fihayd's back indicated that he had been killed in his sleep; and that, even if he had been found sleeping near the girl, however grave the offence, bedouin law required that he be awakened before being killed. They declared that Fihayd had been lying on his left side, his head resting on his folded left arm; and that the bullet, which entered the right side of his back below his rib cage, went through his heart, his left tricep, and his wrist. No tracks were found near the body to indicate a struggle. Convinced by this evidence that Fihayd had been wronged, the Tarābīn declared their intention to take revenge; whereupon the Karādma fled with all their belongings to take refuge with a neutral tribe, far removed from the Tarābīn Ḥasāblah.

Because of the amicable relations between the neighbouring Tarābīn and Aḥaywāt confederations, however, the Tarābīn let it be known that, if the actual killer, Ḥimēd Ibn Kuraydim, or his closest kin would swear that he had awakened Fihayd before shooting him, they would forego their right of revenge. Moreover, if Ḥimēd admitted that he had not awakened him, they would settle for blood money (*diya*)—four times the usual sum, however, since Fihayd had been asleep. But the Aḥaywāt Karādma held firm to their version of the events—and remained in hiding.

Two years later the Tarābīn heard that the paramount chief of all the Aḥaywāt tribes, Sulēmān al-Guṣayyir, in a conversation with a third party had expressed his opinion that the Karādma were dealing wrongly with the Tarābīn. Hoping to take advantage of this expression of remorse by the most prominent member of the Aḥaywāt confederation, the poet ʿAnēz abū Sālim al-ʿUrḍī, of the same tribe as the victim Fihayd, sent a poem to al-Guṣayyir in which he repeated that

Poem 2.2 was heard recited by its author, at Nuwēbaʿ at-Tarābīn, 4 April 1983.

the Tarābīn were still intent on seeing justice done despite the passage of time (lines 1–6), urged him to bring the Karādma section of his confederation to litigation (lines 7–17), and warned him of the revenge that awaited him if the Aḥaywāt persisted in their intransigence (lines 18–19).

One tent stays put while another tent moves,
But, in packing, the loads on the camel aren't straight.[1] 1

Rights are oppressed, but the victims intent;
And in due course they'll get what they want though it's late. 2

Those who die fighting, their dignity keep,
But others lose life as though dead—in their sleep.[2] 3

Some chiefs rejoice at their game being bagged,[3]
While some, by the danger of bloodshed, are nagged.[4] 4

No matter—the backbiting, slander, and tales[5]
Will bring you no joy, but lead you astray. 5

I'm awake till the first morning breeze cools my face;
When I doze—like a wolf in a dangerous place. 6

Yet, with dawn I'd ride out on a plain broad and flat:
The waste from el-'Arīsh to Naga' Rukhēmāt.[6] 7

[1] i.e., although the Karādma removed themselves far from the Tarābīn for fear of retaliation (and also to *demonstrate* this fear, so as not to add insult to injury), justice still remained to be done. This is expressed by the imagery of camel loads, whose 'balance' (*'adl*) is also the word for justice (see poem 1.3, n. 5).

[2] Bedouin believe that a person's soul leaves him when he is asleep. Hence, an avenger must awaken his victim before killing him; otherwise his revenge will be considered invalid, he having 'killed' someone already dead. Moreover, it is thought necessary to awaken the victim so that he may defend himself; otherwise the revenge will have no merit.

[3] i.e. Jum'a Sālim Ibn Kuraydim, chief of the Aḥaywāt Karādma.

[4] i.e. Sulēmān 'Aliyyān Sulēmān al-Guṣayyir, paramount chief of the Shawāfīn division of the Aḥaywāt, and recipient of this poem.

[5] i.e. the claim that Fihayd was shot 'in the act', expressed in bedouin law by the term 'between her four' (*bēn arba'hā*), referring to the woman's two calves and two thighs.

[6] The Aḥaywāt tribal area covers much of barren central Sinai. It does not begin as far north as el-'Arīsh—used here for poetic effect—but near the 30th parallel, from where it extends southwards to the broad flintstone flat called Naga' ar-Rukhēmāt, approximately seventy-five kilometres south of the former pilgrimage way-station, Nakhl.

And approaching near T̲h̲emed,[7] I'd bridle her tight,
   And shorten the tasselled girth-strap a mite.[8]   8

She'd[9] stop at a tribe who's known to be keen,
   They are not Ḥuwēṭāt and they're not Tarābīn;[10]   9

When they fight among themselves for a guest, it's sincere,[11]
   And performing their duty they don't hold sheep dear.[12]   10

She'd stop off with Guṣayyir, whose positions are wise,
   And the virtue one sees in a face never lies.[13]   11

Say:[14] I've suffered this pain more time than one should,
   I whose liver has tried the bitterest of cures;[15]   12

You're a person of judgement, you raise a sound tribe,
   So stop them following erroneous ways.   13

Waste no time, for 'an early excursion is wealth';
   Sleep is putrid and, surely, it never brings health.   14

If the brands on our camels with lies could be hid,
   Many'd have lost, Friend, more herds than they have.[16]   15

[7] T̲h̲emed (properly at̲h̲-T̲h̲amad) is a well near the former Muslim pilgrimage route (*darb al-ḥajj*), half-way between Nak̲h̲l and present-day Eilat. Sulēmān al-Guṣayyir, the recipient of this poem, generally camped nearby during the hot summer season.
[8] Bridling to keep her running quickly; shortening the tasselled girth to avoid a snag.
[9] i.e. the camel bearing the messenger.
[10] This is a form of riddle employed to inject an element of tension into the line, as Aḥaywāt rhymes with Ḥuwēṭāt in the original text.
[11] In bedouin law, 'fighting' among the members of an encampment for the right to provide dinner for a guest is termed g̲h̲alāṭ (lit. 'harsh words'); and conflicting claims to that right can be adjudicated as a specific branch of the law. For example, one member may wish to slaughter one of his sheep for a guest to whom he owes a debt of gratitude. Another member, however, will insist that it is his turn to slaughter and that the other person had already done so for the latest guest at their encampment. He might point out, for example, that one article of their law holds that 'blood cannot flow on blood already spilt' (*dam mā yisīl 'a dam*). If the judge, however, accepts the obligation of the former to be overriding, he will grant him the right while finding a compromise arrangement.   [12] i.e. they slaughter many sheep, which otherwise are closely guarded.
[13] To ensure the poem's positive reception, the poet expresses his high regard for al-Guṣayyir despite the temporary friction between the two tribes.
[14] This is the introduction to the actual message, often uttered in a poem, as if to the messenger.
[15] i.e. in the past we have taken harsh measures when angered (hence the liver—the seat of anger—and the allusion to cures).
[16] The poet compares the clean bullet wound in Fihayd's back to a camel brand that cannot be obliterated by lies.

Your case might be solid if seen on the spot;
Since it's not, bring some proof and witnesses too. 16

Should we go to a judge and each presses his foe,
I'll take oath that you know who's right and who's wrong. 17

If the rifle goes off we'll all hear its sound,
And vultures and kites will hover around.[17] 18

Then together we'll count what Ghanīma has cost,[18]
But we'll bear our fine lightly, though heavily we've lost.[19] 19

1 dārin tiraḥḥilha ū-dārin imgīma ū-fi-š-šēl ma yiṭlig ʿalēhin ʿadīlāt	1 دارٍ ترحّلهـــا ودارٍ مقيمـــة وفي الشيل ما يطلق عليهن عديلات
2 wi-l-ḥagg ẓalma wir-rjāla ʿazīma taṣībaha nōba ū-taxṭīk nōbāt	2 والحـــقّ ظلمة والرجـــالة عزيمـــة تصيبهـــا نوبـــة وتخطيـــك نوبـــات
3 ū-ʿumrin tigaẓẓa fi karāma ū-šīma ū-ʿumrin tigaẓẓa ḥayy min ẓumin al-amwāt	3 وعمـــرٍ تقضّى فـــي كـــرامة وشيمة وعمـــرٍ تقضّى حيّ من ضمن الاموات
4 wi-kbār tifraḥ ʿend ṭayḥ al-walīma wi-kbār tandam ʿendima sēlaha fāt	4 وكبـــار تفـــرح عنـــد طيح الوليمة وكبـــار تندم عندمـــا سيلـها فـــات
5 ū-harj al-gafa wil-wiswisa win-nimīma tinḥāk ʿan dār as-saʿāda misafāt	5 وهـــرج القفـــا والوسوسة والنميمة تنحـــاك عـــن دار السعادة مسافـــات

[17] This is an implied threat that more than one person will be killed if the conflict continues unresolved.

[18] The girl in question (whose real name was Mētha) is sarcastically called 'Ghanīma' ('plunder'), as girls who cause such problems often are. The Tarābīn were also incensed that she was allowed to live, while Fihayd's life had been taken. This situation reminded the poet of the proverb 'Should Klēb have been killed for a she-camel?' (*yibgā klēb sadd fi-n-nāga*)—referring to the pre-Islamic story of Klayb ibn Rabīʿa, chief of the powerful Banī Taghlib tribe, who killed the she-camel belonging to a ward of his brother-in-law Jassās, only to be killed by the latter in revenge (see Nicholson, pp. 56–7).

[19] As bedouin law allows for vengeance against only the same number of persons as those originally violated, any additional victims open new blood-feuds and must either be avenged or compensated for. The poet thus stresses his group's determination to find justice (i.e. rehabilitate their marred reputation) by declaring they will go to any length to achieve their aim, however costly.

6 washar īlimma-l-lēl yubrud nasīma
wanām nōm ad̲-d̲īb fa-rẓ al-maxafāt

6 واسهر لمّا الليل يبرد نسيمه
وانام نوم الذيب في ارض المخافات

7 waṣ-ṣubḥ agāsī kull gabba ġašīma
bēn el-ʿarīš ū-bēn nagaʿ-r-rixēmāt

7 والصبح اقاسي كلّ قبّة غشيمة
بين العريش وبين نقع الرخيمات

8 ū-ʿend at̲-t̲amad l-akrub ʿalēha-ṣ-ṣarīma
wugṣur safayifha in kan hin ṭawīlāt

8 وعند الثمد لاكرب عليها الصريمة
واقصر سفايفها ان كان هن طويلات

9 ū-tilfī ʿala rabʿin lihum d̲āt gīma
lā hum tarabīn ū-lā hum ḥwēṭāt

9 وتلفي على ربعٍ لهم ذات قيمة
لا هم ترابين ولا هم حويطات

10 wiġlāṭhum fa-ẓ-ẓayf mā hū xaṣīma
wi-naʿājhum yōm il-lawāzim raxīṣāt

10 وغلاطهم في الضيف ما هو خصيمة
ونعاجهم يوم اللوازم رخيصات

11 ū-tilfi-l-igṣayyir lah mawāgif disīma
wa-l-jūd fī wijh aĺ-fata lah ʿalamāt

11 وتلفي القصيّر له مواقف دسيمة
والجود في وجه الفتى له علامات

12 witgūl ana ʿendī mawājiʿ gidīma
wal-kibid yāma jarrabat murr dawiyāt

12 وتقول انا عندي مواجع قديمة
والكبد ياما جرّبت مرّ دويات

13 inti fahīm ū-kull rabʿak fahīma
waḥaras ʿalēhum ʿin durūb il-mizallāt

13 انت فهيم وكلّ ربعك فهيمة
واحرس عليهم عن دروب المزلّات

14 wisrī t̲ara sirwāt badrī ġanīma
wan-nōm ʿafn ū-lah ʿawāgib waxīmāt

14 وإسري ثرا سروات بدري غنيمة
والنوم عفن وله عواقب وخيمات

15 win kān ḥaki-z-zōr yiġba-l-wasīma
ya-xūwī yāma kān ġabyit wisīmāt

15 وان كان حكي الزور يغبى الوسيمة
يا اخوّي ياما كان غبيت وسيمات

16 wi-ḥaggin imṣallab ʿend rās al-jarīma
ū-ḥagg yitaṣallab ġēr bi-šhūd wit̲bāt

16 وحقٍّ مصلّب عند راس الجريمة
وحقّ يتصلّب غير بشهود واثبات

17 ū-yōm aĺ-qabal wil-kull yigsī sigīma
wan-ašhad innak ʿārif il-ʿēb min yāt

17 ويوم القبل والكلّ يقسي سقيمه
وانا اشهد انّك عارف العيب من يات

18 wi-yōm it̲mēdī kull yismaʿ ġazīma
wa-ʿugba yiḥawman aŕ-raxam wi-ĺ-ḥidayyāt

18 ويوم الثميدي كلّ يسمع غزيمه
وعقبه يحومن الرخم والحدايّات

19 iḥna nag'ud inḥāsib fī maṣāliḥ aġinīma
winšīl kull iḥmūlha lō ṯigīlāt

احنــا نقعد نحاسب في مصالح غنيمة 19
ونشيل كــلّ حمولهـــا لـــو ثقيلات

2.3

From Salmān, Chief of the Huzayyil to Ibn Busēs, Chief of the Banī ʿAṭiyya

A Poem of Warning

In 1830[1] the Arabian Banī ʿAṭiyya tribe were forced by drought to seek pasture in the Negev. Having no alliance with the intruders, the paramount chief of the Tiyāhā confederation, Salmān ʿAlī ʿAzzām al-Huzayyil, on behalf of the Negev tribes, demanded that they pay him a tribute. His request was not only refused, but the Banī ʿAṭiyya even proceeded to cultivate the fertile Beersheba plain. Thereupon, Salmān gathered a force of warriors of the Tiyāhā, Tarābīn, and Ḥanājra tribes, as well as villagers from the Hebron Hills, and despatched the following poem of warning to the Banī ʿAṭiyya leader, Ibn Busēs.

O Rider on a camel, fast as a flood,
With side-sacks and a saddle that kindle pride, 1

Follow Wādī al-Ghamr to the spring at Ghaḍyān,[2]
Fill your water bag up, then continue to ride! 2

Poem 2.3 was heard recited by Sulēmān Ḍayfallāh Imsāʿid of the Tarābīn Ḥasāblah tribe, in Wādī Ijbēriyya on the ʿIjma plateau, 18 March 1971; l. 5 was also transcribed by ʿĀrif al-ʿĀrif (*Taʾrīkh*, p. 169). Discrepancies between the two texts were resolved according to the judgement of Mūsā al-ʿAṭāwna.

---

[1] In 1869 the guide of the English Orientalist, E. H. Palmer, related (as they passed the wadi where a battle took place at the time that this poem went unheeded) that this episode had occurred when he was a child forty years before. For the background of these events, see Bailey, 'Nineteenth Century', pp. 55–8.

[2] Wādī Ghamr is the northern part of the ʿAraba rift; ʿAyn Ghaḍyān is a spring in the southern ʿAraba (near present-day Yotvata).

Steer him to tents above the wadis Yitām;[3]
From the horses of Karak they hide their camps.[4] 3

Warn Ibn Busēs,[5] who smokes *du<u>khkh</u>ān*,[6]
This brotherly counsel he mustn't deride. 4

Say: your homeland's Tabūk,[7] ours the plain of the <u>Kh</u>ān;[8]
And farming our land will bring you no joy. 5

Before tobacco and melons,[9] you'll meet spears of *zān*,[10]
And mounts champing bits, tugging bridles aside! 6

1 ya rākb<u>in</u> min ʿendina min fōg siḥwān
al-xurj wal-mēṯūr yizhī bi-hinna

1 يـــا راكب,, من عندنا من فوق سحوان
الـــخرج والميثور يزهـــي بهنّـــد

2 yammak ʿal al-ġamr min dūn ġaẓyān
amla ṣamīlak wadhaj ad-darb yamma

2 يمّـك عــل الغمر مــن دون غضيــان
امــلا صميلــك وادهج الدرب يمّـــد

3 sūga ʿal-illī yiskunū rūs al-ītām
muzbūn ʿan xēl al-karak mā yiṭanna

3 سوقــد عــل اللي يسكنو رؤوس الايتام
مزبون عــن خيل الكرك مــا يطنّــد

4 itgūl l-ibn ibsēs šarrāb ad-duxxān
gōlit axāk lā tsāfil bi-hinna

4 تقــول لابــن بسيس شرّاب الدخّــان
قولــة اخـــاك لا تسافــل بهنّـــد

5 dārak tabūk wi-dārna sāḥil al-xān
wi-ḥajrak waṭanna mā-yʿaggib miḥanna

5 دارك تبوك ودارنــا ساحــل الخــان
وحجرك وطنّــا مــا يعقّب محنّـــة

[3] the Yitām wadis are mountain passes leading from Aqaba up to the <u>Sh</u>arā Mountain.

[4] Although the Banī ʿAṭiyya became allies of the dominant Majālī family of Karak after 1860 (see Gubser, p. 16), they may have maintained hostile relations earlier in the century.

[5] According to Frederick Peake (p. 207), Ibn Busēs is a family in the Marāgīn section of the Banī ʿAṭiyya.

[6] Tobacco: this address is a compliment, as only wealthy bedouin, such as chiefs or successful raiders, would smoke from a narghila.

[7] The village Tabūk in northern Ḥijāz was a commercial centre for the Banī ʿAṭiyya (Musil, *Hegaz*, pp. 234–5).

[8] The north-west Negev was known as 'the plain of <u>Kh</u>ān Yūnis'.

[9] Tobacco and melons are summer crops, sown after the winter-pasture season that attracted the Banī ʿAṭiyya to the Negev.

[10] A type of reed grown in Wādī <u>Gh</u>azza (Gaza) and used for spears (Burckhardt, i. 52).

6 at-titin wal-baṭīx dūna xašab zān
ū-xēlin tigargaẓ bal-ḥasak wal-a'inna

6 التتن والبطيـــخ دونـــه خشب زان
وخيـــل„ تقرقض بالحسك والاعنّـــة

2.4

From Jum'a al-Farārja to Jāzī al-'Arādī

A Poem to Notify that Hashish has Arrived

After the First World War, if not before, the bedouin of Sinai formed a vital link in the smuggling route between Syria, Lebanon, and Turkey—where hashish was grown—and the great entrepôt of Cairo. The hashish that the bedouin of southern Sinai smuggled often came to them from the Jordanian port of Aqaba, where it was brought by Syrian and Jordanian smugglers, and from there taken to Sinai in small boats by bedouin fishermen who plied the south-eastern coast of the peninsula.

One such fisherman in the 1950s was Jum'a 'Īd Dakhīlallāh, of the Farārja section of the Tarābīn Ḥasāblah; and one of the ringleaders for whom he worked was his fellow tribesman, Jāzī Ḥamd al-'Arādī from the Rāḥa hills of south-western Sinai just south of Suez, who had the merchandise transported to Cairo. To amuse his employers, such as Jāzī al-'Arādī or 'Anēz abū Sālim al-'Urḍī, both poets of note, Jum'a would occasionally send them messages in verse. In the present poem, which Jum'a sent to Jāzī with a messenger, he informs him in disguised language that he has brought a consignment of hashish over Mt Khlēlāt to the 'Ayn Umm Aḥmad oasis, and reassures his boss that his illegal consignment is large by alluding to a fat camel bearing Jāzī's brand (l. 4).

Poem 2.4 was heard recited by its author, at el-'Arīsh, 19 October 1970.

Lightning flashed over Gōz Khlēlāt;[1]
I saw it and thought it the Pleiades' sign.[2] 1

She poured forth her rain sprouting grasses so high,
Filling wells at the spring after these had run dry.[3] 2

O Rider racing along hidden ways,[4]
Far from all souls, be they friend be they foe, 3

Tell Jāzī a camel passed bearing his sign;[5]
If he thinks that she's thin, assure him she's fine. 4

And to Jāzī and gang my greetings convey;
This news, good or bad, is what I have to say. 5

1 bargin barāg ʿa rās gōz il-xlēlāt
xilti ū-gult imni-ṯ-ṯurayya wasīmi

2 kabbat maṭarha ū-rabbat al-ʿišib zōmāt
wasgat ʿidūd al-ʿayn ʿugb il-gaṭīni

3 yā rākb-illī zarwaʿ fi-l-ixfayyāt
yibʿid ʿan iblād al-maḥibb ū-ẓigīni

4 wi-tgūl li-jāzī faṭrak wasimha fāt
win gāl lak tilfāna gūl-li samīni

5 ū-sallim ʿalā jāzī ū-ʿal al-jamaʿāt
widd ōdaʿak harjī šēni ū-zēni

1 بــرق„ بــراق ع راس قــوز الخليلات
خلتــد وقــلت مــن الثريــا وسيمة

2 كــبّت مطرهــا وربّت العشب زومــات
واسقت عــدود العيــن عقب القطينــة

3 يـــا راكب اللي زروع في الخفيّــات
يبعد عـــن بــلاد المحبّ وضغينــة

4 وتقول لجــازي فاطرك وسمهــا فــات
وان قــال لــك تلفانة قول لد سمينة

5 وسلّــم على جازي وعــل الجماعات
ودّي اودعـــك هرجي شينــة وزينــة

[1] A mountain approximately thirty-five kilometres north of Nuwēbaʿ at-Tarābīn.

[2] The appearance of the Pleiades at sunset in November ushers in the rainy season, necessary for the sprouting of annual pasture and the winter grains planted by the bedouin; the name of the season is 'the sign of the Pleiades': (*wasm ath-thurayya*) (see Bailey, 'Star-lore', pp. 582–91). (Cf. poems 4.20C and 6.18 for further references to the Pleiades.)

[3] i.e. the hashish that has come to the spring of ʿAyn Umm Aḥmad is as beneficial as a heavy rainfall. In the Arabic text dryness is conveyed by the image of *gaṭīna*—a piece of cotton used to soak up the last drops of water in a well.

[4] Smuggling routes inaccessible to the Egyptian desert police.

[5] i.e. his hashish, bearing a specific trade-mark (cf. poem 6.15, l. 11).

2.5

From Jumʿa al-Farārja to ʿAnēz abū Sālim al-ʿUrḍī

A Poem to Notify that Hashish has Arrived

The use of code words and disguised language among smugglers is not only a necessity, but a matter of pride and a sign of cleverness. In the present poem Jumʿa ʿĪd Dak͟hīlallāh, who had brought a load of hashish from Aqaba by boat, informs his ringleader, ʿAnēz abū Sālim, that he can send someone from Riyaʿ Lāmī in Wādī Watīr to pick it up in Wādī Ṭābā near the Israeli frontier. He applies the image of she-camels to hashish (line 3) because its value always multiplies; and *white* she-camels because the hashish is packaged in white oil-cloth. He states that the camels are 'ageing and thin' to signify that the consignment has come a long way, and that its cost, put up front, has made the profit margin slim. However, when taken to Egypt by the usual route—over the remote and safe ʿIjma Plateau and over the Gulf of Suez by skiff (line 4)—their price will increase, just like the price of camels after they have grazed on annual grasses. Continuing the camel image to represent the glutted hashish market that has kept prices down (line 5), Jumʿa compares it to the camel-disease *jaʿām* (intestinal worms caused by unseasonal early rains that bring up annual plants before the ground temperature is cold enough to destroy the worms that are on them); and he alludes to the cures for *jaʿām*—forcing oil into the camel's nostrils[1] and pasturing it on special grass[2]—to imply that the new *ḥas͟hīs͟h* (lit. grass), wrapped in *oil*-cloth, should find a better market.

O Rider, whose mount bears him fleetly through darkness,
On a broad plain speeding, there's no need to prod; 1

If you leave Riyaʿ Lāmī well into the night,
The barbed-wire border you'll reach before light; 2

Poem 2.5 was heard recited by its author, at el-ʿArīs͟h, 19 October 1970.

[1] Ar. *hum yisʿaṭū al-jamal*. About two, small bean-cans of oil are used; and, in order that it 'gets into the body', the camel is prevented from drinking for four days. (Oral communication from Jumʿa ʿĪd Dak͟hīlallāh.)

[2] The bitter plants used in curing *jaʿām* are commonly termed *ḥamḍ* (lit. 'sour') and includes species of Anabasis, Atriplex, Hammada, Salsola, and Suaeda (Bailey and Danin, 'Plant Utilization', p. 149).

And find there white she-camels tended by friends,
But ageing and thin from long journeys. 3

Yet, taken to graze on the ʿIjma plateau,
And then on to Egypt by boat, they will grow; 4

Though they've ached and they've suffered unseasonal rain,
With grass and with oil their weight they'll regain. 5

1 yā rākb-illī šarradạ fiẓ-ẓulāmī
win zarwaʿan fi-l-gāʿ ma gāl-la ḥīt

2 widd ōṣfak mimšā mi-riyaʿ lāmī
waṣbaḥ ar-rawẓ illī tagaḏarab ʿal aš-šīk

3 yalga-l-wuẓayḥiyyāt ʿend iz-zlāmī
wal-fuṭar illī ẓāmri min mašaḥīk

4 wi-nsūgha li-mirbāḥḥa fi-l-ʿijāmī
win rabbaʿat fōg al-gaṭāyir timannīk

5 tilfat ū-minna ṣādha al-jaʿāmī
wa-ʿdōdalat ila ḏāgat al-ʿišib wiz-žēt

1 يـــا راكبِ اللــي شرّدد فــي الظلام
وان زروعن في القاع ما قال لد حيت

2 ودّي اوصفــك ممشا مــن ريــع لامــي
واصبح الروض اللي تقذرب عل الشيك

3 يلقــى الوضيحيّـــات عند الزلام
والفطر اللــي ضــامرة مــن مشاحيــك

4 ونسوقهــا لمرباعهــا فــي العجــام
وان ربعت فوق القطــاير تمنّيــك

5 تلفت ومنــد صادهــا الجعــام
واعدودلت الا ذاقت العشب والزيت

2.6

From a Disappointed Lover to his Friend

A Poem to Share a Burden

As bedouin migrate from one place to another in search of pasture for their livestock, shepherds and shepherdesses frequently become acquainted and perhaps fall in love, only to be separated when their parents decide they must migrate again. The pain experienced by such separation has been a theme in desert poetry from earliest times.

Accordingly, a bedouin girl in north-west Arabia, learning that her family was about to migrate to the vicinity of Khaybar oasis,[1] sent a message to her beloved asking him to come and see her before she moved. By the time the young man received the message and reached her camp, the girl and her family were already gone and he found the camp deserted. He composed the following poem to express his disappointment and sent it as a missive to a friend, Salmān, with whom he could share his burden.

O Rider on one whose spine isn't slack,
  A tawny Sharārī with full lofty back;[2] 1

Keep him straight as you ride him, by night and by day;
  Wadis and flat lands you'll pass on your way. 2

If he feels your heel pressing, he'll take off in flight,
  With the speed of an ostrich chick bolting from fright.[3] 3

He'll stop off with Salmān, for whom the girls pine,[4]
  Whose miseries I know, just as he will know mine. 4

Poem 2.6 apparently originated in north-west Arabia and was heard recited by Ṣabāḥ Ṣāliḥ al-Ghānim of the ʿAgēlī tribe, at Rabʿa oasis, 27 November 1971.

[1] Khaybar is an oasis town in north-west Arabia. According to Doughty (i. 276), it was customary for the Wild Sulēmān division of the ʿAnēza confederation to camp in its vicinity during the summer months.

[2] Sharārī camels, which are considered good stock, were raised by the Sharārāt tribe of north-west Arabia at least as early as the early nineteenth century, as attested by the explorer J. L. Burckhardt in 1831 (ii. 77). Murray (p. 114) states that Sharārī camels were highly regarded in the early twentieth century, too.

[3] Bedouin poets liken a swift camel to an ostrich to emphasize its speed (cf. poems 2.10, 6.1, 6.18).

[4] A common compliment in bedouin poetry (cf. poems 1.4, 6.1, 6.7).

My sigh's like the sigh of a tail-clipped young colt[5]
Whose trainer's sharp stirrups are tearing his coat. 5

My sigh's like the sigh of a young girl betrothed,
Who was forced to wed him whom her heart deeply loathed.[6] 6

My sigh is like one who midst strangers is found,
Who craves to be generous, but's poverty bound.[7] 7

My sigh is like that of an old mother's sigh,
Who sees her son harmed, but can only stand by. 8

My sigh is like that of a camel that's jaded;
Though couched, none will take off the load he's been laded. 9

O girl with white cheeks, whose whiteness is strong,
And with black eyes covered by eye-lashes long; 10

Whose breasts are a bustard's egg in size
When the bustard's still brooding, before she rises. 11

I looked down from a hill near her last camping ground;
Nothing remained there but crows hopping round. 12

I looked down from a hill—O, what's left to say?
I curse Khaybar town and the camps out that way! 13

1 ya rākbin 'allī imdāna fagāra
ašgar šarārī šāmix al-mitn nabī

1 يا راكبٍ عاللي مدانا فقارد
اشقر شراري شامخ المتن نابيد

2 arkab 'alē wigdī lēla wi-nahāra
yigṭa' bak ar-rīẓān wid-daww yaṭwī

2 اركب عليد واقديد ليلد ونهارد
يقطع بك الريضان والدوّ يطويد

[5] Comparing one's personal suffering to a known discomfort in bedouin life is a common poetic device (cf. Shuqayr, p. 392). Bedouin clip the tails of their young horses to train them to hold their tails high, which is considered the hallmark of a good horse (see poem 1.10, n. 14).

[6] Since families arrange marriages for family and clan interests, girls are rarely consulted, or even informed, about whom they are to wed (see Bailey, 'Weddings', p. 114; cf. poem 1.14, n. 1).

[7] This reflects the bedouin aversion to being dependent on others, independence and self-sufficiency being indispensable for one's status and security. For other expressions of this sentiment, cf. poems 3.8, 3.9, 3.11, and 6.14.

3 in ḥass lizzāt al-kaʿb fazz ġāra
farx an-naʿām wilā ḥaṭam min mifalī

3 ان حسّ لزّات الكعب فزّ غارة
فرخ النعام ولو حطم من مفاليه

4 yilfī ʿala salmān šōg al-ʿaḏāra
yaʿrif šikawiyyī wana ʿārif šikawī

4 يلفي على سلمان شوق العذارى
يعرف شكاويّ وانا عارف شكاويه

5 ya wentī wennit jibīb al-mahāra
raʿī bil-irkabāt fi-l-janb kawī

5 يا ونّتي ونّة جبيب المهارة
راعيه بالركابات في الجنب كاويه

6 ya wentī wennit fitāt al-ʿadāra
malzūztin ʿal-jōz ma-l-galb hawī

6 يا ونّتي ونّة فتاة العذارى
ملزوزةٍ عالجوز ما القلب هاويه

7 ya wentī wennit iṣbayyin maʿ ijnāba
ʿārif miʿāni-l-jūd wal-gill ṭawī

7 يا ونّتي ونّة صبيٍّ مع اجنابة
عارف معاني الجود والقلّ طاويه

8 ya wentī wennit ʿajūzin kibīra
tirʿī waladha wal-xalāyig ibtihwī

8 يا ونّتي ونّة عجوزٍ كبيرة
ترعي ولدها والخلايق بتهويه

9 ya wentī wennit itlēb al-jimāla
berik wi-ḥimla fī maṭabba imxallī

9 يا ونّتي ونّة ثليب الجمالة
بارك وحمله في مطبّه مخلّيه

10 abū xidēdin zāydin fī šigāra
wal-ʿayn sōda wi-ġamg ar-rimiš ġaṭī

10 ابو خديدٍ زايدٍ في شقارة
والعين سودا وغامق الرمش غاطيه

11 abū nihaydin kēf bēẓ al-ḥibāra
ū-bēẓ al-ḥibāra yōm turgud taġaṭī

11 ابو نهيدٍ كيف بيض الحبارى
وبيض الحبارى يوم ترقد تغاطيه

12 ašraft ʿal-mišrāf baraʿʿī bi-dyāra
ū-ma-lgēt ġēr al-ġurbān yitnāgazan fī

12 اشرفت عالمشراف بارعّي بدياره
ما لقيت غير الغربان يتناقزن فيه

13 wašraft ʿal-mišrāf gōlī xasāra
ū-baddaʿī ʿala xaybar ū-ʿallī sikin fī

13 واشرفت عالمشراف قولي خسارة
وبادّعي على خيبر وعاللي سكن فيه

2.7

From ʿAnēz abū Sālim of the Tarābīn To Shēkh ʿĪd Muṣliḥ Ibn ʿĀmr of the Tiyāhā

A Poem Meant to Mollify

Six months before Israel evacuated Sinai in March 1982, a young man of the Tarābīn in east-central Sinai ran off with a girl of the neighbouring Tiyāhā tribe, and took refuge with bedouin in Israel's Negev desert. A warning issued by a Tiyāhā delegation to the Tarābīn elders resulted in the girl's return to her family. However, when the couple eloped a second time and the Tiyāhā made representations, the Tarābīn rejected their request to send the girl back, and accused the Tiyāhā of negligence in the moral upbringing of their women.

The Tiyāhā thereupon took the Tarābīn to court, to the most renowned and stringent judges of honour in cases of the sexual violation of women—judges traditionally belonging to the Masāʿīd tribe in north-western Sinai. The first judge to hear the case, al-Ḥājj Salīm Abū Ḥasan, awarded the Tiyāhā forty five-year-old camels, worth some eight thousand Egyptian pounds, for their injured honour, plus three thousand pounds for expenses arising out of the affair. The Tiyāhā, nevertheless, were not satisfied with this judgment, since Abū Ḥasan did not order the Tarābīn to return the girl again. When, however, the Tiyāhā had their chief, ʿĪd Muṣliḥ Ḥamd Ibn ʿĀmr, appeal the case before another judge of the Masāʿīd tribe, Salāma Abū Amīra, this judge, stressing the girl's role in the elopements, reduced the award from forty camels and three thousand pounds to ten camels, pricing them at a total of one thousand pounds. The girl was thereby held to be culpable and unworthy of a large award; and, although the boy was also fined, it was only to indicate that *any* amorous contact with bedouin females is inadmissible. The Tihāyā refused to accept this award and departed.

Concerned lest the Tiyāhā avenge what they considered their injured honour, a delegation of Tarābīn notables asked their fellow confederate, ʿAnēz abū Sālim al-ʿUrḍī, to compose a poem to placate Shēkh ʿĪd Ibn ʿĀmr, his friend and maternal relative. After some initial chiding (line 1), ʿAnēz complied; and, although he did not hesitate to express his opinion that the Tiyāhā were wrong, and to praise the second judge, Salāma Abū Amīra (lines 7–14), he succeeded in restoring the Tiyāhā chief's honour by emphasizing his nobility in not deserting friends and fellow tribesmen, even though they had erred (lines 16–22).

Guests came my way but swore that they would never eat my meat,[1]
And chided me: a bard you are, but tend to lie and cheat. 1

So I set out to find a rhyme that might be right for me
And said to my slim-waisted mate:[2] Go ready me some tea. 2

The cover that your kinsmen give you often makes you cold,
And our hearts refuse to sleep, the more our worries grow.[3] 3

An envoy I'd already sent for news I wished to know,
A lad on whom I could rely, no 'tail-end of a hoe';[4] 4

He rode a strong and sturdy mount, at Ṭāst al-ʿIlū raised,[5]
A pure-bred sired by a stud whose pedigree is praised. 5

I threw upon him saddle-bags, each full with things one needs,
And thought about a route that over hilly desert leads, 6

And steered him toward a man whose reputation is his pride:
A paragon for worthy men, a camel in his stride. 7

Poem 2.7 was heard recited by its author, at Nuwēbaʿ at-Tarābīn, 18 April 1984. The recipient of the poem, ʿĪd Muṣliḥ Ḥamd Ibn ʿĀmr, chief of the Tiyāhā Ṣgērāt since 1953, lived in Wādī Mitmatnī in central Sinai (cf. poem 6.1).

---

[1] To exercise their chagrin at the poet's reluctance to compose the desired poem, the delegation refused to eat the sheep that the poet had extravagantly slaughtered for them. Refusing to partake of another's food is a sign of hostility, one of the steps taken by opponents in a conflict. By contrast, when people overcome their differences, this act of peace (*ṣulḥ*) is marked by their sharing a meal, as reflected in the maxim 'He who is well disposed toward you will eat your food' (*man rādak, akal zādak*). Commensality creates a 'non-aggression pact' between people. The expression 'bread and salt' (*ʿēsh ū-miliḥ*) is one term for a pact of friendship; and to stress the binding nature of commensality a bedouin proverb states 'He who eats the bread of [even] a Christian, will grip his sword in battle' (*man akal ʿēsh an-naṣrānī yiḥārib bi-sēfih*).

[2] i.e. his wife, expressed in the Arabic text as his companion, and in the masculine gender for the sake of propriety (cf. poem 1.14, n. 2).

[3] When the heart is free of cares, it is said to be warm (*al-galb dāfī*). Although kinsmen 'give you support' (*yisnadū ʿalā gafāk*: lit. 'hold your back up') and thus give you 'cover', the support that one must give them in return, even if the trouble is of their own making, is a source of anxiety which makes the heart 'cold', and thus sleepless. Hence, the more cover (ie. kinsmen) you have, the more worries.

[4] Ar. *dhanab fās*; an expression for a worthless person.

[5] Ṭāst al-ʿIlū is a dune area, thirty-five kilometres east of Ismailia. This line is a compliment to the Arabian camels raised there by the Masāʿīd and the ʿAyāyda tribes.

Abū Amīra's sons, as well, are known as men of worth,
For lo! a lion's whelp will not be trampled in the earth.[6] 8

No pails exhaust the fullness of this ever-flowing well;[7]
His judgment's like an ocean, even divers dread its swell.[8] 9

A well so deep that one would tire tugging on its rope,
A well where all the thirsty tribes resort when void of hope. 10

When he decides, a guarded girl can never meet with blame,[9]
While one who's been indecent dare not claim she's put to shame. 11

Defective judges often deem a full or empty womb the same,[10]
And thus a house of honour needs a guard to shield its name.[11] 12

Dishonour is like game, it must be hunted to be found;
But households where just one stain shows, for sure there's
more around. 13

If both the judges judged the same, then justice would have died,[12]
And we'd have said that these are courts where justice is denied. 14

[6] Cf. poem 1.5, n. 7

[7] Beneficent persons are often compared to a perennial well (*ʿidd*), that never goes dry nor disappoints (cf. poems 4.5, 5.11, 7.1).

[8] The judges from the Masāʿīd tribe are called *manāshid* (sing. *manshad*) and their jurisdiction is sought in difficult cases concerning the violation of a woman's honour; they are referred to as 'a sea that drowns' (*baḥar yigharrig*) because of their severe judgments. The allusion to sea (*baḥar*) comes from the rhymed and metaphorical definition of the bedouin legal process as *ṣakhar*, *nahar*, and *baḥar*. *Ṣakhar* (a rock) is the problem to be resolved; *nahar* (a river) is the guarantee of safety and of compliance with the verdict, which bedouin notables give to the respective, contending parties in order to facilitate their coming together to adjudicate their problem; and *baḥar* (a sea) is the judge and his profound knowledge.

[9] The allusion to a guarded girl (lit. a 'hidden' girl (*mukhabbā*)) reflects the proverbial sentiment 'Honour requires watchfulness' (*ash-sharaf widdih inṭāra*).

[10] In bedouin law a serious violation of a girl's honour entails a high fine, as much as forty or fifty camels, paid to her family. If, however, the girl is pregnant—an indication of compliance on her part—the man is only required to pay five camels as a bride-price and to wed the girl. A judge who awarded a pregnant girl's family a large sum would be suspected of ignorance of the law.

[11] i.e., if the law fails to protect the bedouin, they must place guards around their women, an obvious impossibility.

[12] i.e. if Salāma Abū Amīra had confirmed the large sum that al-Ḥājj Salīm Abū Ḥasan had awarded the Tiyāhā.

Take my message, bring me word, let no detail pass,
And clarify how Swēlim got the best of Abū Rās.[13] 15

And say to Ibn ʿĀmr, 'Your reward's on Judgment Day;
For by accepting justice you preserved the bedouin way'.[14] 16

Hearing his award, he spurned the sum as mean,
And praised the Lord he had no need for wealth that was unclean. 17

The Tiyāhā tribe are stallions—battle-stallions shod with shoes,
Stallions who, although held back, the bloody fray would choose. 18

And God has not abandoned even him who abandoned Him:
God who raised this dead man's bones after deep despair;[15] 19

For Ibn Fayyāḍ's adventure, he got his just reward;
Distraught, he's seen another man take his riding mare.[16] 20

A man may wish to help his friends, and that should gain him praise,
But each judge, like a measuring cup, will differ how he weighs.[17] 21

The claim you thought to draw up with your own hands had to fail:
An evil, monstrous claim it was, with neither head nor tail. 22

This poem is meant to make men heed lest such things re-occur,
And to mollify the party that was angered by a slur. 23

Throughout his life a poet's heart is tried and tired, alas,
And he who made this latest poem's an issue of Hirmās.[18] 24

[13] Swēlim Zāyid al-Gunbēzī of the Tarābīn Ḥasāblah (of Jabal Maghāra in central Sinai) was the spokesman ('tongue': *lisān*) for the Tarābīn, and Sulēmān abū ʿĀṭiyya 'Abū Rās' of the Tiyāhā Brēkāt for the Tiyāhā.

[14] This line reflects the bedouin perception of their law being a guardian of their society and way of life.

[15] i.e. Abū Amīra's reversal of Abū Ḥasan's decision saved Ibn Fayyāḍ from paying a large sum.

[16] The girl whom Ibn Fayyāḍ abducted later ran off with a man of the Jahālīn tribe (of the West Bank). The reference to his wife as his 'riding-mare' (*dhalūl*) is an allusion to their sexual escapade (cf. poems 4.8, l. 6; 6.13, l. 10).

[17] In Egypt there are different-sized measuring cups, known as *kēl ad-dibbāsi*, *kēl al-ʿabbāsī*, and *kēl al-garāya*. An Egyptian proverb to the effect that 'all things are not equal' says 'the ʿAbbāsī and the Dibbāsī do not measure the same' (*kēl al-ʿabbāsī mā yiṭabbig ʿalā kēl ad-dibbāsī*).

[18] Hirmās was an ancestor of ʿAnēz and the forefather of most of the Tarābīn Hasāblah living in south-east Sinai.

You won't make someone drink the bitter using means that please;
You'll only make him drink it having brought him to his knees. 25

And if a judge not honour God, nor fear His awesome sway,
He'll twist the law so even wolves to cats fall easy prey.[19] 26

1 jawnī ẓyūf ū-ḥarramū yāklu-š-šā
ū-gāl int šāʿir bass itkawḏib ʿal an-nās

1 جونـــي ضيوف وحرّمو ياكــلو الشاة
وقال انت شاعر بسّ تكوذب عل الناس

2 ū-ṣirt atanaddar ū-kull ḥarf ataḥallā
ū-gult il-naḥīf al-jism gūm sawwī lī kās

2 وصرت اتنــدّر وكــلّ حــرف اتحلّاد
وقلت لنحيف الجسم قوم سوّي لي كاس

3 wal-jism yubrud kull ma yukiṯir ġaṭā
wa-l-galb yishar kull ma zād hilwās

3 والجسم يبرد كــلّ مــا يكثر غطــاد
والقلب يسهــر كــلّ مــا زاد هلواس

4 w-irsalt lī mirsāl ū-ṣirt ataḥarrā
rajili̲n̲ yijīb ar-radd mā hū ḏanab fās

4 وارسلت لـــي مرسال وصرت اتحرّاد
راجــلٍ يجيب الردّ مــا هو ذنب فاس

5 min fawg ʿawdi̲n̲ ṭāst al-ʿịlū mirbā
ḥurri̲n̲ ẓarūba musandīna ʿal asās

5 من فوق عودٍ طــاسة العلــو مربــاد
حــرٍّ ظروبد مسنّديند عــل اساس

6 wurẓum ʿalē al-xurj wil-gašš juwwā
waḥsib iḥsāb in fī ṭalʿa ū-minkās

6 وارضم عليد الخرج والقشّ جوّاد
واحسب حساب ان فيه طلعة ومنكاس

7 waṭurra ʿal illī yirfaʿ ar-rās ṭiryā
ʿawdi̲n̲ imsaṭṭa lar-rajajīl migyās

7 واطرّد عل اللي يرفع الراس طرياد
عودٍ مسطّــى للرجاجيل مقيــاس

8 abū amīra ʿaggab igrūm šarwā
ū-ma ʿumr ʿagb as-sabaʿ bir-rijl yindās

8 ابــو اميــرة عقّب قــروم شرواد
وما عمر عقب السبع بالرجل ينداس

9 ʿiddi̲n̲ rawī mā yanzaḥan jamma idlā
ū-ʿilmi baḥar ʿasri̲n̲ ʿala kull ġuṭṭās

9 عــدٍّ روي مــا ينزحن جمّــد ادلاد
وعلمه بحر عسرٍ على كــلّ غطّــاس

[19] Bedouin regard wolves highly, because they are intrepid and self-sufficient, as is a bedouin in his own eyes. On the other hand, cats, rare in the desert, are scorned because of their timidity and dependence on others for their survival. To imply that cats could get the best of wolves is a way of expressing the extreme danger of ill-considered legal judgments—i.e. they reverse the natural order.

10 ʿiddin ṭawīl ū-yitʿibak ṭillt iršā
tawrid ʿalē ūrūd min kull al-ajnās

10 عدٍّ طويـل ويتعبك طلّـة رشاه
تورد عليـه ورود مـن كـلّ الاجناس

11 ū-ʿend al-magarr itlāg ḥagg aĺ-imxabbā
wal-mijrisa ʿend aĺ-ʿarab mā liha-jrās

11 وعند المقـرّ تلاق حقّ المخبّـى
والمجرسة عند العرب مـا لـها إجراس

12 ū-ʿend al-laṭūḥ al-fāẓya zē-l-imʿabbā
ū-dār aš-šaraf widdhā ʿan al-ʿayb ḥurrās

12 وعند اللطوح الفـاضية زي المعبّـى
ودار الشرف ودّها عن العيب حرّاس

13 wil-ʿayb ṣayd ū-wēn ma kān tilgā
ū-tilga-d-dyār al-ʿāyiba kulliha-lwās

13 والعيب صيد ووين مـا كـان تلقاه
وتلقى الديار العايبة كـلّـها لواس

14 ū-law kān gāl al-ḥagg aḷḷa tiwaffā
la-gult fī ibyūt giṭṭāʿit imrās

14 ولـو كـان قـال الحقّ اللّـه توفّـاه
لقلت فيـه بيوت قطّـاعة امراس

15 ū-xud lī ū-hāt ū-kull ḥarfin tilgā
ū-šūf lī swēlim kēf sawwa fa-bū rās

15 وخذ لي وهات وكـلّ حرفٍ تلقاه
وشوف لي سويلم كيف سوّى في ابو راس

16 ū-itgūl l-ibn ʿāmr in ajrak ʿal aḷḷā
illī raẓī bi-ʿilm raẓyū bi han-nās

16 وتقول لابن عامر ان اجرك عل اللّـه
اللـي رضي بعلم رضيو بـه النـاس

17 illī simaʿ simlān ḥaggi ū-xallā
ū-gām yitaġanna-ḷḷā ʿan māl al-injās

17 اللـي سمع سملان حقّـه وخـلّاه
وقام يتغنّى اللّـه عن مال الانجاس

18 wi-rubʿ at-tiyāha ḥuṣn ū-ḥuṣnin imḥaddā
ḥuṣnin tixūẓ ad-damm maʿ gōlit inḥās

18 وربـع التياها حصن وحصنٍ محذّى
حصنٍ تخوض الدم مع قولة إنحاس

19 aḷḷā mā yinsāk lō kunt tinsā
wi-yiḥya-l-ʿaẓām al-mayyta ʿugb al-iyās

19 اللّـه مـا ينساك لـو كنت تنساه
ويحيـا العظام الميّـتة عقب الياس

20 ū-mišwār bin fayyāẓ yikfā ma jā
xadū ḏalūla minna ū-ẓall miḥtās

20 ومشوار ابن فيّـاض يكفـاه مـا جاه
اخذو ذلولـه منـه وظـلّ محتـاس

21 illī saʿa fi-l-xēr yikfī masʿā
ū-kēl al-garāya yiksiri kēl ʿabbās

21 اللـي سعى في الخير يكـفيه مسعـاه
وكُـيل القرايـا يكسره كيل عبّـاس

22 waṭ-ṭalba illī widdak itsawwiha-swā
ṭalba xabīṯa mā-liha ḏēl maʿ rās

22 والطلبة اللي ودّك تسوّيـهـا سواة
طلبة خبيثة ما لـها ذيل مـع راس

23 wi-hēd̲ī gaṣīda la-rajajīl taw'ā
min xawf tiz'al min sawalīfna an-nās

23 وهيذي قصيدة لرجـاجيل توعـاه
من خوف تزعل من سواليفنا الناس

24 wal-galb al-imgaṣṣid ṭūl 'umri imgasā
waxar gaṣīda gāliha 'agib hirmās

24 والقلب المقصّـد طول عمره مقاسي
واخر قصيدة قالـها عقب هرماس

25 wal-murr mā tisgī lir-rajil bi-rẓā
ala in sigēti-yyā bi-ḥwās wi-dwās

25 والمـرّ مـا تسقيه لراجل برضـا
الا ان سقيته ايّـاه بحواس ودواس

26 wi-law la-l-miḥillī yittigī hēbt aḷḷā
la-'ṭa-d̲-d̲yāba ṣayd l-ūlād al-ibsās

26 ولو لا المحلّـي يتّـقي هيبة اللّـه
لاعطـى الذيابة صيد لاولاد البساس

2.8

From the Slēmiyyīn Section of the Ḥuwēṭāt to their Chief, Muḥammad Abū Ṭugēga

A Poem of Complaint

When the parties to a conflict are unwilling to settle their differences, and there is a danger of the conflict spreading, a notable third party may intervene and impose a truce by declaring that any further act of hostility will be considered a violation of his own honour—and an attack upon himself. The notable is thus said to have 'thrown his face' (*ramā al-wijh*) between the contending parties—face meaning honour. A usual condition of such a truce requires that one or both of the parties relocate, so that they will not normally meet, especially when murder has been committed and retaliation is likely.[1]

Thus it was that the paramount chief of the Ḥuwēṭāt Tihāma tribe of north-west Arabia, Muḥammad Abū Ṭugēga, intervened in a dispute

Poem 2.8 was heard recited by 'Abēdallāh Salām 'Awda, chief of the 'Alēgāt Zmēliyyīn tribe, near Nagb Rakna, 5 April 1971; and by 'Amr Muḥammad aṣ-Ṣāni' of the Tiyāhā Gdērāt, near Tell 'Arād, 20 February 1972. Discrepancies between the two texts were resolved according to the judgement of Mūsā al-'Aṭāwna.

[1] For more on the workings of the enforced truce, see al-'Ārif, *al-Qaḍā'*, pp. 91–4; Jaussen, pp. 204–8; S̲h̲uqayr, pp. 409–10.

that arose when one of the Slēmiyyīn section of his own tribe had been killed by a member of the neighbouring Masāʿīd tribe in a disagreement over the ownership of date-palms in the al-Sharma oasis (about 1910).[2] The contending parties were accordingly separated and forbidden to enter the disputed oasis. The Masāʿīd, however, violated the terms of the truce and entered the oasis to harvest not only their own dates but those of the Slēmiyyīn as well.

Although informed of the violation, Abū Ṭugēga refrained from taking action against the Masāʿīd. The Slēmiyyīn thereupon sent him a poem asking him to act and threatening to blacken his face (*sawād al-wijh*)—defame him by exposing his failure to live up to his word—if he continued to remain inactive.[3] The first seven lines of the poem describe the camel and rider bearing the message, followed by four lines of praise for the recipient, Abū Ṭugēga. These lines, meant to extol the chief and predispose him in favour of the request, are followed by a two-line complaint of the violation and a four-line warning of the consequences should the chief fail to redress the injustice that the Slēmiyyīn have suffered.

O Rider of a pure, unmixed, well-chosen mount,
Perfect of limb and with sires beyond count, 1

Like a fawn that's fleeing over bare, open ground,
Lest a hunter be hiding behind a low mound.[4] 2

His chest-disc chafes not and his legs don't turn out,[5]
For his chest is just right, neither narrow nor stout. 3

[2] The event apparently took place around 1910, for in June of that year the explorer Alois Musil had as his guide a man of the Masāʿīd who refused to proceed with him to meet Shēkh Abū Ṭugēga because 'one of [the guide's] relatives had killed a subject of Abū Ṭugēga who attended to a palm garden in the oasis of Sharma' (*Northern Hegaz*, p. 118). While only the Masāʿīd are mentioned in the poem itself as a party to the conflict (l. 12), Musil's testimony leads us to believe that the other party was the Slēmiyyīn, particularly as Musil, in *Arabia Petraea* (iii. 49), cites the Slēmiyyīn as residents of the Sharma oasis.

[3] Having one's face blackened is greatly feared by bedouin, since the 'blackened' person, in violating the bedouin code of honour, is considered unworthy of bedouin society. The most common way to publicize a person's 'blackness' is to build a cairn of stones at a crossroads or water-source frequented by many people, who will naturally enquire as to the reason for the cairn (cf. poem 6.15). For more on this custom, see Shuqayr, p. 408.

[4] The topographical term used in the Arabic text, *daghrūg*, means a shallow depression in a desert flat.

[5] Two camel defects, called *hanaf* and *janaf*.

His forelegs are tapered from shoulders to feet,
Like his midriff beneath which the saddlebags meet. 4

His hocks are hairless and carry no flaw;
His hind legs are close, though knock-kneed they're not. 5

On the nape of his neck the bridle is rich:
A pattern of sections with leaves done in stitch; 6

And his rider, if seen sitting high on a peak,
Will resemble a scout come to scan Dhaʿālīq.[6] 7

His herds he'd retrieve though the thieves would have fled;
Though they'd gotten away a full three days ahead. 8

He'll stop off with those people who hearten on sight,
Chiefs whom we turn to when matters get tight; 9

They're my people, my strength, Lad, the day when I fear:
Yea, they moisten my spittle the day it goes dry.[7] 10

Their foes they oppose with sword-blades so thin,
Whetted sharp swords cutting bone after skin. 11

Say: O Chief, you have ruled and your ruling's decree;
But while we're to stay put, are the Masāʿīd free? 12

We left our dates ripening as they were, on the trees;
Now our foes go and pick them whenever they please.[8] 13

If you bring us our rights without further lag,
From each pole, in your honour, we'll fly a white flag;[9] 14

[6] Dhaʿālīq (vernacular *dhaʿālīg*) is a place-name, derived from the plant *dhaʿlūg* (Scorzonera musili, Vel.) whose growth characterizes this area. For more on naming places after plants, see Bailey, 'Place-names', pp. 42–57.

[7] Danger and stress are conceived as 'drying of the spittle' (cf. poems 1.11, n. 3; 4.19, 4.20G).

[8] The Arabic text reads 'They are playing with your face [i.e. honour]'—in expectation that the chief would not tolerate such a slight.

[9] 'Whitening one's face' (*bayāḍ al-wijh*) in this manner announces that someone has bestowed an unusual favour (cf. n. 3 above).

But if, from fear, you squirm out of your word,
We'll rip the accord up and leave it in shreds. 15

It's the shaking of water that makes it come clear,
And to chiefs who desert us, we'll never adhere;[10] 16

But we'll bring you the long, black cloak of a knave,
And the tall, pointed cap of a lowly black slave.[11] 17

1 ya rākbin ḥurrin imnaggaḥ ū-ṣāfī
ū-zamli ijyād ū-hū mwaffag tawafīg

1 يـا راكبٍ حـرٍّ منقّـح وصـافي
وزملد جياد وهو موفّـق توافيق

2 tigūl ẓabyin jāflin min kišāfī
min xōf gannāṣin yijī maʿ ad-daġarīg

2 تقـول ظبـيٍ جافـلٍ من كشافِ
من خوف قنّـاصٍ يجي مع الدغاريق

3 ṣadri xaliyyin ʿan al-ḥanaf wal-janāfī
lā hū wisīʿ ū-la-ygūlū bi haẓ-ẓīg

3 صدرد خليٍّ عن الحنف والجنافِ
لا هو وسيع ولا يقولو بـد الضيق

4 wīdē min ʿend al-manākib rihāfī
ū-baṭni tilāgin ʿalēha-l-maʿalīg

4 وايديد مـن عنـد المناكب رهافِ
وبطنـد تـلاقن عليهـا المعاليق

5 jurdin ʿaragībi ū-lā bi xilāfī
yilḥag walā yišraʿ ʿalē hib-talaḥīg

5 جـردٍ عـراقيبد ولا بـد خلافِ
يلحق ولا يشرع عليد بتلاحيق

6 wi-ʿaḏārin fī miʿalbā ḥilwin ū-wāfī
wi-bkār fīhin imwarrigātin tawarīg

6 وعذارٍ في معلباد حلـوٍ ووافي
وبكـار فيهـن مورّقاتٍ تواريق

7 tišūf rakkība ū-hū ʿaš-šafāfī
tigūl haḏa mišrifin ʿaḏ-ḏaʿalīg

7 تشوف ركّيبد وهو عالشفافِ
تقول هذا مشرفٍ عالذعاليق

[10] To clarify murky water the bedouin shake it in a vessel and then let the impurities settle on the bottom. The poet likens his present problem with the chief to this shaking of the water (*khaḍḍ al-mayya*), implying that, just as this problem serves to clarify the chief's attitude towards the Slēmiyyīn, so also will it determine whether they remain loyal to him.

[11] According to Lane (*Manners*, pp. 35–6), slaves in Egypt, in the early nineteenth century (at least), wore 'peculiarly formal turbans, consisting of several spiral twists, one above another, like the threads of a screw'. Bedouin of the Arabian Ḥuwēṭāt Tihāma tribe, such as the present poet, could have been familiar with this headdress, as many of their tribesmen had moved to Egypt and kept up their connection with the parent tribe (see poem 7.1; Burckhardt ii. 225; Musil, *Northern Hegaz*, p. 130).

8 yilḥag wisīg al-gōm linhin migāfi
linhin ṯilāṯt iyyām gabli miwasīg

8 يلحق وسيق القوم لنّهن مقافي
لنّهن ثلاثة ايّـام قبلد مواسيق

9 ū-yilfī ʿal illī ṭayyibīn al-milāfī
aš-šyūx lillī niztibinhum ʿin aẓ-ẓīg

9 ويلفي عل اللي طيّبين الملافي
الشيوخ للّـي نزتبنهم عن الضيق

10 rabʿī ū-izzī ya walad yōm axāfi
rabʿī yibillū ya walad yābs ar-rīg

10 ربعي وعزّي يـا ولد يوم اخافِ
ربعي يبلّو يا ولد يابس الريق

11 willī yiṣīdūni ib-ṭurr ir-rihāfi
ṭurr aḏ-ḏiyāb yiḏalg al-ʿaẓm taḏlīg

11 واللي يصيدوند بطـرّ الرهافِ
طـرّ الذيـاب يذلّـق العظم تذليق

12 ya šēx jibt il-ʿilūm ū-ʿilmak yikāfi
ʿilmak manaʿna wal-masaʿīd aṭalīg

12 يـا شيخ جبت العلوم وعلمك يكافي
علمك منعنا والمساعيد اطاليق

13 futna naxalna fi liḏīḏ il-miṣāfi
wi-l-wišš yilʿab fih bēyin ū-tadrīg

13 فتنا نخلنا في لذيذ المصافِ
والوجد يلعب فيد بيّـن وتدريق

14 win kān kafilna yaʿṭī al-ḥagg wāfi
l-inġuzz li hal-bēẓ ib-rūs al-bawarīg

14 وان كان كفيلنا يعطي الحقّ وافي
لنغزّ لـد البيض برؤوس البواريق

15 win kān kafilna yitimaġras ū-xāfi
ḥana-nmišligha ū-taġda mašalīg

15 وان كان كفيلنا يتمغرس وخافِ
حنا نمشلقها وتغدى مشاليق

16 limma-nxuẓẓ al-mī yiẓhar ib-ṣāfi
ū-min kabbna ma niltiṣig fih talṣīg

16 لمّـا نخضّ المي يظهر بصـافي
ومن كـبّنا مـا نلتصق فيد تلصيق

17 win bāg l-injīb lih ṯōb min is-sūd wāfi
ū-ṭarṭūr malbūs il-ʿabīd ir-ragarīg

17 وان باق لنجيب لد ثوب من السود وافي
وطـرطور ملبوس الـعبيد الرقـاريق

2.9

From Ṣabāḥ al-Ghānim of the ʿAgēlī to a Ẓuwēʿin of the Bayyāḍiyyīn

A Poem of Complaint

In the 1960s Ṣabāḥ Ṣāliḥ al-Ghānim of the ʿAgēlī tribe of north-western Sinai sold a camel to a man called Ẓuwēʿin of the neighbouring Bayyāḍiyyīn tribe. On taking the camel, Ẓuwēʿin gave a down payment and agreed to pay the balance of twenty-five Egyptian pounds on a specified later date, but failed to do so without offering any excuse. Shortly thereafter Ṣabāḥ also heard that the buyer denied owing him any money. Angered by this insolence, Ṣabāḥ sent him the following reprimand.

O Rider of a mount, barren year after year;
Eight years since there's calf to suckle or rear.[1] 1

Generations, her pedigree's too long to keep;[2]
One day out of Cairo in Shār she will sleep.[3] 2

The lad who made her saddle, from the Nile never drank;[4]
He shaped it with a saw, his adze cut the plank. 3

Her side-sacks, not flat nor tilting, are right;
Neither halter nor bridle are required to check flight. 4

Stop off with Ẓuwēʿin, whom travellers desire:
You'll find him midst coffee-pots, near to the fire;[5] 5

Poem 2.9 was heard recited by its author, at Rabʿa oasis, 24 October 1970.

---

[1] See poem 1.1, n. 14.

[2] A camel is considered thoroughbred when its ancestors, on both sides, have been thoroughbred for at least five generations, after which 'the counting stops' (*baṭal al-ʿadd*).

[3] Jabal Shār is in north-west Arabia; this line is hyperbolic to emphasize the camel's prowess and endurance.

[4] i.e. a proud allusion to a bedouin from Sinai, specifically disallowing that he was ever 'corrupted' by a visit to Egypt proper.

[5] A compliment: i.e he is ever preparing coffee in anticipation of thirsty and weary guests.

A chap who greets guests and whose talk is correct,[6]
While the coffee goes round among his guests on a tray. 6

He roasts the beans fast for the more hurried men;[7]
The coffee-cups passed are no fewer than ten.[8] 7

Say: don't lie to Ṣabāḥ; it's bad luck, you will find:
I'd to wait all alone like a dog left behind![9] 8

The sum is so paltry, why deny there's a debt?
Merely five times five is no sum to regret. 9

Let me finish my poem with a prayer for the Fine:[10]
Muḥammad, whose light brightly glows from his shrine.[11] 10

1	ya rākbin min fōg ḥīlin baʿd ḥīl liha ṯamānt is-snīn ma laẓẓha ḥwār	يا راكبٍ من فوق حيلٍ بعد حيل لها ثمانة السنين ما لظّها حوار	1
2	wa-ʿaddha fa-l-gōd jīlin baʿd jīl min maṣr gāmat maraḥat fī jabal šār	وعدّها في القود جيلٍ بعد جيل من مصر قامت مرحت في جبل شار	2
3	šdādha ṭaggit walad ma širib nīl dōsa ib-gadūma wit-tafṣīl minšār	شدادها طقّة ولد ما شرب نيل دوسه بقدومه والتفصيل منشار	3
4	ū-xurjha ma fī ʿadlin wala mīl tinsāg dālʿa la ṣarīma wala ʿaḏār	وخرجها ما فيه عدلٍ ولا ميل تنساق دالعة لا صريمة ولا عذار	4

[6] In the Arabic original 'he who doesn't ask unbecoming questions' (such as, what is your name? what is your tribe? where are you from? or what are you looking for here?—all of which are disparaged in bedouin hospitality). (Cf. poem 4.7, l. 4.)

[7] A compliment for the consideration shown to guests despite his 'natural' desire to have them stay and honour his tent with their presence.

[8] i.e. implying that his hospitable tent is always filled with guests.

[9] A dog that is absent while his master breaks camp and migrates will return to the campsite to find no one there. The contempt for a dog that allows for its abandonment by a migrating owner serves as a strong image for expressing the poet's indignation over Ẕuwēʿin's violation of his honour by not keeping their appointment.

[10] For 'Fine' or 'Beautiful' as an epithet for the Prophet Muḥammad, see poem 1.11, n. 8.

[11] The Prophet Muḥammad's tomb is conceived in popular Islam to be shrouded in a blinding light; thence, no one is allowed to enter. It is also believed that a pillar of heavenly light crowns the sepulchre to direct pilgrims' steps from a three-day walking distance (Burton, i. 316, 341).

5 tilfī ʿala ẓwēʿin fī magʿadin̲ zēn
tilga bakarijhum ʿala jurft an-nār

5 تلفي على ظويعن في مقعدٍ زين
تلقى بكـارجهم على جرفة النـار

6 rajlin̲ yirīd aẓ-ẓayf wi-sʿāla zēn
ū-ṣīniyta allī ʿal al-jamaʿ tindār

6 راجـلٍ يريد الضيف وســأله زين
وصينيّــته اللــي عــل الجمع تندار

7 fī ḥamṣ al-bann mā yiwannūk ʿajlīn
tilga fanajīlhim mi-l-ʿašr wi-kṯār

7 في حمص البنّ مــا يونّــوك عجلين
تلقى فناجيلهم مــن العشر وكــثار

8 gūl lā tikḏib ʿala ṣabāḥ yā kiḏbak al-bēn
xallēta ʿal al-mīʿād kalbin̲ ʿala dār

8 قول لا تكذب على صباح يا كذبك البين
خلّــيته عل الميعاد كلبٍ على دار

9 ʿimli gilīli ma tağiẓẓī bak imn ad-dēn
hin xamis xamsāt mā hin ikṯār

9 عملة قليلة ما تغضّي بك من الدين
هــن خمس خمسات مــا هن كثار

10 waxtim kalāmī bi-ṣalātī ʿal az-zēn
wi-mḥammad illī gabra yizhī bal-anwār

10 واختم كلامي بصلاتي عل الزين
ومحمّــد اللــي قبره يزهي بالانوار

2.10

From the Bilī Tribe to King Ibn Saʿūd

A Poem Pleading for Mercy

In 1932, members of the Bilī confederation of north-western Arabia, led by their chief, Ḥāmid Ibn Rifāda, rebelled against the authority of King ʿAbd al-ʿAzīz Ibn Saʿūd, who had established himself in the Ḥijāz province in 1925.[1] Ibn Rifāda, popularly known as 'One-Eye' (*al-aʿwar*), had reportedly gathered a force of some six thousand

Poem 2.10 was heard from four reciters in central and southern Sinai: ʿĪd Ḥammād Masʿad of the Ḥuwēṭāt ʿAbayyāt tribe, at Jabal ʿUrf, 23 October 1970; Rāḍī Swēlim ʿAtayyig of the Muzēna Darārma tribe, at el-ʿArīsh, 20 March 1971; ʿAwda Sālim ʿAlī of the Muzēna Darārma tribe, at Dhahab oasis, 22 August 1972; and Rabīaʿ Abū Ḥarbī of the Ṣawālḥa ʿAwārma tribe, at Fīrān oasis, 4 September 1972. Discrepancies between the different renditions were resolved according to the judgement of Muṣliḥ Ibn ʿĀmr and Mūsā al-ʿAṭāwna.

[1] Dickson, *Kuwait*, p. 329. Ḥāmid Ibn Rifāda had been friendly to the Hashimites since he first joined them in their rebellion against the Ottoman Empire in the First World War (Lawrence,

mounted men, including sections of the Ḥuwēṭāt Tihāma tribe, under their chief, Aḥmad Abū Ṭugēga; but Ibn Saʿūd, using wireless communication and motor vehicles to transport his troops, was able to defeat him in a surprise attack at the port town of Ḍaba in which most of the Ibn Rifāda clan were reportedly killed, including Ḥāmid himself, and his severed head, according to the oral tradition, was kicked around like a ball (until bought back by a relative for four Egyptian pounds).[2]

The Ibn Rifāda people who remained in the Ḥijāz, being subjected to harsh treatment by the local governor, asked Ḥassān Jawwān of the Ḥuwēṭāt to compose the present poem, requesting King Ibn Saʿūd to restrain his officials and rehabilitate their clan. Most of the poem extols the power and piety of the Saʿūd regime in an attempt to flatter the ruler and to convince him that the Bilī have abandoned all thought of opposing his rule, and have even accepted his strict religious doctrines.

O Riders of ten, on whose hinds ten more rest,[3]
Their forelegs are broad, their forebears pure, 1

Most like an ostrich in beauty and build,[4]
Taking slopes up and down with no pain to endure. 2

They'll stop off with Abū Turkī,[5] foe of our foes,
Sultan of the desert, who knows his obligations; 3

pp. 116, 159), and, according to British Colonial Office records, his rebellion was instigated by the (then) Amīr ʿAbdallāh of Transjordan (see Great Britain, Colonial Office, (CO)831-20/97805-X/K1957, Cox to Cunliffe-Lister, 24 Sept. 1932 (attached Interim Report: Hedjaz Revolt—Origins and Responsibility).

[2] Oral communication from Salāma Ḥimēd ʿĪd al-Ashgar of the Bilī Magābla, at Mazār, 4 March 1974. His account of Ḥāmid's head bandied about as a football is corroborated by Murray (p. 133), who heard of it soon after the event. See l. 17 below.

[3] As a poetic device, ten camels were 'sent' carrying twenty delegates on behalf of the Bilī. In actuality, 'double riding', called *marādif*, did exist, in which the riders would take turns, one riding on the saddle and one behind it.

[4] Cf. poem 2.6, n. 3.

[5] ʿAbd al-ʿAzīz Ibn Saʿūd was commonly known as Abū Turkī, 'the Father of Turkī'. Although this first-born son died in 1919, a victim of the influenza plague, the father's epithet remained. (Cf. poem 1.6, n. 2.)

God help him to fight malevolent Christians,[6]
And to beat down those who betray their commissions.[7]   4

Authority before him was always but token,
Then, like camels who're trained with a stick, we were broken.[8]   5

We'd heard of his reign, but we dwelled far away;[9]
And now, over us, he enforces his sway.   6

He's a hawk who's higher than <u>sh</u>āhīn hawks in flight,[10]
And he scatters feathers whenever he bites.   7

Known wide as a host with slaves that obey,
He 'divorces' young wives to make a guest stay.[11]   8

Yes, that's Abū Turkī, two thousand troops strong:
Woe's him upon whom these armed locusts throng.[12]   9

Where's Duwī<u>sh</u> with his millions of warriors today?[13]
The <u>Sh</u>arīf—where is he and the tribes out his way.[14]   10

[6] Ibn Saʿūd, hoping to extend his kingdom and authority beyond the confines of the Arabian peninsula, came into conflict between 1917 and 1928 with Great Britain in its capacity as the ultimate authority in Kuwait, Iraq, and Transjordan. The reference to Christians as 'malevolent' (<u>kh</u>abī<u>th</u>īn) was common in Arabia, for Doughty heard it fifty years earlier (ii. 284).

[7] An allusion to the members of the Ikhwān religious movement, which rebelled against Ibn Saʿud's authority in 1929–30.

[8] 'Training with a stick' (*ṭabaʿ ba-l-maṭrag*) refers to a mounted trainer who teaches a camel to follow directional signals by riding without reins and holding out a stick; the term does not denote beating with a stick.

[9] The Bilī lived in the remote north-west corner of Ibn Saʿūd's new kingdom.

[10] The <u>sh</u>āhīn hawk cited in the Arabic text is the long-winged Falco tinnunculus variety, native to the Arabian peninsula. The image is used in bedouin poetry to allude to a person's martial prowess (cf. poem 5.1).

[11] In the Arabic text, the young wives are described as 'those with standing breasts' (*zābirāt an-nuhūd*). Ibn Saʿūd, as many another bedouin host, no doubt swore on various occasions that he would divorce one of his wives if a visitor refused to stay for dinner. This allusion to his threats to divorce is a compliment to his generosity. For more on this custom, see poem 1.4, n. 8.

[12] The poet, as is customary among bedouin, uses the word locusts (*jurūd*) to designate soldiers, reportedly because they appear in great numbers and in close formation, and cause great destruction.

[13] Fayṣal Sulṭān Āl Duwī<u>sh</u>, paramount chief of the large Imṭēr tribal confederation of north-central Arabia, rebelled against Ibn Saʿūd in 1929, was defeated, and was executed. 'Millions' of soldiers is hyperbole.

[14] The <u>Sh</u>arīf, Ḥusēn ibn ʿAlī, descendent of the Prophet and custodian of the Holy Places in Mecca and Medina, was expelled from western Arabia by Ibn Saʿūd in 1925, despite the support he received from various tribes in the Ḥijāz.

Where are the Rashīd lads, on horseback so skilled,
From whom none could flee, and by whom they were killed?[15] 11

He returned to our faith those who'd been vain,
From the good things of life he has made them abstain; 12

He has forced many men to drink muddy dregs:
Bravo to ʿAbd al-ʿAzīz bin Saʿūd! 13

But mud, though it sticks, never holds a stone tight,[16]
And fire needs fuel in order to light.[17] 14

God help us from governors who treat us with scorn,
And short-armed ciphers, with rank adorn.[18] 15

They brought Ḥāmid's head to the heart of the market,
And raised it high on a stick in the square. 16

Had they heeded Maḥmūd they'd all now be well,[19]
And Ḥāmid's head, in Gāʿ Sūdī, to sport had not fell. 17

Ḥāmid's clansmen themselves—only thirty remain,
And like apes, on all fours, they walk round in disdain.[20] 18

Though their minds may have erred, don't put them through hell,
And don't deem a mud-hole a rich-flowing well![21] 19

[15] The Ibn Rashīd family, that had ruled north-central Arabia since 1834, began to lose its authority to Ibn Sa'ūd when he took Riyāḍ for his capital in 1901. In August 1921 his army conquered the city of Ḥā'il, the Rashīd capital, putting an end to this dynasty. The Rashīdī reputation for relentlessness in the pursuit of enemies was legendary, for Doughty (ii. 36), writing during the height of their power, recorded, 'None of [Ibn Rashīd's] enemies are taken to quarter until they be destroyed.'

[16] i.e. vile persons may attach themselves to rulers, but cannot provide them with effective support.

[17] i.e. rulers need worthy supporters in order to rule effectively.

[18] The image of 'short-armed' (*gaṣrān*) may denote stinginess or weakness.

[19] 'Maḥmūd', reportedly the military commander of the rebel forces, had counselled them in vain to surrender to Ibn Sa'ūd before their defeat.

[20] Some of the Bilī fled to the Negev where they were destitute; 'Ārif al-'Ārif, then Chief Officer of the Beersheba District, saw them 'wandering about aimlessly' (*Ta'rīkh*, p. 115).

[21] i.e. do not consider those who became influential in our absence as our equals.

O Messenger, tell him these times are too hard;
Ask him whom God favoured, now our good to guard.[22]

1 ya rakbīn ʿašara yizōzin bi-ʿišrīn
gabb al-ʿaẓūd imnaggaḥāt al-jidūdī

1 يا راكبين عشرة يزوزون بعشرين
قبّ العضود منقّحات الجدودِ

2 ašbah naʿāmin bit-tawaṣīf wiz-zēn
ma kādhin hall at-taraj wis-sinūdī

2 اشبه نعامٍ بالتواصيف والزين
ما كادهن هلّ الترج والسنودِ

3 yilfin ʿal abū turkī ʿadū il-ʿadūwīn
sulṭān barr ū-bil-lawāzim sudūdī

3 يلفن عل ابو تركي عدو العدوّين
سلطان برّ وباللوازم سدودِ

4 alla yiʿīna ʿal an-naṣāra al-xabīṯīn
wa-ygaddira ʿal bāyigīn il-ʿuhūdī

4 اللّه يعينه عل النصارى الخبيثين
ويقدّره عل بايقين العهودِ

5 min gabl ḥukmi ma kunna muṭiʿīn
wal-yōm ṭabbaʿna ṭibāʿ al-gaʿūdī

5 من قبل حكمه ما كنّا مطيعين
واليوم طبّعنا طباع القعودِ

6 wa-nismaʿ bi-ḥukma kān wiḥna baʿīdīn
wal-yōm kull ma biyḥakma ʿalēna yizūdī

6 ونسمع بحكمه كان واحنا بعيدين
واليوم كلّ ما بيحكّمه علينا يزودِ

7 ṣagrin taʿalla ʿal aṣ-ṣugūr aš-šayahīn
wallī yiʿaẓẓa sār rīša bidūdī

7 صقرٍ تعلّى عل الصقور الشياهين
واللي يعضّه صار ريشه بدودِ

8 ṣīta kabīr ū-lih xadadīm ṭawiʿīn
yāma taṭallagat min zabrāt an-nihūdī

8 صيته كبير وله خداديم طوعين
ياما تطلّقت من زابرات النهودِ

9 ū-hāḏa abū turkī jurūda alfēn
ya wēl min ṣabbū ʿalē hal-jurūdī

9 وهذا ابو تركي جروده الفين
يا ويل من صبّو عليه الجرودِ

10 wēn ad-duwīš illī jurūda malayīn
wēn aš-šarīf ū-wēn ḏīk al-ibdūdī

10 وين الدويش اللي جروده ملايين
وين الشريف ووين ذيك البدودِ

11 wēn ar-rašīd illī ʿal al-xēl darkīn
wild ar-rašīd imṯaglīn aš-šarūdī

11 وين الرشيد اللي عل الخيل دركين
ولد الرشيد مثقّلين الشرودِ

[22] This line is an allusion to the Qurʾānic dictum (28. 77) 'Be beneficent just as God has been beneficent to you.'

12 illī jahal xallā yimšī ʿal ad-dīn
xalla ḥayāta ʿal ad-dinya zuhūdī

12 اللي جهل خلّاه يمشي عل الدين
خلّا حياته عل الدنيا زهود

13 kam wāḥdiṉ asgā min ġaṯbar aṭ-ṭīn
la bās ya ʿabd al-ʿazīz as-saʿūdī

13 كم واحد اسقاد من غثبر الطين
لا باس يا عبد العزيز السعود

14 ʿumr al-ḥajar ma yiṣṭaʿib fa-ṭ-ṭīn
wan-nār ma tōlaʿ ablayya wugūdī

14 عمر الحجر ما يصطعب في الطين
والنار ما تولع بليّا وقود

15 aḷḷā min ḥukm yahīn al-ʿarībiyyīn
wa-ynōms al-hāmil gaṣīr az-znūdī

15 اللّه من حكم يهين العريبيّين
وينومس الهامل قصير الزنود

16 jābū rās ḥāmid baṭn ad-dakakīn
ū-ġazzū fi-d-dagaʿa ʿala rās ʿūdī

16 جابو راس حامد بطن الدكاكين
وغزود في الدقعة على راس عود

17 la ṭawwaʿū maḥmūd kullhū salīmīn
kān ma laʿib-ib-rās ḥāmid fī gāʿ sūdī

17 لو طوّعو محمود كلّهم سليمين
كان ما لعب براس حامد في قاع سود

18 ya gōm ḥāmid bagīhū ṯalaṯīn
yinaṭṭū ʿal aḏ-ḏurʿān miṯl al-gurūdī

18 يا قوم حامد باقيهم ثلاثين
ينطّو عل الذرعان مثل القرود

19 la taxrabū ya hēl il-ʿugūl al-xarībiyyīn
ʿū-la taḥsabūn al-baẓẓ miṯl al-ʿudūdī

19 لا تخربو يا هيل العقول الخريبيّين
ولا تحسبون البضّ مثل العدود

20 ya mirsalī gūl-li tarā wagitna šēn
ū-man jād ʿalē aḷḷā ʿalēna yijūdī

20 يا مرسلي قول له ترا وقتنا شين
ومن جاد عليه اللّه علينا يجود

2.11

From the Rumēlāt Tribe to
Sh̲ēkh Salmān al-Huzayyil
A Request for Intercession

In the early 1950s many bedouin—some from Sinai, others displaced by the Arab–Israeli War of 1948—crossed illegally into Israel from neighbouring countries in order to smuggle, spy, or engage in sabotage. One such bedouin, of the Rumēlāt confederation of northeast Sinai, crossed the border and was captured and jailed. Shortly thereafter, the Rumēlāt sent a messenger to Salmān ʿAlī Salmān al-Huzayyil, the most prominent bedouin chief in Israel at the time, asking him to ascertain the whereabouts of their kinsman. Salmān's close relations with the military administration in the Negev were well known.

The Rumēlāt made their request in the attractive form of a poem which the messenger learned by heart and recited to Salmān himself. As the poem is intended to engage the chief's interest, most of it relates to themes of recent Negev history with touches of both pain and humour. The poet first describes the bedouins' astonishment to see their familiar world change beyond recognition in such a short time (lines 1–5). Then, to recall the flight of the bedouin during the war of 1948, he mockingly portrays how even the wild animals and the venerated dead saints of the Negev had to flee the war's harshness (lines 6–10). A single line (line 11) suffices to state the subject of the poem—the missing infiltrator (further details being provided by the messenger in conversation). This line is immediately followed by the request that Sh̲ēkh Salmān use his good offices to intervene—a three-line request, of which two contain praise for his station and generosity, and one (line 14) a discreet offer of money. The poet ends with the conventional prayer for the Prophet Muḥammad, intimating that the chief imitate the Prophet's divine intercession on behalf of the dead.

Poem 2.11 was heard recited by its author, Lāfī Faraj Sulēmān, a black appended member of the Rumēlāt Busūm tribe, at el-ʿArīsh̲, 15 October 1970.

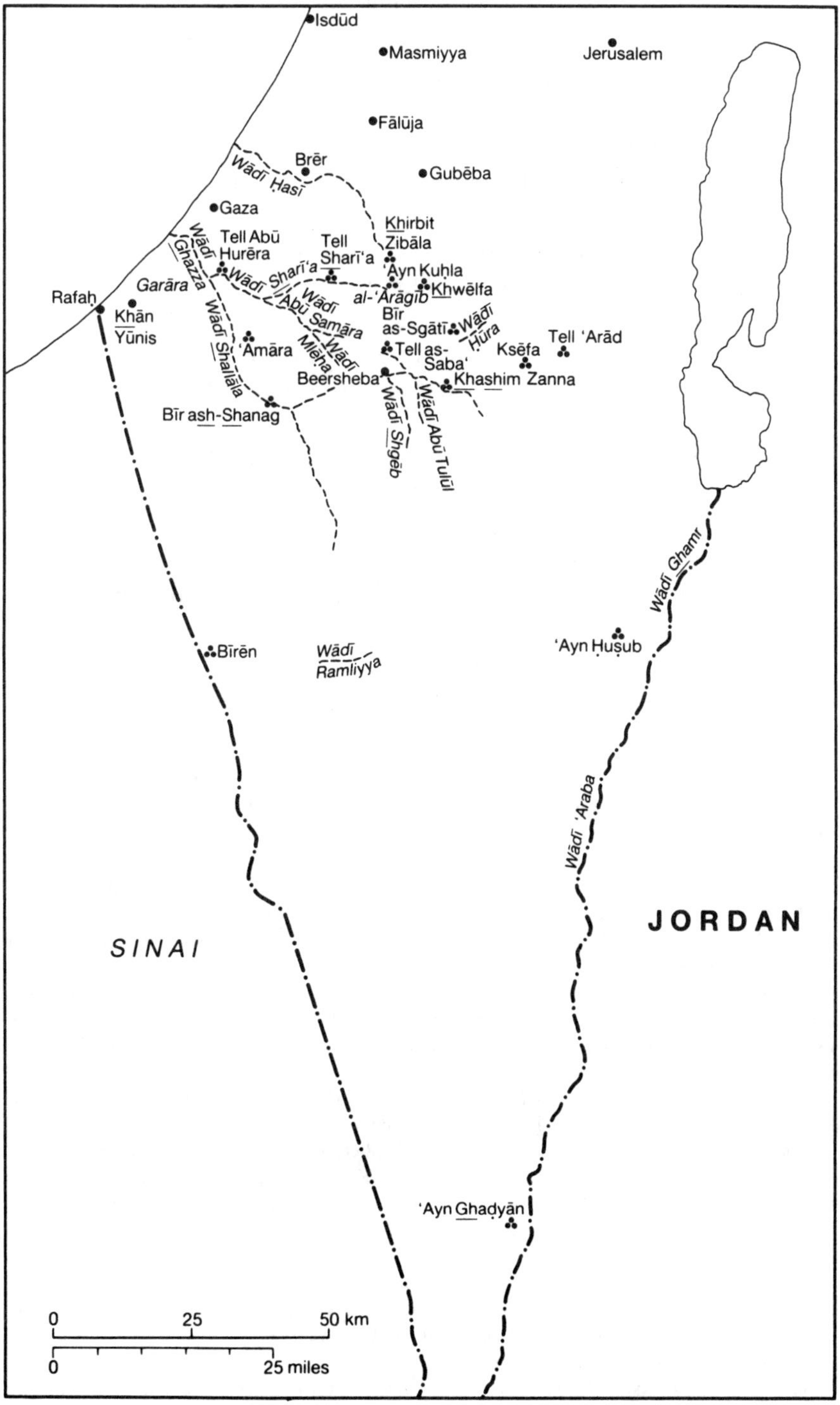

MAP 4. Places in the Negev mentioned in the book.

From Gaza to Beersheba one sees only trees,
In Wādī Sharī'a you get lost with ease;[1] 1

I'm confused by the sight of the buildings I find,[2]
I'm stunned and I feel that I'm losing my mind. 2

Once Wādī Sharī'a was pools and huge stones,
Where a bedouin's camels could water alone;[3] 3

Left and right there were sand-pools whose water was good,
And the herd-lasses scooped it in bowls made of wood.[4] 4

And though Abū Samāra gave a kantar of wheat,[5]
From its peaches today you just pick and eat.[6] 5

The wolf left his whelp—on that day not so brave—
When the bombing and shelling destroyed his small cave. 6

He asked of the fox if he too'd left his place;
He replied: 'Let's just reach Khashim Zanna apace!'[7] 7

[1] Between Gaza and Beersheba is where the chief, Salmān al-Huzayyil (d. 1982), lived, just north of one of the largest wadis, Wādī Sharī'a (present-day Nahal Ha-Besor), which drains the north-west Negev. The actual residence of the chief was called Khirbit Zibāla, presently the bedouin town Rahat.

[2] Tent-dwelling bedouin usually refer to any 'hard' construction, even a one-room storehouse, with the Arabic word for 'palace' (*gaṣr*). Here the poet is referring to the relatively modest immigrant housing that was built in the Jewish agricultural communities established in the north-west Negev between 1949 and 1953.

[3] Generally, camels have to be watered by shepherds, who draw water from otherwise inaccessible sources and pour it into troughs. However, in Wādī Sharī'a, which receives its water from many smaller wadis each year, the rock pools were so full that camels could drink directly from them.

[4] Sand-pools (*thamāyil*, sing. *thamīla*) are formed from rainwater trapped in a deep deposit of sand with a base of non-porous rock such as sandstone or granite; owing to pressure, the water 'seeps up' (*tithmil*), and, by digging in the sand, a shepherd can obtain water that accumulates in the depression, a cupful at a time. The hyperbolic image of scooping up bowlfuls of accumulated water at one stroke is here used to stress the fact that the sand-pools were exceptionally full. The bowls referred to in the Arabic text (*gidāḥ*, sing. *gadaḥ*) are carved out of the wood of desert trees, such as the Acacia or Pistacia, and are primarily used for milking camels.

[5] A kantar (bed. Ar. *gunṭār*) is a dry weight approximating one-third of a ton in the Negev. Such a harvest of winter wheat or barley to a dunam (approx. a quarter acre) would be considered excellent in that area. Wādī Abū Samāra is a branch of the Sharī'a.

[6] i.e. peaches grown by Israeli farmers.

[7] Khashim Zanna is east of Beersheba. Some bedouin of the northern Negev fled there in 1948 and 1949 to escape the hostilities between the Egyptian and Israeli armies.

Even Abū Hurēra fled, leaving his grave,[8]
Consulting Munṭār how they'd weather this storm;[9] 8

While Nūrān on his hilltop[10] a tambourine beat[11]
To gather the Holies and join the retreat. 9

They should go to the Prophet, whose light is a beam,[12]
For a pilgrim to Mecca might wash his sins clean.[13] 10

In times such as these every soul is concerned,
Knowing nothing at all of our boys who're interned. 11

But the tribe of Huzayyil has a chief that is choice;
The entire Tiyāhā pay heed to his voice.[14] 12

He's surrounded by coffee-beans—left and right—[15]
And meanness won't suit him if meant as a slight. 13

[8] Abū Hurēra was a Companion of the Prophet and a fertile source for the Traditions of the Prophet after Muḥammad's death. Although he died in Medina and was probably buried there, he is believed by the bedouin to be buried in the Negev. The tomb of Abū Hurēra in the Negev is just south of the present-day village of Misillot, about eight kilometres west of Tell S͟harī'a. The Malālḥa tribe of the Gaza area and north-eastern Sinai claim him as their ancestor. (For more on Abū Hurēra, see Canaan, *passim*; al-'Ārif, *al-Qaḍā'*, pp. 261–2.)

[9] Al-Munṭār is the name of a holy man whose tomb lies just east of the city of Gaza. One tradition has it that he was a member of the Masā'īd tribe and was killed in a battle against a seventeenth-century governor of Gaza when his tribe was migrating to their present location in north-west Sinai. The tradition is cited in S͟huqayr, p. 118.

[10] S͟hēk͟h Nūrān was a holy tomb visited, in particular, by the Tarābīn of the Negev prior to 1948; its origin is unknown even to the bedouin (see Canaan, *passim*, al-'Ārif, *al-Qaḍā'*, pp. 255–6.)

[11] The beating of tambourines at holy tombs is part of an exorcism rite.

[12] The theme of Muḥammad as a beacon to the faithful is prevalent in Islam. One of his formal designations is 'the Light' (*al-nūr*) (see Ebeid and Young, p. 260); and when he died he was eulogized as 'the brightness and the light that we followed' (*kāna al-ḍiyā' wa-kāna al-nūra natba'uhu*) in a eulogy by Hassān Ibn T͟hābit (Ibn His͟hām, iv. 321; trans. Guillaume, *Life*, p. 690.) Cf. poem 2.9, n. 11.

[13] A pilgrimage (*ḥajj*) to Mecca is considered an effective means for a Muslim to expiate his sins. A common greeting for a returning pilgrim is 'May your pilgrimage be acceptable and your sins forgiven' (*ḥajj mabrūr wa-d͟hanb mag͟hfūr*). The image of sins being washed away derives from Muḥammad's own prayer (*du'ā*): 'O God! Wash me of my sins with ice-water and hail (*allāhumma, ig͟hsilnī bi-mā' al-t͟halj wa-l-barad min al-d͟hunūb*). If the poet was implying that the holy men themselves had sinned, perhaps it was by not preventing the Arab defeat in the 1948 war.

[14] The Huzayyil, being but one tribe in the Tiyāhā confederation, had an on-going rivalry with the 'Aṭāwna tribe over the leadership of the entire confederation (see Bailey, 'Nineteenth Century', *passim*). Attributing 'victory' to Salmān al-Huzayyil in verse was thus a complimentary gesture.

[15] i.e. the large supply of coffee-beans is testimony to Salmān al-Huzayyil's largesse, which attracts many guests.

His words in the palace a thousand pounds cost,[16]
But those who're oppressed never feel that they've lost. 14

So my words I now seal with praise for the Guide,[17]
Who in heaven or hell always takes up our side. 15

1 min ʿend ġazza lis-sabaʿ kullha-šjār wādi-š-šarīʿa rāḥ bintūh ʿinni	1 من عند غزّة للسبع كلّها اشجار وادي الشريعة راح بنتوه عنه
2 šuft il-igṣūr il-ʿālya ū-ṣirt miḥtār waḥiss ʿaglī tāyih il-fikr minni	2 شفت القصور العالية وصرت محتار واحسّ عقلي تايه الفكر منه
3 wādī aš-šarīʿa kān ġudrān wi-ḥjār ḥatta jahām al-badū yatwārdinni	3 وادي الشريعة كان غدران وحجار حتّى جهام البدو يتواردنّه
4 kulli ṯimāyil ṣaff yimīn wi-ysār ahl al-ġanam bi-gdaḥḥin yiġrifinni	4 كلّه ثمايل صفّ يمين ويسار اهل الغنم بقداحهن يغرفنّه
5 abū samāra ḥillti tijīb gunṭār al-yōm kulli xūx tingaṭ minni	5 ابو سمارة حلّته تجيب قنطار اليوم كلّه خوخ تنقط منه
6 aḏ-ḏīb xallā jirāh ū-farr mišwār ẓarb il-ginābil juḥurhin hadaminni	6 الذيب خلّا جراه وفرّ مشوار ضرب القنابل جحرهن هدمنّه
7 gāl lil-iḥṣēnī wi-lēš bithammil ad-dār gāl lih ana wiyyāk ʿal xašim zanni	7 قال للحصيني وليش بتهمّل الدار قال له انا ويّاك عل خشم زنّه
8 abū hrēra hajj miš ʿāyiz ad-dār lagga ʿal al-munṭār biyšāwrinni	8 ابو هريرة هجّ مش عايز الدار لقّى عل المنطار بيشاورنّه
9 wi-nūrān fōg al-ʿālya biydugg aṭ-ṭār biylamlam aṣ-ṣullāḥ wi-yrāfginni	9 ونوران فوق العالية بيدقّ الطار بيلملم الصلّاح ويرافقنّه

[16] Because a *sarāya* (lit. 'palace') was a provincial government building in the Ottoman Empire, the term remained in popular usage among the bedouin for any centre of governmental authority.

[17] 'Guide' is one of the appellations of the Prophet in the sense of 'leader of his people' (see the poems in Ibn Hishām, iv. 317, 322; trans. Guillaume, *Life*, pp. 690, 795).

10 widdhum yilaggū ʿań-nabī kāmil anwār
min zār makka ġassal aḏ-ḏanb ʿinni

10 ودّهم يلقّــو عالنبي كـــامل انوار
من زار مـكّــة غسل الذنب عنـــد

11 hāḏa zimān ū-fīh tahat il-ifkār
willī biyṭubb as-sijin mā-nidrī ʿinni

11 هذا زمان وفيد تاهت الافكار
واللى بيطبّ السجن ما ندري عنــد

12 wamma-l-huzayyil ʿendihum šēx muxtār
kull it-tiyāha ibṯāxiḏ ar-rāy minni

12 وامـّـا الـهزيّــل عندهم شيخ مختار
كـلّ التياها تاخذ الراي منـــد

13 ʿendi-kyās al-bann yimīn wiysār
mū hū m-illī-l-buxul biyšiḥḥ ʿanni

13 عندد كيــاس البـــنّ يمين ويسار
ما هو من اللي البخل بيشحّ عنـــد

14 juwwa aṣ-ṣarāya kilimti balaf dīnār
lin jā li hal-maẓlūm mabsūṭ minni

14 جوّا السرايا كلمتد بالف دينار
لـــن جــا لــد المظلوم مبسوط منـد

15 waxtum kalāmī bi-mdaḥt al-hādī iz-zēn
hū šifīʿ an-nās nārin ū-janni

15 واختم كلامي بمدحة الـهادي الزين
هو شفيع الناس نــارٍ وجنّـــة

2.12

From ʿAnēz abū Sālim to King ʿAbdallāh of Jordan

A Poem to Request a Camel

ʿAbdallāh, King of Jordan (1922–51), was fond of poetry and of bedouin poetry in particular. It was rumoured among the bedouin that when favourably impressed by a poem he would reward the author.[1] Accordingly, ʿAnēz abū Sālim, finding himself in Aqaba in 1950, put his mind to composing a poem in the hope that the king might grant him a camel with its riding paraphernalia. To please the monarch,

Poem 2.12 was heard recited by its author, in Wādī Murēkhī, 26 May 1984; by Rāḍī Swēlim ʿAtayyig of the Muzēna Darārma tribe, at el-ʿArīsh, 20 March 1971; and by Rabīaʿ Abū Ḥarbī of the Ṣawālḥa ʿAwārma tribe, in Wādī Fīrān, 4 September 1972.

---

[1] Also T. E. Lawrence (p. 212) remarked of ʿAbdallāh: 'He was fond of Arabic verses, and the local poets found him a profitable audience.'

eleven of the poem's nineteen lines praise him and his family, their importance, and their generosity; there is even a stated bedouin preference for Jordan to Egypt as a homeland (line 2). A touch of subtle political humour is also not lacking, especially in the detailed description of tea drinking (lines 10–11). Tea, as a beverage, was introduced into the bedouin area by the British between the two world wars; thus, by stressing ʿAbdallāh's excessive use of tea, the poet hinted at his political collaboration with Britain—an allusion the king might appreciate as subtle and clever. The poem was transcribed and then sent to the king by a black scribe, Imsallam Abū ʿĀyid, who at that time provided secretarial services for the bedouin in Aqaba.

O Rider of a mount with muscles well-turned,
The colour of coffee-beans, brown, but not burned: 1

Leave those who manure the land with a hoe[2]
And order back anyone raiding a foe.[3] 2

Stop off with people whose power is real,
And their hailing of 'Welcome' is quick and with zeal: 3

The S͟harīf and his sons, on horseback so skilled;
The riders they chase are doomed to be killed. 4

Ṭalāl and Nāyif,[4] both are the best,
Drinking enemies' blood from the top of the breast.[5] 5

To hear the cry 'Charge!' from their lips is just fine,
As the enemy's horses up front break their line. 6

[2] i.e. the Egyptians, whom the bedouin contemptuously view as a nation of immobile peasants tied down to their intensively cultivated plots which they manure over and over again. This way of life contrasts sharply with that of the bedouin, who place great value on freedom of movement. In Sinai a bedouin expression for 'hard times' is 'working with a hoe' (*as͟h-s͟hug͟hl bi-l-fās*) (cf. poem 6.17).

[3] One bedouin view of Egyptian government as oppressive stems from its efforts to subject them to the laws of the land: e.g. prohibitions on vengeance, raiding, and intertribal hostilities.

[4] The sons of King ʿAbdallāh; Ṭalāl, the father of King Ḥusēn of Jordan (cf. poem 1.6, l. 3).

[5] It was a bedouin custom to drink the blood of a slain enemy, explained (by the author) as necessary to 'dispel the rancour from one's heart' (*yizīḥ al-g͟hill min galbih*) and 'let one's heart cool off' (*yik͟hallī galbih yibrid*) as the rancour 'subsides' (*yifis͟hs͟h*). One expression for 'I'll kill you' is 'I'll drink your blood' (*as͟hrab min damak*). The drinking was done from the *naḥr*, the spot where the throat meets the chest. In the Arabic text the enemy is called 'the stinking one' (*al-muṣannī*).

They've a palace and horse guard, a million men[6] strong,
To deter any plot that might do them a wrong. 7

On all of them seated together I'd gaze,
Just the sight of such monarchs must surely amaze. 8

Say: O Sir, we all stand at your beck and command,
Since the day your army protected our land.[7] 9

Say: O Sir, how you generously offer the glass,
Filled with tea that poets so commonly praise, 10

So strong that it leaves in the glass a dark stain;
Even after it's washed black markings remain. 11

Then you pour fresh coffee over cardamom seeds:[8]
Coffee that stains with henna-red beads.[9] 12

And then when you bring your guests what to eat,
Goat-ghee flows through the rice and the meat.[10] 13

Say: I want a young camel whose ride is a 'high':
Tawny, not whiteness that glares in the eye; 14

With a saddle and saddle-bags fitted just right,
And tassels that sway between his legs when in flight, 15

[6] 'A hundred million' in the Arabic text; hyperbole (cf. poem 2.10, l. 10).

[7] Some southern Sinai bedouin of the poet's tribe, like Salīm ʿĪd Sālim Ibn Jāzī (oral communication, 1974), were in Aqaba on 10 March 1949 when the Israeli army arrived at the Red Sea coast of what was later to become Eilat. Since the Jordanian army under British officers was deployed around Aqaba, the bedouin assumed that this deployment contained the Israelis in the Negev and deterred them from entering Sinai.

[8] Bedouin traditionally use at least two and often three pots for brewing coffee. One pot is used for boiling the coffee, and its pure liquid contents are then poured—without the coffee grounds—into a pot that contains seeds of the cardamom spice and is called the 'spice pot' (*bahārjiyya*); whence, after the brew is sufficiently spiced, it is poured into cups for drinking.

[9] Henna (*ḥinna*) is a reddish powder made from the *Lawsonia inermis* plant and used for staining and dyeing.

[10] In Jordan and the Arabian peninsula rice stacked on a tray and topped with mutton is a semi-festive dish called *mansaf*. For the clarified goat butter (*samn*) poured over the *mansaf* as an act of hospitality, see poem 1.10, n. 7.

And a thigh-rest new, its thongs on his withers,[11]
And reins stitched by hands dyed a henna-red hue.[12] 16

If the king gave me only a pack camel—Fine!
But speedy young mares set me on fire. 17

I am sending these words on a sheet of white paper,
Set in language that's fine by a scribe who can write. 18

So I'll now seal this poem with Allah in mind;[13]
The message is finished, the poet has signed. 19

1 ya rākbin min ʿendina min fōg ḥirsās
aškaḥ šakāḥ al-bunn ma ṣāyidha-n-nī

1 يا راكبٍ من عندنا من فوق حرساس
اشكح شكاح البنّ ما صايدها النّي

2 kuzzi ʿan illi-ytarb al-ġayṭ bil-fās
ū-yāmir ʿal illī yifzaʿū biṯ-ṯinnī

2 كزّه عن اللي يترّب الغيط بالفاس
ويامر عل اللي يفزعو بالثنّي

3 tilfī ʿal illī bāshum bās
wi-gōlit hala ʿendihum mā tiwannī

3 تلفي عل اللي باسهم باس
وقولة هلا عندهم ما تونّي

4 tilga-š-šarīf ū-tilig li wild furrās
willi-ytigaffa xēlhum mā-yṯannī

4 تلقى الشريف وتلق له ولد فرّاس
واللي يتقفّى خيلهم ما يثنّي

5 wildi ṭalāl ū-nāyif kullihum rās
šarrābt ad-damm min naḥīr al-imṣannī

5 ولده طلال ونايف كلّهم راس
شرّابة الدم من نحير المصنّي

6 ya ma-ḥala-lsānhum gōltin ḥās
ū-yaʿṭū wjūh al-xēl yitbaʿziginnī

6 يا ما حلا لسانهم قولةٍ حاس
ويعطو وجود الخيل يتبعزقن

[11] A padded cushion, usually of leather, is hung from the front pommel of the saddle to cover the withers and serve as a leg rest, and is called either 'a place for the thigh' (*mīraka*) or 'little shield' (*duwēraʿ*). Properly, the *duwēraʿ* is longer.

[12] Brides traditionally have their hands stained with henna as an antidote to post-pregnancy barrenness (*kabsa*). As this condition is thought to be caused by an encounter with a menstruating woman, a bride 'immunizes' herself by staining parts of her body with *ḥinna*, which resembles blood. This resemblance constitutes the antidote to the ill effect of menstrual blood—an example of 'sympathetic magic' (i.e. things which are similar influencing each other).

[13] 'Remembering God' (*dhikr allāh*); pronouncing a formula containing God's name is considered necessary in planning, commencing, and finishing an enterprise, to ensure that no evil spirit frustrates it and that it is carried out with good intention (see Bailey, 'Religious Practices', p. 74; cf. poem 3.5, n.6).

7 ilhum gaṣr ʿalē mīt malyūn ḥarrās
min xōf rāyin yijī ʿala ġēr gannī

7 لهم قصر عليه مية مليون حرّاس
من خوف راي يجي على غير قنّ

8 abġa-šūf wujūḥ-ḥar-rabaʿ jallās
šōf al-mulūk yiẓayyiʿ al-fikir minnī

8 ابغي اشوف وجوه الربع جلّاس
شوف الملوك يضيّع الفكر منّي

9 tigūl li ya sīdī amrak ʿal ar-rās
min yōm jēšak min warāna-ygannī

9 تقول له يا سيدي امرك عل الراس
من يوم جيشك من ورانا يقنّي

10 witgūl-li ya sīdī yōm itgadm al-kās
tara šāyin ma sōlaf ʿalē hal-muġannī

10 وتقول له يا سيدي يوم تقدّم الكاس
ترا شايٍ ما سولف عليه المغنّي

11 aš-šāy yiʿaggib fi-l-maʿamīl hilwās
kān min ʿugb iš-širib mā-ynaẓfannī

11 الشاي يعقّب في المعاميل هلواس
كان من عقب الشرب ما ينظّفنِ

12 wal-kēf dabb al-baharjiyya mi-r-rās
kēfin yiʿaggib fi-l-maʿamīl ḥinnī

12 والكيف دبّ البهارجيّة من الراس
كيفٍ يعقّب في المعاميل حنّي

13 wat-tānya tagdīmt az-zād lin-nās
samn al-ġanim fōg al-manāsif yigannī

13 والثانية تقديمة الزاد للناس
سمن الغنم فوق المناسف يقنّي

14 widdī gaʿūd irkūbti burj fa-r-rās
waškaḥ mi-lli-lwānhin yibargannī

14 ودّي قعود ركوبته برج في الراس
واشكح من اللي الوانهن يبرّقنِ

15 urẓum ʿalē haš-šdād wi-xrayj bi-gyās
ū-safāyifa bēn arbaʿa yilʿabinnī

15 ارضم عليه الشداد وخريج بقياس
وسفايفه بين اربعه يلعبنِ

16 wi-dwēriʿin ʿal-mitn li-s-sāʿa mindās
wi-ʿadār sawwinni ṣawābiʿ ib-ḥinnī

16 ودويرعٍ عالمتن للساعة منداس
وعذار سوّنه صوابع بحنّي

17 law innū iydawwir lī riḥūla ū-lā bās
lakin ʿērat anẓa-ylawʿannī

17 لو انّه يدوّر لي رحوله ولا باس
لكن عيرات انضا يلوّعنّي

18 warsil kalāmī fī warag farx girṭās
bi-lisān ḥusn ū-ṣāḥib al-ḥibr yiginnī

18 وارسل كلامي في ورق فرخ قرطاس
بلسان حسن وصاحب الحبر يقنّ

19 waxtim kalāmī bi-dikrit alla ya nās
wiygūl hāda axar kalām al-muġannī

19 واختم كلامي بذكرة اللّه يا ناس
ويقول هذا اخر كلام المغنّي

3
Poems of Instruction

THE BEDOUIN CREDO

It seems anomalous to speak of bedouin poems of instruction. In bedouin, as in other nomadic and pre-literate cultures, a poem with aphorisms on a variety of subjects would be too formal and systematic a method of instruction. Bedouin children or adults learn things in connection with a practical matter of immediate interest or else inadvertently as they listen to other people discussing a particular subject. Many shepherds and shepherdesses, for example, can identify by name as many as three hundred varieties of plants, grasses, flowers, and shrubs that grow in their own area of habitation or migration. Yet, throughout their childhood they had to learn about each and every plant incidentally. No one ever deliberately explained desert vegetation to them as an integral subject as in a modern botany class, listing, for example, four species of plants especially preferred by camels, nine bushes that provide pasture in midsummer, or seven plants that are lethal to goats. An adult at pasture would simply point to a specific plant, telling a child to 'keep the goats away from that poisonous plant'. The same phenomenon exists in law. With no law-enforcement agency in a widely diffused nomadic society, all its members know the laws that govern their relations and what constitutes transgression. Every bedouin is a jurist in his own right. Yet no one is told specifically that there are six laws governing pasture rights, or four ways of determining whether testimony is true or false.

A poem that sets forth the mores of a society for 'theoretical' edification must thus be a sort of anomaly, even if the poet would be gratified were people to find instruction in his composition. Yet, poems in this form do exist, and it is even their stated purpose to impart instruction. It appears, however, that what actually prompts the poet to compose such a poem is less a desire to instruct than an emotional need to express himself, similar to that which gave rise to the poems of Chapter 1. In the 1960s, for example, when ʿAnēz abū Sālim composed a poem of instruction from prison addressed to his young son, ʿIs̲h̲ēs̲h̲ (poem 6.14), he intimated that the inspiration for the poem came to him one night,

> As I woke up from slumber with anguish I sighed
> In a flash I stopped sleeping, my eyes opened wide . . .

What had disturbed his sleep, as later related, was news that his son, ʿIs͟hēs͟h, felt he was being treated with contempt. ʿAnēz was thus naturally moved to anger, but the content of his poem had little to do with ʿIs͟hēs͟h's grievance. Only three of the eleven lines counsel him to maintain his self-respect and be patient; three lines lament the father's own condition; two warn ʿIs͟hēs͟h to be wary when adjudicating conflicts in a bedouin court (which was irrelevant to the boy's immediate condition); two lines serve as an introduction; and the concluding line seeks to cheer the boy by hinting that together father and son would one day settle their accounts with a gun. It seems, therefore, that, while the father did impart something of immediate significance to his son, the true impulse behind his poem came from his anger; and, although this anger arose from the son's discomfiture, what finally found expression were elements of the father's reservoir of perspectives about his personal fallen state and about life in general.

Indications of a variety of emotional stimuli are evident in the otherwise didactic poems of the present selection. Poem 3.1, for example, was composed after its author had been insulted in public. Judging from the opening of poem 3.9, by contrast, it was initially composed upon the birth of a son, and it is followed by another poem of advice (3.10), induced by the anger of the new-born child's uncle, who, hearing no mention of God in his brother's composition, wished to rectify the omission with a religious message. Another, much longer, religious poem counselling a life of ascetic abstention (3.11) was composed after its author's betrothal was annulled by the girl's father.

As the circumstances of life naturally call to mind various principles of living, such principles may find their way into any poem arising from immediate and practical causes. Hence a bedouin poet's personal values may also be found in poems that are not ostensibly didactic. When, after he had been imprisoned, ʿAnez abū Sālim was betrayed by his wives and by two lesser members of his clan who seduced them (see details in Chapter 6), he coined—in poem 1.1—his own aphorism:

> As life must end, so women are lesser than men,
> And the poor take heart when calamities come.

In another poem (2.7), ʿAnēz stressed the difficulty in persuading others to conduct themselves properly, by stating as a principle:

You won't make someone drink the bitter using means that please;
You'll only make him drink it having brought him to his knees.

Similarly, the Bilī tribe, trying to convince King Ibn Saʿūd that he was basing his rule on the wrong people (poem 2.10), stated the metaphorical principle:

Mud, though it stick, never holds a stone tight,
And fire needs fuel in order to light.

In bedouin society, such aphorisms make the rounds, and any original aphoristic line may appear in a subsequent poem composed by someone else who happened to have heard it; it may even become a proverb. For example, the proverb, 'Virtue stems from a woman's ṯhighs just as fire must come from tinder' (*al-ʿizz min awrāk an-nisā, wa-n-nār min migbāshā*), stressing the importance of maternal kin for the qualities of a child, was heard in Syria and Sinai at the turn of the twentieth century,[1] and again in the Negev later in the century,[2] and it may be found as the line of a poem recorded by the German orientalist, Albert Socin, in the mid-nineteenth century.[3] The line appearing in the nineteenth-century poem may be original or, equally, it may be but the incorporation of an earlier proverb; just as, in the present volume, line 4a of poem 5.6—'Woe to the wrongdoer, and woe to his neighbour' (*yā wēl al-māsī ū-yā wēl jārah*)—is a proverb at least as ancient as the second century AD when it appeared in the Mishna in Hebrew.[4] In any case, the bedouin world is replete with lines of poetry that find their way into different compositions in times and places quite remote from each other.

Poem 3.2 offers an example of this phenomenon. It was heard recited in Sinai, in 1971, by a bedouin who claimed that he had composed its five lines. The lines in and of themselves make perfect sense, either as a complete poem or as the introduction to a didactic poem on how to prepare and serve coffee to guests. It is therefore conceivable that, when the reciter put the lines together on some occasion, he thought he was composing an original poem. It seems, however, that he was actually drawing upon a 'reservoir' of lines that existed in the same rhyme scheme—a fact that is confirmed by four other poems, or versions of

[1] See Musil, *Manners*, p. 472; Shuqayr, p. 372.
[2] Oral communication from Mūsā al-ʿAṭāwna, 1972.
[3] Socin p. 73.
[4] Mishna, *Negaʿim*, xii. 6 (via Schwartzbaum, p. 6).

this poem, transcribed between the mid-nineteenth and mid-twentieth centuries, which contain these same five lines—but in very different sequences. The first two were actually similar, but not completely identical, versions of a poem shown to Albert Socin in north-central Arabia;[5] it was said to have been composed by Muḥammad al-Qāḍī, a resident in the town of Ḥā'il, who allegedly composed it when he suspected his wife of infidelity. The third was heard by Alois Musil sometime between 1900 and 1920, not in Arabia but from a member of the Syrian Rawala tribe; and again it was ascribed to a poet 'known as Muḥammad al-Qāḍī'.[6] The fourth version, or poem, was heard in yet another desert—the Negev—by ʿĀrif al-ʿĀrif, when it was recited to him in the 1930s by ʿAyyād Ibn ʿAdēsān of the ʿAzāzma tribe, this time without any ascription to Muḥammad al-Qāḍī.[7] Table 1 gives a comparison of the five lines from Sinai presented as poem 3.2, with their place in other versions, empty spaces indicating that the line was omitted. The longest of these various versions was that recorded by Musil (32 lines), followed by Socin 1 (27 lines), Socin 2 (25 lines), and al-ʿĀrif (7 lines). As some of the lines appearing in the Socin versions were absent in the longer Musil version, we can assume that either the original poem was even longer than Musil's rendition, or that this rendition incorporated lines with the same metre and rhymes that

Table 1. *The varying order of lines in different versions of poem 3.2*

Sinai	Socin version 1	Socin version 2	Musil	al-ʿĀrif
1a	5a	5a	9a	2a
1b	5b	5b	9b	3b
2a	6a	6a		
2b	6b	6b	10b	2b
3a	9a			
3b	9b			
4a	12a	9a		5a
4b	12b	9b		5b
5a	17a	17a	12a	6a
5b	16b	16b	21b	6b

5 Socin, pp. 44–7.

6 Musil, *Manners*, pp. 108–9.

7 Al-ʿĀrif, *al-Qaḍā'*, pp. 206–7.

originated in yet other poems circulating at the same time in the Middle Eastern deserts.

Versions may also differ within the confines of Sinai and the Negev. Poem 3.9, for example, was heard in four different versions, all containing some of the same lines; and three of the four versions containing lines not included in the others. Their reciters came from four different tribes and the lengths of the versions were 19, 11, 7, and 4 lines, respectively. Indeed, in two different recitations, in 1971 and 1975, the same reciter—Ḥamdān abū Salāma Abū Mas'ūd—gave two different renditions in sixteen and nineteen lines. If a reciter can forget some lines of a poem he has already committed to memory, he can certainly forget lines he may once have heard from another reciter, but which he never completely learned.

Poem 3.2 is an instruction on how to prepare and serve coffee; it is followed by four more didactic poems dealing with the rules of proper hospitality. Poem 3.3 recited to one named Salmān, is all instruction of the do/don't variety, telling him how to receive guests, how to prepare coffee, how to behave in a decorous manner, and the importance of generosity. The second poem, addressed to an anonymous Aḥmad, also gives instructions on how to prepare and serve coffee; but only as the background for a moral lesson on the importance of being a generous host and an obliging protector. The next poem, rather than give pointed instruction, reflects on the qualities of good hospitality and worthy company; the purpose again, is to impart a moral lesson—this time, however, on the disabilities that unmanly behaviour may cause one. The last poem in this group, in addition to the instruction about the reception of guests and the importance of decorum, also stresses the importance of self-sufficiency and prudence.

The instruction in these four poems is given in one of four forms. In some cases, we have direct and often specific admonitions, or do/don't instruction, with no reasons provided for the proposed behaviour—as in 'Then ready what's needed of coffee and spice / And roast the grey beans till they're brown on each side'. In other cases, we are given instruction immediately followed by the reason: 'And serve from the right to avoid the guests' spite / If another's served first they may think it's a slight'. Some lines are a statement of principles: 'Largesse won't lessen your wealth one *dīnār* / Whereas avarice acts like a pail never full'; while others describe correct behaviour: 'The host, if he sees you pass by, will rise / And the coffee you sip will help open your eyes.'

Whatever the form, each line constitutes part of a bedouin's beliefs, a conception of life and how it should be lived. The coffee-preparation theme is found throughout poems of instruction—perhaps because it is around the open fire where coffee is prepared and brewed that a bedouin relaxes, reflects, and on occasion is stimulated to compose a poem. Similarly, the almost hallowed ritual of coffee preparation and the related acts of hospitality are so central to bedouin culture that they are ever at hand as a theme with which to introduce other elements of a poet's credo, such as the importance of generosity, humility, or manly behaviour.

A poem entirely about life and the art of living is poem 3.7, in which the poet asks God for the indispensible ingredients of a happy life: a large tent, a well-brought up wife, a swift mare, a rifle, brave sons, power to protect a ward, a good reputation, a flock of goats, a herd of camels, and an opportunity to make the pilgrimage to Mecca—also adding the posthumous privilege of going to Paradise.

This is followed by two longer poems (3.8 and 3.9) with more than twenty-four lines, each poem being a list of aphorisms resembling the biblical Book of Proverbs. Both poems present concrete examples of the social values that the anonymous poets deemed essential to bedouin life: the importance of self-reliance, decorum, prudence, and courage; the importance of being solicitous of paternal kin, neighbours, and guests; and the importance of wedding women of good stock.

The final two poems are religious in inspiration. The first (3.10) is the angry reaction of the uncle of a boy for whom the preceding poem was composed, a poem that had omitted to mention God and the Islamic religion. Reflecting the age-old tension between the institutions of Islam and bedouin culture, he counsels his nephew to ignore bedouin advice and live a good Islamic life. The type of Islamic life he recommends is spelled out in detail in the final poem (3.11), which urges the bedouin to live a life of pious asceticism: to surrender to God's will and abstain from wordly temptations.

The values presented in the poems of this chapter are essential in understanding bedouin culture. The recurrent theme of *hospitality*, for example, tells us that a host must be available to his guests, friendly and patient; that he must light a fire immediately, prepare a drink, roast the coffee-beans carefully, and then dispense the coffee properly. In the poem on the components of a good life (3.7), five are explained in terms of hospitality. Desirable are a spacious tent where riders can meet; a wife of good breeding to attend to the guests; power to help those who come to the tent for protection; goats to provide guests with meat; and camels to provide them with milk.

In the same poem most of the other components of happiness are connected to *power*: a mare, a rifle, brave sons, and a good reputation (which is power derived from status). Hospitality and power, therefore, appear to be the two highest values of bedouin society; that is, unless we consider that hospitality and the reputation for being a generous host may, in themselves, be but another component of power. The disregard for wealth and material possession that is reflected in a display of bedouin generosity is one way by which a person may demonstrate that he enjoys an almost reckless independence of any material bonds that, in the hour of need, might otherwise hinder him from defending his rights or redressing any wrongs perpetrated against him. In other words, generosity is but one more means with which a bedouin enhances his reputation as a relentless defender of his rights ('rights' being defined as the inviolability of person, family, property, and honour)—a reputation that is his first line of defence in a society devoid of law-enforcement agencies.

From this perspective, furthermore, we can understand why certain other social values are also stressed in the poetry of instruction. Economic self-reliance, for example, is an aspect of the independence that a person must enjoy in order to pursue the defence of his rights at any given time. Marriage to women of good breeding enables a bedouin man to delegate to them duties, such as herding, that might otherwise restrict his freedom of movement if he were obliged to attend to them personally. Solicitude towards paternal kin is recommended, because it is they who are bound to help a bedouin defend himself in the framework of his blood-revenge group, the *khamsa*. He is urged to behave in a decorous manner in public so that other men consider him serious and self-possessed. Similarly, he should not gossip nor offend neighbours, because bedouin society gauges his virtue and integrity according to his compliance with its conventions. Finally, he is encouraged to accept death bravely and as a matter of fate, thereby demonstrating a disdain for death that should also enhance his reputation for 'recklessness' in the relentless pursuit of his rights.

Against the background of endemic tribal contention, such as emerges from this observation of bedouin values, it is little wonder that Islamic religious principles are rare in bedouin poems of instruction—principles that would encourage men to concentrate more on their relations with God than on their earthly conflicts, or would counsel moderation and good will rather than suspicion and truculence. Even in the long final poem, which is replete with an ascetic form of Islamic advice, the age-old bedouin virtues—self-reliance, disdain for death, solicitousness for paternal kin, and even the guarding of secrets from one's wife (to prevent her prudent objections from deflecting her husband from recklessly pursuing his rights)—assert themselves, revealing their indelible impression on the bedouin mind.

3.1

On Human Inconstancy

A Poem of Reflection

In the early 1980s ʿAnēz abū Sālim al-ʿUrḍī, of the Tarābīn Ḥasāblah tribe, went to a governmental reception in Cairo, only to be turned away for not having an invitation. The insult was compounded when his companions managed to enter unhindered and barely disguised their joy at his embarrassment. The event inspired the following short poem.

If folks don't invite you, invite not yourself,
  Lest some doorman inquire by what right you're there; 1

He'll utter some words that will ruin your mood,
  And give pleasure to those who resent how you fare. 2

There are folks who will welcome you knowing you're rich,
  But who'll buy and who'll sell you the moment you're poor. 3

Don't think if you're gone this world won't endure,
  Nor will it feel shame, having dashed you, be sure! 4

1 in ma daʿawk an-nās lā tidʿ ḥālak
  ṣafīhum yigūl lak mīn dāʿīk

2 yigūl lak kilma ha-yġayyir zalālak
  ū-šamt-illī yikrahaw lafiytak fīk

1 ان ما دعوك الناس لا تدع حالك
  صفيهم يقول لك مين داعيك

2 يقول لك كلمة هيغيّر زلالك
  وشمت اللي يكرهو لفيتك فيك

Poem 3.1 was heard recited by its author, at Nuwēbaʿ at-Tarābīn, 4 April 1983.

3 ū-fīhum iyrahhib bak 'ala kuṯr mālak
win gall lak imwālak yibī'ak ū-yišrīk

3 وفيهم يرحّب بك على كثر مالك
وان قلّ لك اموالك يبيعك ويشريك

4 ū-dinyāk ma yiṣ'ab 'alēha ziwālak
wila tistiḥī min ramītak yōm tirmīk

4 ودنياك ما يصعب عليها زوالك
ولا تستحي من رميتك يوم ترميك

3.2

A Poem of Advice

On How to Prepare Coffee

The proper roasting of coffee beans, the pounding of the beans in a mortar, and the proper serving of the drink to guests, are themes that often appear in bedouin poetry. A bedouin in central Sinai, Sulēmān 'Īd Dakhīlallāh of the Tarābīn Sarāy'a tribe, claimed to have composed these lines, although evidence may be found to indicate that the poem originated in Arabia (see pp. 122–3).

Roast me three handfuls, friend, one after one;
Let the beans on hot *ghaḍā*-coals[1] waft to the mart. 1

Take care that they neither be burnt nor undone;
While roasting don't let yourself dream, but be smart.[2] 2

The cadence and beat of your grinding should stun,
Even out in the waste, weary travellers will start.[3] 3

Poem 3.2, was heard recited by Sulēmān 'Īd Dakhīlallāh of the Tarābīn Sarāy'a tribe, at 'Ayn Umm Aḥmad oasis, 25 September 1971.

[1] *Ghaḍā* is the Haloxylon persicum bush.

[2] The proper roasting of the coffee-beans, essential in making a good brew, is stressed in many bedouin poems (cf. poems 3.3, 3.4).

[3] The resonance of the coffee-pounding, done with a mortar and pestle to cadence, is intended as a welcoming message to passers-by (cf. poems 3.6, l. 2; 4.9, l. 4).

In a coffee-pot, tall by the fire, heap the grains;
Then the pot, like a crane, will go round with a tray.[4] 4

The coffee, poured, will leave dark reddish stains,
Like the blood of a sheep, heart and lungs cut away.[5] 5

1 iḥmiṣ t̲alāt̲i ya nadībī ʿala sāg
bunnin ʿala jamr al-ġaẓa yafẓaḥ as-sūg

2 wiḥraṣ ilha min nī wi-ḥrāg
walla tṣīr fi-sāʿit al-ḥamṣ maṭfūg

3 ū-duggha ib-nijrin yirīaʿ kull mištāg
wiyrīaʿ ṭārid al-hawa in dann bi-xfūg

4 wi-laggimha ab-bakraj ʿidda mawlaʿ as-sāg
ū-midda ib-ṣīniytin kanna-l-ġarnūg

5 linna d̲alag min mabsama tigūl šibrāg
ya damm jōf ū-minna maʿlūg

1 احمص ثلاثة يا نديبي على ساق
بنٍّ على جمر الغضا يفضح السوق

2 واحرس لهـا مـن نـي وحراق
ولّا تصير فـي ساعة الحمص مطفوق

3 ودقها بنجـرٍ يريع كـلّ مشتاق
ويريـع طارد الهـوا ان دنّ بخفـوق

4 ولقّمهـا ببكرج عدّه مولـع الساق
ومدّد بصينيّـةٍ كـنّـد الغرنوق

5 لنّـد ذلق مـن مبسمد تقول شبراق
يـا دم جوف ومنـد معلوق

[4] A tray with small cups is passed among the guests, before each of which the coffee is separately poured from the pot; long-necked pots are often compared to cranes (cf. poem 1.10, n. 5).

[5] The colour of the fresh blood of animals is often cited as the proper colour of coffee (cf. poem 6.7).

3.3

On Being a Gracious Host

A Poem of Advice

The present poem advises a brother, Salmān, on how to receive wayfarers graciously. It stresses the importance of roasting the coffee-beans just right, urges Salmān to be generous, and, while cautioning him against being indecorous in the presence of guests, yet counsels him to be tolerant of any lapsed behaviour on their part.

Take from me, Salmān, some weighty advice,
And accept it, Salmān, for it's special and clear: 1

If you should spy travellers from lands far away,
Stand in front of the tent till they see you and turn.[1] 2

Then shake out the carpets[2] and make yourself mild,
So your guest may sit down in the tent and feel sure; 3

And kindle a fire, but then let it decline,
To take care while you roast lest the coffee-beans burn,[3] 4

As you toss them between the three blackened stones,[4]
Heedful of him who discreetly discerns. 5

Poem 3.3 was heard recited by Ṣāliḥ Imbārak 'Īd of the Muzēna Shaẓāẓna tribe, at Dhahab oasis, 22 August 1972.

---

[1] When a bedouin hears or sees strangers passing by his encampment, it is proper for him to stand in front of his tent (lit. 'by the front tent-pole' (*'alā migdim al-bēt*)) so that the strangers see him and know that he is welcoming them. Biblical Abraham and Lot greeted visiting angels in a similar manner (Genesis 18.2, 19.1).

[2] The long, narrow carpets on which guests sit are shaken out in order to rid them of dust and harmful insects, such as scorpions, that might have been sheltering underneath. To do this on the very arrival of a guest is seen as a deliberate gesture of personal respect.

[3] The green coffee-beans stored by a bedouin are roasted in a long-handled pan-like utensil called a *miḥmāṣ* or *maḥmaṣa*.

[4] Three stones are placed around a fire on which pots are propped over the flames. Generally, they are called 'keepers' (*ḥafāyiẓ*); in this poem—perhaps owing to their blackness—they are given the name *malāḥ*, usually reserved for black-spotted sheep, or black camels.

And fight for the right to sup the camp's guest,[5]
God made us five fingers[6] and keeps us in store. 6

And if your guests let themselves lapse into jest,
Your eye may laugh with them, but add nothing more.[7] 7

1 xùḏ minna ya salmān naṣīḥa
kān tagbalha ya salmān wa-hī ʿala fann

1 خذ منّا يا سلمان نصيحة
كان تقبلها يا سلمان وهي على فنّ

2 in sŭft mubʿidāt al-masăḥī
awgaf ʿala migdim il-bēt ḥatta-ysakkan

2 ان شفت مبعدات المشاحي
اوقف على مقدم البيت حتّى يسكّن

3 ū-tušš il-frāš ū-xall nafsak simāḥī
abga-ẓ-ẓayf yugʿud ū-yiṭman

3 وطشّ الفراش وخلّ نفسك سماح
ابقى الضيف يقعد ويطمن

4 wawgd an-nār wiḥtiri-ṣ-ṣalāḥī
ū-ḥarriṣ lil-maḥmāṣ la taṣhad al-bann

4 واوقد النار واحتري الصلاح
وجرّس للمحماص لا تصهد البنّ

5 gallibha bēn iṯ-ṯalāṯa il-malāḥī
ū-xaṣṣha li-llī yajxaṣ al-kēf la kann

5 قلّبها بين الثلاثة الملاح
وخصّها للّي يجخص الكيف لو كنّ

6 ū-šidd al-ġalāṭ ū-lā txallak kisāḥī
war-rizig ʿal imfarrg al-xams yiẓman

6 وشدّ الغلاط ولا تخلّك كساح
والرزق عل مفرّق الخمس يضمن

7 win kaṯṯarū aẓ-ẓyūf maʿak al-mizāḥī
iẓḥak ilhum bal-ʿayn wiktim ʿal as-sann

7 وان كثّرو الضيوف معك المزاح
اضحك لهم بالعين واكتم عل السنّ

[5] On 'fighting to provide for a guest' (*ghalāṭ*), see poem 2.2, n. 11.

[6] One Muslim eulogistic appellation of God as the creator of man is 'Separator of the five fingers' (*mufarrig al-khams*); i.e. by this act God differentiated between man and beast. An oath uttered during argumentation is 'I swear by [lit. 'bring you'] He who brings forth the sun and separates the five' (*anā basūg ʿalēk illī biyiẓhar ash-shams ū-biyfarrig al-khams*).

[7] As a host's primary responsibility is to serve and provide, it would be a dishonourable reversal of roles for him to be entertained by his guests. Moreover, decorum is always the recommended behaviour, even for guests (see poems. 3.5, l. 4; 3.8, ll. 12–13).

3.4

Some Remarks on the Reception of Guests

A Poem of Advice

The present poem, composed for a son or a servant, expresses certain guidelines for hospitality: in particular, the preparation of coffee, the proper treatment of travellers and guests, and the importance of generosity.

By God, Aḥmad, rise and light me a fire;
  A fire whose flame will bring brightness and pride. 1

Then ready what's needed of coffee and spice,
  And roast the grey beans till they're brown on each side. 2

Don't forget the proportions you need when they're done,
  And measure the water for six parts to one;[1] 3

And serve from the right to avoid the guests' spite:
  If another's served first they may think it's a slight.[2] 4

Poem 3.4 was heard recited by Ḥamdān abū Salāma Abū Mas'ūd of the Muzēna Darārma tribe, in Wādī aṭ-Ṭūr, 31 March 1971.

---

[1] One coffee-cup (*finjāl*) of unroasted beans (*bunn nay*) and six cups of water is considered the right blend for coffee.

[2] Being served coffee in one's turn as it is dispensed from the pourer's right to left is a bedouin's right. A bedouin proverb says 'Serve from your right though Abū Zēd be on your left' (*liff 'āl-yamīn wi-law abū zēd 'āsh-shimāl*), Abū Zēd being the legendary hero of the bedouin epic, *Sīrat Banī Hilāl* (see Lane, *Manners*, pp. 398–406). A tradition from the Negev tells that, when reinforcements of the Tarābīn and 'Azāzma tribes assembled in the 'Araba valley to aid the local Sa'īdiyyīn tribe against enemies from Transjordan, the 'Azāzma, insulted because the Tarābīn were served their coffee first, demanded that the Sa'īdiyyīn pitch a separate guest tent for them. A poet of the 'Azāzma is remembered for versifying:

wallāhī law tigassimū-l-khēl khēlēn
  wallah innī 'ala gasimhin rāḍī
šarb al-gahāwa muwaddāt
  wiṣrāfhin bil-aghrāḍī

By God, if you made of the horsemen two groups,
  Such a division would please me;
Drinking coffee's an act of mutual love,
  But here it's dispensed with partiality.

But at times with this order you shouldn't comply,
As for thirsty travellers whose throats may be dry;[3] 5

Indeed, if a party that's travelling comes through,
Throw the coffee you're serving away and make new. 6

Largesse won't lessen your wealth one *dīnār*,
Whereas avarice acts like a pail never full; 7

But if you be humble with a guest and a ward,[4]
You'll find that your sustenance comes from the Lord. 8

1 baḷḷa ya-ḥmad gūm waggid lī an-nār
al-wagd innū taġtiwī fī sanāha

1 باللّد يا احمد قوم وقّد لي النار
الوقد انّد تغتوي في سناها

2 ū-ḥaḍḍir lī al-maṭlūb min bunn ū-bihār
waḥmaṣ lī aṭ-ṭabxa ū-ḥarriṣ niyāha

2 وحضّر لي المطلوب من بنّ وبهار
واحمص لي الطبخة وحرّس نياها

3 ū-linnak ḥamaṣt al-bunn xallī bi-miḥkār
sitta lil-wāḥad yōm gannant māha

3 ولنّك حمصت البنّ خلّيه بمحكار
ستّة للواحد يوم قنّنت ماها

4 ū-sūgha ʿal al-ēman ʿan kašf al-asrār
min xawf šakkat xāṭir illī walāha

4 وسوقها عل الايمن عن كشف الاسرار
من خوف شكّة خاطر اللي ولاها

5 wi-ʿawdēn xuṣṣ ibha xaṣṣin ʿala dār
xaṣṣ aẓ-ẓawāmī lēš tagṭaʿ ẓamāha

5 وعودين خصّ بها خصٍّ على دار
خصّ الظوامئ ليش تقطع ظمأها

6 ila lafōk ar-rabaʿ min ʿugb misyār
aṭ-ṭabxa illī ma tigahwī balāha

6 الا لفوك الربع من عقب مسيار
الطبخة اللي ما تقهويد بلاها

[3] Exceptions to the rule may also be made for a very old man in the company, or for a very honoured guest.

[4] The guest of a bedouin is considered to be under his care and responsibility, just as if he were a ward who had specifically sought that bedouin's protection. A proverb says 'The well-being of a guest is part of a host's luck' (*salāmit aḍ-ḍayf min bakht al-miḥillī*). Moreover, because both a guest and a ward are dependent on their host, he must behave humbly in order to dispel any sense of imposition. Hence, the bedouin greet their visitors with the expression *ahlan wa-sahlan*: 'Consider yourself part of the family [*ahl*] and access to us is with ease [*sahl*].' For the rights and obligations of guests and wards, see al-ʿĀrif, *al-Qaḍāʾ*, pp. 190–200.

7 wil-jūd ma naggaṣ min al-xēr dīnār
wil-buxul dalwi ma tijī-bi-mlāha

7 والجود ما نقّص من الخير دينار
والبخل دلو ما تجي بملاها

8 ila xaẓaʿat an-nafṣ laẓ-ẓayf wil-jār
rizgak ʿal illī yiʿtilī fi-smāha

8 الا خضعت النفس للضيف والجار
رزقك عل اللي يعتلي في سماها

3.5

How to Gain Esteem

A Poem of Advice

The present poem, said to originate among the Ḥuwēṭāt of north-western Arabia, contains advice for a son. The child is counselled to gain a good reputation through hospitality, generosity, and dignified behaviour; and is advised to be self-sufficient and prudent.

O son, hear my advice—grandson of Abū Dhān—
Its meaning you may understand after I am gone. 1

When travellers, men of oaths,[1] at your tent one day arrive,
Drop all else[2] and make for them a brew that will revive;[3] 2

Poem 3.5 was heard recited by ʿĪd Ḥammād Misʿad of the Ḥuwēṭāt ʿAbayyāt tribe, at Jabal ʿUrf, 23 October 1970.

[1] In the Arabic text 'people who feel free to take oaths'; i.e. they have nothing to hide.

[2] It is a tenet of bedouin (and, by extension, Arab) hospitality that, when a visitor appears, the host must drop whatever he is doing to show that he is honoured by the visit and considers it more important than any other concern.

[3] Traditionally, bedouin pour for a guest three successive small cups of coffee, explaining (in rhyme) that the first is for 'reviving him from his tired condition' (*kayf*), the second is for his 'dryness' (*hayf*) and the third is 'in honour of the guest' (*ḍayf*).

Whoever sows bounty among his guests will reap a name,
For guests go forth and then their host's largesse they must proclaim.[4] 3

And when you visit other tents, beware no joker seem;
A laugher in the men's *dīwān* will never gain esteem.[5] 4

But if your words you preface with remembrance of God,[6]
They'll be as though inscribed with ink, and others will be awed. 5

And if you're going to a well,[7] don't go without some help,
If you should lack sufficient strength to tug the rope yourself;[8] 6

And bear in mind that if your rope is not nine fathoms long,
Another's rope will not make up for what in yours is wrong. 5

1 awṣīk ya-bnī ya-bn ax abū ḏān
in kān tifham waṣātī min warāya

2 awṣīk linnak jawk ṭulgin al-aymān
ʿajjil-lhum bil-kēf ʿan kull ġāya

3 ila zaraʿt aṭ-ṭīb fi-r-rabaʿ rabḥān
ila mašaw lāzim tijī lak irwāya

1 اوصيك يـا ابني يـا ابن اخ ابو ذان
ان كـان تفهم وصاتي مـن ورايا

2 اوصيك لنّـك جـوك طلقين الايمـان
عجّـل لهم بالكيف عـن كـلّ غاية

3 الا زرعت الطيب في الربع ربحان
الا مشو لازم · تجـي لـك رواية

[4] After leaving a tent where he has received hospitality, it is considered proper for a bedouin to praise his host. The expression used for this act is literally 'to versify' (*yushʿur*); i.e to sing his praises. A host may even unashamedly aid guests to enhance his reputation by daubing the blood of the animal he has butchered for them on their camels (cf. poem 1.5, n. 5).

[5] Bedouin value decorum, believing that, if a person does not overly reveal himself in public, others will not detect his weaknesses. A relevant proverb holds 'Silence inspires dread, whereas loose talk disappoints' (*as-sukūt hayba, ū-kuthr al-kalām khayba*). *Dīwān* is one term for the men's section of the tent; others are *magʿad, shigg*, and *ruba*ʿ.

[6] Bedouin, being Muslims, should remember to mention God's name as the aegis of their thoughts, actions, plans, and talk. When making a plan, or appointment, they say 'If God wills' (*in shā allāh*). When beginning an action they utter 'In the name of God, the merciful and compassionate' (*bi-sm illāh ar-raḥmān ar-raḥīm*); upon completing an action 'May God be praised' (*al-ḥamd l-illāh*). If one were speaking thoughtlessly, he would refrain from this 'remembrance of God' (cf. poem 2.12, n. 13).

[7] The image of a well, here as in other poems, is used as a metaphor for battle (see poem 1.6, n. 4).

[8] The allusion to 'tugging the rope' refers to the use of a pulley (*dāya*) over a well. A bedouin would draw water, using the pulley, by placing the free end of the rope over his shoulder and walking away from the well.

4 awṣīk lā tiẓḥak fī kull dīwān ẓaḥākt ad-dīwān mū hū iḥkāya	اوصيك لا تضحك في كلّ ديوان ضحاكة الديوان ما هو حكاية 4
5 awṣīk xall-al-harj fī naṭig raḥmān irsim kalāmak zē rasim ad-diwāya	اوصيك خلّ الهرج في نطق رحمان ارسم كلامك زي رسم الدواية 5
6 awṣīk lā turd al-bīr min ġēr ʻawwān in kān ma yumnāk timkin ib-dāya	اوصيك لا ترد البير من غير عوّان ان كان ما يمناك تمكن بدايا 6
7 win kān ma ḥablak yijī tisiʻ biyʻān iḥbāl ġērak ma tijī lak ōfāya	وان كان ما حبلك يجي تسع بيعان احبال غيرك ما تجي لك وفايا 7

3.6

On the Pleasure in Sitting with Worthies

A Poem of Advice

In the present poem advice is given through a depiction of desirable hospitality and company rather than through didactic maxims, as in the preceding poems. Its aim is to stress the importance of manly behaviour for social acceptance.

O how pleasant's the coffee, says Ibn ʻĪd,
Which spiced, can rest on the tray for an hour, 1

In two pots[1] that craftsmen from Baghdad have wrought,[2]
While the sound of the mortar a company's brought.[3] 2

The spice has been mixed in a brew clear of grains,
Made from beans one buys from the seekers of gain. 3

Poem 3.6 was heard recited by ʻĪd Ḥammād Misʻad of the Ḥuwēṭāt ʻAbayyāt tribe, at Jabal ʻUrf, 23 October 1970.

---

[1] On the use of more than one pot for preparing coffee, see poem 2.12, n. 8.

[2] In bedouin poems, coffee-pots of Baghdad style or manufacture—those with a wide bottom, short neck, and long spout—are a recurring image for an excellent vessel (cf. poem 6.11).

[3] On pounding coffee as a sign to passers-by, see poem 3.2, n. 3.

The host, if he sees you pass by, will rise,[4]
And the coffee you sip will help open your eyes,[5] 4

In a guest-tent, for worthies a gathering place;
For men whose deeds never brought them disgrace. 5

He who acts like a child gains no welcome nor love,
Neither northwards nor where the Quḍā'a tribes live.[6] 6

He alights from his mount, but none beg him remain;
Thus he'll fare till the Trustee his life doth reclaim.[7] 7

1 ya ma-ḥala-l-finjāl yigūl ibn 'īd
imbahhari<u>n</u> yirgud 'al aṣ-ṣīn sā'a

1 يا ما حلا الفنجال يقول ابن عيد
مبهّرٍ يرقد عل الصين ساعة

2 bi-daltēn kull abūhin baġadīd
ū-bi-nijri<u>n</u> linni dann ḥāš al-jamā'a

2 بدلّتين كلّ ابوهن بغاديد
وبنجرٍ لنّد دنّ حاش الجماعة

3 ū-bihārhī yijī wil-gahawa tizwīd
wana šarēti ū-ṭārid ar-ribḥ bā'a

3 وبهارها يجي والقهوة تزويد
وانا شريته وطارد الربح باعد

4 in jīt ū-šōfak linnak yigūm bi'īd
'ugibha tifakkir wan-nawāẓir awsā'a

4 ان جيت وشوفك يقوم لنّك بعيد
عقبها تفكّر والنواظر وساعة

5 fī-šigg bēti<u>n</u> mag'adi la-l-ajawīd
min fi'l kaffa ma dana' li had-danā'a

5 في شقّ بيتٍ مقعده للاجاويد
من فعل كفّد ما دنع له الدناعة

6 xuṭū aĺ-walad ma li maḥabba ū-la rīd
lā bi-šmāl ū-lā bi-dīrt al-guẓā'a

6 خطو الولد ما له محبّة ولا ريد
لا بشمال ولا بديرة القضاعة

7 'end manzila mā-ykaṯrūn at-tanašīd
limm-astalam 'umra wakīl al-widā'a

7 عند منزله ما يكثّرون التناشيد
لمّا استلم عمره وكيل الوداعة

[4] See poem 3.3, n. 1. [5] See poem 3.5, n. 3.

[6] Quḍā'a is the traditional denomination for the once largest tribal confederation in southern Arabia. Hence, its tribal area is here an allusion to the south.

[7] God—*allāh*—is portrayed in the Qur'ān (4. 86) as the true and exclusive repository of man's trust. Man's death, or departure from this world, is also His trust. Hence, He is referred to in this poem as the 'Trustee of man's departure' (*wakīl al-widā*'a). For more on God's 'reclaiming' of souls, see poem. 1.13, n. 3.

3.7

The Best Things in Life

A Bedouin's Credo

The present poem, in which a bedouin reveals his concept of the important things of life, corresponds with a general bedouin consensus, for it was heard in all parts of Sinai and the Negev. Of the 'ten things' asked of God, three themes predominate: what is necessary for hospitality (lines 2, 3, 8, 9), for status in society (lines 4–7), and for eternal salvation (lines 10, 11). Characteristically, the desire for power and for wealth is depicted in terms of altruistic ends: to help the weak and provide for a guest.

God, grant me the ten things that make life worthwhile,
  Inscribe them for me as my fate: 1

Firstly, a tent held by tent-ropes spread wide,
  Where horsemen will meet when they're out on a ride;[1] 2

Second, a wife of good training and breed,
  Who, when guests come, directly will bring what they need;[2] 3

Third, a mare who'll beat stallions, though bound on one side,[3]
  And a far-shooting rifle to hold while I ride; 4

Poem 3.7 was heard recited by Khlēf Imgēbil al-Hirsh, chief of the Bayyāḍiyyīn Hurūsh tribe, at Raba'a oasis, 27 November 1971; 'Awda Huwēshil Sālim of the Muzēna Jaraba tribe, at Dhahab oasis, 29 March 1971; 'Awda Imsallam Abū Ṣbēḥ of the Ẓullām Abū Grēnāt tribe, near Beersheba, 7 April 1972; and Sulēmān 'Īd Dakhīlāllāh of the Tarābīn Sarāy'a tribe, at 'Ayn Umm Aḥmad, 25 September 1971. Discrepancies between the different texts were resolved according to the judgement of Muṣliḥ Ibn 'Āmr.

---

[1] A tent that worthies ('horsemen') choose to frequent is an asset to the owner's status (cf. poem 5.5, l. 5), and the larger it is, the better. The reference to horsemen in the Arabic text is actually to their horses, termed 'those with flowing tails' (*kābbāt as-sabīb*).

[2] Breeding, in regard to hospitality and generosity, involves both training and nature; if a woman is raised in a family that is naturally hospitable, she will be trained to carry out the duties relating to hospitality. In the Arabic text the poet asks for a wife as beautiful as a *ḥūriyya*: a dark-eyed comely maiden of Paradise (Qur'ān 44. 54).

[3] Hyperbole. Hobbling a horse by *ḥijār*, as in the Arabic text, means binding the two limbs of the same side. Bedouin also hobble by binding the forelegs to one back leg, a method called *shikkāl*.

Fourth, power that's given by sons who are brave,
Whose fire will amaze when the battle's engaged;[4] 5

Fifth, fillies who're fleet and who power afford
For redressing the wrong that's been done to a ward;[5] 6

Sixth, cover[6] for daughters[7] to shield them from shame
Lest talk at a gathering of slanderers stain; 7

Seventh, black goats that will need many shepherds,
To bring our guests meat freshly butchered and fat;[8] 8

Eighth, camels, in herd, that will need many shepherds,
To milk for God's guest:[9] serve him milk for his thirst; 9

Ninth, a pilgrimage made to the Prophet by rite,
To grip there the lattice and see Our Dear's light;[10] 10

And Tenth, O Muḥammad, please save me from Hell,[11]
And at Judgment may Gabriel my good deeds retell.[12] 11

[4] This states the importance of male children, who, when grown, will provide defence for their kin.

[5] Lit. 'to balance a ward's tilted right'. For more on the bedouin image of injustice as 'tilting' (*mīl*), see poem 1.3, n. 6.

[6] The reference to cover (*sitr*) means the protection that God provides against slander (cf. poem 6.9, n. 3).

[7] The word for daughters in the Arabic—*'adhārā* ('virgins')—reflects the concern lest a pre-married girl be suspected of sexual impropriety, and become ineligible for a marriage of interest (see poem 1.14, n. 1). Such a suspicion, moreover, contains criticism of the girl's family for being remiss in its social responsibility to educate its daughters in sexual propriety (cf. poem 1.15, l. 8).

[8] Bedouin feel that a main reason for maintaining livestock is to be able to butcher for an unanticipated guest. Storing meat, as such, is impossible under desert conditions.

[9] One expression of a bedouin's complete deference to a guest is to consider him as a 'guest of God'—it being God that gives him the wherewithal to provide for his guest. Accordingly, instead of thanking a host in whose tent one has been fed, it is proper to say 'May God compensate you' (*allāh yikhlif 'alēk*). If one mistakenly should thank a host, his reply would be 'It was from God's purse' (*min kīs allāh*). Cf. Ibn Hishām (i. 143; trans. Guillaume, *Life*, p. 58), for the alleged pre-Islamic use of the term 'guest of God' (*ḍayf allāh*) for a pilgrim to the Ka'ba in Mecca.

[10] For more on the light emanating from the Prophet's tomb in Medina, see poem 2.9, n. 11.

[11] The appeal to Muḥammad for intercession, while common among the bedouin, is condemned by purist Islam as polytheism (*shirk* (lit 'co-opting others to God's omnipotence')).

[12] Although the angel Gabriel (Jibrīl) does not defend souls on Judgment Day according to Islam, his popular reputation for extending help (see *Encyclopaedia of Islam*, 'Djabrīl'), may have led the present bedouin poet to ascribe him this function.

1 al-ʿašra-llī bi-hin al-ʿumr yinzād
ya alḷa fī-hin tiktib naṣībī

1 العشرة اللي بهن العمر ينزاد
يا اللّه فيهن تكتب نصيبي

2 al-awwala bētin wasīʿ al-aṭnāb
yitwāʿidanna kabbāt as-sabībī

2 الاوّلة بيتٍ وسيع الاطناب
يتواعدنّه كابّات السبيبِ

3 aṯ-ṯānya ḥuriytin biṭ-ṭabaʿ wil-kār
in šāfit aẓ-ẓīfān yammak tijībī

3 الثانية حوريّةٍ بالطبع والكار
ان شافت الضيفان يمّك تجيبِ

4 aṯ-ṯālṯa muhritin talḥag al-xēl bi-hijār
ū-bundigiytin bal-kaff tirmī baʿīdī

4 الثالثة مهرة تلحق الخيل بهجار
وبندقيّةٍ بالكفّ ترمي بعيدِ

5 ar-rābʿa ʿizwitin wawlād jassār
la ṣārit al-kawnāt ṭaxxin ʿajībī

5 الرابعة عزوةٍ واولاد جسّار
لو صارت الكونات طخٍّ عجيبِ

6 al-xāmsa ʿizutin min fōg al-amhār
aʿaddil ibha la māl ḥagg aṭ-ṭanībī

6 الخامسة عزوةٍ من فوق الامهار
اعدّل بها لو مال حقّ الطنيبِ

7 as-sātta sitr al-ʿaḏāra himn-al-ʿār
min magʿad as-siffā harjin yiṣībī

7 الساتّة ستر العذارى من العار
من مقعد السفّاد هرجٍ يصيبِ

8 as-sābʿa ġanmin bi-riʿyān ikṯār
wajīb liẓ-ẓīfān laḥam al-ġaṣībī

8 السابعة غنمٍ برعيان كثار
واجيب لضيفان لحم الغصيبِ

9 aṯ-ṯāmna niyāgin bi-riʿyān ikṯār
waḥlib li-ẓayf alḷa wasgī ḥalībī

9 الثامنة نياقٍ برعيان كثار
واحلب لضيف اللّه واسقيه حليبِ

10 at-tāsʿa amšī li-mḥammad zawwār
wamsik šababīka wašāhid ḥabībī

10 التاسعة امشي لمحمّد زوّار
وامسك شبابيكه واشاهد حبيبي

11 al-ʿāšra tajīrnī mḥammad ʿan an-nār
ū-fi-l-āxira jibrīn yiġdī ḥasībī

11 العاشرة تجيرني يا محمّد عن النار
وفي الاخرة جبرين يغدي حسيبي

3.8

Advice to a Younger Brother

A Bedouin 'Book of Proverbs'

The following poem, a set of proverb-like statements, attributed to an Arabian Sharīf called ad-Dasm,[1] takes up themes such as the harmfulness of gossip, the right choice of wife, the maintenance of good relations with kinsmen, and self-reliance. It also deals with the utility of raising camels rather than goats. This last theme suggests that the poem might have originated sometime after the First World War, when the replacement of camels by the motor vehicle as the main means of transport in the Middle East caused many camel-raisers to change to smaller livestock.

For you, O my brother, I've some counsel direct;
Advice that must touch your mind with effect. 1

Hear your brother's advice, which will bring you no blame,
For my teeth are full grown,[2] and my wit just the same; 2

Hear your brother's advice, which will bring you no blame,
And guide you away from life's many foul ways. 3

The first I advise—by God's duties abide,
Like fasting and prayer, as God did provide.[3] 4

Second, remember a light foot brings shame;
One who seeks out encampments is open to blame. 5

Poem 3.8 was heard recited by Muṣliḥ Ibn 'Āmr of the Tiyāhā Ṣgērāt tribe, at Wādī Munbaṭaḥ, 9 June 1972; 'Īd Ḥammād Mis'ad of the Ḥuwēṭāt 'Abayyāt tribe, at Jabal 'Urf, 23 October 1970; Sulēmān Ḥamd al-'Arādī of the Tarābīn Ḥasāblah tribe, at el-'Arīsh, 30 October 1972; and 'Abdallāh Ḥimēd 'Awwād of the Muzēna Igṣēnāt tribe, at Dhahab oasis, 16 December 1981. Discrepancies between the texts were resolved according to the judgement of Mūsā al-'Aṭāwna.

[1] Oral communication from Muṣliḥ Ibn 'Āmr.

[2] The image of teeth fully grown (*munīb*) comes from camel-lore (cf. poem 1.4, n. 10).

[3] Although there are 'five pillars' or main obligations in Islam, bedouin often refer to the performance of prayer and fasting as the mark of a good Muslim.

If nothing of note should oblige you to leave,
Stay home for your own guests to greet and receive.[4] 6

The passer of gossip, from his camp keep away,
And don't, God forbid, take to heart what he says; 7

He conveys to you gossip, then brings it to me,
Not caring if truth or a lie it may be. 8

And third, do not pass where the goat lasses graze,
Where the paths of their flocks mark clearly the way; 9

None pass there but wolves who are whelped to be sly,
And the sole tracks you'll find are a wolf's just gone by. 10

Let me caution you too if to strange lands you go,
Get the lay of the land though the learning be slow; 11

If one balks at your questions, query him not:
Be as if on a peak far from winds that are hot. 12

Remember that talking too much brings you shame;
He who prates disappoints and is open to blame.[5] 13

And a stalwart's girl marry, though hard she may be;
Her husband, you'll see, finds welcome and worth.[6] 14

But a vile one's daughter forget, though she please;
Her husband enjoys neither welcome nor worth. 15

Keep from chiefs and from rulers, their teeth are full;[7]
They can make one's affairs either rise or fall. 16

[4] In the Arabic text, the word *luzūm* ('obligations') suffices to specify that staying at home to receive unanticipated guests is proper behaviour.

[5] i.e. be reserved and taciturn (cf poem 3.5, n. 5).

[6] On the importance of marrying a girl of good stock, see poem 1.6, n. 7.

[7] In the Arabic text, chiefs and rulers are compared to fully-toothed male camels (*zaml munība*), implying that they bite like male camels do when rutting (cf. n. 2 above).

And their flunky, who'll say what he thinks they would hear,[8]
Through his double-faced talk you'll be felled from the rear.[9] 17

Beware of the rich one whom all would befriend,
Though none has he helped, and on none would he spend. 18

And the poor, in his turn, like a churning-skin smells;
He's the butt of men's scorn wherever they dwell. 19

And do not, O brother, your kinsman revile,
Where others are gathered who'll meddle with guile;[10] 20

For you'll destroy him or he'll destroy you,
And you'll live among strangers, one of the two. 21

Don't tire, though hard, to remain self-sustained;
Even leap over peaks, if your strength you've retained. 22

Be swayed not by butter nor even its curds,
Raising goats and deserting your camel-based herds;[11] 23

The goat-herd gets grey long before he is old,
Just from chasing the wolf all night from the fold. 24

Raise the ship of the desert, whose hocks may be coarse,[12]
But care she dispels, and of pride she's a source; 25

[8] i.e. he will not content himself with saying, 'I do not know . . .', but will make up a story. In the Arabic text, 'I do not know' is expressed by the image *nafaḍ jēbah* ('shaking the chest area of one's shirt'). A bedouin resorts to this gesture before stating a fact of which he is uncertain; at the same time he utters 'I fear God' (*akhāf allāh*). In Egypt proper, however, the word *jēb* means 'pocket', rather than chest area; hence the expression *naffaḍ jēbah* means 'he went broke' (lit. 'he shook out his pocket').

[9] i.e. you'll be felled by backbiting, just as if you had been hamstrung (*gaṣṣ al-ʿarāgīb* in the Arabic text; lit. 'cutting the Achilles tendons').

[10] i.e. the impression of clan solidarity is an important element in each member's security, because paternally related clansmen defend and avenge each other (cf. poem 4.19).

[11] Goat-milk (*laban*) is creamier than camel-milk (*ḥalīb*), and provides a base for making butter and cheese.

[12] 'Coarse of hocks' (*ḥirsh al-ʿarāgīb*) and 'bent-hocked' (*ʿawj al-ʿarāgīb*) are designations of a camel, based on physiological characteristics. For another, see poem 4.12, l. 8.

Even through drought, from her milk she'll provide,
Till you move on to pasturelands wondrously wide.[13] 26

1 ya-xūwī lak ʿendī waṣātin imṣībi
isma' waṣātī talmas al-ʿagl wa-tṣīb

1 يا اخوّي لك عندي وصاةٍ مصيبة
اسمع وصاتي تلمس العقل وتصيب

2 isma' waṣāt axūk mā biha ʿēbi
liʿād innī kāmil al-ʿagl wa-mnīb

2 اسمع وصاة اخوك ما بها عيبة
لعاد انّي كامل العقل ومنيب

3 isma' waṣāt axūk mā biha ʿēbi
tinḥāk ʿan baʿd id-drūb al-adarīb

3 اسمع وصاة اخوك ما بها عيبة
تنحاك عن بعد الدروب الاذاريب

4 awwal waṣātī bal-furūẓ al-yidībi
ṣōm ū-ṣalā wi-tʿidya-bha bil-mawajīb

4 اوّل وصاتي بالفروض اليديبة
صوم وصلاة وتعدية بها بالمواجيب

5 ṯānī waṣātī xift ar-rijil ʿaybi
min laḥag al-furgān yurkuẓ li hal-ʿayb

5 ثاني وصاتي خفّة الرجل عيبة
من لحق الفرقان يركض لد العيب

6 in kān ma lak ḥājtin tigtaẓī bi
tagẓī luzūmak fī salām ū-tarḥīb

6 ان كان ما لك حاجةٍ تقتضي به
تقضي لزومك في سلام وترحيب

7 rāʿi-n-nagīla la tināzil šiʿībi
ū-la tuḥuṭṭ ya-bū zaʿzūʿa bal-jīb

7 راعي النقيلة لا تنازل شعيبه
ولا تحطّ يا ابو زعزوعة بالجيب

8 hāḏa yiwaddīha ū-hāḏa yijībi
wi-hāḏa yisawwīha bi-ṣudgin wi-takḏīb

8 هذا يودّيها وهذا يجيبه
وهذا يسوّيها بصدقٍ وتكذيب

9 ṯāliṯ waṣātī ṭilʿatin mā yinʿadī bi
ū-la yidillak ʿalēha ġēr kiṯr al-masarīb

9 ثالث وصاتي طلعةٍ ما ينعدي به
ولا يدلّك عليها غير كثر المساريب

10 wila ʿadāha ġēr ḏīb min baṭn ḏībi
wi-llī ʿadāha gabl tarā hū ḏīb

10 ولا عداها غير ذيب من بطن ذيبة
واللي عداها قبل ترا هو ذيب

11 wōṣīk ya-xūwī lin jīt min dyārin ġarībi
awṣīk bi-tiritb al-ʿilm tartīb

11 واوصيك يا اخوّي لن جيت من ديارٍ غريبة
اوصيك بترتّب العلم ترتيب

[13] This reflects the rhymed aphorism in which camel-milk is praised as providing 'sustenance that saves one from death' (*ġōt ʿan al-mōt*); camel-hair for providing tent-cloth (*wuhūt*), the dung, for providing fuel (*wugūd*), and the sale-price for providing cash (*nugūd*).

12 ū-min lā yijībak lā tistajībi
xallak kama-llī bi-rās ʿayṭa
ʿin simūm al-lawahīb

12 ومن لا يجيبك لا تستجيبه
خلّك كما اللي براس عيطة عن سموم اللواهيب

13 ū-ḥurṣak tarāha kiṯrit al-ḥakī ʿēbi
ūwʿa kiṯīr al-ḥakī maḏmūm wiyixīb

13 وحرصك تراها كثرة الحكي عيبة
اوعى كثير الحكي مذموم ويخيب

14 wawṣīk ya-xūwī ʿala bint as-sbāʿ aṣ-ṣalībi
tara jōzha yiṣbiḥ ib-xērin ū-tarḥīb

14 واوصيك يا اخوّي على بنت السباع الصليبة
ترا جوزها يصبح بخيرٍ وترحيب

15 wayyāk ya-xūwī ʿan bint ar-radī al-halībi
tara jōzha mā yiṣbiḥ ib-xērin ū-tarḥīb

15 ويّاك يا اخوّي عن بنت الردي الهليبة
ترا جوزها ما يصبح بخيرٍ وترحيب

16 wōṣīk ʿan iš-šyūx wal-ḥukkām
zamlin imnībi
bī-hum ʿamārin lal-gaẓāya wi-taxrīb

16 واوصيك عن الشيوخ والحكّام زملٍ منيبة
بهم عمارٍ للقضايا وتخريب

17 rafīghum ma yirtidī nafaẓ jēbi
yiḥkī ʿal al-wijhēn yiguṣṣ al-ʿaragīb

17 رفيقهم ما يرتدي نفض جيبه
يحكي عل الوجهين يقصّ العراقيب

18 wirʿa kiṯīr al-māl kullin ḥabībi
wilaw inni fī zimāni ma ʿamal ṭīb

18 وارعى كثير المال كلٍّ حبيبه
ولو انّه في زمانه ما عمل طيب

19 wirʿa gilīl al-māl šanan ruwēbi
fī wusṭ al-ʿarab takṯar ʿalē haḏ-ḏaʿarīb

19 وارعى قليل المال شنن رويبة
في وسط العرب تكثر عليه الذعاريب

20 wawṣīk ya axūwī ʿan munāgar garībi
busṭ al-majālis yikṯrōn al-lawaʿīb

20 واوصيك يا اخوّي عن مناقر قريبه
بوسط المجالس يكثرون اللواعيب

21 imma yiblāk aw tibtalī bi
yiṣbaḥ ḥadēkum fī-dyār al-ajanīb

21 امّا يبلاك او تبتلي به
يصبح حديكم في ديار الاجانيب

22 witʿab ʿal al-ʿīša ū-lō hī ṣaʿībi
ma zāl bak ḥaylin yinuṭṭ al-maragīb

22 واتعب عل العيشة ولو هي صعيبة
ما زال بك حيلٍ ينطّ المراقيب

23 wila yiʿijbak az-zibid maʿ rawībi
titbaʿ aẓ-ẓān ū-tutruk an-nīb

23 ولا يعجبك الزبد مع رويبه
تتبع الضان وتترك النيب

24 rāʿi-l-ġanam yišīb min gabl šēbi
ū-ṭūl al-liyālī ṣār hū yuṭrud aḏ-ḏīb

24 راعي الغنم يشيب من قبل شيبه
وطول الليالي صار هو يطرد الذيب

25 rabbī safīnt al-barr ḥirš al-ʿaragīb
al-bil miʿazza tuṭrud al-hamm waš-šēb

26 tiʿīšak fī snīn al-maḥal law min ḥalībi
īlimma tilḥag iblād al-faẓa wit-taʿajīb

25 ربّـــي سفينة البـــرّ حــرش العــراقيب
البــل معــزّة تطــرد الهـــمّ والشيب

26 تعيشك فــي سنين المحــل لــو من حليبه
لمّــا تلــحق بــلاد الفضـــا والتعــاجيب

3.9

Advice to a Newborn Son

A Bedouin 'Book of Proverbs'

Moved by the birth of his son, a bedouin put together a series of ideas that could be termed his secular creed. The subjects are all of bedouin concern, containing no trace of Islamic influence. The poet counsels his son on the importance of independence (line 2), prudence (lines 3–5), clan ties (line 6), the right choice of wife (lines 7–11), disciplining children (line 12), proper relations with one's neighbours (lines 13–14), the proper reception of guests (lines 15–17), the dismissal of gossip (lines 18–19), the care of weapons (lines 20–21), and the acceptance of one's fate (lines 22–24). The poem was recited to the present writer by bedouin from three different confederations in southern Sinai (the Aḥaywāt, Tarābīn, and Muzēna), but its origin and framework apparently stem from the Arabian peninsula and an earlier date. One of its better known phrases (line 15a, recalled by all the reciters) was also incorporated into a poem recorded by Alois Musil in Syria at the turn of the century.

O king, hear this advice from me, you who're born today,
You're small enough to order yet, and vigilance convey: 1

Poem 3.9 was heard recited by Ḥamdān abū Salāma Abū Masʿūd of the Muzēna Darārma tribe, at aṭ-Ṭūr, 30 March 1971, and at Nabik, 28 June 1975; ʿAmmār ʿAbdallāh Sālim of the Tarābīn Ḥasāblah tribe, in Wādī Watīr, 24 September 1971; and ʿAwda Sulēmān ʿAliyyān of the Aḥaywāt Ḥamādāt tribe in Wādī Ṭābā, 10 December 1971. Discrepancies between the texts were resolved according to the judgement of Muṣliḥ Ibn ʿĀmr.

Be mindful of your livestock, they'll shield you from disgrace;
The wealth of anybody else will not afford you face.[1] 2

Though governed by your brother's son, don't settle in a town;
If you should need but five *dīnārs*, he too would turn you
down.[2] 3

When starting on a journey, make provision as behoves:
Prepare sufficient water, a fire-steel and shoes; 4

You never know where night will find you, travelling all the day,
Or if, by chance, some circumstance will lead you off your way. 5

Be mindful of your brother's son and father's brother's boy;
It's they who'll share your worries, take pleasure in your joy.[3] 6

Don't take a wife who'll make you be remiss in social virtue,
And would, if you consult her, even harm your brother, too.[4] 7

[1] Shielding from disgrace refers here to the ability to be both a host and a helper, owing to an independent source of income, such as a flock. A flock-owning bedouin is in a position to entertain a guest with proper respect (slaughtering an animal for him) and possibly have others in his debt by helping them financially. By contrast, being indebted to others is not only demeaning, but dangerous. It may oblige one to defer to others' interests at the expense of one's own, and limits the option of calling upon them for help in the hour of need (i.e. when one's own rights and interests are challenged). Accordingly, bedouin loathe receiving favours, a sentiment expressed in the proverb 'A favour is heavier than a mountain' (*al-maʿrūf athgal min al-jabal*).

[2] Normally, a bedouin would not refuse his relative—especially a paternal relative—the request of a loan. To emphasize the evil and alienation of the city, therefore, the poet asserts that a city-dwelling cousin, even if he ruled the city, would behave like a stranger.

[3] A bedouin man, and his male relatives on his father's side, form a natural self-defence unit, called a *khamsa* (lit. 'fiver'; i.e. the descendants of his grandfather's grandfather, who comprise five generations, including his own). As the members of a *khamsa* are prepared to defend or avenge any other member without question, each bedouin views his paternal relatives as essential to his welfare and security (cf. poems 1.10, n. 10; 3.11, n. 39).

[4] A bedouin man has social obligations that derive from the conventions of bedouin society. These obligations, the fulfilment of which will largely determine the status and reputation of a person and his family in the society, often involve the readiness to sacrifice wealth and even life. Such sacrifice, however, might well clash with the more immediate and more practical considerations of a man's wife. Thus, if he consulted her, and deferred to her inclinations, a bedouin might become remiss ('short-handed' in the Arabic text) in his obligations—to the detriment of his standing in the society. To emphasize this point, the poet asserts that a domineering wife will go so far as to wrong even her husband's brother—which, in bedouin society, is a man's most vital connection (cf. poem 1.10, n. 10). This sentiment is expressed in the proverb 'It is women that split brothers' (*an-nisā fārgāt ikhwān*).

Don't take a wife who'll keep you from the people you hold dear,
Although she shines like sun and moon, beautiful and clear. 8

Desire not some mountain-goat, although you'll be amused,
And surely if she's not been raised by your paternal kin; 9

Rather take a cousin,[5] by her you'll be amused,
She'll not complain when you're away, yet when you're back be pleased.[6] 10

An outside girl will have no mind to soothe you when you grieve,
And if your wealth should disappear, she'll make accounts and leave.[7] 11

Be not loath to strike your son, to have him grow up right;
And keep the upper hand, though it rouse his mother's spite. 12

Keep your children from your neighbour, lest you rouse his scorn;
He may his anger well disguise, but in his thoughts it's borne. 13

Indeed, your neighbour's dog forbear, although he bites your leg,
Even if he tears your shoes, leaving you unshod.[8] 14

Don't show a guest approaching where your neck's two muscles meet;[9]
Look friendly and be cheerful, like he's one you gladly greet. 15

And even if the guest offend you, treat him like a precious friend,
Even if, at times, his prating brings your patience to an end. 16

Guests don't come and tire with a long, eternal stay:
Most will spend the dark of night and leave at break of day. 17

[5] i.e. paternal cousin (*bint 'amm*).

[6] Bedouin men, in pursuit of their interests—herding, raiding, warfare, or attendance at tribal gatherings—must often spend nights and even prolonged periods away from their families.

[7] In-laws that are not part of one's blood-revenge group (*khamsa*) are called 'outsiders' (*ajānib*), and are considered less likely than related in-laws, to compel their daughters to be obedient to their husbands, in accordance with the conventions of bedouin society. In-laws from one's own *khamsa* are believed to be more interested in a successful marriage, because the sons of that marriage will strengthen their own blood-revenge group.

[8] To emphasize the importance of cordial relations with neighbours, the poet exaggerates by counselling restraint even when a neighbour's dog—the most despised of creatures—causes distress.

[9] i.e. do not show him your back!

Don't let men's untrue reports arouse you to concern:
Just as gossips bring you news, they carry yours, in turn; 18

Thus I'll have slandered you, and me you'd denigrate,
I'll have made you angry, and you'll be full of hate. 19

And don't neglect your sword's sharp edge, it's there to save your life;
Your right hand will yet seek its aid, when you're faced
with strife; 20

The sword is not a brother always there to be your shield;
The sword is but a weapon for your own strong arm to wield.[10] 21

Finally, when God wills war and puts us to the test,
And fighters call on you for aid, don't flee from their request. 22

Once the battle has begun, with God's your preservation;
He'll save you from the pit of death, if that's his inclination. 23

Your written fate is bound to reach you, even if you hide;
Another's fate will miss you, though you're standing at its side. 24

1 ya mālik isma' kalāmī wāna-l-yōm bōṣīk
winta ṣuġayyir agdar amirk wanhāk

1 يا مالك اسمع كلامي وانا اليـــوم باوصيك
وانت صغيّـــر اقـــدر امـــرك وانهاك

2 ḥaššim ġanāmk-illī ma' al-badū taḏrīk
ma yinfa'ak hāḏa wala yinfa'ak ḏāk

2 حشّم غنـــامك اللي مـــع البدو تذريك
مـــا ينفعك هـــذا ولا ينفعـــك ذاك

3 ir'a-l-madīna law ḥakamha bin axīk
law tuṭulba xamsa dinanīr ma-'ṭāk

3 ارعـــى المدينة لـــو حكمها بـــن اخيك
لـــو تطلبد خمسة دنانير مـــا اعطاك

4 wila bānat an-niyya darrik ma'anīk
darrik šarābak w-iḏhin az-zind wi-ḥḏāk

4 ولو بانت النيّـــة درّك معـــانيك
درّك شرابك واذهـــن الزند وحـــذاك

5 ū-la ta'raf il-ayyām hī wēn tirmīk
ū-bi-rubbi̲n̲ ma tirmīk 'ala ġēr mašḥāk

5 ولا تعرف الايّـــام هـــي ويـــن ترميك
وبـــربّ„ مـــا `ترميك علـــى غير مشحاك

[10] The sentiment here expressed, that one ultimately lives by the sword, is also reflected in the proverb 'A right not companioned by a sword is lost!' (*ḥaggi̲n̲ mā yibrāh-has-sēf, ḥaggi̲n̲ ḍāya'*).

6 ū-ḥaššim walad ʿammak ū-ḥaššim bin axīk
yiẓīg min ẓīgak wi-yirẓa ʿala-rẓāk

6 وحشّم ولد عمّك وحشّم بن اخيك
يضيق من ضيقك ويرضى على رضاك

7 la tāxiḏ illī tugaṣrak ʿin maʿanīk
lin ṭiʿitha bi-šōr jārat al-axāk

7 لا تاخذ اللي تقصّرك عن معانيك
لن طعتها بشور جارت عل اخاك

8 la tāxiḏ illī tibʿidak ʿin ġawalīk
la kān zē aš-šams aw al-gamr ḏāk

8 لا تاخذ اللي تبعدك عن غواليك
لو كان زي الشمس او القمر ذاك

9 ū-la baġayt lak ġifrin yisallīk
la tāxḏ illī mā marabbī marbāk

9 ولا بغيت لك غفر يسلّيك
لا تاخذ اللي ما مربّيه مرباك

10 la tāxḏ ila bint ʿammak tisallīk
tuṣbur ʿala ṭūl al-liyāli tiḥarrāk

10 لا تاخذ الا بنت عمّك تسلّيك
تصبر على طول الليالي تحرّاك

11 al-ajnabiyya ma dawī mašakīk
in gall ma bēn īdēk tigfī ū-tinsāk

11 الاجنبيّة ما داوي مشاكيك
ان قلّ ما بين ايديك تقفي وتنساك

12 wuẓrub waladak kōd tabġā yišfīk
law tizʿal amma la tixallī yilāk

12 واضرب ولدك كود تبغاه يشفيك
لو تزعل امّه لا تخلّيه يلاك

13 anḥa ṣaġīrak ʿan ṭanībak yizarīk
yungul zaʿāl fī ẓamīra wilaw kān ma warrāk

13 انحى صغيرك عن طنيبك يزاريك
ينقل زعل في ضميره ولو كان ما ورّاك

14 ōṣīk ʿan kalb ṭanībak linna daggar fīk
linnu gaṭaʿ anʿalēk ya walad waḥfāk

14 اوصيك عن كلب طنيبك لنّه دقّر فيك
لنّه قطع نعاليك يا ولد واحفاك

15 waẓ-ẓayf la taʿṭī magran ʿalabīk
xallak ṣaḥība ū-wadīda ila jāk

15 والضيف لا تعطيه مقرن علابيك
خلّك صحيبه ووديده الا جاك

16 ū-xalla ḥabībak ū-ṣadīgak linnu muʿadīk
wilaw al-kalām baʿẓ ōgāt ġaẓāk

16 وخلّه حبيبك وصديقك لنّه معاديك
ولو الكلام بعض اوقات غظاك

17 aẓ-ẓayf mū hū dīmt ad-dōm yiwazīk
yibayyit samār al-lēl waṣ-ṣubḥ xallāk

17 الضيف ما هو ديمة الدوم يوازيك
يبيّت سمار الليل والصبح خلّاك

18 ōṣīk ʿan harj al-ʿarab ya ẓafr yiġwīk
min jāb lak harja yiwaddī li-hḏāk

18 اوصيك عن هرج العرب يا ظفر يغويك
من جاب لك هرجه يودّيه لهذاك

19 ʿendak haraj fīna wi-ʿendī haraj fīk inta baġaẓtūna wiḥna karahnāk	عندك هرج فينا وعندي هرج فيك 19 انتم بغضتونا واحنا كرهناك
20 was-sēf la tirmiṯ bi-ḥaddi yixallīk fī sāʿitin tuṭlub farajha bi-yumnāk	والسيف لا ترمث بحدّه يخلّيك 20 في ساعةٍ تطلب فرجها بيمناك
21 was-sēf mā hū lak xawiyyin yibarīk yikōd ma ẓarabt as-sēf bi-ʿazm yumnāk	والسيف ما هو لك خويٍ يباريك 21 يكود ما ضربت السيف بعزم يمناك
22 wōṣīk yōm aḷḷa fi-l-hawš yiblīk la tinḥarf yōm ir-rajajīl tinxāk	واوصيك يوم اللّد في الهوش يبليك 22 لا تنحرف يوم الرجاجيل تنخاك
23 ṭubb al-madārik hū al-maʿtinī fīk arād lak min nugrit al-mōt najāk	طبّ المدارك هو المعتني فيك 23 اراد لك من نقرة الموت نجاك
24 ū-maktūbak law taġabbayt yatīk maktūb ġērak law tabayyant ma jāk	ومكتوبك لو تغبّيت ياتيك 24 مكتوب غيرك لو تبيّنت ما جاك

3.10

A Rejection of Bedouin Advice

A Poem of Advice

The present poem is said to have originated as an indignant retort to the last poem, which lacked Islamic content. It was composed by the uncle of the child to whom that poem was addressed, and took the rhyme scheme of the earlier composition's first hemistich for that of its own. This poem is entirely Islamic in intention, infused with the basic themes of Islamic asceticism (*zuhd*); namely, that one should shun sinfulness and take heed that the end of life is imminent and awesome.

Poem 3.10 was heard recited by Ḥamdān abū Salāma Abū Masʿūd of the Muzēna Darārma tribe, at Nabik oasis, 28 June 1975.

O heart, hear my words as now I advise you;
My harvest's all over and straw's what remains.[1] 1

What you've heard is unfounded, I hope it won't touch you,
For bedouin counsel a good name may stain. 2

I'll begin by recalling the Name who has made you,[2]
Forming from nothing your flesh and your bones. 3

Permit not the drift of your heart to mislead you
Till into a sea you can't swim, you are thrown.[3] 4

From ignorance, sinfulness comes to mislead you,
Till you're drunk from much drinking and your end is in sight.[4] 5

Take stock of your times; your eye should suffice you
To see how a frog puts an ostrich to flight.[5] 6

The world's full of infidels ready to strike you,
But Muslims, as well, who'll fight till they win. 7

O heart, heed my words as now I advise you;
On that day when we're judged there's a throng and a din.[6] 8

1 ya galb tisma' jābtī yōm bōṣīk
az-zar'-antaha ma bāgī ġēr aṣ-ṣarāmī

2 had̲ūl harj an-nāfila mā yijī fīk
ū-harj al-'arab barẕū yijīb al-malāmī

1 يـــا قلب تسمع جابتي يـــوم باوصيك
الزرع انتهى مـــا باقـــي غيـــر الصرامِ

2 هذول هرج النافلة مـــا يجي فيك
وهرج العـــرب برضـــو يجيب المـــلامِ

[1] i.e. I am old.

[2] For 'recalling God's name' (*d̲h̲ikr allāh*), see poems 2.12, n. 13; 3.5, n. 6.

[3] In the Arabic text this line integrates Qur'ānic and bedouin imagery. The image of being thrown into 'an unfathomable sea' (*lijjit al-baḥr*) as a punishment for sinfulness is an adaptation of the Qur'ānic passage (24. 40) that describes unbelievers as living in darkness, such as that of 'an unfathomable sea' (*baḥrin̲ lujjiyyin̲*). The 'unswimmable' aspect of the sea in the original imagery derives from the bedouin depiction of *mans̲h̲ad*—the branch of bedouin law that deals with sexual offences against women—as a 'fire that burns and a sea that drowns' (*nārin̲ yiḥarriġ ū-baḥrin̲ yig̲h̲arriġ*). (Cf. poem 2.7, n. 8.)

[4] The image *kās al-ḥamām*, in the original text, is a term for 'death'.

[5] i.e. the world has become unnatural.

[6] The allusion to 'throng' derives from the Qur'ān (4. 87): 'He will gather you all together on the Day of Resurrection.'

3 awwal kalāmī aḏkur illī-msawwīk
   ū-min-al-ʿadam minša-l-laḥam wal-aẓāmī

٣ اوّل كـلامي اذكر اللـي مسوّيك
   ومن العدم منشا اللحم والعظام

4 ya galb la titbaʿ hawa-n-nafs tahwīk
   tirmīk fī lijjit baḥar mā yuʿāmī

٤ يا قلب لا تتبع هوى النفس تهويك
   ترميك في لجّة بحر مـا يعام

5 darb al-xaṭa maʿ gilt il-ʿirf taʿṭīk
   taskar ʿan aṣ-ṣaḥwa ū-kās al-ḥamāmī

٥ درب الخطا مع قلّة العرف تعطيك
   تسكر عـن الصحوة وكـاس الحمـام

6 unẓur zamānak ū-bi-ʿaynak tigazzīk
   waẓ-ẓifadaʿ tuṭrud jafīl an-naʿāmī

٦ انظـر زمـانك وبعينـك تقزّيك
   والضفدع تطــرد جفيل النعـام

7 aʿdād kāfr ʿal ad-dinya muʿaddīk
   wa-ʿdād mislim ma ẓarab bil-hizāmī

٧ اعداد كافر عـل الدنيا معدّيك
   واعداد مسلم مـا ضرب بالهـزام

8 wiya galb tismaʿ jābtī yōm bōšīk
   wa-ʿdād xalg alla yōm iz-zḥāmī

٨ ويا قلب تسمع جابتي يوم باوصيك
   واعداد خلق اللـه يوم الزحام

3.11

How to Be a Good Muslim
A Poem of Religious Advice

The present poem, composed by Muṣliḥ Sālim Sulēmān Ibn ʿĀmr of the Tiyāhā Ṣgērāt tribe of east-central Sinai around 1930, is a religious poem, instructing the listener in how to conduct his life as a good Muslim.[1] The religious sentiments that pervade this poem are of an ascetic nature: stressing the transience of life, and the imminence of death with its implied threat of eternal torment ('the Fire') and its

Poem 3.11 was heard recited by its author, in Wādī Munbaṭaḥ, 19 October 1970.

---

[1] Muṣliḥ Ibn ʿĀmr, who claimed to have composed the poem when he was about twenty years old (c. 1930), had had five years of formal schooling (in the town of el-ʿArīsh, where his father as a chief maintained a residence in order to have ready access to the authorities). The poet's ability to integrate lines (although paraphrased) from the Qurʾān and Ḥadīth Tradition into the poem is unusual for a bedouin, and may be due to this brief, but formal, education.

promise of eternal paradise ('the Garden')—each person's destiny determined by his deeds in this life. The poem counsels the bedouin to observe God's commandments, take the successes of this life lightly, walk humbly, and be charitable and merciful to God's creatures.

When Islam is ascetic it appeals to bedouin, because asceticism—compelled, albeit, by natural circumstance—is a central feature of their daily experience. The desert affords little luxury to tempt a bedouin; and, as a matter of survival, he views material possessions as an encumbrance. If a bedouin held the amassing of wealth and possessions in high regard, he would be unable to live in the desert, which is marked by paucity and an unpredictable climate; indeed to migrate in search of pasture and water would itself be impossible if his possessions were many. Moreover, with most of the bedouin wealth in livestock—the danger of whose loss, through drought or an enemy raid, has ever been imminent—the impermanence of life and wealth has always been a familiar theme. Nor does lofty position, disparaged in ascetic theology, make an impression on a nomadic society that has traditionally attached no special privilege or advantage to leadership, aware that each individual desert-dweller must enjoy maximum independence in order to survive. The bedouin's lack of deference to high tribal office is also reflected in a popular proverb 'The leader of a group is the one who serves it' (*gāyid al-gōm khādimhā*).

Several originally bedouin values expressed in this poem, such as patience, self-reliance, and family solidarity, were, along with others, adopted by the Islamic faith at its outset.[2] The bedouin, however, believe that all their values and customs are Islamic in origin and character—even values that are alien to Islamic precepts, such as not divulging secrets to one's wife (line 4c), or not fearing death 'if you're looking for fame' (line 11b). Line 2b, moreover, urging bedouin to seek pride and, by extension, glory (Ar. *ʿizz*, *ʿizza*), stands in contrast to Islam. The Qur'ān (4. 139) specifically disparages such ambitions, saying 'Surely, all glory belongs to God'.

This poem, unlike its predecessors in this book, is composed in quatrains (sing. *marbūaʿ*, in bedouin poetry), in which the first three lines rhyme with each other, and the last line with the fourth line of the other quatrains. The translation has sought to maintain the original scansion of four accentuated feet to a line, and to recapture the rhyme-

[2] See, e.g., the Prophet's sayings on patience ('Victory comes from patience'), self-reliance (' 'Tis better to bear a bundle of branches on your back than to beg'), and family solidarity ('Support your brother, whether oppressor or oppressed') (Wensinck, ii. 242; vi. 284, 461). Cf. stanzas 10, 15, 17, and 18 in the present poem.

scheme of the original quatrains. To rhyme all the fourth lines in one uniform scheme, however, proved beyond the present writer's capacity.

1 God's pardon we ask,[3] beginning our poem,
Lord of all that there is, divine on His throne;[4]
O that He, each error I make, might condone:
One who looks to the Lord, his hope will endure.[5]

2 If only you'll hear the advice I provide,
The length of your life will be lived out with pride,
And the Garden is what you will gain when you've died;[6]
But each follows the path of his own inclination.[7]

3 If by chance you're chosen to judge between men,
Let your judgment not waver though one be your friend;[8]
For the Lord, on His throne, is our judge in the end,[9]
And where can we turn from His stern condemnation?

[3] 'Asking God's pardon' (*istighfār*) for an act of arrogance is common among Muslims (see Piamenta, p. 135); in the present case the arrogance possibly lies in the attempt to set down religious precepts in verse.

[4] The images used in the Arabic text of this line—'Lord of all that there is' and 'divinity of the throne'—indicate how a bedouin poet, semi-literate and with little access to the Qur'ān, might adapt Qur'ānic images to his poem, but confuse them. For example, while the Qur'ān often alludes to 'Lord of the throne' (e.g. Sūra 9. 129), it has no phrase 'divinity of the throne' (although a close collaboration of the terms occurs in Sūra 27. 26 with 'there is no divinity but Him, Lord of the throne'). Similarly, while the term used in the Arabic text of the poem for 'all that there is' (*mulk*) is found in Qur'ānic phrases like 'God's is the possession [*mulk*] of the heavens and the earth and all that is between' (5. 120), the present combination, 'Lord of all that there is', is the innovation of either the present poet or of one of his predecessors along the line of oral transmission.

[5] Cf. Qur'ān, 2. 217: '[The faithful] look to God's mercy, for God is forgiving and compassionate.'

[6] Lines 2b–c form a juxtaposition of bedouin and Islamic aspirations: pride and 'the Garden'.

[7] This statement of free will reflects the saying (*ḥadīth*) of the Prophet with which the thirteenth-century scholar, al-Nawawī, chose to open his revered collection of the forty most essential sayings: 'Actions are done according to inclination; each person has his own inclinations' (al-Nawawī, p. 9).

[8] Judging honestly, always an important ideal in bedouin society, also received the endorsement of the Islamic religion. Muḥammad is reported to have said, 'There are three kinds of judges, one of which is bound for the Garden, while the other two are doomed to the Fire. A judge who knows the law and judges accordingly is bound for the Garden. A judge who knows the law, but does not judge accordingly, is doomed to the Fire; and a judge who knows not the law and judges out of ignorance is doomed to the Fire' (Wensinck, v. 418).

[9] This image derives from the Qur'ān (10. 93): 'And the Lord will judge between them on Judgment Day.

4 Don't rejoice over life though your riches be great,[10]
For what's really at hand is the end of your life;[11]
And your actions keep secret, don't share with your wife:
How often a wife's brought a man to low station.[12]

5 Don't rejoice over life though you've reached highest station,[13]
For the lowest—the grave—is our last habitation;[14]
Envy not others, we're all God's creation:[15]
And those who build dwellings, their shelter is sure.[16]

6 Do not defy God, but obey and be humble;[17]
At your back is the grave, that abode ever hateful,
Where the worm eats your flesh like pasture so tasteful,
While your bones, interred, end in disintegration.[18]

[10] This ascetic admonition not to rejoice over 'this life' because of wealth comes directly from the Qur'ān (28. 76: 'Don't rejoice . . .'). Again, the non-believers are reviled for rejoicing over 'this life' (rendered as 'the near life' (*al-dunyā*) as opposed to 'the after-life' (*al-ākhira*)). Muḥammad, too, is reported to have said: 'Love of this life is the source of all sin'; and: 'Abstain from the things of this life, and God will love you' (Wensinck, ii. 152, 348, respectively).

[11] The imminent transience of this life is a strong image in Islam, as expressed in the following sayings of the Prophet: 'Relate to this life like a foreigner or a passer-by'; and: 'If it is evening, expect not the morning—and if it is morning, expect not the evening' (Wensinck, iv. 473; vi. 228, respectively).

[12] Men in bedouin society are advised to be secretive about their plans and movements, especially not to divulge them to their wives. A bedouin proverb holds 'Consult your wives, but do just the opposite' (*shāwirūhin w-ikhlifū shōrhin*). See poems 3.9, n. 4; 6.2, l. 4.

[13] Cf. Qur'ān (28. 83): 'The Garden is for those who seek not high station.'

[14] Cf. the eighth-century ascetic poet, Abū-l-'Atāhiya, p. 430: 'Even after palaces, their dwellers have but graves for habitation.'

[15] The disaparagement of envy stems from the Prophet's saying: 'Beware of envy; it destroys one's merits as fire consumes wood' (Wensinck, i. 465).

[16] A bedouin proverb corresponding to the English 'You reap what you sow'.

[17] A prevalent Muslim sentiment is that a man's afterlife depends on whether he has been obedient or defiant towards God. The origin is in the Qur'ān (4. 13, 14): 'He who is obedient to God and His apostle will be admitted to the Gardens beneath which eternal rivers flow. He who defies God and His apostle, and transgresses His limits, will be put into the Fire, where he will suffer a harsh, eternal torment'.

[18] Cf. lines by the twelfth-century poet, al-Ḥarīrī, as translated in Nicholson, p. 334; also, 'Nothing will remain but the disintegrating bones', of Abū-l-'Atāhiya (p. 485).

[19] The five religious obligations mentioned in this stanza (the recitation of the Muslim creed, the performance of prayers five times daily, the month-long fast of Ramaḍān, the pilgrimage to Mecca, and the giving of charity) are known as the Pillars of Islam (*arkān al-islām*) because the Prophet viewed Islam as being 'built upon' them (al-Nawawī, no. 3).

7 Render Allah His due with perfect completion:
Pilgrimage, prayer, and the Fast obligation;
The oath—God is one . . .—of the Muslim nation;
And the alms we're commanded to give to the poor.[19]

8 These five are a duty, upon us incumbent,
Taught by Muḥammad,[20] the herald that God sent;
I hope I will always perform His commandment:
An obeying soul's place in the Garden's secure.[21]

9 Don't compel Allah's creatures: instead, treat them kind;[22]
And if you feel strong, in no need, never mind,[23]
For if you should fall within fate's certain bind,
It's the Lord you'll ask to relieve your affliction.[24]

10 Be aware that your heart is your guide as you go:
It will indicate who is your friend, who your foe;[25]
And beautiful patience I advise you to know:[26]
When misfortune befalls it will help you endure.[27]

[20] The image that 'Muḥammad taught us' (*akhbaranā muḥammad*) derives from the *ḥadīth*, which relates how the angel Gabriel visited the Prophet and said: 'O Muḥammad, teach me [*akhbirnī*] what Islam is.' The Prophet complied by enumerating the five Pillars (al-Nawawī, no. 2).

[21] The origin of this line is the Qur'ān (79. 40): 'Those who curb their soul's desires will dwell in the Garden.'

[22] The compassion counselled in this line goes back to the Qur'ān (2. 280): 'If your debtor be in straits, postpone the payment until his situation be eased; and if you waive the debt as alms, it will be a boon for you.' The Prophet, too, is reported as saying: 'God will be merciful to the person who is generous and kind when selling, buying, or collecting a debt' (Wensinck, ii. 164).

[23] Cf. Qur'ān (96. 6, 7): 'A person is impious if he considers himself in need of no one'; and (49. 10): 'God does not love the arrogant and the proud.'

[24] Here one is said to ask *the Lord* to relieve *affliction* (Ar. *balā'*), because, in the language of the Qur'ān (2. 4), it is *the Lord* that brings *affliction*.

[25] This is a bedouin sentiment which affirms the importance of intuition in assessing one's social environment, and is embodied in the pithy proverb 'The heart is a guide' (*al-galb dalīl*). The sentiment is given an Islamic nuance by the bedouin oral tradition that the Prophet, once receiving a protestation of love, replied 'Hearts are their own evidence' (*al-gulūb shawāhid*) (al-Bilādī, p. 184).

[26] When biblical Joseph in the Qur'ānic account (12. 18) was reported to have been devoured by a wolf, his father vowed he would survive the misfortune 'with beautiful patience and God whom we ask for aid'. Again (70. 6), the faithful are told to gird themselves 'with beautiful patience' while waiting to witness God's power. Hence, the phrase 'Patience is beautiful' (*aṣ-ṣabr jamīl*) is proverbially uttered when a bedouin is faced with adversity (cf. poem 1.15, n. 3).

[27] The belief that patience can help against adversity is rooted in the Qur'ānic dictum (2. 153) 'Seek help in patience and prayer for God abides with the patient'. The second half of the dictum (Ar. *allāh ma' aṣ-ṣābrīn*) is also a bedouin expression of comfort (see Piamenta, p. 47).

11 Do not buy cheap goods if you're looking for gain,[28]
And never fear death if you're looking for fame;[29]
And don't commit sins if the Garden's your aim:
Your life will be followed with just compensation.

12 Do bad turns to foes though five hundred in number;
But accede to your wife when asked for a favour;
When delivering evil consider the danger:
Restrain your desires and your soul's agitation.[30]

13 Disappoint not the needy expecting your dole:[31]
Wealth's but a boon come to rescue your soul;[32]
And don't treat men's deeds, as if all equal all:
Each illness requires its own proper cure.

14 Be neither too sad when grief should embitter,
Nor overly happy when gladdened by pleasure;
Life is like that—sometimes sweet, sometimes bitter:
The world is all willed by God the Creator.[33]

[28] This line reflects the bedouin sentiment that dear goods are more worthwhile than cheap ones. Hence the proverbs 'The dear is really cheaper' (*al-ghālī hū ar-rakhīṣ*); and 'The cost of something dear is covered by its worth' (*al-ghālī thamnah fīh*).

[29] For the defiance of death as an important element of one's reputation, see poem 5.1, l. 7.

[30] Although it follows three lines of purely bedouin advice, the inspiration for this line was Islamic (cf. poem 3.10, l. 4, and n. 21 above).

[31] Cf. the bedouin proverb 'Disappointment is only towards him who depends on you' (*mā khāb ghēr man khāb nāṣīh*).

[32] The opportunity that a believer's wealth presents for saving his soul is a Qur'ānic concept found in verses such as 'Take charity from the wealth [of new believers] that they may be cleansed and purified' (9. 103). Infidels, on the other hand, cannot ransom their souls, even with 'a world of gold' (3. 91).

[33] Although 'His is the creation and the command, Allah be blessed' (Qur'ān, 7. 54), the idea that God changes the conditions of life arbitrarily is contrary to the basic Islamic outlook, which promised goodness to the faithful and misfortune to the infidel. Life's vicissitudes are rather a native bedouin thought, as reflected in the proverb 'Good lasts not forever, nor does bad' (*al-khēr mā biydūm, wa-sh-sharr mā biydūm*).

15 Who drinks with his own hand will know when he's slaked,
So look only to God—not to people—for aid;
It is He who sustains whomever He deigns:[34]
If you're needy, appeal not to man's dispensation.

16 Fear not the truth, for the truth is what God sent,[35]
But rather fear God and His warnings of torment[36]
That day when each soul reads his book before Judgment,[37]
When every soul goes through dire trepidation.

17 Find helplessness shameful and wear not its stain;
Cast helplessness off though it takes some pain;
Ask Allah for aid—not who worship His name,
And thus rid your life of base degradation.[38]

18 Be careful to suffer your kinsman's mistake,
Don't hold him a foe in your heart though it ache:[39]
Any shame on your kinsman hurts you in its wake,[40]
So make your heart pure of harsh inclination.

[34] Self-reliance—an aspect of cherished independence—is a bedouin rather than Islamic principle. The first line of this stanza is an improvisation on the bedouin proverbs 'He who drinks not with his own palm is not slaked' (*illī mā yis͟hrab bi-ḥifnitah mā yirtiwī*); 'He who eats not with his own hand will not be sated' (*illī mā yākil bi-īdih mā yis͟hba'*); and 'Other folks' morsel doesn't fill you' (*luqmat an-nās mā tis͟hba'*). The second line, disparaging the recourse to other people for aid, however, also derives from the Islamic tradition reflected in the *ḥadīt͟h*: 'It is better to bear a bundle of branches on your back than to ask it of someone else—who might comply or might refuse (Wensinck, i. 477). The third line, urging reliance on God alone, is a paraphrase of the Qur'ān (28. 82): 'God sustains whomever He will'; the more colloquial verb *yirīd* is used here instead of the Qur'ānic *yis͟ha'* for 'He will'.

[35] Cf. Qur'ān (18. 29): 'Say, "The truth is from your Lord."'

[36] Cf. Qur'ān (2. 196): 'Fear God and know that His punishments are hard.' The word used in this poem for eternal torment (*'ad͟hāb*) occurs in the Qur'ān more than 320 times.

[37] The Qur'ān (17. 16) teaches that each person has a book in which his deeds are recorded during his lifetime, and which he must read in the presence of God on Judgment Day.

[38] Note 34, above, is also relevant to this stanza.

[39] The preservation of solidarity among kinsmen is vital in bedouin society (cf. poems 1.10, n. 10; 3.9, n. 3) One punning proverb holds 'Consider kinsmen a garden though they may craze you' (*al-qarāyib janna wa-law tijanninūk*); another 'Even a snake doesn't bite its own belly' (*al-ḥayya mā bit'uḍḍ baṭinhā*). Paternal kin are essential to one's security; being ready to avenge any insult or injury serves to deter others from acting against one. Maternal kin, on the other hand, may aid one economically in the context of 'consideration for kinship-by-marriage' (*ḥasab ū-nasab*).

[40] While this line may pertain to all one's relatives (see n. 39), it recalls bedouin sayings concerning maternal kin, such as 'Talk that is against your maternal kin is against yourself as well' (*kalām illī fī k͟hālak fīk*). The reasoning behind this saying is that a person's qualities are considered to derive from his mother's family (cf. poem 1.6, n. 7.)

19 Rid yourself for good of an ill-doing friend:
His friendship will lead you to harm in the end;
If his faults, full two thousand, to suffer you tend,
From his ill, you will find, even you're not secure.[41]

20 Throw no stone on the path where you're taking a trip,
It will make either you or a friend of yours slip;[42]
And heed not a foe if your friend he would slur:
Though your friend may have faults, they're for you to endure.[43]

21 For the end of my verse, I, the Prophet recall:[44]
Muḥammad—of those sent to bring us God's call.
God's blessing upon them—upon one and all;
Any law but Muḥammad's, we'll surely abjure.

1 awwal gōlna nistaġfir aḷḷa
ilā al-ʿarš rabb al-milk kulli
yaġfir fī kalāmī kull zalli
nafsin tirjā ma yugṭaʿ rijāha

1 اوّل قولنا نستغفر اللّه
الد العرش ربّ الملك كلّه
يغفر في كلامي كلّ زلّة
نفسٍ ترجاه ما يقطع رجاها

2 ana awṣīk in kan tismaʿ awaṣātī
tiʿīš ib-ʿizz ʿa ṭūl al-ḥayātī
ū-tiksib jinntin baʿd il-mamātī
lakin al-kull li niyti illī nawāha

2 انا اوصيك ان كان تسمع وصاتي
تعيش بعزّ ع طول الحياةِ
وتكسب جنّةٍ بعد المماتِ
لكن الكلّ له نيّته اللي نواها

[41] The subject of bad companions is an Islamic religious concern. A popular *ḥadīth* holds 'A person is considered to hold the convictions of his friend; let each beware whom he befriends' (Wensinck, iii. 257). Among bedouin, however, considerations of kinship-proximity are more important than a friend's character or personality. Still, bedouin are aware of the ill effects of bad behaviour, and, if they suffer from the actions even of a kinsman, they may ostracize him—an act that they call 'exposure to the sun' (*tashmīs*), i.e. no longer enjoying his family's 'cover' or protection. The awareness that a wrong-doer can jeopardize the welfare of his entire group (owing to the principle of mutual responsibility) is also embodied in the bedouin proverb 'One scabby goat can infect the whole flock' (*al-ʿanz al-jarbā tiʿdī al-ghanam kullhā*).

[42] Cf. the Prophet's saying 'Removing a harmful thing from the road is charity' (al-Nawawī, no. 26; cf. Wensinck i. 425, for alternative versions of the same statement).

[43] Bedouin consider it proper to ignore the shortcomings of friends (see poem 2.1, n. 5).

[44] For more on mentioning the Prophet deferentially at the end of a poem, see poem. 1.11, n. 8.

3 in ṣirt bēn an-nās gāẓī
la tiḥkum bēnhum bil-iġtirāẓī
bukra tilga rabb al-ʿarš gāẓī
wēn itrūḥ min gāẓī gaẓāha

3 ان صرت بين الناس قاضي
لا تحكم بينهم بالاغتراضِ
بكرة تلقى ربّ العرش قاضي
وين تروح من قاضي قضاها

4 wila tifraḥ ʿal ad-dinya bi-mālak
tara-d-dinya garīb minha zawālak
wala dirrī nisāk ʿala fiʿālak
yāma-sbāʿin ḏallatha nisāha

4 ولا تفرح عل الدنيا بمالك
ترا الدنيا قريب منها زوالك
ولا درّي نساك على فعالك
ياما سباعٍ ذلّتها نساها

5 wala tafraḥ ʿala ʿilūwi-l-amākin
fa-in al-gabr āwṭa fi-l-masākin
walā taṭmaʿ ʿa xalg allāhī lākin
mā yuskun dār ġēr illī banāha

5 ولا تفرح على علو الاماكن
فان القبر اوطى في المساكن
ولا تطمع ع خلق اللّه لاكن
ما يسكن دار غير اللي بناها

6 wi-lā taʿṣa-l-ilā ū-kūn muṭīʿī
warāk ilḥūd maskinha šanīʿī
warāk ad-dūd laḥamak li rabīʿī
wi-yibga-l-ʿaẓm bālī fī fanāha

6 ولا تعصى الاله وكون مطيعِ
وراك لحود مسكنها شنيعِ
وراك الدود لحمك له ربيعِ
ويبقى العظم بالي في فناها

7 wi-aʿṭ-allā ḥagga bit-tamāmī
ṣalā wi-ḥijj maʿ farẓ aṣ-ṣiyāmī
wi-šihādit muʾminīnin bil-islāmī
wi-zakātin lil-fagīr taʿṭi-yyāha

7 واعطي اللّه حقّه بالتمامِ
صلاة وحجّ مع فرض الصيامِ
وشهادة مؤمنينٍ بالاسلامِ
وزكاةٍ للفقير تعطيه ايّاها

8 hāḏa xams hin ḥaggin ʿalēna
axbarna mḥammad al-mursil ilēna
in kan ana ʿala amra imšēna
an-nafs aṭ-ṭāyʿa al-janna jizāha

8 هذا خمس هن حقٍّ علينا
اخبرنا محمّد المرسل الينا
ان كان انا على امره مشينا
النفس الطايعة الجنّة جزاها

9 warḥam xalg rabbak la tijabbir
win istiġnēt ʿanhum la tikabbar
wi-in wagaʿt fī amrin imgaddar
fa-uṭlub rabbna yihawwin balāha

9 وارحم خلق ربّك لا تجبّر
وان استغنيت عنهم لا تكبّر
وان وقعت في امرٍ مقدّر
فاطلب ربّنا يهوّن بلاها

10 wi-aʿlam in galbak lak dilīlī
yidillak ʿal-ʿadū ū-ʿal-xalīlī
wana-wṣīk ʿal aṣ-ṣabr al-jimīlī
tarā yiʿīn nafsak ʿà balāha

10 واعلم ان قلبك لــك دليلِ
يدلّــك عــالعدو وعــالخليلِ
وانــا اوصيك عــل الصبر الجميلِ
تــراه يعين نفسك ع بــلاهــا

11 in ridt ar-ribiḥ la tišri-r-rizāya
win ridt aṣ-ṣīt la-thāb al-manāya
win ridt al-janna la taʿmil xaṭāya
tarā kull nifs jazwāha warāha

11 ان ردت الربح لا تشري الرزايا
وان ردت الصيت لا تهاب المنايا
وان ردت الجنّة لا تعمل خطايا
تــرا كــلّ نفس جزواها وراهــا

12 bil-matlūf ʿānid xums miyyi
ū-bal-maʿrūf axẓaʿ lal-wiliyyi
wilā taġlaṭ ib-tagdīm ar-radiyyi
wa-hīn an-nafs la titbaʿ hawāha

12 بالمتلوف عــاند خمس ميّــة
وبالمعروف اخضــع للوليّــة
ولا تغــلط بتقديم الرديّــة
وهيــن النفس لا تتبــع هواهــا

13 wala txayyib ṭālbin yirjū ʿaṭāka
fa-in al-māl kulli fī fadāka
walā tiʿāmil ʿamal hāḏa bi-ḏāka
mā yibrī ʿiltak ila dawāha

13 ولا تخيّب طالبٍ يرجو عطاكُ
فان المــال كلّــد فــي فداكُ
ولا تعــامل عمــل هذا بذاكُ
مــا يبري علّــتك الا دواهــا

14 wilā tiḥzin ʿala ḥiznin yimurrī
wilā tifraḥ ʿala farḥin yisurrī
tarā hāḏa ḥālha ḥilwin ū-murrī
bi-amr aḻḻā rabbi-llī nišāha

14 ولا تحــزن علــى حــزنٍ يمرِّ
ولا تفــرح علــى فــرحٍ يسرِّ
تــرا هذا حالها حلوٍ ومرِّ
بامر اللّــد ربّي اللي نشاهــا

15 mā yirwi-s-sabaʿ ġēr aš-šarb bīdi
tarajja-ḻḻā akram min ʿabīdi
yaʿṭi-r-rizig li-min hū yirīdi
ū-bāb al-xalg la tuṭlub rajāha

15 ما يروي السبع غير الشرب بايدد
ترجّــى اللّــد اكــرم مــن عبيدد
يعطــي الرزق لمــن هــو يريدد
وباب الخلق لا تطلب رجاهــا

16 ū-gūl al-ḥagg šarʿan la-thāba
ū-xāf min aḻḻa la tinsa ʿaḏābi
yōm al-kull yagra fī kitābi
ū-tabga-r-rūḥ fī aṣʿab šagāha.

16 وقول الحقّ شرعًا لا تــهابد
وخاف من اللّــد لا تنسى عذابد
يوم الكــلّ يقرا فــي كــتابد
وتبقى الروح في اصعب شقاهــا

17 wila txallī ʿalēk ad-dill bādī
ū-zīḥ ad-dill ʿannak bijtihādī
tarajja-llā la tirja-l-ʿabādī
wi-ʿēš ad-dill utrukha bilāha

17 ولا تخلّي عليك الذلّ بادي
وزيح الذلّ عنك باجتهادِ
ترجّى اللّه لا ترجى العبادِ
وعيش الذلّ اتركها بلاها

18 ū-aḥmal kull zalla min garībak
walā tabgī fī galbak ḥarībak
tara-d-dill law ṣāba yiṣībak
ū-iṣf niytak li min gasāha

18 واحمل كلّ زلّة من قريبك
ولا تبقيد في قلبك حريبك
ترا الذلّ لو صابد يصيبك
واصف نيّتك لد من قساها

19 rafīg as-saw kibbi ʿank marra
mā fī rufigti ġēr al-maẓarra
la taḥmal zallti alfēn marra
nafs as-saw ʿinnak ma naḥāha

19 رفيق السو كبّد عنك مرّة
ما في رفقتد غير المضرّة
لو تحمل زلّتد الفين مرّة
نفس السو عنك ما نحاها

20 walā tirmī ḥaṣātin fī ṭarīgak
in-kan ma tiʿaṯrak tiʿaṯṯir rafīgak
wala-tṣaddig ʿaduwwak fī ṣadīgak
ū-xalg aḻḻā la tʿaddid radāha

20 ولا ترمي حصاةٍ في طريقك
ان كان ما تعثّرك تعثّر رفيقك
ولا تصدّق عدوّك في صديقك
وخلق اللّه لا تعدّد رداها

21 ū-āxir gōlna nudkur nabīna
muḥammad maʿ jamīaʿ-l-mursalīna
ṣalāt aḻḻā ʿalēhum ajmaʿīna
šarīʿit imḥammad ma nitbaʿ sawāha

21 واخر قولنا نذكر نبينا
محمّد مع جميع المرسلينَ
صلاة اللّه عليهم اجمعينَ
شريعة محمّد ما نتبع سواها

4
Poems to Entertain

BEDOUIN HUMOUR

The need to adhere to convention as a requisite of survival in the desert has made the bedouin a highly conventional people. A man's virtue is measured by his observance of convention; and, far from viewing convention as something imposed upon them, the bedouin regard it as natural. In their own terminology, for example, a rutting camel that bites its master is called an *ʿāyib*, or one that has done something unnatural; the name derives from the same root as *ʿayb*—a breach of convention.

This reverence for convention even finds its way into bedouin humour and into poems composed to amuse. Bedouin laugh at breaches of convention, as we see in three poems of the present section. One poem (4.7) is about bedouin who marry Egyptian peasant girls (sing. *fallāḥa*), an act considered shameful by Sinai tribesmen. They regard a *fallāḥa* as stingy, immodest in dress and behaviour, and domineering—things that contravene bedouin values. A bedouin who marries a peasant girl, therefore, becomes an object of derision, as one who puts his carnal desires above convention. Greed that obscures conventional obligations is lampooned in two other poems. One (poem 4.8) is directed against those who, during Israel's occupation of Sinai, sent their wives unchaperoned to Egypt to purchase goods for domestic use or for sale. The poem implies that, while it is normal to have women tend to the livestock, freeing the men to deal with problems of honour and station, they are not to take over the masculine functions, such as marketing or smuggling, merely for the 'undignified' pursuit of gain. The second lampoon (poem 4.9) is directed against a goat-raiser who, because of his inordinate greed, lives alone with his flock far from his tribe's encampments, where he cannot receive guests, where he must perform the women's chores himself, and where he lapses into eccentric and indecorous behaviour.

However, there is one convention that bedouin allow themselves to violate in poetry, at least vicariously: the inhibitions concerning intimate contact between men and women. The inviolability of women is a strict rule of bedouin life in the desert, since women must often be left alone at pasture or at home while the men are away attending to their own duties or to the family's interests. It is therefore a serious transgression for unrelated men to approach, touch, or even gaze deliberately at a mature girl or woman. In this matter, however, the laws of nature are bound to clash with convention, and it is not surprising to find even conventional bedouin seeking relief from these oppressive sexual mores in the delightful medium of humorous and even 'bawdy' verse far removed from the ordinary experiences of real life.

This is illustrated in three poems of the present section. One (poem 4.10) is the description of its author's beloved in which he dwells on parts of the female body, opening for his listeners an imaginary peep-hole forbidden in daily reality. In another poem (4.11), a bedouin guest is seduced by his host's wife during the night, with all the excitement of such an illicit escapade. In the third poem (4.12), an old man recalls a romantic tryst with a shepherdess when he was young.

These anti-conventional poems, while humorous, also exhibit qualities which are necessary for survival in the desert. One such quality, daring, is the theme of poems in which bedouin, again vicariously, defy authority and power. It is a bedouin principle to show outward deference to governmental and tribal authority when necessary, so as not to invite trouble; as one deferential proverb has it, 'He who marries my mother, I'll duly call him "Dad"' (*illī a<u>kh</u>a<u>dh</u> immī, ʿammī*). This prudent attitude has been all the more necessary ever since roads and motor transportation put the bedouin within easy reach of powerful governments they could no longer challenge. Accustomed as bedouin are to independence, which they have always considered vital to their security, they are averse to the encroachment of government into their lives; and, to offset feelings of impotency, they seek release through humour that detracts from its power.

The usual devices are to depict situations in which a bedouin does as he pleases despite governmental prohibitions, or to compose insolent poems which, in elevated language, poke fun at governmental or tribal authority. In one poem, for example, composed during the rule of the puritanical Wahhābī sect in western Saudi Arabia (in the 1920s) (poem 4.13), a young man describes how he ignored the interdictions of government and fell in love with a girl. Another poem (4.14), recited in the presence of senior officers of the Israeli army, subtly ridicules the hypocrisy governing relations between the Negev bedouin and the Israeli state. A third poem (4.15), a mock panegyric to the first king of modern Saudi Arabia, ʿAbd al-ʿAzīz Ibn Saʿūd, satirically depicts many of his religious excesses and cruelties as praiseworthy. These humorous poems enable the authors as well as their audience to retain a modicum of self-respect in the face of the pervasive presence of authority.

The importance bedouin attach to self-respect is evident even in panegyric poems, which, although composed to honour someone, are also a form of entertainment. A bedouin (when he is not specifically asking a favour) is reluctant to show deference without alluding to his own power, either subtly or assertively. In the first poem in this chapter, for example, composed to express deference to President Anwar al-Sādāt of Egypt, and recited at a rally held after Sādāt's historic visit to Jerusalem in 1977, the poet concludes by saying:

Now, Sinai's mountains may, by any soldiery, be taken,
But honour is well-founded there, its pegs remain unshaken.

In another poem (4.2), composed by an indigent but once prominent bedouin to thank a benefactor who had supplied him with flour, the poet injects praise for himself to show that, despite his present condition, he had once been—and still is—a person of quality. He even embellished the poem with an inspired flight of fantasy to remind his listeners of his once renowned skill in poetry. A third panegyric (poem 4.3) describes the fine qualities of a stud-camel that a friend had purchased in order to congratulate him on his precious acquisition. Even in this congratulatory poem to a friend, however, the poet cannot rest unless he too could demonstrate some superiority—which he does with a derisive gibe at one of the favourite butts of bedouin satire: the Egyptian peasant, whom bedouin view as ungainly and uncultured.

Perhaps the most human side of the bedouin as reflected in their poetry is their ability to laugh at themselves—often , indeed, for being excessively 'bedouin' One bedouin quality that is ridiculed, for example, is inordinate pride, which frequently leads a bedouin to reject any intimation of blame for an error or a failure, which he prefers to attribute to someone else. Thus, one poem (4.4) tells of a bedouin in northern Sinai who fell from his camel and broke his leg, and then blames the leg for the pain he is suffering. The leg replies, however, reminding him that it is his own faulty riding that caused him to fall. Another bedouin composed a poem (4.5) in which he challenges his chief to a trial to establish his rights—all because of his rooster, which the chief's wives had stolen. Two other bedouin qualities—the frequent inability to accept reality and the excessive dependence on outside intervention to extricate one from predicaments—led a Sinai bedouin smuggler in an Egyptian prison to compose a poem (4.6), in which he refuses to accept the reality of his confinement and implores his chief to set him free. A veteran inmate counsels him to relax and learn to adapt to the routine of prison life.

The subject of convention also appears in a special type of poem—the poem of repartee—in which someone commits a breach of convention and another puts him in his place. In one seventeenth-century poem (4.16) a bedouin leader attempts to violate the honour of his friend's female ward, and is challenged by the protector's slave; in another poem (4.17) a notable bedouin scolds a slave for daring to slander his hospitality. A third repartee (poem 4.18) is between an insolent ward who praises his benefactor's enemy and someone who rebukes him; while a fourth poem (4.19) contains a bedouin's reply to a public insult by his brother.

As popular as these repartee poems are among bedouin, their authenticity may be questioned. Poems are often improvised on the spot, but the four presented here are far too intricate in rhyme-scheme and content to have been the product of on-the-spot composition. Three explanations are possible. If there is an element of truth to the stories and the poems, we may have reason to believe that the first half of a poem may have been recited in the circumstances described, but that the reply was added later, as is clearly the case in the poem about the insolent slave who slandered a 'pure' bedouin. Another explanation is that the first part of each repartee was indeed recited, and that someone entirely unrelated to the event composed the reply in order to create a tale-in-verse to amuse some listeners. A third possibility is that the entire repartee in verse was fabricated, even if it was based on a real-life conflict between the two parties actually cited. Whatever the case, the genre of stories comprising prose narrative interspersed with poetic passages attributed to the various personalities involved was popular in the deserts of the Middle East. One such part-prose part-poetry episode (4.20), the unconventional romance between a powerful bedouin chief of Iraq and a wealthy female merchant, is presented here in a verbatim translation as heard from several reciters.

4.1

In Praise of Anwar al-Sādāt's Visit to Jerusalem

A Poem of Deference

After Egypt's president, Anwar al-Sādāt, returned from his historic first visit to Jerusalem in 1977, rallies and receptions were organized throughout Egypt to show popular support for his peace initiative. The official responsible for the bedouin in Egypt's Socialist Union Party, Mr Salīm Maḥmūd Abū Yamānī, organized one such reception for his constituents, in ʿAyn Shams, and asked ʿAnēz abū Sālim al-ʿUrḍī of the Tarābīn, who owned a small plantation in that area, to compose a poem in honour of the president.

The poem that ʿAnēz recited at the rally commends the Sādāt initiative (lines 1–3), describes the confrontation in Israel's Knesset between Sādāt and Israel's Prime Minister, Menahem Begin (lines 4–5) refutes the current allegation that Sādāt betrayed the Arab cause in order to recover Sinai without a war (lines 6–7), points out the evils of war (lines 8–9), and extols the President. The end of the poem is devoted to praise for the two Arab leaders who were expected to support the Egyptian initiative: King Ḥusēn of Jordan and King Khālid of Saudi Arabia; finally a proud word for the bedouin of Sinai who were the poet's immediate audience.

The Fiṭr feast[1] returned, how sweet this holiday,
How fine when feast and happiness combine the self-same day; 1

Holiday, well-being and love all came at this one time,
A time precisely chosen by He Whose will's sublime. 2

The will for peace which made Sādāt embark on such a mission
Brought those who ruled along with him to take up his position. 3

In Jerusalem, two doughty men clashed in harsh dispute,
Each rode his horse as hard he could in hope to gain repute. 4

Poem 4.1 was heard recited by its author, at Nuwēba' at-Tarābīn, 5 April 1983; and by Rāḍī Swēlim ʿAtayyiġ of the Muzēna Darārma tribe, at Nagb Shāhīn, 5 October 1980.

[1] The 'breaking the fast' holiday that follows the Muslim month-long fast of Ramaḍān.

Each speech they gave was followed by a din of ululation;[2]
Those who hold the reins received the people's adulation. 5

If someone were a traitor, he would act in ways unknown,
And betray the Arabs' land and borders while he gained his own. 6

But virtue in a good man's face is there for all to see;
And where is virtue when a man has land he will not free? 7

Wars are more than pious words or the playing out of games,
Or the singing of a necklaced lass recalling warriors' names:[3] 8

Families lose their homes in war, and many men are slain;
The losers number many more than those that maybe gain. 9

Anwar is choice, a leader, a healer and saint,
And for his pains we owe him our thanks without restraint. 10

Ḥusēn, too, is a heavyweight, three hundred pounds or more;
But then I may be short, for he has more such weight in store. 11

He himself will take up arms the day the battle's rough,
And force his doughty foes to yield, even though they're tough. 12

And Khālid's there to give support to those whose need is dire,
Behaving in a goodly way in keeping with his sires. 13

Now Sinai's mountains may, by any soldiery, be taken,
But honour is well-founded there, its pegs remain unshaken. 14

I ask God's mercy if my praise was heavy or too light,
Or if I lied or falsified what was some worthy's right. 15

1 yigūl al-ʿīd ʿād ū-gult ma-ḥala-l-ʿīd
wēš ḥāl limma-yṣīr ʿīd ū-saʿāda

1 يقول العيد عاد وقلت يا ما حلا العيد
وايش حال لمّا يصير عيد وسعادة

[2] Ululations (*zaghārīt*) by women express acclaim and are calculated to expel the evil eye on festive occasions.

[3] On festive occasions women and girls sit in rows facing each other and sing improvised songs which may include events of tribal history (see, for example, poem 5.4).

2 ʿīd ū-salāma ū-ḥubb jin fī mawaʿīd
fī wagit ḥākim fī gāẓi-l-irāda

عيد وسلامة وحبّ جن في مواعيد 2
في وقت حاكم فيد قاضي الارادة

3 willa-rġam as-sadāt ʿa-zyārit al-ʿīd
amr yitiḥattam ʿal aṣḥāb is-syāda

واللي ارغم السادات ع زيارة العيد 3
هو امر يتحتّم عل اصحاب السيادة

4 fi-l-guds ṣār aṣdām bēn aṣ-ṣanadīd
willī hawā al-ḥamd yirkab jawāda

في القدس صار صدام بين الصناديد 4
واللي هواه الحمد يركب جواده

5 az-zaġarīṭ itlijj ʿugb al-anašīd
wal-faẓl lillī maskīn al-giyāda

الزغاريط تلجّ عقب الاناشيد 5
والفضل للّي ماسكين القيادة

6 ū-fiʿil al-muxazzaʿ yifʿala ġēr at-talbīd
ū-iymayyil aḥdād al-ʿarab fī iḥdāda

وفعل المخزّع يفعله غير التلبيد 6
ويميّل احداد العرب في احداده

7 wil-xēr fī wij hal-fita lah šawahīd
wilā xēr fi-llī mā yiḥarrir bilāda

والخير في وجد الفتى له شواهيد 7
ولا خير في اللي ما يحرّر بلاده

8 wil-ḥarb mā hū bass kalām ū-tamaṯīl
wila uġniyya marxiyyāt al-gilāda

والحرب ما هو بسّ كلام وتماثيل 8
ولا اغنيّة مرخيّات القلادة

9 wa-l-ḥarb sūga ḏabḥ ʿālam ū-tišrīd
wi-sūg al-xasāra dāyman fi-z-zyāda

والحرب سوقد ذبح عالم وتشريد 9
وسوق الخسارة دايمًا في الزيادة

10 anwar xiyār ū-gāyid ū-ṣāliḥ ū-sīd
ū-yājib ʿalēna nušukra ʿal ijtihāda

انور خيار وقايد وصالح وسيد 10
ويجب علينا نشكره عل اجتهاده

11 wiḥsēn wazna wagam gunṭār wiyzīd
la xass min wazna wala wazn kāda

وحسين وزنه وقم قنطار ويزيد 11
لا خسّ من وزنه ولا وزن كاده

12 yōrid ibi-nafsa yōm tagsa-l-mawarīd
wal-ġānma yuʿrud ʿalēha aʿrāda

يورد بنفسه يوم تقسى المواريد 12
والغانمة يعرد عليها اعراده

13 ū-xālid sanad lillī ma la sawanīd
wil-fiʿil ḥaggin wāriṯa ʿin ijdāda

وخالد سند للّي ما له سوانيد 13
والفعل حقٍّ وارثه عن اجداده

14 wa-haẓāb sīna faẓilha ʿal-maṭalīb
wal-ʿizz fīha mā tizalzal ōṯāda

وهضاب سينا فضلها عالمطاليب 14
والعزّ فيها ما تزلزل اوثاده

15 wadxal ʿaḷḷā ʿan it-tnaggiṣ wit-tazwīd
wi-ʿan ḥagg wāḥdin nuzrufa fi-š-šihāda

15 وادخل عاللّـه عن التنقّص والتزويد
وعن حقّ واحدٍ نزرفه في الشهادة

4.2

In Praise of ʿĪd Aḥamad aṭ-Ṭulēlī

A Poem of Thanks

Rabīaʿ az-Zmēlī (app. 1886–1946) of the ʿAlēgāt Zmēliyyīn tribe was an outstanding personality among the bedouin of southern Sinai during the first half of the twentieth century, as a noted hunter, smuggler, and poet. In his old age, however, he was destitute and dependent on others. Among those who helped him was a prominent chief, ʿĪd Aḥamad Naṣīr aṭ-Ṭulēlī of the Ṣawālḥa Garārsha tribe in Wādī Fīrān, a centre of bedouin life in the south. When the chief had a load of flour brought in from Egypt, he would often put aside a few sackfuls for Rabīaʿ az-Zmēlī.

On one occasion, when a large number of men had gathered in Wādī Fīrān, Rabīaʿ recited the present poem, which he had composed to thank ʿĪd for his generosity. However, not content to play the supplicant with a plain panegyric, as appears in the first five lines, the aged Rabīaʿ decided to divert his audience with some lines of humour (9–13) that demonstrated his skill in prosody, reminding them that he was still a personality to reckon with.

ʿĪd told them: 'Fill the sacks with grain!'—his custom every year:
I praise you, Abū Aḥamad, the son of old Naṣīr. 1

When God bestows his blessings, may he give you ever more;
I hope the Lord is large with you with bounty from his store. 2

Your clan are all nobility, a sharpened, steely sword,
Behaving like true nobles, giving shelter to a ward. 3

Poem 4.2 was heard recited by ʿAwda Ijmēaʿ al-Ajrab of the Muzēna Darārma tribe, at Fīrān oasis, 4 September 1972.

How good to find these worthy men so faithful to their ilk;
They treat one met with dignity, as flawless as silk. 4

If I should speak of deprivation, grant me pardon, ʿĪd;
Though I'm the elder in this group, it's you who give the lead. 5

But once, for hunting and for war my gun was always loaded;
A marksman, how I loved the sound each time the shot exploded. 6

Now, on any giver's hand for nurture I rely,
And, like a beggar, cast about imploring with my eyes. 7

Just thinking of my fallen state has put forth hoary hair;
Yes, I've this greyish turban donned from begging here and there. 8

From dawn until the sun hangs down, sinking from the sky,
I run about and, on your life, if I had wings I'd fly; 9

But fearful lest I'd disappear from flying much too slow,
And others then would laugh and ask: Where'd the old man go? 10

Other poets might then come with poems of lower class,
Accustoming our bedouin to go watering on an ass. 11

But if I then came back, by God, I'd charge them with a crime,
And sentence them to prison for a long and weary time; 12

I'd rouse up all the shepherds, and the wolves I'd shout away
And balance out the saddlebags, so each the same would weigh.[1] 13

1 gāl ʿīd al-imʿawwad wi-ya ʿīd
wi-ʿīd ya-bū aḥamad yā bin naṣīrī

1 قال عيد المعوّد ويا عيد
وعيد يا ابو احمد يا بن نصيرِ

2 waḷḷa yibārik kamān fīk wi-yizīd
ya rēt xērak ʿend rabbak kaṯīrī

2 واللّـه يبارك كمان فيك ويزيد
يا ريت خيرك عند ربّك كثيرِ

3 ū-rabaʿak irjāl al-ʿiz miṯil il-bawalīd
wi-kull minhum zē ad-darrā wal-aṣīlī

3 وربعك رجال العزّ مثل البواليد
وكلّ منهم زي الذرّا والاصيلِ

[1] 'Balance out the saddlebags' means 'to do justice' (see poem 1.3, n. 5).

4 ya ma-ḥala win jīt ʿend al-ajawīd
win jīthum baṭ-ṭīb zē al-ḥarīrī

4 يا ما حلا وان جيت عند الاجاويد
وان جيتهم بالطيب زي الحرير

5 wana daxīlak ʿan hurūj at-tanakīd
wana kabīr al-yōm winti kabīrī

5 وانا دخيلك عن هروج التناكيد
وانا كبير اليوم وانت كبيري

6 wana zimān bawārdi-r-rakb waṣ-ṣayd
ya ma-ḥala win sār ʿendi ṯawīrī

6 وانا زمان بواردي الركب والصيد
يا ما حلا وان صار عنده ثوير

7 wal-yōm barʿa-r-rizig fīd ar-razazīg
warʿī bi-ʿaynī waštahī zē al-gaṣīrī

7 واليوم بارعي الرزق في ايد الرزازيق
وارعي بعيني واشتهي زي القصير

8 ū-min fikir hāḏa wi-ḏīk ʿammēt biš-šēb
wi-ʿammam ʿalayy aš-šēb kuṯr il-xaṭīrī

8 ومن فكر هذا وذيك عمّيت بالشيب
وعمّم عليّ الشيب كثر الخطير

9 ū-min as-ṣubḥ limma tidang aš-šams wi-tġīb
ḥayātkū lin lī jināḥ kunt aṭīrī

9 ومن الصبح لمّا تدنّق الشمس وتغيب
حياتكم لن لي جناح كنت اطير

10 xāyif aṭīr fi-l-jaww babṭī wana-mġīb
xāyif yigūlū wēn lagga-l-kabīrī

10 خايف اطير في الجوّ بابطئ وانا مغيب
خايف يقولو وين لقّى الكبير

11 wi-tjīhum aš-šuʿʿār ʿugbiyy ū-tiʿīb
wi-yawrdū nuṣṣ al-ʿarab bal-ḥamīrī

11 وتجيهم الشعّار عقبي وتعيب
ويورّدو نصّ العرب بالحمير

12 win jīthum l-aʿmal ʿalēhum taratīb
wišzin ʿalehum šizin li-wagtin ṭawīlī

12 وان جيتهم لاعمل عليهم تراتيب
واسجن عليهم سجن لوقتٍ طويل

13 waḥawḥaṭ ʿal ir-riʿyān wazʿag ʿal aḏ-ḏīb
wasawwī lil-ḥaml al-mugallaṣ ʿadīlī

13 واحوحط عل الرعيان وازعق عل الذيب
واسوّي للحمل المقلّص عديل

4.3
In Praise of a Newly Bought Camel
A Poem to Hearten a Friend

In the mid-1960s K͟hlēf Imgēbil al-Hir<u>sh</u>, of the Bayyāḍiyyīn Hurŭ<u>sh</u> tribe of north-west Sinai, bought a thoroughbred male camel. To celebrate the purchase and praise the 'wise transaction', his friend, Ṣabāḥ Ṣāliḥ al-<u>Gh</u>ānim of the neighbouring 'Agēlī tribe, composed a poem which he recited before a gathering of tribesmen. Although the poem was meant for an assembled audience, it begins with the conventional theme of sending the poem as a message on a camel, which is duly described. Ṣabāḥ then praises K͟hlēf's new stud, as well as the new owner as a true bedouin who appreciates the value of a thoroughbred. To emphasize K͟hlēf's virtues the poet concludes with a description of the despised Egyptian peasant, who would not know the difference between a thoroughbred and a mixed-blood camel.

O Rider on one of whose stock none need query:
  No stud of mixed blood had his mother to carry.[1]   1

Bring a saddle that suits him and set it on tight,
  Press its wood on the cushions firmly with might;   2

Then around the four cross-beams and the front pommels bind
  A belt that you will, round the pommel-pins, wind;[2]   3

And the leg-rest, with thongs, is a beauty to see,
  Embellished with tiny tin stars.   4

And four dangling tassels—bought but hand-made:
  When he runs, birds rest there, so straight are they laid.   5

When he races, and riding-mares run alongside,
  He's an officer ordering his soldiers with pride;   6

Poem 4.3 was heard recited by its author, at Rab'a oasis, 24 October 1970.

[1] i.e. his mother was never mated with a non-thoroughbred.

[2] The frame of a camel-saddle comprises a front-pommel (*migdim*) and a back-pommel (*mīk͟hir*), each of two pieces that are joined by a wooden pin (*k͟hābūr*). The pommels are connected by cross-beams (*'awāṭī*).

Or a Mauser with bullets still bright from their case,
The peal from its barrel rocking the place. 7

But the best mount is Khlēf's, his praises are meet,
And soon he'll be sought to seed mares who're in heat; 8

Then the offspring that's born of his loins and his zeal
Will raise dust when they run, like an automobile. 9

If you find a fine male, the earning consider,
And keep your stud fit for a generous bidder. 10

There are those who themselves are of mongrel extraction
Who think riding mixed-bloods no shame or detraction; 11

Wearing head-rope and robe, bedouin dress they enjoy,
But they strut, legs apart,[3] like a circumcised boy.[4] 12

1 ya rākb-illī ma-nsaʿal kīf ʿaddi
amma-l-iġzayyil ma waṭṭanha xawawīr

2 hāt al-ġabīṭ illī-mwāfig ū-šiddi
ū-ruṣṣ al-xašab ʿa gṣayrāt al-mawaṯīr

3 warbaʿ ʿawāṭī wal-magadīm ḥaddi
wa-liff il-ʿaṣab ʿa gṣayrāt al-xawabīr

4 wi-dwēraʿa mēzūn ya zēn šaddi
wal-wājba raṣṣū ʿalē ha-d-dababīr

5 warbaʿ safāyif maštara wi-dōs yaddi
lamma šarad turgud ʿalēha-l-ʿaṣafīr

1 يا راكب اللي مـا انسأل كيف عدّد
امّـد الغزيّـل مـا وطّنها خواوير

2 هات الغبيط اللـي موافق وشدّد
ورضّ الخشب ع قصيرات المواثيـر

3 واربع عواطي والمقاديم حدّد
ولفّ العصب ع قصيرات الخوابيـر

4 ودويرعد ميزون يـا زيـن شدّد
والواجبة رضّـو عليد الدبابير

5 واربع سفايف مشترى ودوس يدّد
لمّـا شرد ترقـد عليها العصافير

[3] An ungainly gait is one of the derisory characteristics that bedouin notice in the Egyptian peasant.

[4] Muslim boys may be circumcised until they are thirteen years old (the age that biblical Ishmael, their reputed ancestor, was circumcised); hence, their ability to walk soon after the operation.

6 ū-linni šarad wil-hijin tišrad ib-ḥaddi
zābiṭ biyilgī ʿa junūdi awamīr

ولنّــد شرد والـهجن تشرد بحدّه 6
ضابط بيلقــي ع جنــوده اوامير

7 zē alamānī izrūfi kasir ʿiddi
tismaʿ ẓabīḥa min ixšūm al-mawaṣīr

زي المــاني زروفــد كسر عــدّة 7
تسمع ضبيحه من خشوم المواصير

8 wal-ġawj ʿend ixlēf wal-gōl gaddi
yitiwāṣifūna li-ligāḥ al-mayasīr

والغوح عند خليف والقول قدّه 8
يتواصفونــد للقـــاح الميــاسير

9 wōlādi allī tinātijin min makaddi
yōm yirkabūhin miṯil ʿajj al-ḥanatīr

واولاده اللي تناتجن مــن مكــدّه 9
يوم يركبوهن مثل عجّ الحناتير

10 wint-in lagēt az-zēn lil-girš ʿiddi
wi-ḥugg ad-ẓarāyib ya-ūlād al-mišayīr

وانت ان لاقيت الزين للقرش عدّه 10
وحقّ الظرايب يــا اولاد المشايير

11 fī an-nās aṣli kīš wil-kīš jiddi
mā yistiḥī šī min irkūb al-xawawīr

في الناس اصله كيش والكيش جدّه 11
مــا يستحي شي من ركــوب الخواوير

12 lābis mirīri ū-binš zēna ū-ʿaddi
ū-mašī tafāhij miṯil maši-l-maṭahīr

لابس مريرة وبنش زينة وعدّه 12
ومشيه تفاهج مثل مشي المطاهير

4.4

An Argument with a Broken Leg

A Poem to Ridicule Swiftness to Anger

When Ṣabāḥ Ṣāliḥ al-Ghānim of the ʿAgēlī tribe was thrown by his camel and broke his leg, he was moved by anger and pain to express himself in verse. However, when he realized that he was composing a poem about the 'treachery' of his own broken leg, he suddenly became aware of his folly. The poem he thereupon composed satirizes a bedouin's characteristic quickness to anger and his readiness to blame others for his misfortunes—both qualities born of bedouin pride.

Poem 4.4 was heard recited by its author, at Rabʿa oasis, 24 October 1970.

In mock seriousness the poet tells his leg that he will bring it to trial in a civil court—and regales his listeners with the details of a civil trial, which bedouin would normally find intimidating and incomprehensible. The leg now replies, bringing the poet back to earth with a threat to try him in the real courts of justice—the black bedouin tents—reminding him that he cannot get along without his leg, and rebuking him for causing the accident by careless riding. Ṣabāḥ then comes to his senses and in mock earnestness promises henceforth to look after his leg's welfare. He concludes by using the *khatm*, the conventional remembrance of the Prophet, as a plea for reconciliation.

THE POET

O God, by your decree, life is narrow or it's wide;
And if you grant us latitude no wrong must we abide.[1] 1

O Leg, whose aching makes the spittle in my mouth go dry,
And makes my hearty appetite the taste of food deny, 2

I'll summon you, and file complaint, and then interrogate,
And have you standing trial before a real magistrate. 3

And then I shall accuse you, and throw you in the dock;
Confront you with a barrister who'll put your words to mock. 4

And if, by chance, the judges should decide to set you free,
I'll cauterize your sore spots with embers from a tree.[2] 5

THE LEG

It's rather I who will try you in three black bedouin tents;[3]
Look here, I've brought my guarantor; now where is your defence?[4] 6

[1] Open spaces (and their pasture for the livestock) are vital to bedouin existence; hence, the term for God-given good fortune is 'spaciousness' (*wusa'*), whereas ill fortune is described as 'confinement' (*ḍīg*) (cf. poem 1.12, l. 1).

[2] Bedouin often resort to cauterization (*kayy*) as a cure. One method is to place a tiny ember on the affected spot. A species of Ephedra is the large bush referred to in the Arabic text.

[3] In serious cases the bedouin judicial system provides for appeal (*istināḍ*). When the parties to a conflict decide to adjudicate, they choose three judges. One party chooses the judge he will appeal to in case he rejects the initial judgment; and the other party does likewise. The remaining judge will be the court of first instance. The three judges are called *makhāṭīṭ* (sing. *makhṭūṭ*: lit. 'those

Remember this: that it is I that takes you here and there,
And brings you to some water when the heat gets hard to bear. 7

It's the devil who's the source of ill: Iblīs, who's used to trick:[5]
He had you, mounted bare-back, give the camel's hump a kick. 8

And further, even God himself can't hold a camel back,
If, pulling at the nose-ring,[6] you should let the reins go slack. 9

Devilish deeds like these, and men who wish to see you err,[7]
Consider not the evil in them something to forswear. 10

THE POET

I'll tread no more upon you, without your being shod,
Or make you, over stones or thorns, by night go on and plod. 11

I'll show you I'm all right, O Leg, if with me you stay,
As out from Egypt on to Shām we wend our common way.[8] 12

From sunshine I will find you shade, and cover you from cold,
When from your foot up to your waist you feel the ache take hold. 13

With blessings for the Beautiful, this poem I now will cease:
Muḥammad, who would always preach that we should live
in peace.[9] 14

1 yaḷḷa yillī bamrak al-wusaʿ waẓ-ẓīg
wi-innak tawassiḥḥa ū-balāš aẓ-ẓulāmī

١ يا اللّــه يللي بأمرك الوسع والضيق
وانّــك توسّعها وبــلاش الظلامِ

for whom lines have been drawn'), because in naming them in turn a line (*khaṭṭ*) is drawn in the sand.

[4] Since there is no neutral law-enforcement agency in bedouin society to ensure that the parties to a dispute comply with the decision of the court, notable members of the society must guarantee their compliance. Such a guarantor is called a *kafīl* (pl. *kafalā*). For more on the *kafīl*, see al-ʿĀrif, *al-Qaḍāʾ*, pp. 86–94, and Jaussen, pp. 195–7.

[5] Iblīs is the personal name of the devil in Islam.

[6] Riders often direct a camel with a rope tied to a nose-ring (*khizām*).

[7] i.e. envious persons, who might cast the evil eye on someone and cause him harm (see Bailey, 'Religious Practices', pp. 78–9).

[8] Bedouin often refer to present-day Israel as *Shām*, an Arabic designation for historical Syria. This line, alluding to the poet's being a smuggler, was included for humorous effect.

[9] For this prayer to the Prophet, see poem. 1.11, n. 8.

2 ya rijil yillī wajadkī nāšif ar-rīg
wan-nafs ʿayyit l-adūg aṭ-ṭaʿāmī

2 يا رجل يللي وجدكي ناشف الريق
والنفس عيّت لاذوق الطعامِ

3 l-aktib ilkī maḥẓar ū-šakwa wi-taḥgīg
wawagfik guddām ḥākim niẓāmī

3 لاكتب لكي محضر وشكوى وتحقيق
واوقّفك قدّام حاكم نظامِ

4 ū-awajjih ilkī tuhma warmīk fa-ẓ-ẓīg
wawaggif ilkī guddām gōlik imḥāmī

4 واوجّد لكي تهمة وارميك في الضيق
واوقّف لكي قدّام قولك محامي

5 kān il-ḥukūma fī ġalaṭkī tibarrīk
l-adawgīk ʿas-sabit jamr al-ʿadāmī

5 كان الحكومة في غلطكي تبرّيك
لاذوّقك عالسبت جمر العدامِ

★ ★ ★

6 gālat hī hāda ṯalāṯ ibyūt widdī agaẓīk
warʿa il-kafīl ū-bass hāt al-lizāmī

6 قالت هي هذا ثلاث بيوت ودّي اقاضيك
وارعى الكفيل وبسّ هات اللزامِ

7 fākir ʿalak wannī bajībak wawaddīk
wawardak fī blād nuṣṣ al-maẓāmī

7 فاكر علك وانّي باجيبك واودّيك
واورّدك في بلاد نصّ المظامئ

8 kulli min aš-šēṭān wiblīs wazīk
tulkiz ibna ʿa ṣifāḥ jurd as-sināmī

8 كلّد من الشيطان وابليس وازيك
تلكز بنا ع صفاح جرد السنامِ

9 isma' waṣātin kān alla bil-hijn yiblīk
irxa-r-rasin wimsik gaṣīr al-xizāmī

9 اسمع وصاةٍ كان اللّد بالهجن يبليك
ارخى الرسن وامسك قصير الخزامِ

10 hāda sawāt iblīs willī taġabīk
ma-btiḥisbin aẓ-ẓulm fīhin ḥarāmī

10 هذا سواة ابليس واللي تغابيك
ما بتحسبن الظلم فيهن حرامِ

★ ★ ★

11 biyikfī innī adhak ʿalēk ġēr wi-nʿālkī fīk
wala baḥuṭṭik fī ʿakāš wa-ʿatāmī

11 بيكفي انّي ادهك عليك غير ونعالكي فيك
ولا باحطّك في عكاش وعتامِ

12 win ṭālat il-midda ya rijl awarrīk
ū-gaṭʿak ma bēn maṣrin ū-šāmī

12 وان طالت المدّة يا رجل اورّيك
وقطعك ما بين مصرٍ وشامِ

13 ʿan aš-šams aẓillik wal-burūda aġaṭṭīk
limma wajʿakī ṣār yōṣil ḥizāmī

13 عن الشمس اظلّك والبرودة اغطّيك
لمّا وجعكي صار يوصل حزامي

14 waxtim kalāmī bi-ṣalātī ʿal az-zēn
wi-mḥammad illī xaṭab lis-salāmī

14 واختم كـلامي بصلاتي عـــل الزين
ومحمّـد اللـي خطـب للسلام

4.5

Litigation over a Rooster

A Poem to Ridicule Contentiousness

In early 1967 a rooster raised by Ḥamdān abū Salāma Abū Masʿūd, of the Muzēna Darārma tribe of southern Sinai, disappeared. After three months Ḥamdān learned that the rooster had been taken by the wives of his chief, Mūsā Sfērān. However, when he broached the subject with Mūsā, the chief became indignant and accused the rooster of causing damage, for which he would ask compensation. The injustice of the situation at first incensed Ḥamdān until he realized that his characteristic bedouin zeal to defend the slightest infringement of a right made him exaggerate the importance of a rooster. His own comical behaviour led him to compose the present poem, in which he portrays himself seeking refuge from his chief with Ṣāliḥ Imbārak ʿĪd, chief of the Shaẓāẓna section of the Muzēna. He was even prepared to force the accused to the extremity of 'licking the red-hot iron'—the bedouin ordeal by fire used mainly in cases of murder and rape—to prove that his rooster had been stolen. Indeed he would not settle for the mediocre bedouin justice meted out in Egypt, but would take his case to Jordan and Saudi Arabia, the source and heartlands of bedouin life!

Those who are humble like you, Chief, are few,
And most chiefs collect from their flock more than you;[1] 1

But a rooster will hardly cause true men to fight,
Unless there's between them some long-standing spite. 2

Poem 4.5 was heard recited by its author, in Wādī aṭ-Ṭūr, 31 March 1971.

[1] Chiefs regularly exact payments from their tribesmen for expenses incurred and effort expended on behalf of the tribe.

When livers are bilious, words will not do;
If your people want evil, I'm tough as a Jew. 3

My rights I'll pursue from morning till night,
Uphill and down on a mount that has might; 4

To Ṣāliḥ I'll go, on whom many rely:
Abū-Imbārak, that well never dry.[2] 5

He's surrounded by followers ever on call,
And each obligation is met by them all. 6

A wolf is not someone it's easy to cheat,
Without licking the iron no case is complete.[3] 7

But no trial will I hold in this Pharaonic land:[4]
For my trials I'll go to Saʻūd or Amman.[5] 8

Our rooster which went missing three months ago:
Why, we sleep through our prayers if he doesn't crow![6] 9

And ninety old hens infertile remain,
From crowding the cock his bottom hangs low. 10

If owing to fast talk I lose my just case,
I'll appeal to the Generous who gives out of grace. 11

[2] For the image of a well for a munificent person, see poem 2.7, n. 7.

[3] In grave cases of rape, murder, and other crimes for which there are no witnesses, the bedouin could require that one or both of the parties undergo the ordeal called *bis̲h̲ʻa*, the licking of a red-hot iron implement, called, as in the Arabic text, 'licking the fire' (*laḥs an-nār*). Bedouin in Sinai and the Negev resorted to persons from two tribes for this ritual: the ʻAyāyda ʻAwāmra tribe of western Sinai and the Suez Canal Zone, and the Ḥuwēṭāt Dubūr tribe of southern Jordan and northern Arabia. For more on *bis̲h̲ʻa*, see al-ʻĀrif, *al-Qaḍā'*, pp. 95–101; for the ʻAyāyda, see Bailey and Shmueli, *passim*.

[4] Bedouin in Egypt, including Sinai, refer to themselves proudly as Arabs (Ar. *ʻarab*, i.e. stock originally stemming from the Arabian peninsula). In conversation among themselves they refer to the non-bedouin population of Egypt as Pharaonics (*farāʻīn*, sing. *farʻūnī*), i.e. people of Pharaoh. When speaking to sedentary Egyptians, they refer to them with the more respectful designation 'natives' (*al-ahālī*). For more, see Bailey and Shmueli, pp. 35–8.

[5] i.e. places that respect the bedouin and their culture. Bedouin often personalize the name of Saudi Arabia by calling it '[the land of] as-Saʻūd', i.e. the Saʻūd family.

[6] The first of the five mandatory daily Muslim prayers is the *fajr* or dawn prayer. The allusion to sleeping through prayers is a humorous touch, as neither the author nor many other men in his society at the time of this composition were fastidious about praying at the ordained hour.

1 yā šēx miṯlak mā-ylaggi-š-šaxatīr
wila ʿād miṯlak ʿan ir-raʿiyya yizūdī

1 يـا شيخ مثلك مـا يلقّـي الشخاتير
ولا عـاد مثلك عــن الرعيّــة يزودِ

2 wiṭ-ṭayr ma ʿumri yizaʿʿil rajajīl
ġēr kān ʿilli min gadīm ij-jdūdī

2 والطير مـا عمـرد يزعّـل رجاجيل
غير كـان علّــة من قديم الجدودِ

3 wil-harj ma yišfi kibād al-maʿalīl
ṣurba nāwī ʿal-buṭul wana yahūdī

3 والـهرج مـا يشفي كـباد المعـاليل
سربة نـاوي عالبطـل وانا يـهودي

4 nijrī maʿ-l-jarāy min aṣ-ṣubḥ lil-lēl
min fōg jiyyid ʿāt-taraj wis-snūdī

4 نجري مـع الجراي مـن الصبح للـليل
مــن فوق جيّـد عـالترج والـسنودِ

5 ū-yilfin ʿala ṣāliḥ zibūn al-masayīr
abū-mbārak miṯil jamm il-ʿudūdī

5 ويلفـن علــى صالح زبون المسايير
ابـو مبـارك مثـل جـمّ العدودِ

6 ʿendihū nišāma lil-lawāzim maḥaẓīr
wil-kull minhū lil-lawāzim sidūdī

6 عندهـم نشامـة للـلوازم محاضير
والكـلّ منهـم للـلوازم سدودِ

7 wad-dīb ma yimšin ʿalē hal-maḥayīl
min dūn laḥs an-nār tubṭul išhūdī

7 والذيب مـــا يمشن عليد المحاييل
مــن دون لحس النار تبطـل شهودِ

8 wilā aṭīḥ lahū sūg barr al-faraʿīn
amma ʿala ʿammān walla-s-siʿūdī

8 ولا اطيح لـهم سوق بـرّ الفـراعين
امّـــا علــى عمّـان ولّا الـسعودِ

9 wa-dīkna illī rāḥ giṭʿat mahalīl
lil-farẓ yiṣḥa wal-xalāyig urgūdī

9 وديكنـا اللـي راح قطعـة مهـاليل
للفـرض يصحـى والخـلايق رقـودِ

10 tisʿīn ʿutgiyya hiyẓallin imḥayīl
ṣiʿibin ʿal-aṯ-ṯullāb marxi-l-juʿūdī

10 تسعيـن عتقيّـة يظـلّـن محـاييل
صعبـن عـل الثـلّاب مرخـي الجعودِ

11 wiykūd ḥaggi-yrūḥ ʿugb al-bawaṭīr
ugṣud karīm illī-bi-xayra yijūdī

11 ويكـود حقّـي يـروح عقب البـواطير
اقصد كـريـم اللـي بخيـرد يجـودِ

4.6

A Conversation in Prison

A Poem to Ridicule the Rejection of Reality

Sa'd abū Sālim, of the 'Alēgāt Zmēliyyīn tribe of south-west Sinai, was imprisoned in Egypt on the charge of smuggling. He suffered greatly during his internment and appealed to his chief, among others, to use his influence to effect his release. However, he soon realized the folly of relying on others, as bedouin often do, and of not coming to terms with reality. This realization gave rise to the present poem, in which Sa'd relates how on entering prison he immediately sent his chief a plea requesting aid, only to be counselled by a fellow-inmate to relax and adapt himself to the dull routine of prison life. He died in prison in 1955.

SA'D ABŪ SĀLIM:

Now that I've greeted you magazine readers, allow me to vent my dismay. 1

O Life, who has sat me down square on hot ashes—why have you dashed me this way? 2

Curses upon you for flinging me down, for prison's the lowest disgrace; 3

With troop after troop out there guarding the gate, no one breaks out of this place. 4

Oh, just to stroll about freely and build me a house in the hills far away! 5

So, chief, if you'd help a dear friend who's in need, come see me with no more delay. 6

Muḥammad and Abū Miẓ'ān[1] and the gang are all here, and their wishes convey. 7

Poem 4.6 was heard recited by 'Aṭiyya Miẓ'ān 'Awwād of the 'Alēgāt Zmēliyyīn tribe, near Abū Rudēs, 11 November 1971.

---

[1] 'Aṭiyya Miẓ'ān 'Awwād, the reciter.

A FELLOW-INMATE:

Welcome and greetings to Abū Sālim, sit down and relax in the shade; 8

Here is a jug you can use for ablution, and here's where the prayers are said. 9

This is the spot where al-Sayyid would sleep; he served out his time and then went; 10

And I, who was here before you, must abide with more than a year not yet spent. 11

Jail's like a man's *jalabiyya*[2] got stuck, but no chief can unstick you a jot; 12

There's no other course but ask Allah above to come down and unravel the knot. 13

بعد السلام عليكم — يا قرّائين المجلّة 1
1 ba'd is-salām 'alēkum—ya garrayīn al-majalli

ولَيد يا دنيا ترميني — وتقعّديني ع ملّة 2
2 ū-lē ya dinya tirmīnī—witga''idīnī 'a malli

رمتني الدنيا الملعونة — وما عقب السجن مذلّة 3
3 ramatni-d-dinya-l-mal'ūna—ū-mā 'ugb is-sijn maḏalli

والحرس ع باب السجن — وشلّة من ورا شلّة 4
4 wal-ḥaras 'a bāb is-sijn—ū-šilli min wara šilli

هواي في الدنيا اتنزّه — وابني لي في الجبل فلّة 5
5 hawāy fi-d-dinya-tanazzah—wabnī lī fa-í-jabal filli

كان هواك في حبيبك — لا تطولد ولّا تقول لد 6
6 kan hawāk fī ḥabībak—lā-tṭūla walla tagūl la

يوم جيت لاقيت ابو مظعان — ومحمّد وباقي الشلّة 7
7 yōm jīt lagēt abū miẓ'ān—ū-muḥammad ū-bāgi-š-šilla

[2] A gown worn as the main garment in Egypt and by the bedouin of Sinai.

مرحبا بابو سالم – اقعد وتهنّى في الظلّة 8
8 marḥaba babū sālim—ug'ud ū-thanna fiẓ-ẓilli

وهذا ابريق الوضو – وهذا مكان المصلّة 9
9 ū-hād-ibrīg il-waẓū—ū-hāḏa makān al-imṣalli

هذا منام السيّد – اخذ حقّه من هذا وولّى 10
10 hāḏa manām as-sayyid—axaḏ ḥagga min hāḏa ū-walla

وانا قدّامك مستنظر – ولي سنة وقريطلّة 11
11 wana guddāmak mustanẓir—ū-layy sana wa-grayṭalli

واللي بينتشب ثوبه – لا شيخ ولّا جعيدي يحلّه 12
12 willī biyintišib ṯōbi—la šēx walla ji'aydī yiḥilli

ونطلب من اللّه اللي فوق – يبعث للعقدة محلّة 13
13 wi-nuṭlub min aḷḷā-llī fōg—yib'aṯ lil-'ugda maḥalli

4.7

On Marrying Peasant Girls

A Lampoon on a Breach of Convention

Bedouin coming into close contact with Arab peasant society often marry a peasant woman or *fallāḥa*. These men are usually wealthy chiefs and smugglers, but they might be the common run of bedouin who work among peasants. In the past there were chiefs who might marry in order to strengthen ties with neighbouring settled communities (e.g. Sulēmān Sālim al-'Aṭāwna in the Negev; cf. poem 5.6, n. 10), but most bedouin marry peasants for reasons of domestic material comfort (cf. poem 7.7, lines 14, 15). Peasant girls are desired for their superior cooking, for the trappings of sedentary life that they bring to a home, and for their softer (often plumper) bodies.

To introduce a peasant wife into bedouin society, however, is considered a breach of convention, for the bedouin would suspect her of being contemptuous of bedouin customs, such as hospitality,

Poem 4.7 was heard recited by its author, at St Catherine's Monastery, 5 November 1978.

modesty in dress, co-operation with the women regarding chores, and submissiveness to her husband. Thus, Ṭuʿēmī Mūsā ad-Dagūnī of the Jabāliyya Awlād-Jundī tribe of southern Sinai composed a lampoon on this digression from custom to remind his fellow tribesmen (whose traditional service to St Catherine's Monastery at Mt Sinai obliges many to spend long periods working for the same monastic order in Egypt proper) of the disgrace that attends marriage with a peasant woman.

Those who wed *fallāḥa*-girls are bound to break convention: 1

They keep their house-door locked with key—a measure of prevention;[1] 2

So if a guest arrive one day, they'll hardly hear him call, 3

Or maybe ask the guest, Who's there?—the meanest word of all.[2] 4

The *fallāḥa*'s like a lamb that's skinned,[3] her arms exposed to sight;[4] 5

She's bare to knee and elbow, like an apple shining bright. 6

Looking at her gets it up, he wants to lay her flat; 7

From so much ease and sitting still, her treasure's plump and fat. 8

She brings no wood nor waters, nor sees the flock be grazed, 9

Just laundering and housework; maybe cook, if she be praised.[5] 10

[1] Bedouin believe that *fallāḥīn* try to discourage guests by locking the door. A bedouin tent, by contrast, is always open to wayfarers and guests.

[2] According to bedouin convention, anyone who approaches a tent is to be welcomed and encouraged to stay. A host does not ask his guest to identify himself, for hospitality is to be given indiscriminately. Bedouin thus ridicule sedentary Arabs who customarily ask a visitor who he is ('*Mīn?*'), even before he enters their house.

[3] The skinning of a goat or sheep begins by removing the skin from the hind legs.

[4] Bedouin women must be covered from head to toe so as not to attract the attention of men, but *fellāḥa*-women, because much of their work is done along the canals and rivers, or in alluvial soil, are accustomed to roll up their sleeves and skirts, a habit regarded by the bedouin as immodest.

[5] Bedouin women are supposed to do their chores automatically, and this is taken for granted by a bedouin man. In any case, praise is not considered necessary to motivate them.

But if, alas, his cash runs out, his 'weapon' she'll ignore; 11
She'll snort and tear her clothes,[6] with her finger scold him sore; 12
And whip his sides with cane stick, if he utter one word more.[7] 13
And if you ask him: What's the meaning of this noisy war? 14
He'll tell you: It's that peasant girl, no better than a whore! 15

يترك كلّ القوانين ـ اللي يتجوّز فلّاحة 1
1 yutruk kull il-gawanīn—illi-ytijawwaz fallāḥa

ياخذ طبع الفلّاحين ـ الباب تملّي بمفتاحه 2
2 yāxiḏ ṭabaʿ al-fallaḥīn—il-bāb tamallī bi-miftāḥa

الضيف ان طقّ على بابك ـ بختك لو عرفت صراخه 3
3 aẓ-ẓēf in ṭagg ʿala bābak—baxtak la ʿaraft iṣrāxa

لن عرفته تقول لد مين ـ كلمة تلحقها القباحة 4
4 lin ʿarafti tigūl li mīn—kilmi tilḥagha-l-gabāḥa

تجيك مقشّطة الذرعان ـ خروف موجّه لسلاخة 5
5 tijīk imgašṭit aḏ-ḏurʿān—xarūf imwajjah li-slāxa

من حدّ الاركب والكيعان ـ تلمع زي قشر التفّاحة 6
6 min ḥadd al-arkab wal-kīʿān—talmaʿ zē gišr it-tuffāḥa

تفكّر فيهن بتهويك ـ وتشهيك للبطاحة 7
7 itfakkir fīhin bitahwīk—wi-tašhīk lal-baṭāḥa

راعية الخزنة النديانة ـ من كثر المقعد والراحة 8
8 rāʿiyt al-xazni-n-nidiyāna—min kiṯr il-magʿad war-rāḥa

لا حطب ولا وريد ـ ولا بتهمّم سراحة 9
9 la ḥaṭab walla wirīd—walla bithammim sarāḥa

[6] In Egypt women rend their clothes as a sign of grief (see Blackman, p. 124).

[7] A bedouin woman would not be allowed to scold her husband as the *fallāḥa* described in this line.

غير الغسيل والكشاني ـ واذا يشكرها طبّاخة
ġēr al-ġasīl wal-kašānī—wiḏa yiškurha ṭabbāxa

الميتة ان قلّت فلوسه ـ واللّه رمهن سلاحه
al-mīta in gallit iflūsa—walla ramhan islāḥa

تخرّفه باصبع حماسة ـ تدي له شخرة وشلاحة
itxarfa bi-uṣbaʿ ḥamāsa—tadī la šaxra wi-šlāḥa

وان زاد عليها بالكلام ـ بخيزران عل صفاحه
win zād ʿalēha bil-kalām—ib-xayzirān ʿal iṣfāḥa

وان قلت ايش الهيّة اللي قبيلان
win gult ēš il-hayya-lli-gbēlān

يقول شرموطة فلّاحة
iygūl šarmūṭa fallāḥa

4.8

Sending Women to Egypt for Shopping

A Lampoon on a Breach of Convention

Following Israel's conquest and occupation of Sinai in 1967, the bedouin of Sinai were cut off from Egypt proper and its markets. The following year, moreover, Israel took a census of the Sinai population, which limited the ability of the inhabitants to move in and out of Sinai. As a result, the bedouin became dependent on products originating in Israel, the West Bank, or the Gaza Strip, which were more expensive than Egyptian products and beyond the means of many.

With the end of the so-called War of Attrition between Egypt and Israel in September 1970, an arrangement was made under the auspices of the International Red Cross whereby bedouin, mainly women, could visit Egypt proper for humanitarian reasons. A motor launch was acquired to make weekly crossings between Suez and Rās aṣ-Ṣadr, a landing in Sinai, south of Suez. These launch-crossings became a

Poem 4.8 was heard recited by its author, at Dhahab oasis, 10 June 1973.

shopping junket for bedouin women, who were sent by their husbands to bring back basic commodities for domestic use or for sale. Israel relied on the tribal chiefs to recommend which women were to go for 'humanitarian visits'—for which recommendations the chiefs exacted a tax of three Egyptian pounds for each package the women brought back.

After one such crossing the poet ʻAṭiyya Miẓʻān ʻAwwād of the ʻAlēgāt Zmēliyyīn tribe tried to buy a set of underwear from some returning women at the landing, but was pushed aside by their eager husbands. The result was a poem lampooning the undignified husbands and chiefs who, for material goods and slight profit, were willing to disregard convention and send their women abroad unattended. To highlight the importance that was attached to these missions, he mockingly depicts the women as heroines.

Why not sing praises to our girls?
  I've filled the tape with tripe before! 1

We'd have died naked from the cold
  But for our women since the war! 2

They've shown that they've the pluck of men,
  Who, since the census, move no more, 3

For, since the road to Egypt closed,
  It's they came forward and enrolled. 4

The girls themselves would never cheat,
  Their honesty's impugned by none; 5

The chief's good word secures their pass,
  They guarantee them one by one. 6

The chiefs make gain from every trip,
  They tax each box on their return. 7

Whilst, at the pier, her old man waits,
  With sleeves rolled up and great concern: 8

He's waiting for a change of clothes,
And blankets fringed with hanging thread. 9

And as if her favours weren't enough,
He's quick to ride her into bed.[1] 10

ليش ما تغنّو في البنات ــ مليت المسجّل ثرد 1

1 lēš ma tiġannū fil-banāt
malēt al-imsajjil ṯard

لو لا هن من الحرب وجاي ــ عريتم وقتلكم البرد 2

2 law lā hin min al-ḥarb ū-jāy
ʿarētū ū-katalku-l-bard

وبانت مرجلة البنات ــ يوم صار الحصي والجرد 3

3 ū-bānit marjilt il-banāt
yōm ṣār al-ḥaṣī wa-l-jard

يوم لزّت الدرب وضاقت ــ ينسردن بالمشي سرد 4

4 yōm lazzat ad-darb ū-ẓāgit
yinsardan bil-mašī sard

عمرهن ما اكلن واحد ــ ريحتهن برّا زي الورد 5

5 ʿumrhin ma-kalan wāḥad
rīḥithin barra zē-l-ward

يمشن على حسّ المشايخ ــ على ممشاهن بالفرد 6

6 yimšin ʿala ḥass al-mašāyix
ʿala mimšāhin bil-fard

شافو ع جرّتهن خير ــ لهم مصالح عالطرد 7

7 šāfū ʿa jurrithin xēr
lihum maṣāliḥ ʿaṭ-ṭard

تلقى شيبتها في الموقف ــ متقشّط لها زي القرد 8

8 talga šēbitha fil-mawgif
mitgaššaṭ liha zē-l-gird

[1] Bedouin often refer to sexual intercourse as a man 'riding' a woman (cf. poem 6.13, l. 10).

جايبة لد طقم غيارات ـ وبطاطين من امّ هرد 9

9 jāyibi li ṭagm ġayarāt
ū-baṭaṭīn min umm hard

بعد جميلها دا كلّـد ـ لنفسد يمردها مرد 10

10 baʿd jimīlha dā kulla
li-nafsa yimradha mard

4.9

Living in the Wilds like an Animal

A Lampoon on a Breach of Convention

In the 1950s military restrictions forbade bedouin from dwelling and grazing in the highlands of the central Negev. Most of the ʿAzāzma tribe that normally grazed that area were concentrated on reserved lands just south of Beersheba. The chief of the ʿAzāzma, who had been appointed by Israel, aided the army in enforcing these restrictions, hoping that the gathering of his tribe near his residence would strengthen his authority. There were, however, sections of the ʿAzāzma—the Sarāḥīn and the ʿAṣiyyāt—who defied both his authority and the government, and infiltrated into their former grazing lands by hiding in some remote wadi. Raising goats for a livelihood was their main occupation. The need to hide, however, compelled them to leave their tents and their household belongings in the reserved area in the care of their womenfolk.

A friend of the chief and fellow member of the Masʿūdiyyīn section of the tribe, Sulēmān ʿAwwād Ibn ʿAdēsān, composed a poem mocking these herdsmen for the breaches of bedouin convention brought about by their abnormal existence. In this poem he attacks all by describing the indecorous and vile behaviour of a single individual who keeps away from bedouin society, is unprepared to receive guests, does not dress or ride a camel like a bedouin, and even neglects the essential precepts of Islam, such as washing after sexual intercourse. And the ostensible justification for all this shameful behaviour? To sell a few goats!

Poem 4.9 was heard recited by its author, in Wādī Shgēb, 18 February 1972.

Don't boast on the back of a mount of mixed breed,
He'll never run well though you add to his feed.[1] 1

Like a babbler who sits among men as their chief,
And cites different ways to bring trouble relief, 2

And even midst stalwarts, he goes on and rants;
But when faced with adversity shits in his pants. 3

He possesses no roasting pan, coffee to heat,
Nor a mortar, some travellers to call with its beat.[2] 4

No tent has he pitched in whose shade men could rest:
Men far from home, of their camels in quest. 5

Like an ibex, his pasture's untrod and remote,[3]
With only a daughter to water the goats. 6

He escorts the kids to be suckled all day,
He'll even knead cheese should the girl be away.[4] 7

As if it would pour, a rain-cap he wears,[5]
And none but the she-goats his company shares, 8

With the goats he will sleep where the high bushes grow,
Bushes that shield him from friend and from foe. 9

But his only true foe is the wolf out for prey,
And he'll spend the night waiting to shout him away. 10

[1] To a bedouin the riding capacity of a horse or camel derives from its breed, a pedigree animal being the best. From this the poet concludes that a person, such as the subject of this poem, cannot be improved through cultivation, as nature is too compelling (cf. poem 4.18. l. 8).

[2] Cf. poem 3.2, n. 3.

[3] Ibex (sing. *badan*) keep as far as possible from humans, fearing attack.

[4] Bedouin women knead and salt curds churched from goat's milk in making the cheese they call *'afiq*. The kneaded balls are then left to dry in the sun. Kneading cheese and attending to the suckling of goat-kids are conventionally female tasks.

[5] Among the first trappings of modern, non-bedouin civilization that bedouin adopt are items of Western dress, often worn out of their original context. Thus, a bedouin, when alone, might wear a Western-type waterproof cap, perhaps found discarded in the desert, as protection against the hot rays of the sun.

Riding an ass he may come by some night,
But he'll sleep and be off to the souk before light; 11

Then at dusk he will visit his wife in the brush,
And they'll join without washing, as he's in a rush.[6] 12

For his true joy's when traders come out to his place,
And he asks, 'What's the price?', with a serious face.[7] 13

1 awṣīk la tabjaḥ ʿala mitn xawwār
ma-yʿijbak linnak tazīd al-ʿalīgī

1 اوصيك لا تبجح على متن خوّار
مــا يعجّبك لنّــك تزيد العليق

2 zē-l-haytigān illī in gaʿad gult muxtār
wi-mṣalliḥin xaṭṭ ar-radī li ṭarīgī

2 زي الـهيتقان اللي ان قعد قلت مختار
ومصلّــحٍ خــطّ الردي لـــــه طريقٍ

3 allī in gaʿad bēn al-ajawīd faššār
win ṣābin imṣībāt laga-l-xarīgī

3 اللي ان قعد بين الاجاويد فشّار
وان صابن مصيبات لقى الخريقٍ

4 la li miḥmāṣin yiṣālī sina-n-nār
wila li nijrin yinādī margīn aṭ-ṭarīgī

4 لا لـــه محماصٍ يصالي سنا النار
ولا له نجــرٍ ينادي مــارقين الطريقٍ

5 wila li bētin ba haẓ-ẓill mindār
yitnaḥḥarana imṭalbāt al-wasīgī

5 ولا لــه بيتٍ بــه الظــلّ مندار
يتنحّرنــه مطــلّبات الــوسيقٍ

6 zē al-badan yirʿa ʿaḏiyyāt al-agfār
ū-ʿendi fatā imnaššila lin-naʿīgī

6 زي البدن يرعى عذيّــات الاقفار
وعنده فتــاة منشّلــة للنعيقٍ

7 gāṭiʿ zimāni bēn rāyim ū-naffār
win ġābit al-ʿaḏra yiʿajn il-ʿafīgī

7 قــطّــاع زمــانه بين رايم ونفّــار
وان غابت العذرى يعجّن العفيقٍ

8 gubaʿa ʿala rāsa ʿan ġarīzāt al-amṭār
mā li bala miʿzā ḥayy ū-ṣadīgī

8 قبعة على راسه عن غريزات الامطار
مــا لــه بلا معزاه حــيّ وصديقٍ

[6] After sexual intercourse Muslims are enjoined to perform the *ghusl*—the washing of the entire body, which has become impure through contact with sexual excretions (see *Encyclopaedia of Islam*, 'Djanāba', and Bailey, 'Religious Practices', p. 80).

[7] Lit. 'like a livestock breeder of profound understanding'.

9 yimriḥ ibhin fī ġarīzāt al-ašjār
mitigiyyāta ʿan al-baġīẓ ū-ṣadīgi

9 يمرح بهن في غريزات الاشجار
متقيّاته عن البغيض وصديقِ

10 ū-ma li ʿaduwin ġēr ḏībin ila dār
yimẓa ʿagāb al-lēl yizʿag zaʿīgī

10 وما له عدوٍ غير ذيبٍ الا دار
يمضى عقاب الليل يزعق زعيقِ

11 ū-ya suriʿ ma yumrug ʿalēk ḥammār
yimarriḥ ū-min bākir yijīb id-dagīgī

11 ويا سرع ما يمرق عليك حمّار
يمرّح ومن باكر يجيب الدقيقِ

12 wal-maġrib byitilāgū ʿala-d-dār
yitjāmaʿū ma-ytṭahharū bil-barīgī

12 والمغرب بيتلاقو على الدار
يتجامعو ما يتطهّرو بالابريقِ

13 ū-yifraḥ ila ṭalaʿū min as-sūg tujjār
yisʿal ʿan il-asʿār sāyis ġamīgī

13 ويفرح الا طلعو من السوق تجّار
يسأل عن الاسعار سايس غميقِ

4.10

The Description of a Beautiful Girl

A Poem of Cheek

As a young man in the 1930s or 1940s Ḥamdān abū Salāma Abū Masʿūd of the Muzēna Darārma tribe, fell in love with a shepherdess whom he saw at a well in southern Sinai. In the present poem, inspired by his infatuation, he applied his creative abilities to a motif often found in bedouin poetry—the description of a girl, using similes to emphasize her features. Since it is improper for bedouin men to take overt notice of women, to do so in a poem is considered bold and entertaining. At the end of the poem Ḥamdān challenges the girl's fiancé (ʿAṭiyya) to do battle, and rebukes her father (Salāma) for insisting that his daughter does not wish to marry our poet.

Poem 4.10 was heard recited by its author, in Wādī aṭ-Ṭūr, 31 March 1971.

For three full days I've not touched food,
Nor did my mount his own teeth scrape:[1] 1

At a clear well watering, there she was,
As luck had brought her—no escape. 2

I tried to bind my eager heart,
But, having seen his love, he reared, 3

And like a horse with stirrup urged,
His arms outstretched, at her careered. 4

Her ankles are of amber hue,
This maiden is not meet to mock; 5

I can't describe what's under clothes:
White!—like fresh milk from a pastured flock.[2] 6

Her waist is like a thin, rolled fag,
And drawing near you meet your fate. 7

The breasts that rest upon her chest:
A little bunch of ripened dates. 8

Her fingers—stamens of a date-palm,
When the shepherd's flute they play.[3] 9

Her long neck's like a silver jug;
Though bare of necklace, still she'd slay. 10

Around her mouth are stars tattooed,[4]
Like Venus bright some cloudless night; 11

[1] The camel is comically portrayed as fasting out of solidarity with its master; hence, its teeth were not scraping, as they do at night when he is chewing the cud.

[2] The milk of a freshly pastured animal is the whitest and most pure; hence the allusion to the shepherdess's covered skin.

[3] The *shabbāba*, a piece of metal pipe, between one and two feet long, into which holes are perforated to act as keys, and which is played like a flute by blowing into one end, holding it sideways.

[4] On tattooing women, cf. poem 1.1, n. 5.

Her eyes are like a summer pool,
Their beauty is the suitor's plight. 12

Her eyebrows are connected straight;
Blacker than a written word. 13

Her hair spread out in silk array,
Within my heart a fire stirred. 14

So if you meet ʿAṭiyya, say:
Gather men, prepare for war, 15

And bring your flintlocks on your shoulder,
Powder by your side in store. 16

At that clear well we'll sit and wait,
And when they come we'll deftly hit. 17

O People tell Salāma this:
Take your lies back, every bit! 18

Let Zēna wed her heart's desire:
I'll pay her price, although it's higher.[5] 19

1 ṯalāṯt ayyām wana ṣāyim
ga'ūdī ma ṣarak nāba

1 ثلاثة ايّـام وانا صايم
قعـودي مـا صـرك نابد

2 waradna al-ʿidd al-garāḥ
ṣadafta wal-baxat jāba

2 وردنا العـدّ القراح
صدفتـد والبخت جـابد

3 ū-gumt aʿaggil ʿa galbī
ʿayyānī yōm šāfit iḥbāba

3 وقمت اعقّل ع قلبي
عيّـاني يوم شافت احبابد

4 yijrī bīdēn il-fuwārig
ḥiṣānin hizzēt irkāba

4 يجري بايدين الفوارق
حصانٍ هزّيت ركـابد

[5] Normally, the bride-price (*siyāg̣*) paid by a groom to the father or brothers of the bride is higher if the families are not related (see Bailey, 'Weddings', pp. 110–11).

5 sīgāna zē al-kahramān ma ḥad biylāwim aṣḥāba	سيقانه زي الكهرمان ما احد بيلاوم اصحابه 5
6 ma jibna waṣfa mitġaṭṭa al-hagwa zē dirr al-ḥallābi	ما جبنا وصفه متغطّى الهقوة زي درّ الحلاّبة 6
7 ṣulbi zē laff al-isgāra wiygarrib lil-ʿumr isbāba	صلبه زي لفّ السقارة ويقرّب للعمر اسبابه 7
8 ū-yā-bū-n-nuhūd ʿaṣ-ṣadr gāʿūd yišdih min ṭarḥ ar-riṭāba	ويا ابو نهود عالصدر قاعود يشده من طرح الرطابة 8
9 aṣabiʿi zē aš-šamarīx yiẓrubū xrūṭ iš-šibbābi	اصابعه زي الشماريخ يضربو خروط الشبّابة 9
10 wi-rgēbti zē-brīg al-fuẓẓa wi-tuktul min ġēr iglādi	ورقيبته زي ابريق الفضّة وتقتل من غير قلادة 10
11 ʿala-l-xarṭūm maxaṭṭ injūm zuhra ū-ma fīha rihāba	على الخرطوم مخطّ نجوم زهرة وما فيها رهابة 11
12 ʿiyūnha zē ġadīr aṣ-ṣayf ū-yā ʿaḏḏāb al-xaṭṭāba	عيونها زي غدير الصيف ويا عذّاب الخطّابة 12
13 ya-bū ḥawājib magturnāt šuhra ʿa xaṭṭ al-iktāba	يا ابو حواجب مقترنات شهرة ع خطّ الكتابة 13
14 ū-ya-bū šuʿūr ḥarīr manšūr xalla fī galbī šaʿlābī	ويا ابو شعور حرير منشور خلاّ في قلبي شعلابة 14
15 man wājih ʿaṭiy-ygūl li biylimm ar-rjāl il ḥarābi	من واجد عطيّة يقول له بيلمّ الرجال لحرابة 15
16 yijīb al-banādig fitāyil kull wāḥad li kuḥl fī ġāba	يجيب البنادق فتايل كلّ واحد له كحل في غابة 16
17 ū-nugʿud ʿal al-ʿidd al-garāḥ min jāna nidrik ṣawwāba	ونقعد عل العدّ القراح من جانا ندرك صوّابه 17

18 ya 'ālam gūlū salāma
biylimm al-baẓ'a kaddābi

18 يــا عالـم قولـو سلامة
بيلمّ البضعــة كـذّابة

19 ū-ya'ṭī zēna ṭalabha
win jānī ba'ṭī iḥsāba

19 ويعطــي زيــنــة طلبـها
وان جاني باعطيد حسابه

4.11

A Nocturnal Tryst with the Host's Wife

A Poem of Insolence

A tale is told among the bedouin concerning one of their number from Egypt, who, journeying in the Nejd region of north-central Arabia, stopped for the night at the tent of a chief. Left to sleep alone in the men's sitting section of the tent after the others had retired, he was surprised by his host's wife Marādī, who crept into his compartment from the other side of the tent and demanded that he lie with her. Frightened by the prospect of being killed by her husband and kinsmen if this became known, he rejected her advances. Marādī thereupon threatened that, if he did not comply with her wish, she (like Potiphar's wife in the Bible) would divulge that he had made advances towards her, and would leave him to the mercy of her menfolk.

Marādī's intrigue did not cease, even after the hapless guest had lain with her. As dawn broke she said: 'Now you must tell them all that has transpired between us or I shall say that you violated me!' Accordingly, when he took his morning coffee with the hosts, he recited the following poem. After the first four lines, which faithfully relate the night's events, the offended husband drew his sword, only to hear in the fifth and final line that the whole affair had been a dream.

In addition to the danger that any bedouin would fear in such a situation, the poem entertains by its frank depiction of the love scene.

Poem 4.11 was heard recited by Sālim Swēlim al-Wajj of the Ẕullām Janābīb tribe, in Wādī Ramliyya, 15 December 1968; Muṣliḥ Mabrūk Imbārak of the Tiyāhā Ṣgērāt tribe, at Bīr al-Mālḥa, 4 April 1971; and Imsallam Sālim Abū Nīfa of the Tarābīn Ḥasāblah tribe, at Nuwēba' at-Tarābīn, 4 April 1983. Discrepancies between the different texts were resolved according to the judgement of Mūsā al-'Aṭāwna.

I'd a visit last night by a girl called Marādī,[1]
Of impeccable features and beautiful body. 1

Her braids hung loose like a saddle's long strap:
In length as long; and when wound, a sure trap. 2

I first, with my arms, drew her close in embrace;
Then I pressed her to enter the disallowed place. 3

From her firm, upturned breasts I tore open the shirt,
And watered her parched loins with seed in a spurt. 4

But when I woke up, and away languor edged,
Why, she was in Egypt, whilst I was in Nejd. 5

1 al-beriḥa bal-lēl jānī marādī
zēn al-ḥalāya ū-kāmlin bil-awṣāf

2 umm igrūn miṯil ḥabl iš-šdādī
baṭ-ṭūl wāfī ū-bal-gudr zāfin baṯar zāf

3 awwal ẓabbēthī ẓabb al-ayādī
ū-ṯānī ẓabbēthī ẓabb al-azrāf

4 xallēt gamīṣhī ʿal inhūdhī badādī
wasgēt zarʿin fi-l-ḥaša ʿugib ma hāf

5 ū-yōm innī waʿēt ū-ṭār ʿinni-r-rgādī
linnī bi-nijd ū-ṣāḥbī yamm al-aryāf

1 البارحة بالليل جاني مرادي
زين الحلايا وكامل بالاوصاف

2 امّ قرون مثل حبل الشداد
بالطول وافي وبالقدر زاف باثر زاف

3 اوّل ضبّيتها ضبّ الاياد
وثاني ضبّيتها ضبّ الازراف

4 خلّيت قميصها عل نهودها بداد
واسقيت زرع في الحشا عقب ما هاف

5 ويوم انّي وعيت وطار عنّي الرقاد
لنّي بنجد وصاحبي يمّ الارياف

[1] In the Arabic text the woman is randomly referred to in both the feminine and masculine gender (cf. poems 1.15, n. 2; 2.1; 2.6; 4.10).

4.12

Three Illicit Trysts

A Poem of Audacious Young Love

In the following poem ʿĪd Imfarrij Imsāʿid, of the Tarābīn Ḥasāblah tribe in south-eastern Sinai, already advanced in years, relates how he and his future wife had spent three illicit nights together before they were wed. The bold escapade described by the poet was entertaining to his younger listeners.

Do you remember, O Dallāl, that afternoon we met, 1
And descended to the wadi's head before the sun would set? 2
We found green bushes everywhere to gather all around, 3
And used up all our charcoal for three nights on the ground.[1] 4
We parted when we felt the dew, then met upon the stony plain; 5
Oh, how my legs refused to budge until we'd meet again. 6
I asked our Lord a small request and then it was attained: 7
A beauty having thick, split lips,[2] and a baby boy to heed. 8
'Leave off this herding goats,' I said. 'One kid is all we need.' 9

1 mintī xābra ya dallāl
al-ʿaṣr yōm talagēna

2 al-ʿaṣr ḥīn al-masiyya
ʿa rās al-wādī kittēna

1 ما انتي خابرة يا دلّال
العصر يوم تلاقينا

2 العصر حين المسيّة
ع راس الوادي كتّينا

Poem 4.12 was heard recited by its author, at Sēl ar-Ruwēg on the ʿIjma plateau; 12 March 1971.

[1] Bedouin make charcoal from acacia, tamarisk, and genista—usually, however, for sale to settled communities.

[2] i.e. a camel, referred to here by one of its peculiar features (cf. poem 3.8, n. 12).

3 fīha al-xaẓāẓir kiṯīra ū-min laṭāna ḥaššēna	3 فيها الخضاضر كثيرة ومن لطانا حشّينا
4 ṯalāṯt ayyām imbayyatīn wi-min il-habša wafēna	4 ثلاثة ايّام مبيّتين ومن الهبشة وفينا
5 šilna maʿ an-nidāwī ū-ʿal-ḥamād talagēna	5 شلنا مع النداوي وعالحماد تلاقينا
6 ʿayyit rijlī la timšī ya dābī limma-ltagēna	6 عيّت رجلي لا تمشي يا دابي لمّا التقينا
7 ṭālib mi-rabbī ṭilba wiṭ-ṭilba ṣārit bīdēna	7 طالب من ربّي طلبة والطلبة صأرت بايدينا
8 ṭālib furg al--baraṭīm wa-ʿiwayyil yimšī ʿalēna	8 طالب فرق البراطيم وعويّل يمشي علينا
9 fuẓẓī minkī ar-raʿiyya wi-zlēyiṭ wāḥad yaġnīna	9 فضّي منكي الرعيّة وزليّط واحد يغنينا

4.13

In Love in Wahhābī Arabia

A Poem of Natural Defiance

When King ʿAbd al-ʿAzīz Ibn Saʿūd took control of the Ḥijāz district of western Arabia in 1925, he introduced the rigid moral laws of his puritanical and fundamentalist Wahhābī creed. Never the less, a young bedouin found himself enamoured of a girl he had seen, and declared himself willing to accept the consequences and endure the punishment of the powerful regime.

Poem 4.13 was heard recited by Muṣliḥ Ibn ʿĀmr of the Tiyāhā Ṣgērāt tribe, in Wādī Munbaṭah, 15 November 1972.

O eye, by the way that you follow desire,
  To be an Ik̲h̲wānī[1] you hardly aspire. 1

By God, what a maiden I've just now beheld:
  Her cheeks, like a well, are with liveliness swelled; 2

With black *koḥil*-powder she darkened her eyes,
  Her lashes—the plumes of a crow when it flies; 3

And over her shoulder she let down her braid,
  Why, as long as both belly- and girth-straps arrayed! 4

O Girl, whose teeth are like new-fallen hail,
  This craving for you is surely my bale. 5

1 ya ʿayn ilkī ba-l-hawa lafti
mintī ʿala dīn al-ixwānī

2 yaḷḷā min ṣaḥbin̲ šufti
xaddi min az-zēn rawyānī

3 wal-kuḥl bal-ʿayn dāʿijti
wir-rimš ya rīš ġirbānī

4 wal-garn ʿal-mitn ḥād̲ifti
yilḥag maḥagīb wi-bṭānī

5 ya-bū t̲ināya barad hallī
ḥibbak ʿal al-mōt waddānī

1 يا عين لكي بالهوى لفتة
ما انتي على دين الاخوانٍ

2 يا اللّه من صاحبٍ شفته
خدّه من الزين رويانٍ

3 والكحل بالعين داعجته
والرمش يا ريش غربانٍ

4 والقرنٍ عالمتن حاذفته
يلحق محاقيب وبطانٍ

5 يا ابو ثنايا برد هلٍّ
حبّك عل الموت ودّاني

[1] i.e. a member of the 'brotherhood' (*ik̲h̲wān*) that adhered to the Wahhābī creed.

1. Two successful, young, bedouin smugglers (*c.* 1950). 'Anēz abū Sālim, the poet (right) and Sulēmān Ibn Jāzī, future paramount chief of the bedouin of central Sinai

2. ‘Anēz aḅū Sālim al-‘Urḍī of the Tarābīn Ḥasāblah tribe. The most prominent poet in Sinai

Mūsā Ḥasan al- ʻAṭāwna, chief of the Tiyāhā Nutūsh
›e, Negev

4. Muṣliḥ Sālim Ibn ʻĀmr, poet and chief of the Tiyāhā Ṣgērāt tribe, Sinai

5. Ṣabāḥ Ṣāliḥ al-Ghānim, poet of the ʻAgēlī tribe

6. Sulēmān ʻAwwād Ibn ʻAdēsān, poet of the ʻAzāzma Masʻūdiyyīn tribe

7. Ḥamdān abū Salāma Abū Masʻūd, poet of the Muzēna Darārma tribe

8. Ṭu'ēmī Mūsā ad-Dagūnī, poet of the Jabāliyya Awlād-Jundī tribe

9. Jum'a 'Īd al-Farārja, poet of the Tarābīn Ḥasāblah tribe

10. Lāfī Faraj Sulēmān, poet of the Rumēlāt Busūm tribe

11. 'Īd Imfarrij Imsā'id, poet of the Tarābīn Ḥasāblah tribe

12. 'Īd Ḥammād Mis'ad, reciter of the Ḥuwēṭāt 'Abayyāt tribe

13. 'Awda Sulēmān 'Aliyyān, reciter of the Aḥaywāt Ḥamādāt tribe

14. Ṣāliḥ Imbārak ʻĪd, reciter of the Muzēna Shaẓāẓna tribe (holding a *ghalyūn*-pipe)

15. Musliḥ Mabrūk Imbārak, reciter of the Tiyāha Ṣgērāt tribe

16. Khlēf Imgēbil al-Hirsh, reciter of the Bayyāḍiyyīn Hurūsh tribe

17. Rāḍī Swēlim 'Atayyig, reciter of the Muzēna Darārma tribe

18. Sulēmān Salīm Ibn Sarīa', chief of the Tarābīn Sarāy'a tribe

19. Swēlim Sulēmān Abū Biliyya, of the 'Azāzma Sarāḥīn tribe

20. Sulēmān 'Īd Ibn Jāzī, chief of the Tarābīn Ḥasāblạh tribe

4.14

Aspects of Bedouin Life in Israel

A Poem of Impudence

In 1971 senior officers in the Israeli army, including the General-Commander of the Southern Front, paid an official and ceremonial visit to the chief of the ʿAzāzma tribe, ʿAwda Abū Muʿammar, in recognition of his successful efforts to enlist bedouin into service for the army as trackers. For the occasion the chief asked a fellow tribesman, Sulēmān ʿAwwād Ibn ʿAdēsān, to compose a poem.

Sulēmān could have acquitted himself of the obligation by composing a simple panegyric poem, as is often done under similar, ceremonial circumstances. Knowing, however, that the Jewish and even the Druze soldiers would not understand the unfamiliar dialect and idiom of his poem, he decided to address himself primarily to the bedouin guests who were the majority and, in doing so, entertain them with some bold comments on the Israeli government and the tribal chiefs. The result was a parody on panegyric poems in general, satirizing the insincerity behind the good will that was said to underlie bedouin–Jewish relations and which this visit of senior officers to a bedouin tent was intended to demonstrate.

Accordingly, although the first subjects which Sulēmān chose—the Prime Minister, Golda Meir, and the Defence Minister, Moshe Dayan—give the impression of a straight panegyric, the choice was in fact ironical: that bedouin should be subjected to taking orders from a woman; and that Moshe Dayan (who had limited the bedouin grazing areas when he was Chief of Staff in the 1950s) could be expected to take an interest in bedouin rights. The poet then mentions two Arab leaders: King Ḥusēn of Jordan (whom he could afford to praise before Israeli officers, since the king had recently expelled the PLO from his kingdom), and President Anwar al-Sādāt of Egypt, whom he cautions not to imperil his life for Palestine, as ʿAbd al-Nāṣir had done, since the effort, he implies, will prove fruitless.

Sulēmān then turns to his chief and host, ʿAwda Abū Muʿammar. While ostensibly commending the chief for having established a bedouin-tracker unit for the army, he amused his bedouin audience by asserting that this achievement was based on the bedouins' respect for him—rather than on the pressures he exerted or on his offers of sundry rewards. This was an amusing gibe, however, that the chief could

Poem 4.14 was heard recited by its author, in Wādī Shgēb, 16 February 1972.

tolerate since, ironically, it affirmed his power within the tribe; the poet, moreover, was quick to add a purely panegyric stanza. He then turns his attention to the recruitment activity of another bedouin chief, Ḥammād Abū Rubēʿa of the Ẓullām Abū Rubēʿa tribe of the northern Negev, satirizing his efforts by using the term *jihād* (a Muslim holy war) for the act of sending bedouin soldiers to fight Muslim Egypt on behalf of Jewish Israel.

Sulēmān continues his satire by giving vent to the current bedouin grievance; namely, that the chiefs were exploiting the authority that the government had granted them over their tribes for their own personal interests. He then concludes the poem with a mock oath to Ibrāhīm—biblical Abraham who, as the father of Isaac and Ishmael, is said to be the common ancestor of both Jews and Arabs, and whose memory both parties hypocritically invoke whenever they wish to emphasize an underlying affinity. The ultimate irony, however, lies in what the poet swears to; namely, that Israel has dealt fairly in giving everyone his share, punning on the word 'share' (Ar. *ḥagg*) to imply praise for Israeli justice (as understood by his Jewish audience) but also undeserved oppression (as understood by his bedouin listeners).

I'll begin by remembering the Lord.[1]
Bring a pad, and some words we'll record;
Fine words in the past I've had written. 1

But fellows, please let me explain,
To lie is not something we deign;
And if from the truth we refrain,
Each lover of truth will be bitten. 2

Of Golda Meir we should say,
Midst medals and crowns in array,
If she sent all her troops to the fray,
With obedience we all would be smitten. 3

Now Moshe Dayan all revere,
To do battle he's always in gear,
And my rights he will always hold dear;
No one's been able to beat him. 4

[1] For 'remembering God' at the outset of a poem, see poem 3.5, n. 6.

King Ḥusēn always comes between foes
And brings all the nations repose;
For his fine inclinations we greet him. 5

To Anwar Sādāt we would say:
Why harp on what's past every day?
Recall when Jamāl passed away,
No one at all could retrieve him.[2] 6

For such is Palestine,
Where life in the past was just fine,
. . . .[3]
And we thanked and commended the Lord. 7

Now our chief has a troop to inspect;
They joined not from force but respect;
May the Lord, ʿAwda's luck, not neglect,
His command we have never ignored. 8

He has given us all that we own,
But we scoundrels are his, as we've shown;[4]
And the Fates,[5] may they leave him alone:
We ask God to ensure his reward. 9

Ḥammād Abū Rubēʿa, he too,
(I believe what I say to be true)
Made *jihād* on the side of the Jew,[6]
Sending men to the Suez Canal. 10

[2] Jamāl ʿAbd al-Nāṣir (in the West known as Nasser) ruled Egypt from 1953 until 1970., when he died from a heart attack following Jordan's defeat of the PLO in the 'Black September' hostilities. He was succeeded by Anwar al-Sādāt.

[3] When asked for this apparently missing line, the poet protested that it had never existed. There are two possible explanations: either he considered it prudent not to record the rhyme-word, which was probably 'devils' (Ar. *s̲h̲ayāṭīn*), referring to Israel (e.g. 'until the devils came'); or he deliberately omitted the line from his original composition: as the line would obviously have ended with 'devils', its omission might have been stronger and more humorous. '

[4] i.e. we joined the army, as trackers, for the chief's benefit.

[5] Fates (Ar. *manāyā*) here mean fated death (see poem 1.12, n. 1).

[6] The central point of the gibe ('on the side of the Jew') does not appear in the original text. Being understood by the bedouin audience, it required no statement.

But if I'm to tell the whole truth,
All of our chiefs are no use;
Their handing out permits a ruse
  Lest the army their goat-herds assail.[7] 11

But by Ibrāhīm[8] I would swear
That Israel's rule one can bear;
To the tall and the short it is fair:
  In the end, each gets his without fail. 12

1 awwal gōlna fī rabbī
hāt daftar win'abbī
  gōli̲n̲ zēni̲n̲ katabnā

1 اوّل قولنا في ربّيْ
هات دفتر ونعبّيد
قولٍ زينٍ كتبناه

2 ya jamā'a čēš ingūl
widdna nkaḏḏib miš ma'gūl
in ma ḥikēna bal-uṣūl
  kull ṣādig ġaššēnā

2 يا جماعة ايش نقول
ودّنا نكذّب مش معقول
ان ما حكينا بالاصول
كلّ صادق غشّيناه

3 widdna-ngūl fī gūlda me'īr
ib-tājāt ū-dababīr
lin gālat lil-jēš yisīr
  ṭayiḥḥa inti wānā

3 ودّنا نقول في قولدا مئير
بتاجات ودبابير
لن قالت للجيش يسير
طايعها انت وانا

4 mūsī dayān al-muta'aẓẓam
ila sūg al-jabha mitnaẓẓim
ma'ayy 'al-ḥagg mitiḥattim
  kullna ma ḥakamnā

4 موسي ديان المتعظّم
لسوق الجبهة متنظّم
معي عالحقّ متحتّم
كلّنا ما حكمناه

[7] Grazing lands for bedouin have nearly always been limited in Israel, for military and other reasons (see poem 7.8). Chiefs, however, were given special grazing privileges.

[8] The name Ibrāhīm appears in the Arabic text as al-Khalīl (lit. 'the friend'), another Arabic name for Abraham, whom 'God took as a friend', according to the Qur'ān (4. 125). Hence, Arabs also call Hebron, the city in which Abraham is buried, by the name al-Khalīl.

5 al-malak iḥsēn il-mitiwassiṭ
il kull dōla biybassiṭ
'a ḥisn ifkāra šakarnā

5 الملك حسين المتوسّط
لكلّ دولة بيبسّط
ع حسن افكاره شكرناه

6 gūlū li-anwar as-sadāt
lēš tiḥkī fi-llī fāt
'abd an-nāṣir yōmin māt
kullna ma raddēnā

6 قولو لانور السادات
ليش تحكي في اللي فات
عبد الناصر يومٍ مات
كلّنا ما ردّيناه

7 li-in hāḏī falasṭīn
'išna fīh'a mabsūṭīn
. . . .
ū-ḥamadna-ḷḷā ū-šakarnā

7 لئن هذي فلسطين
عشنا فيها مبسوطين
— — — — — —
وحمدنا اللّه وشكرناه

8 abū mu'ammar li katībi
baš-šaraf mā hī ġaṣībi
aḷḷa-ygawwī naṣībi
gōla kulla sama'nā

8 ابو معمّر له كتيبة
بالشرف ما هي غصيبة
اللّه يقوّي نصيبه
قوله كلّه سمعناه

9 mālna min bēn īdē
wal-hamal fadwin 'alē
wil-manāya ma tijī
ib-jāh rabbin naxēnā

9 مالنا من بين ايديه
والهمل فدوٍ عليه
والمنايا ما تجيه
بجاه ربٍّ نخيناه

10 amma-bū-rbē'a ḥammād
baftikir niṣfa wakād
lamm rab'a lil-jihād
fa-ṭ-ṭawābī 'al-ganā

10 امّا ابو ربيعة حمّاد
بافتكر نصفه وكاد
لمّ ربعه للجهاد
في الطوابي عالقناة

11 ū-iḏa ḥakēna-ṣ-ṣaḥīḥ
fi-l-mašāyix nāyim rīḥ
kull naṣba 'at-taṣrīḥ
l-il-mīm la yāxiḏ ma'zā

11 واذا حكينا الصحيح
في المشايخ نايم ريح
كلّ نصبه عالتصريح
للميم لا ياخذ معزاه

12 wi-ḥayāt abūna-l-xalīl
ikwayyis ḥukm isra'īl
al-gaṣayyir waṭ-ṭawīl
kull wāḥad ḥagga yignā

12 وحياة ابونا الخليل
كويّس حكم اسرائيل
القصيّـر والطـويل
كلّ واحد حقّه يقناه

4.15

ʿAnēz abū Sālim on King Ibn Saʿūd

A Poem to Satirize Panegyrics to the King

ʿAbd al-ʿAzīz Ibn Saʿūd, who conquered and united most of the Arabian peninsula in the 1920s and then put down some menacing rebellions against his authority, was often praised in panegyric poetical compositions. One such poem was the appeal for mercy which the Bilī tribe sent him in the early 1930s, after their rebellion against his authority had been suppressed (poem 2.10). When the king died in 1953, ʿAnēz abū Sālim, of the Tarābīn Ḥasāblah tribe, wishing to amuse some friends, adopted the second hemistich rhyme of the earlier Bilī poem in order to ridicule the usual panegyrics composed for the king. Thus, after nine lines of conventional treatment, referring to the fine camel that would 'bear the message', and praise for the recipients of the poem (the Saʿūd clan), the poet—perhaps led on by his need to find matching rhymes—breaks off into five unrelated and certainly undignified lines (10–14); and these he rounds off with two mock-heroic lines ridiculing the praise that other poets had heaped on Ibn Saʿūd for his religious fanaticism and his ruthless treatment of the bedouin (lines 15–16). ʿAnēz ends his poem with the hope that after Ibn Saʿūd's death, when the bedouin no longer need fear his troops, he be granted whatever he desires in paradise (line 17), and that those who succeed him be no worse than he (line 18).

O God who maintains agriculture with rain,
And dry lands with thunder and cloud doth sustain: 1

Poem 4.15 was heard recited by its author, at Nuwēbaʿ at-Tarābīn, 20 April 1984.

All through the night my confusion was deep,
My eye hardly tasted that sweetness of sleep; 2

I tossed and I turned as though on a flame,
Hard times smash our bones, leaving us lame. 3

When dinner was over I saddled a mount,
A Sharārī and white, beyond pedigree count.[1] 4

Four others, as well—firstlings with speed—
A male and three mares, marked by excellent breed; 5

Faster than those who flutter and fly:
Iraqi geese led through the sky;[2] 6

On hearing their hoofbeats: drums one would think;
When they turn they're like grouse sweeping down for a drink. 7

They'll visit where coffee-pots tire the fire:[3]
The Saʿūdīs who spurn all but purebreds. 8

Respectful and generous, the weak they defend,
Achieving their goals down to the end. 9

So pure are their deeds, whisky bars they eschew,
(For no one would enter a bar but a Jew).[4] 10

My wish is to visit their bountiful land,
And find me a thoroughbred, youthful and grand; 11

From India to Sind I've gone round and around,
But the likes of my own mount I still haven't found. 12

Yet in travelling so much, I stepped on a nail:
Blood poured from my foot and caused me to ail. 13

[1] For Sharārī camels, see poem 2.6, n. 5; for the determination of pedigree, see poem 2.9, n. 3.

[2] According to the author of this poem, what the Sinai bedouin call 'Iraqi geese' fly over Sinai on their supposed way to Ethiopia

[3] A compliment to the Saʿūdī's hospitality (their coffee pots are ever by the fire in anticipation of guests) and station (they are ever being visited).

[4] This is mock praise for the puritanical Saʿūdīs, who strictly enforced the Muslim injunction against alcoholic drinks. The author of this poem, himself, was not abstemious.

So they fetched me the nine finest doctors in town;
With knives they proceeded to flay my skin down. 14

How ʿAbd al-ʿAzīz, when in power, was brave;
How many men's corpses he cast in the grave! 15

He forced bedouin chieftains to drink cups of bile,
And shirkers at prayer to kneel down in file. 16

How I wish him two castles in Wādī Azhār,
And two thousand Houries—his troops being far.[5] 17

May God grant his children the thoughts they will need,
And may he who takes over be no worse in deed. 18

1 aḷḷā ya mihnī garāya bal-amṭār
ya mirzig al-ʿafra bi-mizn ar-ruʿūdī

1 اللّه يا مهني قرايا بالامطار
يا مرزق العفرا بمزن الرعودِ

2 al-beriḥa fi-l-lēl bitt miḥtār
wil-ʿayn ma ḏāgit laḏīḏ ar-rugūdī

2 البارحة في الليل بتّ محتار
والعين ما ذاقت لذيذ الرقودِ

3 agalb ʿal al-janbēn kannī ʿal an-nār
yōm az-zamān aš-šēn gaṣam ʿuẓūdī

3 اقلّب عل الجنبين كنّي عل النار
يوم الزمان الشين قصم عضودي

4 ʿugb al-ʿaša šaddēt min fōg bēṭār
ašgar šarārī ḥurr ʿagb il-judūdī

4 عقب العشا شدّيت من فوق بيطار
اشقر شراري حرّ عقب الجدودِ

5 šaddan maʿayī arbaʿa wiṣift imhār
ṣufī ṯalāṯ abkār ū-minhin gaʿūdī

5 شدّن معي اربعة وصفة امهار
صفي ثلاث بكار ومنهن قعودي

6 asbag min illi-ysafsaf bi-jināḥa ū-ṭār
wazz al-ʿarāg ū-lahū dalīla tigūdī

6 اسبق من اللي سفسف بجناحه وطار
وزّ العراق ولهم دليلة تقودِ

7 tismaʿ waḥiyyithin tigūl dagdagit aṭ-ṭār
yilfin kama yilfi-l-gaṭa ʿal-ʿudūdī

7 تسمع وحيّتهن تقول دقدقة الطار
يلفن كما يلفي القطا عالعدودِ

[5] Palaces in paradise (here, 'the Flowered Wadi' (Wādī al-Azhār)) are promised to the devout Muslim. Each palace will have 4,900 rooms, each room provided with a dark-eyed *ḥūrī* (pop. houri) (see poem 3.7 n. 2) for the pleasure of the occupant. (See Klein, pp. 93–4, n. 2).

8 ū-yilfin ʿallī dlālhum tajhad an-nār
rikkābt al-ʿayrāt wild as-saʿūdī

8 ويلفن عاللي دلالهم تجهد النار
ركّابة العيرات ولد السعودِ

9 hayl ad-dyāna waz-zakā wi-ʿiẓzit il-jār
nābī zaharhum ʿa jimīaʿ al-bunūdī

9 هيل الديانة والزكاة وعزّة الجار
نابي زهرهم ع جميع البنودِ

10 ma ʿumrhum gālū daxalna ʿala-l-bār
ū-la yudxul al-barāt ġēr al-yahūdī

10 ما عمرهم قالو دخلنا على البار
ولا يدخل البارات غير اليهودي

11 ibġī ašugg iblād har-rabaʿ zawwār
ʿašan anaggī min an-nẓa lī gaʿūdī

11 ابغي اشقّ بلاد هالربع زوّار
عشان انقّي من النضا لي قعودِ

12 laffēt kull al-hind was-sind dawwār
ma šuft wāḥid jāb̩ waṣfit gaʿūdī

12 لفّيت كلّ الهند والسند دوّار
ما شفت واحد جاب وصفة قعودي

13 min kiṯr laffī dagg bir-rijl mismār
xalla dimūmī yiskibin ʿa znūdī

13 ومن كثر لفّي دقّ بالرجل مسمار
خلّى دمومي يسكبن ع زنودي

14 jawnī dakātrit al-balad tisʿa akbār
ū-ba-hal-mawāsa šarraḥū bī-jlūdī

14 جوني دكاترة البلد تسعة كبار
وبهالمواسة شرّحو بجلودي

15 abū-s-saʿūd illī ʿal al-ḥukm jabbār
rama dagašīm il-lḥa lil-liḥūdī

15 ابو السعود اللي عل الحكم جبّار
رمى دقاشيم اللحى للحودِ

16 wasga-l-mašāyix kasāt al-imrār
ʿallam gilīlīn aṣ-ṣalā lis-sijūdī

16 واسقى الشيخان كاسات الامرار
علّم قليلين الصلاة للسجودِ

17 ya rayt li gaṣrēn fī wād al-azhār
walfēn ḥūriyya ibdāl al-jinūdī

17 يا ريت له قصرين في وادي الازهار
والفين حوريّة بدال الجنودِ

18 aḷḷa yisāʿid kull wilda ʿal-afkār
willī tiwalla-l-ḥukm minhum sdūdī

18 اللّه يساعد كلّ ولده عالافكار
واللي تولّى الحكم منهم سدودِ

4.16

A Hard Conversation between a Libertine and the Slave of a Trustworthy Man

A Poem of Repartee

In the seventeenth-century large sections of two tribes from western Arabia—the Masāʿīd and the Banī ʿUgba—migrated up the ʿAraba rift that separates the Negev from southern Transjordan, and encamped near the spring called ʿAyn Ḥuṣub (present-day ʿĪr ʿOvot). According to the oral tradition, the Negev tribes, then led by the Wuḥēdāt, were concerned lest this formidable force invade the Negev and conquer new pasture lands. (Similar invasions by Arabian tribes into neighbouring Transjordan had been taking place over the past century.)[1] The oral tradition relates that, to avert this possibility, al-Wuḥaydī, the paramount chief of the Negev tribes, resorted to a ruse.

Al-Wuḥaydī had been informed that the leaders of the Masāʿīd and Banī ʿUgba tribes—Saʿūd Ibn Masʿūd and Da'ūd, respectively—were totally different in character; Saʿūd was a vile libertine, while Da'ūd was sober and trustworthy. With the aim of setting the two leaders against each other, al-Wuḥaydī sent a beautiful girl in the company of her brother, both from the Imṭēr tribe, to take refuge with Da'ūd, expecting that Saʿūd, on seeing her beauty, would attempt to violate her honour. When this attempt was indeed made, Saʿūd was challenged by Da'ūd, whereupon their respective tribes fought each other to a finish, so that they no longer posed a threat to the tribes of the Negev.

When relating this oral tradition, the bedouin include the following poetic passage, which contains the conversation that precipitated the mutual destruction. This conversation took place between Saʿūd and Da'ūd's slave, as they were reclining under the well-known 'tree of Ḥuṣub' playing the floor-game, *sīja*;[2] Da'ūd's beautiful ward came to water her camel at the adjacent spring and, letting her veil slip, was observed by Saʿūd.

Poem 4.16 was heard recited by Sālim Muḥammad Sālim al-ʿUgbī of the Tiyāhā Banī ʿUgba tribe, in Wādī Ḥūra, 12 February 1972. Other renditions of the poem may be found in Shuqayr, pp. 117–18, and al-ʿĀrif, *Ta'rīkh*, pp. 118–19. Discrepancies between the texts were resolved according to the judgement of Mūsā al-ʿAṭāwna.

[1] See Peake, pp. 216–19; also Blunt, pp. 371 ff., for Iraq and Syria.

SAʿŪD

Ibn Masʿūd has seen an exceptional sight:
  A doe; and Oh, how his heart has been split. 1

DA'ŪD'S SLAVE

But Prince, she's not ours, but a lass of Imṭēr,[3]
  And a ward of Da'ūd, who'll cause her no shame; 2

O Prince, she's not ours, but a lass of Imṭēr,
  We can't bring her to you, she's under our care. 3

SAʿŪD

We'll take her with mounted young men bearing spears,
  And a blow her protector and neighbour will feel. 4

DA'ŪD'S SLAVE

Before taking her, Prince, many spears will be thrown,
  And many fine riderless mares left alone; 5

Before taking her, Prince, many spears will be thrown,
  And many breasts pierced with blades sharply honed; 6

Before taking her, Prince, many spears will be thrown,
  And lovers will weep for those whom they loved; 7

To Ḥisma, Naʿima, Shigrā and ʿAjāt we'd go,[4]
  To shield her from scum, so she'd not be brought low. 8

[2] *Sīja* is a bedouin game played in the sand. A 'board' is sketched out on the ground, on which each side puts his 'men'—those of one side being stones, those of the other camel droppings. The goal is to remove the men of one's adversary by trapping them on both sides with men of one's own.

[3] Imṭēr (properly, Muṭēr) is a pure, respected tribe in north-central Arabia (see Dickson, *Arab*, pp. 563–7). According to the oral tradition, the girl in question was not of the Imṭēr as such, but of an appended outcast tribe (a 'Hitēm' tribe). In the seventeenth century there were members of such a Hitēm tribe called Banī ʿAṭā living in the Gaza area and aligned to the dominant Wuḥaydāt tribe (see Heyd, pp. 67, 78, 85, where the Wuḥaydāt are called Banī ʿAṭiyya). In the twentieth century the Banī ʿAṭā are known mainly by the name Dawāghra, and live near the Barduwīl Lagoon in northern Sinai; both are aware that their 'parent tribe' is the Arabian Imṭer. Hence, the reference in the poem to a woman of Imṭēr.

[4] The places referred to are located in the Banī ʿUgba tribal area of north-west Arabia (see Musil, *Northern Hegaz*, *passim*; Philby, *passim*).

SAʿŪD

Who chides me will die from my sharp poisoned spear,[5]
Or snake-bite, in flight through the sand-dunes out there. 9

If two sons has he, may the better be slain,
The other unable a stick to regain;[6] 10

If two daughters has he, may the better abscond,[7]
And the other her guardian rape on the ground![8] 11

SAʿŪD

1 ibn masʿūd šāf naẓra
ġazālin ū-ma bēn al-ḥināya šigī-bha

سعود :

1 ابن مسعود شاف نظرة
غزالٍ وما بين الحنايا شقي بها

AL-ʿABD

2 imṭēriytin ya amīr mā hī lina min gabīla
ṭanība li-da'ūd illī ma yiʿībha

3 imṭēriytin ya amīr mā hī lina min gabīla
wilā hī min ḥimāna lak injībha

العبد :

2 مطيريّةٍ يا امير ما هي لنا من قبيلة
طنيبة لداود اللي ما يعيبها

3 مطيريّةٍ يا امير ما هي لنا من قبيلة
ولا هي من حمانا لك نجيبها

SAʿŪD

4 nijībha bas-sird wal-murd wal-gana
ū-ẓarbin yiʿaddī jārha maʿ ṭanībha

سعود :

4 نجيبها بالسرد والمرد والقنا
وضربٍ يعدّي جارها مع طنيبها

AL-ʿABD

5 ya ma dūnha ya amīr min ṭaʿan sābig
wi-kam ʿawdtin fi-l-mīdān ma yinsaḥī-bha

العبد :

5 يا ما دونها يا امير من طعن سابق
وكم عودةٍ في الميدان ما ينسحي بها

[5] According to present-day bedouin, their ancestors would dip arrowheads and spearheads into poison while tempering them, in order to render them lethal (cf. poem 5.3, l. 6).

[6] i.e stricken with paralysis and thus useless for the protection that a son should provide.

[7] A marriage in which a woman absconds with a man for romantic reasons is called 'a marriage of destruction' (*jīzit ʿadam*), implying the destruction of her family's honour and reputation (cf. poem 1.1, n. 8). Although the verb 'be destroyed' (*yaʿdam*) is repeated at the end of the first hemistiches of ll. 10 and 11, its meaning differs in regard to a man and a woman.

[8] Being a ward, in itself, is a demeaning acknowledgment of dependence; to be violated by a protector is a manifestation of abject helplessness.

6 ya ma dūnha ya amīr min ṭaʿan sābig
wi-ḥarba tigidd al-jōf ḥāmī lihību̲ha

6 يا ما دونها يا امير من طعن سابق
وحربة تقدّ الجوف حامي لهيبها

7 ya ma dūnha ya amīr min ṭaʿan sābig
wi-ʿaynin̲ tiruẓẓ al-bukā ʿala ḥabībha

7 يا ما دونها يا امير من طعن سابق
وعينٍ ترضّ البكـــا على حبيبها

8 narʿa biha ḥisma ū-s̲h̲igrā ū-naʿima ū-ʿajāt
ū-nint̲inī winʿaddīha ʿan kull wabšin̲ yirīdha

8 نرعى بها حسمة وشقرا ونعمة وعجات
وننثني ونعدّيها عن كلّ وبشٍ يريدها

سعود :

SAʿŪD

9 min lāmnī yabla bi-ḥarba imsammama
walla bi-ḥayya nāymi fī kat̲ībha

9 مـن لامنـي يبلـى بحربة مسمّمة
ولاّ بحيّـة نـايمـة فـي كـثيبها

10 win kān li waladēn yaʿdam ixyārhum
wit̲-t̲ānī tugruṭ la hal-ʿaṣa ma yijību̲ha

10 وان كان له ولدين يعدم خيازهم
والثاني تقرط له هالعصا ما يجيبها

11 win kān li bintēn yaʿdam ixyārhin
wit̲-t̲ānya yilga ʿalēha ṭanību̲ha

11 وان كان له بنتين يعدم خيارهن
والثانية يلقى عليها طنيبها

4.17

An Exchange of Insults over Hospitality

A Poem of Repartee

A chief of the Ḥuwēṭāt named Suḥaymān was once invited to a feast given by another chief in Wādī Giṭān in north-west Arabia, a grand feast in which ninety *manāsif*—platters laden with meat and rice—were served to the guests.

Shortly thereafter one of the host's slaves who had been at the feast was travelling in the district where Suḥaymān was chief, and sought shelter for the night in his *dīwān* or one-room guest-house. When he reached the *dīwān*, however, he found it locked, so that he was obliged to find shelter at the guest-room of the nearby Saʿūdī police post. On

Poem 4.17 was heard recited by Muṣliḥ Ibn ʿĀmr of the Tiyāha Ṣgērāt tribe, in Wādī Munbaṭaḥ, 15 November 1972.

resuming his journey the next day, the slave composed four lines of verse in which he upbraided Suḥaymān for having locked his guest-house, accused him of parsimony, and compared him unfavourably to his own generous master.

When the poem finally reached the ears of Suḥaymān he was indignant at being insulted by a slave. Borrowing the same rhyme scheme, the chief immediately composed a retort in which he not only defended his reputation for generosity but brought the full force of his invective to humiliate the slave.

THE SLAVE

'Tis shameful, this breach of convention, Suḥaymān;
A disgrace and dishonour to lock your *dīwān*.[1] 1

Must Ikhwānī police feed the guests that you send?
Quite a few on their bounty already depend. 2

Our own tents appease the pangs of the hungry,
Of those who from want and from poverty flee; 3

In Giṭān ninety platters were teeming with meat,
While your guests cost nothing; they'd nothing to eat. 4

SUḤAYMĀN

O artful at slander and wounder of pride,
Why should you, of all people, my bounty deride? 5

The expense we incur is a price very dear,
A price such as people of less pride would fear. 6

I've witnesses come from the north of Amman,
And from far Jabal Shār[2]—ask in any *dīwān*. 7

This posing as though you're important is shame;
There's nothing you've done that could earn you a name. 8

[1] 'To lock your guest-room [*dīwān*]' in the original text is 'to prevent access to the coffee-pot'. On the importance of a host's accessibility to travellers and guests, cf. poem 3.8, n. 4.

[2] Jabal Shār is in north-west Arabia, twenty-five kilometres north of the coastal village of Ḍabā.

What's secret or hid is of no value deemed,
  Even virtue, unseen, often goes unesteemed.[3] 9

Don't roll up your sleeves without first taking care,
  Lest one sees that you're less than your cover when bare. 10

Yesterday morning I heard of your guile:
  Contemptible slander that's stirred up my bile; 11

My heart started quivering quite like a bell,
  Or scales delicately balanced. 12

Had you lied to my face I would not have been tried;
  I would just have stopped roasting, the beans put aside, 13

And fanned not the fire till worthies came by,
  Though the shadows of dusk had turned dark in the sky.[4] 14

Did you think you could hamstring me, ass-like clown?
  One had better climb heights ere one dares to look down.[5] 15

AL-ʿABD

1 al-ʿayb wal-ʿayb ya sḥaymān
  al-ʿayb itsakkir ʿala-d-dalli

2 ẓayfak tasikka ʿal al-ixwān
  rabbēt lak ʿendihum šilli

العبد :

1 العيب والعيب' يا سحيمان
العيب تسكّر على الدلّة

2 ضيفك تسكّد عل الاخوان
ربّيت لك عندهم شلّة

[3] i.e. things that are secret do not help one. A reputation for commendable acts of bravery, hospitality, generosity, and altruism is important for a bedouin's status and security, and neither he nor those whom he has benefited refrain from dwelling on them in public. A host will take trouble to publicize his generosity to his guest (see poem 1.5, n. 5; cf. poem 3.5, n. 4). By contrast, gifts that a guest may give to his host are given discreetly, so as not to detract from the host's own generosity, it being his duty to give rather than to receive.

[4] A host is obliged to provide a wayfarer with food and drink as a matter of basic hospitality. To show his contempt for the insolent slave, the poet declares that, had he come to him and insulted him to his face, he would have ignored him as a human being by refusing to prepare coffee or light a fire for him, fundamental acts to which anyone is entitled among bedouin.

[5] i.e. prove your own worth before criticizing others.

3 ibyūtna tihjī al-ji'ān
lin jan hawārib imn al-gilli

3 بيوتنا تهجي الجوعان
لن جن هوارب من القلّة

4 tis'īn mansaf galaṭ fī giṭān
maṣrūfkū ma-ntagaṣ kulli

4 تسعين منسف قلط في قطان
مصروفكم ما انتقص كلّه

SUḤAYMĀN

سحيمان :

5 ya bānī al-garaḥ wal-gīfān
wēš haś-sabab tijrim ad-dalli

5 يا باني القرح والقيفان
ويش هالسبب تجرم الدلّة

6 maṣrūfha ġālī al-at̲mān
ma yiḥaṣṣili šārib ad̲-d̲illi

6 مصروفها غالي الاثمان
ما يحصّله شارب الذلّة

7 wi-šhūdha min warā 'ammān
willī sakan šār bal-ḥilli

7 وشهودها من ورا عمّان
واللي سكن شار بالحلّة

8 'aybin 'al illī banā li šān
ma-ybayyin al-'ilm wi-yidilli

8 عيب عل اللي بنا له شان
ما يبيّن العلم ويدلّه

9 ma yanfa' ad-dass wal-xifyān
al-bayyin an-nās bitḥilli

9 ما ينفع الدسّ الخفيان
البيّن الناس بتحلّه

10 la tisḥab at̲-t̲ōb bal-irzān
fī ṭūl ġērak kubr jilli

10 لا تسحب الثوب بالاردان
في طول غيرك كبر جلّة

11 ams aẓ-ẓaḥa bān lī ma bān
min harj al-and̲āl bē 'illi

11 امس الضحى بان لي ما بان
من هرج الانذال بي علّة

12 galbī tadāraj tigūl jirsān
walla mawazīn mintalli

12 قلبي تدارج تقول جرسان
ولاّ موازين منتلّة

13 la šuft fi'lak mānī bilšān
l-aturk al-bann ma-zilli

13 لو شفت فعلك ماني بلشان
لاترك البنّ ما ازلّه

14 walla ašibbha li-jēyt iẓ-zurmān
la ṭarraḥ al-'aṣr baẓ-ẓilli

14 ولاّ اشبّها لجيّة الظرمان
لو طرّح العصر بالظلّة

15 'agartnī lēš ya zmētān
min ašraf ar-rīa' laytilli

15 عقرتنـــي ليش يـــا زميتان
مـــن اشرف الريـــع ليطلّـــه

4.18

An Exchange of Praises for Rival Chiefs

A Poem of Repartee

At the turn of the century a member of the Syrian Rawala tribe, called Abū Zuwayyid, fled from blood revenge and took refuge with his chief's arch-enemy and the ruler of most of northern Arabia, the Amīr, Muḥammad Ibn Rashīd.[1] Ibn Rashīd, whose capital was in the town of Ḥā'il, enjoyed the company of Ibn Zuwayyid and his poems. One evening, however, when he called upon the poet to come to his guest-tent and compose a poem, he was surprised and indignant when Abū Zuwayyid made verses in praise of his Rawala chief, Nūrī Ibn Sha'lān,[2] the rival of Ibn Rashīd. According to the oral tradition, a member of the Rashīd clan present at the recitation immediately composed a rejoinder to Abū Zuwayyid to defend the injured honour of his own chief. The reply may have been composed on a later occasion, but it is taken to be an on-the-spot composition, perhaps to heighten interest in the episode.

ABŪ ZUWAYYID

O Rider of one like a wolf in her pace:
She's reddish, and calf never nursed of her grace;[3] 1

Poem 4.18 was heard recited by 'Amr Muḥammad aṣ-Ṣāni' of the Tiyāhā Gdērāt tribe, at Tell 'Arād, 13 January 1973.

[1] Muḥammad ibn Ṭalāl Ibn Rashīd (d. 1922) was the last ruler of the Rashīd dynasty (see Musil, *Negd*, pp. 251–3).

[2] Nūrī Hazzā' Ibn Sha'lān (d. 1936) was a very powerful chief of the large Rawala tribe that migrated between southern Syria and northern Arabia (see Musil, *Arabia Deserta*, *passim*).

[3] i.e. she is 'barren', and therefore strong (cf. poem 1.1, n. 14).

When racing, her forelegs come near to her hocks,
As she raises her right legs the left pound the ground.[4] 2

The fat on her back makes the saddle beams tight,[5]
And her sharp canine teeth are already in sight.[6] 3

The tent of Shaʿlān is a nest for the stranger;
O luck of his wife and those fleeing from danger.[7] 4

A son whom a mother no better begets,
From the sun-rise east to the west where it sets. 5

He's loved by a girl who's spurned others with scorn;
She'd have wed no one else whatever the tribe.[8] 6

He kills camels full-grown, should the hungry arrive –
Even camels whose milk keeps his tribesmen alive. 7

ONE OF THE RASHĪD

O Abū Zuwayyid, your mare has defects,[9]
Faults coming to pure-breds won't help to correct. 8

Ibn Shaʿlān is to us but one branch of our tree;
And it's our chief to whom the oppressed always flee.[10] 9

The dates that we give after lunch for good cheer,
Are as many as he serves his guests in a year. 10

Ibn Rashīd rears horses that limp when told: Back!
But when set on the foe, they race to attack. 11

[4] Unlike horses, camels, while running, raise both limbs of one side as they lower those of the other side, the forelegs and rearlegs of the same side always moving in unison.

[5] As the fat of a camel is stored in its hump (*sināma*), its well-being is judged by the hump's size, large being good.

[6] For the importance of canine teeth, see poems 1.4, n. 10; 3.8, n. 2.

[7] This is a reference to the help he gives to the weak, which is a source of pride to his wife (whose name in the text is ʿAliyā).

[8] Another wife (cf. n. 7) named Shaghā

[9] i.e. your poem is full of untruth, which even your sojourn with the Rashīd will not alter (untruth being part of one's nature (cf. poem 4.9, n. 1)). Just as poets use the theme of sending poems-as-missives with the riders of camels, so this allusion to a camel refers to a poem.

[10] Lit. 'he's at home [even] mid-morning to receive the needy' (cf. poem 3.8, l. 6).

Wanting nothing, I've said what I wished to declare.
Tell Ibn <u>Sha</u>ʿlān what I've said; I don't care! 12

ابو زويّد :

ABŪ ZUWAYYID

1 ya rākb-illī mišīha xirwiʿ aḏ-ḏīb
ḥamra wa-la ʿumri-l-iḥwayyir ġaḏī ba

1 يا راكب اللي مشيها خروع الذيب
حمرا ولا عمره الحويرّ غذي به

2 ḥamra itsūg akwāḥha bal-ʿaragīb
bitḥūš bil-yimna ū-taxbaṭ janība

2 حمرا تسوق اكواعها بالعراقيب
بتحوش باليمنى وتخبط بالجنيبة

3 ḥamra wi-tugṣum min ʿayyāha-l-maṣalīb
ḥamra wi-taww ibʿayyigha manība

3 حمرا وتقصم من عيّاها المصاليب
حمرا وتوّ بيعيّقها منيبة

4 ya bēt ibn šaʿlān ʿišš al-ajanīb
ya niʿim bil-ʿaliya ū-min yiltijī ba

4 يا بيت ابن شعلان عشّ الاجانيب
يا نعم بالعليا ومن يلتجي به

5 ya šēx yillī ma ḥamal bak walla jīb
min šargī muḏirr aš-šams wi-ġarbī muġība

5 يا شيخ يللي ما حمل بك ولاّ جيب
من شرقي مذرّ الشمس وغربي مغيبه

6 ya šōg min ʿayyat ʿala kill xaṭīb
ū-ġērak ʿala kill al-gabāyil ʿaṣība

6 يا شوق من عيّت على كلّ خطيب
وغيرك على كلّ القبايل عصيبة

7 ya mišbiʿ al-jiʿān min šimmax an-nīb
illī yiʿīšin al-ʿarab min ḥalība

7 يا مشبع الجوعان من شمّخ النيب
اللي يعيشن العرب من حليبه

واحد من الرشيد :

WĀḤID MIN AR-RA<u>SH</u>ĪD

8 ya-bū zwayyid fāṭrak bi ḏawarīb
jıytak ʿala ḥurri<u>n</u> tizawwid hiḏība

8 يا ابو زويّد فاطرك به ذواريب
جيّتك على حرٍّ تزاود هذيبه

9 amma-bn šaʿlān šiṭna-mn-al-jīb
magīm aẓ-ẓaḥa lil-minhazim la tijība

9 امّا ابن شعلان شطنة من الجيب
مقيم الضحى للمنهزم لو تجي به

10 bass at-tamr illī ʿala-l-ġada yijīb
ḥawliyti<u>n</u> lillī karamhum iḥkī ba

10 بسّ التمر اللي على الغدا يجيب
حوليّةٍ للّي كرمهم حكي به

11 xayla ʿan aš-širdāt ʿirj ibhin ʿayb
wamma ʿala-r-raddi sarīaʿ al-haḏība

11 خيله عن الشردات عرج بهن عيب
وامّا على الردّة سريع الهذيبة

12 mā giltha ū-mānī bāḡī maṭalīb
ū-mānī bi-ḥāl illī zi'il law dirī ba

12 ما قلتها وماني باغي مطاليب
وماني بحال اللي زعل لو دري به

4.19

Insults between Two Brothers

A Poem of Repartee

The present poem of repartee between Sulēmān Ibn Rifāda, the chief of the north-west Arabian Bilī tribe, and his brother Fuhaymān early in the twentieth century is one of the best-known Arabian poems to be found among the bedouin of Sinai and the Negev. In the poem the chief, imputing unworthy behaviour to his brother who had just come to visit his guest-tent, orders his slave to pass Fuhaymān up, although seated on the right, and to serve his guest Abū Rutēma, chief of the Juhayna tribe, first. He then compounded the insult by stating that his brother was not worthy of having fresh coffee made in his honour.[1] Fuhaymān responds by expressing dismay at his brother's indiscretion in airing a family quarrel in public, as any division in family ranks betrays a weakness that rivals might exploit.[2]

SULĒMĀN

O you who serves the coffee, dispense it now by cup;
Serve certain of the persons, pass others of them up. 1

Serve those who get around and know the taste of every well;[3]
Who save their friends in battles when their tongues from dryness swell.[4] 2

Poem 4.19 was heard recited by Ṣāliḥ Imbārak 'Īd of the Muzēna Shaẓāẓna tribe, at Dhahab oasis, 22 August 1972; 'Īd Iṣbēḥ Sālim al-Imṭērāt of the Ẓullām Abū Rubē'a tribe, at Ksēfa, 17 March 1973; and Salāma Ḥimēd 'Īd of the Bilī Magābla tribe, at Mazār, 4 March 1974. Discrepancies between the texts were resolved according to the judgement of Mūsā al-'Aṭāwna.

[1] Cf. poem 3.4 for the importance of brewing fresh coffee for a guest.
[2] Cf. poem 3.8, ll. 20–1.
[3] i.e. raiders and warriors, men of stature.
[4] Lit. 'when the spittle was dry' (cf. poems 1.11, n. 3; 2.8, n. 7).

Serve those who're not remiss in their social obligation;
Who, even as they're feeding guests, will show no ostentation.[5] 3

Yet there are those among us whom I would fain eschew:
Fresh coffee don't prepare for them; reboiled dregs will do. 4

FUHAYMĀN

O woe the tent that's just been rent where it was tightly sewn;
While some things may a secret stay, others will be known.[6] 5

And where are we to find some shade, the day of our disgrace;
A day whose sun is burning both our liver and our face?[7] 5

Of him who's wasted forbears' fortune, what are we to deem,
Though, shamelessly, he lets himself behave with self-esteem? 7

Even were a camel his saddle pad to bite,
No worthy here would silent stay, pretending it was right.[8] 8

But having neither power nor a carbine to extend,
Nor proudly with a whetted sword my enemy to rend; 9

Insult must make me take my leave, like thunder looses rain:
I'll be alone, yet I'll be far from lies and from disdain. 10

سليمان :

SUḶĒMĀN

1 ya-mbahr al-finjāl baḷḷa tisūga
ū-tiʿaddī ʿala nās ʿan nās

1 يا مبهّر الفنجال باللّـد تسوقد
وتعدّيد علـى نـاس عـن ناس

[5] On the importance of humility in a host, see poems 3.3, l. 4; 3.4.

[6] The tent is an image for secrecy because it keeps the faults and defects of a family or clan hidden from the eyes of outsiders, enabling it to maintain a reputation for loyalty and solidarity (as in the present case). (Cf. poems 1.1, n. 8; 3.8, ll. 20–1; 3.11, l. 18.)

[7] Just as the tent represents secrecy, the sun refers to unwelcome exposure that impairs one's reputation and hence strength; therefore the poet alludes to the 'liver', the source of an individual's strength, and to the 'face', i.e. reputation (cf. poems 1.15, n. 1; 2.8, n. 3).

[8] A rutting camel that bites its master or its saddle cushions is metaphorically called an *ʿāyib* (lit. 'a breaker of convention'). The present allusion is meant to compound the shamefulness of the present company for tolerating an actual breach of convention.

2 sūga ʿal illī kull ʿiddin̲ yid̲ūga
fakkāk rabʿa yōm ar-rīg yabbās

2 سوقه عل اللي كلّ عدٍّ يذوقه
فكّاك ربعه يوم الريق يبّاس

3 sūga ʿal illī yaʿraf ḥugūga
rafiẓin̲ ū-la gaddam az-zād lin-nās

3 سوقه عل اللي يعرف حقوقه
رفضٍ ولو قدّم الزاد للناس

4 ū-nuṣṣ al-ʿarab ʿendī sahīla iḥgūga
tikfāhum at̲-t̲anwa ū-la šaṭṭab ar-rās

4 ونصّ العرب عندي سهيلة حقوقه
تكفاهم الثنوة ولو شطّب الراس

FUHAYMĀN

فهيمان :

5 aḷḷa min bētin̲ bānin ʿalēna futūga
šayin̲ xafa ū-šayin̲ tidrī bi han-nās

5 اللّه من بيتٍ بانن علينا فتوقه
شيٍ خفاً وشيٍ تدري به الناس

6 yaḷḷa min d̲arāna yōm bānat igdūda
šamsi gawiyyi ū-taṣhad al-kabid war-rās

6 يا اللّه من ذرانا يوم بانت قدوده
شمسه قويّة وتصهد الكبد والراس

7 ēš rāyak fi-llī mākil mawārit̲ ijdūda
wil-yōm imʿawwid ʿala šōmt ar-rās

7 ايش رايك في اللي ماكل موارث جدوده
واليوم معوّد على شومة الراس

8 ū-kayf al-jamal yākil mawāt̲ir ibdūda
ma ḥad yanham al-jamal ʿan dagt al-wit̲ir ya nās

8 وكيف الجمل ياكل مواثر بدوده
ما احد ينهم الجمل عن دقّة الوثر يا ناس

9 waḷḷā ma lī ḥīla timidd al-barūda
walla bi-šad̲rit as-sēf ʿabbās

9 واللّه ما لي حيلة تمدّ البارودة
ولّا بشذرة السيف عبّاس

10 ila agfi miznin̲ tigāfat irʿūda
ṣabrī ʿala nafsī walā harj al-amkās

10 الا اقفي مزنٍ تقافت رعوده
صبري على نفسي ولا هرج الامكاس

APPENDIX

4.20 (A–I)

The Romance of Jidēaʿ Ibn Hadhdhāl

A Story in Prose and Poetry

Bedouin appreciate the four preceding poems, in which two persons 'duel' in verse, primarily for the dexterity they display in assaulting and defending honour; and poems 4.4, 4.6, and 7.11 (which also contain repartee) because they reveal the humour in bedouin behaviour. For such poems to be meaningful to an unfamiliar audience, however, their recitation must be preceded by prose explanations of their background, the presentation of which creates a story, however brief, comprising a bit of prose narrative and the poem. The interest that such poems arouse also stems from their similarity to a kindred genre of prose–poetry story-telling that was popular in the deserts under study until shortly after the First World War. Itinerant reciters told such stories, which were longer than the preceding poems, and in which the settings and characters were more remote and less identifiable.

This genre is the *sīra* literature. *Sīra* (pl. *siyar*) is often rendered as 'biography', because many such stories deal with a single person's life; literally it means 'an ongoing story', which is what many *siyar* are: a series of episodes concerning various personalities. The genre goes back to the early centuries of Islam, when such stories were compiled in Classical Arabic on the constant wars (the *ʿayyām al-ʿarab*) that characterized pre-Islamic bedouin life in Arabia, and on the life of the Prophet Muḥammad.[1] By the thirteenth century AD this genre became known in the vernacular oral tradition as well, with professional and other reciters performing the lengthy *sīra* of the Banī Hilāl concerning a tribe that had migrated from Arabia to North Africa in the tenth century and the exploits of Abū Zēd, its leader.[2] Another popular

Renditions of the present story and poems were heard recited by Mūsā Ḥasan ʿAli al-ʿAṭāwna of the Tiyāhā Nutūsh tribe, at Bīr as-Sgātī, 25 November 1970; ʿĪd Sālim al-Ḥimēdī of the Aʿsam section of the Tiyāhā Gdērāt tribe, in Wādī Abū Tulūl, 30 October 1971; Ṣāliḥ Imbārak ʿĪd of the Muzēna Shaẓāẓna tribe, at Dhahab oasis, 22 August 1972; Salāma Abū Isbēt of the Tiyāhā Gdērāt tribe, at Tell as-Sabaʿ, 15 September 1973; and Salāma Ḥimēd ʿĪd al-Ashgar of the Bilī Magābla tribe, at Mazār, 4 March 1974.

---

[1] See Nicholson, pp. 54–70, 356; also Ibn Hishām and Guillaume, *Life*, *passim*.

[2] See Lane, *Manners*, pp. 396–406, for a description of this story; and Connelly, *passim*, for a socio-anthropological study based upon it; a reputedly complete Arabic version was published in Cairo in 1963. For the ʿAntar story, see Lane, *Manners*, p. 420, and Nicholson, p. 459.

story dealt with the pre-Islamic poet and warrior, ʿAntar ibn Shaddād. What lent credibility to these integrations of poems with a prose narrative was not only their occurrence in a familiar bedouin milieu but their reflection of the practical role that poetry plays in everyday bedouin life—a role that will become apparent in Chapters 5 and 6.

By the late 1960s, when I began collecting poetry in the Sinai and the Negev, only snatches of a few poems from the Abū Zēd or ʿAntar stories were to be heard, even among the oldest bedouin; and these fragments were devoid of any narrative context. Only one story of this genre could still be reconstructed from the fragments of nine poems that were heard, together with prose explanations, as recited by five different persons. It was the story of a prominent bedouin chief called Jidēaʿ Ibn Hadhdhāl, who married Irgayya, a beautiful and wealthy female merchant—who also composed poetry, which is considered shameful for women, because of the irreverent and sexually suggestive themes that often appear in women's verse. Jidēaʿ thus warned his bride that, if she ever recited poetry again, he would divorce her; and, when a spy working for Ibn Hadhdhāl's jealous bedouin wives revealed that she had defied his warning, Jidēaʿ kept his oath. Irgayya, indignant, went to her former husband's arch-enemy, Khlēf al-Ḥantashī, and told him that she would consent to marry him on condition that he bring Jidēaʿ Ibn Hadhdhāl as a prisoner. When fortune enabled Khlēf to do so, however, he realized that Irgayya still loved her former husband; he therefore set Jidēaʿ free to remarry her.

There was much in this story to fascinate bedouin. Firstly, it offered them a glimpse into the life of an urban woman unfettered by tribal conventions. It is of interest to note that Irgayya's sexually suggestive poems (in particular 4.20 A, D, and E) were especially popular among the bedouin, who were also fascinated by the notion that a bedouin was able to marry such a woman. Furthermore, there was the motif of honour that compelled Jidēaʿ to divorce a woman he loved because of an oath he had taken; or compelled Khlēf al-Ḥantashī to concede his beloved Irgayya to his enemy. Finally, there was the envy and intrigue of the bedouin wives to amuse (at least) the men.

It is difficult to ascertain how much of the story is true and how much fantasy. Yet we know that there was a chief called Jidēaʿ Ibn Hadhdhāl, who led the ʿAmārāt section of the great ʿAnēza confederation, the largest in the Middle East, out of northern Arabia to new lands in Iraq west of the Euphrates River during the second half of the eighteenth century.[3] Moreover, there are elements in the narrative and

[3] Musil, *Manners*, p. 85. Similarly, Von Oppenheim (i. 90, n. 3) cites a Jidēaʿ Ibn Hadhdhāl

poems that serve to identify the name *Jidēaʿ* Ibn Ha<u>dh</u>dhāl with the Ibn Ha<u>dh</u>dhāl tribe of Iraq—for example, the name of his enemy, <u>Kh</u>lēf al-Ḥantashī, who would have belonged to the Ḥanātish section of the Fidʿān tribe, the immediate northern neighbours of the Ibn Ha<u>dh</u>dhāl.[4] Poem D furthermore, refers to Jidēaʿ as 'the brother of Batla' (*akhū batla*), which is indeed the war-cry of the Iraqi Ibn Ha<u>dh</u>dhāl;[5] and poem E has a reference to a garment sold by merchants from the Iraqi town of Kubēsa, which is in the heart of Ibn Ha<u>dh</u>dhāl territory.[6]

Furthermore, if the story was current in the nineteenth century—that is after the death of the historical Jidēaʿ Ibn Ha<u>dh</u>dhāl—it would have time to spread and take root in the bedouin world, including the widely separated parts of Sinai and the Negev[7] where the five men who related it to the present writer were born early in the twentieth century. There would also have been enough time for well-known lines of the poems to be integrated into other unrelated poems, such as those transcribed by Alois Musil, early in this century.[8] Finally, sufficient time had elapsed to explain why ʿAnēz abū Sālim, born in remote Sinai in 1920, was unable to identify Jidēaʿ Ibn Ha<u>dh</u>dhāl specifically, and knew only enough to cite him in a poem (1.1) as 'a great hero':

> And I, once a wolf that preys inside camps,
> Who charged upon non-bearing mares like Jidēaʿ . . .

The story as reconstructed below contains elements related by the five different people, who lived in three different parts of Sinai and the Negev. There are several similarities between the various renditions. They all agree on the basic general outline of the story and on certain details. All recognize that both Jidēaʿ and Irgayya were poets, and that the shepherd who betrayed Irgayya by revealing that she had recited a

leading a battle that took place in 1781. Spoer (p. 179) has it that the renowned Transjordanian poet–chief, Nimr al-ʿAdwān, was married to the sister of a Jidēaʿ Ibn Ha<u>dh</u>dhāl—which was chronologically possible, as Nimr died at a very advanced age in 1823 (Merrill, p. 275; cf. Peake, p. 170). Spoer's attribution of Jidēaʿ to the Banī Ṣakhr tribe was unfounded, as that tribe contains no Ibn Ha<u>dh</u>dhāl section (see Peake, pp. 215–19; Musil, *Arabia Petraea*, iii. 112–19).

[4] Musil, *Arabia Deserta*, p. 56.

[5] al-ʿAzzāwī, i. 268.

[6] Musil, *Euphrates*, pp. 29–31.

[7] i.e. southern and northern Sinai; and three different tribal groups in the northern Negev. Fragments of these poems were also heard (but not incorporated here) among the Aḥaywāt, Badāra, and Tarābīn Nadāyāt (central Sinai), and the ʿAgēlī (northern Sinai).

[8] Musil (*Manners*, pp. 147–8) includes the two lines of poem G in a poem in which the wounded man is not of the Ibn Ha<u>dh</u>dhāl, as in the present story, but was brought to an Ibn Ha<u>dh</u>dhāl tent; Sowayan (p. 107) includes these lines in a poem in which the wounded man is an enemy of Ibn Ha<u>dh</u>dhāl. Lines from poem I were also included out of context, in another poem of Musil (ibid. 177).

poem was a member of an outcast Hitēmī tribe[9]—some of the raconteurs placing him in the north-west Arabian Hitēmī tribe, the Sharārāt (of whose existence they knew), while the raconteur from northern Sinai had him belonging to a Hitēmī tribe of northern Sinai, the Dawāghra.

Certain key phrases were also common to all five raconteurs: the expression *dhikr allāh ʿalēkī* ('the name of God be upon thee', i.e. against the evil eye[10]), which was uttered by the old woman who counselled the jealous wives of Jidēaʿ, when she visited Irgayya to lay a trap for her; the expression 'whoever knows poetry got his camels back' (*radd abāʿirah*), with which the shepherd betrayed Irgayya to Jidēaʿ; and the angry husband's 'You are divorced' (*intī ṭālig*). These three expressions and the context in which they were uttered apparently made an impression on those who related the tale.

It is not surprising that differences, too, exist in both the narrative and the poetry. In the narrative, there are differences in regard to length, specific details, purpose, and the importance given to different aspects of the story. The bulk of the narrative, for example, was rendered by Mūsā al-ʿAṭāwna, who was the only source to give the 'stocking-up trip' background to the story, including details that he would not have related to a bedouin listener but which he thought necessary for the present writer, and entailing some unnecessary improvisation that might not have been part of the original story. For example, the name of Baghdād as the market where the Ibn Hadhdhāl stocked up for the winter, is based on little more than its being in the same country as the Ibn Hadhdhāl tribe and a city that the listener would surely know. Furthermore, to make the story up to date, anachronisms were introduced, such as the buying of flour (the current practice) rather than unground wheat; the stocking up of tea, which bedouin began to drink only after the First World War (cf. poem 2.12); or the 'honeymoon' that Jidēaʿ and Irgayya supposedly took, despite there being no such institution in traditional bedouin life.[11]

The poems, like the prose, were recited by different people at different times (the first four poems were recited by one person alone, poem E by four, poem F by two, poems G and H by four, and poem I by one), so that neither uniformity nor purity could be hoped for. The

[9] For more on the Hitēm, see poem 4.16, n. 3.

[10] See Bailey, 'Religious Practices', pp. 78–9.

[11] It is customary, however, for newly married bedouin either to go off into the desert and camp by themselves or to remain in the privacy of their bridal tent, usually for two to three days (see Bailey, 'Weddings', p. 129; Shuqayr, p. 388).

perceptible errors that appeared in the various renditions of the poems were: whole lines deleted; the sequence of lines jumbled; hemistiches mismatched; words changed; the same events described in different words; and the contexts of certain poems confused. As it is not the purpose of this chapter to analyse the discrepancies in these versions but merely to present a version that might resemble the original version, a final rendition of each was produced by applying the criteria of metrical suitability, logic, and most recurrent usage (in those poems with more than two recitations). Most of the narrative is presented verbatim, as told by Mūsā al-ʿAṭāwna. Where other raconteurs added important detail, their account, also verbatim, was integrated into the narrative, although without accreditation.

The Story

1. Jidēaʿ Ibn Ha<u>dhdh</u>āl, one of the bedouin chiefs who lived in Iraq, was known for his power and his wealth and was a poet as well. Once, Jidēaʿ Ibn Ha<u>dhdh</u>āl and some companions went to the market in Baghdad to buy what they needed from the city. They may have needed coffee and sugar and tea, and such. These were things they always used to store up, because the bedouin in those days did not go to town every day, or even every month. When they did come, therefore, they would buy the bread and flour they needed. Then they would go off to the places where they could find pasturelands, which would be far from the town—maybe five or ten days' distance; maybe twenty or more. Therefore the bedouin had to buy large quantities so as not to come in every few days for a kilogram of coffẹe or a bag of sugar. No. They would buy enough for four or five months—until they finished the winter pasture and came to other areas closer to the city, at which time they would visit it again. The bedouin called this 'stocking up' (*kayl*), i.e. buying what they needed for a long period.

2. Fine. <u>Sh</u>ē<u>kh</u> Jidēaʿ Ibn Ha<u>dhdh</u>āl went to the city of Baghdad with his companions, wanting to buy, or stock up with, all the goods that they and their tribe needed. When they arrived it was morning, so they walked around town—for Jidēaʿ Ibn Ha<u>dhdh</u>āl had friends there who knew him. It was his custom to visit one of his friends—eat lunch, sleep, drink—along with his companions.

3. As they were walking through one of the streets, there was a very beautiful girl sitting by the door of a shop, and beside her were coffee-pots glistening brightly. As the bedouin were passing down the street she, noticing that their leader was quite a man, said 'O shēkh, please have a cup of coffee. Drink a cup of coffee; the coffee is prepared. God grant you long life. Welcome, chief of the bedouin!'

4. Shēkh Jidēaʿ Ibn Hadhdhāl wished her long life, too. Favourably disposed, he uttered words of greeting, sat down on the carpets and drank a cup of coffee. Together with the girl were other owners of the shop and others who had come to buy and sell. And after he had drunk the coffee, the beautiful girl, seeing that the shēkh was quite a man, a person of great stature and dignity, said: 'By God, O shēkh, I would like to know something about you. Who are you?' 'I am Jidēaʿ Ibn Hadhdhāl,' he said. 'Welcome, O shēkh, welcome. I have heard about you. And as you are Jidēaʿ Ibn Hadhdhāl, you and your companions will be my guests today.'

5. He said, 'But who are you?' and she answered, 'I am Irgayya.' 'Irgayya? By God, I have heard of your renown. You are a poet, Irgayya, are you not?' 'Yes,' she answered, 'I compose poems.' And she said:

4.20A

IRGAYYA

Jidēaʿ, my eyes have never seen your like;
I'm sure that from love's path you hardly stray. 1

O stay and let us tailor you two shirts;
And taste our food before you go away. 2

JIDĒAʿ

I have a wife more bountiful than you,
Whose dowry twenty camels I'd to pay.[12] 3

While you are people used to settled life,
We bedouin bake our bread in ashes grey.[13] 4

[12] In the Arabic text 'twenty camels young and old'. For more on the kinds of camels designated for the payment of bride-price, cf. Bailey, 'Weddings', p. 112, n. 18.

[13] For other examples of the definition of bedouin as those who bake bread in the camp-fire, cf. poems 5.6, l. 13, 7.7, l. 15; for the antiquity of this definition, see Chapter 9.

My tribe's departed calling Allah's name,[14]
Waving reins above their heads in play.

IRGAYYA

1 ya jdēa' inti ma lak fī ma šāfit al-'ayn
walla inti ya jdēa' 'an darb al-hawa mistazilli

2 gīm 'endina limma-nfaṣṣil lak gimīṣēn
windawwigak fī ṭabaxna ya-l-imwallī

JIDĒA'

3 ana lay ḥalīltin minnik wa-xayr
sugt fīha 'išrīn min ḥašwin ū-jallī

4 intum ḥaẓrun ū-kārku-l-garāya
wamma-ḥna badwin janb nāra yamillī

5 raba'ī rikibit waxzit kull šīṭān
ū-šawšaḥat li-rsūnhin bit-ti'illī

رقيّة :

1 يا جديع انت ما لك في ما شافت العين
ولّا انت يا جديع عن درب الهوى مستزلّ

2 قيم عندنا لمّا نفصّل لك قميصين
ونذوّقك في طبخنا يا المولّي

جديع :

3 انا لي حليلةٍ منك واخير
سقت فيها عشرين من حشوٍ وجلّي

4 انتم حضرٌ وكاركم القرايا
وامّا احنا بدوٍ جنب ناره يملّي

5 ربعي ركبت واخزت كلّ شيطان
وشوشحت لرسونهن بالتعلّي

6. Then Irgayya played a trick on Jidēa'. She sent a slave and two maidservants ahead to prepare lunch—food and drink. Then she took the chief and his companions to her palace. Irgayya had built a palace about one or one-and-a-half kilometres out of town, and around it had made a garden with all sorts of good things in it—like fruit; all the pleasantness that Allah has created for man.

7. Jidēa' entered Irgayya's guest-room—a dignified guest-room, like that of the greatest chiefs; like that of a king; like that of a minister. Chairs and tables and carpets and pillows on which to recline—everything suitable for guests.

8. They came and they lunched. Irgayya brought them a generous meal. She had lambs slaughtered—more than enough; and even camels, for her guests were many. Then, after the meal, Jidēa' said, 'All

[14] Lit. 'confounding the devil', i.e. by calling God's name—as 'Satan fears nothing but the name of Allah' (see Bailey, 'Religious Practices', p. 79; cf. poem 7.3, l. 2b). Hence, when starting on a journey, bedouin, as other Muslims, pronounce, 'In the name of Allah, the merciful and compassionate' (cf. poem 3.5, n. 6).

right, Irgayya, we have to go now. Thank you. May God compensate you.[15] May God grant you much goodness.'

9. Irgayya answered him, 'O shēkh Jidēaʿ, will you, Jidēaʿ Ibn Hadhdhāl, Irgayya's guest, eat and run?' Three and one-third days (that was the custom in that period; the receiving of guests was defined—three and a third days).[16] 'You are with Irgayya! Irgayya is a well-known woman; and you are a renowned man. Impossible!'

10. He tried to depart but she stopped him—with reasonable words, of course. So Jidēaʿ Ibn Hadhdhāl and his companions, numbering some forty or fifty people, ate and drank at Irgayya's house for three and a third days. They still had not bought the things they needed from the market—sugar, rice, coffee, dates; perhaps some cloth for children's clothes—they still had not got what they wanted. So they said, 'Fine, we've finished the three and a third days. We would like your leave to go and buy our goods.'

11. She said: 'Listen. It is a simple matter. Why tire yourselves out at that market, and why let those merchants cheat you with high prices. No. We'll bring my scribe forthwith and he'll write up a list of all the things you want. My slaves will go and load the animals with whatever you want and bring it here. Then you can go. That will save you money.'

12. They said, 'We don't want to trouble you.' She answered, 'No trouble at all. I do it to honour you, O respectable chief.' So the worthy woman Irgayya wrote down all the things that Jidēaʿ and his companions wanted, and sent people to the market to prepare these things.

13. When, after two or three hours, they brought everything—and it cost a great sum of money—Shēkh Jidēaʿ Ibn Hadhdhāl asked her, 'How much is the bill, so I can give you the necessary dirhems.' She replied, 'The bill is paid. I paid the bill, and that, too, out of regard for you. That too is part of my hospitality. You are my guest and I have paid for all these things. By God, I won't take a penny from you.' Naturally, Jidēaʿ and his friends were embarrassed. What could they do?

14. During these two or three nights Jidēaʿ and Irgayya amused themselves after all the guests and the household had gone to sleep. They stayed awake long into the night, and Irgayya asked him, 'What do you think, fellow? By God, I want to marry you. What do you think?'

[15] *Allāh yikhlif ʿalēkī* (cf. poem 3.7, n. 9).

[16] Actually, the period for which a guest is *entitled* to stay.

15. He said, 'Well, if you want to marry me, I want you, too. God grant you long life. I'll be very happy to have you. You are of good stock, and have a good reputation, and are good at everything. However, Irgayya, I am laying down one condition.' 'What condition?' she asked.

16. 'If you become my wife,' he replied, 'that is, if I marry you tomorrow and you become the wife of Jidēaʿ Ibn Hadhdhāl but continue to recite *gaṣīd*[17] or other poems, it will be a disgrace to me. I am prepared to marry you, but on the lifelong condition that you no longer recite a poem. If I ever hear of you reciting a poem, it will be your writ of divorce. Do you agree?' Irgayya replied, 'I agree entirely. I shall never recite a poem . . . Fine . . . But tomorrow, when your companions go on their way—may God ease their path[18]—you stay here with me a while.'

17. The next day the companions of Shēkh Jidēaʿ Ibn Hadhdhāl took their goods, and headed for home, riding their female camels, while their male camels carried the sugar, coffee, and cloth. Jidēaʿ remained behind, telling them, 'I'll catch up with you—may God ease your way. I am going to stay with my Irgayya a few days.'

18. So they understood, recognizing that Jidēaʿ would stay there until he had finished his honeymoon.[19] They returned to their tribesmen, and when they were asked, 'Where is Shēkh Jidēaʿ Ibn Hadhdhāl?' they said, 'By God, Jidēaʿ has married Irgayya and taken up residence in the city.'

19. Fine. Jidēaʿ Ibn Hadhdhāl remained immersed in pleasure, happy and having a good time on his honeymoon—but instead of taking one month he took a three-month honeymoon. Then, one night, when they were sleeping high up in the palace, he suddenly woke up, as one often wakes up at night. The window was open, and when he awoke he saw lightning—lightning that flashed over the area in which his own tribe resided. When the lightning flashed, he thought of his tribe, and remembered his children and wives. He remembered everything, and said:

[17] The vernacular plural of *gaṣīda*, the 'serious' poem.
[18] *Allāh yisahhil ʿalēhum*, a common farewell blessing.
[19] An anomalous term (see n. 11, above).

4.20B

Lightning flashed and was over Rās Bannā seen,[20]
Drenching dry pastures that tired our mares. 1

White are the withers that cumber my mount,[21]
Shoulders protruding from loads she would bear; 2

Grazing on new grass that fills her with milk,
Her rear teats alone feed the calf from their swell. 3

When he who draws water raises his voice,[22]
She jostles the other parched mares from the well; 4

When he who draws water raises his voice,
Like sharp driven nails is the sound of her moan.[23] 5

Leaving the well like a pigeon she'll roll,
Slaked she will walk as with calf, fully blown.[24] 6

A troop of swift riders is mine to protect her,
Pig-faced they wait their horses[25] to prod. 7

A swift sorrel mare is mine to protect her:
A mare that can run with the best horses shod. 8

1 bargin barāg ū-bi-rās banna naxīla
yirwī mafālī mitʿibāt al-maʿašīr

1 برقٍ براق وبراس بنّا نخيلد
يروي مفالي متعبات المعاشير

2 layyi fāṭrin mišhabb ʿāli ẓahīra
ḥumm al-iktūf ū-marsala lil-xaṭaṭīr

2 لي فاطرٍ مشهبّ عالي ظهيرة
حمّ الكتوف ومرسلة للخطاطير

3 tijī min al-mafla wihī mistidīra
turẓiʿ waladha min iġlūg al-mawaxīr

3 تجي من المفلى وهي مستديرة
ترضع ولدها من غلوق المواخير

[20] For the same device of auguring good fortune, cf. poem 2.4.

[21] Cf. poem 1.1, n. 9.

[22] i.e. calling the camels to drink.

[23] The 'moan' (*ḥinīn*) of a camel-mare when she wants to nurse her calf has a staccato rhythm; for camel sounds, see poem 6.16, n. 1.

[24] Cf. the image in poem 5.6, l. 7.

[25] Lit. 'the hard-hoofed ones'.

4 win simʿit al-mayyāḥ yiʿlī zaḥīra
bi-ʿuẓūdha tanḥa-ẓ-ẓawāmī ʿin al-bīr

4 وان سمعت الميّاح يعلي زحيره
بعضود ها تنحى الظوامئ عن البير

5 win simʿit al-mayyāḥ yiʿlī zaḥīra
tirxī ḥinīn miṯil dann al-masamīr

5 وان سمعت الميّاح يعلي زحيره
ترخي حنين مثل دنّ المسامير

6 win ṣadarat miši-l-ḥamām al-ʿamīra
win ṣadarat tišdī ṣadīr al-maʿašīr

6 وان صدرت مشي الحمام العميرة
وان صدرت تشدي صدير المعاشير

7 layyi min dūnha ṣurbtin miʿajliyya
ʿala ṣumm al-ḥawāfir zē wujūh al-xanazīr

7 لي من دونها سربةٍ معجّليّة
على صمّ الحوافر زي وجوه الخنازير

8 ū-layyi min dūnha ḥamra ṯiniyya
tudxul ribāʿ imṭabbaga bil-misamīr

8 ولي من دونها حمرا ثنيّة
تدخل رباع مطبّقة بالمسامير

20. During this period he had forgotten everything. So, when he recalled these things at night, he cried. When he cried, a tear dropped from his eye upon sleeping Irgayya's cheek, a burning tear which woke her up to find Jidēaʿ crying. She said, 'Jidēaʿ, what is the matter? why are you crying?'

21. He said, 'By God, woman, I saw lightning flash—lightning over our country—and I remembered our tribal lands. Truly, I am going to leave this morning—go home and see what has been happening with the tribe. I'm a person with responsibility for my tribe and my kin. I cannot go on this way—forgive me. It is not that I am dissatisfied with you or dislike you, but rather that this is a necessity requiring me to check up.

22. Irgayya replied, 'Fine, if that is the way things are. Tomorrow you will go, but we will do without sleep tonight. We two will stay awake and talk, for tomorrow you go.' She lit the fire and made fresh coffee and tea, and so on; and they remained talking together until the sun rose.

23. In the morning, Jidēaʿ ate and drank, and went to saddle his camel-mare. But, because his mount had been fettered for three months, eating and drinking, she had developed a layer of fat. Thus, when Jidēaʿ came up to put the saddle on her, the saddle would not go on. So he began pulling the padding out of the saddle cushion. He pulled and pulled until the saddle went on with no padding at all.

24. Meanwhile, Irgayya prepared everything for him, sending everything they had. She said, 'Truly, I want to see you off. I'll walk with you a while, just until I see you off.' 'Fine,' he said; so she began walking, and Jidēaʿ began walking, holding the rein of his mount, which he led behind him. Each time they walked a bit he would say: 'Enough, good-bye. Go home, Irgayya . . . Enough Irgayya. You have gone far from the house.'

25. She would say, 'No, O shēkh. Another hundred metres . . . another hundred metres.' Every time they would walk another hundred metres, he would say to her 'You have gone far from the house; go back home, good-bye.' But she would say, 'No. Just a little more.' She thought she would walk a long distance—two, three, four kilometres—seeing Jidēaʿ Ibn Hadhdhāl off. Finally, he said: 'That's that. Enough. Up to here and no more.'

26. He couched his camel, mounted her, and said a final good-bye; and after the camel had passed and walked a few steps, she called out: 'O, Jidēaʿ, may God ease your way.' Then she remembered that she hadn't asked him how long he would be away, and wanted to stop him; but, as is known among bedouin, when one has received the parting words and has begun going on one's way, it is forbidden to call him back or to continue speaking to him at length. The bedouin see that as an evil omen. She said, 'Good-bye. How long will you be absent from me?'

27. Jidēaʿ merely raised his hand, his fingers upward, and kept going. Irgayya thought this might mean five days or five weeks. In any case, she went home. Naturally, five days passed; then five weeks. She said, 'All right, there is still five months. But when five months passed and Jidēaʿ Ibn Hadhdhāl did not return, she took it into her head that he meant five years. Irgayya became worried and began walking back and forth. Her mother said, 'Daughter, Jidēaʿ is involved in wars among the bedouin. Be patient. Patience is the key to relief.' Irgayya then composed this poem.

4.20C

O Lord who lets strangers go back to their land,
Like the waves he lets roll to and fro as they will 1

Steadfast my mother entreats me to be;
Patience, she says, is the key to relief.[26] 2

[26] 'Patience is the key to relief' (*aṣ-ṣabr miftāḥ al-faraj*) is a popular proverb.

Steadfast my mother entreats me to be,
But autumn's now gone and the Pleiades bring lightning.[27] 3

Jidēaʿ Bin Ha<u>dhdh</u>āl is astringent in strife,
Accustomed to charge coats of mail in the fight.[28] 4

I made you, Jidēaʿ, an ostrich-plumed pillow,
For your head that finds rest on my midriff, O Knight! 5

1 ya rabb ya midʿī kull ġarīb yirawḥ iblāda	١ يا ربّ يا مدعي كلّ غريب يروّح بلادده
ū-ya miʿṭī mawj al-baḥar yidlij idlāj	ويا معطي موج البحر يدلج ادلاج
2 wammī tigūl lī bi-ʿilm aṣ-ṣamāda	٢ وامّي تقول لي بعلم الصمادة
wuṣburī waṣ-ṣabr miftāḥ al-ifrāj	واصبري والصبر مفتاح الافراج
3 ammī tigūl lī bi-ʿilm aṣ-ṣamāda	٣ امّي تقول لي بعلم الصمادة
wal-gēẓ gayyaẓ ū-yibrag al-wasm liʿʿāj	والقيظ قيّظ ويبرق الوسم لعّاج
4 ū-jdēaʿ bin ha<u>dd</u>āl <u>d</u>awbi<u>n</u> ʿalāja	٤ وجديع بن هذّال ذوبٍ علاجة
<u>d</u>irbi<u>n</u> ʿala hēl al-malabīs daʿʿāj	ذربٍ على هيل الملابيس دعّاج
5 ana ya jdēaʿ sawwēt lak rīš an-naʿām wisāda	٥ انا يا جديع سوّيت لك ريش النعام وسادة
ū-baṭnī lak ya fāris al-xēl mishāj	وبطني لك يا فارس الخيل مسهاج

28. Irgayya waited until a year had passed, and when lightning flashed over their land, she remembered and said:

4.20D

Lightning flashed and was over Rās Bannā seen;
I hope that new clouds poured rain on their land. 1

They duel on horseback, they always fight keen;
They slaughter with swords of Indian brand.[29] 2

[27] The Pleiades appear in the evening sky in mid-November (cf. poem 2.4, n. 2).

[28] Traditionally, bedouin wore coats of mail in warfare (cf. Doughty, ii. 36, 480).

[29] An Indian sword, the *hindī*, was considered second in quality only to that of Persia, the *ʿajamī* (Doughty, i. 265, 505).

Lucky is he who sits firm on his mount,
  A spear neath his armpit the moment they charge. 3

Batla's brother:[30] Trust and you will surmount;
  You, for whom slender and scented girls wait.[31] 4

May he who mocks me[32] meet his fate,
  And the angel of death[33] snatch at his breath. 5

1 bargin barāg ū-bi-rās banna naxīla
  ya rayt jidīd al-mizn ʿal iblādhum ṭāḥ

2 nazzālt al-garbūṣ hayl al-maʿārik
  ẓarrabtin bil-hind ya wēl man ṭāḥ

3 ya hanī man aʿtadal fōg mārid
  yōm al-hidāya bēnhum ʿabṭ al-irmāḥ

4 ʿal aḷḷā ya-xū batla šaharhum yifārig
  ya šōg maṣlūb al-ḥašī ū-ṭīb al-aryāḥ

5 ū-man lamnī yabla bi-ʿumra yifārig
  walla bi-ʿizrayīn gabbāẓ al-arwāḥ

1 بــرقٍ بــراق وبراس بنّــا نخيلد
يا ريت جديد المزن عل بلادهم طاح

2 نزّالــة القربوس هيــل المعارك
ضرّابــةٍ بالـهند يــا ويل من طــاح

3 يا هني من اعتدل فوق مارد
يوم الـهدايا بينـهم عبط الارماح

4 عل اللّــد يا اخو بتلة شهرهم يفارق
يا شوق مصلوب الحشي وطيب الارياح

5 ومــن لامنــي يبلــى بعمرد يفارق
ولّا بعــزراييــن قبّــاض الارواح

29. Irgayya sent him a letter with someone, saying: 'What do you think sir? I am distressed! You said five and you would be back, but I have already counted five months. and you have not returned.'

30. He then sent her a letter, this Shēkh Jideāʿ Ibn Hadhdhāl, saying, 'Forgive me, by God, Irgayya. I respect you and want you, but I cannot come and live in the city, leaving my tribe behind. We bedouin are living in a dangerous land—pillaging and being pillaged. It will be disgraceful if I leave for a woman, deserting my family and tribe. However, if you come here you will stay with me as my wife. Come

[30] *Akhū Batla* was the war-cry of the Ibn Hadhdhāl tribe, called by the warriors in battle (al-ʿAzzāwī, i. 268).

[31] Cf. poem 1.4, n. 8.

[32] i.e. for my uncontrolled passion.

[33] 'ʿIzrāʾīl' (in the colloquial text, ʿIzrāyīn): the angel of death in Islam.

to me. Welcome. With all due respect, God grant you long life, I will not divorce you. However, if you want to stay there, and wish that I grant you a divorce—that is up to you. The decision is yours. You are free. I love you, and if you come, I will welcome you.'

31. When the letter came to Irgayya, she realized that nothing would help. So she prepared herself to travel. She wanted to go to Jidēaʿ Ibn Hadhdhāl. She took along presents not only for Jidēaʿ, however, but for all his bedouin. She took plenty, for she was very rich. She had no children and lived in a palace alone. Then she went off, not knowing whether she would return or not, and took along much of her wealth as presents.

32. Irgayya travelled for several days before she arrived at the place where Jidēaʿ Ibn Hadhdhāl was. When she arrived he greeted her and slaughtered an animal in her honour. He also honoured her by convening all the elders of his tribe who greeted her, too. Thus, Irgayya had great pleasure from the very first day; and on the second day they pitched her a large goat-hair tent like those of the bedouin.

33. Then Irgayya began making tea and coffee in the tent from early in the morning on, and she made her tent a meeting-place for men. Men began coming to the guest-section of Irgayya's tent to drink coffee every day, so that her tent became a main meeting-place. This one would see that one there; they would drink coffee and enjoy themselves.

34. Shēkh Jidēaʿ had married bedouin women before Irgayya, but when people started coming to Irgayya's tent, their meeting-place became nullified. She had taken all the men away by her charm and by her being forthcoming. She acted as if she were the bedouin's leader. The other wives of the *shēkh* grew angry from all this regard for Irgayya. It was as if they were neglected or abandoned.

35. The bedouin wives of Jidēaʿ grew jealous, each saying, 'My tent was the meeting-place where everyone came, and now she acts as if she is the very leader of the bedouin.' They went to an old woman—very old—saying, 'O granny, what are we going to do?' She said, 'You know that Irgayya is a poet and Jidēaʿ is a poet—both of them are poets. But Jideāʿ swore that if she recited poetry she would be divorced. I will work out a plan whereby she will recite poetry so that she gets divorced.'

36. The next day the old woman came to Irgayya, saying, 'The mention of God is upon your house.[34] By God it is nice, and by God

[34] *Dhikr allāh ʿala bētkī*, an invocation against the evil eye (cf. n. 14, above).

this and by God that. Only one thing is missing: livestock—camels—homing toward your tent like bedouin women have. Irgayya said, 'That is simple. I have money and I will get some camels.'

37. When Jidēaʿ came to her to amuse himself in her company (sleep with her at night, etc.), she made a request of him. She said, 'I have noticed that all the bedouin have camels—female and male—whereas I have none to return to my tent in the evening. O, Jidēaʿ, I want to go down to the market of Muzērīb[35] to buy me some camels. I have money and will do the buying myself.' Jidēaʿ replied, 'There is no problem. I'll engage a shepherd for you. We can hire the old Sharārī woman's son.'

38. Meanwhile the wives of Ibn Hadhdhāl began to give instructions to the boy, saying to him: 'O honourable Sharārī, we are going to do you a favour and give you some money. You are going to accompany Irgayya when she goes to the market. Only, we implore you, inform us of whatever you hear of Irgayya's doings. Bring us bits of information. Maybe she will make a mistake, maybe she will do something, maybe she will sing to someone or maybe someone will stare at her and laugh with her. That is to say, you must inform us of every movement, and of every aspect of Irgayya's behaviour, and we will give as much money as you wish.'

39. 'Fine,' the Sharārī said, and he made an agreement with these women that, when Irgayya prepared her journey in two or three days, he would say, 'I will go along with you on your way. I'll entertain you, sing for you; and I'll help you, too. But, by God, only buy me a young camel.' So the Sharāri went along with Irgayya together with a few other people—slaves and guides. And, for the camels she would buy, she also took along some shepherds. So she went to the market, and when she got there she bought some wonderful camels, and said to the Sharārī, 'Come here, O Sharārī! Buy whichever young camel you like from this market and I will pay its price right away.' The Sharārī saw a young camel and said, 'I want this one,' and bought it. Then they took her she-camels and the Sharārī 's young camel and began the journey home, to the tribe of Jidēaʿ Ibn Hadhdhāl.

40. For two or three days on the road they had not seen anyone. Then, suddenly, a party of raiders attacked them and stole their camels. In addition, one snatched Irgayya's necklace from off her neck and another stole the cloak that she had wrapped herself in. One of the raiders, however—a young lad—when he noticed how pretty Irgayya

[35] A town on the *ḥajj* route, sixty kilometres south of Damascus.

was, began to parade his mount back and forth in front of her. He neither took anything nor did he seem to care about anything. She said, 'Boy, who is the head of your party, the commander of your party?' He said, 'Khlēf al-Ḥantashī.' 'Where is he?' she asked. 'Sitting atop that mountain, there,' they said. 'Why did your leader remain sitting there instead of coming with you?' she asked.

41. One answered, 'He did not want to make battle with you, because you are only four or five men and a woman with you. So he told us, "Go take the camels of that group and come back." He did not come with us, because there would be no battle, no enemies for us to be fighting. So he stayed up on that mountain, waiting and watching.'

42. She said, 'Fine, but I want to go to him. Won't you take me to him?' she said to the boy. 'I would love to do so,' he said. So he put her behind him on the waist of his camel, and dashed off, taking her to Khlēf, and letting her down right in front of him.

43. Now, between the Ḥantashī and the Hadhdhāl, acts of plundering, looting, and hostility had been going on for years. So when Khlēf al-Ḥantashī asked her, 'Who are you?'—and she answered, 'I am Irgayya and married to Jidēaʿ Ibn Hadhdhāl'—he said, 'By God! There is nothing between us and him but plundering and looting!'

44. Irgayya, upon hearing these words, said, 'I would like to talk to you, O notable chief. Would you have me address you in poetry or just like this?' He said, 'Poetry? Do you know poetry? Well, let's hear some poetry from you. I did not know there were women talented in poetry.' So Irgayya began this poem.

4.20E

O Khlēf, you're not the type to fight with lovers,
Letting some grey-beard snatch my cloak; 1

And my necklace which the raiders took
Was purest gold in braids unbroke. 2

How I wish I were a camel in the market,
And you a bidder pushing men away; 3

And with you bare, unclad I'd lie at night,
Or in a thin Kubēsī gown I'd stay.[36] 4

[36] This highly unconventional and shameful allusion and the preceding line reflect the attraction

1 ya xlēf min mit̲lak yiḥārib ahl aš-šōg
ū-ta'ṭī ḥitīt aš-šēb yāxid̲ 'abātī

1 يا خليف من مثلك يحارب اهل الشوق
وتعطي حتيت الشيب ياخذ عباتي

2 ya xlēf ana ṭawgī ma' al-gōm manhūb
silāsla muxx ad̲-d̲ahab mabrimātī

2 يا خليف انا طوقي مع القوم منهوب
سلاسلة مخّ الذهب مبرماتٍ

3 ya xlēf min ḥaṭnī lak bakratin̲ wāgfa fi-s-sūg
winti-s-swīm illī tfidd aš-šarātī

3 يا خليف من حطّني لك بكرةٍ واقفة في السوق
وانت السويم اللي تفدّ الشراةٍ

4 ya hanī man nāwamak jardin̲ bila t̲ōb
aw t̲ōbin̲ ikbēsiyyin̲ min an-na'imātī

4 يا هني من ناومك جردٍ بلا ثوب
او ثوبٍ كبيسيٍّ من الناعماتٍ

45. These were very pleasant words, and Shēkh Khlēf al-Ḥantashī rejoiced in this affair. He wanted her, saw that she was pretty, and that her talk was very nice; that is to say, she had said, 'We will sleep together naked'—without a dress. And if a dress, only a thin one—a transparent one; called a dress, but in fact hiding nothing.

46. Khlēf called to his raiders, saying, 'Listen, raiders. Return the camels. The camels are mangy. They have the mange.' So the camels were brought in. Naturally, they could not contradict his words. But they returned all the plundered camels except the young camel of the Sharārī. Apparently, the one who had taken the Sharārī's camel was either a fool or hard of hearing, who did not hear them say, 'Return the camels.' So the Sharārī did not have his young camel returned.

47. But when all the others were returned, and Khlēf said to her . . . she excused herself saying, 'I, Irgayya, am wed to Jidēa' Ibn Hadhdhāl and only came to buy some she-camels. That's the whole story.' 'All right,' said Khlēf. 'You are welcome, anyway. We have returned all your camels to you and you can go on your way.'

48. So they departed. But after they had gone a way, the Sharārī saw that his young camel was not there. He said, 'My young camel is missing.' She said, 'Listen, fellow. Take for yourself the best of all these she-camels. If your camel was worth ten pounds, take one that is worth twenty.' But he retorted, 'My young camel is worth all the others. It is better than all the she-camels together. I want nothing but mine.'

that the figure of Irgayya held for the reserved bedouin. A Kubēsī gown is one sold by the itinerant merchants of the Syrian desert, who come from the oasis village of Kubēsa, a few kilometres west of the Euphrates river, between al-Rumādī and Ḥīt (see Musil, *Euphrates*, pp. 24–30).

49. In any case, as they were approaching their camp, she tried again saying, 'Take anything in place of your camel, but don't tell any tales. No one heard me recite poetry except you. I am afraid that Jidēaʿ will divorce me.' He said, 'I will say nothing.' But the women had bribed him, and he had promised them that, if she recited poetry, he would tell.

50. Well, they reached the camp, exchanging greetings with the people there, and Shēkh Jidēaʿ Ibn Hadhdhāl got up and greeted Irgayya, 'May God bestow good health upon you.[37] Congratulations. You have bought some fine she-camels. And you have been away from us too long.' In other words, he uttered some nice words, and she went on.

51. The Shārārī meanwhile came to the men's quarters and sat down, pretending he was sad and distressed; he covered the lower half of his face with his head-cloth and scowled. The shēkh asked him, 'O Sharārī, aren't you well? Why aren't you pleased? What has happened?'

52. He said, 'By God, O Jidēaʿ, whoever knows poetry got his camels back; and whoever does not know poetry lost his camels.'[38] Jidēaʿ asked, 'What is the story?' The Sharārī replied, 'The story is that the raiders of Khlēf al-Ḥantashī plundered us, and Irgayya recited a poem. And after she recited a poem her camels were restored. Whereas I, not knowing how to recite, lost my young camel. Because Irgayya recited to Khlēf a poem, her camels came back missing neither tail nor a single hair.'[39]

53. Jidēaʿ went to Irgayya and asked, 'Did you recite a poem?' She said, 'Truly, I did recite. Necessity has its own rules.[40] If I had not recited the poem, I would not have got back any of the camels.'

54. He said, 'OK. But you know there is a condition between you and me. You have become forbidden to me. You are divorced. I cannot sleep with you.' She said, 'Is that what you think?' He said, 'Yes. We agreed upon it, and what was forbidden has occurred. It is a disgrace. It is not that I hate you; to the contrary, I love you. But this was forbidden. Now you have become like my sister. If you want to stay here as my sister, you are welcome—but not as my wife; according to the condition we agreed to when we married.'

[37] *Allah yaʿṭīkī al-ʿāfiya*, a common blessing said to someone who is at work, or immediately thereafter.

[38] In the Arabic text, *illī maʿah g̣ōl radd abāʿirah, w-illī mā maʿah g̣ōl rāḥat abāʿirah*, a line that became a proverb for 'He who has the means succeeds'.

[39] In the Arabic text, *lā dhēl walā shaʿra*, an expression for 'nothing whatever'.

[40] '*Aḍ-ḍarūra lihā aḥkām*', a proverb.

55. Irgayya was angry. She sat there, in her tent, for a day or two, and then said, "All right, let me have your leave to go. If I am divorced, and not your wife, and you are going to consider me as your sister, I would rather go away.' Jidēaʿ said, 'May God ease your way. Wherever you want to go I will send people with you to see that you get there.' So one or two people went off with her, those who could take her to where she wanted. And Irgayya composed the following poem.

4.20F

Our leaving was followed by rain-clouds and thunder,
  Our feet are in water, yet thirst dries our spit.[41] 1

When loved by my dear one, I loved him in turn,
  And picked him from numerous suitors less fit. 2

But as he rejects me, so I'll leave him too,
  Like a deer that bolts from a hunter's shell. 3

Please listen, O Lord, who first brought him to me,
  As you bring pregnant mares to lush pastures to dwell: 4

Redeem me with one at whose tents travellers stop,
  Who'll serve guests fresh coffee and their morning's first bite; 5

He'll illumine the men's tent, and I'll light up his,
  And at day's end we'll meet and then revel all night. 6

1 agfa ẓaʿanna miznin tagāfat ar-raʿūdī
  ar-rijl bil-ma waẓ́-ẓama yabs ar-rīg

2 šōgī yōm inna hawānī hawayti
  walla-xtirt ʿin šōgī kiṯīr al-ʿašašīg

3 wal-yōm inni jafānī jafayti
  jaflit wiẓayḥī wi-ramū hayl ad-dafafīg

1 اقفى ظعنّا مزن تقافت الرعود
الرجل بالما والظمأ يبس الريق

2 شوقي يوم انّد هواني هويتد
ولّا اخترت عن شوقي كثير العشاشيق

3 واليوم انّد جفاني جفيتد
جفلة وضيحي ورمود هيل الدفافيق

[41] For the drying of spittle, cf. poem. 2.8, n. 7.

4 ya rabb yaḷḷā yillī aʿṭayta
ya maʿṭī al-xalfāt ib-rōẓ al-ʿašašīb

4 يـا ربّ يـا اللّـه يللـي اعطيته
يـا معطي الخلفات بروض العشاشيب

5 ʿiẓnī bi-ṣabiyyin tanḥar al-hijn bēta
ū-mgadm ad-dalla wi-fṭūr al-marayīg

5 عضني بصبـيّ„ تنحر الـهجـن بيته
ومقدّم الدلّـة وفطـور المراييق

6 hū nūr al-majlis wāna nūr bēta
waḷḷa limma-ltammēna kama lēlt al-ʿīd

6 هو نور المجلس وانا نور بيته
واللّـه لمّـا التمّينا كما ليلة العيد

56. When Irgayya's guides asked her where she wanted to go, she answered, 'Take me directly to Shēkh Khlēf al-Ḥantashī.' And, since the whole affair had taken less than a month, Khlēf recognized Irgayya on sight when she came. 'Hey, Irgayya,' he said. 'What brings you here? How are you?' She said, 'I am divorced and I have come to marry you, if you will have me.' He said, 'You are welcome, by God. I should hope I will marry you! I shall be happy to marry you.'

57 Then Irgayya said, 'Look here. I will marry you, but on one condition. When a battle takes place between you and Jidēaʿ Ibn Hadhdhāl, you must bring him to me. You must bring him as my prisoner and let me see him humiliated.' Khlēf replied, 'At your service. I agree, and, by God, if a battle takes place and I catch him alive, I will bring him to you.'

58. When Jidēaʿ Ibn Hadhdhāl learned that Irgayya had camped with Khlēf, he got up a raiding party to make a surprise raid. The raiders came upon a party of Khlēf's and sent spies out to its watering place. This place, where the camels were watering, was full of horsemen, posted there with the livestock, out of fear. One spy crept up to get a look at the watering place, and saw fighting-men there as numerous as dust. He came back to Jidēaʿ and said, 'The watering place is full of people. There is no chance of taking it. Let us get out of here before they see us.' They began taking counsel. Should they attack or should they flee. Someone said, 'Let's attack today. There is no escaping it. Whoever comes out safe will be safe. Whoever dies will die.'

59. They attacked and met in a fierce battle, a cursed battle, in which some people were killed. Jidēaʿ Ibn Hadhdhāl himself broke his leg, and Khlēf al-Ḥantashī's party caught him alive. They put him on a horse and brought him back home with them. The bedouin of Khlēf al-Ḥantashī were happy—nay, overjoyed, for they had won the battle and captured Shēkh Jidēaʿ Ibn Hadhdhāl, who, moreover, was wounded in

the leg. As you know, when a raiding party comes home successful, it is the greatest joy, and the greatest bedouin celebration. Some sing and some trill. The young men and women dance and race on horseback and camelback.

60. In the midst of such a celebration, Irgayya stood watching. Then after a while they dismounted the prisoner into the men's compartment, his leg broken. Irgayya looked and behold it was Jidēaʿ Ibn Hadhdhāl. When she saw him lying there wounded, a prisoner and degraded; she composed the following poem about him.

4.20G

Greetings, O shield of the high-tailed horse,[42]
Who has lightened the load off many a purebred.[43] 1

O Lord, blight instead the base and the coarse,
Let my own poor friend's leg its painfulness shed. 2

1 salāmtak ya ḏārī kull mišwāl
ya mxaffif ʿan jard al-aṣāyil ṯagalha

2 ya rayt šarrak yingisim bēn al-anḏāl
ya rabb rijil ṣwēḥbī ʿiff ʿanha

1 سلامتك يا ذاري كلّ مشوال
يا مخفّف عن جرد الاصايل ثقلها

2 يا ريت شرّك ينقسم بين الانذال
يا ربّ رجل صويحبي عفّ عنها

61. Irgayya proceeded to fetch water and to clean the wound. She behaved like a doctor, and composed this poem:

4.20H

This fighter, who once could fill out a saddle,
Could not fill the bowl of a stone pipe today;[44] 1

This fighter, who once could fill out a saddle,
Now gingerly walks like a cat out for prey. 2

[42] i.e. any horse that he is riding is safe. [43] i.e. who has felled their riders.

[44] The bedouin smoke pipes (*ghalāyīn*, sing. *ghalyūn*) comprising a small, hollowed out, stone bowl attached to a long reed or wooden stem.

Why didn't you, Jidēaʿ, send a scout out to spy,
A lad to discern if there's foe round the well? 3

I did, said Jidēaʿ, send a scout out to spy,
Who'd watch enemy bedouin pitch tents and come tell. 4

Some of us said, Let's escape to the plain,
The foe is distracted in filling the skins;[45] 5

Some of us said, Let us leave; let's turn round,
Before their armed riders to gird do begin. 6

Others said, No; we will trample the foe,
Be our gain but to stab and be stabbed in return; 7

Those swaying on high humps must sure win the day,
While death is what those at the well-spring will earn. 8

Black horses with riders then fell on the foe,
The Governor of Syria had fewer to lead. 9

Indian swords made a clash and a clang,
The swaying of spears seemed a madman's stampede. 10

Then felled, I saw Frēja[46] was limping away,
Afraid lest the foe mount a counter-foray. 11

1 al-maṣʿab illī kān ḥašū aš-šdādī
al-yōm ma yidibb d̲ēl ġalyūn

1 المصعب اللي كان حشو الشداد
اليوم ما يدبّ ذيل غليون

2 al-maṣʿab illī kān ḥašū aš-šdādī
al-yōm zē al-giṭṭ yimšī ʿala hūn

2 المصعب اللي كان حشو الشداد
اليوم زي القطّ يمشي على هون

3 lēš ya jdēaʿ ma-ṭlagt min rabʿak
ṣabyi-l-wakādī
ḥurrin tiramram nugrit al-jōf magṭūn

3 ليش يا جديع ما اطلقت من ربعك صبيّ الوكاد
حرٍّ ترمرم نقرة الجوف مقطون

4 gāl ana-ṭlagt min rabʿī ṣabyi-l-wakādī
wi-yirgab byūt al-badū yōm yibannūn

4 قال انا اطلقت من ربعي صبيّ الوكاد
ويرقب بيوت البدو يوم يبنّون

[45] i.e. skins for storing water. [46] Jidēaʿ Ibn Had̲hd̲hāl's horse.

5 fīhum yigūl fuẓẓū-bna ʿal-ḥamādī
ma zālhum ʿinna ʿal aṣ-ṣamamīl yilhūn

5 فيهم يقول فضّو بنا عالحمادِ
ما زالهم عنّا عل الصماميل يلهون

6 ū-fīhum yigūl xallūna ʿanhum intanni
gabl iytiḥazzam ʿendihum kull mazyūn

6 وفيهم يقول خلّونا عنهم نثنّي
قبل يتحزّم عندهم كلّ مزيون

7 ū-fīhum yigūl xallna-ndūs al-aʿādī
la ṣār kasabna al-yōm ṭāʿin ū-maṭʿūn

7 وفيهم يقول خلّنا ندوس الاعادي
لو صار كسبنا اليوم طاعن ومطعون

8 al-hawš ʿend imṣalfaḥāt at-tawadīd
wal-mawt ʿend illī ʿal al-bīr yisgūn

8 الهوش عند مصلفحات التواديد
والموت عند اللي عل البير يسقون

9 taṭallagat zurg ar-ramak bil-ʿayālī
ʿaskar wizīr aš-šām ʿendma-yʿiddūn

9 تطلّقت زرق الرمك بالعيالِ
عسكر وزير الشام عندما يعدّون

10 tasmaʿ sagīṭ imsaggiṭāt al-hinādī
nadḥ al-ʿarūg ū-la rakaẓ kull majnūn

10 تسمع سقيط مسقّطات الهنادي
ندح العروق ولو ركض كلّ مجنون

11 ib-ʿaynī šuft frēja tarta' bil-ayādī
min xawf ahayl ar-ramak ʿanha yišfūn

11 بعيني شفت فريجة ترثع بالايادِ
من خوف اهيل الرمك عنها يشفونِ

62. Jidēaʿ Ibn Hadhdhāl stayed there for a month, maybe more, until he was better and the fracture healed; until that which was broken got better.

63. Then Khlēf al-Ḥantashī came by and said to Irgayya, 'By God, I have felt from the first day on that your heart favours Jidēaʿ. You composed a poem about him and have been doctoring him during all these days, treating him until he was better. Listen, Irgayya, if you want to return to him and marry him, I will divorce you now and you will be ritually proper for him and prohibited for me.[47]

64. Irgayya answered: 'Thank you, if you put it that way. By God, I truly want him with all my soul. I will return to him.' He said, 'Fine. You are released from my custody: free, divorced from me, and proper to return to Jidēaʿ Ibn Hadhdhāl.

65. So she returned, and there was now a reason for peace between the Ḥantashī and the Hadhdhāl. Jidēaʿ Ibn Hadhdhāl said, 'By God, O

[47] If a Muslim divorces his wife by proclaiming 'You are divorced' (*intī ṭāliq*) three times (as Jidēaʿ must have done), he can only remarry her if she has been wed to another man in the interim.

Khlēf, after what has happened let us cover up the blood of Muslims[48] and let us make a peace that will last until Judgment Day.[49] I wish to settle accounts: you have lost and we have lost; you have plundered and we have plundered. So, whatever is lost is dead.[50] Whatever is lost is like a cliff come down on its own shadow.[51] We from this day forward will be in sacred covenant—brothers.' And the tribesmen of Jidēaʿ came forth when they learned of the reconciliation. They celebrated and flew white flags, and peace was established through this event. Then Jidēaʿ parted from Khlēf and he, Irgayya, and his tribesmen returned home.

66. Eventually Jidēaʿ Ibn Hadhdhāl died, and they say that Irgayya bore a child from him. But when Jidēaʿ died, she went back to the city to live with her child. The child was young—two years old. Because he was young he did not know his father when he died. Growing up from infancy in the city, he naturally thought that his father was from the city—not a bedouin. But when the child grew up and began asking his maternal uncles and his mother, 'Where is my father?' they said, 'Your father is dead.' 'Then where are my paternal uncles and my paternal cousins?'—and, as he continued to ask such questions, his mother began telling him at length. 'Listen,' she said, 'your father was the chief of a tribe called Ibn Hadhdhāl, and he died. Your brothers, relatives, tribe, and kin are all in such and such a place. Whereas I, your mother, am from the city.'

67. He said, 'I would like to meet my brothers and kinsmen and make the acquaintance of my tribe.' The boy had always lived in the city, and never saw bedouin or areas outside the city. Then one of the maternal uncles of the son of Jidēaʿ said, 'I will go with you.' So they came to Irgayya and took provisions. Then, the uncle of Irgayya's son put him behind him on a camel, and they journeyed, composing poems all the way. The proverb says 'Children of mice dig holes too'.[52] Thus, the son of Jidēaʿ Ibn Hadhdhāl was also a poet; he composed poems. Just as his mother was a poet and his father, too, he also turned out a poet without ever seeing his father or the bedouin.

68. Finally, he and his uncle, trying to get to the Hadhdhāl tribe, through wadi and over mountains, approached some tents in order to ask directions. He said, 'Let us ask that girl, herding the camels, the way to the tribe of Jidēaʿ and the tribesmen of Jidēaʿ Ibn Hadhdhāl.' As

[48] *Nahjab dam hal-misilmīn*, i.e. 'let's settle the conflict'.

[49] *Ṣulḥ daydāma limmā tigūm il-giyāma*, said to stress the permanence of the reconciliation.

[50] *Illī fāt māt*, said to stress the completeness of the reconciliation.

[51] *Al-jurf inhadam ʿalā ẓillah* (as in n. 50).

[52] *Ibn al-fār ḥaffār*, a proverb.

they slowly approached the girl alongside the hill, the boy saw that she was pretty. A pretty bedouin girl! Her face, her hair, her eyes—all pretty. Like a fawn in the desert. He went 'out of his mind', and addressed her with this poem.

4.20I

1 Greetings my friend;
I would not offend,[53]
But rather commend:
Ninety good wishes to you.

2 I saw her though coy,
My heart filled with joy,
My pain was no ploy;
My health I may never renew.

3 Out grazing I passed her,
For eyes she's a pasture,
A mare without master;
Ibn Hadhdhāl raised her too.

4 I saw her discreet,
With neck-plumes replete;
All I would eat
Is her spittle, like dew.

5 Were she sitting inclined,
On my camel behind,
'Twere better I'd find—
Mother's brother—than you.

6 My uncle I'd give for her sake,
With his bones her eye-paint I'd make;
This kinsman of mine you could take,
If you only allow me to woo.

[53] In the Arabic text '[Allow me] a word from close by'; it is forbidden for non-related men to approach a girl or woman at pasture—hence the excuse 'I would not offend'.

7 When my love smiled,
I felt my heart split,
And then when she laughed,
I said: God help me through![54]

8 Her midriff is fine;
On two dates she dines,
And drink she declines,
But one sip of water or two.

9 Her cheeks are white,
Her muscles are tight,
'Tween her breasts upright,
Lies a tiny mole, amber of hue.

1 gaww al-ḥabayyib kilmi min garayyib ū-tisʿīn ma bēn al-ʿawāfi wal-aḥwāl	قـوّ الـحـبيّـب كـلمة مـن قريّب وتسعين مـا بين العوافـي والاحـوال 1
2 šufti ib-šarḥa wamtala-l-galb farḥa min kubr jarḥa ma gidirt angal al-ḥāl	شفـتـه بشرحـة وامتلا القلب فرحة مـن كـبر جرحة ما قدرت انقل الحال 2
3 ū-šufti ib-wādī ya rabīaʿ-l-fuwādī muhra itgādī min imhār ibin haddāl	وشفـتـه بـوادي يـا ربيع الفوادي مـهـرة تقـادي من امهار ابن هذّال 3
4 ū-šufti imkīša lābis ʿal al-ʿung rīša mā lī ʿīša ġēr rīgha ila sāl	وشفتـه مـكـيشة لابس علٰ العنق ريشة مـا لـي عيشة غير ريقها الا سال 4

[54] In the Arabic text 'O He who shields us!' (*yā sātir al-ḥāl*), the most common Muslim exclamation when one suddenly meets danger or hears bad news.

5 rayta radīfa
fōg wirk al-ʿasīfa
alad̲d̲ waḥala
min imrādifk ya xāl

5 ريتـه رديفـة
فوق ورك العسيفة
الـذّ واحلـى
من مرادفك يا خال

6 xālī fadāha
waṣḥana fī dawāha
wi-yifdi-l-ḥabayyib
alf ʿammi̲n̲ ū-miyt xāl

6 خالـي فـداها
واسحند فـي دواها
ويفـدي الحبيّـب
الف عمٍّ وميّـة خال

7 yōm al-ḥabīb tabassam
ḥassēt galbī tagassam
wi-lamma ẓiḥik
gult ya sātir al-ḥāl

7 يوم الحبيب تبسّم
حسّيت قلبي تقسّم
ولمّـا ضحـك
قلت يا ساتر الحال

8 ẓāmir ḥašāha
tamrtēni̲n̲ ʿašāha
šurbha min al-mā
bass rubaʿ finjāl

8 ضامـر حشاهـا
تمرتيـنٍ عشاهـا
شربهـا مـن الما
بسّ ربع فنجال

9 bēẓi̲n̲ ixdūda
mabrimāti̲n̲ ʿaẓūda
ma bēn inhūda
ya ʿanbar al-xāl

9 بـيـضٍ خـدوده
مبـرمـاتٍ عضوده
مـا بين نـهوده
يـا عنبـر الخال

69. The girl laughed and said, ‘The bedouin are just ahead of you.’

70. When they arrived, no one knew the boy or his uncle. But after they were seated awhile, the guests introduced themselves. Thus the boy met his brothers and kinsmen, and stayed on living with the Ibn Had̲h̲d̲h̲āl.

5
Episodes in Poetry I

Poems from the War of Zāriʿ al-Huzayyil (1875–1887)

THE NEGEV IN THE NINETEENTH CENTURY

The Tarābīn and Tiyāhā tribes,[1] who jointly invaded the Negev from Sinai during Napoleon's occupation of Palestine in 1799,[2] spent most of the next century plunged in internecine war as the sections of these tribes fought each other for better lands and political predominance. The first such war (1813–16) pitted the leaders of the 1799 invasion, the ʿAṭāwna section of the Tiyāhā, against a coalition comprising the Tarābīn and two other sections of the Tiyāha: the Huzayyil and Gdērāt. All parties to this coalition had received lands in poorer parts of the Negev, south of Wādī Shallāla (see Map 4), and now wanted to take the more fertile and rainfed lands to the north of that wadi that had been occupied by the invading ʿAṭāwna and other sections of the Tiyāhā. Following hostilities, the Huzayyil crossed and settled beyond the more northerly Wādī Sharīʿa, but leadership of the Tiyāhā, which they also coveted, remained in the hands of the ʿAṭāwna.

The Huzayyil's opportunity for predominance within the Tiyāhā did not come until much later (in 1842). In a feud over the honour of women between ʿAwda, the chief of the ʿAṭāwna, and his brother ʿĀmr, the latter, as the offended party, turned for protection and support to his brother's arch-enemy and rival, Salmān ʿAlī ʿAzzām al-Huzayyil. Salmān, pleased to play a role in a conflict that might sap the strength of the ʿAṭāwna, took up ʿĀmr's cause and rallied the Tarābīn around their banner. This stubborn war lasted twenty-two years until the ʿAṭāwna were defeated and at the mercy of their enemy. However,

[1] While both the Tarābīn and Tiyāhā should each be considered a tribal confederation composed of member tribes each with its own chief or *shēkh*, they will, in this chapter, be referred to as tribes, in the general or historical sense. Accordingly, a sub-confederation such as the Ghawālī of the Tarābīn will be referrerd to as a division, while the group led by a chief—normally a tribe—will be called a section: hence, the Abū Sitta section of the Ghawālī division of the Tarābīn tribe.

[2] See Bailey, 'Nineteenth Century', for the dating and verification of the main historical events mentioned in this chapter.

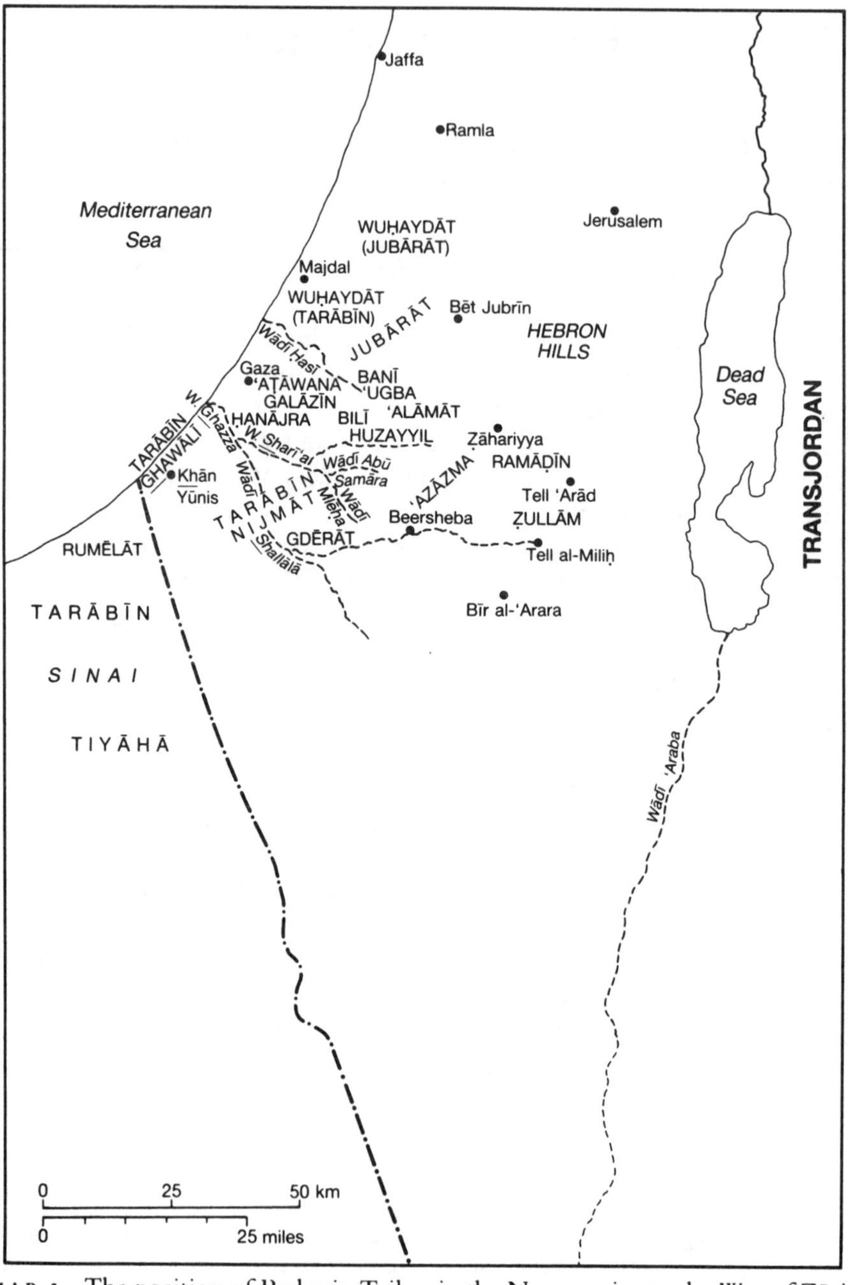

MAP 5. The position of Bedouin Tribes in the Negev prior to the War of Zāri' al-Huzayyil.

when S̲h̲ēkh Fihayd al-Huzayyil (Salmān's successor) was urged by the Tarābīn to divide between them the Tiyāhā territories they had so long fought for during twenty-two years, he realized that territory was a sacred matter to a tribal confederation such as the Tiyāhā—indeed, its very *raison d'être*³—and that he could not cede any part of it to the Tarābīn. Accordingly, despite an alliance of sixty-two years, he rejected the Tarābīn proposal, saying 'Your land is the S̲h̲allāla, not the S̲h̲arī'a', whereupon the leadership of the Tiyāhā finally reverted to the Huzayyil.

Soon after the struggle for leadership within the Tiyāhā was settled, a similar struggle took place within the Tarābīn. Now, however, the Abū Sitta section of the Tarābīn was supported by the Tiyāhā in its struggle against the Ṣūfī section of that tribe, just as the Huzayyil had been supported by the Tarābīn in their struggle against the 'Aṭāwna. According to the oral tradition, this involved relationship between the Tarābīn and the Tiyāhā began when Dahs̲h̲ān Ṣagr Abū Sitta murdered Muḥammad aṣ-Ṣūfī and took refuge with the Tiyāhā military leader ('agīd), Zāri' al-Huzayyil. Eager to embroil Zāri' in the conflict, Ṣagr Abū Sitta, the father of Dahs̲h̲ān, then urged their protector to annex the territory adjoining his own—al-'Arāgīb—inhabited by the 'Azāzma tribe, the ally and protégé of Hammād aṣ Ṣūfī, who had succeeded his murdered father as chief. Dahs̲h̲ān's intrigue succeeded and the twelve-year War of Zāri' al-Huzayyil broke out in 1875. In the middle of the conflict, however, the Abū Sitta rejoined the Tarābīn camp, so that the war became a bloody, if inconclusive, struggle between the Tarābīn and all the Tiyāhā, ending only when the Turkish authorities in Jerusalem themselves intervened and imprisoned the major chiefs of both camps, in 1887. In the course of this war, the following poems were composed to threaten and ridicule enemies and rivals, to celebrate victory, and to lament defeat.

---

³ By right, every tribe ('*as̲h̲īra*) belonging to a tribal confederation (*gabīla*) enjoys free access to all the pasturelands and natural water sources (old wells, springs, rainpools) to be found anywhere in the common confederal territory. This right is embodied in the saying 'We are equal at the trough and in the little meadow' (*iḥna wāḥad fi-l-ḥawḍ wi-r-rawḍ*). Hence, a bedouin's prime duty to his confederation consists in preserving its territorial integrity wherever it may be threatened. Accordingly, while Fihayd al-Huzayyil could fight against others of his own tribal confederation, the Tiyāhā, and still remain a member, he had to stop short of allowing any of its territory to come under the possession of another confederation.

5.1

From Muṣṭafā al-ʿUgbī to Muḥammad aṣ-Ṣūfī

A Poem of Warning

As noted above, the War of Zāriʿ al-Huzayyil began when Dahshan Abū Sitta of the Ghawālī division of the Tarābīn killed Muḥammad aṣ-Ṣūfī of the Nijmāt division, took refuge with Zāriʿ al-Huzayyil, and succeeded in inciting his host to conquer the adjacent area called al-ʿArāgīb and drive out the ʿAzāzma, the allies and protégés of the Ṣūfī. Upon receiving this news, Ḥammād aṣ-Ṣūfī, son of the murdered Muḥammad and chief in his place, declared war on the Tiyāhā. According to the oral tradition, Hammād swore an oath that he would defeat his enemy, the Tiyāha, pitch his tent at Khwēlfa in the ʿArāgīb region and fill his coffee-pot with water from the well of Khwēlfa. Upon hearing of Ḥammād aṣ-Ṣūfī's oath, the Tiyāhā–Ghawālī coalition[1] prepared itself to meet his assault. One of their number was the poet, Ḥājj Muṣṭafā Zaban al-ʿUgbī of the Banī ʿUgba tribe that had appended itself to the Tiyāhā at the beginning of the century.[2] As related by the reciter, Sālim Muḥammad al-ʿUgbī, the Tiyāhā came to Ḥājj Muṣṭafā and said: O Ḥājj Muṣṭafā, as-Ṣūfī has sworn[3] he would fill his coffee-pot from Khwēlfa (*ṭallag ghēr yisharrib al-bakraj min khwēlfa*)'. Ḥājj Muṣṭafā told them that this would never happen and 'sent off a poem [lit. utterance] to aṣ-Ṣūfī' (*shayyaʿ liṣ-ṣūfī gōla*).

The intention of the poem was to dissuade Ḥammād aṣ-Ṣūfī from embarking on hostilities. Thus, in lines 4–6 the poet praises him, pointing to his resolve, his generosity, and his military skill, hoping thereby to relieve him of the need to restore his challenged honour by war. The rest of the poem, however, is a threat intended as a further inducement to Ḥammād to desist from war. For example, lines 7–10 relate the prowess of those sections of the Tarābīn that will be fighting

Poem 5.1 was heard recited by Sālim Muḥammad al-ʿUgbī of the Tiyāhā Banī ʿUgba tribe, in Wādī Ḥūra, 12 February 1972. In addition to the version of the poem recited by al-ʿUgbī, a longer version in al-ʿĀrif (*Ta'rīkh*, pp. 184–5) was referred to, making possible the inclusion of ll. 3 and 9, which al-ʿUgbī had deleted. Discrepancies between the texts were resolved according to the judgement of Mūsā al-ʿAṭāwna and Muṣliḥ Ibn ʿĀmr. Accordingly, the reader will find corrections to the al-ʿĀrif text in regard to ll. 2, 3, 4, 10, 11, 13, and 14.

[1] The Abū Sitta were the main section of the Ghawālī division of the Tarābīn, all of which joined the Tiyāhā against the rest of the Tarābīn.

[2] The Banī ʿUgba were already resident in the Negev when the Tiyāhā conquered it in 1799 (see Bailey, 'Nineteenth Century', pp. 47 ff.).

[3] Lit. 'swore he'd divorce his wife' (cf. poems. 1.4, n. 8; 2.10, l. 8).

alongside the Tiyāhā—the 'Uwēlī, Abū Sitta, and Maghāṣba sections of the Ghawālī division—and of their Wuḥaydāt neighbours who had appended themselves to the Tarābīn early in the century.[4] Likewise, lines 11–14 affirm the might of the Tiyāhā themselves and their resolve to defend their lands. The beginning of the poem (lines 1–3) is the traditional opening, directing the camel-borne messenger to his destination.

O Rider on a mount, pure for untold generations,[5]
Tawny as bred by the Sharārāt Ḍabā'īn.[6] 1

Tighten his body-girth and ready provisions,
And let him fly as if he'd stepped on hot embers, 2

Ridden by a lad used to mirage-strewn spaces;
'Arār, if directed, will complete every charge. 3

Spur him on toward Ḥammād, whom we highly commend,
Whom you'll find sitting taut as a long-winged hawk 4

In a long, black tent with spacious sections,
By coffee-pots glistening from the fire's hot glow. 5

To Abū Muḥammad, foe of yellow-fanged fighters,[7]
Give my greetings, Panther,[8] and do not delay. 6

Say: Naṣṣār Abū 'Uwēlī is a pouncing eagle,
Fearing only that in meeting-tents they say he failed; 7

[4] Until the Tiyāhā–Tarābīn conquest of the Negev, the Wuḥaydāt had been the dominant tribe there. After their defeat, however, they split into two tribes, one that moved northward and appended itself to their former allies, the Jubārāt, and one that remained on its land and appended itself to its new neighbours of the Ghawālī division of the Tarābīn. For more on the affiliations of these sections, see al-'Ārif, *Ta'rīkh*, pp. 82–90.

[5] Lit. 'of whose numerous pedigree ancestors we have lost count' (cf. poem 2.9, n.2).

[6] The Ḍabā'īn are a section of the north-western Arabian tribe, the Sharārāt, who raise fine camels (see poem 2.6, n. 2). According to Burckhardt (i. 30), writing in the early nineteenth century, the Sharārāt used to sell their camels in Gaza, which may explain their use by the Negev bedouin. Tawny (*ashgar*) is a favourite colour for camels among bedouin.

[7] Here, noted warriors are likened to wild animals (*wuḥūsh*), who are thought to have canine teeth yellowed by the blood of their prey.

[8] It is complimentary to address someone by the name of a beast of prey, such as wolf (*dhīb*), lion (*saba'*), or panther (*nimr, fahad*) (cf. poem 2.7, n. 19).

And the sons of Abū Sitta fight like the Zaghāba,[9]
Men of valour whenever horse-riders clash; 8

And Abū Mughayṣīb's four sons fight like wolves,
Dashing to the clash like young camels; 9

And Ḥumūd al-Wuḥaydī, chief of red-clad bedouins,[10]
Mounted: a suckling she-camel searching for grass. 10

And we Tiyāhā are a sword ever gripped at the hilt,
Providing profit to the camel-merchant, although we are few.[11] 11

Our lands are lands of plenty, whose harvests we glean,
And those sent forth to scout them out are quickly met 12

By lads firing weapons unrestrained,
Forming ranks round Khwēlfa two thousand strong. 13

By the life of Him who makes it rain from the clouds,
We'll not concede our land while we sit square on a mount. 14

1 ya rākb-illī ma liḥigna ʿadādi
ašgar šarārī mi-rkāb aẓ-ẓabaʿīn

1 يا راكب اللي ما لحقنا عدادد
اشقـر شراري من ركـاب الضباعين

2 ukrub ibṭān al-hēj ū-haḍḍir zihābi
ū-xallī miṯil illī ʿal al-jamr yaṭīn

2 اكرب بطـان الـهيج وحضّر زهابد
وخلّـيه مثل اللي عل الجمر ياطين

3 fōga ṣabīy yigṭaʿ ifjūj as-sarāba
ʿarār lin waddēti bil-ʿilm yišfīn

3 فوقـه صبـيّ يقطع فجوج السرابة
عرار لن ودّيته بالعلم يشفين

4 kizzi ʿala ḥammād ya niʿimnā bi
tilgā mikniz miṯil ṣagr aš-šiyahīn

4 كـزّه علـى حمّـاد يـا نعمنا به
تلقـاه مكـنـز مثـل صقـر الشياهين

[9] The Zaghāba were a section of the Banī Hilāl tribe that migrated from Arabia to North Africa in the tenth century. They were reputed, from the legend of their leader, Abū Zēd, to be intrepid fighters.

[10] Wearing clothes made of fine woollen broadcloth (*jūkh*), customarily dyed red, was a sign of wealth.

[11] i.e. by capturing the mounts of their enemies.

5 ib-bētin wasīaʿ imfahhigātin ibwābi
wi-dlāl tawhij min ṣala-n-nār tiškīn

5 ببيتٍ وسيع مفهّقاتٍ ابوابه
ودلال توهج من صلا النار تشكين

6 labū mḥammad ẓidd ṣufr an-niyābi
balliġ salāmī ya fahad lā tiwannīn

6 لابوِ محمّد ضدّ صفر النيابة
بلّغ سلامي يا فهد لا تونّين

7 gūl naṣṣār abū ʿuwēlī miṯil saṭu-l-ʿagāba
min xawf harjāt al-fašal fa-d-dawawīn

7 قول نصّار ابو عويلي مثل سطو العقابة
من خوف هرجات الفشل في الدواوين

8 wi-ʿayāl abū sitta miṯil az-zaġāba
fi maṣādam al-firsān irjālin sijīʿīn

8 وعيال ابو ستّة مثل الزغابة
في مصادم الفرسان رجالٍ سجيعين

9 ūlād abū muġaṣīb arbaʿithum ḏiyābi
yittallagū ʿal-hawš miṯil al-gaʿadīn

9 اولاد ابو مغاصيب اربعتهم ذيابة
يتطلّقو عالهوش مثل القعادين

10 wi-ḥimūd šēx al-ʿarab ḥumurin iṯyābi
xayyāl šawla lil-mafalī-tkazīn

10 وحمود شيخ العرب حمرٍ ثيابه
خيّال شولا للمفالي تكازين

11 ū-ḥana kama sēf angabaẓ mi-nṣāba
inrabḥ al-fuwwād linna gilīlīn

11 وحنا كما سيف انقبض من نصابه
نربّح الفوّاد لنّا قليلين

12 ū-ninzil idyār al-ʿizz ū-nijna xaṣāba
willi-yḥūf ad-dyār najī ʿajlīn

12 وننزل ديار العزّ ونجنى خصابه
واللي يحوف الديار نجيه عجلين

13 bi-ʿayāl tuẓrub baḍ-dafak ma tihābi
nunṣub ʿarāẓī dūnha wagam alfēn

13 بعيال تضرب بالدفك ما تهابه
ننصب عراضي دونها وقم الفين

14 wi-ḥayāt min ṣawwar maṭar bi-saḥābi
ma-nfūtha wāḥna ʿal al-xēl ʿadlīn

14 وحياة من صوّر مطر بسحابة
ما نفوتها واحنا عل الخيل عدلين

5.2

From the Dūdēn to the Tarābīn

A Poem to Threaten

Since Ḥammād aṣ-Ṣūfī proved to be implacable, the war broke out despite al-ʿUgbī's poetic endeavour. Thereupon, the Tiyāhā enlisted the support of their immediate neighbours, the villagers who lived on the western slopes of Mount Hebron: they had collaborated with the Tiyāhā in the earlier wars of the century and now feared that a Tarābīn conquest of Tiyāhā territory would endanger their own lands. On joining the Tiyāhā again, these villagers—known collectively as the Gaysiyya, descendants of Gays, the patronymic ancestor of the northern Arabian tribesmen who had settled in this area during the early years of Islam—dispatched their own poem of warning to the enemy in the apparent hope of intimidating them. The surviving fragment, composed in the name of the leading family of Dūrā village, the Dūdēn, reads:

O Wind, bear my greetings to the Tarābīn
And tell them Dūdēn has entered the fray; 1

For this war that you've started, O Tarābīn
You will yet have dearly to pay! 2

1 ya rīḥ sallim ʿat-tarabīn
wi-gūl-lhum dūdēn xašš al-ḥarāba

2 wi-ḥarbin gawwamtūha ya tarabīn
ya wēlkū min ʿagāba

1 يـــا ريـــح سلّـــم عالترابين
وقول لـهم دودين خشّ الحرابة

2 وحرب„ قـــوّمتوهـــا يـــا ترابين
يـــا ويلـــكـم مـــن عقـــابه

Poem 5.2 was heard recited by Mūsā Ḥasan al-ʿAṭāwna, at Bīr as-Sgāṭī, 1 October 1973 (cf. Musil, *Arabia Petraea*, iii. 385, for a similar version; the next lines presented by Musil, however, appear to be a confusion of Ḥammād aṣ-Ṣufi's oath (poem 5.1, n. 3) and an oath uttered sixty years earlier in the War of Abū Sirḥān (cf. Bailey, 'Nineteenth century', p. 52)).

5.3

From the Tarābīn to the Gaysiyya

A Poem to Threaten

The Tarābīn replied with a poem composed by their chief poet, Swēlim Abū Haddāf, and recorded by Alois Musil. In what was probably only a fragment of the original, the poet insults the Gaysiyya and attempts to intimidate them. The first line is an insult embodied in the description of an obviously haggard camel that the poet 'chose' to bear the message, implying that the Gaysiyya are not worthy of receiving messages on better camels (cf. poem 6.15). Line 2 simply mentions the one for whom the poem is intended; line 3 tells them that they have no just cause to be in this conflict, and lines 4–8 warn them of what awaits them should they be so foolhardy as to intervene. Another insult is delivered by the poet in line 5, recalling a previous battle at Brēr village in the north-western Negev when the Tarābīn and their allies, the Ḥanājra, pursued the Gaysiyya northwards to Masmiyya village in such a humiliating defeat that it was recalled in songs sung by the girls of Brēr.[1] The final lines contain an ancient motif in which absurd expectations are compared to unnatural phenomena. Here the poet tells the Gaysiyya that, if they join the war, it would be absurd of them to expect a reconciliation without their total defeat.

O Rider upon a scrawny mount with neck drooping,
And belly flesh twisted from so many trips; 1

Convey my regards to ʿĪd and ʿAwda,[2]
And these words to the people whom we call Gaysiyya: 2

Water your herds in Wādī Ḥasī,[3] and pasture in the Hebron Hills,
But at Wādī Sharīʿa[4] you have nothing to find! 3

Poem 5.3 was transcribed by Musil, *Arabia Petraea*, iii. 238–9, and read aloud by Mūsā al-ʿAṭāwna, at Bīr as-Sgātī, 1 October 1973.

[1] When in the exclusive company of women, such as at wedding and circumcision feasts, or at pasture, women and girls will sing improvised ditties to amuse themselves. Such ditties recall events from the tribal history (cf. poems 1.8, 4.1, and 5.4), relate to the present celebration (cf. poem 8.1), or comprise romantic and sexually suggestive themes (cf. Abu-Lughod, *passim*, who bases a study of the role of women in bedouin society on such compositions).

[2] Leaders from Dūrā village.

[3] A wadi in the northern Negev.

[4] A northern border of the Tarābīn.

We Tarābīn are like a ring in a rutting camel's nose,[5]
  Famous among the bedouin as the Zag̲hāba.[6] 4

Ask the maidens of Brēr what happened at the threshing floor,
  When you fled on horseback all the way to Masmiyya. 5

And surely you couldn't forget the Ḥanājra,
  Their lance-blades dipped in viper's poison?[7] 6

We will grant you no peace, no peace will you see, 7
. . . .

Until the wolf recites rhymes at our night-time dances,
  Or an ostrich bitch suckles a jackal. 8

1 ya rākbin̲ min fōg ġawjin̲ imẓammar
  sīṭān baṭni min as-safar maṭwiyyi

1 يـا راكبٍ مـن فوق غـوجٍ مضمّر
سيطان بطند من السفر مطويّـة

2 sallim lī ʿala ʿīd wa-ʿawda
  waṣṣil kalāmī ġād ʿal-gaysiyya

2 سلّـم لـي علـى عيد وعودة
وصّل كـلامي غـاد عالقيسيّـة

3 al-ḥisī mākū wil-ijbāl maflākū
  wilā ẓall likū ʿal aš-šarīʿa niyya

3 الحسي ماكـم والجبال مفلاكم
ولا ظـلّ لكـم عـل الشريعة نيّـة

4 guddāmkū ṣaldam ixzām al-ʿāyib
  zē az-zaġāba bal-ʿarab masmiyya

4 قدّامكـم صلدم خـزام العايب
زي الزغـابة بالعرب مسميّـة

5 isʾal banāt brēr bil-jurn wēš ṣār
  ū-xuyūlkū laggat ʿal-masmiyya

5 اسأل بنات برير بالجرن وايش صار
وخيولكـم لقّـت عالمسميّـة

6 ū-ḥanājratin̲ mā nisītūhum
  ḥirābhum samm al-afʿa masgiyya

6 وحنـاجـرةٍ مـا نسيتـوهـم
حرابـهم سمّ الافعة مسقيّـة

[5] i.e. the Tarābīn bend their enemies to their will just as a rider controls a rutting camel by pulling at a special rein (*k̲hizām*) fastened to a ring in the camel's nose. In the Arabic text the Tarābīn are referred to by one of their names, Ṣaldam; another name is ʿAyāl Ṣaldam: the offspring of Ṣaldam (cf. poem 5.6, l. 5).

[6] See poem 5.1, n. 9.

[7] See poem 4.16, n. 5.

7 yiḥram ʿalēk aṣ-ṣulḥ mā tišūfū — 7 يحرم عليك الصلح ما تشوفوه

. . . . — — — — — — —

8 ila ad̲-d̲īb yirzaʿ bas-sāmir
ū-ila-n-naʿāma tarẓaʿ-l-wawiyya — 8 الا الــذيب يــــرزع بـــالسامر
والا النعـــامــة تـــرضـــع الـــواويّـــة

5.4

Women of the Tiyāhā Tribe

A Poem to Ridicule a Shameful Marriage

The following four years of warfare did not go well for the Tarābīn aṣ-Ṣūfī. Three major battles were fought at Abū Samāra, ʿAyn Kuḥla, and Bīr as̲h̲-S̲h̲anag, victory going to the Tiyāhā in the first and third. Ḥammād aṣ-Ṣūfī then realized that he could not defeat the Tiyāhā as long as Ṣagr Abū Sitta and his people were fighting in their ranks. He therefore granted the G̲h̲awālī a reprieve, which permitted them to return to their own lands near K̲h̲ān Yūnis. To seal the agreement, Ḥarba, the beautiful daughter of Ḥusēn Abū Sitta, was given to Ḥammād aṣ-Ṣūfī in marriage.[1]

News of the G̲h̲awālī defection from their camp naturally dismayed the Tiyāhā. Thus, to divert their thoughts from the threat posed by the marriage between Ḥammād and Ḥarba, they bemused themselves by treating it primarily as a disgrace. They asserted it was a shame for the Abū Sitta to surrender their finest maiden to purchase peace, and that it was disgraceful for Ḥammād aṣ-Ṣūfī to leave his father's blood unavenged for the sake of a woman. To entertain themselves with these themes, women of the Tiyāhā composed ditties that they would sing to each other in groups, for example, one group playing the part of the Ṣūfī section, and another giving Ḥarba's reply.

Poem 5.4 was heard recited by Mūsā al-ʿAṭāwna, at Bīr as-Sgātī, 20 April 1979.

---

[1] The family responsible for the murder of a man (*al-madmiyya*, lit. 'the blood-stained') may compensate by giving one of its girls in marriage to a man of the injured family (*aṣḥāb ad-dam*, lit. 'possessors of spilled blood'), without the latter family paying a bride-price (*siyāg*). Such a girl is then called a *g̲h̲urra* (lit. 'a marked one').

THE ṢŪFĪ
O Ḥarba, O worthless
  O you whom we got free! 1

ḤARBA
Though we slaughtered you with spears
  We've appeased you with pudenda! 2

AṢ-ṢAWAFA
1 ya ḥarba ya šinlāš
  yillī axadnākī balāš

ḤARBA
2 dabaḥnākū bal-aḥrāb
  ū-ṭayyabnākū bal-aksās

1 يا حربة يا شنلاش
يا اللي اخذناكي بلاش

2 ذبحناكم بالحراب
وطيّبناكم بالاكساس

5.5

A Poem by Swēlim Abū ʿArgūb

Praise for the Tarābīn Leaders

In the Tarābīn camp happiness reigned when it was realized that the marriage between Ḥammād aṣ-Ṣūfī and Ḥarba Abū Sitta would confer great advantages upon the Tarābīn and their allies. To celebrate these advantages Swēlim Abū ʿArgūb of the ʿAzāzma Farāḥīn composed a panegyric poem in Ḥammād aṣ-Ṣūfī's tent, perhaps on the occasion of the wedding itself. The first four stanzas are in praise of Ḥarba and her father, Ḥusēn Abū Sitta; the next six in praise of Ḥammād: his generosity (5–7), nobility (8), and wisdom in returning the Ghawālī to the fold (9). The poet apparently included stanza 6 as a hint to Ḥammād that he expected a reward for his poem.

Poem 5.5 was transcribed by Shuqayr (pp. 586–7) and (with a few changes) by al-ʿĀrif, *Taʾrīkh*, p. 188. Discrepancies between the two texts were resolved according to the judgement of Mūsā al-ʿAṭāwna and Muṣliḥ Ibn ʿĀmr.

1 Ḥarba is a crystal,
Shining like a light,
  In the dark of night.

2 She walks with a swing,
Dignity surrounds her,
Her eyes are black
  Without antimony.

3 Her father is a protective wall;
Even among hawks he's a leader,
Shielding young women
  From slander.

4 His sword is refined silver,
And good for slashing skulls;
When war is grinding,
  It's active as a bee.

5 The meeting-room of Ḥammād's tent
Is where excellent men gather.
Yes, Ḥammād is virile
  As a stallion used for stud.

6 This is Ḥammād,
Who gives finest wool,
And I will dress wonderously
  Among my people.

7 This is Ḥammād,
Who slaughters sheep,
Feeding meat to honoured guests
  As well as paupers.

8 He is a hawk to his friend
And, in support of his ward,
Will run over fire
  Even in flame.

9 When Allah so decreed,
Ḥammād came to our aid
And brought the good people
Back from the plain.[1]

10 So I've seen the young men
Shaking spears of *zān*[2]
Asking aid at the graves of Nūrān
And Awlād ʿAlī.[3]

1 ḥarba ballūr
tazī zē-n-nūr
fi-l-liyālī al-ʿatmi

1 حربة بلّور
تضي زي النور
في الليالي العتمة

2 ibtimšī hazz
yibrāha-l-ʿizz
ʿayūnha sumur
bila kuḥilī

2 بتمشي هزّ
يبراها العزّ
عيونها سمر
بلا كحل

3 abūha sūr
yigūd aṣ-ṣgūr
ḥammāy al-ḥūr
ʿan aḏ-ḏillī

3 ابوها سور
يقود الصقور
حمّاي الحور
عن الذلّ

4 sēfi rūbās
biyigṭaʿ ar-rās
yōm aḏ-ḏirrās
miṯil an-naḥalī

4 سيفه روباص
بيقطع الراس
يوم الذرّاس
مثل النحل

[1] i.e. by his marriage to Ḥarba, Ḥammād brought the Ghawālī, who lived mainly in the coastal plain south of Gaza, back to the fold.

[2] See poem 2.3, n. 10.

[3] Two holy tombs where the Tarābīn offer sacrifice. For Shēkh Nūrān, see poem 2.11, n. 10. Awlād, ʿAlī, in Sinai, is forty kilometres south of el-ʿArīsh, at Riwāfʿa (see Shuqayr, 581; al-ʿĀrif, *al-Qaḍāʾ*, p. 258).

5 rab'at ḥammād
malamm ijyād
ū-fī d̲immitī
inni faḥalī

5 ربعة حمّاد
ملمّ جياد
وفي ذمّتي
انّد فحل

6 hād̲a ḥammād
biya'ṭī jūx
albas 'ajaban
fī bēt ahalī

6 هذا حمّاد
بيعطي جوخ
البس عجباً
في بيت اهلي

7 hād̲a ḥammād
yid̲baḥ xirfān
yigri-ẓ-ẓīfān
ma'-l-hit̲alī

7 هذا حمّاد
يذبح خرفان
يقري الضيفان
مع الهثل

8 ṣagr al-ġālī
'izz at-tālī
yurkuẓ 'an-nār
ū-hī ša'alī

8 صقر الغالي
عزّ التالي
يركض عالنار
وهي شعل

9 yōm al̤la 'ād
jāna ḥammād
radd al-ajwād
imin ad-daḥalī

9 يوم اللّد عاد
جانا حمّاد
ردّ الاجواد
من الدحل

10 šuft aṣ-ṣubyān
biyhizzū az-zān
biyanxū nūrān
wūlād 'alī

10 شفت الصبيان
بيهزّو الزان
بينخو نوران
واولاد علي

5.6

From the Tarābīn to the Huzayyil

A Poem to Offer an Alliance

Before resuming the war, however, the Tarābīn made an effort to win their former allies, the Huzayyil, over to their side, and thus divide the Tiyāhā. As part of this plan Swēlim Abū Haddāf, a Tarābīn poet, addressed a poem to Fihayd al-Huzayyil, chief of the Huzayyil tribe.[1] The description in the first three lines of the fine horse (presumably fit to carry a message to the Huzayyil) is calculated to convince Fihayd that the Tarābīn are well disposed towards him. He then warns him, however, not to join the ʿAṭāwna-led Tiyāhā (line 4), boasting that the Tarābīn are invincible (lines 5–9). Abū Haddāf goes on to remind Fihayd that the old Tarābīn alliance had brought great benefit to the Huzayyil (line 10), and chides him (in line 11) for befriending his former enemies, the ʿAṭāwna, who, by making false accusations against Salmān al-Huzayyil (Fihayd's predecessor), had precipitated his hanging by the Turks. The last two lines are satirical, suggesting that the Huzayyil may prefer to follow the example of the ʿAṭāwna and forego their bedouin character; and, like them, consent to provide men to guard the grain grown by villagers in the northern Negev (line 12). Finally, he uses the image of bread to symbolize the difference between bedouin and *fallāḥ* culture, stating that the Tarābīn, as 'true bedouin', prefer the unleavened and dry bedouin bread (*khubz nāshif*) grown on their own land to the fluffy village bread (*khubz raṭīb*; lit. moist bread) eaten by the ʿAṭāwna chiefs who had been so imprudent as to marry *fallāḥa*-women from the village of Brēr.

O Rider of a swift steed, one with compact spine,[2]
In his six years no defect has blighted his forelegs; 1

Poem 5.6 was heard recited by ʿAwda Imsallam Abū Sbēḥ of the Ẓullām Abū Grēnāt tribe, near Beersheba, 7 April 1972, and Mūsā al-ʿAṭāwna; l. 9 was transcribed by al-ʿĀrif, *Ta'rīkh*, p. 185.

[1]Fihayd was reportedly the most powerful chief in the Negev: when the chiefs were summoned to meet with the Turkish authorities, Fihayd was the first to enter. After his death, a poet composed an elegy in which he said:

ash-shuyūkh ba'd fihayd surbit jadāwīn
bayāʿhum fi-s-sūg mā tirbaḥ minnih

After Fihayd, all the chiefs are a flock of kids,
Whose sale in the market would bring you no gain.

[2] For the desired qualities of a horse, see poem 1.10, n. 14.

Ride him by rope and temper his gait,
As his shod hoofs tread upon rocky terrain. 2

Feeling your spurs nicking hiṣ skin,
He'll raise his tail arching over his hinds. 3

Say: woe to the wrongdoer, and woe to his neighbour,[3]
Woe to all on whom horses descend in foray. 4

The offspring of Ṣaldam,[4] on fillies so lithe,
Their gunshot as thick as the smoke of steamships; 5

Horses weak before watering, but then spring to the fray,
And, like pregnant young camels, they bear their tails high; 6

Coming toward you they look like the doves at ʻAmāra;[5]
From behind they resemble a herd of fine colts. 7

The Tarābīn have a chief who knows how to lead them,
Famous for tents lighted all through the night.[6] 8

Kuḥla was revenge for Abū Samāra,
And the infamy of Shanag we yet will erase.[7] 9

O Fihayd, we've raised you to the tower of greatness,
And let you parcel Lafag and near Nakhābīr;[8] 10

But where's the revenge you should have for Salmān,
From those whose false witness led to his death?[9] 11

[3] This hemistich is a well-known proverb. Its application here is intended to dissuade the Huzayyil from joining forces with the ʻAṭāwna, whom the Tarābīn consider their main enemies.

[4] i.e. the Tarābīn, as called after one of their ancestors (cf. poem 5.3, n. 5).

[5] Doves have broad chests. ʻAmāra is a spot in Wādī Shallāla, some twenty-five kilometres south of Gaza.

[6] i.e. guests visit him throughout the night, thus attesting to his boundless generosity.

[7] The three places mentioned were the scenes of the most important battles fought until then in the war. The Tiyāhā won the first and third, the Tarābīn the second.

[8] Places in the north-west Negev near Gaza that the Huzayyil had captured from the ʻAṭāwna.

[9] According to the information recorded by ʻĀrif al-ʻĀrif (*Ta'rīkh*, p. 107), Shēkh Sulēmān Sālim al-ʻAṭāwna and Muḥammad Abū ʻAlī ash-Shawā of Gaza reported to the Turkish authorities in Gaza that Salmān al-Huzayyil had forcibly deflowered forty virgins, extracted money from other bedouin tribes, and withheld taxes he had collected on behalf of the government. Consequently, the Turks took him to Syria (*ash-shām*) and hanged him. According to Mūsā

By God, maybe each has a natural calling,
  And yours is to guard the fellaheen's grain.[10] 12

When we eat salad, it's with bedouin bread sown in our own Garāra,[11]
  Which is better than fluffy fellaheen bread baked in the ovens of Brēr.[12] 13

1 ya rākbin ǵōjin imdāna fagāra
  sadās ū-ma ṭabban a'ẓūdi 'awaṯīr

1 يا راكبٍ غوجٍ مدانى فقاره
سداس وما طبّن عضوده عواثير

2 ya rākbi baṣ-ṣur' wazzin ihjāra
  yāṭī 'ala ṣamm aṣ-ṣaxar bal-masamīr

2 ويا راكبه بالسرغ وزّن هجاره
ياطي على صمّ الصخر بالمسامير

3 lin ḥass lakzāt al-ka'ab wi-ntišāra
  yirmī sibībi 'a gaṭāti ba'aṯīr

3 لن حسّ لكــزات الكعب وانتشاره
يرمــي سبيبــه ع قطــاته بعاثير

Ḥasan al-'Aṭāwna, his great-grandfather Sulēmān involved the Turkish authorities in order to prevent an impending attack by the Huzayyil on his own tribe in the War of 'Awda and 'Āmir. Upon hearing of the planned attack, Sulēmān went to Brēr village and from there summoned the Governor of Gaza. Among the Huzayyil there is a tradition that Salmān's innocence regarding the accusation of having raped 'forty-five girls [*sic*]', was demonstrated by the instant dessication of the tree upon which he was hanged, thenceforth known as 'the tree of al-Huzayyil' and reportedly still standing in 1978 near Sidon, Lebanon (which was part of Syria in the nineteenth century). (Oral communication from Jaddūa' Salmān 'Alī Salmān al-Huzayyil, great-grandson of the Salmān in question.) During prolonged periods that the present writer spent in Sidon between 1982 and 1984 he found no one who could identify such a tree.

[10] The shēkh Sulēmān Sālim al-'Aṭāwna (see n. 9) 'protected' villages such as Brēr and Fālūja in the northern Negev, for which he received tribute in grain. He is reportedly also the first bedouin in the Negev to have his own lands cultivated, which became a common practice towards the end of the nineteenth century.

[11] Garāra, a fertile area near the Mediterranean coast just north of Khān Yūnis, was conquered by the Tarābīn Abū Sitta from the Rumēlāt tribe during the conquest of the Negev (1799) or during the War of Abū Sirḥān (1813–16). The Rumēlāt then emigrated to north-east Sinai between Rafaḥ and Abū Ṭwēla, where they have remained until the present. Their initial refusal to acquiesce in the loss of Garāra to the Abū Sitta was expressed in a poem of which the following fragment (from Shuqayr, p. 582) survives:

aṣūm 'an kull iṭ-ṭa'āmāt
  wagṭa' al-garāra fi-ẓ-ẓlāmāt

I'll henceforth fast from every food,
  Unless I pass through Garāra, though by night.

[12] The unleavened bread of the bedouin is baked on a metal disc (*ṣāj*) over an open fire or in its hot ashes (*malla*). The villagers bake their leavened bread in a rough oven called *ṭābūn*.

4 gūl ya wēl al-māsī ū-ya wēl jāra
ū-ya wēl min jati aŕ-ramak bat-tašawīr

4 قول يا ويل الماسي ويا ويل جارة
ويا ويل من جتد الرمك بالتشاوير

5 wi-ʿayāl ṣaldam fōg jurd al-muhāra
wal-bizir maʿahum mitil ʿajj al-buwabīr

5 وعيال صلدم فوق جرد المهارة
والبزر معهم مثل عجّ البوابير

6 yirdin hidīl ū-yuṣdurin yamm ġāra
wi-duyūlhin šibh al-ibkār al-maʿašīr

6 يردن هذيل ويصدرن يمّ غارة
وذيولهن شبه البكار المعاشير

7 win agbalin yišdin ḥamām al-ʿamāra
win agfan šibh al-ibkār al-muġatīr

7 وان اقبلن يشدن حمام العمارة
وان اقفن شبه البكار المغاتير

8 wi-ʿayāl ṣaldam gōm šēxin amāra
ū-buyūthum tuẓwī bi-šamaʿ ū-fananīr

8 وعيال صلدم قوم شيخٍ امارة
وبيوتهم تضوي بشمع وفنانير

9 ū-yōm kuḥla sadd fa-bū samāra
wamma šanag nistaddha ḥad hal-mašawīr

9 ويوم كحلة سدّ في ابو سمارة
وامّا شنق نستدّها احد هالمشاوير

10 ya fhayd waṣṣalnāk burj al-kibāra
ū-xallēnāk tigsim ʿal-lafag wań-naxabīr

10 يا فهيد وصّلناك برج الكبارة
وخلّيناك تقسم عاللفق والنخابير

11 willī katal salmān ma jibt ṯāra
wi-ḥaṭṭaw ʿalē ixtūmhum bat-tazawīr

11 واللي قتل سلمان ما جبت ثارة
وحطّو عليه ختومهم بالتزاوير

12 walḷa l-inxallī al-kull yirjaʿ la-kāra
witṣīrū ʿala gamḥ al-garāya nawaṭīr

12 واللّه لنخلّي الكلّ يرجع لكارة
وتصيرو على قمح القرايا نواطير

13 winġams as-salaṭa ib-xubz al-garāra
axēr min xubz aṭ-ṭawabīn fi brīr

13 ونغمّس السلطة بخبز القرارة
اخير من خبز الطوابين في برير

5.7

From the Tiyāhā Banī ʿUgba to the Tarābīn Wuḥaydāt

A Poem to Chide

The Huzayyil rejected the Tarābīn overtures and war again broke out in 1882. One result was that the Wuḥaydāt, having returned to the Tarābīn camp along with the Ghawālī, now found themselves at war with the Banī ʿUgba, a tribe traditionally considered to be their 'maternal uncles'.[1] One day, according to the oral tradition as related to the present writer by Sālim Muḥammad al-ʿUgbī, Nimr Wākid al-Wuḥaydī boasted that, if he met his maternal uncle, Ḥājj Muṣṭafā al-ʿUgbī, he would take him prisoner (*gāl: wallāhī, lin lagēt khālī, ghēr ākhidhih yisīr*). Ḥājj Muṣṭafā, upon hearing this report, said: 'That is nonsense. No one will take me prisoner unless I am dead.' Then he sent Nimr a poem, admonishing him for thinking that the Tarābīn could overtake riders of the Tiyāhā (line 5). The following fragment survives:

O Riders riding on barren camels,[2]
  Heading southwards from northern lands, 1

From colder climes with plundered mounts,[3]
  You'll yet reach a tent full of coffee-pots fine.[4] 2

Poem 5.7 was heard recited by Sālim Muḥammad al-ʿUgbī, in Wādī Ḥūra, 12 February 1972.

[1] A bedouin considers two categories of relatives as 'maternal kin' (*khawal*, sing. *khāl*): (1) his mother's family or (2) the families (including descendants) of the wives of his paternal grandfather, great-grandfather, etc. Accordingly, one may assume that the poet, Ḥājj Muṣṭafā al-ʿUgbī, was the brother of Nimr al-Wuḥaydī's mother or that one of his paternal aunts or grandaunts was Nimr's paternal grandmother or great-grandmother. In any case, intermarriage between the Banī ʿUgba and the Wuḥaydāt began when the former first came to the Negev (see al-ʿĀrif, *Ta'rīkh*, p. 120). Oral tradition has it that the established Wuḥaydāt deigned to 'take' girls of the newcomer Banī ʿUgba as wives but would not 'give' them their girls to wed. This expression of superiority—often heard among the bedouin in regard to marriage with neighbouring peasant communities, for example—is not commensurate with the common conception that it is a wife's family that determines the qualities of the children (see poem 1.6, n. 7).

[2] For barren she-camels, see poem 1.1, n. 14.

[3] The plundering of camels being virtuous in bedouin society, the depiction of riders as raiders enhances the positive image with which the poet wished to open his poem.

[4] i.e. a tent where wayfarers may find rest and coffee; by implication a tent that attracts worthy men is itself worthy (cf. poem 3.7, n. 1).

Say: O Nimr, your life is all wind and nought else,
Of those who wear anklets and bangles the lust;[5] 3

Unlike Wākid, your father, in war a fierce hawk,
A wolf who'd kill non-bearing ewes for his guests.[6] 4

Take the word of your uncle—you never will catch
Riders on camel-mares kept without calf. 5

1 ya rakbīnin̲ fōg ḥīl aṭ-ṭararīš
mitgaṣdātin̲ min blād iš-šimālī

2 ū-min dīrt aš-šinb bal-arkāb al-maxarīš
ib-rubʿatin̲ yalgan milīḥ ad-dilālī

3 gūl ya nimr dunyāk huffin̲ wala fīš
ya šōg min talbas iḥjūl ū-dalālī

4 abūk wākid bil-ʿada ġallab ar-rīš
ya d̲īb ya d̲abbāḥ šāt al-ḥiyālī

5 min gōl xālak gaṭṭ ma-btalagīš
rukkāb gabbin̲ maḥṣanātin̲ ḥiyālī

1 يا راكبينٍ فوق حيل الطراريش
متقصّداتٍ من بلاد الشمالِ

2 ومن ديرة الشنب بالركاب المخاريش
بربعةٍ يلقن مليح الدلالِ

3 قول يا نمر دنياك هفٍّ ولا فيش
يا شوق من تلبس حجول ودلالِ

4 ابوك واكد بالعدا غلّب الريش
يا ذيب يا ذبّاح شاة الحيالِ

5 من قول خالك قطّ ما بتلاقيش
ركّاب قبٍّ محصناتٍ حيالِ

[5] By alluding to Nimr's attractiveness to women, the poet is chiding him gently. Nimr's dalliance may not be admirable as compared to his father's prowess in war but, in bedouin poetry, it is not a negative image (cf. poem 1.4, n. 7).

[6] Keeping a sheep barren in order to fatten it for a future guest means sacrificing the gain that might accrue from its lambs. Its slaughter is thus considered a mark of great generosity.

5.8

Ḥammād aṣ-Ṣūfī to the Tiyāhā Gdērāt

A Poem to Boast of Victory

One of Ḥammād aṣ-Ṣūfī's first actions when hostilities resumed was to move against the Gdērāt section of the Tiyāhā, traditional allies of the Huzayyil, some of whom lived in eastern Sinai and others near Beersheba. Ḥammād accordingly prevented the Sinai Gdērāt from watering their livestock at the wells of Bīrēn and from pasturing in Wādī ʿAmr, places near their own Wādī Gdērāt.[1] Then he informed them of his move in a poem, of which the following fragment survives:

O Wind, tell the Gdērāt
  That Ḥammād has kept his vow: 1

Bīrēn now belongs to Ibn Krīshān,
  And al-ʿAmr to Ibn Jahāma.[2] 2

1 ya rīḥ gūl lil-gdērāt
  ḥammād waffa kalāma

2 bīrēn libn krišān
  wal-ʿamr libn jahāma

1 يا ريح قول للقديرات
حمّاد وفّى كلامه

2 بيرين لابن كريشان
والعمر لابن جهامة

Poem 5.8 was transcribed by Shuqayr (p. 586), and recited by Mūsā al-ʿAṭāwna.

[1] Bīrēn and Wādī ʿAmr straddle the Negev–Sinai border respectively, just south of the Byzantine ruin, Nitzana. Wādī Gdērāt is twenty kilometres further to the south.

[2] Ibn Krīshān is a section of the ʿAzāzma Ṣubḥiyyīn; and Ibn Jahāma a section of the Tarābīn Nabaʿāt (cf. poem 1.6, n. 8).

5.9

An Anonymous Tiyāhā Poet

A Poem of Relief after Victory

The ensuing hostilities appear to have been very momentous, for they inspired at least five compositions (poems 5.9–5.13) that survived into the twentieth century. The first was composed by an anonymous poet of the Tiyāhā, who apparently witnessed a battle on the banks of Wādī Sharīʿa in which his tribe successfully repulsed a Tarābīn attack—and this induced him to put his impressions into rhyme.

A lad is singing whom sadness has steeled;
Tiyāhā, O glory of the desert outstanding. 1

On the banks of the Sharīʿa they resisted with force,
That pool-studded wadi, which waters parched throats. 2

The Tiyāhā won't cede their homeland to others,
Like a State[1] standing guard over all that is hers. 3

How many mounts have their painful fate met,
Which must now be replaced from the horse broker's stock! 4

How many fair dames will spend sleepless nights,
Complaining of the widowhood that has orphaned their
young! 5

1 yuġannī ṣubīyin ʿālij al-bēn xāṭri
tiyāha ya ʿizz al-bawādī igbālha

1 يغنّي صبيٍّ عالج البين خاطره
تياها يا عزّ البوادي قبالها

2 ʿayyū ʿala janb aš-šarīʿa ib-guwwi
ya ʿagultin tirwi-l-maḥarīg jā-lha

2 عيّو على جنب الشريعة بقوّة
يا عقلة تروي المحاريق جا لها

Poem 5.9 was heard recited by Muṣliḥ Ibn ʿĀmr of the Tiyāhā Ṣgērāt tribe, in Wādī Munbaṭaḥ, 17 July 1974. Another version was transcribed by al-ʿĀrif (*Taʾrīkh*, pp. 187–8). Discrepancies between the two texts were resolved according to the judgement of Mūsā al-ʿAṭāwna.

[1] The bedouin term used in the Arabic text for 'state'—*ghuzz*—derives from the ruling *mamlūk* cast of Turks (specifically Oġuz Turcomans) in the Ayyūbid Sultanate (1186–1260). See Ayalon, pp. 10 ff.

3 tiyāha dārhum ma y'iffūha-l-ġērhum
tigūl ġuzz wāg'a dūn mā-lha

3 تياها دارهم ما يعفّوها لغيرهم
تقول غــزّ واقعة دون ما لـها

4 ya kam 'awdtin sūg al-manāya 'adābha
ū-min sawag ad-dallāl yišrū-bdālha

4 يا كم عودةٍ سوق المنايـا عذابـها
ومــن سوق الـدلّال يشرو بدالـها

5 ū-kam xawdtin ṭūl al-liyālī sihīri
tiškī mi-r-rumla yatāma 'ayālha

5 وكم خودةٍ طــول الليالي سهيرة
تشكي مــن الرملة يتــامى عيالـها

5.10

An Anonymous Poet of the Tarābīn

A Poem of Excitement after Battle

The second poem, heard among the Tarābīn in 1977, was composed by an anonymous poet who was moved by the Battle of Gubēba[1] to philosophize on the subject of war and warriors. Judging by references to women and the *daḥiyya* dance[2] (lines 3 and 14), the following verses were composed as a song to accompany the dancers' movements. As versifying in these dances is done at intervals, verses are often marked by incongruity, the content of some lines standing independently of all the other lines. Accordingly, the verses in this poem are independent statements by one who apparently participated in the battle of Gubēba and was stimulated to poetic activity by its fury. They are a random collection of impressions and thoughts, expressed as they occurred to the poet in the course of the dance. Only three lines (10–12) relate consecutively to the same event: how Sulēmān ibn Ṭallāg of the 'Aṭāwna refrained from killing Ḥusēn Abū Sitta of the Tarābīn when the latter had fallen from his horse.

Poem 5.10 was heard recited by 'Anēzān Sālim Swēlim al-'Urḍī of the Tarābīn Ḥasāblah tribe, at Rās ar-Ridādī, 25 February 1977.

[1] According to an account of the War of Zāri' related to the present writer by Sulēmān 'Aṭaywī Imsallam of the Tarābīn Ḥasāblah, an important battle did take place at Gubēba in the northern Negev.

[2] Descriptions of the *daḥiyya* may be found in Shuqayr (pp. 348–9); also Bailey, 'Weddings', p. 123.

The sword of Abū Sitta is good for slaughter. 1

The night of the Gubēba battle ended many a worthy life. 2

Upon fillies of the ʿUbayyāt,[3] O daughter of the loosened
head-band.[4] 3

One a stubborn foe for the other, their saltpeter melting with heat. 4

Drive the mount on as you should; all death is decreed by fate. 5

Upon the fillies of the ʿUbayyāt, nightfall and the slaughter's
still raging. 6

Throwing one down upon the other, as they cut through each
other's ranks. 7

The worthless have no resolution, while a hero comes forth
like a lion. 8

Many bones have been crushed; ground into the dust. 9

Sulēmān Ibn Ṭallāg[5], his stallion dashing to the slaughter, 10

They said: Kill Abū Sitta; he said, 'Leave me off that course.' 11

A hero is dear to a hero, O girl with perfect lashes. 12

Many riders have fallen; many well-groomed lads have died. 13

Go on dancing, O pigeon, you with the trim waist. 14

[3] The *ʿubayya* is one of the five main strains of thoroughbred Arabian horses, so-called because the ancestress of the line allegedly held her tail so high that, when the cloak (*ʿabāya*) of a galloping rider once flew off, it was caught by the horse's upraised tail (Blunt, pp. 433–40; cf. poem 1.10, n. 13).

[4] Women must keep their hair covered and 'in place'. Married women wrap around their forehead a black cloth called *ʿaṣāba*. On certain occasions, however, they may let their hair down and 'act without propriety' (*bilā ḥayā*)—e.g. at a wedding celebration (*faraḥ*) when the bedouin dance the *daḥiyya*.

[5] Forefather of the Ṭalālga lineage belonging to the Tiyāhā Nutūsh, and a noted warrior.

There is no relief in this world, and only the stories remain.[6] 15

Some wear belts made with goat-hair; while others must wear palm fibres round their waist.[7] 16

امّا سيف ابو ستّة – هو اللي للذبح طايب 1
1 amma sēf abū sitta—hū illī liḏ-ḏabiḥ ṭāyib

ليلة نهار القبيبة – وياما يا طاوت شايب 2
2 lēlt nahār al-gubēba—wi-yāma ya ṭāwit šāyib

قال ع بنات عبيّنات – ويا مرخيّة العصايب 3
3 gāl ʿa banāt iʿbayyanāt—ū-ya marxiyt al-ʿiṣāyib

قال هذا يا عنيد هذاك – راعي الملح الذايب 4
4 gāl hāḏa ya ʿinīd haḏāk—rāʿī al-milḥ aḏ-ḏāyib

قال سوقو السوق النظيف – وامّا الموت بسبايب 5
5 gāl sūgū as-sūg an-naẓīf—wamma-l-mōt ib-sibāyib

قال ع بنات عبيّنات – العصر والذبح طايب 6
6 gāl ʿa banāt iʿbayyanāt—al-ʿaṣr wi-ḏ-ḏabiḥ ṭāyib

قال يرمن هذا ع هذاك – يفتح لدارب شقايق 7
7 gāl yirmin hāḏa ʿa haḏāk-yiftaḥ lad-darib šigāyig

والهامل ما منه نيّة – والسبع في الذبح يوايق 8
8 wal-hāmil ma minna niyya—was-sabaʿ fi-ḏ-ḏabḥ iywāyig

قال ياما طحن عظامي – وطاحن عند الترايب 9
9 gāl yāma ṭaḥan ʿaẓāmī—ū-ṭaḥan ʿend at-tirāyib

[6] This line echoes a bedouin sentiment about the importance to a group's reputation of such qualities as bravery, dependability, and generosity. Bedouin life is a constant struggle to maintain a good reputation, which every individual wishes to leave behind. This is reflected in the saying 'Everyone dies, but the good deed [and its renown] lives on' (*kullu biyrūḥ bass al-maʿrūf bāgī*). The word for good deed (*maʿrūf*) means 'what is known'; in Islam good deeds are called *bāgiyāt* (lit. 'that which remains' (e.g. Qur'ān 18. 46)).

[7] In bedouin culture the imagery for being down and out is 'to gird oneself with dry palm fibres' (*mitḥazzim bi-līf*); i.e. one does not even have a flock to provide sufficient goat-hair for a belt.

قال امّـا سليمان ابن طلّاق ـ حصـانه للذبح موايق 10
10 gāl amma slēmān ibin ṭallāg—ḥiṣāna liḏ-ḏabḥ imwāyig

قال قال اذبح ابو ستّـة ـ قال فضّوني من الطرايق 11
11 gāl gāl iḏbaḥ abū sitta—gāl faẓẓūnī min aṭ-ṭirāyig

السبع للسبع غالي ـ يا راعية الرمش النظيف 12
12 as-saba' lis-saba' ġālī—ya rā'īt ar-rimš an-naẓīf

قالّ ياما طاح الركايب ـ وياما راحن غنادير 13
13 gāl yāma ṭāḥ ar-rakāyib—ū-yāma rāḥan ġinadīr

قال العبي يا حمامة ـ ورعية الصلب النظيف 14
14 gāl il'abī ya ḥamāma—ū-rā'īt as-ṣulb an-naẓīf

قال ما عالدنيا راحة ـ ما تبقى غير الخراريف 15
15 gāl ma 'ad-dinya rāḥa—ma tabga ġēr al-xararīf

قال فيهم يا حبلد شعر ـ وفيهم يا وين حبلد ليف 16
16 gāl fīhum ya ḥabla ša'ar—ū-fīhum ya wēn ḥabla līf

5.11

Salāma Abū Swēriḥ to Shēkh 'Alī al-'Aṭāwna

A Poem to Request Intercession

The same battle was sufficiently eventful to inspire the imagery of another poem, perhaps at a somewhat later date. The poet, Salāma Abū Swēriḥ of the Suwārka tribal confederation,[1] sent his poem to the chief, 'Alī Sulēmān al-'Aṭāwna, as part of a request that 'Alī intercede with the Turkish authorities on the poet's behalf (line 14). Hoping to please

Poem 5.11 was heard recited by Mūsā al-'Aṭāwna (the grandson of the person to whom it was addressed), at Bīr as-Sgāṭī, 3 October 1973.

[1] The Suwārka of the Negev were a branch of the tribe by that name in Sinai (see al-'Ārif, *Ta'rīkh*, pp. 148–9). Before the War of Abū Sirḥān (1813–16) they lived between the Wādīs Shallāla and Sharī'a, but were then driven northwards with their confederates, the Jubārāt, to take up residence along the Mediterranean coast between Wādī Ḥasī and Isdūd village (present-day

the chief, he reviews instances of Tiyāhā bravery, recounting, too, a theme of the previous poem—how Ḥusēn Abū Sitta's horse was cut down by Sulēmān Ibn Ṭallāg of the Aṭāwna (lines 4–7).

O Rider setting off on a fleet winged bird,
A beige Nubian camel[2] that bolts from its shadow: 1

Take this letter from me, upon your life,
Convey it to a chief of whom few are his like; 2

To Ibn ʿAṭiyya—heir of chiefly stock,[3]
A well never dry, though the ropes grow worn.[4] 3

Once Ḥusēn Abū Sitta, drunk with daring,
Gathered his warriors and attacked him at dawn; 4

But Ibn Ṭallāg appeared with his singular rifle,
Took aim, and Abū Sitta was downed with a shot. 5

As his horse with the rearguard fell, he was trampled,
But the Offspring of Ṣaldam turned round to retrieve him. 6

I say Bravo to the Tarābīn; good for them:
They returned to fetch Ḥusēn after passing him by. 7

And Gāsim Ibn ʿAṭiyya,[5] so stringent with a spear,
That even horses cowered on seeing his shadow. 8

And Jabr al-ʿAṭāwna,[6] stout heart and a hero,
Jabr who bequeathed his prowess to his sons; 9

Ashdod). In that earlier war, too, the Suwārka and Jubārāt were aided by the ʿAṭāwna, with whom they were on friendly terms.

[2] Nubian camels bred in Upper Egypt (*aṣ-ṣaʿīd*) by the Bishārīn tribe are prized for their speed (Burckhardt, ii. 77; Murray, p. 113).

[3] ʿAlī al-ʿAṭāwna (also Ibn ʿAṭiyya), chief during the War of Zāriʿ, was the fifth chief of the Tiyāhā Nutūsh in the Negev according to the following descent: (1) Salīm; (2) son Sālim; (3) Sālim's brother ʿAwda; (4) Sālim's son Sulēmān; (5) Sulēmān's son ʿAli. ʿAlī was chief until 1917, when he was succeeded by his son Ḥasan, who in turn was succeeded by his own son Mūsā in 1948.

[4] For the image of a well for a munificent person, cf. poems 2.7, n. 7; 4.5; 7.1.

[5] A son of ʿĀmr, renowned for his role in the War of ʿAwda and ʿĀmr (1842–1854) (see Bailey, 'Nineteenth Century', pp. 61–7).

[6] A brother of the previous chief Sulēmān.

When he attacked the Tarābīn, 'twas like ancient Jassās,[7]
Their horses cowered and they were dismayed, 10

The Tiyāhā horsemen butting their mounts in the fray,
And whoever fell, forever was lost. 11

The ʿAzāzma were a pack of fleeing curs,
The cloaks of Slēma's offspring were flapping behind them.[8] 12

Like the worthless Jarāwīn, with no lineage of note,
Be not impressed by their prowess in hoeing the ground.[9] 13

Whereas ʿAlī Ibn ʿAṭiyya treads on government carpets;
He snorts at the rulers, who say: What is your wish? 14

1 ya rākbi͟n min ʿendina fōg nisnās
ašgar ṣaʿīdī jāfli͟n min ziwāli

1 يا راكبٍ من عندنا فوق نسناس
اشقر صعيدي جافلٍ من زوالد

2 xu͟d minnī al-maktūb ʿal-ʿayn war-rās
waddī liš-šēx illī gilīli͟n imṯāli

2 خذ منّي المكتوب عالعين والراس
ودّيه للشيخ اللي قليلٍ مثالد

3 ibin ʿaṭiyya šēx mabnī ʿal asās
ʿiddi͟n ma yinniziḥ ila tigaṭṭaʿ ḥibāli

3 ابن عطيّة شيخ مبني عل اساس
عدٍّ ما ينّزح الا تقطّع حبالد

4 wi-ḥsēn abū sitta kama šārib al-kās
lamlam ijrūdi ū-ṭalʿat aš-šams jā li

4 وحسين ابو ستّة كما شارب الكاس
لملم جرودد وطلعة الشمس جا لد

[7] A reference to the pre-Islamic bedouin warrior Jassās, whose slaying of Klēb, the chief of Bakr bin Wā'il, brought on the celebrated War of Basūs (Nicholson, pp. 55–60). (Cf. poem 2.2, n. 18.)

[8] This description of how the ʿAzāzma deserted the battle is a satire in three respects: (1) they are compared to dogs; (2) their cloaks are described as horse-blankets (rather than the customary *ʿabāya*-cloak), implying poverty; (3) they are dubbed the offspring of a woman (Slēma) i.e. of a 'bastard' lineage with no known forefather. Indeed, one tradition relating to their origins tells only of a mother and her son ʿAzzām (see al-ʿĀrif, *Ta'rīkh*, pp. 94–6); another that one section of the ʿAzāzma, the Zurāba, is descended from an illegitimate child.

[9] The Jarāwīn, an appended section of the Tarābīn who were engaged in agriculture before the other Tarābīn, were suspected to be of *fallāḥīn* origin (see al-ʿĀrif, *Ta'rīkh*, pp. 91–3), and were not, therefore, eligible to marry purely bedouin women. Hence, the allusion to their absence of 'lineage' (*asās*) refers to maternal kin, from whom bedouin children are believed to derive their characteristics and social qualities (cf. poem 1.6, n. 7).

5 kun jā ibin ṭallāg bal-bundagī xāṣṣ
ū-min malhaẓ aš-šawwāf bal-bizir šāli

5 كن جاه ابن طلّاق بالبندقي خاصّ
ومن ملحظ الشوّاف بالبزر شاله

6 ṭāḥat jiwādi tālī al-xēl winḥās
wi-ʿayāl ṣaldam farrakūhin igbāli

6 طاحت جواده تالي الخيل وانحاس
وعيال صلدم فرّكوهن قباله

7 la bās ʿāwlād at-tarabīn la bās
raddū ū-jābū-ḥsēn baʿd irtiḥāli

7 لا باس عاولاد الترابين لا باس
ردّو وجابو حسين بعد ارتحاله

8 ū-gāsim ibin ʿaṭiyya bēnhum baĺ-gana gās
wal-xēl gaffat yōm šāfit ziwāli

8 وقاسم ابن عطيّة بينهم بالقنا قاس
والخيل قفّت يوم شافت زواله

9 jabr al-ʿaṭāwna gawī al-bās dawwās
jabr illī warrat̲ al-ḥarb ila ʿayāli

9 جبر العطاونة قويّ الباس دوّاس
جبر اللي ورّث الحرب الى عياله

10 yōm karr ʿaṫ-tarabīn itgūl jassās
gaffat ixyūlhum wil-kull mašdūḥ bāli

10 يوم كرّ عالترابين تقول جسّاس
قفّت خيولهم والكلّ مشدوح باله

11 ʿayāl at-tiyāha tanṭaḥ al-xēl furrās
willī wigaʿ bēnhum ẓāʿ ḥāli

11 عيال التياها تنطح الخيل فرّاس
واللي وقع بينهم ضاع حاله

12 wamma ʿazāzimtak kama gōm hirbās
ʿayāl islēmi al-kull ṭāyir jilāli

12 وامّا عزازمتك كما قوم هرباس
عيال سليمة الكلّ طاير جلاله

13 wamma jarawīn aĺ-gašal mā-lhum sās
la yiʿijbak bal-fās kit̲rit ifʿāli

13 وامّا جراوين القشل ما لهم ساس
لا يعجبك بالفاس كثرة افعاله

14 ʿalī ibin ʿaṭiyya ʿal frāš il-wizir dās
yinxaṭ ʿal al-ḥukkām waĺ-kull yisāli

14 علي ابن عطيّة ع فراش الوزر داس
ينخط عل الحكّام والكلّ يساله

5.12

Saʿīd of the Tiyāhā Gdērāt

A Poem of Relief after Good News

Another poem composed under the circumstances of the War of Zāriʿ is attributed to a poet named Saʿīd, who reportedly grew up among the Gdērāt division of the Tiyāhā. While in Transjordan he was told by someone coming from the Negev that the Tarābīn had routed the Tiyāhā and slaughtered their best men. In despair over the news of these sad events, Saʿīd decided to verify them himself. He mounted a camel and rode to a Tiyāhā encampment near Jabal Khwēlfa,[1] where he found a gathering of Tiyāhā warriors—some from the ʿAṭāwna section (lines 4–5), others from the Gdērāt (lines 6–8)—all of whom he had been told were killed. His relief impelled him to compose a poem of which we have the following fragment:

Yesterday night I slept not a wink;
My heart felt pricked as if cauterized with nails.[2] 1

He said: ʿAyāl Ṣaldam[3] are baring their heads,[4]
Rushing to battle like pregnant camels to a well. 2

But today, what joy is mine to find a full camp!
Tents pitched in circles at Khashm al-Jubēl.[5] 3

And so long as Ibn Ṭallāg is here we needn't fear,
Mounted and wielding his steel *jawhar* sword.[6] 4

Poem 5.12 was heard recited by two members of the Gdērāt division of the Tiyāhā tribe: ʿĪd Ḥimēdī al-Aʿsam, in Wādī Abū Tulūl, 1 October 1971; and ʿAmr Muḥammad aṣ-Ṣāniʿ, at Tell ʿArād, 20 February 1972. Discrepancies between the two texts were resolved according to the judgement of Mūsā al-ʿAṭāwna and Muṣliḥ Ibn ʿĀmr.

---

[1] Jabal Khwēlfa is approximately fifteen kilometres north of Beersheba.

[2] Cf. poems 4.4, n. 2; 6.12, n. 1.

[3] For ʿAyāl Ṣaldam, see poem 5.3, n. 4.

[4] In battle, bedouin bared their heads to hear well and not be seized by their head-cloths.

[5] One edge (*khashm*) of Jabal Khwēlfa.

[6] Sulēmān Ibn Ṭallāg was noted for his *jawhar*-type sword, made in Damascus (for *jawhar*, see Musil, *Arabia Petraea*, iii. 372).

And Frēḥ Ibn Ṭallāg raging on the battlefield,
Bent-beaked birds hovering above him.[7] 5

And Abū Rigayyig racing his horse to the weary;
Ibn ʿAyyāda is like a wall when they break in retreat. 6

And Abū Khubēza attacks, though the foe be many,
Butting roan mares that he meets straight on. 7

And Nabhān aṣ-Ṣāniʿ attacks, though the foe be many,
And they hear his halter of bells as he charges straight at them.[8] 8

1 al-beriḥa bil-lēl ma bitt ġāfī
aḥiss ib-galbī miṯil laḏʿ al-masamīr

1 البارحة بالليل ما بتّ غافي
احسّ بقلبي مثل لذع المسامير

2 gāl ʿayāl ṣaldam yṭawwaḥūn al-kifāfī
yirdū ʿal al-kōnāt wird al-maʿāšīr

2 قال عيال صلدم يطوّحون الكفافي
يردو عل الكونات ورد المعاشير

3 ya hanī min wāyig an-nizil ẓāfī
xašm al-jbēl imbanyīn ad-dawawīr

3 يا هني من وايق النزل ضافي
خشم الجبيل مبنّيين الدواوير

4 ma zāl ibin ṭallāg lak la tixāfī
ʿal aŕ-ramak yungul ḥadīd al-jawahīr

4 ما زال ابن طلّاق لك لا تخاف
عل الرمك ينقل حديد الجواهير

5 frēḥ abin ṭallāg fi-d-daww hāfī
ḥāmin ʿalē iṭyūr hidf aṣ-ṣanagīr

5 فريح ابن طلّاق في الدو هافي
حامن عليه طيور هدف الصناقير

6 amma-bū-rgayyig yihajri lit-tilāfī
ibin ʿayyāda sūr lin jan baʿaṯīr

6 امّا ابو رقيّق يهجّرد للتلاف
ابن عيّادة سور لن جن بعاثير

7 ū-abū xubēza hadd wil-jamīaʿ ẓāfī
yinaṭḥ aš-šagrā wujūh ad-daʿaṯīr

7 وابو خبيزة هدّ والجميع خاف
ينطّح الشقرا وجود الدعاثير

8 wi-nabhān aṣ-ṣāniʿ hadd wil-jamīaʿ ẓāfī
ū-brayšimin tismaḥḥa yōmin bitġīr

8 ونبهان الصانع هدّ والجميع خاف
وبريشم تسمعه يوم بتغير

7 Frēḥ Ibn Ṭallāg was allegedly so adept at killing that the scavenger birds used to follow his movements in battle, knowing that he would provide them with victims.

8 Such bells (*brayshim*) were worn to frighten the enemy.

5.13

Swēlim Abū ʿArgūb of the ʿAzāzma Farāḥīn

A Poem of Relief after Victory

A poet of the opposite camp, Swēlim Abū ʿArgūb of the ʿAzāzma, also composed a poem out of relief. Just when he feared that the Tarābīn camp might fall apart because some of the warriors were deserting it (lines 1–3), a battle took place at Wādī al-Mlēḥa in which his allies fought bravely and won (lines 5–8). He therefore concluded his poem with a boastful taunt to his enemy that Ḥammād aṣ-Ṣūfi will never let them cross Wādī Sharīʿa into his territory, as he had crossed into theirs.

If the enemies of the Tarābīn never crossed Wādī Sharīʿa, however, it was because the Turkish governor decided to halt the twelve-year hostilities that had unsettled the Negev. In 1887 Ra'ūf Pasha sent for twelve of the leading bedouin warriors and imprisoned them to compel the warring parties to reconcile their differences, which they promptly did. It was thus that the War of Zāriʿ al-Huzayyil came to an end.

1 Yesterday my heart pained me, and I was afraid
Of a war that has sated the sections of all tribes,

2 Which seems set on parting the dearest of friends;
So I ask your opinion, for in counsel there's truth.

3 I saw Nabhān of the Ḥanājra[1] aiming to betray us,
His warriors retreating before it was dawn,
Like wolves who attacked a flock but got no plunder.

4 But then I saw dust rise over al-Mlēḥa,[2]
Broad daylight—not a treacherous attack before dawn;[3]
You could hear the clang of swords, even of the hilts!

Fragments of Poem 5.13 were transcribed by al-ʿĀrif, *Ta'rīkh*, pp. 186–7, and heard recited by Muṣliḥ Ibn ʿĀmr, in Wādī Munbaṭaḥ, 15 August 1973, who also recommended revisions in al-ʿĀrif's text.

[1] The Ḥanājra, to the south and east of Gaza, had been traditional allies of the Tarābīn since the beginning of the nineteenth century (cf. poem 5.3, l. 6).

[2] Wādī Mlēḥa is a southern tributary of Wādī Ḥasī.

[3] Usually an attack is mounted just before dawn, according to the dictum 'Attack when the stars have set' (*hijūm wi-ghuyūb an-nujūm*). Although such an attack takes the sleeping victims by surprise, it ensures that women and children will be distinguished from men (i.e. warriors) and spared.

5 And then the Ḥanājra came to the fray,
Their rifles sounding like thunder in the air.

. . . .

6 And the sons of Ibn Ḥammād[4] riding thoroughbreds,
Each rider butting the mounts of the attackers,
Upright as a tent's central pole when you tighten the rope.

7 The offspring of Abū Ismāʿīn[5] joined us, as if racing to a well,
Each rider butting mounts that wished to get away;
Oh for a hundred Zaghāba-like[6] men such as they!

8 The sons of Abū ʿUwēlī,[7] wanting nothing but battle,
Left the enemy's wives on a cold winter's night
To complain of their calamity before those who might avenge it.

9 This is the Sharīʿa, but, like glorious girls,
You won't be able to taste of its goods
So long as aṣ-Ṣūfī fans the flames of war
And blights you as though you'd been plagued with locusts.

1 al-beriḥa galbī šakā lī ū-xāyif
min ḥarābtin kafat injūʿ aṣḥāba

1 البارحة قلبي شكا لي وخايف
من حرابةٍ كفت نجوع اصحابد

2 fi bālha tifrug ʿazīz al-walāyif
wēš rāykū waš-šor ʿārif maṣāba

2 في بالها تفرق عزيز الولايف
وايش رايكم والشور عارف مصابد

3 ašūf ibin nabhān al-ḥanjūrī
ʿal al-bōg nāwī
jamāʿta ʿagāb al-lēl yimšū ʿagbāwī
ḏībin ʿada ʿal-māl waxṭa maṣāba

3 اشوف ابن نبهان الحنجوري عل البوق ناوي
جماعتد عقاب الليل يمشو عقباوي
ذيبٍ عدا عالمال واخطا مصابد

4 wādī al-mlēḥa šuft ana al-ʿajj fōga
aẓ-ẓuhur mā hū ṭalʿat aš-šams bōga
jākū silīl as-sēf wa-gbal inṣāba

4 وادي المليحة شفت انا العجّ فوقد
الظهر ما هو طلعة الشمس بوقة
جاكم سليل السيف واقبل نصابد

[4] The 'sons of Ibn Ḥammād' are the Ḥamāmda section of the ʿAzāzma.
[5] The present writer was unable to establish the identity of the 'offspring of Abū Ismāʿīn'.
[6] See poem 5.1, n. 9.
[7] The ʿUwēliyyīn are a section of the Ghawālī division of the Tarābīn.

5 ḥanājra fōg al-marawīḥ lin jaw
bawarīdhum mitil ar-rawa'īd fi-l-jaww

. . . .

6 ūlād ibin ḥammād fōg as-salāyil
xayyālhum yanṭaḥ wujūh ad-dabāyil
hum 'amūd al-bēt yōm iktirāba

7 'ayāl abū-sma'īn jōna wirīdī
xayyālhum yanṭaḥ wujūh aš-šarīdī
'al-yōm linhum wagam miyya zaġāba

8 'ayāl abū 'uwēlī šifāhum 'al-kōn
xallū ḥarīm aẓ-ẓidd fī lēl kanūn
yiškin bilāhin min siddād aṭ-ṭlāba

9 hāḏī aš-šarī'a zē al-banāt al-'ujāba
yaḥram 'alēkū ma-tḏūgū waṭanha
ma dām aṣ-ṣūfī-ygawwim zaḥanha
miṯil al-jarād yilgī 'alēkū maṣāba

5 حناجرة فوق المراويح لن جو
بواريدهم مثل الرواعيد في الجوّ

— — — — — —

6 اولاد ابن حمّاد فوق السلايل
خيّالهم ينطح وجود الدبايل
هم عمود البيت يوم اكترابة

7 عيال ابو اسماعين جونا وريدِ
خيّالهم ينطح وجود الشريدِ
عاليوم لنّهم وقم ميّة زغابة

8 عيال ابو عويلي شفاهم عالكون
خلّو حريم الضدّ في ليل كانون
يشكن بلاهن من سدّاد الطلابة

9 هذي الشريعة زي البنات العجابة
يحرم عليكم ما تذوقو وطنها
ما دام الصوفي يقوّم زحنها
مثل الجراد يلقي عليكم مصابة

6
Episodes in Poetry II

Poems Sent from and to the Sinai Smuggler–Poet ʿAnēz abū Sālim during a Prison Term (1962–1970)

SMUGGLING IN SINAI

By the end of the nineteenth century intertribal wars in Sinai and the Negev had become a thing of the past, and even camel-raids between groups had ceased by 1925 as a result of effective governmental control in those areas.[1] The passing of organized large-scale hostilities, however, did not mean that courage was no longer highly valued in bedouin society; its manifestations were simply transferred to other areas. One such area was smuggling hashish and other contraband items, an activity that involved certain risks, such as crossing international borders illegally. As the source of these drugs was either Turkey, Syria, or Lebanon and their major market Egypt, the bedouin of Sinai and the Negev served as a vital link in their conveyance. There were four main routes prior to the Six Day War of 1967: some contraband was brought by sea to the Gaza Strip or the Mediterranean coast of Sinai and then smuggled into Egypt proper on camelback by the bedouin of northern Sinai; some came over the Syrian–Jordanian border and down to the southern West Bank, where it was picked up by bedouin of the northern Negev and smuggled into Gaza or northern Sinai, there to be given to local bedouin for transshipment; some was brought from Syria through Jordan to the border opposite the central Negev, where it was smuggled across the central Negev into central Sinai by the bedouin of these two areas; and some was brought down to southern Jordan where the bedouin of southern Sinai either took it by camel across the southern Negev or by small boats from the Jordanian port of Aqaba over to the eastern coasts of Sinai. Once taken across Sinai, the contraband entered Egypt proper either by camel over the Suez Canal or by small boats over the Gulf of Suez (see poem 2.5).

[1] Jarvis, p. 82.

The danger involved in smuggling was an aspect of the trade that appealed to its practitioners. They might be ambushed by an army patrol while crossing an international border or passing through the Negev, or they might encounter the Egyptian police while moving the contraband across Sinai by night. The night hours, the time of the smugglers' greatest activity, were traditionally feared by bedouin as an unwholesome time, when evil spirits lurk in the dark, not to mention the wild beasts of the desert. Thus, the excitement and daring of smuggling led bedouin in general to regard it as highly rewarding. This is reflected in the laudatory line of poetry 'Take note of those who've travelled far and near / Take note of those who smuggle without fear' (*ʿaynak ʿal-illī rawwaḥū kull dīra / ʿaynak ʿal illī mā yihāb il-mashāwīr*).[2]

No less compelling than the adventure, however, was the economic advantage of smuggling, which constituted an important part of a bedouin's income, providing in years of drought the difference between what he derived from his livestock or his primitive agriculture and what he needed to cover his expenses, however meagre; in making up the 'difference', smuggling afforded a bedouin the increment he had formerly derived from raiding. In Sinai prior to 1967, bedouin claim, there was hardly a family of which at least one member was not involved in smuggling, either in the actual conveyance, the leasing of camels, the storage of the contraband along its route to Egypt, investment in a smuggling venture, or serving as a lookout against police or army patrols.

Like the others, the small Ḥasāblah section of the vast Tarābīn confederation (37,500 in 1974)[3] also followed the contraband trade, exploiting the remoteness of their seventy-kilometre stretch of coast opposite Aqaba and their mountain-rimmed wadis that rise from the Gulf of Aqaba into the interior, just as they exploited the presence of their widespread fellow Tarābīn confederates throughout the peninsula. The structure of the Tarābīn, with the genealogical position of the Ḥasāblah, is shown in fig. 1.

One member of the Ḥasāblah in particular, ʿAnēz abū Sālim of the ʿArayḍa clan (therefore called al-ʿUrḍī), was reputedly one of the leading smugglers in all of Sinai, organizing several rings and operations in which many bedouin participated in one form or another for a livelihood. ʿAnēz had been experienced in the ways of the world since early youth and was generally looked up to for his wit, daring,

[2] Poem by Ḥamdān abū Salāma Ạbū Masʿūd of the Muzēna Darārma tribe; the complete poem is not presented in this book.

[3] According to censuses taken by Israel (as in Bailey and Peled, p. 116).

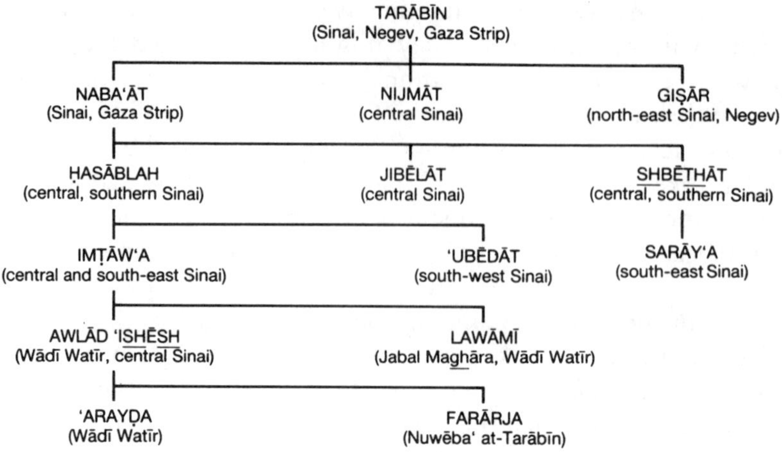

Fig. 1. The Ḥasāblah Section in the Tarābīn Tribal Genealogy

generosity, and success. He was equally admired as a skilful poet whose compositions could both sting and amuse. His fabled earnings from smuggling enabled him to buy a modest plantation in Egypt, to dig a motor-powered well and cultivate palms and gardens at the oasis called ʿAyn Umm Aḥmad in south-east Sinai, and at the same time to maintain three wives.

On 11 March 1962, however, ʿAnēz's good fortune seemed to come to an end. He was arrested by the Egyptian police on suspicion of smuggling and of spying for Israel, subsequently convicted for smuggling, and sentenced to fifteen years in prison. To the bedouin of almost all the tribes and regions of Sinai, ʿAnēz's internment was a source of great sorrow. The confinement of one who had conferred such benefit on so many bedouin was bound to arouse sympathy among a nomadic people accustomed to freedom of movement and wide horizons. Moreover, ʿAnēz's tragedy was intensified in that after his imprisonment two of his three wives ran off with other men—men, moreover, who were close kinsmen, thus compounding the shame. The deceit of fellow clansmen in this sensitive area was the ultimate insult to a man of power and social standing, whom fate had unexpectedly brought low.

ʿAnēz's tragedy came to the attention of his fellow bedouin in Sinai through the poems he composed in prison and sent to friends. ʿAnēz would recite his missive-poems to a literate prison-mate, who would write them down. He would then entrust the message to a visitor to be delivered to a merchant friend in the town of el-ʿArīsh, one Fu'ād Ṣāliḥ

Ismāʿīl, who traded by truck among the bedouin of south-east Sinai. Fu'ād, in turn, would read the poem to the bedouin recipient—two or three times if the recipient wished to memorize the poem. The recipient himself would later recite it to others who were eager to obtain news of ʿAnēz; and they, in turn, would also learn it and recite it to others. In this way ʿAnēz's poems enjoyed considerable currency throughout Sinai; the present writer heard his poems recited by members of eleven different tribal confederations, representing almost every major area of the peninsula.

ʿAnēz's poems not only aroused great interest and admiration among his listeners; they also elicited replies, either from the original recipients or from one of the bedouin along the line of transmission. Some were poems of encouragement, some of reprimand, others messages with specific themes—especially those about the infidelity of his wives. Bedouin who wished to send ʿAnēz a poem would have it transcribed by a passing merchant, who would then take care that it arrived at ʿAnēz's prison. On receiving the poem, ʿAnēz would ask a literate prison-mate to read it to him aloud.[4]

6.1

From ʿAnēz abu Sālim to Sulēmān Ibn Sarīaʿ

A Poem about Being Tortured

ʿAnēz was accused of spying and underwent rigid interrogation with torture at the Military Prison in ʿAbbāsa. At some time during the interrogation he composed a poem which he sent to Sulēmān Salīm Muḥaysin Ibn Sarīaʿ (see poem 1.5), the chief of the small Tarābīn Sarāyʿa tribe, that camped alongside the Tarābīn Ḥasāblah in south-east Sinai. Ibn Sarīaʿ was one of ʿAnēz's smuggling partners, as well as his father-in-law. ʿAnēz sent him this poem primarily to report on himself,

Poem 6.1 was heard recited by ʿAwda Ṣāliḥ Imbārak, of the Muzēna Shaẓāẓna tribe, in Wādī Gharandal, 11 November 1968; and Sālim Muḥammad Salāma Ibn ʿĀmr of the Tiyāhā Ṣgērāt tribe, at Guṣēma oasis, 20 September 1971. The poem was reviewed with its author in Wādī Murēkhi, 26 May 1984.

[4] Just before his release from prison in 1970 (after his term was commuted to eight years), ʿAnēz learnt the rudiments of reading and writing.

but also on the courageous and helpful testimony given on his behalf by the chief of the Tiyāhā Ṣgērāt tribe, ʿĪd Muṣliḥ Ḥamd Ibn ʿĀmr (see poem 2.7), and by a member of the Aḥaywāt Nijmāt tribe of central Sinai, Muḥammad Salāma ʿAliyyān al-Guṣayyir, a police officer at the small east-central Sinai post of Kuntilla.

The first three lines are the traditional description of the imaginary camel that is to bear the message, and instructions to the 'messenger' himself. Lines 4–6 are a subjective portrayal of the poet's feelings; lines 7–8 an expression of fatalism; line 9 a condemnation of those who informed against him to the police; lines 10–13 a description of ʿAnēz's sufferings from interrogation and torture; lines 14–15 praise for the testimony of Muḥammad Salāma ʿAliyyān; and the final line an intimation that Shēkh ʿĪd Ibn ʿĀmr should be rewarded for his testimony.

O Rider on a bay-hued and bolting camel:
An ostrich that's spotted men searching for prey;[1] 1

Put up a saddle and other fine gear,[2]
Bring plenty of food and water that's clear. 2

Then show her the desert route empty and wide,[3]
On which you'll meet doughty men worthy of pride; 3

And if they should ask, give them news as it's sought;
Say: Fellows, our friend's like a hawk that's been caught. 4

His heart is a well, drained dry by concern;
Though ninety cares leave, eighty more come in turn. 5

While other folks slumber, awake he remains,
And wearied, his liver from eating abstains.[4] 6

Though we hid among stars in the heavens so vast,
Fate's rope must ensnare us wherever it's cast;[5] 7

[1] Cf. poems 2.6, n.3; 2.10, l. 2.

[2] The other gear comprises colourful woven saddlebags, an embroidered girth strap, an embroidered bridle, and a leather leg-rest with thongs.

[3] In this poem the route chosen between the prison in the Egyptian Delta and the recipient of the poem in south-eastern Sinai was over the broad Tīh desert of central Sinai.

[4] Cf. poem 1.15, n. 1.

[5] Cf. poems 1.1, n. 6; 1.12, n. 2.

Though we all became birds flying freely about,
In time we would witness God's will carried out. 8

And those chiefs who impressed against me their seal:[6]
Chiefs of those you'd curse on your way, and with zeal,[7] 9

They couched me where men must be tough or undone;
I'm beat on the soles—twice mornings, once noon.[8] 10

Then at dusk if they[9] mount yet another attack,
And their whips make a smithy's clack clack on the rack, 11

Their *kurbāj*[10] raised high in its serpent-like shape:
From Allah's harsh judgment, O where's the escape? 12

Then your night's in cold water, naked and sick,
You sleep on your stomach, crouched like a tick.[11] 13

But Muḥammad, for whom the perfumed ladies long,[12]
Could not have been better, his statement was strong. 14

This Abū Salāma's a camel that leads,
And he'd trek under load to Baghdad were there need. 15

Ibn ʿĀmr, as well, may wear robes that will trail;[13]
This chieftain who knows how to free men from jail. 16

[6] Although those who helped the police develop a case against ʿAnēz were not chiefs, but lesser people reportedly envious of his success, he mocks them by calling them chiefs, thereby highlighting their vileness and pretensions. The allusion to seals, to complete the image, refers to signets that the government gave to the usually unlettered chiefs for signing documents.

[7] i.e. men who could only be chiefs of people so vile that one would curse them wherever one met them.

[8] The form of torture called *maṭrād*, reportedly used in Egyptian prisons during interrogations, is to hang the prisoner upside down and administer twenty-five lashes on the bottom of his feet.

[9] i.e. the jailers.

[10] A leather whip.

[11] Another form of torture reportedly used in Egyptian prisons is to have the tired prisoners spend the night on a cell floor covered with an inch of cold water. The prisoner thus cannot sleep lying flat and has to sit or crouch on his stomach, in which positions he will sleep fitfully because of the cold and his fear of breathing in water.

[12] Cf. poems 1.4 and 2.6 for the same compliment.

[13] Until the mid-twentieth century prominent chiefs wore cloaks and coats that were superfluously long as a sign of wealth. The allusion to this custom here is the poet's way of subtly expressing his regard for ʿĪd Ibn ʿĀmr by wishing him this sort of good fortune. Had ʿAnēz bluntly stated his intention that Ibn Sarīaʿ make him a present (e.g 'Ibn ʿĀmr is worthy of reward'), he would have felt that he had slighted him.

1 ya rākbin̲ min fōg ḥamra gaḥūmī
tigūl naʿāma wargabat zōl ṣayyād

يا راكبٍ من فوق حمرا قحومِ 1
تقول نعامة وارقبت زول صيّاد

2 urẓum ʿalēha gaššha wal-hidūmī
wimla-lha hal-girba ū-kat̲t̲ir ilha-z-zād

ارضم عليها قشّها والهدومِ 2
واملا لها هالقربة وكثّر لها الزاد

3 ū-laggī ṭarīg al-barr maʿ al-ixrūmī
wi-sbidd ma tadhaj ʿala darbak ajwād

ولقّي طريق البرّ مع الخرومِ 3
واسبدّ ما تدهج على دربك اجواد

4 win naššadūk ibd̲al ʿalēhum ʿilūmī
wi-gūl ya har-rabaʿ hū ṣagir winṣād

وان نشّدوك ابذل عليهم علومي 4
وقول يا هالربع هو صقر وانصاد

5 ū-lih galbin̲ mawrad al-himūmī
tisʿīn miṣdār ū-t̲amanīn mīrād

وله قلبٍ مورد الهمومِ 5
تسعين مصدار وثمانين ميراد

6 ū-lih ʿayn tishar wal-maxalīg nūmī
ū-lih kibid min kut̲r as-sihir ʿāfit az-zād

وله عين تسهر والمخاليق نومِ 6
وله كبد من كثر السهر عافت الزاد

7 ū-la ṣirt ma bēn as-sama wan-nujūmī
ḥabl al-manāya wēn ma-tigurṭa ṣād

ولو صرت ما بين السما والنجومِ 7
حبل المنايا وين ما تقرطه صاد

8 ū-la ṣirt ṭayr ṭūl ʿumrak tiḥūmī
wa-ḥkām rabbak ġēr tinfid̲ ib-mīʿād

ولو صرت طير طول عمرك تحومِ 8
واحكام ربّك غير تنفذ بميعاد

9 šēxānna-llī ḥaṭṭat ʿalēna-l-ixtūmī
mašāwix illī tilʿana winti gaṣṣād

شيخاتنا اللي حطّت علينا الختومِ 9
مشاوخ اللي تلعنه وانت قصّاد

10 win barrakūna fī manāx al-juzūmī
waṣ-ṣubḥ maṭradēn waẓ-ẓuhr maṭrād

وان بركّونا في مناخ الجزومِ 10
والصبح مطرادين والظهر مطراد

11 wal-ʿaṣr law šannū ʿalēna-l-hujūmī
tismaʿ ranīnithum tigūl ṭarg ḥaddād

والعصر لو شنّو علينا الهجومِ 11
تسمع رنينتهم تقول طرق حدّاد

12 win jāk bil-kurbāj zē al-hamm yūmī
min wēn lak min ḥikmit al̲l̲ā mašrād

وان جاك بالكرباج زي الهمّ يومي 12
من وين لك من حكمة اللّه مشراد

13 win nawwamū-l-wāḥad bilayya hidūmī
yurgud ʿala baṭna tigūl nōmt igrād

وان نوّمو الواحد بليّا هدومِ 13
يرقد على بطنه تقول نومة قراد

14 ū-mḥammad ʿašīr imʿaṭrāt al-hidūmī
wil-kilma-llī-yḥuṭṭhī ma-btinzād

14 ومحمّد عشير معطّرات الهدوم
والكلمة اللي يحطّها ما بتنزاد

15 abū salāma zē al-jamal bass yizūmī
zamlin tiwaddi-ḥmūlha law kān baġdād

15 ابو سلامة زي الجمل بسّ يزوم
زملٍ تودّي حمولها لو كان بغداد

16 waš-šēx ibin ʿāmr yijurr al-hidūmī
šēxin ʿala fakk al-maḥabīs maʿtād

16 والشيخ ابن عامر يجرّ الهدوم
شيخٍ على فكّ المحابيس معتاد

6.2

From ʿĪd Imfarrij to ʿAnēz abū Sālim

A Reprimand for Surrendering

On hearing the poem sent by ʿAnēz to Sulēman Ibn Sarīaʿ, one of the older members of the Tarābīn Ḥasāblah in south-east Sinai, ʿĪd Imfarrij Imsāʿid—himself a veteran smuggler and a third cousin of ʿAnēz's father—sent the following poem to rebuke ʿAnēz for not having made a greater effort to resist arrest, since he had apparently been given sufficient warning. The allusion to the ignominy of consulting wives (line 4) is a reference to the allegation believed by many of his tribesmen that ʿAnēz, in deferring to the request of his third wife Shēkhā (the daughter of Sulēmān Ibn Sarīaʿ) to be taken to Egypt for medical care before giving birth, precipitated his own arrest. According to these tribesmen, it was well-known that the chief of the police post (*ma'mūr al-qism*) of Nakhl, from whom a permit for leaving Sinai was required, was seeking an occasion to arrest ʿAnēz; and that ʿAnēz acted against his better judgement in wishing to please his wife. Some tribesmen also contend that Shēkhā's need for medical care was a ruse, and that she intended to leave ʿAnēz once she reached her father's plantation in Egypt.

In a personal communication ʿAnēz himself insisted that he had had no reason to suspect the police-chief, Rashād Hāshim, of ill will, and that he believed he was being summoned to meet him in order to receive the permit he had requested. If ʿAnēz is right, the story of

Poem 6.2 was heared recited by its author, in Wādī Shbēḥā, 25 September 1971.

Shēkhā's intrigue may have stemmed from a wish to absolve her greatly admired husband of poor judgement.

'Anēz, what brought you down from yonder hill
To yield to sons of beltless tarts by will?[1] 1

The old Martini gun why didn't you take,
And riding, side-sacks flying, make your break? 2

Why didn't you crouch inside some distant cave,
A shelter only animals would crave? 3

Consult a wife and hang your withers low;
For women are the source of every woe![2] 4

And since you've gone and implicated all,
None will come to see you lest they fall. 5

1 wēš jābak ya 'anēz min gafa-l-gōz min ġād
wi-zagaf nafsak lūlād al-muraffilātī

1 وايش جابك يا عنيز من قفا القوز من غاد
وزقف نفسك لاولاد المرفّلاتِ

2 lēš ya 'anēz ma lagaṭṭ bīdak 'adīla
ū-rikibit min fōg al-murafrifātī

2 ليش يا عنيز ما لقطت بايدك عديلة
وركب من فوق المرفرفاتِ

3 lēš ma ṭawayt rijlak fī 'ujra ṭawīla
guddāmak rabbat ūlād al-'aṣiyyātī

3 ليش ما طويت رجلك في عجرة طويلة
قدّامك ربّت اولاد العصيّاتِ

4 lakin man šāwaṙ an-niswān dangar ġurāba
wi-ṯra-n-niswān min jimī' al-masiyyātī

4 لكن من شاور النسوان دنقر غرابه
وثرا النسوان من جميع الماسيّاتِ

[1] A bedouin woman, outside her tent, must be belted (*mitḥazzma*). The bedouin view this custom as a religious injunction and a way to preserve sexual modesty among women, by indicating whether they are pregnant. They accordingly consider the custom of Egyptian peasant women to appear unbelted as both immodest and heretical. Hence, wishing to refer to the Egyptian policemen as 'bastards', the poet in the Arabic text calls them 'offspring of the unbelted women'.

[2] This common sentiment was heard by Doughty a century earlier in Arabia as 'All torments in men's lives be along of the cursed hareem!' (i. 218). A bedouin proverb states 'Women come from Satan's sling' (*an-nisā min miglā' iblīs*).

5 janaḥt rabʿak ū-kull al-gabīla
li-ḥadd jēb al-mirasilātī

5 جنحــت ربعـــك وكــلّ القبيلة
لحـــدّ جيـــب الــمــراسلاتِ

6.3

From ʿAnēz abū Sālim to Sulēmān Ibn Sarīaʿ

After Intercession Failed

After his arrest ʿAnēz received a message from a prominent member of the Aḥaywāt Ṣafāyḥa tribe, Salām a<u>sh</u>-<u>Sh</u>uhaybī, to the effect that he could secure his release if ʿAnēz composed a poem for a certain official. He was later told by the same Salām that his poem was not well-received. Angered and disappointed, ʿAnēz composed the present poem to express his contempt for people who foster false hopes in order to gain other people's confidence and gratitude. He sent the poem to Sulēmān Ibn Sarīaʿ, his friend and father-in-law. In contrast to the deceit and hollow boasts that had led him to believe he might obtain his freedom, the poet (lines 6–9) gives us a description of something he regards as the quintessence of truth and honesty: a smuggling mission by night through southern Israel, from Jordan to Sinai, over mountainous terrain.

O Writer,[1] rise and write some pleasant words,
Whose meaning's like a cure to one that's ill. 1

He says my poems of random scraps are made,
But I say they're a pure *salīmī* blade.[2] 2

Poem 6.3 was heard recited by ʿAwda Ṣāliḥ Imbārak of the Muzēna <u>Sh</u>aẕāẕna tribe, in Wādī <u>Gh</u>arandal, 11 November 1968. The poem was reviewed with its author at Nuwēbaʿ at-Tarābīn, 18 July 1985.

---

[1] i.e. the poet's prison cell-mate.

[2] A *salīmī* was a type of sword commonly found among the bedouin of Sinai and said to be named after the Ottoman Sultan Salīm I who conquered Egypt. It was a straight sword only bent at its head. <u>Sh</u>uqayr (p. 376) reported it to be the most inferior sword in Sinai. The author of the poem considered its steel the best. For more on swords, see poems 1.6, n. 12; 4.20D, n. 29.

I have some thoughts I'd say that make me sigh:
   Don't turn to men, but only God, for aid. 3

Our asking him who cannot help was vain,
   As vain as telling women of our pains;[3] 4

Though many take a boaster at his word,
   I hate the boasts that I have lately heard. 5

O give me camels, their chests dark from sweat,[4]
   With limestone mountains up and back beset;[5] 6

Reins tapping on the pommels is all you hear
   And camels, untrained, fill your heart with fear;[6] 7

The guide gets lost among the mountains high,[7]
   Night's dark, our water-skins are tinder dry; 8

But with the dawn we pass Mt Yaḥāmīm,[8]
   And on across the stony flats we stream.[9] 9

1 gūm ya xatībī iktib lina hat-tanaʿīm
   maʿnāthin miṯil ad-dawa ʿas-sagīmī

1 قوم يا خطيبي اكتب لنا هتناعيم
معناتهن مثل الدوا عالسقيمِ

2 intum tigūlūn gaṣīdī ramarīm
   wana gaṣīdī miṯil ṭurr as-salīmī

2 انتم تقولون قصيدي رماريم
وانا قصيدي مثل طرّ السليمي

3 lī kilimtēn agūlhin kull ma-zīm
   wi-bdāl ma-gṣud ʿabid l-agṣud karīmī

3 لي كلمتين اقولهن كلّ ما ازيم
وبدال ما اقصد عبد لاقصد كريمي

[3] i.e. psychological or social problems (cf. poem 3.9, n. 4).

[4] In the Arabic text, blackness comes from the allusion to black ostriches (*aẓālīm*).

[5] i.e. Jabal ash-Shuʿēra and Jabal Rās an-Nagb, respectively.

[6] Bedouin train smuggling-camels not to emit sounds when on the move. After the camel is one year old, they fasten a ring of wire, called a *zināg*, around its neck to prevent it from grumbling (*yiraghghī*) when frightened. This 'necklacing' (verb: *zannag*) is usually continued for a period of three months, and, if necessary, longer.

[7] The Arabic text also has the image of the camels slipping in the mire of the narrow, rocky wadis, apparently after winter rains.

[8] The Yaḥāmīm Hills are located twenty-two kilometres east-north-east of the Themed wells in east-central Sinai.

[9] The 'stoney flats' (*ḥamād samīm*) are sought out, because they leave no tracks.

4 šikwāk ʿallī ma-yfikk al-maẓalīm
zē-llī yiškī wajʿata ʿal-ḥarīmī

4 شكواك عاللي ما يفكّ المظاليم
زي اللي يشكي وجعته عالحريم

5 wal-fašr nuṣṣ an-nās tāxiḏi sīm
wana-kruh illī yifšurū min gadīmī

5 والفشر نصّ الناس تاخذه سيم
وانا اكره اللي يفشرو من قديم

6 arīd yōm iṣdūrhin zē al-aẓalīm
guddāmhin ḥazm ū-warāhin ḥazīmī

6 اريد يوم صدورهن زي الاظاليم
قدّامهن حزم ووراهن حزيم

7 tismaʿ šilīl irsūnhin fa-l-magadīm
wiydibb galb illī ḏalūla ġašīmī

7 تسمع شليل رسونهن في المقاديم
ويدبّ قلب اللي ذلوله غشيم

8 tāh ad-dalīl ū-waḥḥalan bēn al-laḥaṭīm
wal-lēl ẓulma waĺ-gurab zē al-hašīmī

8 تاد الدليل ووحّلن بين اللحاطيم
والليل ظلمة والقرب زي الهشيم

9 waṣbaḥ ʿalēna aṣ-ṣubḥ bēn al-yaḥamīm
windawr ib-hinna-l-ḥamād aṣ-ṣamīmī

9 واصبح علينا الصبح بين اليحاميم
وندوّر بهن الحماد الصميم

6.4

From ʿAṭiyya Miẓʿān ʿAwwād to ʿAnēz abū Sālim

A Poem of Sympathy

The ʿAlēgāt confederation that straddles an extensive coastline in south-west Sinai often participated in smuggling operations with the Tarābīn by conveying the contraband across the Gulf of Suez to Egypt by boat. To strengthen the bonds of co-operation between the two groups, marriages were arranged between their respective members. It was not surprising, therefore, that the news of ʿAnēz's internment was received with amazement and dismay by the ʿAlēgāt, to many of whom he was a generous friend. ʿAṭiyya Miẓʿān ʿAwwād of the ʿAlēgāt Zmēliyyīn tribe, on hearing of ʿAnēz's misfortune, immediately composed a poem

Poem 6.4 was heard recited by its author, at Abū Rudēs, 25 November 1971.

to express his sympathy and loyalty. After the introduction describing the 'camel' and its trappings, which was intended to embellish the simple message, ʿAṭiyya (lines 5–7) alludes to another current rumour about the circumstances of ʿAnēz's arrest—namely, that he had been betrayed by kinsmen. In the last line ʿAṭiyya intimates that he has not visited ʿAnēz so as to avoid any suspicion of complicity in his alleged crimes.

O Rider on a camel lank as a sailing skiff,[1]
His girth and his belly-strap tighten up stiff! 1

Some wire binds the saddle with mare-skin, in strands;
A braided lad's love wove the side-sacks by hand;[2] 2

And girls with bright hair-pins the leg-rest made[3]
From the skin of an ibex felled from high hills. 3

There are times when a man his own brother can't trust,
As Ḥassān al-Yamānī once cautioned.[4] 4

I've heard, O ʿAnēz, that your kin would impede
Your escape by their warning: From danger take heed! 5

[1] A reference to the *sanbūk* traditionally used for Red Sea coastal traffic (Philby, p. 225) and described by Burton. i. 188.

[2] Until the mid-twentieth century men braided their hair. For the fashion of four braids on each side, as in the text, see Burton, ii. 81, fig. 1.

[3] For the use of a leg-rest, see poem 2.12, n. 11.

[4] Ḥassān al-Yamānī (the Yemenite) refers to the fifth-century legendary ruler of Himyarite Yemen, Ḥassān ibn Tubbaʿ, who was murdered by his brother ʿAmr (see Nicholson, p. 25). According to legend, Ḥassān, before his death, made some dire predictions about the future, based on the perfidy of his own times. One of them was:

yijīkū wagit yā sitār minnih
al-akhū mā yāmin li-khāh
yijīkū wagit yā sitār minnih
al-ʿayla tiḥālif min taḥit al-ghaṭā

A time will come, O God give us cover,
When one brother will not trust another;
A time will come, O God give us cover,
When siblings take oath before sleeping together.

(Oral communication from Salīm ʿĪd Sālim Ibn Jāzī of the Tarābīn Ḥasāblah, at ʿAyn al-Furṭāga, 4 October 1984.)

But then you were trapped through their craft and deceit,
Like they'd dash an old camel to slaughter for meat.[5] 6

Were it not for the jaws our loose tongues would just spill,
For few are the folk who can keep their tongues still.[6] 7

I've waited, ʿAnēz, for the air is unclear;
But surely I'll come when there's no cause for fear. 8

1 ya rākb-illī baṭna tigūl sanbūk
ugšaṭ ʿalē al-ḥagab wal-biṭānī

1 يا راكب اللي بطند تقول سنبوك
اقشط عليد الحقب والبطانِ

2 ġabīṭa imʿaṭṭa bi-julūd niyāg wi-sulūk
ū-xurja sawāt šōg marxi-ṯ-ṯimānī

2 غبيطه معطّى بجلود نياق وسلوك
وخرجه سواة شوق مرخي الثماني

3 wi-dwayraʿa sawāt illī fī janābhin šōk
ū-min jild illī ṭāḥ rūs al-ganānī

3 ودويرعه سواة اللي في جنابهن شوك
ومن جلد اللي طاح رؤوس القنانِ

4 ū-fī wagitna ya ʿanēz ma-yʿizzak axūk
zē wagtin yigūla ḥassān al-yimānī

4 وفي وقتنا يا عنيز ما يعزّك اخوك
زي وقتٍ يقوله حسّان اليماني

5 ʿalimt ya ʿanēz rabʿak ibyanḥūk
ʿan maši-l-xaṭa wal-muxṭarānī

5 علمت يا عنيز ربعك بينحوك
عن مشي الخطا والمخطرانِ

6 wi-dārū lak bil-wils wi-ramūk
ramiyt illī šābik an-nāb ṯānī

6 ودارو لك بالولس ورموك
رمية اللي شابك الناب ثاني

7 al-lisān habir ū-ḥakmāta ḥanūk
ū-nuṣṣ an-nišāma ma yiṣīnin lisānī

7 اللسان هبر وحاكماته حنوك
ونصّ النشامة ما يصينٍ لسانه

8 waḷḷā ya ʿanēz law-la-l-jaww markūk
l-ajīk fī saʿt is-saʿa wal-iṭminānī

8 واللّه يا عنيز لولا الجوّ مركوك
لاجيك في ساعة السعة والاطمنانِ

[5] In the Arabic text, an old camel is referred to as 'having got his second set of canine teeth'; i.e. it is in its eighth year (cf. poem 3.8, n. 2).

[6] The phrase 'one doesn't guard his tongue' (*mā yiṣīn lisānah*) comes from the proverb 'Your tongue's like your steed. If you guard it, it guards you; if you abuse it, it abuses you' (*lisānak ḥiṣānak. in ṣuntah ṣānak; in huntah hānak*).

6.5

From ʿAnēz abū Sālim to Jumʿa al-Farārja

An Expression of Despair

Like other bedouin prisoners before him who composed anguished poems on prison life[1] and sent them to friends at home, ʿAnēz sent such poems to several friends back in Sinai. One was Jumʿa ʿĪd Dakhīlallāh of the Farārja section of the Tarābīn Ḥasāblah, a fisherman in the Gulf of Aqaba who had been bringing contraband over to Sinai from Aqaba in his boat (see poems 2.4 and 2.5): hence, the gibing allusions to motor skiffs and the wadis Jumʿa frequented, north of Nuwēbaʿ. In this poem ʿAnēz concludes from his own fall from power that fate has turned the world upside-down, raising the unworthy to prominence and vice versa. Lines 3b, 4, 9, and 10 refer to the inevitability of cruel fate, while lines 5–8 deride the ascent of the vile.

O Rider who's riding a Masāʿīd mare,[2]
Much faster than motor skiffs, double the power,[3] 1

At the end of the night seek out Jumʿa ibn ʿĪd,
'Tween Ḥuwayyiṭ, Imḥāshāt, and Bīr aṣ-Ṣwēr. 2

When you meet him fishing the edge of the sea,[4]
Tell him that fortune has thrown us down, 3

As fortune has often jailed men of good name,[5]
Though tending one's interests is hardly a shame.[6] 4

Poem 6.5 was heard, in 1971, from a recording made by its author at Birshāg, Egypt.

[1] These precedents will be discussed in Chapter 8.

[2] The small Masāʿīd confederation, partly in north-west Sinai and partly in north-west Arabia, are know to raise fine camels (cf. poem 2.7, n. 5).

[3] In the Arabic text: a motor boat put into double gear.

[4] The reference is to a method of fishing called 'with an *ishāʿa*-net'—a small circular net lined with lead weights (originally stones) that is carried on one shoulder as the fisherman walks along the shore looking for fish feeding on the nearby coral reefs. He then flings (*yishayyiʿ*) the net (lit. 'that which is flung' (*ishāʿa*)) over the fish, closing them in.

[5] Hence the proverb 'Prison is for men' (*al-ḥabs li-rijāl*) (cf. poem 6.13, l. 17).

[6] Bedouin look upon smuggling as a legitimate occupation, it being one of the few sources of income that the desert affords. Therefore, taking advantage of it is neither shameful nor insulting; nor is being imprisoned for it a disgrace.

These are times when a child may be named to be chief,[7]
While those who should normally lead are now lost; 5

These are times when masters say 'Sir' to their slaves,
When, wells being dry, folks to mud-puddles go;[8] 6

Nay, they've hewn for them troughs, all white-washed and bright,
By which many have watered and yet others alight.[9] 7

When it's safe you can teach even tykes to be game,
Like we learn how to hunt on beasts that are lame.[10] 8

As the world endures, and the sky moves by plan,[11]
So the rope of fate snares you wherever it can;[12] 9

And I have seen purebreds that once ran without binds,
Later couched, with loads on their backs and their hinds.[13] 10

1 ya rākb-illī min niyāg al-masa'īd
asbag min illī sakkabat bad-dabal-gīr

1 يا راكب اللي من نياق المساعيد
اسبق مــن اللــي سكّــبت بالدبل جير

[7] 'Child' is used in the sense of someone lacking mature wisdom and experience. This is a reference to people—obviously not the 'smuggling crowd'—to whom the Egyptian government had granted authority. The reference to 'a child' in this connection reflects the bedouin proverb 'A child stays a child though he rule a town' (*al-walad walad, wi-law ḥakam balad*).

[8] The poet compares himself and other imprisoned smugglers to 'wells of living waters', i.e. underground sources that never go dry; but likens those who have replaced them as important people in the tribe to sand-pools (*thamīla*, pl. *thamāyil*) that trap only a limited amount of rainwater and dry up before summer (cf. poems 2.7, n. 7; 2.10, l. 19).

[9] i.e. many people come to the new leaders seeking benefit.

[10] One bedouin method of teaching children to hunt is to wound an animal or to find an injured animal and have them hunt it down.

[11] In the Arabic text, 'the heavenly order [*falak*] has its fixed times'. The order of celestial bodies, each moving in its own orbit, is understood in Islam to be a result of God's action and a manifestation of his power. In the Qur'ān (21. 33) we have 'and He it is that created night and day, and the sun and the moon—each to glide in its own orbit' (. . . *kullun fī falakin yasbaḥūna*). Again (36. 39) 'it is not fit that the sun overtake the moon, or night outstrip day—for each glides in its own orbit'. In addition, the bedouin adhere to snatches of what they call 'the science of the heavenly order' (*'ilm al-falak*), according to which acts of fate (*magādīr*) are 'permitted by the heavenly order' (*bi-idhn al-falak*). Hence, while God is responsible for the big issues, like birth, death, and sustenance, the *falak* 'controls one's coming and going' (*yammshīk ū-yijībak*).

[12] For more on fate, see poems 1.1, n. 6; 1.12; 1.14; 6.1.

[13] The poet here compares himself to a free, pure-bred camel that has been broken and reduced to a life incommensurate with its nature.

2 tuġša ʿagāb al-lēl jumʿa ibn ʿīd
bēn al-iḥwayyiṭ wal-imḥašāt waṣ-ṣwēr

2 تغشى عقاب الليل جمعة ابن عيد
بين الحويّط والمحاشات والصوير

3 tilgā ʿala šaṭṭ al-baḥar yuṭrud aṣ-ṣayd
witgūl li ḥina ramanna-l-magadīr

3 تلقاه على شطّ البحر يطرد الصيد
وتقول له حنا رمنّا المقادير

4 ū-yāma ramat ġubr al-liyālī ṣanadīd
wal-maṣlaḥa mī hī iḥkāyit maʿayīr

4 وياما رمت غبر الليالي صناديد
والمصلحة ما هي حكاية معايير

5 ū-šāxat ʿala rūs al-badāwa walalīd
ū-rāḥat ʿal illī kān hum al-bawaṭīr

5 وشاخت على رؤوس البداوة ولاليد
وراحت عل اللي كان هم البواطير

6 wis-sīd sār yigūl lil-ʿabid ya sīd
wal-bīr miẓmī waṯ-ṯamīla ġadat bīr

6 والسيد صار يقول للعبد يا سيد
والبير مظمئ والثميلة غدت بير

7 ū-ṣāran ilha ḥīẓān abyaẓ min aš-šīd
wilha mawarīd wilha maṣadīr

7 وصارن لها حيضان ابيض من الشيد
ولها مواريد ولها مصادير

8 ū-darb al-amāna tiʿalm al-hayf il-fēd
ū-biyjasrak ʿaṣ-ṣayd ṭard al-makasīr

8 ودرب الامانة تعلّم الهايف الفيد
وبيجسّرك عالصيد طرد المكاسير

9 wal-kōn ʿāmir walʻ-falak lah mawaʿīd
wa-ḥabl al-manāya wēn ma dirti hēdīr

9 والكون عامر والفلك له مواعيد
وحبل المنايا وين ما درته يدير

10 ū-liḥigit ʿal illī kān ma yiḥmilin al-gēd
yibarkin bēn al-aḥmūl al-ganaṭīr

10 ولحقت عل اللي كان ما يحملن القيد
يبرّكن بين الحمول القناطير

6.6

From Jumʿa al-Farārja to ʿAnēz abū Sālim

A Warning about his Wives

Jumʿa ʿĪd Dakhīlallāh's reply to ʿAnēz opened a new episode in the imprisoned smuggler–poet's life. In keeping with his means ʿAnēz had three wives when he entered prison: Ṣubḥiyya, the daughter of Faraj Saʿīd of the Farārja section of the Ḥasāblah; his cousin Khaḍrā, the daughter of Ḍayfallāh Imfarrij Imsāʿid, a kinsman from ʿAnēz's own blood-revenge group—his *khamsa*; and Shēkhā, the daughter of his friend and colleague, Sulēmān Salīm Muḥaysin Ibn Sarīaʿ. Once he was in prison, however, his wives proved to be less than devoted. It was said that Shēkhā wished to be divorced, but was dissuaded by her father; however Ṣubḥiyya and Khaḍrā allowed themselves to be seduced by two of their husband's kinsmen: the former by a fellow tribesman of Sulēmān Ibn Sarīaʿ, ʿĀyd ʿAbēd; the latter by ʿAnez's paternal first cousin, Amīra ʿAbdallāh Swēlim.

This information was delicately conveyed to ʿAnēz in the present poem. The images (lines 6–7) to denote infidelity are those of sown fields and houses being destroyed, implying that the manifestation of ʿAnēz's honour and power—his wives' inviolability in his absence—had been effaced. A man's honour is what gives him security, relieving him of the need to be constantly on guard, as the bedouin proverb says 'If a man's back won't protect him, neither will his face' (*in mā ḥamāh gafāh, mā ḥamāh wijhah*). Since the exigencies of bedouin life often require women to be left on their own, the sanctity of their persons is a reflection of the social status and power of their husbands. As previously explained (poem 1.1, n. 8), a man's honour is thus likened to a tent in that it 'shelters' him from any unseemly exposure—in particular, of weakness; and, since his wife's decent behaviour is a main element in his honour, she is depicted as 'holding the tent up'. A popular bedouin proverb says 'The wife is a tent's main pole' (*ʿammār al-bēt al-marā*); and, conversely, a common curse—'May your tent be destroyed!' (*yikhrab bētak!*)—means 'May your women be disgraced!'

My heart from worries and care cannot keep:
Last night I missed the sweet savour of sleep; 1

Poem 6.6 was heard recited by its author, at Nuwēbaʿ at-Tarābīn, 30 April 1972.

My heart departed on hearing they're caught—
Abū Sālim! Ḥājj Jāzī![1] Two of my friends . . . ! 2

Since guile among rulers usurped honour's place,
You're seen as vile, your clan's lost its face: 3

Even an ass-herder met on the track,
When greeted by us will not answer back. 4

O ʿAnēz, drop those whose first love is clothes.
Heed me, ʿAnēz, as I tell you your woes: 5

Your spring's a pasture for oxen become—
They ruin what's sown free to go and to come; 6

These unscrupulous scum have demolished your home—
It's a motley mass, like the offspring of Rome.[2] 7

How vile this devilish breed that would cheat,
Prowling with long beards like ibex in heat.[3] 8

1 ya galb yillī kull hammak hawajīs
wal-beriḥa ma d̲ugit lid̲d̲ al-manāmī

1 يا قلب يللي كـلّ همّـك هواجيس
والبارحة مـا ذقت لـذّ المنامِ

2 galbī ġadā bī yōm gālū maḥabīs
al-ḥājj jāzī wabū sālim izlāmī

2 قلبـي غـدا بـي يوم قالو محابيس
الحـاجّ جـازي وابـو سالـم زلامي

3 min yōm sāyir ḥukm mū hū nawamīs
tabga d̲ilīl ū-mā li-zilmak magāmī

3 من يوم صاير حكم ما هو نواميس
تبقـى ذليل ومـا لزلمـك مقامِ

[1] 'Ḥājj Jāzī' is Jāzī Imsallam Ḥamd al-ʿArādī, a prominent member of the Tarābīn Ḥasāblah in the Jabal Rāḥa area of south-west Sinai and a smuggling partner of ʿAnēz ('Abū Sālim'). He was arrested one year after ʿAnēz, in 1963, and served a six-year detention term.

[2] Bedouin view the rest of the world as a vaguely defined conglomeration of peoples, unlike themselves with their pure lineage. This is especially true of the European or Christian world, referred to here as 'the offspring of Rome'. The present image for destroyed honour—substituting a stone house for a tent (ʿAnēz actually had such a house at the spring of ʿAyn Umm Aḥmad)—stresses the severity of the blow to ʿAnēz's honour.

[3] According to the bedouin, the beard of a male ibex grows when he ruts (in early February).

4 ar-rā'ī illī kān lil-'ēr gādūs
in gult gawwak ma-yrudd is-salāmī

4 الراعي اللي كان للعير قادوس
ان قلت قوّك ما يردّ السلامِ

5 ya 'anēz fuẓẓ illī hawāhin malabīs
win ṭa'atnī ya 'anēz adhan kalāmī

5 يا عنيز فضّ اللي هواهن ملابيس
وان طعتني يا عنيز اذهن كلامي

6 al-'ayn ṣārat mirta'a lil-jawamīs
tasraḥ ū-tiẓwī wil-mazāri' 'adāmī

6 العين صارت مرتعة للجواميس
تسرح وتضوي والمزارع عدامِ

7 'ugb al-'amār xarabūha-ṭ-ṭawasīs
ū-ṣārat xilēṭa zē 'iyāl ar-ruwāmī

7 عقب العمار خربوها الطواسيس
وصارت خليطة زي عيال الروامِ

8 azwal 'alayy al-gadr ū-xulfit iblīs
digna ṭawīli zē-il-badan fi-l-ḥiyāmī

8 ازول عليّ القذر وخلفة ابليس
دقند طويلة زي البدن في الحيامِ

6.7

From 'Anēz abū Sālim to Sulēmān Ibn Sarīa'

Seeking News of his Wives

When he received the versified message from Jum'a 'Īd Dakhīlallāh, 'Anēz was in solitary confinement (*az-zinzāna*). While meditating on a reply and a request for further information, he was reminded by the appearance one day of a bird on his high cell-window of a genre of poem often composed in prison, in which the poet addresses a bird, questioning it about news from the outside. He thus composed and sent the poem to Sulēmān Ibn Sarīa', whom he duly praises (lines 1–6) and asks for information about his wives ('she-camels': line 7)—especially Ibn Sarīa''s daughter Shēkhā (lines 8–10). The last three lines allude to the sufferings of his mother and sister, with the inference that Ibn Sarīa' should care for them.

Poem 6.7 was heard recited by 'Awda Ṣāliḥ Imbārak of the Muzēna Shaẓāẓna tribe, in Wādī Gharandal, 11 November 1968; and by Ṣabāḥ Ṣāliḥ al-Ghānim of the 'Agēlī tribe, at Rab'a oasis, 24 October 1970. The poem was reviewed with its author, in Wādī Murēkhī, 26 May 1984.

O Bird, you're unbearable since your long flight;
How horrid this habit of croaking all night. 1

O Bird, I am longing; yes, even for word;
My heart, you're aware, is in turmoil, O Bird! 2

And say, while away, did you visit Birshāg,[1]
Or come to Ẓalal or the Hills of Zilāg;[2] 3

And alight at a camp where the food's steeped in ghee,[3]
A camp travellers seek, where the wronged always flee;[4] 4

Where coffee-pots shine in the fire, copper red,
Pouring brown like the blood of a camel just bled?[5] 5

Did you stop off to drink at our hill-rimmed spring,[6]
The realm of my friend for whom slim lasses long;[7] 6

And flying about did you spy tracks below,
Of mares in Liṯḥī or where four wadis flow?[8] 7

I've a special young mare with the herd gleaming white;
I'd to leave her with calf, in spite of myself, 8

That night, when the grief and the pain tore my heart:
God spare us from nights on which loved ones must part. 9

[1] Birshāg is a village in the 'Abbāsa subdistrict of Sharqiyya province of Egypt, where 'Anēz owned a plantation.

[2] Jabal Ẓalal and Wādī Zalaga are about 100 kilometres south-west of Eilat, an area where the Tarābīn Ḥasāblah and Saray'a often graze their livestock during the winter.

[3] Cf. poems 1.10, n. 8; 2.12, l. 13.

[4] In the Arabic text 'where they hearten the needy'; to encourage and reassure people in need of help is one of the highest values in bedouin society (cf. poems 1.10, 3.4, 3.7).

[5] The blood referred to in the Arabic text is of the *filāg*: an overworked and ill camel. To relieve a camel, a bedouin will bleed it by snapping a capillary (*rīsh*) in its nose with his finger. The blood then has a dark-red, almost brownish hue. (Cf. poem 3.2, l. 5.)

[6] The spring referred to is 'Ayn Umm Aḥmad in south-east Sinai where 'Anēz owned date-palms and a small plantation.

[7] For more such complimentary allusions, see poems 1.4, 2.6, and 6.1; the reference here is to Ibn Sarīa'.

[8] Wādī Liṯḥī is in south-east Sinai, north of 'Ayn al-Furṭāga. The 'junction' of the four wadis (*al-malāgī*) drains the Ḥaysī, Shbēḥa, Ṣawwāna, and Khurayyiṭ wadis at Bīr aṣ-Ṣawra.

She's firm in the foreleg and thin in the shank;
Her tears must have filled a bottomless well.[9] 10

And mother plies every new driver for word,[10]
Even strangers the asking of whom is absurd. 11

My sister once laughing stopped laughing to shout,
Shedding tears so profuse her eyes emptied out. 12

Finding tracks of the camel corps[11] cutting the plain,
Her heart blazed afire and still will not wane. 13

1 ya ṭayr min ʿugb itiġiybak mint minṭāg
ma šēn ṭabʿak ṭūl lēlak itigāgī

2 ya ṭayr ana mištāg lil-ʿilm mištāg
galb al-xaṭa ya ṭayr zē mint hāgī

3 ya ṭayr ma ṭabbayt li-yamm biršāg
walla-ẓ-ẓalal jīta wi-rūs az-zilāgī

4 ū-ẓift al-farīg illī biha as-samin dafāg
ʿizz aṭ-ṭanīb ū-minwatin min yilāgī

5 hayl id-dilāl aš-šugr ma ṣādha ḥirāg
yisgūk minhī lōn damm al-filāgī

6 walla waradt al-ʿayn ū-hadīk al-iṭbāg
madāj xallī ṣadīg ad-digāgī

7 ya ṭayr ma gaṣṣēt lī jurtin niyāg
fi-l-liṭḥ walla-mgōṭrāt il-malāgī

1 يا طير من عقب تغيّبك ما انت منطاق
ما شين طبعك طول ليلك تقاقي

2 يا طير انا مشتاق للعلم مشتاق
قلب الخطا يا طير زي ماانت هاقي

3 يا طير ما طبّيت ليمّ برشاق
ولّا الظلل جيتد ورؤوس الزلاقِ

4 وضفت الفريق اللي بها السمن دفاق
عزّ الطنيب ومنوةٍ من يلاقي

5 هيل الدلال الشقر ما صادها حراق
يسقوك منها لون دم الفلاقِ

6 ولّا وردت العين وهذيك الطباق
مداج خلّي صديق الدقاقِ

7 يا طير ما قصّيت لي جرّةٍ نياق
في اللطح ولّا مقوطرات الملاقي

[9] Lit. 'Her tears flowed so, the drawers of water couldn't exhaust them.'

[10] A reference to itinerant merchants from el-ʿArīsh, who brought merchandise to the bedouin of south-east Sinai by truck, passing through Wādī Watīr, where the poet's tribe lived.

[11] The Egyptian desert police, who arrested ʿAnēz.

8 lī bakratin šagra maʿ ad-dōd milhāg
ġaṣbin ʿalayya xallētha wi-hiya milāgī

لي بكرةٍ شقرا مع الذود ملهاق 8
غصبٍ عليّ خلّيتها وهي ملاقي

9 fi-l-lēla illī šarrha ma biyinṭāg
wālla la yibla bi-lēl al-firāgī

في الليلة اللي شرّها ما بينطاق 9
واللّه لا يبلى بليل الفراق

10 imdamlaj ad-durʿān ū-rgayyig as-sāg
dimʿa badār ma yinzaḥanni-s-sawāgī

مدملج الذرعان ورقيّق الساق 10
دمعه بذار ما ينزحنّه السواقي

11 wammi-tiḥarra-l-ʿilm maʿ kull sawwāg
wi-tinašd-illī manšida ma yiṭāgī

وامّي تحرّى العلم مع كلّ سوّاق 11
وتنشّد اللي منشده ما يطاق

12 wuxtī warāy itbadl aẓ-ẓaḥk bi-ziʿāg
wi-dmūaḥḥa ma ẓallat ilhin bawāgī

واختي وراي تبدّل الضحك بزعاق 12
ودموعها ما ظلّت لهن بواقي

13 in ligyit aṯārhin gāṭiʿ ar-rawẓ mišlāg
ū-ya galbha maḥrag ū-zāda ḥirāgī

ان لقيت اثارهن قاطع الروض مشلاق 13
ويا قلبها محرق وزاده حراق

6.8

From Jumʿa al-Farārja to ʿAnēz abū Sālim

On the Disloyalty of ʿAnēz's Wife, Khaḍrā

After hearing ʿAnēz's poem from Sulēmān Ibn Sarīaʿ, Jumʿa ʿĪd Dakhīlallāh decided to detail the trysts that ʿAnēz's cousin, Amīra ʿAbdallāh Swēlim, was having with ʿAnēz's wife, Khaḍrā, bringing her presents in the remote Wādī Samrā where she was pasturing her flock. After deriding Amīra as a fox with a fox's paltry and cowardly characteristics (line 5), the poem becomes lyrical in an effort to comfort ʿAnēz in his distress.

He said: What sort of news have you heard, O Lad?
I said: I'll drink, then you'll hear all the news that I've had. 1

Poem 6.8 was heard recited by its author, at el-ʿArīsh, 20 October 1970.

I chanced in the Ḥamrā[1] on tracks made by shoes:
One laden with dresses and jewels had passed through, 2

On the way to his in-law who camps near the bend,
Alone in the Samrā—toward her he would wend. 3

None but a lecher his in-law would woo,
Bringing her dresses and other things too. 4

But a fox, when he weds, serves but jackal and hare,
And the tiniest stir makes him hide in his lair. 5

Last night, O ʿAnēz, when alone with your bane,
I'd have come to protect you from peril and pain. 6

Be strong through the torment of night after night,
Be strong though the torment of night shows its claws. 7

O Rider of one running swift on a plain:
On a broad, bare plain a wolf's howl made him start. 8

Tell ʿAnēz that with relish they eat what he's sown:
A harvest of darkened-eyed girls he'd once known. 9

1 wi-ygūl ʿilūmak kayf ya haṣ-ṣbāwī
gult limm-atagahwa tāxud̠ al-ʿilm tirtīb

2 lagēt fi-l-ḥamrā jurrit iḥd̠āwī
yadbaḥ dabīḥa baĺ-xaraz waĺ-jalalīb

3 waddi ḥimāti nāzla fi-l-ḥināwī
darba ʿala-s-samrā ṣawb al-maʿazīb

4 ma yāxid̠ il-ḥimyāt ġēr az-zināwī
wi-yjīb min zēn al-malabīs wi-yjīb

1 يقـول علومك كـيف يـا هالصباوي
قلت لمّـا اتقهوى تاخذ العلم ترتيب

2 لاقيت فـي الحمـرا جـرّة حذاوي
يدبـح دبيحـة بالخـرز والجلاليب

3 ودّه حمـاته نـازلة فـي الحناوي
دربه على السمرا صوب المعازيب

4 مـا ياخذ الحميات غيـر الزناوي
ويجيب من زين الملابيس ويجيب

[1] The wadis Ḥamrā and Samrā mentioned in the text flow into the upper reaches of Wādī Watīr.

5 lakin ʿirs al-iḥṣēnī ḏabiḥ arnab ū-wāwī
win ḥass ḥirki yindirig fa-ḏ-daġalīb

5 لاكن عرس الحصيني ذبح ارنب وواوي
وان حسّ حركة يندرق في الدغاليب

6 al-beriḥa ya ʿanēz winta xalāwi
wanḥāk ʿan darb al-xaṭar wal-maṣaʿīb

6 البارحة يا عنيز وانت خلاوي
وانحاك عن درب الخطر والمصاعيب

7 wuṣbur ʿala ġulb il-liyālī liyālī
wuṣbur ʿala ġulb il-liyālī maxalīb

7 واصبر على غلب الليالي ليالي
واصبر على غلب الليالي مخاليب

8 ya rākb-illī šarrada fī siḥāwī
fī gāʿ xālī ū-jaffala ʿawiyt aḏ-ḏīb

8 يا راكب اللي شرّدد في سحاوي
في قاع خالي وجفّلد عوية الذيب

9 zarʿak xaṣāb ū-māklīni šihāwī
sumur al-ʿiyūn imkaḥḥalāt al-ḥawajīb

9 زرعك خصاب وماكليند شهاوي
سمر العيون مكحّلات الحواجيب

6.9

From ʿAnēz abū Sālim to his wife, Khaḍra

A Poem of Reprimand

The unhappy news he received from Jumʿa about his wife Khaḍrā angered ʿAnēz, increasing his resentment that months had passed since his arrest without a visit from any of his kinsmen or wives, all of whom feared to appear lest they be implicated in his accusation of spying; they even stayed away from his trial demonstrating little concern for his welfare. He addressed this poem to Khaḍrā.

O Rider of one who's white-haired on her back,
White-haired having long been laden with pack;[1] 1

Poem 6.9 was heard recited by ʿAwda Ṣāliḥ Imbārak of the Muzēna Shaẕāẕna tribe, in Wādī Gharandal, 11 November 1968. The poem was reviewed with its author, in Wādī Murēkhī 26 May, 1984.

[1] Cf. poems 1.1, n. 9; 4.20B, l. 2.

Rush her these words ere I hear more of her,[2]
Quick: as though the whirr of bright bullets were heard. 2

They tell me it seems that she's losing her mind,
That she's having trysts of a secretive kind. 3

In my absence my name only God can maintain:
May Allah not sully my name with a stain.[3] 4

There are camels, though galled, who bear loads but don't cry;
Others shy, though the fat in their humps is stacked high.[4] 5

And my kin missed my trial; to come none would dare;
They ran off, tails high, like a calf-bearing mare.[5] 6

My eyes from much watching are losing their sight;
I look out for cars by day and by night. 7

And my wives, may God their luck dispel,
Don't bring me so much as pitch from a well.[6] 8

1 ya rākb-illī šāyiba min ẓaharha
min kuṯr ma yirmū ʿalēha-l-mawaṯīr

2 tiwaddī l-xabr guddām yōṣil xabarha
win ṣār ḥiss imṣaggalāt al-masamīr

3 yitawāṣafūha yōm yōgaf zaḥarha
win ṣār šī min xafiyyāt al-mašawīr

1 يا راكب اللي شايبة من ظهرها
من كثر ما يرمو عليها المواثير

2 تودّي الخبر قدّام يوصل خبرها
وان صار حسّ مصقّلات المسامير

3 يتواصفوها يوم يوقف زحرها
وان صار شي من خافيّات المشاوير

[2] i.e. before detrimental consequences are allowed to develop, which the poet will hear about.

[3] Bedouin, like other Muslims, are ever hopeful that, if one is unable to defend his reputation, God will provide 'cover' (*sitr*) from shameful exposure (cf. poem 3.7, l.7). A popular sentiment is that '[the ultimate] cover is from God' (*as-sitr min allāh*). Accordingly, when turning down an invitation—which puts a host's generosity and hospitality in question (by depriving him of the chance to demonstrate these virtues)—one must immediately say 'God will cover your tent [from shame]' (*allāh yustur bētak*), or 'God will cover you' (*allāh yusturak*), implying that the invitation in itself is sufficient to uphold his reputation.

[4] Here, the poet uses camel behaviour as a metaphor to imply that, if his wife's nature was good, there would be no reason for not persevering with him.

[5] Cf. Musil, *Manners*, pp. 549–50, for the fright of calf-bearing camels.

[6] 'Pitch from a well' (*ğīr min bīr*) is a rhyming expression for something worthless.

4 win ma satarha-ḷḷā mā ḥad satarha
walḷa ma yiktib ʿal ʿabdi ʿawaṯīr

4 وان ما سترها اللّـه ما احد سترها
واللّـه ما يكتب عل عبده عواثير

5 zamlin tiwaddi-ḥmūlha ʿa dabarha
ū-zamlin tirawwiz law šaḥamha ṭanaṭīr

5 زمـلٍ تودّي حمولهـا ع دبـرها
وزمـلٍ تـروّز لـو شحمهـا طناطير

6 willī simiʿ bi-ṭalābtī ma ḥaẓarha
iz-zilm tigfī zē-n-nyāg al-maʿašīr

6 واللي سمـع بطلابتي مـا حضرها
الزلـم تقفـي زي النيـاق المعاشير

7 ʿayni min it-tafkīr kammal naẓarha
wana ataraggab ʿa durūb al-ḥanatīr

7 عيني مـن التفـكير كمّـل نظرها
وانـا اتـرقّب ع دروب الحناتير

8 ḥatta-l-ḥarīm aḷḷa ġayyab zaharhin
ma fīhin illī-tjīb lī gīr min bīr

8 حتّى الحريم اللّـه غيّـب زهرهن
ما فيهن اللي تجيب لي قير من بير

6.10

From ʿAnēz abū Sālim to Amīra ʿAbdallāh Swēlim

A Poem of Reprimand and Disdain

After a while ʿAnēz vented his anger against his first cousin, Amīra ʿAbdallāh, for philandering with Khaḍrā. Having little regard for Amīra's worth to begin with, he ridicules him for his audacity in betraying someone as prominent as the smuggler–poet himself. He emphasizes his worthlessness (in line 2) by citing his poverty ('a man with one camel and curs'), implying that he lacks the courage to earn a substantial living by smuggling. He satirizes him for his pretentions, depicting him as a worm that would bite like a snake, and a dog that would prey like a wolf; and he upbraids him for his deceit and shamelessness, which must reflect adversely on their clan (line 5). He expresses his amazement at Amīra's behaviour and warns him that the final settling of accounts will be graver than his amorous escapade!

Poem 6.10 was heard, in 1971, from a recording made by its author at Birshāg, Egypt.

I arrived after effort atop a high peak,
One whose climb and descent leave you equally weak.[1] 1

There I sighted a man with one camel and curs:
He was making his way to the camp of my wife. 2

Well, one friend was home, the other away,
So the hostess gave each guest his portion that day.[2] 3

There are friends who respect me although I'm in jail,
While others behave like their senses would fail; 4

He who shames with a slut, his disgrace is the same,
Though for some men disgrace isn't really a shame.[3] 5

And taking no note of what strangers might say,
They'll appear in our camps with a wife gone astray.[4] 6

So, the little blind worm's now sprung teeth and can bite,
And what once was a cur's now a wolf out at night. 7

Why, this world is all treachery, a frock with two sides,
While exposing what's down, the up-side it hides. 8

It replaces a head-man[5] with one who's a tail:
Such are the signs of these times of travail. 9

The hard knocks of life make one sit up in wonder,
But the end is a reckoning—no quick raid for plunder! 10

[1] This imaginary ascent to a high place is a device used to indicate perspective and an emotional experience over and above the scope of daily life (cf. the first lines of poems 1.10 and 1.14).

[2] The author here puns on the word 'portion' to infer that his wife gave her guest more than obligation required (cf. poem 4.14, stanza 12, l. 4).

[3] This line reflects the sentiment in a popular bedouin proverb 'A family used to acting contrary to bedouin convention will not consider their actions unconventional' (*al-ʿēb min ahl al-ʿēb mū hū ʿēb*).

[4] A family's reputation for behaving according to bedouin convention is an important component of their status, and hence security (cf. poem 4.19, n. 6).

[5] In the Arabic text, 'necks' (*al-ʿunūg̦*), reflecting the image of social responsibilities being hung on the necks of leaders. Accordingly, the person who is responsible for knowing the state of relations between his tribal confederation and others is called the *g̦alīd*—'he who wears the necklace' (*g̦ilāda*); i.e. the responsibility.

1	al-yōm ana wayagit ʿa rās mirgāb mirgāb la ṭalʿa ū-nizla ṣaʿībi	اليوم انا وايقت ع راس مرقاب مرقاب لد طلعة ونزلة صعيبة
2	wi-rāyabt lī rāʿī zmāli ū-kilāb ū-darbi ʿala miskān ahalna tijība	ورايبت لي راعي زماله وكلاب ودربه على مسكان اهلنا تجيبه
3	xallān mayjūda ū-xallān ġayyāb wi-ʿend al-miʿazzib kull yiṭlab naṣība	خلّان موجودة وخلّان غيّاب وعند المعزّب كلّ يطلب نصيبه
4	wi-xallī tiḥallānī wana wara-l-bāb wi-xallin maʿ al-badwān ʿagla ġadī bi	وخلّي تحلّاني وانا ورا الباب وخلٍّ مع البدوان عقلد غدي به
5	al-ʿayb ʿayb illī maʿa ṣāḥba ʿāb ū-nuṣṣ ir-rjāl al-ʿāyba ma tiʿībi	العيب عيب اللي مع صاحبه عاب ونصّ الرجال العايبة ما تعيبه
6	ū-mā yaḥaṣa harj ar-rajajīl al-ajnāb yajlib ʿal al-ʿarbān gašra nasība	وما يحصى هرج الرجاجيل الاجناب يجلب عل العربان قشرة نسيبه
7	wad-dūda hal-ʿamya tarabba ilha nāb wal-kalb ṣār bi-xilf il-ayyām ḏība	والدودة العميا تربّى لها ناب والكلب صار بخلف الايّام ذيبة
8	wa-dinyāk ġaddāra ilha ṯōb gilāb illī ʿalēha min taḥitha tijībi	ودنياك غدّارة لها ثوب قلاب اللي عليها من تحتها تجيبه
9	wi-tbadl ʿunūg ar-rajajīl bi-ḏināb ū-hēḏī ʿalamāt al-umūr aṣ-ṣaʿībi	وتبدّل عنوق الرجاجيل بذناب وهيذي علامات الامور الصعيبة
10	ū-maṣāyib ad-dinya tiwarrīk al-aʿjāb wal-ʿumr lih mīʿād mā hū nihībi	ومصايب الدنيا تورّيك الاعجاب والعمر له ميعاد ما هو نهيبة

6.11

From ʿAnēz abū Sālim to Sulēmān Ibn Sarīaʿ

A Poem to Announce his Divorces

Eventually it became clear to ʿAnēz that the information he had been receiving was true, and he decided to divorce all three of his wives in order to save his prestige. He sent them a writ of divorce through a letter to Ḥājj Ḥimēdān, a member of the Tarābīn resident in Aqaba, naming for each wife a warrantee who was to return her to her father's tent.[1] He declared his decision in the present poem (line 11), which he composed on the morning of the first Feast of the Sacrifice (*ʿīd al-aḍḥā*) that he spent in prison. The poem was prompted by his recollections of the happy celebrations of the holidays that take place in the desert oases (see poem 1.1) as contrasted with the gloomy holiday season in prison. He sent the poem, transcribed by his cell-mate (line 2), to Sulēmān Ibn Sarīaʿ.

O God, O Creator of servant and lord;
Who orders all things as firm or just fleeting.[2] 1

To write down some poems, my mate I implored,
Poems composed by one whom the nights have been cheating. 2

Greet those who pour coffee out of pots from Baghdād,[3]
And tell them—if asked of my state—that it's bad. 3

The news I don't want has been proved to be right;
I bear the oppression of dark thoughts each night. 4

The feast day's returned, but I am all hate;
I hate even feast days, because of my fate. 5

Poem 6.11 was heard recited by ʿAwda Ṣāliḥ Imbārak of the Muzēna Shaẓāẓna tribe, in Wādī Gharandal, 11 November 1968 and ʿAṭiyya Miẓʿān ʿAwwād of the ʿAlēgāt Zmēliyyīn tribe, at Abū Rudēs, 25 November 1971. The poem was reviewed with its author, at Nuwēbaʿ at-Tarābīn, 25 May 1984.

---

[1] According to the bedouin custom (see Shuqayr, p. 417).

[2] On 'remembering God' as the aegis of a poem, see poem 3.5, n. 6.

[3] For Baghdad-made coffee-pots, cf. poem 3.6, n. 2.

Remembering those mornings, the sounds of a gun,
The girls ululating, their braids loosely hung.[4] 6

My heart is a thunder peal ready to burst;
My body, acacia coals burning with thirst. 7

They[5] said: Come drink coffee; I cannot, I said;
They asked: What's the matter? I said: I'm like dead! 8

I'm now like a dog at the well left behind,[6]
No longer that shotgun whose wood brightly shines. 9

No doubt if I live long, some feast I'll yet share,
But if my life's shortened—by God, I won't care. 10

And, lest every Zēd and ʿAbēd[7] laugh at me,
I've set my three non-bearing she-camels free. 11

1 yaḷḷa ya xālg al-ʿabd was-sīd
bi-umrak tiṯabbitha ū-bumrak tizālī

1 يا اللّـه يـا خالق العبد والسيد
بامـرك تثبّتها وبامـرك تزالِ

2 gūm ya xaṭīb iktib lina hal-gawaṣīd
gaṣīd min ḥālit ʿalē hal-liyālī

2 قوم يا خطيب اكتب لنا هالقواصيد
قصيد مـن حالت عليـه الليالي

3 ū-sallim ʿala hayl ad-dlāl al-baġadīd
win naššadōk ōṣif lihum kēf ḥālī

3 وسلّـم علـى هيل الدلال البغاديد
وان نشّدوك اوصف لـهم كيف حالي

4 hāḏī al-ʿulūm illī biha xāṣṣ ma-rīd
waṣbur ʿala ġulb al-liyālī liyālī

4 هذي العلوم اللـي بهـا خاصّ ما اريد
واصبر على غلب الليالي ليالي

5 al-ʿīd ʿād ū-ṣirt ana-krah al-ʿīd
wakrah nahār al-ʿīd min ma jarā lī

5 العيد عاد وصرت انا اكره العيد
واكره نهار العيد مـن مـا جرى لي

[4] On holidays and at other celebrations women may wear their hair loose, which is considered improper on ordinary days (cf. poem 5.10, n. 4). For shooting contests at holiday time, see poem 1.1. ll. 2–4.

[5] i.e. the poet's prison-mates.

[6] See poem 2.9, n. 9.

[7] 'Zēd and ʿAbēd' is the equivalent of 'Tom, Dick and Harry'.

6 yōm atatarra-ṣ-ṣubḥ ū-ḥiss al-bawarīd
ma' zaġarāṭ imraxxiyyāt al-madālī

6 يوم اتطرّى الصبح وحسّ البواريد
مع زغراط مرخّيّات المدالي

7 awḥī bi-galbī miṯil gaṣf ar-rawa'īd
wawḥī bi-jismī miṯil jamr as-siyālī

7 اوحي بقلبي مثل قصف الرواعيد
واوحي بجسمي مثل جمر السيالِ

8 gālū tagahwa gult wal̲l̲āhī ma-rīd
gālū mā lak gult ya raba' mā lī

8 قالو تقهوى قلت واللّهِ ما اريد
قالو ما لك قلت يا ربع ما لي

9 aṣbaḥt za-llī ẓall 'al-mawarīd
ū-mānī bi-ḥāl illī xašabhin iylālī

9 اصبحت زي اللي ظلّ عالمواريد
وماني بحال اللي خشبهن يلالي

10 win ṭawwalat la budd ma-naḥẓar al-'īd
win gaṣṣarat wal̲l̲ā mānī masālī

10 وان طوّلت لا بدّ ما نحضر العيد
وان قصّرت واللّه ماني مسالي

11 ū-min xawf la-yiẓḥak 'alēy zēd wa-'abēd
bayya't 'ayrāt an-nyāg al-ḥiyālī

11 ومن خوف ليضحك عليّ زيد وعبيد
بيّعت عيرات النياق الحيالِ

6.12

From 'Anēz abū Sālim to his Wife, Ṣubḥiyya

Castigation after her Marriage

Although he had divorced his wives, the news of Ṣubḥiyya's subsequent marriage to her illicit suitor 'Āyd 'Abēd Muḥammad enraged 'Anēz anew. He sent the present poem cursing the eyes that were first attracted by her beauty, and scolding her for her mischievous frolicking with 'Āyd while he was being tortured and interrogated.

O Life, why so bold do you suddenly appear,
After I was your brother, your friend, and your dear? 1

Poem 6.12 was heard, in 1971, from a recording made by its author at Birshāg, Egypt.

And these eyes! I'll chastise you! That would be meet!
And by cauterization! By nails red with heat![1] 2

Yes, Eyes, you are cheats, may your own hopes abort;
May God curse those who lie about whom we should court.[2] 3

For we get our reward when we follow love's lure;
And, though drinking pure poison, we never seek cure.[3] 4

From your wandering, O Eyes, my heart's now in pain;
I must stay up and soothe it until the moon wanes. 5

All that I built has come down stone by stone,[4]
But this latest affliction's the worst that I've known. 6

Some friends hear you cry but aren't moved by your plight,
Whereas some come apart from not sleeping at night. 7

But you, fancy dresser! By your news I'm dismayed:
Why, the black dress I left you in still hasn't frayed![5] 8

Those who sold you and bought you[6] are subject to blame,
But you surpass all in behaving with shame. 9

You let down your hair tassels loose on your back[7]
While they hung me and beat me on rack after rack.[8] 10

[1] For cauterization as a cure, see poem 4.4, n. 2. As alluded to here, nails and other iron fragments may be used as the cauterization instrument.

[2] Here the poet compares his eyes to the women who pay visits to a prospective bride in order to appraise her suitability for marriage to one of their kinsmen. This appraisal is called *nagd* (the term for literary criticism in the cities); and the person, *naggād*.

[3] Pure poison, in the Arabic text, is called 'the poison of Socotra' (*as-samm aṣ-ṣagaṭrī*). This is a poison used against animals and is an image for anything exceptionally potent. A very assertive person may be likened to it (*fulān zē as-samm aṣ-ṣagaṭrī*). Socotra, here, is the island at the southern entrance to the Red Sea.

[4] i.e. my honour has been stained by my wives' infidelity (see poem 1.1, n. 8, and the introduction to poem 6.6).

[5] i.e. you are not yet needy, contrary to what you claim (see poem 1.1, n.7); a black dress is the standard apparel for an adult bedouin female.

[6] A bride-price (*siyāg*) is paid by the groom to the bride's father or guardian (see Bailey, 'Weddings' pp. 110–11).

[7] i.e. you were having a 'festive' time (cf. poem 6.11, n. 4; on festive occasions women adorn their braids with tassels (*sharāshīb*, sing. *shirshiba*)).

[8] Cf. poem 6.1, n. 8.

1 ʿal ēš ya dinya tigillī ḥayākī
min ʿugib maḥna-xwān waṣḥāb waḥbāb

2 biygūl tistahlī ya ʿayn hāḏa jizākī
gāl āh wakawwīkī ṯamanīn dūlāb

3 ya ʿayn xibtī ū-xayyib aḷḷa rajākī
waḷḷa yilʿan kull min nagadha xāb

4 hāḏa jizāki-llī titbaʿ hawākī
yišrab min as-samm aṣ-ṣagaṭrī ū-mā ṭāb

5 yiškī ʿalēy galbī nuṣṣ al-mašākī
wi-tammēt asajjid fīh limma-l-gamr ġāb

6 ū-ya dār kull al-ġulb ʿallī banākī
wal-ġulb al-axar ma ḥasabna li ḥisāb

7 xallān ma yiṣʿab ʿalēhum jafākī
ū-xallān min kiṯr as-sahr jisimhum ḏāb

8 ya-mm ad-dalāl az-zēn jānī nabākī
wal-asmar illī futkī fīh ma ḏāb

9 al-ʿayb ʿallī bāʿkī wištarākī
wintī taʿaddētī ʿala kull min ʿāb

10 tarxī garamīl al-ġawa ʿa gafākī
wiḥna-ngāsi-l-ġulb min bāb li-bāb

1 عل ايش يا دنيا تقلّي حياكي
من عقب ما احنا اخوان واصحاب واحباب

2 بيقول تستاهلي يا عين هذا جزاكي
قال اه واكوّيكي ثمانين دولاب

3 يا عين خبتي وخيّب اللّه رجاكي
واللّه يلعن كلّ من نقدها خاب

4 هذا جزاكي اللي تتبع هواكي
يشرب من السمّ الصقطري وما طاب

5 يشكي عليّ قلبي نصّ المشاكي
وتمّيت اسجّد فيه لمّا القمر غاب

6 ويا دار كلّ الغلب عاللي بناكي
والغلب الاخر ما حسبنا له حساب

7 خلّان ما يصعب عليهم جفاكي
وخلّان من كثر السهر جسمهم ذاب

8 يا امّ الدلال الزين جاني نباكي
والاسمر اللي فتكي فيه ما ذاب

9 العيب عاللي باعكي واشتراكي
وانتي تعدّيتي على كلّ من عاب

10 ترخي قراميل الغوى ع قفاكي
واحنا نقاسي الغلب من باب لباب

6.13

From Ḥamdān abū Salāma to ʿAnēz abū Sālim

A Poem of Encouragement

The present poem sent to ʿAnēz by a bedouin who did not personally know him reflects the concern felt for the smuggler–poet throughout Sinai. Ḥamdān abū Salāma Abū Masʿūd of the Muzēna Darārma tribe, being a poet, felt a special affinity for ʿAnēz, and he composed this poem to comfort and encourage ʿAnēz on hearing that he had divorced his wives and that they had remarried. The introductory themes of the poem (lines 1–8) are unusually rich in imagery for bedouin compositions from Sinai and the Negev. Ḥamdān then goes on to add his condemnation of the behaviour of ʿAnēz's kinsmen (lines 9–11), to stress the loss to bedouin society as a result of ʿAnēz's absence (line 12), to state his belief in ʿAnēz's innocence (lines 13–16) and to express the bedouin disdain for prison ('Jail for a hero is no source of shame'). In maintaining ʿAnēz's innocence, Ḥamdān reveals the bedouin's permissive attitude to smuggling ('All he earned was for guests, so they'd spare him their blame'), asserting that, since he had not spied (line 15), he was essentially blameless. The bedouin contempt for the settled Egyptian (whom they term a *fallāḥ* whether agricultural or urban) is pointedly expressed in line 16.

O ʿAnēz, as it's likely you're longing for word,
Let's bring paper and ink and write down some verse. 1

After dinner we'll open our windows and doors,
Till the poem comes down like a cloudburst—pours, 2

As if Antares appeared with huge cumulus clouds
To sweep ibex down rushing ravines. 3

O Rider of one who has cut canine teeth,[1]
Whose hoof-beats on the broad plain[2] will stimulate fear; 4

Poem 6.13 was heard recited by its author, at aṭ-Ṭūr, 30 March 1971.

[1] On the virtue of a camel's receiving canine teeth, see poem 1.4, n. 10.

[2] Lit. 'a standing plain' (*gāʿ wāgif*). Although riding swiftly, a rider feels he is standing, because of the vastness of the plain.

She's plundered from herdsmen of a thoroughbred herd,
So pure it's needless to count out her sires.[3] 5

No broker'd take her to the souk for sale,
For her mother's milk would not fill a cup.[4] 6

Her foreleg is lithe, her thigh is taught,
And her waist is slim as the bow of a *rabāba*;[5] 7

She bears side-bags that shine, so fine is their wool,
And a carbine that kills the most stubborn of wolves. 8

For his gray hair and cross heart not ʿAnēz is to blame,
With kin who themselves ruined his tent without shame;[6] 9

Some saw him dismounted and quick rode his mares[7]
While other kin sold them for new clothes to wear; 10

They're heedless that time changes spell after spell,
And that blame, in the end, stains in-laws as well. 11

When a lion has gone, it's like Pleiades' demise,[8]
For those who'd then lead us are those we despise. 12

O Allah, who's higher than all mountain peaks,
Watch ʿAnēz and send the relief that he seeks. 13

Lord of all, you can see that ʿAnēz did no shame:
All he earned was for guests, so they'd spare him their blame.[9] 14

[3] On reckoning camel pedigree, see poem 2.9, n. 2.

[4] Thoroughbred camel-mares are known to give little milk. In the Arabic text the 'cup' referred to is the smallish *hināba* bowl, holding roughly a litre; it is used for kneading dough and holding a soup of milk and *samn*, rather than for drinking (Shuqayr, p. 373; Musil, *Arabia Petraea*, iii. 138).

[5] The one-string violin of the bedouin.

[6] On the imagery of the tent as honour, see poems 1.1, n. 8; 4.19, l. 5; 6.6, introduction; 6.9, n. 3.

[7] i.e. fornicated with his wives: (cf. poem 4.8, n. 1).

[8] The short absence of the Pleiades (*thurayyā*, but also *an-nijm* ('the Star') as in the present text), which occurs in June, is considered the worst and most unhealthy period of the year. Even the Prophet Muḥammad is recorded as expressing this view: 'When the Pleiades rise, all harm rises from the earth' (Bailey, 'Star-lore', p. 591, n. 41).

[9] This line reflects the logic behind the bedouin resentment of Egyptian efforts to curb their smuggling: the bedouin consider smuggling a legitimate way to earn a living as if it were a natural

He who squealed on ʿAnēz is a liar;
To dispel his untruth I'd myself "lick the fire".[10] 15

Follow not the *fallāḥ* who's fond of his drink:[11]
That fat-bottomed breed from the Land of the Nile.[12] 16

To greet an old friend with a poem was my aim:
Jail for a hero is no source of shame.[13] 17

1 ya ʿanēẕ kōd innak ʿal al-gōl mištāg
hāt al-warag wal-ḥibr wiktib iktābi

1 يا عنيز كود انّــك عل القول مشتاق
هات الــورق والحبــر واكــتب كتابة

2 wi-ʿugb al-ʿaša naftaḥ šababīk wi-bwāb
mitl it-tiʿūl illī-stihallat saḥābi

2 وعقب العشا نفتح شبابيك وابواب
مثل الثعــول اللي استهلّــت سحابة

3 walla-l-uḥaymir la-jā maʿ rijid saḥāb
waṣ-ṣayd min rūs al-xalaxīl jāba

3 ولّا الاحيمر لو جا مــع رجد سحاب
والصيد مــن رؤوس الخلاخيل جابد

4 ya rākb-illī taww šāriḥ an-nāb
fī gāʿ wāgif war-radiyya tihāba

4 يا راكب اللي تــوّ شارح الناب
فــي قــاع واقــف والرديّــة تهابد

5 ū-rāʿī jāba jabiḏ min ṭōgit rikkāb
mū hū min illī ʿadd zamli ḥisābi

5 وراعيد جابد جبذ من طوقة ركّــاب
ما هو من اللي عــدّ زملد حسابد

6 ma sāga-d-dallāl lis-sūg jilāb
amma labanha ma yidibb al-hināba

6 مــا ساقــد الدلّال للسوق جلاب
امّــد لبنهــا مــا يدبّ الـهنابة

7 madmūjt iḏ-ḏurʿān ū-mabrūmt is-sāg
waṣ-ṣulb ẓāmir mitil gōs ar-rabāba

7 مدموجة الذرعان ومبرومة الساق
والصلب ضامر مثل قوس الربابة

way to utilize what they view as 'their' desert. The desert's inaccessibility and its geographical situation between centres of civilization are two characteristics favourable for smuggling (cf. poem 6.5, n. 6).

[10] Licking a red-hot iron implement to establish innocence is often referred to as 'licking the fire'; for more details, see poem 4.5, n. 2.

[11] i.e. alcoholic drinks, which are forbidden in Islam.

[12] For further expressions of the contempt that Sinai bedouin feel for Egypt's government and settled population, see poems 1.6; 2.9; 2.12, n. 2; 4.3; 4.7; 7.9; 7.10.

[13] Cf. poem 6.5, n. 6.

8 wal-xurj maṣgūlin ʿala kēf ma ṭāb
wi-mʿaddili tirmī ʿinūd aḏ-ḏiyāba

8 والخرج مصقولٍ على كيف ما طاب
ومعدّلة ترمي عنود الذيابة

9 ma-lūm galb ʿanēz war-rās la šāb
min rubʿata xallū buyūti xarāba

9 ما الوم قلب عنيز والراس لو شاب
من ربعته خلّو بيوته خرابة

10 ū-xallū ṭraygī ū-ṣārit ar-rabaʿ rikkāb
bāʿū-r-raḥāyil ū-faṣṣalūhum iṯyābi

10 وخلّوه طريقي وصارت الربع ركّاب
باعو الرحايل وفصّلوهم ثيابِ

11 ma yaḥsabū in al-wagit bal-ḥukm gallāb
wal-lōm barẓū ma yifūt an-nisāba

11 ما يحسبو ان الوقت بالحكم قلّاب
واللوم برضو ما يفوت النسابة

12 wis-sabaʿ ila ġāyib kama-n-nijim la ġāb
wan-niḏil ʿugbi iyṣīr gāyid ʿaṣāba

12 والسبع الا غايب كما النجم لو غاب
والنذل عقبه يصير قايد عصابة

13 yaḷḷā yā ʿālī ʿala kull mirgāb
xall aṅ-naẓr li-ʿanēz winha ṭilāba

13 يا اللّه يا عالي على كلّ مرقاب
خلّ النظر لعنيز وانهى طلابه

14 inti-īlā al-kull tara ʿanēz ma ʿāb
min šān sutr il-ḥāl hāḏa asbāba

14 انت اله الكلّ ترا عنيز ما عاب
من شان ستر الحال هذا اسبابه

15 willī fitin fī ʿanēz bil-ʿilm kaḏḏāb
walḥas ʿalē an-nār wiṯbit ikḏāba

15 واللي فتن في عنيز بالعلم كذّاب
والحس عليه النار واثبت كذابه

16 ū-la titbaʿ al-fallāḥ lil-xamr šarrāb
marbā wādi-n-nīl kubrit jaʿāba

16 ولا تتبع الفلّاح للخمر شرّاب
مرباه وادي النيل كبرت جعابه

17 hāḏa salāmī barsali yamm al-aṣḥāb
wal-ḥabs liṣ-ṣanadīd mū hū maʿāba

17 هذا سلامي بارسله يمّ الاصحاب
والحبس للصناديد ما هو معابة

6.14

ʿAnēz abū Sālim to his Son, ʿIshēsh

Advice to Console a Son

Some years after divorcing his wives and their remarriages, ʿAnēz received news that his son by Khaḍrā, ʿIshēsh (b. 1958), who was raised by ʿAnēz's elder brother ʿAnēzān, felt he was being treated with contempt. This upset ʿAnēz, and he composed a poem of instruction to his son in imitation of the genre that is current in the desert (as presented in Chapter 3). The lines that are relevant to 'Ishēsh's annoyance (lines 3, 6, and 7) counsel him to behave with self-respect and patience. Lines 4 and 5—offering advice on how to present a case to a bedouin court—were included by the poet, although of little practical use to a boy barely in his teens, in order to leave ʿIshēsh with some 'lasting advice' (*waṣāh imgīma*), as stated in line 2. The next three lines (8–10), lamenting the poet's fallen state, are meant as a personal confession to his distant son. To end the poem on an elevated note, however, and leave his son with a sense of pride in his father, he counsels ʿIshēsh to look after their rifle so that one day they will be able to settle their accounts with others like men, reminding him proudly that the rifle itself was stolen from no less an important figure than an Egyptian army officer.

As I woke up from slumber with anguish I sighed,
In a flash I stopped sleeping, my eyes opened wide; 1

O ʿIshēsh, let me give you some lasting advice,
Advice that's all mine, who's drunk gall once or twice. 2

I'd advise you, don't eat the remains of a feast,
And when sitting midst men don't behave like their least. 3

Beware of those people who'd judge between foes;
Take care they're not hungry behind the just pose. 4

Poem 6.14 was heard, in 1971, from a recording made by its author at Birshāg, Egypt. The poem was reviewed with its author, in Wādi Murēkhī, 26 May 1984.

When defining the claims and interring the gravel,
Be sure there's a witness to block any cavil.[1] 5

I advise you against taking insults to heart;
Seek revenge when you're fledged, wait till then, though you smart. 6

Be steadfast and firm, though you stand all alone;
Be content with your share, though its only a bone.[2] 7

Your father's worn out like an old jaded mare,
His face a used cartridge-shell—grey from much care. 8

After gaining respect and rich clothes of thick wool,
After mortars and pestles and coffee-pots full, 9

We've lost all our worth; on us none rely:
O Life, why'd you deal with me so? Tell me why! 10

Just take care that the gun that feeds hungry folk's fine;[3]
That gun on whose number some officer signed. 11

1 ya wentī wannētha ʿugib nīma
wal-ʿayn titnawwiš min an-nawm tanwīš

1 يا ونّتي ونّيتها عقب نيمة
والعين تتنوّش من النوم تنويش

[1] In the absence of writing skills, bedouin society has had to devise means to ensure the maintenance of a judicial process without the advantage of referring to the written word. A problem arises in connection with defining a claim in such a way that a party to a conflict cannot change his original position in his favour as the trial progresses. To eliminate this difficulty, the bedouin resort to two devices. One is a symbolic act, 'the burying of the gravel' (*dafn al-ḥaṣā*), as mentioned in the poem. When originally stating a claim, the contestant will take some stones and inter them in a small hole that he will have dug; and by announcing 'This is my gravel', he calls the attention of those present to his claim. Secondly, to corroborate this act, someone present serves as a witness; it is his duty to record by memory all the details mentioned and then testify to what he has heard in the event of any subsequent discrepancy. Such a witness is called a *marḍawī* (lit. 'he who receives satisfaction', as he is compensated for appearing and testifying).

[2] For the importance of self-reliance, see poems 3.7, 3.8, 3.9, 3.11.

[3] The bedouin have two terms defining people in different but equally common conditions of hunger. The one in the present Arabic text is *magwī* (pl. *magāwī*), someone who has spent the night without having eaten supper; the other is *maryūg* (pl. *marāyīg*), someone who has gone through a day without eating (lit. 'someone who still has not "broken his dry spittle"' (*fakk ar-rīg*), an expression for breakfasting).

2 ya ʿišēš lak ʿendī wiṣātin imgīma
wasiyt illī jarrab al-murr ya ʿišēš

2 يا عشيش لك عندي وصاةٍ مقيمة
وصيّة اللي جرّب المرّ يا عشيش

3 awṣīk la tākil ʿagāb al-walīma
wilā timattil lir-rjāl ad-darawīš

3 اوصيك لا تاكل عقاب الوليمة
ولا تمثّل للرجال الدراويش

4 wawṣīk ʿa lamm as-sagīm li-sagīma
ū-ḥurṣak min illī magṣada lugimt al-ʿēš

4 واوصيك ع لمّ السقيم لسقيمه
وحرصك من اللي مقصدد لقمة العيش

5 wawṣīk ʿa dafn al-ḥaṣā as-salīma
ū-maskak kafīl al-harj gabl at-tafatīš

5 واوصيك ع دفن الحصاة السليمة
ومسكك كفيل الهرج قبل التفاتيش

6 wawṣīk la tiṣʿab ʿalēk aš-šatīma
wuṣbur iylimma yitikammal lak ar-rīš

6 واوصيك لا تصعب عليك الشتيمة
واصبر لمّا يتكمّل لك الريش

7 ū-xallak ṣabūr ū-xall ʿendak ʿazīma
wirẓa bi-kawmak law aʿṭawk al-karakīš

7 وخلّك صبور وخلّ عندك عزيمة
وارضى بكومك لو اعطوك الكراكيش

8 abūk ṣāyir zē ḏalūl aẓ-ẓalīma
wiššna lōna zē zihāb al-xaraṭīš

8 ابوك صاير زي ذلول الظليمة
وجهنا لونه زي زهاب الخراطيش

9 ʿagb al-maʿazza waṯ-ṯiyāb ad-dasīma
ū-raṣṣ az-zbēdiyyāt janb al-mahabīš

9 عقب المعزّة والثياب الدسيمة
ورصّ الزبيديّات جنب المهابيش

10 ṣirna hafāya ma-lna ḏāt gīma
ū-bass lēš ya dinya ʿamaltī kiḏī lēš

10 صرنا هفايا ما لنا ذات قيمة
وبسّ ليش يا دنيا عملتي كذي ليش

11 yigūl ʿasa mʿaššiyt il-magāwī salīma
illī maẓa ʿa ragimha gāyid al-jēš

11 يقول عسى معشّية المقاوي سليمة
اللي مضى ع رقمها قايد الجيش

6.15

From ʿAnēz abū Sālim to Sulēmān ad-Dilaydim

A Threat over an Unpaid Debt

In addition to his marital problems ʿAnēz still had some unfinished business relating to smuggling. One was an unpaid debt owed him by an associate, a Sulēmān ad-Dilaydim (known as Daldūm) of the Maʿāza Slēmāt tribe that inhabits the western side of the Gulf of Suez. Many of the smuggling operations by bedouin from southern Sinai were carried out in co-operation with the Maʿāza, to whom they would convey the contraband in small boats over the Gulf of Suez for transshipment to Cairo and other markets along the Nile. Upon selling the drugs the Maʿāza would normally deduct their own share of the profits, remitting the balance to the bedouin smuggler of Sinai, who would deal similarly with his associates in Jordan.

However, when ʿAnēz was arrested, Daldūm refused to pay him the money he owed him, despite repeated demands. Finally, ʿAnēz decided to 'blacken his face' (see poem 2.8, n. 3) by sending him an insulting poem of warning, that he also made known to bedouin throughout Sinai. The first eight lines of the poem are pure insult. Instead of honouring the recipient, Daldūm, by depicting a fine camel that would bear him the message—a camel commensurate with the recipient's station—ʿAnēz sent him an old, worn-out mount (lines 1–3); one, moreover, that was black (line 2)—as was the messenger and his attire (line 4), and the black cairns he said he would build at various crossroads (lines 7–8), a device employed to defame one who causes harm by violating bedouin conventions. In lines 9–14 ʿAnēz gives a graphic description—amusing in its frankness—of Daldūm's offence against him. At the same time, he disguises the true subject—hashish—with the euphemism 'white camel-mare', so called because the hashish comes packaged in white oil-cloth and because its worth multiplies like a calf-bearing mare. ʿAnēz ends the poem with a warning of retaliation if the debt is not paid forthwith.

Poem 6.15 was heard recited by ʿAwda Ṣāliḥ Imbārak of the Muzēna S͟haẓāẓna tribe, in Wādī G͟harandal, 11 November 1968. The poem was reviewed with its author, in Wādī Murēk͟hī, 26 May 1984.

O Rider upon a sickly camel that slacks,
Hardly staggering with only some cushions and sacks, 1

As black as can be, with a sore, scabby hide,
All his life has been errands, all roads he has plied; 2

If sent on a trip, like a wolf's is his trot:[1]
A wolf that slinks upon hearing a shot. 3

In your stead seat the black man, Mas'ūd, dressed in black;
Jet black as can be, no black does it lack. 4

Mount him and point him the way to Daldūm,
Let the goodness that brightens his face turn to gloom. 5

Say: Stop at his camp site at dawn and be crass,
And immediately curse him with, 'Up your wives' ass!' 6

Say: I'm sent by 'Ānez to build cairns of black stones,[2]
From uppermost Egypt to the heights behind Bāyir;[3] 7

And from India to Europe[4] let your blackness be known,
And westward to Malta and far al-Jazāyir.[5] 8

If you're really a man, then with no more ado—
With the quickness of vengeance—just pay me what's due![6] 9

You're devouring the value of camels marked clear,
White mares, whose grazing on skiffs made them dear. 10

[1] In the Arabic text the wolf alluded to is a 'wolf of the open spaces' (*dhīb al-khurūm*), considered to be cowardly (as indicated in the second hemistich), especially in comparison with 'a wolf that preys in camps' (*dhīb al-g̣arāya*) (cf. poem 1.1, l. 10a).

[2] On the significance of a black cairn (*rijm aswad*), cf. poem 2.8, n. 3.

[3] A small desert settlement in eastern Jordan.

[4] The word *Rūm* used in the Arabic text refers to Europe rather than the city of Rome, an ancient usage deriving from the name of the Eastern Roman Empire.

[5] i.e. Algeria

[6] The reference to 'the quickness of vengeance' in the Arabic text is 'as if your blood was boiling' (*wad-dam fāyir*). Bedouin call the first three days following a murder 'the boiling of the blood' (*fawrit ad-dam*), the period in which the victim's clan is allowed to commit various excesses not permitted afterwards.

A crescent and stars are my she-camel's brand,[7]
Whose milk, at year's end, meets my children's demand.[8] 11

You've devoured their worth with treachery that's bold;
Don't you fear for God's wrath when your sins are told?[9] 12

With the gain from my camels you feed on minced meat,
And get mangoes, bananas, and cigarettes; 13

With the change you acquire fine clothing and shoes,
Tea, sugar, and scents—for your women to use. 14

Though we wait generations, revenge we will take:[10]
The Maʿāza too often have caused us to lose. 15

We can wait till the grass on our hilltops grows tall,
And the she-camels graze after winter rains fall.[11] 16

Tell Furāḥī:[12] ʿAnēz wields a powerful stick,
On which all of the tribes are inscribed.[13] 17

[7] 'A crescent and stars' was the 'trade-mark' stamped on packages of hashish grown in the Lebanese Biqāʿ valley and marketed through the town of Zahle.

[8] The end of the year means late spring and the end of the annual pasture season (i.e. when the annual plants dry up from the heat). In the Arabic text this season is termed *as-sawāyir* (lit. 'the bracelets') referring to the practice of curing livestock struck with the disease *jaʿām* (intestinal worms) by watering them from troughs in which silver bracelets are placed. For more on *jaʿām*, see poem 2.5.

[9] In the Arabic text God is termed 'Lord of the great' (*rabb al-kabāyir*), explained as deriving from the ubiquitous liturgical exclamation 'God is greater [than other gods]!' (*aḷḷāhu akbar!*)

[10] Lit. 'A violated party is bent on vengeance, and the offspring of a violated party are bent on vengeance.' A violated party is bound not to forget a violation until he has received justice from the offender. This is especially true in regard to murder, even if the conflict remains open for generations. One proverbial story relates how a bedouin avenged a relative's blood forty years after his murder and proclaimed that he had acted with haste (*astat͟hart baʿd arbaʿīn ʿām; astaʿjalt*). Another proverb has it that 'Blood neither disintegrates nor gets worm-eaten' (*ad-dam lā yiblī wa-lā yisawwis*), i.e. it remains subject to vengeance.

[11] The season of winter rains (*an-naw*, as in the Arabic text) begins in November with the appearance of the Pleiades on the eastern horizon at nightfall. The annual grasses that these rains bring are essential to the welfare and strength of the bedouin's livestock; hence, the use of winter rains here as a metaphor for the anticipated renewed ability of ʿAnēz and his clan to take vengeance.

[12] Huwēmil al-Frāḥī, Daldūm's father-in-law and a member of the Maʿāza.

[13] i.e. we remember our accounts with everyone and have the power to settle them in our favour.

Grave talk is direct, not the tales of some clown;
Grave talk makes men throw their *kūfiyya*-ropes down![14] 18

1 ya rākbin min ʿendina min fōg mayhūm dōba haygašši' baĺ-gaba wal-ġarāyir	يا راكب„ مـن عندنا من فوق ميهوم 1 دوبـه يقشّع بالقبـا والغراير
2 azrag zarag ū-gušʿati ya gušʿati šūm ū-ṭūl ʿumri ʿal-maxalīg dāyir	ازرق زرق وقشعتد يا قشعتد شوم 2 وطـول عمـرد عالمخاليق داير
3 in baʿat̲ti mišwār zē d̲īb al-xrūm illī ʿalēh imṣaggal al-miliḥ t̲āyir	ان بعثتد مشوار زي ذيب الخروم 3 اللـي عليـد مصقّـل الملح ثاير
4 arkab ʿalē hal-ʿabd masʿūd bi-hdūm zurg zurg ma ʿalēhin ašāyir	اركب عليـد العبد مسعود بهدوم 4 زرق زرق مـا عليهـن اشاير
5 arkab ʿalē ū-ṭarga yamm daldūm wal-xēr fi wij haĺ-fata lah dalāyil	اركـب عليـد وطرّقد يـمّ دلدوم 5 والخير في وجد الفتى لد دلايل
6 ilfi ʿalēh aṣ-ṣubḥ ya lafiyt aš-šūm wi-šmām sammī la iṭyāz aẓ-ẓarāyir	الفي عليد الصبح يا لفيـة الشوم 6 وشمام سمّي لـد طيـاز الضراير
7 gūl baʿat̲nī ʿanēz l-abnī lak irjūm min aṣ-ṣaʿīd la-mašarīf bāyir	قول بعثني عنيز لابني لك رجوم 7 مـن الصعيـد لمشاريف بايـر
8 wanšur xabr sawdāk fi-l-hind wir-rūm ū-fi barr maṣr ū-malṭa wal-jazāyir	وانشر خبر سوداك في الهند والروم 8 وفي بـرّ مصـر وملطة والجزاير
9 in kān ʿendak marjala widdak itgūm idfaʿ fulūs ʿanēz wid-damm fāyir	ان كـان عندك مرجلة ودّك تقوم 9 ادفـع فلـوس عنيـز والدم فاير
10 tākul at̲mān aš-šugr zahiyyāt al-wusūm šugrun tarabbaʿ fi ẓuhūr al-gaṭāyir	تاكل اثمان الشقر زاهيّـات الوسوم 10 شقـرٌ تربّـى فـي ظهـور القطاير

[14] Wearing the head-rope (*marīra*; ʿ*agāl*) is a sign of manhood and the ability to uphold the obligations of men. In an extreme case of frustration a man is likely to throw his head-rope to the ground as if to say, in an uttered oath, 'I'll either solve this problem to my satisfaction, or I'm not a man!'

11 al-bakra illī wasimhī hilāl ū-nujūm
hēḏi ḥulūbit ʿayltī fi-s-sawāyir

11 البكرة اللي وسمها هلال ونجوم
هيذي حلوبة عيلتي في السواير

12 tākul ṯaminha bōg ya-klak aš-šum
ma-txāf min mawlāk rabb al-kabāyir

12 تاكل ثمنها بوق يا اكلك الشوم
ما تخاف من مولاك ربّ الكباير

13 tākul ṯamin zamlī ʿala-s-sīkh mafrūm
ū-manja ū-mōz ū-min-aʿlab has-sagāyir

13 تاكل ثمن زملي على السيخ مفروم
ومنجاد وموز ومن اعلب هالسقاير

14 wi-tjīb bi-llī ẓall jazmāt wi-hdūm
ū-sukkar ū-šay ū-lal-ḥarayyim ʿaṭāyir

14 وتجيب باللي ظلّ جزمات وهدوم
وسكّر وشاي وللحريّم عطاير

15 al-gōm gōm ū-xilf al-gōm ilak gōm
ū-yāma al-maʿāza kabbadūna xasāyir

15 القوم قوم وخلف القوم لك قوم
وياما المعازة كبّدونا خساير

16 wi-nuṣbur limma yṣīr ʿašb aš-šafa kōm
wi-tirabbaʿ al-jagmā ʿala naw dāyir

16 ونصبر لمّا يصير عشب الشفا كوم
وتربّع الجقما على نو داير

17 gūl il-frāḥī ʿanēz ʿenda ʿaṣa šūm
maktūb fīha ism jimīaʿ al-ʿašāyir

17 قول لفراحي عنيز عند عصا شوم
مكتوب فيها اسم جميع العشاير

18 harj aḋ-darak mā hū tasarīg wi-ʿilūm
harj aḋ-darak biyrammi-r-rjāl al-marāyir

18 هرج الدرك ما هو تساريق وعلوم
هرج الدرك بيرمّي الرجال المراير

6.16

From ʿAnēz abū Sālim to Slēm Imsallam Ṣāliḥ al-ʿUrḍī

A Poem to Reprimand Negligent Kin

Daldūm ignored ʿAnēz's warnings and his power to harm him. ʿAnēz, seeking to enlist the aid of his paternal kinsmen in upholding their prestige, sent them a poem in which he reviewed in metaphor his fruitless efforts to stir them to action (lines 3–6), reiterating the age-old principle of the need for mutual defence among paternal kinsmen if they are to survive in the desert (lines 7–8).

O Rider on one graced with sinuous limbs,
I want word, and I want you to bring it with haste. 1

Quick, like what scatters small birds in mid-flight:
A hawk, when a flock of white doves comes in sight. 2

I've screamed like a warrior whose leg has been cut,
Lying helpless in crossfire as though he's the butt. 3

My teeth I have ground like a camel on sale,[1]
Whose price none will pay, for they fear he's not hale; 4

His herdsman would sell him because he's been slack,
And he's meagre, no fat's formed a hump on his back. 5

Like a wolf I have wailed, like an owl I would shriek,
But the owls hear no call, so their torpor bespeaks.[2] 6

Poem 6.16 was heard recited by ʿAwda Ṣāliḥ Imbārak of the Muzēna Shaẓāẓna tribe, in Wādī Gharandal, 11 November 1968, and by Rabīaʿ Abū Ḥarbī of the Ṣawālḥa ʿAwārma tribe, at Fīrān oasis, 4 September 1972. It was reviewed with its author in Wādī Murēkhī, 26 May 1984. The recipient of the poem was a member of the ʿAlāwna section of the poet's ʿArayḍa clan.

[1] A camel being examined in the market surrounded by people will be restive and scrape its teeth (*yiṣrik*), and is likely to 'emit an angry cry' (*yirghī*). Other camel sounds: a rutting male will call for a mate (*yihaddir*); a milking mare will call for her calf (*tiḥinn*).

[2] i.e. the poet compares his clansmen to owls, because of their inaction despite his call—which is believed to be characteristic of this bird.

As birds without wings are confined to the plain,
So I, without relatives, meet with disdain. 7

For one whose males back him is free from attack:[3]
Wolves never spare sheep that are left on the track.[4] 8

That said, if I now climb a high peak and peer,
I should see, through my field-glasses, someone appear. 9

1 ya rākbin min ʿendina fōg mabrūm
widdī al-ʿilūm ū-hāthin bil-wilāmī

2 wi-asraʿ min illī fi-ś-sama yifrid al-ḥawm
ṣagrin ū-malāyim la jirīmit ḥamāmī

3 aṣrax ṣarīx allī mi-r-rijl magṭūm
ḥālin ʿalē imṭōṭḥāt al-marāmī

4 aṣruk ṣarīk illī imbarrak lis-sūm
wiš-šura ġubr yiksirūn al-ʿaẓāmī

5 wi-mbarka rāʿī min šān mayhūm
ḥarsūs ma rawjim ʿalē has-sināmī

6 aʿwī ʿawī ad-dīb waṣrax kama-l-būm
wal-būm ma yifham maʿāni-l-kalāmī

7 ṭayrin bila jinḥān ma yidrak al-ḥawm
ū-rajulin bila rabaʿ galīl al-magāmī

1 يا راكبٍ من عندنا فوق مبروم
ودّي العلوم وهاتهن بالولامِ

2 واسرع من اللي في السما يفرد الحوم
صقرٍ وملايم لد جريمة حمامِ

3 اصرخ صريخ اللي من الرجل مقطوم
حالن عليه مطوطحات المرامي

4 اصرك صريك اللي مبرّك للسوم
وشراة غبر يكسرون العظامِ

5 ومبرّكه راعيه من شان ميهوم
حرسوس ما روجم عليه السنامِ

6 اعوي عوي الذيب واصرخ كما البوم
والبوم ما يفهم معاني الكلام

7 طيرٍ بلا جنحان ما يدرك الحوم
وراجلٍ بلا ربع قليل المقامِ

[3] The number of adult males who will automatically come to one's defence as part of one's blood-revenge group (*khamsa*) (see poem 3.9, n. 3), largely determines how safe one is and how assertive he may be.

[4] The nineteenth-century English explorer Charles Doughty (i. 319) was warned by friendly bedouin: 'thou art alone, and if thou wast made away, there is none would avenge thee . . . There is not, Khalīl [i.e. Doughty], a man of us all that sit here, that meeting thee abroad in the *khalā* [emptiness] had not slain thee. Thy camel-bags, they say, are full of money, but, *billāh*, were it only for the beast which is under thee; and lucky were he that should possess them. *The stranger is for the wolf!*'

8 willī warā rijāl ma yilḥaga-i-lawm
dīb al-ġanim ḥukmi ʿalčhin ʿadāmī

8 واللي وراه رجال ما يلحقه اللوم
ذيب الغنم حكمه عليهن عدامِ

9 ū-min ʿugib hāḏa ašraft min fōg kartūm
bi-marabbaʿan šōfa yizīḥ al-ʿaṣāmi

9 ومن عقب هذا اشرفت من فوق كرتوم
بمربّعٍ شوفه يزيح العصامِ

6.17

From Jumʿa al-Farārja to ʿAnēz abū Sālim

A Poem to Protest an Insult

ʿAnēz also tried to arouse his former associate, the fisherman–bedouin Jumʿa ʿĪd Dakhīlallāh of the Tarābīn Ḥasāblah, to take action on his behalf. When he received no response, he sent Jumʿa a message saying 'You belong at the back of the men!' Such an insult from the most daring member of his society stirred Jumʿa to compose a reply, in which he tells ʿAnēz how he was cut by his remark, and how desolate life has been in his absence.

O Rider on one that has ever been hale
And whose upper chest never was seared with a nail;[1] 1

Over broken and hilly land making your way,
You'll come by men drinking[2] before break of day; 2

Poem 6.17 was heard recited by its author, at el-ʿArīsh, 19 October 1970.

[1] Overworked camels may develop a chest ailment (*giṭṭūʿ*, *magṭūʿ*) marked by coughing, and treated by cauterization with a nail, stone, or firebrand (*mighās*, as in the Arabic text).

[2] i.e. drinking coffee.

And when your path leads to ʿAnēz, this declare:
Since you're gone all our work's with the hoe,[3] and we're bare.[4] 3

But I lost my bearings and suffered a pang
When you told me, ʿAnēz, I'm the least of the gang. 4

1 ya rākb-illī ma jārat li maʿalli
walla-nẓarab bēn al-bawādir ib-migbās

2 hāti ʿala rūs aṭ-ṭabāga itsilli
ū-tilfi-l-jamāʿa talgāhū aṣ-ṣubiḥ jillās

3 win jat darbak ʿābū sālim itgūl la
gūl la ʿarāya wa-kṯar aš-šuġl bil-fās

4 galbī ġadā bī maʿ ad-durūb al-mazalli
min gōltak ya ʿanēz tugʿud gafa-n-nās

1 يا راكب اللي ما جارت له معلّـة
ولّا انضـرب بيـن البـوادر بمقباس

2 هاتـد علـى رؤوس الطباقة تسلّـد
وتلفي الجماعة تلقاهم الصبح جـلّاس

3 وان جت دربك عابو سالم تقـول له
قـول لـه عرايا واكـثر الشغل بالفاس

4 قلبي غدا بـي مـع الدروب المزلّـة
من قولتك يا عنيز تقعد قفا الناس

6.18

From ʿAnēz abū Sālim to Sulēmān Ibn Sarīaʿ

A Poem to Notify his Impending Release

After serving eight years of his fifteen-year prison sentence, ʿAnēz was successful in proving to a medical commission of inquiry that he had been tortured during interrogation, and he was therefore released from prison on 25 June 1970. Before his release, he composed a poem and sent it to Sulēmān Ibn Sarīaʿ, hinting in disguised language (line 8) that

[3] In Sinai, the expression 'working with the hoe'—a bedouin allusion to the agricultural work of Egyptian peasants—is a bedouin way of saying that life is drudgery because there is no smuggling (cf. poem 2.12, n. 2).

[4] An allusion to the loss of status and face in the absence of their most prominent member. In another poem, not presented in this book, Jumʿa says to ʿAnēz 'The earth, in your absence is dry of its moisture' (*al-arḍ ʿugbak nāshfi ʿan tharāhā*).

Poem 6.18 was heard, in 1971, from a recording made by its author, at Birshāg, Egypt.

he was coming home. He realizes that he will be returning to a changed world that could tolerate the deceit of his faithless and estranged wives, but intimates that he is willing to let bygones be bygones (satisfied, apparently, that ʿĀyd ʿAbēd had divorced Ṣubḥiyya (line 12)). What interests ʿAnēz most is his imminent freedom—proud, none the less, that he has been able to endure the trying conditions of internment for years (line 15).

O Rider on one like an ostrich in flight,[1]
One whose forelegs require no fire to be right;[2] 1

His mother's full udders three years went unbound,[3]
Nor has he been couched to lift loads off the ground. 2

Through the desert direct him o'er the peaks of Samār,[4]
Leaving Jebel-Riḍāwī on the right not too far; 3

And the chalky white ridge circumvent on your left,
Through badlands by hand lead him on, but with care. 4

You'll come to a camp where they greet with respect;
No sheep-herder's flock do their fleshpots neglect.[5] 5

Greet all in my name going round from the right;[6]
To those who are wise, tell but part of my plight.[7] 6

Tell them we're aching in many a part,
And between my two kidneys they won't find a heart. 7

[1] For the allusion to ostriches to emphasize the swiftness of camels, cf. poems 2.6; 2.10; 6.1.

[2] The forelegs of a camēl are sensitive to fracture as a result of stumbling or being overladen. Such fractures are often treated by cauterization (cf. poem 6.17, n. 1).

[3] Young camels are believed to derive strength from their mother's milk, so that allowing them to suckle for three years—not uncommon—is commendable.

[4] All the places mentioned in the following lines are in Sinai on the route between ʿAnēz's prison and Wādī Watīr, where the intended recipient of the poem, Sulēmān Ibn Sarīaʿ, lived. The 'chalky white ridge is the western approach to the ʿIjma plateau near Jabal al-Mughēra.

[5] Every member of this hospitable camp contributes to the reception of guests by slaughtering one of his flock (cf. poem 2.2, n. 1).

[6] Greeting an assembly, like serving them, should be from the right (see poem 3.4, n. 2).

[7] i.e. that will suffice to those of understanding.

Say: News will arrive though it's brought you by bird;
Like a camel that's homing, I'm restless and stirred. 8

Say: A bird will soon come who once couldn't fly,
Though he comes to a home where wolves howl and cry. 9

Time's passed and my homestead gave way to another,
My house is impoverished, no wife, no mother. 10

I'm told there are mothers in Jōf al-Biyār,
And the tracks of men's shoes would approach from afar.[8] 11

In the caves he went hunting, a hare he would find;
What he found was a blind, side-winding snake. 12

May God, who gives cover to all whom he's made,[9]
Cover the shame of those asking his aid.[10] 13

O Creator of Heaven, Creator of Hell,
Who for every ill made a way to get well; 14

Bring ease to this body, it would melt as in fire;
How many a stalwart survives though it's dire! 15

1 ya rākb-illī zē an-naʿāma ila ġār
minṣān ma ṭabbat ʿuẓūdi makāwī

2 amma t̲ilāt̲ isnīn ma ṭabbha-ṣrār
walla barraka rāʿī bēn al-ʿarāwī

3 laggī ṭarīg al-barr gardūd al-asmār
ū-xallī ʿala yimnāk gōz ar-rẓāwī

4 waz-zagm al-abyaẓ mink wi-ysār
wi-tgawwida limma tifūt al-maṭāwī

1 يا راكب اللـــي زي النعامة الا غــار
منصان مـا طبّت عضودد مكـاوي

2 امّــد ثلاث سنين مـا طبّها اصرار
ولاّ برّكـد راعيـد بيـن العراوي

3 لقّـيد طـريق البـرّ قردود السمار
وخلّـي علـى يمناك قـوز الرضاوي

4 والزقـم الابيـض منـك ويسار
وتقـوّدده لمّـا تفـوت المطـاوي

[8] This is a reference to information that ʿAnēz had once received from Jumʿa al-Farārja (see poem 6.8, l. 2). Jōf al-Biyār is immediately south-east of the ʿIjma plateau.

[9] On God's 'cover', see poems 3.6, n. 7; 6.9, n. 3; also Piamenta, p. 101.

[10] This line states ʿAnēz's forgiveness for his former wives and the men who seduced them.

5 ū-tilfī farīg iygablūnak ib-migdār
wi-gdūrhum guṭʿa ġanim kull šāwī

5 وتلفي فريق يقابلونك بمقدار
وقدورهم قطعة غنم كلّ شاوي

6 ū-sallim ʿalēhum kullhum dīr ma dār
wiškī ʿal al-ʿaggāl nuṣṣ aš-šakāwī

6 وسلّم عليهم كلّهم دير ما دار
واشكي عل العقّال نصّ الشكاوي

7 witgūl lihum ḥana mawajīʿna iktār
wal-galb ma tilgā bēn al-kilāwī

7 وتقول لهم حنا مواجيعنا كثار
والقلب ما تلقاه بين الكلاوي

8 witgūl ṭayrin yijīb axbār wi-ywaṣṣil axbār
wana-taṣaggal zē-l-baʿīr al-mināwī

8 وتقول طيرٍ يجيب اخبار ويوصّل اخبار
وانا اتصقّل زي البعير المناوي

9 witgūl ṭayrin yiṭīr ma la jahad ṭār
wad-dār ṣārat lid-diyāba maʿāwī

9 وتقول طيرٍ يطير ما له جهد طار
والدار صارت للذيابة معاوي

10 dār az-zmān ū-dārna-ṣbaḥat dār
wi-dārin ʿala sukkānha-l-fagr ẓāwī

10 دار الزمان ودارنا اصبحت دار
ودارٍ على سكّانها الفقر ضاوي

11 yiṭrūn lī xalfāt fī jōf al-ibyār
ū-biydīrhin fi-l-jōf jurrit iḥdāwī

11 يطرون لي خلفات في جوف البيار
وبيديرهن في الجوف جرّة حذاوي

12 ū-muṣṭād la xarnūg min bēn al-ōkār
fī ḥiddin ū-ṭāliʿ minna ḥāmin ʿamāwī

12 ومصتاد له خرنوق من بين الاوكار
في حدٍّ وطالع منه حامٍ عماوي

13 yāḷḷa yillī lil-maxalīg sitār
tustur ʿuyūb illī ʿal as-sitir nāwī

13 يا اللّه يا اللي للمخاليق ستار
تستر عيوب اللي عل الستر ناوي

14 ū-ya xālg al-janna wiya xālg an-nār
wi-yillī jaʿalt ilkull ʿilla imdāwī

14 ويا خالق الجنّة ويا خالق النار
ويا اللي جعلت لكلّ علّة مداوي

15 tufruj ʿal illī dāb jisma min an-nār
ū-yāma nišāma ṣābra ʿal-balāwī

15 تفرج عل اللي ذاب جسمه من النار
ويما نشامة صابرة عالبلاوي

7
Poems on the Margin of Historic Events (1882–1982)

THE BEDOUIN TESTIMONY

For the past century governments have pursued their national interests in Sinai and the Negev as if there were no local population to take into account. In 1882 Great Britain invaded and occupied Egypt, including the Sinai peninsula. The Negev at the time belonged to the Ottoman Empire; but in the First World War Britain defeated Turkey and ruled the Negev for the next thirty years. At that time the Zionist movement was making headway in British Palestine and purchasing land in the Negev, as a result of which the Negev was incorporated into the State of Israel in 1948. In the late 1940s Britain's authority in Sinai was transferred to Egypt; Egypt then lost two wars to Israel, which, in turn, governed that peninsula for some months in 1956–7 and for fifteen years from 1967 to 1982, when peace between the two countries restored Egyptian authority. These events took place in complete disregard of the local bedouin population. Throughout their long history and down to the War of Zāriʿ al-Huzayyil (Chapter 5) the bedouin had been masters of the desert and of their own fate. Now they were obliged to adjust to whatever situations these non-bedouin powers might create.

If only from the viewpoint of Fourth World history, it is interesting to know how the bedouin were affected by the events that encompassed them and determined the destinies of their desert areas. It is also of interest to know to what extent they were aware of these events and their ramifications, and how they reacted to them. However, as no one consulted the bedouin about the historical changes taking place in their midst nor sought their opinions, we would have had no information to record about the past century were it not for poems composed, as it were, on the margins of momentous events. Not that a bedouin would have composed a poem inspired by an historical event—as if to immortalize it; on the contrary, it was the personal rather than the historical significance of an event that would induce him to versify on it. Thus, the only difference between the poems of expression in Chapter 1 and the poems in the present chapter is that the emotional stimulus of these poems was provided by events that we now know to have had historical dimensions. In both cases, however, it was the authors' emotions of despair, resentment, hope, fortitude, or timidity that found expression in a poem.

The British decision in 1884 to transport Muslim pilgrims to Arabia in greater comfort by ship down the Red Sea rather than by camel over Sinai angered those bedouin who had been earning a great part of their livelihood by providing camels and services to the pilgrimage caravan (poem 7.1). When Britain and Turkey in 1906 delimited the border between their respective domains of authority, Sinai and the Negev, a poet of the Rumēlāt tribe felt relief to know that his more powerful enemies would henceforth inhabit the far side of the new line (poem 7.2). Britain's conquest of the Negev from the Turks in 1919 angered a bedouin poet who believed that the Turkish commander had been bribed to surrender to the British infidels (poem 7.3). The starvation throughout Sinai during that war moved a bedouin to compose a poem of despair (poem 7.4); and anger at the Sharīf of Mecca for raising the banner of revolt against the Muslim Ottoman Empire moved an anonymous bedouin to compose a short poem lampooning his ambitions (poem 7.5).

From a poem composed in criticism of an exaggerated tax appraisal on crops we learn that there were bedouin who regarded British rule in the Negev as oppressive and a threat to their freedom (poem 7.6). Another poem reveals that, during the British Mandate, there were bedouin who scorned certain tribal chiefs for selling land for Jewish settlement (poem 7.7). Bedouin later composed poems of resentment against Israel's efforts to settle them and against their chiefs' collusion in those efforts (poem 7.8), as well as poems resenting Egypt's contemptuous attitude towards them and the measures it took to stop them from smuggling through Sinai (poem 7.10). After 1967 at least one bedouin was angry enough to versify against the oppressively high cost of living under Israel's rule in Sinai (poem 7.11).

It was bedouin attitudes and reactions to historical events that gave rise to these poems; but, in determining the authenticity of these attitudes, one must exercise caution. A poem may on occasion employ mock attitudes in order to satirize a situation. During the Suez War of 1956, for example, ʿAnēz abū Sālim, to amuse his friends, made a mock display of distress at the success of the Israeli, French, and British armies—but only to show the comedy in a bedouin's professing loyalty to his own government in order to obtain something: in this case, arms (poem 7.9). The poet's attitude in the last line of the poem ('we're bedouin and do only what our government says / And if not called to prayer, none of us prays'), was one of satisfaction at the discomfiture of the Egyptians, whom the poet and his audience both regarded as arrogant. One can determine the true attitude of a poem only by identifying the original reason for its composition.

The degree to which a bedouin is aware of the activities of outside powers, as reflected in the poems, is also of historical interest. The poet who described the Turkish defeat on the Sinai–Negev front in the First World War, for example, had considerable knowledge of the fighting that took place. The author of the poem about land sales to the Jews had sufficient foresight to sense that these seemingly innocuous transactions of the mid-1940s might one day oust the bedouin from their ancestral lands. The poet that composed a panegyric to celebrate the signing of a peace agreement between Israel and Egypt (poem 7.12) was well aware of the concurrent Arab boycott of Egypt, and of Egypt's annoyance with it.

As in the case of attitudes, however, restraint should be exercised in regard to the factual matter of the poems as well. Certain facts are of course self-evident. A bedouin poet would not have composed a poem decrying British land taxation, if there were no such taxation; there would have been no poem of despair about starvation during the First World War, if there had been no such hardship; there would have been no poem about land sales, if the Jews had not offered to buy land at high prices, and chiefs had not sold it. When, however, the author of the panegyric poem that celebrated the Israeli–Egyptian peace accord before an assembly of both government officials and bedouin chiefs boasted that each ten Egyptian soldiers fought five hundred Israeli troops or that the bedouin themselves fought for the liberation of Sinai, we may suspect that these are exaggerations introduced to please the respective groups of honoured guests, to strike a hyperbolic effect, or to make a convenient rhyme.

7.1

The Closing of the Pilgrim Route through Sinai, 1884

A Poem to Suggest Rebellion

For six hundred years Muslim pilgrims from North Africa and Egypt went to Mecca in an organized caravan that set out from Cairo each year, crossing 'The Pilgrimage Road' (Ar. *darb al-ḥajj*) over central Sinai before turning south into Arabia towards the holy places. The passage of thousands of people through their barren territory provided many bedouin of Sinai with welcome income from the provision of camels and services to the caravan. In 1884, however, the newly established British rulers of Egypt (as of 1882), put an end to the Sinai pilgrim route, so that pilgrims henceforth were transported down the Red Sea toward Mecca in British steamships. The pretext for this sudden change was the murder the previous year by Sinai bedouin of the Orientalist E. H. Palmer, who had been sent by the British government on a mission to buy the allegiance of the Sinai chiefs, whom he knew from the field research he had done for his book, *Desert of the Exodus*, published in 1872.[1]

Britain's arbitrary decision had a disastrous effect on the economy of the Sinai bedouin: until then governments had never been able to wreak such widespread havoc among the population. Hence, a member of the Ḥuwēṭāt tribe that had been responsible for servicing the pilgrim caravan from Cairo up to the 'Mitla' (*Umm I<u>th</u>la*) Pass in western Sinai dispatched a poem to his paramount chief in north-west Arabia, Muḥammad Abū Ṭugēga,[2] advocating some form of rebellion lest the bedouin acquiesce in what he foresaw as permanent subjection to outside authority.

O Riders on barren mares gliding along;[3]
Under Allah's protection,[4] prod them with song. 1

Poem 7.1 was transcribed by <u>Sh</u>uqayr (p. 555) in 1906. The present rendition, based on a recitation of <u>Sh</u>uqayr's version by Muṣliḥ Ibn ʿĀmr, at Guṣēma oasis, 15 June 1973, includes changes made according to his judgement.

---

[1] <u>Sh</u>uqayr, pp. 547–55.

[2] For the Abū Ṭugēga, see Musil, *Hegaz*, pp. 129ff; Lawrence, p. 175. Also cf. poem 2.8.

[3] See poem 1.1, n. 14, on barren mounts. The 'gliding' image derives from the allusion to young gazelles (*ʿufūr*) in the Arabic text.

[4] 'Under Allah's protection' (*fī jīrit allāh*) is a common blessing said to someone embarking on a journey.

Go to Abū Ṭugēga, that well widely known;[5]
O what barren sheep's fat to his guests he has thrown![6] 2

Say: Word has been heard that all bedouin reject—
Even our women have sworn to object.[7] 3

They're changing the Ḥajj pilgrims' caravan trail;
In those 'pipes of the sea' must the pilgrim now sail.[8] 4

O, woe from a world that contains seven seas,[9]
And by screwing in bolts you have ships made with ease. 5

Whoever minds laws, like a bull will be led,
And endure till they lower the yoke from his head. 6

1 ya rakbīn min fōg ḥiyāl wi-ʿafūr
fī jīrit al̤l̤ā ġannū-lhinni

1 يا راكبين من فوق حيال وعفور
في جيرة اللّد غنّو لهنّ

2 tilfū ʿal abū ṭgēga ya ʿidd mad̲kūr
ū-kam ḥiyālin̲ yirmī šaḥamhinni

2 تلفو عل ابو طقيقة يا عدّ مذكور
وكم حيالٍ يرمي شحمهنّ

3 gūlū lafāna ʿilm mā hū ʿal al-badū mamrūr
ḥatta banāt al-badū ʿayyan la yignaʿinni

3 قولو لفانا علم ما هو عل البدو ممرور
حتّى بنات البدو عيّن لا يقنعنّ

4 wil-ḥajj ṣabbaḥ ʿan mašaḥī madḥūr
wi-ṣārat ġalayīn al-baḥr yingilinni

4 والحجّ صبّح عن مشاحيد مدحور
وصارت غلايين البحر ينقلنّد

5 wall min dinya lak sabʿa buḥūr
ū-lak lawalīb bass tabram ib-hinni

5 ولّ من دنيا لك سبع بحور
ولك لواليب بسّ تبرم بهنّ

[5] For the image of wells for bountiful people, cf. poem 2.7, n. 6.

[6] On slaughtering barren sheep as a mark of generosity, see poem 5.7, n. 6. As Bedouin consider the fat (*s̲haḥam*) of a sheep's tail a great delicacy, a host's throwing it on top of a bowlful of freshly cooked meat, as portrayed here, is also an act of largesse.

[7] Although there are exceptions, women, as protected persons, generally take no active role in conflict. Hence, this line is introduced as much for humorous effect as for emphasis.

[8] Bedouin likened steamships to their own types of pipe (*g̲halāyīn*, sing. *g̲halyūn*), because of the steam they emitted.

[9] For the connection of seven with seas, cf. Doughty (i. 319), who reports that his bedouin friends thought that the Christians 'dwelt behind seven floods'.

6 min ṭā' lin-nimra gawad zē-ṯ-ṯōr
wiyuṣbur limma yinzil an-nīr 'inni

6 مـن طـاع للنمـرة قـود زي الثور
ويصبـر لمّـا ينـزل النيـر عنـده

7.2

Drawing the Border between Sinai and the Negev, 1906

A Poem of Praise and Relief

When Great Britain became the true suzerain of Egypt in 1882, it was not clear how far her authority extended eastwards. Technically, Sinai still remained part of the Ottoman Empire (as did Egypt proper), but, as Istanbul had previously delegated the Egyptian viceroy ('*Khedive*') to assume responsibility for policing Sinai, the question arose of whether the Ottomans or the British would henceforth predominate there. The problem persisted for twenty-four years until, in 1906, Britain forced the Turks to negotiate by using gunboat diplomacy—sending a frigate to the Ottoman-held port of Aqaba at the head of the Red Sea. The result was an agreement to delineate their respective domains between the town of Rafaḥ on the Mediterranean coast and Ṭābā, a spot on the Red Sea opposite Aqaba.[1]

This agreement between the two great empires had an effect on the lives of the bedouin who lived on each side of the new border. To one confederation at least, the Rumēlāt, it promised a formal disengagement from the larger and stronger Tarābīn confederation. The Tarābīn, who had been harrassing the Rumēlāt for a century,[2] were now to be confined mainly to the Ottoman–Negev side of the line.

At the ceremony to celebrate the agreement held at Rafaḥ in the presence of the bedouin notables of northern Sinai, Faraj Sulēmān, a black slave of the paramount Rumēlāt chief, Sulēmān Ma'yūf, composed the following poem. Although intended to be a panegyric to

Poem 7.2 was transcribed by Shuqayr (p. 614) at the time of the event that gave rise to the poem. The present rendition, based on a recitation of Shuqayr's version by Muṣliḥ Ibn 'Āmr, at Guṣēma oasis, 15 June 1973, includes changes made according to his judgement.

[1] Shuqayr, pp. 558–616.

[2] Ibid. 582–5.

those who participated in the negotiations, it also gave expression to the relief sensed by his tribe.

When I was born our borders were blurred;
Even Rafaḥ[3] itself we'd not seen, only heard. 1

Then the Pashas[4] convened between their two lines,
While we waited with patience till all was defined. 2

At last we've a border as straight as a gun,
And every tribe knows where its borders now run. 3

The Governor[5] was there, Naʿūm Bey[6] at his side,
Fatḥāt Pasha,[7] as well, his troops alongside; 4

Then Fihmī, Muẓaffar, and Asʿad came by,[8]
All of them Beys! What a joy to the eye! 5

On Sunday they left us by Allah's good grace,
And with flags marked the border in each distant place. 6

May Allah preserve them and strengthen their states:
Now the bedouin can rest after long dire straits. 7

1 fa-wwal daharna ma-lna ḥadd mazbūṭ wamma rafaḥ fa-ḏ-ḏikir nismaʿ bi-tiryā	1 في اوّل دهرنا ما لنا حـــدّ مضبوط وامّـا رفـح في الذكر نسمع بطرياد
2 altammat al-bašāt bēn al-maḥadīd wiḥna ṣabarna bēnhum lil-imdaʿā	2 التمّت البـاشات بيـن المحاديد واحنـا صبرنـا بينهـم للمداعاة
3 wal-yōm ṣār iḥdādna baṭin al-barūd wil-kull min ḥadda yirjaʿ la-mimšā	3 واليوم صار احدادنا بطن البارود والكـلّ مـن حدّد يرجـع لممشاد

[3] A town on the present border between Sinai and the Gaza Strip.
[4] i.e. the high officials of both parties.
[5] Lt. Col. A. C. Parker, governor of Sinai, 1907–23.
[6] Naʿūm Shuqayr.
[7] Col. Ibrāhīm Fatḥī of the Egyptian service.
[8] Turkish representatives.

4 na'ūm bē wal-mudīr al-imsamma
ū-fatḥāt bāša wal-'asākir ibtibrā

4 نعوم بيك والمدير المسمّى
وفاتحات باشا والعساكر بتبراد

5 jāhum imẓaffar ū-fihmī wa-s'ad
al-kull minhum bē ya ni'im malgā

5 جاهم مظفّر وفهمي واسعد
الكلّ منهم بيك يا نعم ملقاد

6 yōm al-aḥad mišyū 'ala xērit aḷḷā
ū-ġizzū 'alāyim ḥaddhum bal-amwatā

6 يوم الاحد مشيو على خيرة اللّد
وغزّو علايم حدّهم بالمواتاد

7 ya rabb tiḥmīhum ū-tunṣur idwalhum
irtāḥat al-'arbān ba'd al-imgasā

7 يا ربّ تحميهم وتنصر دولهم
ارتاحت العربان بعد المقاساة

7·3

First World War Battles in Sinai and the Negev

A Poem of Anger

The First World War, in which a Christian power, Great Britain, defeated the Muslim Ottoman Empire, had far-reaching consequences for the people of the area who were to come under European domination or influence—in particular for the Arabs of what was to become known as Palestine, including the bedouin of the Negev. Indeed, in the early stages of the war, 1,400 bedouin irregulars from the Negev joined the Turkish forces in their planned attack on the Suez Canal (called by the bedouin 'the Canal War' (*ḥarb at-tur'a*)).[1] Once that attack was repulsed, however, the way was open for the British forces to march over all northern Sinai, and eventually to take Palestine.

One unnamed bedouin irregular, angered over what he understood as a *Muslim* defeat, was moved to compose the present poem, in which

Poem 7.3 was heard recited by Muṣliḥ Sālim Sulēmān Ibn 'Āmr of the Tiyāhā Ṣgērāt tribe, in Wādī Munbaṭaḥ, 15 June 1972.

[1] Al-'Ārif, *Ta'rīkh*, pp. 250–1. Each bedouin volunteer brought his own camel, but was supplied with provisions and provender. Furthermore, the bedouin were guaranteed retention of all the camels, light weapons, and ammunition they could capture; cannon and machine-guns, however, had to be submitted to the Turkish army.

he relates various episodes from the Ottoman–British front in Sinai and the Negev. However, in emphasizing the episodes that would be significant for a bedouin, the poet condenses, into one seemingly unbroken sequence, events that in reality spread over three years, such as the participation of the bedouin volunteers in the assaults on British positions at Gaṭiya oasis (November 1914) and the Suez Canal (February 1915), the fall of the border town, Rafaḥ (January 1917), and the fall of Beersheba (October 1917), which became famous because the city was taken by surprise from the east. His anger at the defeat, moreover, was intensified by the rumour that Jamāl Pasha, the Turkish Governor of Syria (including Palestine), had been paid by the British to lose the war and surrender.[2] The high point of the poem comes when he accuses Jamāl of treachery and holds him responsible for the Turkish débâcle.

1 Before I start this poem to say,
For Prophet Ṭaha let us pray,[3]
As he's our hope on Judgment Day.

2 Toward el-ʿArīsh our army came,[4]
Against Iblīs we called God's name;[5]
We came in force to gain our aim.

3 Ahead the Turkish Pasha went,
At Gaṭiya stopped and pitched his tent,[6]
The cannon to their place he sent.

4 The English Pasha then advanced
(You'd know he's learned, at a glance);
He dug in at Ḥabwa, not by chance.[7]

[2] The accusation of treason, apparently unfounded, was perhaps induced by Jamāl's infamous suppression of Arab nationalism during the war (for which see Antonius, pp. 184–90).

[3] The vocative, Ṭaha, with which Sūra 20 of the Qur'ān opens, is considered one of Muḥammad's appellations in popular Islam. On the reason for the opening prayer, see poem 3.5, n. 6.

[4] In November 1914.

[5] For the idea of confounding *Iblīs* (the devil), see poem 4.20, n. 14.

[6] The first clash with British forces took place at Gaṭiya oasis on 15 November 1914 (al-ʿĀrif, *Ta'rīkh*, p. 251).

[7] Al-ʿĀrif (ibid. 252) claims that it was the Turks who were camped at Ḥabwa near the Suez Canal, north-east of the Great Bitter Lake.

5 The first attack felled Sulēmān,[8]
Who'd led his bedouin in the van
In wars that o'er our history span.

6 The next round found the brave ʿAgēl:
They moved by night toward the Canal
Atop their camels trained and hale.[9]

7 The Mitrailleuse[10] then caused their rout,
All black and with an ugly snout,
While planes above dropped bombs about.[11]

8 The Pasha fled with the Wazīr,
Their units gave up out of fear;
The bedouin scattered far and near.[12]

9 The infidel proceeded on
And brought the town of Rafaḥ down;[13]
His units everywhere were found.

10 But then they met three companies,[14]
Whose officer could fight with ease:[15]
He'd learned his warfare by degrees.

[8] Sulēmān Abū Sitta was one of five bedouin volunteers killed in the battle at Gaṭiya, which otherwise was a Turkish victory (ibid. 251).

[9] Lawrence (p. 410) states that the ʿAgēl participated in an attack which agrees with al-ʿĀrif's description of the attack on Gaṭiya (see above, note 6). It is thus likely that they also participated in the attack on the Suez Canal which took place on 3 February 1915. For more on the ʿAgēl, see poem 1.8.

[10] Mitrailleuse, the French designation for a machine-gun, probably entered bedouin usage through contact with the Ottoman army. In the present context it does not refer to the French weapon, La Mitrailleuse, of the Franco–Prussian War, which was not used by the British army in the First World War. (Communication from Prof. Edward Luttwak, Washington DC.)

[11] While the British resistance was obstinate, there is no mention of the use of war planes in either al-ʿĀrif (*Taʾrīkh*, p. 252) or Wavell (pp. 24–5).

[12] This description tallies with that of the sources consulted (see above, n. 11). Al-ʿĀrif, moreover, notes that, after this attack on the Canal, the bedouin irregulars from the Negev participated in no further operations.

[13] The British surrounded Rafaḥ on 9 January 1917 and encountered a stout defence before subduing the Turkish garrison (Dawney, p. 816). It is likely that the town sustained considerable damage.

[14] ʿIṣmet Bey (later ʿIṣmet Inönu, Prime Minister of Turkey), the commander of Turkish forces in Beersheba, sent three cavalry squadrons with an auxiliary unit of machine-gunners to defend Beersheba from the east. They fought bravely but were overwhelmed (al-ʿĀrif, *Taʾrīkh*, p. 260).

[15] Asʿad Bey.

11 But even they fell to the foe,
Who led their leader off in tow;
The hero's tears stopped not to flow.

12 'Beersheba they won't reach by land,
For As'ad Bey is in command,[16]
And to the West he'll make his stand.'

13 Like it or not, Beersheba fell.
The Turkish luck did not go well;
Their fort is now a ruined shell.[17]

14 At Khwēlfa sat a small platoon—
Its officer's shoulders with stars were strewn;
He caused the infidel some ruin
With light artillery fired soon.[18]

15 They circled around him from every side,
And though their numbers he defied,
They took him captive in their stride;
His soldiers fled to save their hide.

16 The last big clash was at Haddār:[19]
The cannon dust was seen afar;
Nothing was left without a scar,
The bombs they dropped marred and charred.

17 This whole misfortune's from Jamāl,
He put the Muslim faith on sale.
May God betray this coward frail
For orphaned maidens left to wail.[20]

[16] As'ad Bey is apparently a mistaken reference to 'Iṣmet Bey (see above, n. 14).

[17] Tell as-Saba'. Beersheba fell on 31 October 1917.

[18] According to al-'Ārif (*Ta'rīkh*, p. 262), the battles around Khwēlfa were the most severe of the Beersheba campaign, lasting three days and causing the British considerable losses (cf. Pirie-Gordon, p. 820).

[19] A fortified hill near the tomb of Abū Hurēra (holy to the bedouin; see poem 2.11, n. 8). The British broke through on 6 November 1917, and captured Gaza the next day.

[20] An unmarried maiden without a father to conclude a proper marriage for her, and subsequently safeguard her marital interests, is considered unfortunate. Consequently, it is said of a girl whose living father neglects her interests that the daughter of so-and-so is an orphan' (*'awrat fulān yitīma*).

1 awwal ma nibdī wingūl
insallī ʿa ṭaha-r-rasūl
yišfiʿ alna yōm aẓ-ẓīgāt

1 اوّل ما نبدي ونقول
نصلّي ع طـه الـرسول
يشفع لنا يوم الضيقات

2 maddat al-jurda ʿal-ʿarīš
taxza ʿanhum ʿayn iblīs
bil-hamāyim al-guwiyyāt

2 مدّت الجردة عالعريش
تخزى عنهم عين ابليس
بالهمايم القويّات

3 agdam al-bāša guddām
fī gaṭiya bana-l-xiyām
wal-madāfiʿ imdarrasāt

3 اقدم الباشا قدّام
في قطية بنى الخيام
والمدافع مدرّسات

4 agdam bāšt al-inglīz
wi-ṯrāta gārī farīz
fī ḥabwa sawwa-stigamāt

4 اقدم باشة الانقليز
وثراته قارئ فريز
في حبوة سوّى استقامات

5 awwal hawj ṭāḥ islēmān
jisir mabnī ʿal-ʿurbān
fi-l-ḥarāyib al-gidīmāt

5 اوّل هوج طاح سليمان
جسر مبني عالعربان
في الحرايب القديمات

6 wi-ṯānī hawj lafat bi-ʿagēl
yanḥarū-t-turʿa fi-l-lēl
ʿaz-zmūl al-gadīrāt

6 وثاني هوج لفت بعقيل
ينحرو الترعة في الليل
عالزمول القديرات

7 walammhum bi-mitir-al-lōz
azrag ya šinīʿ al-būz
min fōga tirmī ṭayyarāt

7 والمّهم بمتر اللوز
ازرق يا شنيع البوز
من فوقد ترمي طيّارات

8 šarad al-bāša wal-wazīr
wi-rāḥat kull aṭ-ṭawabīr
wal-ʿarab ṣārat šatāt

8 شرد الباشا والوزير
وراحت كلّ الطوابير
والعرب صارت شتات

9 agdam al-hālik guddām
aʿṭa blād rafaḥ ʿadām
baṭ-ṭawabīr al-maʿdūdāt

9 اقدم الهالك قدّام
اعطى بلاد رفح عدام
بالطوابير المعدودات

10 ligī ṯilāṯ ṭawabīr
ū-zabithum mā hū ḏilīl
ū-lih ʿal al-ḥarb ʿadāt

10 لقي ثلاث طوابير
وضابطهم ما هو ذليل
وله عل الحرب عادات

11 axaḏ iṯ-tilāṯ ṭawabīr
ū-zābiṭhin maḥḥin yisīr
dmūʿ ʿayni sāylāt

11 اخذ الثلاث طوابير
وضابطهن معهن يسير
دموع عيند سايلات

12 gulna aś-sabaʿ ma yijī
asʿad bēk imwaggaʿ fī
ġarbiyyi imsawwa-stagamāt

12 قلنا السبع ما يجيد
اسعد بيك موقّع فيد
غربيّـد مسوّى استقامات

13 rāḥ as-sabaʿ ġaṣb ū-ṭīb
ma lit-turk fīha naṣīb
aʿṭū gilāʿa xarabāt

13 راح السبع غصب وطيب
ما لترك فيـها نصيب
اعطـو قـلاعد خرابات

14 ʿa xwēlfa ṭabūr ṣaġīr
maḥḥum zābiṭ ib-dababīr
kassar al-hālik taksīr
bil-madāfiʿ ar-ribaʿiyyāt

14 ع خويلفة طابور صغير
معهم ضابط بدبابير
كسّر الـهالك تكسير
بالـمدافـع الربعيّـات

15 dārū ʿalē dāyir ma-ydīr
ū-walyū bil-jamaʿ al-kiṯīr
waxaḏū-z-zābiṭ yisīr
ū-bāgi-l-ʿaskar rāḥ šatāt

15 دارو عليد داير ما يدير
ووليو بالجمع الكـثير
واخذو الضابط يسير
وباقي العسكر راح شتات

16 waxar ḏabḥa ʿal-haddār
ṣārat il-madāfiʿ ʿiṣār
rāḥat al-ʿālam damār
min kiṯir ramī aṭ-ṭayyarāt

16 واخر ذبحة عالـهدّار
صارت المدافع عصار
راحت العالم دمار
من كــثر رمي الطيّـارات

17 kulli mi-l-bāša jamāl
wālas ʿa dīni bi-māl
alla yixūna hal-baṭṭāl
kuṯr ma yattam ʿawrāt

17 كـلّـد من الباشا جمال
والس ع ديند بمال
اللـد يخوند هالبطّال
كـثر ما يتّم عورات

7.4

Stagnation in Sinai during the First World War

A Poem of Despair

The First World War and its attendant events caused great hardship among the bedouin of Sinai. Near its end a poet from the ʿAyāyda confederation reviewed the condition of his people in the following lines of verse, an expression of despair.

For seven years the world has been at war;
It's hard to earn a wage or find a chore. 1

Folks sell belongings, which to them were dear,
To buy some beans for coffee and some clothes to wear. 2

In their tents you'll hardly find some bread,
And dust has veiled each face up to the head. 3

Folks either beg just sitting by a wall,
Or else they steal or go with nought at all. 4

And should anyone smuggle who isn't fleet,
By major and by sergeant he'll be beat. 5

1 sabaʿ snīn wad-dinya ḥarāba
wi-kadd al-yadd̈ ma gaẓẓa-l-maʿāš

2 bāʿū mā-lhum illī kān ġālī
bēn al-bann ū-ma bēn il-igmāš

3 tilga-byūthum mi-l-ʿēš xālī
ū-wujūh an-nās ġašīha ġabāš

1 سبع سنين والدنيا حرابة
وكدّ اليد ما قضى المعاش

2 باعو ما لهم اللي كان غالي
بين البنّ وما بين القماش

3 تلقى بيوتهم من العيش خالي
ووجوه الناس غشيها غباش

Poem 7.4 was heard recited by Ḥusēn Salīm Ḥasan of the ʿAyāyda Salāṭna tribe, at Ḥamādit Baghdād, 8 March 1972.

4 ya gaʿadū fī janb ḥayṭa
ya saragū ya rāḥū balāš

5 willī yiharrib iyjībū
wiyẓrabū aš-šawīš wil-bimbāš

4 يـا قعدو في جنب حيطة
يـا سرقو يـا راحو بلاش

5 واللـي يهـرّب يجيبود
ويضربـود الشاويش والبمباش

7.5

The Sharīf of Mecca's Rebellion against the Turks, 1915

A Poem of Contempt

Another aspect of Britain's involvement in the Middle East during the First World War was the rebellion it encouraged of the Sharīf of Mecca, Ḥusēn ibn ʿAlī al-Hāshimī, against the Ottoman Empire, as described and made famous by T. E. Lawrence (Lawrence of Arabia) in his book *Seven Pillars of Wisdom*. The British intention was to divert Turkish troops from the Palestine front. While, as Lawrence relates, many bedouin in Arabia and Transjordan joined the rebellion, the composer of the present short satire, perhaps of the Bilī tribe,[1] was among the many who did not. After Ḥusēn ibn ʿAlī proclaimed his rebellion against the Turks and declared himself King of the Ḥijāz, the bedouin poet expressed his indignation over the Sharīf's betrayal of Iṣlam; when the rebellion began, a holy war or *jihād* against the British had already been declared. He thus ridiculed the presumption of the Sharīf, whose function had always been religious ('Keeper of the Holy Places'), in believing he had the qualities, such as generosity or courage, necessary for a king.

Poem 7.5 was heard recited by Muṣliḥ Sālim Sulēmān Ibn ʿĀmr, in Wādī Munbaṭaḥ, 15 June 1972.

[1] The chief of the Ḥijāzian Bilī, Sulēmān Ibn Rifāda, maintained close relations with the Turkish authorities and opposed the rebellion (Lawrence, pp. 116, 158, 161).

A Sharīf you may be, but you're hardly a king; 1

Though you kill barren camels, their fat you don't fling;[2] 2

Though you carry long spears, you don't enter the ring; 3

Though you'd battle,[3] a fox's howl makes you take wing; 4

Though you're quick on the trigger, no bullets ping.[4] 5

شريف ما لا انت شريف ـ لكن ما تهيا ملك 1

1 šarīf ma-la inti šarīf—lakin ma tihya malik

ذبّاح للحايل السمين ـ لكن ما ترمي ودك 2

2 ḏabbāḥ lil-ḥāyil is-samīn—lakin ma tirmī wadak

نقّال للرمح الطويل ـ لكن ما توطا درك 3

3 naggāl lir-ramḥ iṭ-ṭawīl—lakin ma tawṭā darak

فزّاع للصوت البعيد ـ ان شفت حصيني جفّلك 4

4 fazzāʻ liṣ-ṣawt il-baʻīd—in šuft iḥṣēnī jaffalak

بارودتك سريعة الثوير ـ لكن ما ترمي فشك 5

5 barūdtak sarīʻa-ṯ-ṯawīr—lakin ma tirmī fašak

[2] 'Throwing the suet' (*ramī al-wadak*) over the platter of camel-meat being served is viewed as a sign of generosity; especially if the butchered animal is barren (i.e. kept from calving) (cf. poems 1.1, n. 14; 2.9; 7.1, n. 6).

[3] Lit. 'You'd charge off in response to a distant call for help.'

[4] i.e. he is a liar; bedouin often call a liar one who 'shoots without bullets' (*biyṭukhkh bilā fashak*).

7.6

British Agricultural Taxes in the Negev

A Poem to Request a Reduction

An unwelcome feature of British rule in the Negev after the First World War was the imposition of taxes on cultivated land. While, under the Turks, taxes had been imposed on the tribe as a whole, the British authorities in the Negev went out and assessed harvests and counted livestock in order to tax the individual. They were assisted in this task by the expert opinion of bedouin assessors whom they trusted.

One year, in which the harvest was poor, the bedouin assessors came to the plot which Faraj Sulēmān, of the Sinai Rumēlāt, had rented on a share-crop basis from a member of the Tarābīn aṣ-Ṣūfi, an ad-Dibārī; and they assessed his crop to be ten kilograms per *dūnam* (approx. one quarter of an acre)]. Feeling cheated, Faraj availed himself of an occasion when one of the assessors, the influential chief of the Ḥanājra tribe, Frēḥ Abū Middēn, visited Faraj's own chief, Sulēmān Maʿyūf. He composed a poem describing the injustice that was done (lines 1–6), praising Frēḥ Abū Middēn and his companion, chief of the Rumēlāt ʿAjālīn (lines 7–11), and cautioning all who would hear of the dangers lurking in the new British rule (lines 12–16). As a result of this recitation, Abū Middēn waived the taxes that had been levied against the poet's poor harvest.

The harvest was meagre and Dibārī got half,[1]
But Jirwānī assessed it, for luck did a gaffe.[2] 1

Approaching, we deemed it a cavalry troop;
'Twas the Tarābīn agent, Ḥājj Ghēth, come around.[3] 2

When they left us we felt as if stabbed with daggers;
Had they stayed on a bit, we'd have paid thirty more.[4] 3

Poem 7.6 was heard recited by Lāfi Faraj Sulēmān (the son of the author) of the Rumēlāt Busūm tribe at el-ʿArīsh, 15 October 1970.

[1] The ad-Dibāriyyīn clan is part of the Tarābīn aṣ-Ṣūfi; the poet cultivated their land on a share-cropping basis.

[2] i.e. a member of the Jarāwīn tribe, which was appended to the Tarābīn, although its bedouin origins were questioned (see poem 5.11, n. 9).

[3] 'Ḥājj Ghēth' was an assessor in government employ. The insinuation here is that he was 'recommended' by the Tarābīn landlords so that he would assess the crop high and increase their share.

[4] i.e. thirty kilograms more per *dūnam*.

Had I wanted to market this crop, none would buy;
So what should we say when the taxes are high? 4

If Barkil that day to my left had been seated,
He'd have gone by the law, and I'd not have been cheated;[5] 5

Or had I some coins and riyals but a few,
Then the ten kilograms would have gone down to two.[6] 6

Frēḥ Abū Middēn's been appointed a chief,
And his word with the British meets with belief.[7] 7

For his word with the governors people will pay,
And if someone needs help he sets out straightaway.[8] 8

He can ride a wild horse though her four legs are bound;[9]
She'll go forth though they're ambushed by fire all around. 9

And he who brings she-camels,[10] plundered, relief,
Is Sālim Farāj, the new ʿAjālīn chief.[11] 10

When he dons a wool cloak and goes out for a walk,
He's compared by the folk to a proud Shāhīn hawk.[12] 11

[5] Lt. Col. A. C. Parker, governor Sinai (1907–23), enjoyed a quasi-legendary reputation for justice and for an appreciation of the bedouin.

[6] i.e. he would have bribed the assessors.

[7] According to the oral tradition, Abū Middēn, who had been a donkey-thief before the First World War, was discovered suffering from malaria by the British troops advancing under General Allenby, in the summer of 1917. Because of his helpful instructions on how to attack Beersheba from the east, the British appointed him chief in his tribe, judge on the government-sponsored tribal court, and assessor of crops. During the Second World War they further rewarded him with construction contracts; which ultimately led to his founding, together with a fellow tribesman, Frēḥ al-Muṣaddar, one of the largest construction companies in Egypt.

[8] Cf. these lines to poem 2.11, l. 14.

[9] The horse binds referred to here are the *hijār* which connect the front and rear legs on one side. The hyperbolic image is of both sides being bound.

[10] 'Camels' in the Arabic text are depicted as 'those whose teats are bound with cords' (*mukammashāt aṣ-ṣarār*), i.e. those whose calves are being weaned.

[11] The ʿAjālīn are an appended section of the Rumēlāt, originating in the Banī ʿUgba of the Ḥijāz.

[12] Cf. poems 2.10, n 10; 5.1, l. 4.

The new State, each man's name to record doth now seek;[13]
It has taken our arms, so like women we're weak.[14] 12

It's a wall that surrounds all the land where we've been,
All our bedouin to even the far Jahālīn.[15] 13

Some things are clear, some remain under sheath,
But this State's like pliers fastened tight on our teeth. 14

Already they're taxing our land everywhere,
Even figs, watermelon, and wild prickly pear. 15

Nor our chiefs, can they help us, they're worthless today!
They're like chaff when its winnowed by children at play.[16] 16

1 zarʿa zaʿāb ū-nuṣṣhī lid-dbārī tāh ad-dalīl ū-gaddarūha-l-jarawīn	زرعة زعاب ونصّها للدباري 1 تاد الدليل وقدّروها الجراوين
2 hallū ʿalēna tigūl ʿaskar ṣawārī wal-ḥājj ġēṯ imwaklīna-t-tarabīn	هلّو علينا تقول عسكر صواري 2 والحاجّ غيث موكّليند الترابين
3 wigfū kama-mladḏaʿīn ib-šibārī wila rayyaẓū ḥīnēn zādū ṯalaṯīn	واقفو كما ملذّعين بشباري 3 ولو ريّضو حينين زادو ثلاثين
4 wa-law kān widdna inbīʿ mā fī šārī waġlū ʿalēna-l-māl wiḥna masakīn	ولو كان ودّنا نبيع ما فيد شاري 4 واغلو علينا المال واجنا مساكين

[13] Bedouin, considering secrecy one of their main assets in the constant struggle for survival, resent the ability of governments, since the First World War, to break their prized anonymity and register them (cf. poems 4.8, l. 2; 7.10, l. 9).

[14] Traditionally, women were unarmed because they were a 'protected' section of society. As each bedouin man is jealous of the right to defend himself, and proud of his ability to do so, a 'protected' person is considered inferior. Among others traditionally 'protected' were blacks and the Hitēm tribes (see poem 4.16, n. 3).

[15] The Jahālīn traditionally inhabited the northern Negev and Judaean Desert areas abutting the Dead Sea.

[16] The chaff mentioned in this metaphor for unimportance is the very lightest, the 'flying chaff' (*ṭiyūr at-tibn*). Heavier, in ascending sequence, is the regular winnowed chaff (*tibn*), the threshed, pre-winnowed chaff (*gaṣl at-tibn*), and the grain (*ḥabb*).

5 wi-law kān barkil bē gā'id yisārī
li-kān xalla ma-lhī 'al-gawanīn

5 ولو كان بركل بيك قاعد يساري
لكان خلّى ما لها عالقوانين

6 wa-law ṣaḥḥan riyalēn warba' 'ašārī
kān al-'ašar kīlāt raddū 'ala tnīn

6 ولو صحّن ريالين واربع عشاري
كان العشر كيلات ردّو على ثنين

7 ū-frēḥ abū middēn šēxin garārī
briṭānya tāxiḏ kalāma ib-taymīn

7 وفريح ابو مدّين شيخ قراري
بريطانيا تاخذ كلامه بتيمين

8 harji 'al al-ḥukkām 'ạdd al-maṣārī
win jā li hal-maẓlūm biygūm fī ḥīn

8 هرجد عل الحكّام عدّ المصاري
وان جا لد المظلوم بيقوم في حين

9 ḥiml il-ijmūḥ in rabba'at bil-hijārī
tiṭla' wi-law lazzat 'alēha-l-makamīn

9 حمل الجموح ان ربّعت بالهجار
تطلع ولو لزّت عليها المكامين

10 willī bifikk imkammašāt aṣ-ṣrārī
sālim walad farāj šēx al-'ajalīn

10 واللي بيفكّ مكمّشات الصرار
سالم ولد فراج شيخ العجالين

11 ū-limma timašša bil-'abā-š-ša'ārī
waṣfi kama waṣf aṣ-ṣgūr aš-šayahīn

11 ولمّا تمشّى بالعباد الشعاري
وصفد كما وصف الصقور الشياهين

12 wal-ḥukim yuṭlubna kutūbit anfār
ṣirtū min ġēr slāḥ zē an-nisawīn

12 والحكم يطلبنا كتوبة انفار
صرتم من غير سلاح زي النساوين

13 wal-ḥukm ḥāyiṭ 'al jimīa' al-xibārī
ḥatta 'al badwānhī wil-jahalīn

13 والحكم حايط على جميع الخباري
حتّى على بدوانها والجهالين

14 ū-fi-n-nās ma yidrī ū-fi-n-nās dārī
kalbat ḥadīd wi-šabakat 'aṭ-ṭawaḥīn

14 وفي الناس ما يدري وفي الناس داري
كلبة حديد وشبكت عالطواحين

15 wi-ṣārit ibtirmī 'a jamīa' al-ixbārī
ḥatta 'ala-l-baṭīx waṣ-ṣabir wat-tīn

15 وصارت بترمي ع جميع الخباري
حتّى على البطيخ والصبر والتين

16 ū-xallak min illī ma 'alē i'tibārī
ṭayūr tibin maḏriyyīna-ṭ-ṭanawīn

16 وخلّك من اللي ما عليد اعتبار
طيور تبن مذريّيند الطناوين

7.7

Selling Bedouin Land in the Negev to the Jewish Agency

A Poem to Castigate and to Warn

In the 1940s the Jewish Agency, which acquired land for Jewish settlement, was interested in purchasing lands in the Negev and offered unusually high prices. In the early part of the decade the lands acquired included a spot called Magbūla near the well of ʿAṣlūj. It was bought from the chief of the ʿAzāzma Masʿūdiyyīn, Salāma Ibn Saʿīd, for the establishment of the kibbutz Revivim in 1943.

Dismayed by what he considered irresponsible behaviour on the part of the ʿAzāzma chiefs, ʿAyyād ʿAwwād Ibn ʿAdēsān, also of the ʿAzāzma Masʿūdiyyīn, composed a poem which he recited at one encampment after another in order to denigrate the selling of land and those chiefs who had done so; he stressed in particular the danger of the bedouin being disinherited from their own living space and freedom. He mocked the uses to which the chiefs put their newly found wealth, ending with the taunt that one of the sellers, az-Zirbāwī, found he no longer had space to defecate.

O Rider on one who keeps a fast pace,
As if she'd been pricked and appears to be leaping; 1

Like a gazelle who's the lookout ahead of its herd,
As hunters it spies on the plain, and is stirred.[1] 2

O Rider, if you want to urge him to speed,
My advice is: don't let the halter get freed. 3

Stop off with our chieftains, each one of them brave,[2]
Fellows sitting in council, you'll find them all grave; 4

You'll hear a chief belch as he comes forth to greet,
A belt he won't wear, having too much to eat. 5

Poem 7.7 was heard recited by the author's brother, Sulēmān ʿAwwād Ibn ʿAdēsān of the ʿAzāzma Masʿūdiyyīn tribe, in Wādī Shgēb, 16 February 1972.

---

[1] For a similar image, see poems 2.6, 2.8, 6.1.

[2] Ll. 4–5 are intended to ridicule.

Say: Last night, how I felt in my heart a great pain,
For the chiefs aren't aware of what I would complain. 6

I sighed when I saw them, their faces so cool,
Making deals in the market, led on like a fool. 7

They told: 'Sell off your farmland, there's someone who'll buy;
You'll get all you want, for the price of land's high.' 8

Sell your freedom to raid virgin long-necked camels!
Sell pastures where camel herds graze without trammels! 9

Yes, spend on yourselves for one month, maybe more;
Spend freely on clothes for a few nights decor. 10

Your sale in the end is of roots you'll have torn;
You'll yet wander 'tween Egypt and Shām[3] till you're worn. 11

The land that was spacious, yet narrow will be,
You'll find nowhere to rest 'tween the hills and the sea. 12

Look at Ibn Sa'īd and Rabī'a, O my![4]
They've built houses of stone, painted red and so high![5] 13

They've wed daughters of peasants who spice spoiled meat[6]
And spurned those whose fathers spice coffee-pots.[7] 14

Their wives stand around in a thin chemise gown,
Fried foods and soft bread are their only renown.[8] 15

[3] Syria.

[4] The chiefs Salāma Ibn Sa'īd of the 'Azāzma Mas'ūdiyyīn and 'Īd Ibn Rabī'a of the 'Azāzma Zaraba—both of whom sold land.

[5] i.e. they built houses in Beersheba. For use of the term 'palaces' (*gusūr*) for ordinary houses, as in the Arabic text, see poem 2.11, n. 2.

[6] Bedouin believe that peasants, not owning livestock, are constrained to eat non-fresh (hence, unhealthy) meat. By contrast, the meat that they eat is always freshly slaughtered.

[7] i.e. prospective bedouin brides. The reference to 'spicing coffee-pots', denoting hospitality, is cited in the text with pride.

[8] Soft bread is often a symbol of settled as opposed to bedouin life (see poems 4.20A, l. 4; 5.6, l. 13; also Chapter 9).

Even Zirbāwī this life couldn't abide,[9]
When, after shitting, it stuck to each side.[10] 16

1	ya rākb-illī fi-l-mašāḥī sarī'i talad̲d̲a'at taṭra 'alēha-l-jifālī	يا راكب اللي في المشاحي سريعة تلذّعت تطرا عليها الجفالِ
2	mit̲il al-ġazāl ila-šaraf baṭ-ṭalī'i lin rāyab al-gannāṣ fī daww xālī	مثل الغزال الا اشرف بالطليعة لن رايب القنّاص في دوّ خالي
3	ya rākbi in kān widdak tizī'i awṣīk la tirxa 'alē-hal-iḥbālī	يا راكبد ان كان ودّك تزيعد اوصيك لا ترخى عليد الحبالِ
4	tilfī 'ala-š-šēxān zilmi̲n̲ sijī'i zilmi̲n̲ tilgāhum bal-majālis it̲gālī	تلفي على الشيخان زلمٍ سجيعة زلمٍ تلقاهم بالمجالس ثقالِ
5	aš-šēx linni jāk tisma' tirī'i tilgā yimši fī hidūmi irfālī	الشيخ لنّد جاك تسمع تريعة تلقاد يمشي في هدومد رفالِ
6	al-beriḥa ṣārat bi-galbī wijī'i ū-ma yidrū aš-šēxān ēš hū bi-bālī	البارحة صارت بقلبي وجيعة وما يدرو الشيخان ايش هو ببالي
7	wannēt min šōf ad-digūn aṣ-ṣigī'i yiṣaffigū fi-s-sūg mit̲l il-himālī	ونّيت من شوف الدقون الصقيعة يصفّقو في السوق مثل الهمالِ
8	biygūlū lihum ya nišāma-llī la mazra' yibī'i tilāḥagū bis-si'r wil-milk ġālī	بيقولو لهم يا نشامة اللي لد مزرع يبيعد تلاحقو بالسعر والملك غالي
9	tibī'ū šaddkū bil-bikār aṭ-ṭalī'a tibī'ū maḥās imdawrāt al-mafālī	تبيعو شدّكم بالبكار الطليعة تبيعو محاس مدوّرات المفالي
10	iṣrafū 'al arwāḥkū illi-yhill ū-tibī'i wi-tibanḥaṭū fi-l-labs jimlit liyālī	اصرفو عل ارواحكم اللي يهلّ وتبيعد وتبنحطو في اللبس جملة ليالي

[9] Az-Zirbāwī, originally from Rafaḥ, owned and sold land just south of Beersheba, where he was a merchant in the 1940s.

[10] Bedouin camping in tents are accustomed to defecate and urinate out-of-doors, and must have enough space for privacy away from the eyes of others. Hence, the proverb that suggested the jibe of this line 'He who has no land will shit in his hand' (*illī mā lih arḍ, yik̲h̲rā bi-kaffih*).

11 bāgī maba'itha 'alēkū giṭī'i
tigaṭṭa'ū ma bēn maṣir ū-š-šimālī

11 باقي مباعتها عليكم قطيعة
تقطّعو ما بين مصر والشمال

12 wi-ẓāgit 'alēku ba'd ma hī wisī'i
ẓāgit 'alēkū min al-baḥar lil-jabālī

12 وضاقت عليكم بعد ما هي وسيعة
ضاقت عليكم من البحر للجبال

13 fakkirū fi-bn sa'īd wibn rabī'i
bannū guṣūr imḥanniyyātin 'awālī

13 فكّرو في ابن سعيد وابن ربيعة
بنّو قصور محنيّاتٍ عوالي

14 taba'ū banāt imkalfīn il-wigī'i
wi-xallū banāt imbahhrīn ad-dilālī

14 تبعو بنات مكلّفين الوقيعة
وخلّو بنات مبهّرين الدلال

15 tōgif gibāla bil-ihdūm ar-rifī'i
ū-tislā bil-xubz aṭ-ṭarī wit-tigālī

15 توقف قباله بالهدوم الرفيعة
وتسلاه بالخبز الطري والتقالي

16 ḥatta-z-zirbāwī farfarat xalī'i
'ugb al-xara yiẓrab 'ala kull jālī

16 حتّى الزرباوي فرفرت خليعد
عقب الخرا يظرب على كلّ جال

7.8

Expelling Flocks from Pasturelands in the Negev

A Poem to Request Intercession

In the 1950s, when the Negev was under military administration, one regulation required the bedouin to vacate their pasturelands in the central Negev and move closer to the city of Beersheba (cf. poem 4.9). In particular, this order affected the 'Azāzma and Ẓullām Janābīb tribes.

The enforcement of these regulations was entrusted to a sergeant-major named Shlomo Kadosh, whose name—'Kādūsh' to the bedouin—became proverbial for cunning and arbitrariness, among other things for using bedouin trackers in order to ferret out bedouin herdsmen in the unfamiliar expanses of the Negev. The present poem, composed by Sulēmān 'Awwād Ibn 'Adēsān of the 'Azāzma Mas'ūdiyyīn tribe after

Poem 7.8 was heard recited by its author, in Wādī Shgēb, 16 February 1972.

Kadosh and his trackers had raided and seized his flock, was sent as a plea to the chief of the Tiyāhā Natūsh tribe, Mūsā Ḥasan al-ʿAṭāwna, asking him to use his good offices with the Israeli army to relieve his tribesmen of the distress caused them by Kadosh.

Any land where Kādūsh is found,
Though high with grass, is out of bounds. 1

He fills command-cars full of scum,[1]
Over every mountain ridge they come. 2

Don't let your fez be cocked and sway;
Each man has a fate that awaits him![2] 3

I brought forth a camel,[3] the pride of the herd,
A mare never mated by an untrammelled stray.[4] 4

Behind the saddle my rifle[5] was bound:
On my life, its shot could bring anything down. 5

And a water-skin, stitched so tight at the fold,
That its water, so cold, formed crystals of ice. 6

O girl, weave no curtain for a tent that's all rags
Now that we've put our honour behind.[6] 7

[1] 'Scum' are the trackers who worked against their fellow bedouin.

[2] This line is a threat against Kadosh and his pride. [3] A 'reddish mare' in the Arabic text.

[4] i.e., as she had sufficient virtues for breeding pure-bred camels, she was being guarded against an unsuitable stud.

[5] In the Arabic text, rifle is called 'cartridge' (*kharṭūsh*, often corrupted in the colloquial as *khaṭrūsh*), a remnant of the original bedouin designation of a rifle as 'father of the cartridge' (*abū kharṭūsh*).

[6] This is a statement of the bedouins' dismay at their weakness in the face of Kadosh's ability to violate them with impunity. First, the image, in the Arabic text, of a *summer* tent (*kharbūsh*), which is made of rags and deemed unworthy of the elaborate woven curtain that separates the men's and women's sections in a proper winter tent, implies that their society is in tatters and unworthy of consideration. Second, the injunction against weaving a dividing curtain is also meant to imply that, as the bedouin have lost their power, they cannot even protect their own women—the ultimate weakness (cf. poems 1.1, n. 8; 6.6, introduction); thus they might dispense with the façade of being able to do so—i.e. hanging the curtain that shields women from the eyes of male visitors in the tent. For other expressions of bedouin impotence in the face of modern government, see poem 7.6, l. 16; 7.10).

Only Ibn ʿAṭiyya[7] serves as our wall,
And he'd give his life for one and all. 8

And like the moon that shines at night,
He brings the troubled tribesmen light. 9

He who's desired by a glass-bangled lass,[8]
A lass no worthless man could slander. 10

1 ad-dīra halli-bha kādūš
law rabbaʿat ma sakannāha

1 الديرة اللي بها كادوش
لو ربّعت ما سكنّاها

2 dabb al-kamankar ʿayāl habūš
maʿa kull irgēba tamaṯnāha

2 دبّ الكمنكر عيال هبوش
مع كلّ رقيبة تمثناها

3 ya hāmil la tinks aṭ-ṭarbūš
min la miniyyi byitnāha

3 يا هامل لا تنكس الطربوش
من لد منيّة بيتناها

4 dannēt ḥamra tizīn al-bōš
ʿumr al-falit mā tamaṯnāha

4 دنّيت حمرا تزين البوش
عمر الفلت ما تمثناها

5 ardif ʿala ṣulbha xaṭrūš
aẓmin ʿala-r-rūḥ mirmāha

5 اردف على صلبها خرطوش
اضمن على الروح مرماها

6 wi-grayba xarrāzha nadūš
imgaṭṭam aṯ-ṯalj fī māha

6 وقريبة خرّازها نادوش
ومقطّم الثلج في ماها

7 ya bint la tʿandi-l-xarbūš
kull al-maʿānī taraknāha

7 يا بنت لا تعنّدي الخربوش
كلّ المعاني تركناها

8 abin ʿaṭiyya ʿalēna ḥawš
rūḥa ʿan iš-šaʿb yifdāha

8 ابن عطيّة علينا حوش
روحه عن الشعب يفداها

9 miṯil al-gamr la ṭilaʿ bi-duġūš
ẓulma ʿan an-nās jallāha

9 مثل القمر لو طلع بدغوش
ظلمة عن الناس جلّاها

[7] The names Ibn ʿAṭiyya and al-ʿAṭāwna are interchangeable (see poem 5.11, n. 3).

[8] The poet refers here specifically to a type of bracelet worn only by peasant women, alluding to the reputation of the ʿAṭāwna for maintaining close contacts with several villages in the northern Negev and for marrying peasant women (see poem 5.6).

10 ya šōg min hī zahat bil-ġawš
ma nōba han-nidil ḥakāha

10 يا شوق من هي زهت بالغوش
ما نوبة هالنذل حكاها

7·9

Thoughts on the Suez War, 1956

A Poem to Ridicule Bedouin Sympathies for Egypt

Seeing the Israeli army pass down Wādī Watīr on its way to capture Sharm al-Shēkh on 30 October 1956, ʿAnēz abū Sālim experienced a moment of sweet revenge on learning that the Egyptians, regarded by many bedouin to be arbitrary and arrogant, were being defeated and in retreat. To entertain a few friends he composed the following poem, feigning solidarity with Egypt in the first six lines, but revealing his sense of alienation in the last.

Jamāl, Ibn Saʿūd, and Ḥusēn the king,
May God rout their enemies, and victory bring![1] 1

I slept all night rolling around to and fro,
As on fires from whose flames no relief could I know. 2

Great Britain and France, the faithless two;
They raided Egypt, but will meet with woe.[2] 3

And with them Ben Gurion, the infidel Jew,
His men fight our faith, but we're a tough foe. 4

My eyelids turned white[3] seeing those infidel bands,
Their rifles glistening between their hands. 5

If Egypt had armed us, what joy we'd have seen;
To charge alongside them that day we were keen! 6

Poem 7.9 was heard recited by Fu'ād Ṣāliḥ Ismāʿīl of el-ʿArīsh, at el-ʿArīsh, 19 October 1970. It was reviewed with its author, at 'Ayn Umm Aḥmad, 17 March 1988.

[1] Only Jamāl (ʿAbd al-Nāṣir) was actually at war with Israel. Neither King Saʿūd Ibn Saʿūd of Saudi Arabia nor King Ḥusēn of Jordan joined the hostilities.

[2] Lit. 'God was not alongside them', i.e. to give them victory.

[3] i.e. from vexation.

But we're bedouin and do only what our government says,
And if not called to prayer, none of us prays.[4] 7

1 jamāl wibn is'ūd wi-ṯ-ṯāliṯ iḥsēn
alḷa yunṣurhum ū-yiksir a'dāhum

2 al-beriḥa bayyit ma bēn nārēn
ya šūm ḥālī min tiḥimmil sināhum

3 bariṭānya ū-farānsa hal-kala'īn
lamma ġazaw 'ala maṣr ma-ḷḷā ḥaddāhum

4 ū-maḥḥum ibn guryūn al-kāfir aš-šēn
jēši 'adū ad-dīn wiḥna a'dāhum

5 šābit rimūšī yōm šuft al-kala'īn
barūdhum yitlāmi'an bēn īdāhum

6 la sallaḥūna kān ḥina 'āgdin
yōm an-nahār aš-šēn nafza' ma'āhum

7 lakin iḥna šu'ūb lil-ḥukūma muṭī'īn
ū-zē ma biyṣallū binā inṣallī warāhum

1 جمال وابن سعود والثالث حسين
اللّـد ينصرهم ويكسر اعداهم

2 البارحة بيّـتّ مـا بيـن نارين
يا شوم حالي من تحمّـل سناهم

3 بريطـانيا وفـرانسة هالكـلاعين
لمّـا غزو على مصر ما اللّـد حدّاهم

4 ومعهم ابن غريون الكافر الشين
جيشه عدو الدين واحنا اعداهم

5 شابت رموشي يوم شفت الكلاعين
بارودهم يتلامـعن بيـن ايداهم

6 لو سلّـحونا كـان حنا عاقدين
يوم النهار الشين نفزع معهم

7 لكن احنا شعوب للحكومة مطيعين
وزي مـا بيصلّـو بنـا نصلّـي وراهم

7.10

Egypt's Efforts to Halt Bedouin Smuggling through Sinai

A Poem to Express Anger

In the 1950s and 1960s Egypt's authorities viewed hashish smuggling into Egypt over Sinai as a double menace: it exacerbated the high use of drugs in Egypt proper; and it opened the door to possible spying on their country. In the early and mid-1960s, therefore, they took measures to curb this smuggling, especially after 'Abd al-Ḥakīm 'Āmr became Minister of War in 1959 and assumed ultimate authority for the administration of Sinai.

[4] i.e. the bedouin would no more consider fighting for Egypt than Egypt would think of enlisting or arming them.

Poem 7.10 was heard recited by its author, at Rab'a oasis, 27 November 1971.

The bedouin, for their part, resented any measures which jeopardized a source of income as lucrative as smuggling. They even felt themselves entitled to smuggle (and to spy), being the inhabitants of an impoverished area whose plight the authorities did little to alleviate. This sense of victimization by the Egyptians moved Ṣabāḥ Ṣāliḥ al-Ghānim, of the ʿAgēlī tribe of north-west Sinai, to compose a poem to express his anger and despair. Several lines reflect the contempt and estrangement that the bedouin feel towards Egypt and its people; indeed, the poem is addressed, although only sentimentally, to King Ḥusēn of Jordan and his brother Prince Ḥasan, with whom the bedouin found it natural to identify and from whom they would have expected true sympathy had the poem in reality been sent.

I'd ask you, O God, who doth make the world wide,[1]
Who sets things in order, and all doth decide; 1

A young, reddish camel-mare is what I would like[2]
Her limbs like a water-jet stretching in flight. 2

Though bearing two riders she'll never go slow;
Even faster than those who ride motor cars go. 3

Ascend the Yatim,[3] to a bountiful land,
Stop with those from whose faces the light shineth grand; 4

Visit men who the Hashimite ancestry bear:
Ḥusēn and the prince,[4] to whom bedouin chiefs swear. 5

Say: We feel we're of Jordan, though in Egypt we're bred:
A bedouin need not wear black ropes on his head.[5] 6

[1] For the image of spaciousness for welfare, see poem 4.4, n. 2.

[2] The occasional device of requesting the gift of a camel when addressing a poem arises here from the reputation held by King Ḥusēn's grandfather, King ʿAbdallāh, for rewarding bedouin poets (see poem 2.12, n. 1).

[3] Wādī Yatim is the route from Aqaba up to the plateau on which Jordan's capital, Amman, is located; someone coming from Sinai would take this route.

[4] i.e. Prince Ḥasan, the king's brother.

[5] Bedouin in general consider the *kūfiyya*-cloth and *ʿagāl*-rope that they wear as a head-dress to be proper attire for a bedouin man (cf. poem 6.15, n. 14). An element of Egyptian cultural influence on the bedouin of Sinai is apparent in the way the latter often wear their *kūfiyya* as a turban (*ʿimāma*), as Egyptian peasants do, rather than flat on the head and held down by a short rope.

The decrees in Sinai have all become evil,
Since ʿAbd al-Ḥakīm was awarded the rule. 7

On our sons they descend with the aim of conscription,[6]
And our pictures they take with the aim of restriction; 8

Then they make ID cards, each one in his clan;
Naming wives, infants, grandsires, and friends, to the man.[7] 9

They have forced our chiefs to betray their own wards,
And on our smuggling routes have stationed swords. 10

So pity the soul who buys himself land;
For no crime at all they'll put him in chains.[8] 11

It's the crime of the rich—it's they who should pay;
The small man is clean, yet they'll put him in chains. 12

And they'll take him away without warning or word,
And confiscate both his flock and his herd.[9] 13

He'll howl and he'll cry like some helpless young lass,
But he'll sit till the piles have split open his ass. 14

These are times when the worthless and cowards feel sure,
But when lions and hawks can hardly endure.[10] 15

But he who's called bedouin, whose lineage is pure,
Swears to cut off from Egypt although it is near; 16

[6] Compulsory conscription, which removes an adult male from his kin, is abhorrent to bedouin. As every male is a potential combattant for his own blood-revenge group, or *k̲hamsa* (see poem 3.9, n. 3), his presence is considered indispensable to the group security (cf. poem 1.10, n. 10).

[7] While the poet uses hyperbole for comic effect in listing those who appear on the ID card, the bedouin detest being identifiable, as stressed here (cf. poem 7.6, n. 13).

[8] As part of their effort to curb smuggling, Egyptian authorities reportedly kept a close watch on unusual buying habits among bedouin. Anyone suspected of acquiring goods normally beyond his means would be subjected to an interrogation.

[9] Anyone found guilty of smuggling could reportedly have his capital, such as livestock, sequestered.

[10] Bedouin poets often use the imagery of predatory animals and birds of prey to allude to bravery.

So throw down your saddle, don't urge on your steed,
While mixed-breeds,[11] on pure studs like us, have the lead. 17

1 yalla ṭalabtak ya wissīʿ al-bariyyi ya xālg ad-dinya ʿalēk at-tadabīr	يا اللّه طلبتك يا وسّيع البريّة 1 يا خالق الدنيا عليك التدابير
2 ya rabb ana ṭālbak bakratin ḥumriyyi ḏarʿānha fa-r-rakaẓ zē aš-šaxatīr	يا ربّ انا طالبك بكرةٍ حمريّة 2 ذرعانها في الركض زي الشخاتير
3 win zarfalat bir-ridif mā hī winiyyi asraʿ amn illī yarkabūn al-ḥanatīr	وان زرفلت بالردف ما هي ونيّة 3 اسرع من اللي يركبون الحناتير
4 tilfī ʿa wād al-yitim dīri miriyyi ū-tilfī ʿal illī wujūhhū zē-l-fananīr	تلفي ع وادي اليتم ديرة مريّة 4 وتلفي عل اللي وجوهّم زي الفنانير
5 tilfī ʿal illī ijdūdhū hašmiyyi iḥsēn ū-ḥasan ya-mšayyixīn al-maxatīr	تلفي عل اللي جدودهم هاشميّة 5 حسين وحسن يا مشيّخين المخاتير
6 gūl aḥna rabbēna-b-maṣir waḥna urdniyyi kull al-ʿarab la yalbisūn al-marayīr	قول احنا ربّينا بمصر واحنا اردنيّة 6 كلّ العرب لا يلبسون المراير
7 wa-ḥkamna hal-ḥēn ṣārat radiyyi wi-ʿabd al-ḥakīm illī bi-yidda-l-awamīr	واحكامنا هالحين صارت رديّة 7 وعبد الحكيم اللي بيده الاوامير
8 biynazzilū fa-wlādna ʿaskariyyi wiḥna bidfātir šābka fa-t-taṣawīr	بينزّلو في اولادنا عسكريّة 8 واحنا بدفاتر شابكة في التصاوير
9 wi-ʿawdān sawwū-lna baṭāga ʿayliyya bism al-mara waṭ-ṭifil wal-jidd wal-ġēr	وعودان سوّو لنا بطاقة عيليّة 9 باسم المراة والطفل والجدّ والغير
10 ū-biyxatmū fī šuyūxna ʿar-raʿiyya ū-ḥaṭṭū ʿala darb al-miharrib nawaṭīr	وبيختّمو في شيوخنا عالرعيّة 10 وحطّو على درب المهرّب نواطير
11 wal-mōt mōt illī šara la wisiyya min ġēr ḏanb biyilḥagū al-janazīr	والموت موت اللي شرى له وسيّة 11 من غير ذنب بيلحقوه الجنازير

[11] 'Mixed-breeds' is an expression of contempt for the settled population of Egypt. For others, see poems 1.6; 2.12, n. 2; 4.3; 4.7; 6.13; 7.9. For more on bedouin pride in pure lineage, see poem 6.6, n. 2.

12 wad-danb danbi ʿar-rjāl al-ġaniyya
min ġēr danb biyilḥagū al-janazīr

12 والذنب ذنبه عالرجال الغنيّة
من غير ذنب بيلحقوه الجنازير

13 ū-ma yinwixid ʿugb an-nadīra ʿaniyya
ū-yirūḥ māla lal-madāyin maṣadīr

13 وما ينوخذ عقب النذيرة عنيّة
ويروح ماله للمداين مصادير

14 la-yṣīr yibkī mitil bakī al-waliyya
yaṭlaʿ ū-xarga fātḥāt al-bawaṣīr

14 ليصير يبكي مثل بكي الوليّة
يطلع وخرقه فاتحات البواصير

15 wal-wagit hāda sār wagt al-hafiyya
was-sabaʿ ma yaẓhar ib-rūs aṣ-ṣanagīr

15 والوقت هذا صار وقت الهفيّة
والسبع ما يظهر برؤوس الصناقير

16 willī-mnaggaḥ jiddata was-samiyya
igṣād aṣ-ṣaʿīd iyḥilf mā yiʿarf yisīr

16 واللي منقّح جدّته والسميّة
قصاد الصعيد يحلف ما يعرف يسير

17 irmū-l-ašidda la thittū maṭiyya
fātat ʿal ixšūm aẓ-ẓarāyib xawawīr

17 ارمو الاشدّة لا تحتّو مطيّة
فاتت عل خشوم الظرايب خواوير

7.11

The High Cost of Living under Israeli Occupation

A Poem of Self-Ridicule

During Israel's occupation of Sinai after 1967 the rise in the price of basic commodities in the peninsula, due to rising inflation in Israel, put the bedouin at a disadvantage. This poem, composed as a satire of the current situation by a worker in the oilfields near Abū Rudēs in south-west Sinai, complains of how little he has to bring to his family after a week's work away from home. To emphasize the bedouin's economic plight, the poet ʿAṭiyya Miẓʿān ʿAwwād of the ʿAlēgāt Zmēliyyīn tribe consoles his angry wife by assuring her that even the chiefs earn nothing, since hashish smuggling, too, has come to a halt.

Poem 7.11 was heard recited by its author, at Abū Rudēs, 25 November 1971.

I want a pack of cigarettes from old Ḥasūna's shop, 1

Where goods stand piled high in stacks, right up to the top. 2

We all know every client well, the boss to someone said;[1] 3

His pen moved like a barber's razor on a shaven head. 4

A sack of flour, a box of goods, will cost a hundred pounds—[2] 5

And then at home his wife complains, and he asks why she hounds. 6

She answers: After nights away, you can't bring more than this? 7

He says: If you saw us at our work, you'd think we've gone amiss. 8

The whole day long we drown in oil reaching to our eyes, 9

No longer knowing what we are, as time, God curse it, flies. 10

She asks: But what about our chiefs, their teeth are bright with gold? 11

He says: That too's from long ago, when drugs they bought and sold. 12

ودّي علبة سقاير ـ ومن دكّانة حسونة 1

1 widdī ʿilbit sagāyir—ū-min dukkānit ḥasūna

يوم توقف قدّام الدكّان ـ وكنّك واقف في شونة 2

2 yōm tōgif guddām ad-dukkān—ū-kannak wāgif fī šūna

ابو فتيح بيقول لسبيّل ـ كلّ منّا عارف زبونه 3

3 abū-ftēḥ biygūl li-sbayyil—kull minna ʿārif zbūna

يوم يدرج القلم في ايده ـ زي الموس ما يعقّب زيونة 4

4 yōm yidrij al-galam fī-di—zē-l-mūs ma-yʿaggib ziyūna

[1] i.e. they buy on credit because they do not have ready cash.
[2] Israeli pounds; or US$25 in the late 1960s.

والحساب بيقفّل عالميّة ــ ع كيس دقيق وكرتونة 5
5 wil-ḥisāb biygaffil ʿal-miyya—ʿa kīs dagīg ū-kartōna

والحرمة تكاون في الرجال ــ ويقول علامك مجنونة 6
6 wal-ḥurma tkāwin fa-r-rijāl—ū-yigūl ʿalāmik majnūna

تقول غايب عنّي ليالي ــ لا فجلة ولّا لامونة 7
7 tigūl ġāyib ʿinnī liyāli—la fijla walla limōna

قال لنّكي شفتي شغلتنا ــ تقولي دا غلطة مفدونة 8
8 gāl linkī šuftī šuġlitna—itgūlī da ġalṭa mafdūna

طول النهار وهو الواحد ــ غرقان في الزيت لعيونه 9
9 ṭūl an-nahār ū-hū al-wāḥad—ġargān fi-z-zēt il-ʿiyūna

واحنا ما بندري عن انفسنا ــ وسارقنا الوقف الله يخونه 10
10 wiḥna ma-bnidrī ʿan unfusna—ū-sarigna al-wagt aḷḷa yixūna

قالت ايش معنى المشايخ ــ الذهب يلمع في سنونه 11
11 gālat ēš maʿna al-mašāyix—ad-dahab yilmaʿ fi-snūna

قال هذا من مدّة زمان ــ يوم كان بيتاجرو حنونة 12
12 gāl hāda min muddit zimān—yōm kān biytājrū ḥanūna

7.12

The Egyptian–Israeli Peace Agreement, 1979

A Poem in Praise of Peace and President Sādāt

On 3 March 1980, one year after the signing of the peace treaty between Egypt and Israel, President Anwar al-Sādāt entertained 219 bedouin chiefs and notables from Sinai at the Intercontinental Hotel in Cairo for seven days. On the first day the company was treated to a poem, composed and recited by an inhabitant of the northern town, el-ʿArīsh. Not to be outdone, several prominent bedouin of the south approached

Poem 7.12 was heard recited by Rāḍī Swēlim ʿAtayyig of the Muzēna Darārma tribe, at Nagb Shāhīn, 15 October 1980. It was reviewed with its author at Nuwēbaʿ at-Tarābīn, 5 April 1983.

ʿAnēz abū Sālim al-ʿUrḍī of the Tarābīn Ḥasāblah and asked him to compose a poem that would rescue the honour of the south. On the fourth day, at a reception held in the military arms factory (*al-maṣnaʿ al-ḥarbī*), in the al-ʿAbbāsiyya district of Cairo, ʿAnēz recited his composition in the presence of the Minister of War, Muḥammad Ṣādiq. After praising the peace and its author, President Sādāt, the poet answers the critics of that peace; namely, that Egypt, far from deserting the Arab cause, was merely paving the way to regain other Arab lands from Israel.

We ask God who sends us rain with the clouds
  To shield Anwar Sādāt from all evil. 1

God showed us the way, so that victory we'd find,
  For war's evil cords put the folk in a bind. 2

With praise for the Prophet, my poem I'll begin,
  We're the flock of Muṣṭafā, who's free of all sin.[1] 3

I've seen banners of triumph wave over the squares,
  And our troops celebrating, relieved of all cares; 4

I saw peace with my own eyes come in through the door,
  And it comes from them only who're fighting the war.[2] 5

Sixty-seven[3] was bitter with what it revealed;
  Troops hiding behind one another for shield. 6

But then we stood firm in seventy-three[4]—
  The stand all have heard of wherever they be. 7

How we dealt with them harshly, the air filled with dust,
  Till we took back our rights, even more than was just: 8

[1] 'Muṣṭafā' ('the Selected') is one of the Prophet Muḥammad's names.

[2] In the context of his polemic with the Arab world, which criticized Egypt for betraying the Arab and Palestinian cause, the poet includes this line to point out that Egypt was not remiss in its obligations; on the contrary, she actually fought Israel while others only talked.

[3] i.e. the war of June 1967, in which Israel took the Gaza Strip and the Sinai peninsula from Egypt in five days.

[4] i.e. the war of October 1973, in which Egypt succeeded in taking part of the East Bank of the Suez Canal from Israel and establishing a bridgehead in Sinai.

Sinai and Egypt and Gaza, as well;[5]
They're our rights and we wished to retrieve all that fell. 9

Filasṭīn and Jerus'lem, think not I forgot,
But Ṭābā and Sharm are better first got.[6] 10

Anwar did promise a few years ago:
'Everything that was robbed, we'll take back from the foe.' 11

As he was our leader, we wished to accede,
Then Allah brought triumph, and let him succeed. 12

His army and nation, as one, hold him dear,
For his fine moral virtues and vision that's clear. 13

And we of the Sinai, who've two shares of luck;[7]
Don't imagine that we ever heeded the ruck![8] 14

He who brought us our rights from the teeth of the foe
Is better than those who'd see brothers brought low.[9] 15

And whenever the sharp din of gunfire cracked,
We were ready to die so our lands stayed intact. 16

We have opened the field, not it's your turn to win;
If your rival gets tough, give it back on the chin. 17

We're with you as always, but give us a while;
In the end, if we all act alone, we'll be vile.[10] 18

[5] Included for the sake of hyperbole. Gaza was in fact not part of the territory recovered by Egypt in the peace agreement: it was left to subsequent negotiations to determine the future of the West Bank and Gaza Strip.

[6] This line again is meant to answer the accusation that Egypt deserted the Palestine cause. Egypt's position was that it must recover whatever Arab lands are accessible at the time; hence, Sharm ash-Shēkh and Ṭābā in Sinai must be acquired first.

[7] i.e. peace and Sinai.

[8] i.e. those who incited against Sādāt or doubted his motives.

[9] i.e., while Egypt was acting in support of the Arab cause by restoring Arab lands, its critics were weakening that cause by dividing the ranks. In the Arabic text, 'ruck' is 'dry' (*ḥāyif*).

[10] Cf. above, n. 9. This line also expresses the tacit sentiment that eased the conscience of many Egyptians concerning the peace with Israel; namely that, after Egypt recovered its land, it would help the Arab cause by assuming anti-Israel positions.

So Saʿūd we would chide, and we'd say to Ḥusēn:
This cutting relations is slightly a pain.[11] 19

What's the cause of the boycott? Our record is clean;
All our actions were helpful, and surely not mean. 20

Of the triumph God gave us, we made two things more:
The ending of bloodshed and evil of war. 21

Recall, O Ḥusēn, at Khartoum what they said:[12]
'The problem of getting back land's at the head!' 22

'Twould be better to thank those who fought for our sakes,
Lads making our foe drink the venom of snakes. 23

Like Shāhīn[13] hawks they fought till the battle was ceased,
Each ten of them fighting five hundred, at least.[14] 24

When I drew near to Sinai, its hills could be seen,
Those hills poets sang of, the finest there've been. 25

God bestowed on it manna, the fig, and some oil,
And whoever was reared on its bounty stays loyal. 26

And her stalwarts and chiefs will forever be bent,
To repel those who eye her with evil intent. 27

A Sinānī Turbānī, this poem I now give;
Down south, up in Wādī ʿAṭiyya we live.[15] 28

[11] Saudi Arabia cut off diplomatic relations with Egypt after the signing of the Camp David Accords (September 1978); Jordan did so with the final signing of the peace agreement (March 1979).

[12] i.e. the fourth Arab Summit Conference in Khartoum, in August 1967, at which the Arab States jointly defined their post-Six Day War policy.

[13] For Shāhīn hawks, see poem 2.10, n. 10.

[14] Hyperbole.

[15] The poet 'signed' his historic poem by giving credit to his tribe, the Tarābīn; by stating proudly that they originated in the Sinān section of the Begūm tribe of western Arabia (cf. Kaḥḥāla, i. 89 ff., who does not mention a Sinān section of Begūm); by attributing the poem to the southern Sinai bedouin; and by specifying that these are the southern Tarābīn who live in Wādī Watīr. The upper reaches of this wadi are often called Wādī ʿAṭiyya after the alleged forefather of the Tarābīn in Sinai, whose tomb in that wadi is a pilgrimage site.

1 naṭlab min illī yursil al-mī maʿ al-ġēn
yaḥma lina-s-sadāt min kull siyya

1 نطلب من اللي يرسل المي مع الغين
يحمى لنا السادات من كلّ سيّة

2 aḷḷa hadāna wi-ntiṣarna baʿd ḥīn
ū-ḥabl al-xaṭa yajīb ʿal an-nās ṭayya

2 اللّد هدانا وانتصرنا بعد حين
وحبل الخطا يجيب عل الناس طيّة

3 abdī kalāmī bi-ṣalātī ʿal az-zēn
wal-maṣṭafa-llī kullina la raʿiyya

3 ابدي كلامي بصلاتي عل الزين
والمصطفى اللي كلّنا لد رعيّة

4 šāyif aʿlām an-naṣir fōg al-mayadīn
wal-jēš fī farḥa ū-fī fantaziyya

4 شايف اعلام النصر فوق الميادين
والجيش في فرحة وفي فنتزيّة

5 ū-šuft as-salām yuṭrug al-bāb bal-ʿayn
salām yinbaʿ min iṣḥāb al-gaẓiyya

5 وشفت السلام يطرق الباب بالعين
سلام ينبع من اصحاب القضيّة

6 awwal širibna murr sabʿa wi-sittīn
yōm al-xawiy yindirig fī xawiyya

6 اوّل شربنا مرّ سبعة وستّين
يوم الخوي يندرق في خويّد

7 ū-minna wagafna fī ṯalāṯa ū-sabʿīn
al-wagfa-llī al-kull yismaʿ bi-hiyya

7 ومند وقفنا في ثلاثة وسبعين
الوقفة اللي الكلّ يسمع بهيّ

8 ū-ṣirna-ngasīhum nahār ʿajj ū-šēn
lamma xaḏēna al-ḥagg ū-fōga išwayya

8 وصرنا نقاسيهم نهار عجّ وشين
لمّا خذينا الحقّ وفوقد شويّة

9 wi-sīna ū-maṣir wi-sāḥil al-xān yikfīn
ū-ḥugūgna wiḥna raẓēna bi-hiyya

9 وسينا ومصر وساحل الخان يكفين
وحقوقنا واحنا رضينا بهيّ

10 wala nisīt al-guds ū-bāgī falasṭīn
ū-ṭābā ū-šarm aš-šēx rās al-liwiyya

10 ولا نسيت القدس وباقي فلسطين
وطابا وشرم الشيخ راس اللويّة

11 anwar waʿadna waʿd min biẓʿat as-snīn
lāzim yirudd al-kull maslūb šayya

11 انور وعدنا وعد من بضعة السنين
لازم يردّ الكلّ مسلوب شيّة

12 zaʿīmna waḥna li-ḥukma imṭaʿīn
wa-mwafga lan-naṣir rabb al-bariyya

12 زعيمنا واحنا لحكمد مطاعين
وموفّقد للنصر ربّ البريّة

13 ū-jēši ū-šaʿba kullihum lah maḥabbīn
min ḥusn rāya wal-axlāg az-zakiyya

13 وجيشد وشعبد كلّهم لد محبّين
من حسن رايد والاخلاق الزكيّة

14 wiḥna lina fī habbit ar-rīḥ nōbēn
wal-hāyfa maḥna zabāyin il-hiyya

14 واحنا لنا في هبّة الريح نوبين
والهايفة ما احنا زباين لهيّ

15 illī saḥabna al-ḥagg ma bēn ḏirsēn
aḥsan min illī ṭamaʿta fī xawiyya

15 اللي سحبنا الحقّ ما بين ذرسين
احسن من اللي طمعته في خويّه

16 win ṣār ḥiss imʿaddilāt in-nawašīn
ḥina nimōt ū-dārna tiẓall ḥayya

16 وان صار حسّ معدّلات النواشين
حنا نموت ودارنا تظلّ حيّة

17 ḥina fataḥna al-būb liz-zēn wiš-šēn
win māl xaṣmak kūn mayyāl zēya

17 حنا فتحنا البوب للزين والشين
وان مال خصمك كون ميّال زيّه

18 ḥina lakum wintum lana law baʿd ḥīn
win-nās mā hī ʿan baʿẓha ġaniyya

18 حنا لكم وانتم لنا لو بعد حين
والناس ما هي عن بعضها غنيّة

19 ū-inʿātib asʿūd wi-ngūl li-ḥsēn
imgaṭaʿātkū mitʿabitna šwayya

19 ونعاتب سعود ونقول لحسين
مقاطعاتكم متعبتنا شويّة

20 tigaṭiʿūna lēš wiḥna bariyyīn
ḥina binaṣliḥ ma-rtakabna jiniyya

20 تقاطعونا ليش واحنا بريّين
حنا بنصلح ما ارتكبنا جنيّة

21 willī aʿṭāna nigismi hal-widd widdēn
šarr al-ḥarawb ū-manaʿ safk ad-damiyya

21 واللي اعطانا نقسمد الودّ ودّين
شرّ الحروب ومنع سفك الدميّة

22 fī jalst il-xarṭūm ma ṣār ya-ḥsēn
radd an-nawāgiṣ hū ʿamūd al-gaẓiyya

22 في جلسة الخرطوم ما صار يا حسين
ردّ النواقص هو عمود القضيّة

23 willī ʿalēna faẓilhum ʿaskariyyīn
awlād yisgū xaṣamhum samm ḥayya

23 واللي علينا فضلهم عسكريّين
اولاد يسقو خصمهم سمّ حيّة

24 yōm al-maʿārik zē aṣ-ṣgur aš-šayahīn
al-xamstēn yikawnū xams-miyya

24 يوم المعارك زي الصقور الشياهين
الخمستين يكوّنو خمس ميّة

25 wi-haẓāb sīna šufthin yōm yibdīn
ū-ʿalēhin min zēn at-tawaṣīf ġaniyya

25 وهضاب سينا شفتهن يوم يبدين
وعليهن من زين التواصيف غنيّة

26 aḷḷa wahhabha az-zēt wil-mann wat-tīn
willī šibaʿ min xērha wa-haniyya

26 اللّـد وهّبها الزيت والمنّ والتين
واللي شبع من خيرها وهنيّة

27 wa-šuyūxha ū-baṭṭālha mustaʿidīn
li-radaʿ min yanwa liha bi-suw niyya

27 وشيوخهـا وبطّـالـهـا مستعـدّين
لردع مـن ينوي لـهـا بسو نيّـة

28 wāna sinānī wal-gabīla tarabīn
sakkānt al-jinūb wādī ʿaṭiyya

28 وانـا سنـاني والقبيلة ترابين
سكّـانة الجنـوب وادي عطيّـة

8

Composing Bedouin Poetry

Art and Technique

We have seen the pervasiveness of poetry in bedouin society and the important roles it plays as a vehicle for preserving cultural values and as a means of expression, communication, and entertainment. We have also had a glimpse of the variety and intricacy of the bedouin poems themselves. The question naturally arises of how an illiterate bedouin is able to compose a poem often of more than twenty lines and containing two rhymes for each line.

THE ILLITERATE POET AND HIS RESOURCES

A Culture of Rhyme

At first glance it would appear that a bedouin's aptitude for poetry comes from the fact that he lives in a culture replete with rhymes. From the time a child becomes aware of his environment he is exposed daily to proverbs on ever aspect of life, many of which are in rhyme. As part of the common wisdom he will hear, for example, that *al-walad walad, law ḥakam balad* ('A child is a child, though he rule a town'); *jār wi-law jār* ('You must live with a neighbour, though he oppress you'); and *illī fāt māt* (What's done is done'). When a person grows up, rhyming proverbs instruct him in his economics: *wagt a<u>th</u>-<u>th</u>urayyā, wagt ar-rimāya* ('When the Pleiades appear it is time to sow'); *fī <u>sh</u>ahr <u>kh</u>amīs, kull ʿūdi<u>n</u> yabīs* ('In April the annual plants dry up'); and *ar-rāʿī, ikrāh yōm wafāh* ('Pay the shepherd when the season's done').

Proverbs in the form of legal maxims serve to remind the bedouin of their laws. *<u>Gh</u>ulām maktūf warbaʿīn wugūf* ('A manacled lad or forty camels') calls to mind the severe consequences of rape: death or restitution. To stress that justice must be dispensed where people are present to hear it, a trial is called *diwān ū-bakraj milyān* ('An assembly and a full coffee-pot') or *ḥiniyya ū-rukba ma<u>th</u>niyya* ('A semi-circle of kneeling men'). In matters of religion the merits of a sacrificial meal 'shared' with one's ancestors, for example, will be explained by a proverb: *lugimtēn fī baṭn jāy'a, yiẓahhirak yōm al-wagāy'a* ('Two morsels in a hungry stomach will support you the day you fall'). And if a bedouin is to swear an oath in order to settle a dispute, he will most likely chose a rhyming formula like *bi-ḥayāt al-'ūd, wa-r-rabb al-ma'būd* ('By the life of the annual plant and our worshipped Lord').

In the light of this comprehensive exposure to rhyming proverbs it is not surprising to find ordinary bedouin often trying their hand at making their own rhymes; for example, when they water their camels, they make a simple rhyme called a *ḥidā* (literally 'urging'), sung over and over again while urging the camels to drink. Two *ḥidās* heard in southern Sinai are *ya 'idd kuththir khērak, bukra indawwir ghērak* ('O Well, many thanks for your goodness; tomorrow we'll look for another'); *ya marḥaba w-irḥābī, w-itsūg fīhā rikkābī* ('I greet you and greetings again; riders will yet ride them').

Unnatural Stress

Celebrations offer other occasions for making rhymes: women and girls, dancing in front of the tents or seated in facing rows, make up short rhyming ditties that they sing repeatedly and responsively. Singing these verses to a set tune facilitates the poetic effort, because the convention of such singing allows one to stress the syllables of the words unnaturally in keeping with the requirements of the tune.

8.1

See, for example, the words of the following ditty, heard at a wedding in the Negev in 1973.[1]

A bird in the sky whose wings are clipped,
Tell 'Awda we congratulate his bride.

ṭērin fi-s-samā jināḥi magṣūṣ
gūlū li-'awdi mabrūk al-'arūs

طير في السما جناحه مقصوص
قولو لعودة مبروك العروس

[1] Poem 8.1 was sung by women of the 'Azāzma Mas'ūdiyyīn tribe, in the Negev, March 1973.

Accented naturally, this line would be pronounced as follows (capital letters constituting accented syllables):

ṬĒR fi-s-saMĀ jiNĀḥi magṢŪṢ
GŪlū li-ʻAWda maBRŪK al-ʻaRŪS.

Sung, however, it was accented:

ṬĒriṉ FI-S-samā jiNĀḥi MAGṣūṣ
GŪlū LI-ʻawda maBRŪK al-ʻArūs.

8.2

The simplest type of song–poem with successive rhyming lines is the *bidaʻ* or 'improvised poem', which is often composed at celebrations by one or more men during the course of the *daḥiyya* dance.[2] Generally (but not always, cf. poem 5.10), the *bidaʻ* composed during a dance will comprise light subjects, such as flirtation, dealt with in a playfully suggestive rather than forthright manner, as in this song heard in southern Sinai.[3]

Dance young girl, for in the dance there is no blame. 1

Step forward lad, whose face must cast you to Hell's flame. 2

All dancers give a full hand-clap, players in the *daḥiyya* game. 3

العبي لا يا بنيّة ـ اللعب ما فيه رزيّة 1

1 ilʻabī la ya banayya—al-liʻib ma fī raziyya

وقرّب اللي خيالك ـ يرميك في النار الجهيّة 2

2 ū-garrib illī xayalak—yirmīk fi-n-nār al-jahiyya

ودّوني ضرب الخواميس ـ يا ضرّابين الدحيّة 3

3 waddūnī ẓarb al-xawamīs—ya zarrabīn ad-daḥiyya

Each successive dancer (the men are should-to-shoulder in a line opposite a swaying and dancing girl) wishing to compose a line must

[2] For the *daḥiyya* dance, see poem 5.10.

[3] Poem 8.2 was heard sung by members of the Tarābīn Ḥasāblah tribe, at Nuwēbaʻ at-Tarābīn, March 1971.

make it rhyme with the preceding ones; to facilitate his effort a meaningless refrain (*raḥanī gōl arīda*) is sung between each improvised line. This affords the dancer a few extra seconds to think; but even more helpful, as we saw in poem 8.1, is the licence given him not to stress the words naturally. For example, the first line of poem 8.2, if naturally stressed, would sound like:

IL'abī la ya baNAYya—al-LI'ib MĀ fi raZIYya;

whereas it was actually sung with the following stress:

il'abĪ la YA baNAYya—al-LI'ib MĀ fi RAziyya.

8.3

Another example of a *bida'* song, one in which the metrical freedom enabled quick improvisation on a guest's name ('Sh̲ū'a', Arabic nickname for a person named Yehoshua Cohen) was composed in the mid-1960s by Sālim Abū Furth̲ēn al-Wajj of the Ẓullām Janābīb tribe, when three members of Sde Boker, a kibbutz in the central Negev, attended a bedouin celebration.[4]

Go back and go forth as you dance and you sway, O girl who is short but not frail; 1

O Rider remember, while you're on your way, Yehoshua and Raphie to hail; 2

You'll find Mikha'el going round night and day, for his gang like a wolf on the trail. 3

1 لوجي عليهم لوجي ـ يا قصيرة مربوعة

1 lūjī 'alēhum lūjī—ya gaṣīra marbū'a

2 يا ولد راكب عل قعود ـ سلّم ع رافي وشوعة

2 ya walad rākib 'al ga'ūd—sallim 'a rāfi ū-šū'a

3 تلقى مخائيل زي ذيب الليل ـ تملّي يخدم ربوعه

3 tilga mixa'ēl zē d̲īb al-lēl—tamallī yixdim rubū'a

[4] Poem 8.3 was heard recited by its author, Sālim Abū Furth̲ēn al-Wajj, in Wādī Ramliyya, 15 March 1972.

8.4

The longest sequence of rhymed lines sung to a tune requiring unnatural stress on the syllables is often found in a type of poem called *imwēlī*, which a bedouin may improvise and sing in very high tones while travelling on camel-back or, now, in a truck or jeep. The poem usually tells of the places seen and persons met along the way, alluding to some of their notable characteristics in fact or in jest. The language, as in the sung *bida'*, is simple, and composition is facilitated by the repetition of certain words; by the frequent use of personal and place-names; by the use of assonance for rhyming lines when a word containing the final consonant of the dominant rhyme-scheme does not immediately come to mind; and, as mentioned, by employing unnatural stress. The following lines were part of a poem composed by Swēlim Sālim 'Alī, of the Muzēna Ighṣēnāt tribe, while he was travelling north up the eastern Sinai coast in the late 1960s on a tribal pilgrimage to the tomb of a Muzēna saint, Ḥamdān, at Nuwēba' al-Muzēna.[5]

I came along the Dhahab way, the winds we met were hot; 1

I came along 'Amayyid way, and met there lots of friends. 2

When to al-'Ugda we came down, a hag there beat her man;[6] 3

When to the crossroads we came down, into good folks we ran. 4

To Zghārāt we came to drink, their water was aflow;[7] 5

And Frēj as-Sākhin there we met, he thinks the world's his foe. 6

And to Ḥubēk when we came down, our mounts like sheep we led; 7

I asked the Lord who made us all to thwart the Eye we dread.[8] 8

[5] Poem 8.4 was heard recited by its author, Swēlim Sālim 'Alī, in Wādī aṭ-Ṭūr, 31 March 1971.

[6] This humorous allusion refers to Ḥājj Ḥimēd Slēm Imbārak of the Muzēna Ighṣēnāt, who had dug a well and planted a garden in the remote mountain oasis of Bīr 'Ugda, near Rās Abū Galūm.

[7] Zghārāt is commonly known as Bīr Zghēr, fifteen kilometres south of Nuwēba' al-Muzēna. Frēj as-Sākhin belonged to the Muzēna Sakhāna, who inhabit Nuwēba' and the eastern Sinai coast for 50 kilometres to the south.

[8] The descent from Bīr Zghēr to Ḥubēk on the coast is very sharp and rocky. For bedouin concepts of the evil eye, see Bailey, 'Religious Practices', pp. 78–9.

We came to drink at Nuwēbaʿ, a truly wondrous place; 9

And when we came to Ḥamdān's tomb, the mounts were there to race.[9] 10

1 جيت ملقّي عالذهب ـ ولانا بيمّ السمايم

1 jīt imlaggī ʿaḏ-ḏahab—walāna b-yamm as-samāyim

2 جيت ملقّي عميّد ـ ولانا بصدفة حبايب

2 jīt imlaggī ʿamayyid—walāna bi-ṣudfa ḥabāyib

3 يوم هردنا العقدة ـ عجوز بتلطم في شايب

3 yōm haradna-l-ʿugda—ʿajūz ibtalṭum fī šāyib

4 يوم هردنا الملاقي ـ ولانا بعزّ الطنايب

4 yōm haradna al-malāgī—walāna b-ʿizz aṭ-ṭanāyib

5 يوم وردنا الزغارات ـ لاقينا ماهم بزايد

5 yōm waradna az-zġarāt—lagēna māhum ib-zāyid

6 لاقينا فريج الساخن ـ تملّي عروقد عتايب

6 lagēna ifrēj as-sāxin—tamallī ʿurūga ʿatāyib

7 يوم كتّينا عل حبيك ـ قدناهم قود الجلايب

7 yōm kattēna ʿal iḥbēk—gudnāhum gōd al-jalāyib

8 اطلب الربّ اللي خلق ـ مكفينا شرّ المصايب

8 aṭulb ar-rabb illī xalag—makfīna šarr al-maṣāyib

9 يوم وردت النوابعة ـ ويا ملمّ الغرايب

9 yōm waradt an-nawābʿa—ū-yā malamm al-ġarāyib

10 جينا لقبر حمدان ـ ويا ملمّ الركايب

10 jīna li-gabr ḥamdān—ū-yā malamm ar-rakāyib

The difference between the lines stressed naturally and as they are in the poem can be perceived by an examination of the first line. Stressed naturally this would be

[9] Traditionally, camel races have been a part of most bedouin celebrations.

jīt imLAGgī ʿaḏ-ḎAhab—waLĀna b-yamm as-saMĀyim.

However, in the song it is stressed:

JĪT imLAGgī ʿAḎ-ḏahab—waLĀna b-YAMM as-SAmāyim.

Irregular metre

Although the sung verses of the above poems could ignore the natural stress and bend any of their component words to the dictates of the tune, they were not devoid of scansion. Both the *bidaʿ* and the *imwēlī*, when sung, comprised three stressed syllables to a hemistich, six to a line. Even *bidaʿ* poems not composed to music, such as poems 1.5 (anger at disrespect for a deceased kinsman), 1.12 (anger at the loss of livestock to a panther), and 1.15 (love for a shepherdess met at a well), are generally careful to keep a six-foot line, despite their not being sheltered by the tune of a song to relieve them of the need to accent the poem's words naturally. The composition of a non-sung *bidaʿ*, like its sung counterpart, is none the less facilitated in composition by the device of irregular metre. This characteristic of bedouin poetry manifests itself in two ways. First, the feet of any given line are rarely—and if so, inadvertently—all of the same metre. For example,

min ʿUgib MĒTT abū-mḤAYsin ma BAGbal LAẒ-ẓalal ŠĪfa

(1.5)

consists of iamb/iamb/anapaest/anapaest/iamb/feminine anapaest, while

LĒŠ ma tiĠANnū fi-l-baNĀT—maLĒT al-imSAJjil ṮARD

(4.8)

has dactyl/trochee/anapaest/iamb/anapaest/iamb. Secondly, the irregularity of metre that is apparent in nearly every line may and usually does change to a different irregularity in consecutive lines. The first three lines of poem 1.9 illustrate this principle:

gumt ṭaLAʿT al-JAbal al-YĀbis MA yaṬĀ al-xaẒĀR
ḥaṬĒT inʿĀlī fi-rijLĪ MĀšī li-riʿĪ dawWĀR
niZILT ʿala JAbal ġaDĪR imṬALlag BI-L-išJĀR.

The feet of these three consecutive lines are:

anapaest/iamb/anapaest/iamb/iamb/anapaest
iamb/iamb/long anapaest/trochee/anapaest/iamb
iamb/anapaest/anapaest/iamb/iamb/iamb.

The unsung *bidaʿ* poem is the simplest verse that the bedouin themselves consider poetry. It is not, however, considered a 'serious' poem. One reason is that, to their mind, it is associated with a certain playfulness, even naughtiness. Moreover, its lines contain only one rhyme; and this rhyme is often 'the easiest' because it is built on a pronominal suffix (e.g. 'its' or 'her' (*hā*) as in poem 1.15: *ẓamāhā, bilāhā, mijrāhā, xallāhā*, etc.); the diction is rather commonplace; and each line has only six feet, which gives it a quick pace and 'light' feeling. Thus, poets who are mainly known for their composition of *bidaʿ* (such as ʿAṭiyya Miẓʿān az-Zmēlī and Tuʿēmī Mūsā ad-Dagūnī), are generally denied the respectful and often revered appellation for a poet *per se, sh̲āʿir*, and are relegated to the inferior distinction of *baddāʿ*, creator of *bidaʿ*. This is even the case with versatile poets who can compose poems in both genres, such as Ḥamdān abū Salāma Abū Masʿūd (e.g. *bidaʿ*, poem 1.15), whose *gaṣīda* sent to ʿAnēz abū Sālim in prison (poem 6.13) is considered by several bedouin to be one of the finest poems in the present collection. There are also *bidaʿ*-poems on serious subjects, such as anger at disrespect shown for one's deceased kinsman (poem 1.5), simply because the composer is not capable of creating a more intricate piece owing to his limited talent or (as in the case of Ṭuʿēmī ad-Dagūnī) to his temperament.

However, while more challenging rhymes and more elevated diction make a bedouin feel justified in regarding other types of poetry superior to *bidaʿ*, the irregular metre which eases the task of composition is none the less found in these other types, too. The present collection of poems contains, in addition to various *bidaʿ* poems, five examples of the strophic poem called *marbūaʿ* (3.11, 4.14, 4.20I, 5.5, 7.3), some *hijēnī* poems (e.g. 1.14, 4.13, 4.17), and many *gaṣāyid*, all of which have irregular metre.

The lighter strophic poems—one on the Ibn Hadhdhāl shepherdess (4.20I) the other on the marriage of Ḥarba Abū Sitta (5.5)—are, in keeping with their light themes, composed of three or four short lines with two, sometimes three, feet each:

ū-ŠUFti ib-WĀdī
ya raBĪaʿ-l-fuWĀdī
MUHra itGĀdī
min imHĀR ibin hadḎĀL

(4.20I)

and

SĒfi rūBĀS
biYIGṭa' ar-RĀS
YŌM aḏ-ḏirRĀS
MIṯil an-NAḥalī.

(5.5)

On the other hand, a *marbūa'* with a more serious theme—like the poem on how to be a good Muslim (3.11), or that on battles in the First World War (7.3)—has longer verses containing three and four feet each. Hence

KULli mi-l-BĀša jaMĀL
WĀlas 'a DĪni bi-MĀL
AḶḷa yiXŪna hal-baṭṬĀL
KUṮr ma yatTAM 'awRĀT

(7.3)

and

AWwal GŌLna nisTAĠfir AḶḷa
Ilā al-'ARŠ RABB al-milk KULli
YAĠfir fi kaLĀmi KULL ZALli
NAFsin tirJĀ ma YUGṭa' riJĀha.

(3.11)

The *hijēnī*, too, differs from poem to poem between six and seven feet to a line with variations in the metrical structure from line to line. Hence

ṭalLĒT Ana 'Alī-l-mirGĀB—ašRAFT min FŌG mašḎŪbi
ABkī ṣaḤĪbī ziMĀnin ĠĀB—DAM'ī šahaLĪL maṣBŪba

(1.14)

and

al-'AYB wal-'AYB ya sḥayMĀN—al-'AYB itSAKkir 'ala-d-DALli
ẒAYfak taṢIKkah 'al al-ixWĀN—rabBĒT lak 'ENDihum ŠILli.

(4.17)

The *gaṣīda*, which is the form of most of the poems in this book, is only distinguished from the *marbūa'* and the *hijēnī* by the fact that every line has eight feet (four in each hemistich) and because most *gaṣāyid* are double-rhymed (although they need not be; e.g. poems 1.2 and 1.3 with single monorhymes, a form called *abū zēdī*). The first two lines of poems 1.1 and 1.3 will demonstrate the eight-foot line and the irregularity of metre within each line and between the lines. In the first poem the hemistiches are rhymed; in the second only one.

al-BEriḥa fi-l-LĒL BITna giSĀya
ū-giLĪL min NIŠkī ʿaLĒ hal-mawaJĪeʿ
ya MA-ḥala-l-finJĀL BĒN il-wiDĀya
ū-ḤISS alamaniyYĀT fī ḤINwit ir-RĪeʿ

(1.1)

Ana-llī ẒAYFkū min gabl ṢĀliḥ yiẒĪFkū
wal-YŌM ṢĀliḥ ʿala ʿaRABkū niZĪL
BUGʿud bila HIŠmi ū-BĀkil bila ḤAya
ū-SIRT ila-hilBĀJ ir-rJĀL hiBĪL.

(1.3)

In addition to the use of irregular metre to aid the illiterate bedouin in composing a poem, the creative task of the poet is facilitated by devices or licences, such as mixing the two genders to enable the construction of a metre or a rhyme; the rhyming of diphthongs with long vowels (e.g. poem 1.4: *mašēna* with *fīna*; *jēb* with *nīb*); the resort to assonance for rhyming when a word with the rhyming consonant cannot be found (e.g. poem 2.5: *hīt* with *šīk*; poem 4.7: *ṭabbāxa* with *tuffāḥa*); and the changing of the form of a word to make it fit the rhyme: *wasm* to *wasīm*, *nahār* to *nahāra*, *nihba* to *nahība*, *margab* to *mirgāb*.

THE AESTHETIC INPUT

Elevated Diction

These devices notwithstanding, there are aspects of bedouin poetry that testify to the aesthetic resources of a bedouin poet. For an illiterate person to achieve a double-rhyme in poems often of over twenty lines is a remarkable feat in itself; but there are additional features. In most of the double-rhyme poems in this collection the poet has put one rhyme of one hemistich in the feminine and the other in the masculine—as in poem 1:1, which has *gasāya* (fem.) against *mawajīeʿ*; *widāya* with *ar-rīeʿ*. Some rhymes, moreover, are designed to be the same for both hemistiches (e.g. both ending with the letters *īb*), except for this difference in gender—thus producing *imṣībi* (fem.) and *tṣīb*, or *yidībi* and *mawajīb*, as in the twenty-six line poem, 3.8. And the poet of the twenty-four line poem, 3.9, uses another common device, which is to rhyme the two hemistiches with the same letter but to precede the rhyming consonant with a different vowel (*boṣīk/wanhāk*; *mašakīk/tinsāk*). Rhymes are often embellished by backing them up with penultimate words that have both the same metrical value and a pleasant alliterative and assonantal effect. Thus, in poem 2.2, for which the rhyme-scheme of the first hemistiches is based on the letters *īma*, lines 11 and 12 end respectively with *mawāgif dasīma* and *mawāji' gadīma*.

Bedouin poems also abound with internal rhymes and alliteration:

lēha šawīš 'a ktāfi rīš . . . (plays on *īš*)
(1.15)

yaḻḻā ya 'ālī 'ala kull mirgāb . . . (plays on *a*, *ā*, and *l*)
(6.13)

dār az-zmān ū-dārna-ṣbaḥat dār
wi-dārin 'ala sukkānha-l-fagr ẓāwī (plays on *dār* and *ān*).
(6.18)

In another double-hemistich

ya winntī wannētha 'ugib nīma
wal-'ayn titnawwiš min an-nawm tanwīš
(6.14)

the sound 'n' occurs in eight out of ten words; the sound 'wi' occurs five times; the sound 'a' ends three words in the first hemistich; the sound 't' occurs three times in the second hemistich; the sound 'sh' occurs twice in the second hemistich; and the long vowel 'ī' occurs in the rhyme-word of each hemistich.

In the *gaṣīda*, in particular, the diction is quite select. When, for example, 'Anēz abū Sālim heard that others had recited poem 6.18 using (in line 4b) the first conjugation verb *yigūd* (to lead an animal), he was indignant. He insisted that he had composed the poem with the rarer second conjugation form of the same verb, *yigawwid*, for it had a more deliberate character and could more effectively convey the image of 'leading camels by hand over difficult terrain'. For the identical image in the lighter *imwēlī* poem (8.3, l. 7), by contrast, the first conjugation was sufficiently eloquent for the itinerant singing composer. Correcting renditions of poem 6.10 recited by others, 'Anēz insisted on using the rarer verb *rāyah*, rather than the more commonplace *shāf*, to convey the idea of 'to sight someone' (line 2), and in poem 6.7 he rejected the simple *ghēbtak* ('your absence'), transmitted by reciters, in favour of the more intricate fifth conjugation verbal-noun, *itigiybak* (line 1).

The first line of poem 1.10 is a particularly rich example. In addition to the assonance created by the recurrence of the sounds 'r' (twice), 'sh' (four times), 'l' (twice), and 'g' (four times), and the same rhyme ('īg') in masculine and femine for the two hemistiches—we have an example of elevated and intricate diction with the use of two uncommon words for 'high peaks' (*imšamrix, šawahīg*) in the first hemistich and two equally rare words for 'splitting' (*tišagga, šīg*) in the second:

ana ʿaddēt rūs imšamrixāt aš-šawahīg
alḷā min galbin tišagga bi-šīgī.

Rich Imagery

The integration of imagery from the natural environment is another facet of the art of bedouin poets drawn from their own observation and thought. For example, in describing the camel chosen to bear a message-cum-poem (the conventional theme of many poems), poets employ metaphors and similes rich in animal imagery, whether the chosen camel be slow or fast.

If sent on a trip, like a wolf's is his trot:
A wolf that slinks upon hearing a shot.

(6.15)

Quick, like what scatters small birds in mid-flight:
A hawk, when a flock of white doves comes in sight.

(6.16)

Animal metaphor is also used widely to depict human situations.

You sleep on your stomach, crouched like a tick.

(6.1)

But then you were trapped through their craft and deceit,
Like they'd dash an old camel to slaughter for meat.

(6.4)

Whose breasts are a bustard's egg in size
When the bustard's still brooding, before she rises.

(2.6)

Like a camel that's homing. I'm restless and stirred.

(6.18)

How vile this devilish breed that would cheat.
Prowling with long beards like ibex in heat.

(6.6)

The imagery of metaphor may also come from everyday experience.

> Her mother's like a Mauser shot whose range is very far.
> (1.15)
>
> Dishonour is like game; it must be hunted to be found.
> (2.7)
>
> Why, this world is all treachery, a frock with two sides.
> (6.10)

The bedouin poet also excels in finding images that rely on the listeners knowledge and that please with the satisfaction of the initiated. Only bedouin, for example, would understand the expression 'her mother's milk would not fill a cup' (6.13) as a complimentary depiction of a thoroughbred camel (known to produce little milk); or immediately grasp the significance of 'The cover that your kinsmen give you often makes you cold' (2.7)—a reference to one's accountability for a kinsman's misdeeds, which must be accepted along with the protection that the same kinsman affords one, owing to the system of mutual guarantee. Similarly, it would take a bedouin to know that the attainment of justice is referred to metaphorically as 'My side-heavy saddlebag's now been put right' (1.3).

THE TECHNIQUE OF CREATIVITY

The Use of Formulas

Bedouin poetry is not devoid of aesthetic quality, as we have seen, but the question arises concerning the originality of this rich imagery and apt metaphor. How creative is the bedouin poet? To what extent is his composition original?

The question of originality arises because of the oral nature of bedouin poetry. The subject of oral poetry has been dominated since the mid-twentieth century by the theory developed by the two Harvard University scholars, Milman Parry and Albert Lord, who studied the long epic poems recited publicly in Yugoslavia. Observing how illiterate reciters sing between ten and twenty six-syllable lines per minute, they found it unlikely that the memorization of such poems could account for their retention and transmission, and concluded that, instead of memorizing the lines of an epic poem, the reciters, through intensive contact with the poetry of this genre and through deliberate training, familiarized themselves with a vast reservoir of formulas and formulaic expressions that could be recalled in an instant to continue a recitation.

Each such formula or group of words, moreover, was suited to a specific metrical condition, to which it could be adapted, when required, to express 'a given essential idea'. On occasion the reciters would use formulaic expressions that might occupy a full or half a line. In addition, incidents and descriptive passages that were repeated as themes in a variety of compositions could be assimilated into different recitations. Interruptions during performances, intermittent audience interest, or a sudden need to end a poem prematurely would often compel a reciter to improvise, so that the actual renditions of a story-cum-poem might vary from one performance to another, and this led Parry and Lord to conclude that each poem was actually created as a new composition *during* its recitation; and that each reciter, therefore, is himself a poet. They also concluded that in oral poetry there is no such thing as an original version of a poem, but only a general story that is versified anew in each recitation, at least partially.[10]

The conclusions of Parry and Lord seem to preclude any claim of bedouin poetry to originality as the term is understood in regard to written Western poetry. Indeed, one cannot deny the abundance in bedouin poetry of formulas and of recurring images that fit the definition of a formulaic expression. In the present collection the expressions for 'O Rider . . .' (*ya rākib; ya rākbin̲*), for example, clearly constitute a formula that introduces many poems which, in reality or as a literary device, are conveyed by a cameleer. Similarly, the phrase 'he'—either the camel or its rider—'will stop off with . . .' (*yilfī*), appearing a few lines after the beginning of several poems, occurs so frequently that it, too, must be considered formulaic. Various images for worthy camels are also repeated throughout: camels that have cut canine teeth (e.g. poems 1.4, 4.4, 4.18, 6.13), are barren (e.g. 1.1, 2.9, 7.1), are of thoroughbred lineage beyond count (e.g. 2.8, 2.9, 5.1), are bred by the S̲h̲arārāt tribe (e.g. 2.6, 5.1[11]), or are 'the best thoroughbred she-camels' (*ʿērāt anḍā*) (e.g. 2.12[12]). Similarly, men are complimented in many poems for being desired by perfumed or slim-waisted women (e.g. 1.4, 2.6, 6.1, 6.7).

There are further examples of formulaic usage. Poems composed by the northern Sinai poet, Ṣabāḥ Ṣāliḥ al-G̲h̲ānim (e.g. 1.11, 2.9, 4.4,

[10] See Lord, pp. 4–5 and *passim*.
[11] Also found in Socin, p. 41, and Musil, *Manners*, pp. 165, 291, 298.
[12] Cf. Socin, p. 41; Musil, *Manners*, p. 243.

7.10), often begin by 'mentioning God' (*dhikr allāh*) and/or end with praise for the Prophet Muḥammad (*al-khatm*), a theme that goes back in bedouin poetry at least as far as the once well-known medieval epic of Abū Zēd and his Banī Hilāl tribe,[13] and is found in more recent bedouin poetry as far distant as Ḥaḍramawt, in southern Arabia.[14] To describe the blows inflicted in battle, ʿAnēz abū Sālim, composing his poem in praise of the Egyptian–Israeli peace treaty of 1979, compared them to viper poison, an allusion which we also find in a Negev war-poem (5.3) a hundred years earlier. Furthermore, a clear indication of 'borrowing' among bedouin poets is the fact that entire lines of poetry that the present writer heard in Sinai and the Negev may also be found in at least fifteen poems presented in Alois Musil's *Manners and Customs of the Rwala Bedouins* (1928); in some cases, the lines transcribed in Musil bear no contextual resemblance to those heard by the present writer.

It may also be said of these formulaic words and expressions that they play a certain, if limited, generative role in the creation of a poem. For the most part, this role is to expedite composition. For example, since he knows that a poem can be 'sent' on a camel, a poet has certain formulas and images ready at hand: e.g. 'O Rider'; 'upon a white Sharārī'. If he chooses this type of prologue, moreover, he will then know that he should prescribe a route for the camel—whereupon a suitable formulaic word for 'lead him . . .' should quickly come to mind. Similarly, when the camel-rider 'arrives' at the recipient's camp, several more possibilities present themselves, such as complimenting the recipient's martial prowess—perhaps evidenced by the fact that 'birds of prey' follow him to battle; or his hospitality—as manifest in his readiness to 'pour clarified butter profusely' on the gruel, or serve the visitor 'blood-red coffee' from 'pots made in Baghdād'. These handy formulas and recurrent themes make it easier for an illiterate bedouin poet to compose a poem; they also help a listener learn it by heart. The immediate, even automatic, emergence of familiar themes and images to the forefront of one's memory makes it easier to concentrate on the novel facets of a poem. Similarly, it may be owing to these devices that bedouin frequently report their ability to learn a poem composed by someone else after only one, two, or three hearings.

[13] *Sīrat Banī Hilāl, passim.*

[14] See Serjeant, p. 6.

The Limits of Formulaic Usage

Although the bedouin poem falls short of the standards for originality found in Western written poetry, the bedouin poet is less dependent on formulas in generating a new poem than the Yugoslav reciter of epic poems.[15] An ordinary bedouin would find it technically impossible to create poetry on the basis of formulaic composition as defined by Parry and Lord, even if that were the only creative method open to him. The nomadic and often secluded lives of bedouin keep them from hearing poems frequently; and then they hear a far smaller selection (of total lines if not individual poems) than a Yugoslav or other towndweller might be exposed to. Even bedouin of today's older generation, who mainly learned the poems of others, tell of a very limited exposure to new poems, mostly poems brought by travellers from the east (i.e. Syria, Jordan, or the Arabian peninsula), who passed through Sinai and the Negev on their way to or from the markets of Beersheba, Gaza, or Cairo, and whom they rarely saw for more than a day, or more than once. Under such circumstances a bedouin can hardly undergo the deliberate and accumulative stages of training that a poetic aspirant in Yugoslavia could.[16]

Even if so desultory an exposure to poems still leaves a bedouin with a certain fund of formulaic devices, he fails to develop it. The bedouin poet's initiation into poetry is much more casual than that of the Yugoslav reciter. ʿAnēz abū Sālim who, as an active young smuggler, had a chance to hear more poems than the average bedouin, relates that, when he was about nineteen years old, he and a friend—impressed by the poems they had heard from others, such as a noted smuggler from the Aḥaywāt Ṣafāyḥa, ʿAliyyāṇ Imṭēr—began to compose poems to each other for amusement. When people were pleased on hearing ʿAnēz's poems, however, and requested that he compose poems for fun, on one occasion or another, he refused, claiming that he had to have a subject—'a chair' (*kursī*)—on which to rest a poem: 'a subject with its own beginning and ending'.[17] In other words, ʿAnēz was talking about a talent that, once discovered, was sparingly used; not a skill which had to be developed.

The use of formulas as the main instrument of composition was also

[15] In an attempt to prove that bedouin poetry is essentially formulaic, Alwaya (pp. 62–76) compared different renditions of the same poems as if they were individual creations, in keeping with the Parry–Lord concept that each new recitation constitutes a separate and original poem.

[16] Cf. Lord, pp. 21–9.

[17] Personal communication from ʿAnēz abū Sālim, at Nuwēbaʿ at-Tarābīn, 19 April 1984.

technically impossible for bedouin. By Lord's definition, a formula is a group of words repeated in a specific metrical situation; and there is no standard metrical situation in bedouin poetry. Claims made by some scholars that the metre in oral bedouin poetry is quantitative, as in Classical pre-Islamic poetry,[18] have not been substantiated by any of the poems in the present collection, despite the fact that nearly all the poems were transcribed as heard from live recordings with the aid of bedouin knowledgeable in both their poetry and their culture. Occasionally one finds a line that fits a quantitative syllabic metre, but the poem to which it belongs as a whole does not. Poem 1.14, for example, has more hemistiches following quantitative metre than any other poem in the collection. It is a *hijēnī* poem and its first and second hemistiches may be seen to correspond to two quantitative patterns that the Saudi Arabian scholar, Sowayan, presented as *hijēnī* metres (shown, in the following diagram, by a capital 'X' and capital letters for a long syllable, and a small 'x' and lower-case letters for a short one). Even in this poem, however, only nineteen of the thirty-four hemistiches actually fit these patterns. For example, while both hemistiches of lines 2 and 3 fit:

hemistich 1									hemistich 2								
X	X	x	X	X	x	X	X	X	X	X	x	X	X	x	X	X	X
AB	KĪ	ṣa	ḤĪ	BĪ	zi	MĀ	NIN	ĠĀB	DAM	ʿĪ	ša	HȦ	LĪ	l	MAṢ	BŪ	BA
GAL	BĪ	ti	ʿAL	LAG	ma	ʿAL	AḤ	BĀB	WAJ	DĪ	b	HUM	WAJ	d	MAN	HŪ	BI

the quantitative metres for lines 11 and 12 do not:

ṢAG RIN FIL AW WAL ti LĀ HAʿ GĀB / GUL TAL xa BAR ma ʿAK HAN NŌ BI
BAḶ ḶĀ Ū WID d AS ʿa LAK YĀ ʿa GĀB / ʿAN ṢAḤ BĪ WĒ n ga DŌ BI

One possible explanation for this inconsistency is that a literate person originally composed the poem, part of which was subsequently corrupted; another is that a literate person put part of it into quantitative metre at some stage of the poem's transmission. Whatever the explanation, it seems unlikely to the present writer that an illiterate person can compose poetry according to quantitative metre, since this requires a knowledge of too many rules that can only be

[18] Especially Sowayan (pp. 156–60), who gives an 'inventory' of fifty-one quantitative metrical patterns, which he claims to have identified in the bedouin poetry that he examined in central Arabia (where it is called Nabaṭī poetry). Sowayan, however, presents no consecutive lines of poems of one pattern or another to establish that any given pattern was used in an entire poem. Furthermore, most of the poems that he examined were, by his own admission (pp. 11–12), from the written page rather than from live recordings, and could have been put into quantitative metre by literate people who thought it more respectable than accentual metre.

comprehended by seeing the written word on the page. How, for example, could an illiterate person be expected to build a metre based on long and short syllables when he has no way of knowing that certain vowels pronounced as short are actually long—such as the penultimate long vowel of certain words (e.g. the second 'a' in *mawājīb* or *ṭawāḥīn*), or the vowel that precedes a first person imperfect verb at the beginning of a hemistich (e.g. the first 'a' in *ajarrib*)? Could such a person know that the word *kull* (a word that ends with a double, or *mushaddad*, letter) constitutes a long and a short syllable (*kul/l*), if he does not know what a *mushaddad* letter is; and is thus unable to discern the independence of the second 'l' sufficiently—by only hearing it—to let it stand unvowelled on its own as a short syllable (in a phrase such as *kull ṣāḥib*)? Or, finally, how could an illiterate be expected to take metathesized or elided vowels into consideration in determining the syllables of a hemistich when all he knows is the words in their metathesized or elided form as spoken in his vernacular? It is highly unlikely that a simple bedouin could ever have possessed or developed an 'instinctive feeling' for quantitative rhythm.

By contrast, while an illiterate bedouin poet would be incapable of composing poems comprising quantitative metres, he could well have composed accentual verse, in which metre is measured, as shown above, by stressed syllables in keeping with the natural stress of conversation. Even though the number of unstressed syllables in the feet of a hemistich is irregular and there is no consistency in the type of feet appearing in consecutive lines, neither the poet nor his audience are annoyed by this lack of regularity or consistency so long as the number of stressed syllables is the same in all the lines and so long as the last accents in each hemistich remain constant throughout. Thus, for example, they find the first two lines of poem 2.7 pleasing, despite what we might consider the irregularity:

jawnī ẓYŪF ū-ḤARramū YĀKlu-š-ŠĀ
ū-GĀL int ŠĀ'ir bass itKAWḏib 'al an-NĀS
ū-ṢIRT ataNADdar ū-kull ḤARF ataḥalLĀ
ū-GULT il naḥīf al-JISM gūm SAWwī lī KĀS.

Owing to this irregularity in the constituency of a metrical foot, a bedouin poet, unlike a Yugoslav bard, would be encumbered if he had to build his poem from formulas suited to specific metrical conditions. Naturally, in choosing a word or group of words for any specific line, he may need a rising effect as of iambic or anapaestic or a falling effect as of trochaic or dactylic; but in this he would be no more likely to make the wrong choice than an English poet. Indeed, the actual mechanics of choice may be observed in the way one bedouin tried to compensate for a lapse of memory in trying to recite a poem not of his own making. In poem 4.20E, for example, different reciters used synonyms having different metrical value to express the same idea. The first hemistich of line 1 ('O Khlēf, you're not the type to fight with lovers') was rendered in varying metre thus:

ya XLĒF min MIṮlak yiḤĀrib ahl aš-ŠŌG
ya XLĒF MIṮlak ma yiḤĀrib ahl aš-ŠŌG.

Although the second foot (*min MIṮlak—MIṮlak ma*) was given in the first rendition as short/long/short and in the second as long/short/short, it did not matter. What mattered was that the hemistich contained four stressed syllables (*XLĒF/MIṮ/ḤĀ/ŠŌG*) and four accented feet.

In the second hemistich of the same line ('Letting some grey-beard snatch my cloak'):

ū-TA'ṭī ḥitīt aš-ŠĒB YĀxiḏ 'aBĀtī
wi-tXALlī ḥitīt aš-ŠĒB YĀxiḏ 'aBĀtī

the fact that 'letting' was rendered as *TA'ṭī* (long/short) in one version, and as *itXALlī* (short/long/short) in the other, was also insignificant for the same reason; namely, that the hemistich was considered complete because it had its four stressed syllables. Similarly, in line 3 of poem 4.20H ('Why didn't you, Jidēa', send a scout out to spy?') the word for scout (literally 'lad') could be rendered as an iamb (*ġuLĀM*) and a trochee (*ṢAbī*) with no adverse effect on the metre.

The final and most significant reason why an original bedouin poet cannot rely on formulas to the same extent as a Yugoslav reciter of traditional epic poems is that his poetry is truly individual; he composes against an original background of novel events for which he may not have heard many formulas. When 'Anēz abū Sālim composed a poem on the Egyptian–Israeli Peace Treaty, he had to deal with unprecedented circumstances, such as the anger of the other Arab states and the reasons for it. In other poems by 'Anēz, anger at his unfaithful wives and kinsmen was not a hackneyed theme, either. When Sulēmān Ibn Sarīa' died in 1973 and his memory met with disrespect, it was a real and unanticipated situation that his maternal cousin's poem had to express. A century earlier the relief expressed when Ḥarba Abū Sitta was married to Ḥammād aṣ-Ṣūfī during the War of Zāri' in the Negev also arose from an actual event; as did a poet's anger over the sale of bedouin land for Jewish settlement in the Negev seventy years·later. Indeed, all the abductions, murders, and insults portrayed in the present collection of poems were specific occasions for which a bedouin poet had to invent at least some original expressions.

Creativity and the Role of Memory

If, then, it is not from formulas that a bedouin builds his poem, what is the source of his poetic content? The answer, despite Parry and Lord's negation, is his memory. In all illiterate societies memory assumes the larger part of the recording function, and the capacity of the illiterate is no less considerable in bedouin society than in others. Although formulaic expressions do appear in bedouin poetry and, as shown, even alleviate the task of composing a poem, it is not their manipulation that constitutes the main generative apparatus. Rather, in the course of casually hearing poems recited over many years, a poet builds up a fund of poetic expressions and idioms that come to mind under special circumstances, in much the same way that people anywhere may be reminded of a song, poem, or joke by some subconscious stimulus or association.

Even the use of a formula in the composition of a poem arises more out of a passive process of association than an active one of manipulation. The opening phrase of poem 4.20E from the romance of Jidēaʿ Ibn Hadhdhāl just cited begins with the direct address, 'O Khlēf, you're not the type' or 'one like you wouldn't . . .' (*ya xlēf miṯlak ma . . .*), which is apparently a formula for an appeal to someone in a superior position but with whom one can be somewhat intimate—the very situation of Irgayya *vis-à-vis* Khlēf al-Ḥantashī, whose men had just robbed her. Accordingly, when Ḥamdān abū Salāma (poem 4.5) had a dispute with his chief over the trifling matter of a rooster and was induced by it to compose a poem, he came upon an opening that was quite similar except for the substitution of the word *shēkh* (chief) for Khlēf. What brought it to mind, however, was not the need for a formula to suit a certain metrical situation but the association in his mind between his own dispute with his chief and other poems composed over such disputes beginning with *ya šēx miṯlak ma*—poems that he had probably heard at least once, and an example of which is included in the nineteenth-century collection of Socin (p. 73).

Even a less similar situation may conjure up associations in a bedouin poet's memory. When ʿAnēz abū Sālim composed a poem of anger against those who had falsely claimed that they could secure his release from prison (poem 6.3) and included, by way of contrast, lines describing a 'true' undertaking—a night-time smuggling operation from Jordan to Sinai over the southern Negev—one of the expressions he used was *tāh ad-dalīl* ('the guide lost his way'). Guides do lose their way, but in this case there was a poem composed in the late nineteenth century by a poet from the neighbouring tribe to the north, the Aḥaywāt, that included the expression *tāh ad-dālil* in describing a raiding party's return from Transjordan to Sinai. It was a popular poem in the part of Sinai inhabited by the Tarābīn Ḥasāblah and the Aḥaywāt, and parts were even heard and transcribed by Shuqayr (p. 578). Thus, although ʿAnēz was thinking of his smuggling adventure and not a raid on camels, the fact that both parties of riders were returning to safety in Sinai over the same terrain suggested this expression to the later poet.

Similarly, when the fisherman–smuggler, Jumʿa ʿĪd Dakhīlallāh (poem 2.4), wished to inform others about the arrival of a consignment of hashish near Jabal Khlēlāt, associations related to the subject of hashish also occurred to him: white camels (the euphemism for hashish), marked with the owner's brand (*wasm*); *wasm* ('sign'), as in 'the Sign of the Pleiades' (the rain season); rain; lightning; 'Lightning flashed, and was over Rās Bannā seen' (*bargin barāg ū-bi-rās banna naxīla*) (from two of the popular Jidēaʿ Ibn Hadhdhāl poems, 4.20B and 4.20D). Hence, the idea for his own first line—*bargin barāg ʿa rās gōz il-xlēlāt*—replacing only the present tense form of the verb *xāl* (to see: hence, *naxīla*) at the end of his prototype poem's first hemistich, with the past tense *xilti*, with which he began his second hemistitch. When Ṣabāḥ Ṣāliḥ al-Ghānim (poem 7.10) complained about the menacing deeds of a modern and powerful government, Egypt in the 1960s, he focused on its taking a census and its issuing of ID cards, much as another northern Sinai poet, Faraj Sulēmān (poem 7.6), had done in criticizing the British forty years before, even though he used entirely different language.

Prison experiences can also arouse associations from past poetry. When ʿAnēz abū Sālim was nostalgic for his people's encampment at holiday time, and composed poem 1.1, the first hemistich of the second line, 'O how pleasing's the cup one sips under palms' (*ya ma-ḥala-l-finjāl bēn il-widāya*), was, almost verbatim, a line used a century earlier in a poem composed by a powerful Arabian chief, Rākān ibn Falāḥ Ibn Hithlēn, who was imprisoned by the Turks in Istanbul when he also remembered his tribe's encampment at holiday time.[19]

[19] The poem may be found in al-Kammālī, p. 367.

This sort of mental association aroused by similar circumstances could equally have led ʿAnēz to use just one line, or one expression, or one word. For example, when ʿAnēz was in solitary confinement and distressed by the news he had received of his wives' unfaithfulness, the appearance of a bird on his cell window, one day, reminded him of an earlier poem composed in prison by his fellow tribesman and friend, Jāzī Imsallam Ḥamd al-ʿArādī, in which Jāzī addressed his thoughts and wonderings to a bird ('O bird looking down on this slave enduring': (*yā ṭayr yā mis̲h̲rif ʿal ar-ragg ṣabbār*). Thus, ʿAnēz opened his own poem with 'O Bird' (*ya ṭayr*), just as Jāzī had, but quoted nothing more from Jāzī's poem.

Another imprisoned poet of the nineteenth century was a Syrian Druze called S̲h̲iblī al-Aṭras̲h̲, who composed bedouin-style poems from a Turkish prison, poems that were eventually published and made their way to Sinai and the Negev, where they enjoyed immense popularity. ʿAnēz confessed that S̲h̲iblī's poems were a source of comfort and encouragement to him in prison; and when he wished to compose a poem to Sulēmān Ibn Sarīaʿ (poem 6.11) to announce his decision to divorce his unfaithful wives and had already decided on the 'punch-line' (And, lest every Zēd and ʿAbēd laugh at me, / I've set my three non-bearing she-camels free'), he was reminded, by the rhyme-word of the first hemistich, *ʿAbēd*, and by the dismal atmosphere of holiday time in prison, of a poem that S̲h̲iblī composed from prison at holiday time which contained a similar hemistich rhyme (e.g. *sīd*, in line 1).[20] He therefore began his own poem, as S̲h̲iblī had, with the line, *yaḷḷa ya xālg al-ʿabd was-sīd* ('O God, O Creator of servant and lord'), incorporating, also, yet another full hemistich from S̲h̲iblī's composition, *awḥī bi-galbī mitil gaṣf ar-rawaʿīd* ('My heart is a thunder peal ready to burst' (line 7a)). ʿAnez viewed these adaptations neither as plagiarism nor as a diminution of his own creative talents but as one way of enriching his own creation with expressions of true feeling and understanding, in the same way that a scholar might quote a passage from another study, finding it as apt as anything he himself could say. Furthermore, although ʿAnez adopted S̲h̲iblī's 'My heart is a thunder peal ready to burst' as the first hemistich of a line, he still had the task of completing that line with 'My body, acacia coals burning with thirst', which did not come from S̲h̲iblī's poem.

How a theme and a rhyme may combine to form a memory association is also demonstrated by a comparison between poems 2.10

[20] Al-Aṭras̲h̲, p. 108.

and 4.15. The first is an appeal for mercy sent to King ʿAbd al-ʿAzīz Ibn Saʿūd by the Bilī tribe in the early 1930s—a poem that was popular and often recited in Sinai. As an appeal for mercy, more than half of its lines were panegyric. Twenty years later ʿAnēz abū Sālim wished to amuse some friends with a parody on the many panegyric poems that bedouin were accustomed to send to King Ibn Saʿūd. Thus, either inspired to composition by poem 2.10 or else reminded of it by the subject chosen independently, he adopted the rhyme-scheme of the first poem's second hemistich for his own poem's first hemistich.

Similar associations may even emerge from within a poet's own works. When ʿAnēz was prevented from meeting Jordan's King Ḥusēn in 1985 and composed poem 1.6 to express his indignation, the double-rhyme that he had used in a poem he sent to Ḥusēn's grandfather, King ʿAbdallāh, thirty-five years earlier (poem 2.12), naturally came to mind. Two other poems by ʿAnēz, although composed under contrary circumstances—holiday time in prison (6.11) and President Anwar al-Sādāt's historic visit to Jerusalem during the al-Fiṭr holiday (4.1)—both cite the holiday time of the two occasions with the same words *mutatis mutandis*:

> *al-ʿīd ʿād ū-ṣirt ana-krah al-ʿīd*
> The feast day's returned, but I am all hate
> *al-ʿīd ʿād ū-gult ya ma-ḥala-l-ʿīd*
> The Fiṭr feast returned, how sweet this holiday.

Associations arising from within the same poem also serve to aid the poet in his creative task. In poem 1.15, line 6, for example, the use of the verbs *aʿṭī* and *tāxiḏ* suggested to the author that the following line could also be built around the same two verbs, though used in a completely different sense. Thus:

> I'll let (*aʿṭī*) the young kids drink up first, till they take (*tāxiḏ*) their fill;
> I'll set (*aʿṭī*) a date with her, [that will take] (*tāxiḏ*) late summer till it rains.

In the same poem, moreover, the fact that lines 11–13 each begin with the same verb and image (*ibtiswī*: she's worth . . .) suggests that lines 12 and 13 each took their cue from the preceding line. The same phenomenon seems to have taken place in poem 1.11, where the use of the rhyme-word *rmāḥ* (spears) in line 5 ('with spears in their hands') suggested the rhyme-word *slāḥ* (arms) for the not-very-imaginary parallel of line 6 ('with arms in their hands').

However, in making his own 'individual' poem and suiting his composition to the immediate circumstances that inspire it, the bedouin poet is not limited to poetry, neither his own nor that of others, for his raw material. He can equally search his memory and choose imagery and ideas from the surrounding culture and environment, just as poets in other cultures do. When ʿAnēz abū Sālim was in prison and was tortured by being put for the night in a bedless cell with water on the floor so that he could not lie down, he did not have to get the image of 'sleeping crouched like a tick' (6.1) from another poem. Similarly, on a different level, life's experience was a sufficient source for lines (of poem 2.7) like:

You won't make someone drink the bitter using means that please;
You'll only make him drink it having brought him to his knees.

The adaptation of proverbs is one example of how a bedouin poet draws upon non-poetic materials. The present collection is full of thoughts that arise from known proverbs. In using them the poet has to adapt them to the rhyme and metre of his poem; and some of these adaptations are ingenious. 'Poor folk take heart when calamity comes' (poem 1.1) is no less pithy than the original proverb 'The misfortunes of fighters are the common man's gain'. Equally clever is the concluding line of poem 7.7 that protested bedouin land sales—'Even Zirbāwī this life couldn't abide/ When, after shitting, it stuck to each side'—used to stress the main point of the poem as embodied in the proverb 'He who has no land will shit in his hand'.

In short, the bedouin poet, though illiterate, does not approach his art empty-handed. He is first of all a person adept at living through his eyes and as such can draw upon rich experience, replete with observation of his physical and human environment. In introducing this material into a poem he is aided by a life-long familiarity with rhyme, by flexible canons of versification that allow for irregular metre and considerable poetic licence, and, finally, by a rich poetic idiom that comes down to him from a long poetic tradition. Unlike the Yugoslav bards, the study of whose art by Milman Parry and Albert Lord led to the formulaic theory of oral poetic composition, bedouin poets are not public reciters of long poems with set traditional themes. They are the occasional creators of relatively short poems that arise out of novel circumstances. In composing a poem, therefore, a bedouin relies less on the rapid manipulation of set formulas than on the quick workings of his own memory, which, through associations stimulated by the background circumstances that give rise to the creative urge, suggest both the form and content of his new poem.

To contrast the quick and manipulative creative process with the deliberate process of creating a 'serious' poem (e.g. *gaṣīda, marbūaʿ, hijēnī*), we have a description by Jumʿa ʿĪd Dakhīlallāh of how he composed a *gaṣīda* after being overturned in his felucca boat at sea:

> My clothes were ruined. I changed them and brought whatever I needed for the fire and made some tea. I sat quietly for a while, thinking. I had been in a bad situation, in danger; and I was lucky not to die at sea. I sat with my little pot-stove from the felucca and drank tea. When I had drunk tea I thought quietly to myself, for perhaps two or three hours, remembering what had happened. *I gathered up words from here and there and pressed them together, and I made a poem* . . . I was alone.[21]

As we have seen, the bedouin poetry composed by illiterate persons is neither as slavishly formulaic as the epic poems recited publicly in Yugoslavia nor as original as the written poetry of modern Western civilization. It is somewhere in between, with a character and value of its own. To appreciate that value it might be well to consider what was said of poetry from the ancient world: 'It is not the strikingly original but the meaningful manipulation of the long familiar that constitutes the apex of poetic technique.'[22]

[21] Personal communication from Jumʿa ʿĪd Dakhīlallāh, of the Tarābīn Ḥasāblah, at Nuwēbaʿ at-Tarābīn, 30 March 1972.

[22] Gevirtz, p. 5.

9
Perspective on Bedouin Poetry

A Cultural Document for the Ages

AN ANCIENT CULTURAL HERITAGE

If the art of the bedouin poet is 'the manipulation of the long familiar', he has much to manipulate. An illiterate bedouin who sets out to compose a poem unwittingly calls upon a cultural heritage thousands of years old—not a forgotten heritage that has survived in the fabric of the present as a barely perceptible thread; but one that lives much as it always has, with the same surroundings, artefacts, technology, economics, and social and political conditions. In the nineteenth-century 'War of Zāriʿ al-Huzayyil', when the Tarābīn wished to dissuade the Huzayyil from fighting against them in alliance with the ʿAṭāwna (poem 5.6), they deprecated the ʿAṭāwna as degenerate by alluding to their eating of 'fluffy fellaheen bread baked in the ovens of Brēr' (a village with which the ʿAṭāwna had cultivated close relations) instead of eating 'bedouin bread', the unleavened bread that was and still is baked in the hot ashes of a campfire. In the 1940s, when a Negev poet wished to ridicule the chiefs who had sold off bedouin land (poem 7.7), he alluded to the easy life they chose in marrying peasant girls whose only renown, he alleged, are 'fried foods and soft bread'. Similarly, when Jidēaʿ Ibn Ha<u>dh</u>d<u>h</u>āl in the eighteenth century argued that the cultural gap between himself and Irgayya was too wide to be bridged by marriage (poem 4.20A), he said

While you are people used to settled life,
We bedouin bake our bread in ashes grey.

Unknown to the unlettered bedouin poets of these three relatively recent poems, the choice of bread-types as the determinant of cultural difference was not novel. Three thousand years before, in the Akkadian Poem of Erra, the urban god Erra was challenged by nomads with the boast: 'The rich bread of the city cannot compare with bread baked in the embers.'[1]

Many other examples of Middle Eastern nomadic material culture from the book of Genesis have survived for thousands of years—such as the black tent, the water-skin, and the nose-ring worn by women. The survival of this culture in an unlettered society is also apparent in the biblical designations for desert trees and bushes, such as the tamarisk, the acacia, and the genista, that are still being used with only slight Arabic variations by lone, illiterate shepherdesses (with no knowledge whatever of the Bible) in the most remote wadis of Sinai and the Negev; as are the names of at least forty-five other plants and grasses mentioned in pre-Islamic bedouin poems composed fifteen hundred years ago, poems of which these shepherdesses and their menfolk are also totally ignorant.[2] Similarly, the anticipation of rainfall with the yearly appearance of the Pleiades in the winter sky, as alluded to by the seventh-century Arabian poet, ʿAmr ibn al-Ahtam ('the Pleiades . . . and lightnings flash out of the depths of a rain cloud heavy with water . . . gushing forth in frequent showers'),[3] was still active in the mid-twentieth century when the bedouin fisherman, Jumʿa ʿĪd Dak͟hīlallāh, began poem 2.4 with

Lightning flashed over Gōz K͟hlēlāt;
  I saw it and thought it the Pleiades' sign
She poured forth her rain sprouting grasses so high,
  Filling wells at the spring after these had run dry.

The customs of desert life, which appear amply in the present collection of bedouin poems, are also part of a long legacy. The custom of threatening to divorce one's wife unless others fulfil a condition bearing no connection with the wife (poems 1.4, 2.10, 5.1) goes back at least thirteen hundred years to the first century of Islam when the poet Farazdaq threatened to divorce his wife if his rival, Jarīr, could surpass one of his poems with a line of his own.[4] The bedouin custom of standing in front of the tent, suggested in poems 3.3 and 3.6 as the proper way to greet passers-by, is even older, having been practised at least as early as the patriarch Abraham, who went out of his tent to

[1] Cagni, p. 28. I am indebted to Dr Joanna Firbank, of London, for calling my attention to the Akkadian antecedents of the bread phenomenon.

[2] Bailey and Danin, 'Desert Plants', pp. 47–8, based on a comparison of plants mentioned in the *Muʿallaqāt*, the *Mufaḍḍalīyāt*, and the poems of ʿAmr ibn Qamiyya, with three hundred species personally collected in Sinai and the Negev.

[3] *Mufaḍḍalīyāt*, p. 84.

[4] Sowayan, pp. 200–1, for the citation.

greet the three disguised angels sent by God to announce the birth of Isaac (Gen. 18. 2).

The social concepts of desert life are equally ancient, especially those concerned with security. The importance of clan solidarity to a person's security, for example, as expressed in poem 6.16:

For one whose males back him is free from attack:
Wolves never spare sheep that are left on the track—

is currently considered no less that it was in pre-Islamic times when, during the famous War of Basūs, neglect by patrons was rebuked with

These people for their clients have no care . . .
The wolf comes, 'tis my sheep he comes to tear.[5]

Conversely, the notion that contact with someone who does evil may prove contagious is also of ancient vintage. The bedouin proverb 'Woe to the wrongdoer, and woe to his neighbour' (*yā wēl al-māsī, ū-yā wēl jārah*), which was incorporated verbatim as a line in poem 5.6, is found in the second-century *Mishna*,[6] and may even antedate it. Another abiding subject often manifest in desert poetry is the belief in the indispensability of force in resolving conflict. The concomitant of a life in which people must ultimately rely on their own resources for protection, its expression has hardly changed from the sixth century—

'Tis wooing contumely to meet wild actions with humane
By evil thou may'st win to peace when good is tried in vain[7]—

down to 1984 (poem 2.7):

You won't make someone drink the bitter using means that please;
You'll only make him drink it having brought him to his knees.

Even a religious concept such as fatalism, itself borne of experience in the dangerous and defenceless desert, has always served the requirements of security by stimulating courage and a contempt for death. Thus, in the same vein that a sixth-century bedouin poet boasted

Never I reck—if war must be—
What Destiny hath preordained,[8]

[5] See Nicholson, p. 57.
[6] *Mishna Nega'im*, xii. 6, cited in Schwarzbaum, p. 6.
[7] See Nicholson, p. 59.
[8] Ibid. 57.

his twentieth-century descendents are told (poem 3.9):

> Finally, when God wills war and puts us to the test,
> And fighters call on you for aid, don't flee from their request.
> . . . .
> Your written fate is bound to reach you, even if you hide;
> Another's fate will miss you, though you're standing at its side.

THE ANCIENT POETIC HERITAGE

Imagery

As the culture of a distant past is reflected in the everyday lives of contemporary bedouin through their poetry, so their poetry itself, in both content and form, is heir to the poetic genres of the past. This phenomenon is apparent in the imagery of the poems.

For example, not only does one term for fate (*manāyā*), often used by contemporary bedouins (poems 1.12, 1.14, 3.11, 6.1, and 6.5), stem from the pre-Islamic period, but also the image of how it works—with ropes and snares (*aḥbāl*, *asbāb*)—as well as the futility in trying to escape it, remain vital in bedouin poetry today. Thus, whereas the seventh-century Zuhayr ibn Abī Salma, in his famous *Mu*ʿ*allaqa* ode, said

> Whoever fears the snares of fate (*asbāb al-manāyā*) will be taken
> Though he ascend by a ladder to heaven,[9]

the twentieth-century ʿAnēz abū Sālim (poem 6.1), who had never heard of the ode, knew nothing of its author, and mainly used different vocabulary, aphorized with

> Though we hide among stars in the heavens so vast,
> Fate's rope (*ḥabl al-manāyā*) must ensnare us wherever it's cast.

In 1977 ʿAnēz abū Sālim chose 'pegs' as an image for the indispensability of people when he composed a poem praising Anwar al-Sādāt's visit to Jerusalem (poem 4.1):

> Now Sinai's mountains may, by any soldiery, be taken,
> But honour is well-founded there, its pegs remain unshaken.

This image was used in the context of the same culture as that of a pre-Islamic bedouin, who, composing a poem on the importance of co-operation between a chief and his people for the welfare of their tribe, was led to say

[9] Zūzanī, p. 120.

Only with poles the tent is reared at last
And poles it hath not, save the pegs hold fast.[10]

Battles are depicted as 'wells' and 'pools' (where death is drunk), danger as 'the drying of the spittle', destiny as the 'ropes of fate'; these are but a few of the many images common to contemporary and pre-Islamic bedouin poems, images of a common culture, not clichés slavishly repeated. To express the gravity of warfare, for example, the seventh-century Zuhayr, in the aforementioned ode, said 'War . . . is not a tale told at random, a vague conjecture';[11] ʿAnēz abū Sālim, expressed the same sentiment, in poem 4.1, with

Wars are more than pious words or the playing out of games,
Or the singing of a necklaced lass recalling warriors' names.

Just as the imagery of security and of warfare in the desert poetry of the Middle East has not changed for millennia, that of female beauty has also remained the same. In describing the attractive features of women, bedouin poets in Sinai and the Negev, like their pre-Islamic forbears (for example, al-Mukhabbal in the seventh century[12]), cite the whiteness of their skin and compare the size of their breasts to the eggs of big birds, such as the ostrich or the bustard (poem 2.6); they also imagine drinking their saliva, an image that was already known to the desert poets in the Bible, the authors of the Song of Songs, where we find, too, beautiful eyes compared to pools of water and breasts to clusters of dates, just as in poem 4.10 by Ḥamdān abū Salāma Abū Masʿūd.

The detailed imagery of the camel was especially common to both the pre-Islamic and the more recent bedouin poets. The theme of depicting the appearance of a camel from the front as he comes towards one, and from the back as he moves away, as in poems 4.20B and 5.6, may be found in a poem by the well-known seventh-century poet, Bashāma.[13] Similarly, the virtues of a 'barren' camel, sung in several poems of the present collection, were also appreciated in the pre-Islamic era as evidenced in the following lines by al-Aswad ibn Yaʿfūr:

And oft have I followed after friends departing, my beast
a stout she-camel, well-knit, that yields no calves nor milk,
Strong as a wild-ass: the Spring has filled out the chinks of her frame—smooth
now the surface, whereon no tick can find room to lodge.[14]

[10] See Nicholson, p. 83.
[11] Arberry, *Odes*, p. 116.
[12] *Mufaḍḍalīyāt*, p. 76.
[13] Ibid. 26.
[14] Ibid. 163.

Fourteen images from the most famous camel-description in pre-Islamic poetry, that of the *Muʿallaqa* ode of Ṭarafa,[15] may be found in the present poems from Sinai and the Negev:

swift, lean-flanked

Like his midriff beneath which the saddlebags meet; (2.8)

she vies with the noble, hot-paced she-camels, shank on shank

Even purebreds, though barebacked, she'd take on the run; (1.10)

in Spring, cropping the rich heights green in the gentle rains

We can wait till the grass on our hilltops grows tall,
And the she-camels graze after winter rains fall; (6.15)

perfectly firm is the flesh of her two thighs—

Her foreleg is lithe, her thigh is taut; (6.13)

tightly knit are her spine-bones

O Rider on one whose spine isn't slack; (2.6)

ribs like bows

And her waist is slim as the bow of a *rabāba*; (6.13)

widely spaced are her elbows

His chest-disc chafes not and his legs don't turn out; (2.8)

broad the span of her swift legs

His hind legs are close, though knock-kneed they're not; (2.8)

her legs are twined like rope uptwisted

O Rider on one graced with sinuous limbs; (6.16)

her forearms thrust slantwise

His forelegs are tapered from shoulders to feet; (2.8)

her shoulder blades high-hoisted

Shoulders protruding from loads she would bear; (4.20B)

the scores of her girths chafing her breast-ribs are water-courses

And belly-flesh twisted from so many trips; (5.3)

her split lip a tanned hide of Yemen . . . its slit not bent crooked

A beauty having thick, split lips; (4.12)

fleet as a male ostrich,

O Rider on one like an ostrich in flight. (6.18)

[15] Arberry, *Odes*, pp. 83–5.

The imagery of virtue is also common to the panegyric and hortatory lines of pre-Islamic and contemporary bedouin poems. Of the famous panegyric on his tribe, the Bakr, composed by the seventh-century poet Suwayd,[16] imagery from twelve lines appears in the present collection of poems:

they stretch out their hands generously when they are asked

And if someone needs help he sets off straightaway; (7.6)

no hasty foul speech or unseemly impatience

And even if the guest offend you, treat him like a precious friend,
Even if, at times, his prating brings your patience to an end; (3.9)

they recognize what is incumbent on them, and are not weary in doing it

He's surrounded by followers ever on call,
And each obligation is met by them all; (4.5)

they deal forth food from full cauldrons, crammed with meat

No sheep-herder's flock do their flesh-pots neglect. (6.18)

platters . . . filled full with the flesh of fat-humped camels

In Giṭān, ninety platters were teeming with meat; (4.17)

he who seeks their protection fears no treachery

A camp travellers seek, where the wronged always flee; (6.7)

generous are they in giving what other men cling to

The expense we incur is a price very dear,
A price such as people of less pride would fear; (4.17)

they restrain their soul from the stain of covetousness

Envy not others, we're all God's creation:

. . . .

Find helplessness shameful, and wear not its stain; (3.11)

fair are they of face, light-coloured of skin, lords to see

On all of them seated together I'd gaze,
Just the sight of such monarchs must surely amaze; (2.12)

lions are they of whose fury men stand in awe

Turmoil takes place when you seek revenge.

. . . .

A lion rallies . . .; (1.6)

[16] *Mufaḍḍalīyāt*, p. 142.

when they have burthens loaded on them, they halt not beneath them—
when . . . the rich are lamed by their weight

There are camels, though galled, who bear loads but don't cry;
Others shy, though the fat in their humps is stacked high; (6.9)

the good among their coevals are their friends

The meeting-room of Ḥammād's tent
Is where excellent men gather. (5.5)

Themes

Besides imagery, Middle Eastern desert poetry possesses a fund of thematic devices common to the many ages of its long history. To signify emotional turmoil in the present collection of poems, whether caused by longing (1.1), love (1.15), grief (5.12), or worry (6.13), some poets began their compositions complaining of a sleepless night, just as the seventh-century poetess, al-Khansā, had done on hearing of her brother's death in battle: 'I was sleepless, and I spent the night keeping vigil.'[17] When Ṣabāḥ Ṣāliḥ al-Ghānim (poem 4.4) wished to mock his own misplaced anger at breaking a leg, he employed the ancient device of scolding a non-human object (his leg), just as biblical Balaam scolds his ass for leading him astray (Num. 22. 28–30). The very defence used by Balaam's ass ('Am I not your ass, upon which you have ridden all your life to this day? Was I ever accustomed to do so to you?') is the same defence adopted by Ṣabāḥ's leg:

> Remember this: that it is I that takes you here and there,
> And brings you to some water when the heat gets hard to bear.

A similar poetic device of using the obviously unnatural to stress an impossible expectation has likewise been present in desert compositions for millennia. Thus, as the prophet Amos used the figures of speech 'Does the lion roar in the forest when he has no prey?' and 'Does a bird fall in a snare on the earth, when there is no trap for it? to show how unrealistic it was to expect anything that God did not will, so al-Khansā promised her murdered brother

> I shall never make my peace with a people with whom you were at war,
> Not till the black cooking-pot of the good host turns white;

and Swēlim Abū Haddāf in the nineteenth-century Negev threatened his enemies (poem 5.3) with

[17] Arberry, *Poetry*, p. 38.

We will grant you no peace, no peace will you see,
. . . .
Until the wolf recites rhymes at our night-time dances,
Or an ostrich bitch suckles a jackal.

Considering the basic lack of governance in the desert, hostilities have—not unnaturally—been a central theme in its poetry, at least since the biblical period. To express their relief after the rout of Pharoah (Exodus 15.9), Moses and Miriam retold the events:

'The enemy said, I will pursue, I will overtake,
I will divide the spoil, my desire shall have its fill of them.
I will draw my sword, my hand shall destroy them.'
'Sing to the Lord, for he has triumphed gloriously;
the horse and his rider he has thrown into the sea.'

Again, after gaining victor over the Canaanites (Judg. 5), the Israelites expressed relief by retelling it in a poem, the Song of Deborah:

From Ephraim they set out thither into the valley,
Following you, Benjamin, with your kinsmen;
from Machir marched down the commanders,
And from Zebulun those who bear the marshal's staff; . . .
The kings came, they fought;
then fought the kings of Canaan. . . .
Then loud beat the horses' hoofs
with the galloping, galloping of his steeds . . .
Most blessed of women be Yael . . .
She put her hand to the tent peg
and her right hand to the workmen's mallet;
she struck Sisera a blow
she crushed his head
she shattered and pierced his temple.
He sank, he fell,
He lay still at her feet . . .

In pre-Islamic bedouin poetry battles are also 'replayed': some, as in the biblical examples, to celebrate victory; some to lament defeat. For example, to lament his tribe's defeat to the coalition of Bakr and Qurēsh at the Battle of 'Ukāẓ the sixth-century poet, Khidāsh ibn Zuhayr, expurgated his trauma with the following retelling of the events:

And Bakr did not cease to swarm and shout battle cries,
and the first and the last of them pressed on together,

From morning until night came on, when the cloud cleared away
of a day whose evil was manifold, layer upon layer;
And this manner of things continued until Hawāzin withdrew . . .
in flight and Sulaym and ʿĀmir were scattered hither and thither;
And Quraish were as though their keenness would split a rock,
when stumbling fortunes sap the strength of other men.[18]

In the present collection of poems from Sinai and the Negev, battles were also retold in poems composed either to rejoice or to lament. A member of the Tiyāhā, present at the fierce battle of Wādī al-Mlēḥa, and relieved at its outcome, described the turning-point thus (poem 5.13):

But then I saw dust rise over al-Mlēḥā,
Broad daylight—not a treacherous attack before dawn;
You could hear the clang of swords, even of the hilts!

By contrast, Jidēaʿ Ibn Hadhdhāl, personally defeated in battle, lamented in the following account (poem 4.20H):

Black horses with riders then fell on the foe,
The Governor of Syria had fewer to lead.

Indian swords made a clash and a clang,
The swaying of spears seemed a madman's stampede.

Then felled, I saw Frēja was limping away,
Afraid lest the foe mount a counter-foray.

To curry favour is a further reason for retelling the tales of past battles won. A notable example was the sixth-century poem composed by ʿAlqama ibn ʿAbāda requesting the King of Ghassān, al-Ḥārith ibn Jabala, to free his brother Shaʾs who was taken prisoner-of-war. To ingratiate himself with the king, ʿAlqama describes scenes from the battle of ʿAyn Ubāgh in which the king killed the prince of al-Ḥīra, the other major desert kingdom:

Thou pushest [the horse] on till the white rings are hid in blood,
while ever thou rainest blows on helmets of men in mail.
Two hauberks of steel enwrap thy body, and from them hang
two choicest of blades, well named 'Keen-cutter' and 'Sinker-in'.
Thou smotest them till they put before them their champion
to face thee, when near had come the moment of sun-setting.
There battled all Ghassān's best, the bravest that bear the name,
and with them were Hinb and Qās, stout fighters, and bold Shabīb:
The men of al-Aus stood serried there 'neath his charger's breast,
and all the array of Jall, and with them ʿĀtib their kin.[19]

[18] *Mufaḍḍalīyāt*, p. 305. [19] Ibid. 329–31.

Similarly, 1,300 years later, hoping to persuade the Negev chief, ʿAlī al-ʿAṭāwna, to intervene on his behalf with the Turkish authorities, Salāma Abū Swēriḥ sent him a poem (5.11) in which he extolled the military prowess of the chief's kinsmen at the nineteenth-century battle of Gubēba:

> But Ibn Ṭallāg appeared with his singular rifle,
> Took aim, and Abū Sitta was downed with a shot.
>
> . . . .
>
> And Gāsim Ibn ʿAṭiyya, so stringent with a spear,
> That even horses cowered on seeing his shadow.
>
> And Jabr al-ʿAṭāwna, stout heart and a hero,
> Jabr who bequethed his prowess to his sons;
>
> When he attacked the Tarābīn, 'twas like ancient Jassās,
> Their horses cowered and they were dismayed.

Roles

Battle descriptions in bedouin poetry for purposes of rejoicing, lamenting, or currying favour are all natural and legitimate, but the true connection between hostility and poetry lies in the role that the poem plays in the conduct of conflict. When the Tarābīn threatened to go to war against the Tiyāhā in 1875, persons of this tribe immediately came to Muṣṭafā Zabn al-ʿUgbī asking him to compose a poem (5.1) that would dissuade the Tarābīn from their course. A century later in 1984 the Tarābīn, fearing that the Tiyāhā had been insulted and might open hostilities against them, came to ʿAnēz abū Sālim al-ʿUrḍī asking him to compose a poem (2.7) that would dissuade the Tiyāhā from their course. By turning to a poet—one who could wield words—the tribesmen were acting in a traditional manner. In Transjordan, two and a half millennia before then, the Moabite chief Balak summoned Balaam to say things—in this case curses in elevated language—against the Israelite tribes who had recently left Sinai and were camped on his border: 'Come now, curse this people for me, since they are too mighty for me; perhaps I shall be able to defeat them and drive them from the land; for I know that he whom you bless is blessed, and he whom you curse is cursed' (Num. 22. 6). Having studied this phenomenon from several sources, the noted Orientalist, Ignaz Goldziher, commented that it was believed in ancient days that 'a heavenly power was revealed in poetic speech', and that the poet could harm the enemy through his invective and threats no less than the combattant with his weapon.[20]

[20] Goldziher, pp. 24–7.

In pre-Islamic bedouin poetry this invective (*hijā'*, in Arabic)—whether in the form of a curse, a boast, an insult, or a threat—was part and parcel of the armoury of warfare. Describing one battle, the poet ʿĀmir ibn aṭ-Ṭufayl said, 'There came upon us an overwhelming mass, full of boastful words.'[21] Another poet, Muzarrid, defined these words as 'arrows' and 'spears'.[22] *Hijā'*, however, was not confined to battles. Any conflict with another person was a suitable arena for its use. A scornful rhyme could adhere to one forever, like 'a collar round his neck'; 'conspicuous as a mole on his face'. Being rhymed it would be heeded, as one poet attested:

Yea, many the folk that looked at me askance,
with their eyes blinded by hatred,
Have I aimed at with an ode that brought upon them shame
while the people listened intent, and thou mightest have heard the slightest sound![23]

The damage he could thus cause to an enemy's reputation was relished by a poet, as revealed by Muzarrid:

I warrant to him with whom I contend that my words shall be so striking that the night-traveller shall sing them as he fares along, and the caravans be urged forward by them on their road;
Well remembered are they, cast forth with multitudes to bear them about: their sound is gone forth in full sunshine into every land;
They are repeated again and again, and only increase in brilliancy, when the diligent lips of men test my verse by repetition.

In the contemporary world of bedouin, conflict and security are as dominant as they have always been in the desert, so it is not surprising to find *hijā'* a conspicuous aspect of the poetry. Although unfamiliar with the term, ʿAnēz abū Sālim, when asked about the essential components of a poem, said, 'Its message should slaughter!' (*in maʿnāhā yidhbaḥ*).[24] Another Sinai poet, ʿAṭiyya Miẓʿān ʿAwwād, who was given to composing lampoons (e.g. poems 4.8 and 7.11), said that he composed them when angry with someone and that an essential element in such a poem was its ability 'to harm him with artful machinations' (*tikīdih*).[25] In the present collection of poems, therefore, we find curses flying about like arrows, in war (poem 4.16):

21 *Mufaḍḍalīyāt*, p. 299.
22 Ibid. 61.
23 ʿĀmr ibn al-Ahtam, in ibid. 347.
24 Personal Communication, at Nuwēbaʿ at-Tarābīn, 19 April 1984.
25 Personal Communication, at Abū Rudēs, 25 November 1971.

If two sons has he, may the better be slain,
The other unable a stick to regain;
If two daughters has he, may the better abscond,
And the other her guardian rape on the ground;

and in 'peace' (poem 6.9):

And my wives, may God their luck dispel;
Don't bring me so much as pitch from a well.

In war you also have insults (poem 5.3):

Ask the maidens of Brēr what happened at the threshing floor,
When you fled on horseback all the way to Masmiyya;

threats (poem 2.3):

Before tobacco and melons, you'll meet spears of *zān*
And mounts champing bits, tugging bridles aside.

and boasts (poem 5.1):

And we Tiyāhā are a sword ever gripped at the hilt,
Providing profit to the camel-merchant although we are few.

Likewise, in 'peace' you find insults (poem 7.7):

You'll hear a chief belch as he comes forth to greet,
A belt he won't wear, having too much to eat;

threats (poem 2.2):

If the rifle goes off we'll all hear the sound
And vultures and kites will hover around;

and boasts (poem 1.6):

Many stallions we've chased, and from many we've run,
Spirited stallions who charge when told: Turn!

Genres

Flyting—the impromptu exchange of boasts and taunts—is one ancient form of *hijā'* still characteristic of bedouin poems. Thus, as Goliath said to David (1 Sam. 17), 'Come to me, and I will give your flesh to the birds of the air and to the beasts of the field', and David answered, 'I will strike you down and cut off your head; and I will give the dead bodies of the host of the Philistines this day to the birds of the air and to the wild beasts of the earth', so Sa'ūd said to the slave of Da'ūd (poem 4.16):

We'll take her with mounted young men bearing spears,
And a blow her protector and neighbour will feel,

and was answered by the slave with,

Before taking her, Prince, many spears will be thrown,
And many fine riderless mares left alone.

In the present collection, poems 4.16 through 4.19 represent a genre of poetry in which a responsive *hijā*'-argument between two figures of acknowledged poetic skill takes place, presented as an on-the-spot exchange for entertainment's sake. This is also a tradition of the desert, going back at least to the famous *hijā*'-contests of counter-poems, between the seventh-century poets, Farazdaq and Jarīr.

Other ancient genres of poetry are also still present among the bedouin of Sinai and the Negev. The assemblage of admonitions and other maxims as one integral poem—such as the poems of Chapter 3 and poem 6.14—or as the major part of a poem was common among the pre-Islamic bedouin. Although the ancient poems are fragmentary, examples have survived; these not only reveal that the genre of instruction-poems extant among contemporary bedouin is part of a long heritage, but, when studied in conjunction with the contemporary poems, also confirm the historical depth of social concepts. Thus, for example, we find that the opprobrium of gossip, detailed at considerable length in poems 3.8 and 3.9, was treated at no less length by pre-Islamic poets such as ʿAbda ibn aṭ-Ṭabīb and al-Mut͟haqqib.[26] The older compositions also confirm impressions about various bedouin attitudes and motives gained from the contemporary poems. When we read in poem 3.5, for example,

Whoever sows bounty among his guests will reap a name,
For guests go forth and then their host's largesse they must proclaim,

we might wonder if the vaunted custom of hospitality is not observed, after all, in order to gain a reputation. This impression is strengthened when we read a poem by the pre-Islamic ʿAbd al-Qays ibn K͟hufaf, who counselled,

And the guest—honour him! his night's entertainment is a thing due:
become not an object of cursing to those who alight at other tents;
And know that the guest carries news to his people of his night's lodging,
even though he be not asked thereof;[27]

[26] *Mufaḍḍalīyāt*, pp. 101 and 233, respectively. [27] Ibid. 322.

or the poem of ʿAmr ibn al-Ahtam who counselled his son on the protection of wards with:

Do no despite to my protected stranger and my guest
what time the camel-saddle is set down behind the tent:
Visit him with generosity, and guard him well from harm . . .
for surely his report will travel abroad.[28]

Some of the cultural values that pre-Islamic poems mention and thus confirm as being bedouin in origin are found in poem 3.11—which nevertheless purports to be a poem of *Islamic* religious advice. To a bedouin there is no difference and hence no conflict between Islamic and bedouin customs. The proverb 'He who lacks honour, lacks religion' (*illī mā lih sharaf, mā lih dīn*) closes the gap, since the observance of custom and convention ensures one's honour which of itself must needs be sanctioned by religion. Thus the admonitions in poem 3.11 against suffering contempt and poverty, against doing an ill deed with haste, against being impatient with one's close kin, and against clinging slavishly to life, might be mistakenly attributed to a non-bedouin, perhaps Islamic, influence were these values not also defended in the pre-Islamic poems. In ʿAbd al-Qays ibn Khufaf,[28] for example, we find,

The abode of contempt belongs to him that chooses to dwell therein;
When thou fallest into poverty, grovel not, waiting for generosity;
When thou hast in mind to do an evil thing, be slow about it;[29]

and in ʿAbda ibn aṭ-Ṭabīb and ʿĀmr ibn al-Ahtam, respectively:

'Hatreds should be laid aside where kinship exists'

and

Never wilt thou attain to glory until thou give liberally of that which the heart
most clings to—thy life or thy wealth.[30]

Even the Islamic prescriptions for a good life in poem 3.11, however, may be seen as part of the oral, unlettered tradition of the desert. Although most of the ideas originated in the written poems of the eighth-century poet Abū-l-ʿAtāhiya from southern Iraq, these poems, because of their simple style and ascetic content, appealed particularly to the unlettered bedouin who were then visiting and settling in the new Muslim towns of Baṣra and Kūfa.[31] The bedouin, already

[28] *Mufaḍḍalīyāt*, pp. 347.
[29] Ibid. 321–2. [30] Ibid. 102, 347. [31] Guillaume, 'Abū'l-ʿAtāhiya', pp. 107–8.

accustomed to a hard existence that in any case comprised some of the main tenets of asceticism (Ar. *zuhd*), were inclined to accept asceticism as the *bona fide* version of Islam. Therefore, hearing lines of Abū-l-ʿAtāhiya's poetry from local street-preachers, they took them to the desert, where they provided a basis for the Islamic content of their own oral compositions down to the present.

Abū-l-ʿAtāhiya's themes and lines, notwithstanding the adaptations and improvisations that inevitably occurred in the process of oral transmission throughout the ages, still emerge clearly in poem 3.11, which was composed in the 1930s. There is little difference, for example, between

> Don't rejoice over life [*dunyā*] though your riches be great,
> For what's really at hand is the end of your life [*zawālak*],

and Abū-l-ʿAtāhiya's

> Even if you've come by this life [*dunyā*] easily, isn't it your significant fate to disappear [*zawālak*]?[32]

Similarly,

> Be neither too sad when grief should embitter,
> Nor overly happy when gladdened by pleasure;
> Life is like that: sometimes sweet, sometimes bitter . . .

has almost the identical imagery of Abū-l-ʿAtāhiya's

> Many a matter saddens and then gladdens
> Such is life—sometimes sweet and sometimes bitter;[33]

just as

> Don't rejoice over life though you've reached highest station,
> For the lowest—the grave—is our last habitation,

reflects closely the imagery of Abū-l-ʿAtāhiya's

> For you've seen even those who in palaces dwell
> After palaces have but a grave to inhabit.[34]

In at least one instance, moreover, the actual wording of Abū-l-ʿAtāhiya and poem 3.11 is almost the same. While Abū-l-ʿAtāhiya wrote of 'nothing remaining but the bones decaying' (*lam yabqa ilā al-ʿiẓām bāliya*),[35] the contemporary poet from Sinai (line 6d) employs the

32 Abū-l-ʿAtāhiya, p. 338.
33 Ibid. 167.
34 Ibid. 437.
35 Ibid. 485.

same image, stated in the same words—only placed in the affirmative and the singular: *yibgā al-ʿaẓm bālī*.

One significant difference between poem 3.11 and the *zuhdiyyāt*-poems of Abū-l-ʿAtāhiya pertains to style. The latter's poems are mainly in quantitative metre and rhyming couplets, whereas poem 3.11 is accentuated metre, composed in quatrains in which the first three lines rhyme with each other, and the last line with the fourth line of the other quatrains. Significantly, however, the closest models for this form in the classical tradition were the popular *maqāmāt*-verses of the early twelfth-century poet, al-Ḥarīrī, who composed them in quatrains and rhymed prose or *sajʿ*.[36] One of the best known of these *maqāmāt* [the Eleventh Assembly] consists of ascetic preachings in the spirit of Abū-l-ʿAtāhiya and, like the latter's verses, seems to have passed into the oral tradition, as indicated by the similarity of at least one al-Ḥarīrī quatrain,

> In the grave shall thy limbs be laid
> A feast for the worms arrayed
> Till utterly decayed
> Are wood and worms withal[37]

with lines (6b–d) of poem 3.11,

> At your back is the grave, that abode ever hateful,
> Where the worm eats your flesh like pasture so tasteful,
> While your bones, interred, end in disintegration.

Looking for the antecedents of bedouin poems of instruction, however, one can go back beyond early-Islamic or pre-Islamic Arabic poetry to the biblical Book of Proverbs. Not only do various sections of Proverbs begin like the contemporary bedouin poems of instruction (e.g. Hear, my son, your father's instruction; My son, if you receive my words . . .; My son, do not forget my teaching . . .); but elements of the biblical advice, such as disciplining children and consideration for neighbours, are echoed in the present poems:

> Chasten thy son while there is yet hope,
> And let not thy sole spare for his crying
>
> (Prov. 19. 18)

[36] For al-Ḥarīrī's *Maqāmāt* and his use of *sajʿ*, see Gibb, pp. 123–6; Nicholson, pp. 329–36; and Von Grunebaum, pp. 105–9.

[37] Nicholson, p. 334.

Be not loath to strike your son, to have him grow up right;
(3.9)

or

Keep thy foot from thy neighour's house
Lest he be wary of thee and hate thee
(Prov. 25. 17)

Keep your children from your neighbour, lest you rouse his scorn.
(3.9)

Style

Another aspect of the desert heritage, going back as far as Ugaritic poetry and widespread in both biblical and contemporary bedouin poetry, is the use of parallelism, the device whereby the thought or construction of a line or hemistich of poetry is echoed in the next, positively, negatively, or as the development of an idea.[38] In the first instance, called synonymous parallelism, a thought is stressed by repeating it in different words. Whereas in Exodus 15. 5, for example, we have in Moses' song:

The floods cover them;
They went down into the depths like a stone,

poem 2.7 compares the judge Salāma Abū Amīra to an 'ever-flowing well', and continues

A well so deep that one would tire tugging on its rope,
A well where all the thirsty tribes resort when void of hope.

Negative or antithetic parallelism, on the other hand, is employed to stress an idea by contrasting it, or the image conveying it, with another. Thus the biblical proverb

A son who gathers in summer is prudent
But a son who sleeps in harvest brings shame

bears the same construction as these lines from poem 6.12:

Some friends hear you cry but aren't moved by your plight,
Whereas some come apart from not sleeping at night.

[38] Gevirtz, *passim*.

Finally, in what is called synthetic parallelism, an idea is developed, often through explanation, in the succeeding line or lines. Thus,

> Leave the presence of a fool,
> For there you meet no words of knowledge;
> (Prov. 14.7)

and

> And when you visit other tents, beware no joker seem;
> A laugher in the men's *dīwān* will never gain esteem.
> (3.5)

Still, the similarity between contemporary bedouin poems and pre-Islamic bedouin poetry is greater than that between either of the two and the poetry of the biblical period. This is because the former were composed in Arabic rather than Hebrew, and because much of the latter was probably lost in the long time-span before it was written down—and then underwent considerable religious editing, which deleted contents considered either irrelevant or inimical to the editor's goals.

In terms of style the main legacy that survived from the pre-Islamic period to the present was in metre and in rhyme-pattern. In particular, the contemporary *bidaʿ*-poem is close to being the direct descendent of poems composed in the early pre-Islamic period in the *rajaz* metre, which, like today's *bidaʿ*, was considered beneath the dignity of the *qaṣīda*. Several common features characterize both.[39] Their rhythm resembles iambic in its quickness and, at the same time, allows for irregularity. There are four to six feet to a line, and each line, undivided into hemistiches, is an unbroken whole rhyming with the line that precedes it, so that all the lines rhyme with each other. The *rajaz*, like the *bidaʿ*, moreover, was uttered extempore, a few verses at a time, expressing some feeling, emotion, or experience. While it is difficult to know how deep this expression was in the pre-Islamic *rajaz*, that of the *bidaʿ* is generally light, even playful, though the present collection contains notable exceptions, such as the expression of anger at an insult to a deceased kinsman's memory (poem 1.5), and an expression of release after fierce fighting (poem 5.10).

In contemporary bedouin poetry deep feelings and other serious subjects are generally the domain of the *gaṣīda*, which is more suited to deal with them because of its deliberate process of composition and the

[39] For *rajaz*, see Nicholson, pp. 74–5.

elevated language of its lines, wherein it resembles its ancient namesake. Yet even today's *gaṣīda*, like the *bidaʿ*, is structurally more similar to the *rajaz*-rhymes than to the Classical pre-Islamic *qaṣīda*. First, the double-rhyme of each line, one for each hemistich, found in most contemporary *gaṣāyid*, was the rhyme-pattern used in one (apparently less common) form of pre-Islamic *rajaz*-poem, called *ma<u>sh</u>ṭūr* (literally, 'with hemistichs'),[40] whereas the Classical *qaṣīda* had only one rhyme in all but the first line. Secondly, the use of irregular metre in the contemporary *gaṣīda*, although of eight rather than six feet, was in ancient days allowed in *rajaz* more readily than in the more intricate metres used in most Classical *qaṣīda*-poems.

DESERT POETRY AND THE PRE-ISLAMIC QAṢĪDA: A PERSPECTIVE

Whatever the specific structural identity between the contemporary poems and those of fourteen hundred years ago, it is clear from the foregoing that in content and form they are both products of the same bedouin culture. Bedouin culture as a whole may be defined as a response to the peculiar difficulties and dangers of desert life arising from both nature and man; and as life *within* the desert has hardly changed over the millennia, a view of bedouin life as afforded by the poems in the present collection should tell us about the desert life and bedouin culture of other periods, however remote.

Can the poems of the present collection also tell us something about the bedouin poetry of other times, such as pre-Islamic poetry? Judging from the difference in literary quality alone, the answer would seem to be no. While pre-Islamic poetry is rightly considered one of the greatest accomplishments of Arabic literature, the bedouin poems of Sinai and the Negev are considered inferior even to the contemporary poems composed in other deserts; a disparagement shared, moreover, by the inhabitants of Sinai and the Negev themselves. One of their own sayings maintains:

<u>sh</u>uʿr a<u>sh</u>-<u>sh</u>arg gaṭ<u>fin</u> min zuhur;
Poems from the east [Syria, Jordan, Iraq] are like a bouquet of flowers;
<u>sh</u>uʿr al-gibla nag<u>shin</u> min ḥajar;
Poems from the south [Arabia] are like engravings in stone;

[40] Wright, ii. 362.

ū-shu'r al-gharb fattin min ba'r; .
Poems from the west [Negev, Sinai, Egypt] are like grindings of camel dung.[41]

Migrating shorter distances than their bedouin neighbours to the east and south and being relatively sheltered from the more frequent wars and raids that plagued the centres of bedouin life (the Syrian and Arabian deserts), the scope of exposure and skill needed for commanding rich imagery, even in matters pertaining to the camel, was bound to be missing when a poet from Sinai or the Negev composed a poem.

As a cultural document, however, the bedouin poem from Sinai and the Negev is of value even for the study of pre-Islamic poetry. Composed in the context of desert life, poems from Sinai and the Negev constitute one aspect of bedouin adjustment to living under desert conditions. The rhymed poem as a missive, for example, is necessary in any dispersed and illiterate society. The poem of expression is necessary in a society where a man's security requires him to repress his emotions in normal social intercourse. The poem of entertainment, which is often a natural demonstration of individualism and courage, is necessary in a society whose survival requires a strict compliance with convention. To ensure, furthermore, that a poetic missive will command the attention of a distant recipient, it is embellished with descriptions of the camel that 'bears' it and praises for the recipient or his kin. If the poem is intended to intimidate the recipient, as in wartime, it might contain boasts or replays of previous battles that demonstrate the prowess of the poet's group; even a poem of expression, as on the death of a daughter from snakebite, may have a replay of events, perhaps to justify the poet's emotional expression. As one of the most stringent conventions of bedouin society requires the inviolability of females, it is not surprising to find persons seeking relief in accounts, mostly fabricated, of illicit contact with women.

In the light of the circumstances that necessarily prevail in all Middle Eastern deserts, it is inconceivable that the motivation for poetic composition was ever different from what is portrayed in the present collection of poems, even in the pre-Islamic period. Indeed, some of the surviving poems of that period do show signs of having been composed within a realistic context. The poem in which 'Alqama ibn 'Abāda asked the king of Ghassān, al-Ḥārith ibn Jabala, to release his brother Sha's from captivity[42] is a genuine poem of request, not unlike

[41] Communication from Muṣliḥ Ibn 'Āmr, at Guṣēma oasis, 19 October 1970. For a statement on the superiority of central Arabian poetry by a native scholar, see Sowayan, p. 1.

[42] *Mufaḍḍalīyāt*, pp. 329–31.

poem 2.10, which asked King Ibn Saʿūd for mercy, or poem 2.11, which asked the *shēkh* Salmān al-Huzayyil to intercede with the Israeli authorities on behalf of an imprisoned infiltrator. The poem alluded to above, in which the poetess al-Khansā grieved for her murdered brother Ṣakhr, is not unlike poems 1.12, 1.13, and 1.14, which express grief for a lost daughter, brother, and husband, respectively. And the well-known poem by the pre-Islamic Jewish poet, al-Samaw'āl ibn ʿAdīya',[43] composed out of relief after having survived a siege in which he lost a son, resembles in inspiration (as well as its boastful content) the poem from the War of Zāriʿ al-Huzayyil (5.13) composed by a poet of the Tarābīn after the fierce battle of Wādī Mlēḥa. Of those examples of pre-Islamic poetry that have survived, it is the earlier poems (of which few remain) that mostly reflect genuine bedouin inspiration and thereby resemble in content, as in their irregular *rajaz* metre, the contemporary bedouin poems composed under the same cultural circumstances.

Modern scholars like Nicholson and Gibb expressed surprise over the phenomenon of the Classical Pre-Islamic *qaṣīda*, with its quantitative metres 'emerging full-fledged', and conjectured that a long period of experimentation, of which there are few traces, must have taken place.[44] However, on the assumption that the desert defines its own poetry and that it defines it according to the categories of creative impetus set out in this book, it seems unlikely that most of the known pre-Islamic, Classical *qaṣā'id* were created in the desert. It seems more probable that

1. bedouin poetry—similar to that found in Sinai and the Negev, sometimes richer—was being composed in the desert in keeping with the exigencies of life there;
2. at some point rulers in settlements bordering the desert, like Mecca, al-Jābiya, and al-Ḥīra, decided that they could attain prestige by patronizing poetry, which they appreciated either as former bedouin or as persons living in a bedouin culture-area;
3. the bedouin poets that were consequently patronized brought with them the devices of genuine bedouin poetry—such as camel descriptions, battle scenes, *hijā'*, and panegyric—and turned them, out of context, into the themes of a new poetry of entertainment: an 'art for art's sake';
4. the patronized poets, learning how to write in their seats of patronage, began to compose in quantitative metre, 'having received knowledge of Greek metrics through Aramaic–Christian intervention' (as suggested by

[43] Arberry, *Poetry*, pp. 30–3.
[44] Nicholson, p. 75; Gibb, p. 13.

the Austrian Orientalist, Tkatsch, in the 1920s, albeit without substantiation);[45]

5. competition among the patronized poets, and the introduction of poetry contests at fairs, such as al-'Ukāẓ at Mecca, produced an excellence in poetic skill that has given Classical pre-Islamic poetry the critical acclaim alluded to earlier.

Thus, while the pre-Islamic poetry known to us today was poetically superior, it was culturally artificial. The frequent allusions to heavy drinking, for example, and the detailed dalliance with women which characterize much of this poetry, reaching their pinnacle in the magnificent *Mu'allaqa*-ode of 'Imru al-Qays,[46] are, in reality, allusions to impossible behaviour in bedouin society of the desert. Of all the requirements for survival in the desert, sobriety and the inviolability of women must head the list. If then, as occasionally now, bold escapades with women could be fabricated for a company's entertainment (cf. poem 4.11), it is doubtful that they reflected reality. As if to confirm the degree to which pre-Islamic court poetry diverged from the bedouin norm, we have the fact that, based on all the extant examples, the poetry which bedouin continued to compose in the desert remained sober and decorous, whereas dissoluteness often made an appearance in civilized Arab poetry even after the institution of Islam.

The illiterate culture of the Middle Eastern deserts, which has survived almost intact for nearly four thousand years with a tenacity known to no literate culture, is finally reaching its finale with the end of the twentieth century. Modern times have broken into the ancient sanctuary of the desert, with motor vehicles, highways, radios, schools, and non-traditional livelihoods—all of which provide exposure to alternative life-styles and an opportunity to attain them. Even those bedouin who might still prefer to pursue a familiar and often profitable nomadic or semi-nomadic existence are finding that most Middle Eastern governments discourage this option. These governments aspire to have their bedouin settled, so that they can lay claim to the desert vastness and control a population that traditionally evaded effective supervision through dispersion and mobility. Faced with the overwhelming potential for coercion possessed by modern governments, the bedouin have ceased to be masters of their own deserts and destinies.

[45] *Encyclopaedia of Islam*, "Arūḍ'. Conceivably, it was at this stage that poets began to develop Classical Arabic as a poetic koina (cf. Zwettler, ch. 3).

[46] Translation in Arberry, *Odes*, pp. 61–6.

But even if the present collection of poems from Sinai and the Negev comes too late to advance the live study of traditional bedouin society, it was fortunately accomplished before the knowledge of these poems, or even the art of their composition, died with the last people that knew them. As a result, we have a document that reveals the people of the desert as the possessors of a unique culture, a culture which, despite its own constraints, enabled them, and their ancestors before them, to survive under the conditions of the desert for millennia. Finally, we are shown that this rude and unlettered people had poetry with metre and rhyme; that they loved their poetry; and that they wove poetry into the fabric of their isolated lives with the same grace and naturalness that marked much of what they did. With the bedouin episode of human history now ending, we have at least one affirmation of Macauley's famous dictum: As civilization advances, poetry declines.

Glossary of Bedouin Words and Usages

ilā if (3.3, etc.)

illī, allī which , that (*passim*)

ēsh what? (4.14, 6.2, 7.11); *ēsh ḥāl* how wonderful! how great! (4.1)

ء ب ش *wabsh (wubūsh)* a bum, scum (4.16)

ء ب ل *bil* camels (1.10)

ء خ ر *mīkhir (mawākhīr)* one of camel's rear teats (4.20B)

ء د ى *waddā* to bring, convey (3.8, 4.4, 5.11, 6.9, 8.3); to lead (4.13); *waddā bi-ʿilm* to direct (5.1)

ء س س *asās, sās* maternal ancestors (1.6, 5.11)

ء ك د *wakād* certain (4.14)

ء ل س *wils* treachery, deceit (6.4)

ء ل ف *walīf (walāyif)* a friend (5.13)

ء ل م ن *almānī (almāniyyāt)* a Mauser rifle (1.1, 1.15)

ء ن ن *wann* to sigh (1.11, 1.13, 2.6, 6.14, 7.7)

—— *wanna* a sigh (1.11, 1.13, 2.6, 6.14)

ء ن ى *wannā* to delay someone (2.9); to tarry (2.12, 5.1)

—— *tiwannā* to tarry (1.11)

ء ه ل *ahl, hayl (ahālī)* the owners or possessors (of a thing, a quality, a characteristic) (1.1, 2.10, 4.20E, 4.20F, 6.7)

—— *[ahlan] yā halā!* Welcome! (2.12)

ء و ى *wāwī (wāwiyya)* a jackal (5.3, 6.8)

ء ى د *īd* see ى د

ب

balayyā without (2.10, 6.1)

ب ء س *lā bās!* Bravo! (5.10)

ب د د *badd (budūd, badād)* a tribe (2.10); a cushion (4.19)

—— *isbidd* no doubt (6.1)

ب د ر *bādr (bawādir)* the upper extremity of a camel's chest (6.17)

ب د ن *badan (budūn)* an ibex, mountain goat (4.9, 6.6)

ب د و *badāwa* the bedouin (6.5)

ب ر ر *barr (burūr, barārī)* a desert (6.1, 6.18); a country (4.5)

ب ر ش م *burayshim* a necklace of little, closed bells (sing. *jaras imbarsham*) worn in battle (5.12)

ب ر ض و *barḍū* also, in addition (from the Egyptian dialect) (3.10, 6.13)

ب ر ط م *barṭūm (barāṭim)* a camel's thick lip (4.12)
ب ر ق *barrag* to shine, glisten (2.12)
ب ر ى *barā (yibrā), bārā* to escort (3.9, 5.5, 7.2)
—— *barrā* outside (4.8)
ب ز ر *bizir* gunshot (5.11)
ب س م *mabsam (mabāsim)* the tip of a spout (3.2)
ب ض ض *baḍḍ (buḍūḍ)* a mud-hole (2.10)
ب ض ع *baḍ'a* words, talk (4.10)
ب ط ر *bayṭār (bawāṭīr)* a person adroit at legal talk (4.5); an excellent riding camel (4.15); a person of experience, discernment (6.5)
ب ط ل *buṭul* falsehood, evil (4.5)
ب ط ن *biṭān (ibṭina)* a stomach-girth for camels (4.13, 6.4)
—— *baṭṭāniyya (baṭṭāniyyāt, baṭāṭīn)* a blanket (4.8)
—— *baṭīn (buṭnān)* a low mountain, mountain range (1.15)
ب ع ث ر *taba'thar* to disperse in disarray (5.6)
ب ع ر *ba'r* camel dung (3.8)
ب ك ر *bakra (bikār, bawkrī)* the section of a hand-stitched band (distinguished from other sections by its colour) (2.8)
—— *bākūr (bawākīr)* a staff, riding stick (1.7)
ب ك ر ج *bakraj (bakārij)* coffee-pot (2.9, 3.2, 5.1)
ب ل ش *balshān* confused, embarrassed (4.17)
—— *balāsh* without anything . . . , there won't be . . . (4.4, 7.4)
ب ن ح ط *tabanḥaṭ* to spend freely, have a good time (7.7)
ب ن ش *binsh (binshāt)* a cloak with wide sleeves (4.3)
ب ن ن *bann, bunn* coffee-beans (2.11, 3.2, 3.3, 3.4, 4.17, 7.6)
ب ه ر *bahhar* to spice coffee with cardamum (4.19, 7.7)
—— *bahārjiyya (āt)* the pot in which the coffee is spiced (2.12)
ب و ج *bāj (yibūj)* to plunge (a dagger), to puncture (1.3)
ب و ش *bōsh* camels in herd (7.8)
ب و ق *bōg* treachery (5.13, 6.15)
—— *bāyig (bawwīg)* a traitor, treacherous person (2.10)
ب ى ت *bēt (buyūt)* a bedouin tent (1.1, 1.8, 1.10, 3.6, 3.7, 4.4, 4.19, 6.13, 6.18)
—— *bayyat* to spend the night, sleep (2.1, 3.9, 7.9)
ب ى ن *bānat an-niyya* to decide to travel (3.9)
—— *bēn* adversity, evil (2.9, 5.9)

ت

ت ت ن *titin* narghila-tobacco (2.3)
ت ر ج *tarjī (taraj, matārij)* decline from a hill or mountain (2.10, 4.5)
ت ر ع *tirī'a (āt)* a belch (7.7)
ت ل ف *tilfān* worn out, emaciated (2.4, 5.12)
ت ل ل *muntill* heavily loaded (4.17)
ت م ل ى *tamallī* always (from the Egyptian dialect) (4.7, 8.3, 8.4)

ت م م *tamm (yitimm)* to persevere at an action, continue, remain (6.12)
ت ن ى *tanā (yitnā)* to await (7.8)
ت و و *taww* just now, just before (4.18, 6.13)

ث

ث ر د *thard* nonsense (4.8)
thrā, tharā behold! (1.3, 2.2, 1.9, 6.2, 7.3)
ث ع ل *thu'ūl* a localized cloudburst (6.13)
ث ل ب *thilb, thullāb (thulūb)* an old animal (2.6, 4.5)
ث ل ث *thalāthī* a three-calibre bullet (1.10)
ث م د *thumēdī (thumēdiyyāt)* a firearm, rifle (2.2)
ث م ل *thamīla (thamāyil)* a water-hole in the sand (2.11, 6.5)
ث م ن *thamāmī* eight braids, four on each side, worn by bedouin men (6.4)
ث ن ى *thannā, anthanā* to return, double back, go back on one's tracks (1.6, 2.12, 4.16, 4.20H)
—— *tamathnā* to come down the slope of a mountain saddle, to mount from behind (7.8)
—— *muthannā* bound with shank against thigh (1.6)
—— *thaniyya (thanāya)* front teeth (1.1, 4.13); a two-year-old horse (4.20B)
—— *thanwa* old (not fresh) coffee or food (4.19)

ج

ج ب ب *jabīb* clip-tailed (horse) (2.6)
ج ب ذ *jabdh* by force (6.13)
ج خ ص *jakhaṣ (yijkhaṣ)* to discern (3.3)
ج ذ م *jadhm (judhūm)* a root of the teeth (1.11)
ج ر ج ع *jarjū' (jarājī')* a rocky stretch of terrain, unsuitable for walking animals (1.1)
ج ر د *jird* slim (4.20G, 5.1)
—— *jarda* army (7.3)
—— *jurdī (jurūd)* a soldier, fighter (2.10, 5.11)
ج ر ر *jurra (āt)* track, footprint (4.8, 6.7, 6.18)
ج ر س *ijrās* licentiousness (2.7)
—— *mijrisa (āt)* a licentious girl (2.7)
ج ر ف *jurfit an-nār* the edge of the tent-fire pit (2.9)
ج ر م *ajram* to slander, falsely accuse (4.17)
—— *jirīma* a flock (of birds) (6.15)
ج ر ن *nijr (jurūn)* a mortar for pounding coffee (3.2, 3.6, 4.9)
ج ر ى *majrā (majrayāt)* a place (1.15)
ج ز ر *jazūr (juzur)* a fat animal (fit for slaughter) (1.4)
ج س ر *jassār* intrepid (3.7)
ج ع ب *ja'ba (ja'āb)* buttocks, posteriors (6.13)
ج ع د *ja'd (ju'ād, ju'ūd)* coat of an animal, feathers of a bird (4.5)

—— *juʿaydī (juʿaydiyya)* a miser, a contemptible person (4.6)
ج ع م *jaʿām* animal disease of intestinal worms (2.5)
ج ف ى *jafā (yijfī)* to mistreat, reject (4.20F)
ج ق م *jagmā (jagam)* an untrainable camel-mare (6.15)
ج ل ل *jilāl (ajilla, jilālāt)* a rough cloth tied around a camel to protect it from flies; a cloak worn by destitute bedouin (5.11)
—— *jallī* mature (camel) (4.20A)
ج ل ب *jalab (yijlib)* to bring (6.10)
ج ن ب *ajnabī (ajānib)* someone not included in one's blood-revenge group (*khamsa*) (3.9)
janīb left (side, direction) (4.18)
ج ن ح *janaḥ (yijnaḥ)* to implicate someone in a crime (6.2)
ج ن ز ر *janzīr (janāzīr)* handcuff (7.10)
ج ن ف *janaf* a camel defect wherein the chest-disc rubs the forelegs when walking (2.8)
ج ن ى *janā (yijnā)* to glean (1.6, 5.1)
ج و د *jawād Allāh (ajāwīd)* a generous, worthy man (3.6)
ج و ر *jār (yijūr)* to oppress (3.9)
—— *jār (jīrān)* a ward, protected person (3.4)
ج و ز *jōz (jawāz)* [from *zawj*] husband (3.8)
—— *jōziyya (āt)* a wooden bowl (1.10)
ج و ف *jōf (jīfān)* the interior chest and midriff (1.14, 3.2); a large canyon or depression (4.20H, 6.18)
ج و ل *jāl (jīlān)* a side (7.7)
ج و ى *jiwā, jiwī (jiwāyāt, jiwīyāt)* a scabbard (1.3)
juwwā inside (2.7, 2.11)
ج ى ء *jāy* this side of, before (e.g. the bridge: *al-jisr ū-jāy*); since (e.g. the war: *al-ḥarb ū-jāy*) (4.8)
jiyya (āt) the coming or arriving at a place (4.17, 4.18)
ج ى ب *jāb (yijīb)* to bring (1.4, 4.8, 4.9, 6.2 6.3, 6.10, 6.13); to revive, 'bring around' (4.18)
—— *jēb (juyūb)* the open neckline of a bedouin dress or gown (1.4, 3.8)

ح

ح ب ث *ḥubth* deceit (1.6)
ح ت ت *ḥitīt* scraggly (4.20E)
ح ج ر *ḥajar (yiḥjar)* to clear a field of stones, to sow a field (2.3)
ح د د *ḥaddā* alongside (7.9)
ح د ر *ḥaddar* to topple, cause to fall (1.8)
ح ذ ف *ḥadhaf (yiḥdhaf)* to throw (4.13)
ح ر ب *ḥarīb* a contender, enemy (3.11)
ح ر ر *ḥurr* a thoroughbred camel (2.7, 2.8, 4.18); a free and noble bedouin (4.20H)
ح ر س س *ḥarsūs* thin, weak (a camel) (6.16)

ح ر ش *ḥirsh* rough (a camel's hocks) (3.8)

ح ر ص *ḥurṣak* take care! (3.8, 6.14)

ح ر ف *taḥarraf* to shirk (3.9)

ح ر ق *maḥrūg (maḥārīg)* a person having a parched throat (5.9)

ح ر ى *ḥarrā* to look forward to, anticipate (3.9)

—— *taḥarrā* to wish (1.11); to anticipate (2.7, 6.7)

—— *aḥtarā* to wait (3.3)

ح ز م *ḥazm (ḥuzūm)* a limestone mountain ridge (6.3)

ح س س *ḥass* reputation (4.8)

ح س ك *ḥasak (ḥasakāt)* a horse's bit (2.3)

ح ش ش *ḥashsh* to gather grass (4.12)

ح ش م *ḥashsham* to respect, be solicitous of (3.9)

ح ش ى *ḥāshī (ḥashū)* a young, weaned camel (4.20A)

ح ص ن *ḥuṣēnī (ḥuṣēniyyāt)* a fox (2.11, 6.8, 7.5)

—— *muḥṣan* guarded against pregnancy (camel-mare) (5.7)

ح ص ى *ḥaṣā (yiḥṣā)* to reckon, consider (6.10)

ح ط ط *ḥaṭṭ (yiḥuṭṭ)* to encamp (1.9)

—— *man ḥaṭṭnī* How I wish! (4.20E)

ح ط م *ḥaṭam (yaḥṭam)* to bound forward (1.6, 2.6)

—— *ḥāṭim (ḥuṭm)* an attacker (1.6)

ح ق ب *ḥagab (ḥigbān), miḥgāb (maḥāgīb)* the chest-girth (4.13, 6.4)

ح ق ق *ḥagg (ḥugūg)* a share (4.14)

—— *ḥugg!* Think carefully! (4.3)

ح ل ب *ḥalīb* camel-milk (3.8)

ح ل ل *ḥall (yiḥill)* to sight, see, perceive (4.17)

—— *ḥalla (āt)* a guest-section of the tent, sitting space, guest room (in Arabia) (4.17)

—— *ḥilla (ḥilāl)* a stack of grain (2.11)

ح م د *ḥamāda (ḥamād)* a stony plain (4.12, 6.3)

ح م ر *uḥaymir* Antares (star) (6.16)

ح م ص *ḥamaṣ (yiḥmaṣ)* to roast coffee-beans (3.2, 3.4)

—— *miḥmāṣ (maḥāmīṣ)* a coffee-roasting implement (3.3, 4.9)

ح م م *ḥumm* protruding (4.20B)

—— *ḥimma (yaḥāmīm)* a black (flint-covered) surface (6.3)

ح م ى *ḥāmī* sharp (of blade, etc., perhaps from being tempered under heat) (4.16)

ح ن ت ر *ḥantūr (ḥanātīr)* an automobile (6.9, 7.10)

ح ن ف *ḥanaf* a crook-leg deformity in camels (2.8)

ح ن ن *ḥann (yiḥinn)* to emit a call for one's calf (camel-mare) (4.20B)

—— *ḥinīn* a camel-mare's call for her calf (4.20B)

—— *ḥanūna* flowers (by extension, hashish) (7.11)

ح ن و *ḥinwa (ḥināwī)* a bend (in a wadi) (1.1, 6.8)

ḥannā to smear with blood (1.5)

ح و ح ط *ḥawḥaṭ (yiḥawḥaṭ)* to cry out loudly (4.2)

ح و ر *ḥuwār, ḥuwayyir (ḥīrān)* a young, unweaned camel (1.10, 2.9, 4.18)
ح و س *miḥtās* agitated (1.6)
—— *inḥās* trampled upon (5.11)
—— *ḥās! inḥās!* a command to turn and charge given to a horse in battle (1.6, 2.12); a command to withdraw from battle (4.18)
ح و ش *ḥash (yiḥūsh)* to gather, assemble, persons or things (3.6, 4.18)
—— *ḥawsh (ḥīshān)* the wall of a courtyard (7.8)
ح و ف *ḥāf (yiḥūf)* to protect, look after (5.1)
—— *ḥawf* care, attention, concern (1.7)
ح و ل *ḥayl, ḥāyil (ḥiyāl, ḥīl)* barren camel-mare (1.1, 2.9, 5.7, 6.11, 7.1, 7.5)
ح و ى *ḥāwī (ḥawāya)* one who sucks poison out of scorpion and snake bites (1.12)
ح ى ى *ḥayy (aḥyā)* an encampment (4.9)

خ

خ ب ء *mukhabbā (mukhabbāyāt)* a girl whose honour is well guarded (2.7)
خ ب ر *khābir* (participle) remember (4.12)
—— *khibra (khabārī)* an area inhabited by bedouin (7.6)
خ ر ب ش *kharbūsh (kharābīsh)* a summer tent made of rags (7.8)
خ ر ج *khurj (kharaja)* one side of a camel's saddle-bag (1.3); a camel's saddle-bag (2.3, 2.7, 2.9, 2.12, 6.4)
خ ر ش *makhrūsh (makhārīsh)* pursued (by persons whose camels one has plundered) (5.7)
خ ر ط ش *khartūsh, khatrūsh (kharāṭīsh)* the shell of a bullet (6.14); a rifle (from French: *cartouche*) (7.8)
خ ر ط م *kharṭūm (kharāṭīm)* the nose and surrounding area (4.10)
خ ر ف *khurāfa (kharārīf)* small talk, reputation (1.5, 5.10)
خ ر ق *kharg (khurūg)* rectum opening (7.10)
خ ر م *khirm (khurūm)* open stony desert, like Wādī el-ʿArīsh (6.1, 6.15)
خ ر ن ق *kharnūg* pudenda (lit. rabbit) (6.18)
خ ر و ع *kharwaʿ (yikharwiʿ)* to pace, run quickly (4.18)
خ ز ع *mukhazzaʿ* treacherous (4.1)
خ ز م *khizām (khizāmāt)* the rope connected to a camel's nose-ring (4.4, 5.3)
خ ز ن *khazna* 'posteriors' (lit. treasury) (4.7)
خ ص ب *khaṣāb* a good crop, a good year (5.1, 6.8)
خ ص ص *khāṣṣ* genuine, true (6.11)
خ ص م *khaṣīm* unwilling (2.2)
خ ط ء *khaṭā (galb al-khaṭā)* an angry heart (6.7)
خ ط ب *khaṭṭāb (khaṭṭābīn), khaṭīb (khaṭaba)* a suitor (4.10, 4.18); a scribe (6.3)
خ ط ر *khaṭar (yukhṭur)* to bear provisions a distance (a camel) (4.20B)
خ ط ط *makhaṭṭ* tattooed (4.10)

خ ف ق *khufūg* an open desert (3.2)

خ ل خ ل *khalkhūl (khalākhīl)* a steep ravine (6.13)

خ ل ف *khalfa (āt)* post-natal camel-mare (4.20F, 6.18)

—— *khilf* offspring, calves (1.10, 6.6, 6.15)

خ و د *khawda (āt)* a beautiful woman (5.9)

خ و ر *khawwār (khawāwīr)* a non-thoroughbred camel (4.9, 7.10)

خ ى ش *khēsha (khēsh)* a tent made of rags (1.15)

خ ى ل *khāl (yikhīl)* to spot, see (2.4, 4.20B, 4.20D)

د

د ب ب *dabb (yidibb)* to fill (2.12, 4.20H, 6.13, 7.8); to palpatate (6.3)

د ب ح *dabaḥ (yidbaḥ)* to walk under a heavy load, trudge (6.8)

د ب ر *dabra (dabar, dabarāt)* an ulcer on a camel's back (6.9)

—— *dabbūr (dabābīr)* a star denoting an officer's rank (4.14, 7.13)

—— *dabbūra (dabābīr)* metal stars for ornament (4.3)

د ب ل *dabbal* to attack (5.13)

د ح ر *madḥūr* changed, redirected (7.1)

د ح ل *daḥal* coastal plain (5.5)

د ح ى *daḥiyya* a type of bedouin dance (8.2)

د ر ب *darb (durūb)* a road, path (3.8, 4.8, 4.20A, 5.10, 6.1, 6.8, 6.9, 6.10, 6.17)

د ر ج *daraj (yidrij)* to crawl (7.11)

—— *tadarraj* to tremble, palpatate (4.17)

—— *dirja* a moment (1.11)

د ر ر *dirr* the whitest milk (obtained directly after pasture) (4.10)

د ر س *mudarras* emplaced, put in place (7.3)

د ر ع *duwēra' (duwēra'āt)* thigh-rest (on front of hump) (2.12, 6.4)

د ر ق *andarag* to seek shelter, scramble for shelter (6.8, 7.12)

—— *tadrīg* under cover, by stealth (2.8)

د ر ك *darak (yidrik)* to know (4.10, 6.16)

—— *darrak* to tend to (3.9)

—— *darak* honour (6.15); a fray (7.5)

—— *madārik* a battle (3.9)

د ر و ش *darwīsh (darāwīsh)* a beggar, poor man (6.14)

د ر ى *darrā* to inform (3.11)

د س م *dasīm* weighty, notable (2.2); rich, costly (6.14)

د ع ث ر *da'athar* to roll downwards (5.12)

د ع ج *da'aj (yid'aj)* to blacken the eyes (4.13); to attack (4.20C)

د غ ر ق *daghrūg (daghārīg)* a slight depression in a flat plain (2.8)

د غ ش *daghūsh* darkness (7.8)

د غ ل ب *daghlūb (daghālīb)* a slight depression in a flat plain (6.8)

د ف ق *dafag (dafāfīg)* rifle (from Turkish: *tüfek*) (4.20F, 5.1)

د ق ر *daggar* to bite (a dog) (3.9)

د ق ش م *dagshūm (dagāshīm)* a corpse (4.15)

د ق ع *dag'a (āt)* a market square (2.10)

د ق ق *dagg (yidigg)* to pound coffee (3.2)

—— *dagg, dagga (daggāt)* a shot (1.15)

—— *digga (āt)* a make, brand (1.3)

—— *dagīg* flour (4.9, 7.11); pounding of steps (4.15)

د ق ن *digin ṣagī'* a cool face (lit. a cold beard) (7.7)

د ك ت ر *duktūr (dakātra)* doctor (from English) (4.15)

د ل ج *dalaj (yidlij)* to roll (4.20C)

د ل ع *dāli'* ridden unbridled (2.9)

د ل ل *dalla (dilāl)* a coffee-pot (1.6, 3.4, 4.15, 4.17, 4.20F, 7.7)

—— *dalīl* luck (7.6)

—— *dalāl zēn* fancy apparel (6.12)

د ل ه *dallah* to soothe, be kind to (1.10)

د ل ى *madlā (madālī)* a braid (6.11)

د م ج *madmūj* thin, sinewy (6.13)

د م ل ج *imdamlaj* shapely, firm (6.7)

د م ى *madmī (madmiyyīn)* a person or group responsible for murder (lit. 'blood-stained') (5.4)

د ن ق *dannag* to hang down (4.2)

د ن ق ر *dangar (yidangar)* to let hang low (head, shoulders) (6.2)

د ن ن *dann* ringing (3.6, 4.20B)

د ه ج *dahaj (yidhij)* to pass along the way, to go along (2.3, 6.1)

د ه ك *dahak (yidhak)* to tread (4.4)

د و ب *dābī, dōbī* barely (4.12, 6.15)

د و ج *madāj* a 'hang out', 'stomping ground' (6.7)

د و ر *astadār* to look for her calf (a camel) (4.20A)

—— *dār (diyār)* tent (4.9); household (2.2, 2.7, 2.9, 6.12, 6.18)

—— *dīra (dīrāt)* tribal territory (1.7); general area (7.8, 7.10)

—— *dawwār (dawāwīr)* a circular camp (5.12)

—— *mindār* ever present (4.9)

د و س *dōs* handwork (1.9, 2.9)

—— *mindās* made by hand (2.12)

—— *dawwās* one who tramples others (5.11)

د و ل ب *dūlāb (dawālīb)* a thin iron rod used for cauterizing (6.12)

د و ن *dūn, min dūn* before, in front of (2.3, 4.16, 4.20B)

—— *dīwān (dawāwīn)* a guest house, guest section of a tent (3.5, 4.17)

د و و *daww (dawwān)* open desert (2.6, 5.12, 7.7)

د و ى *dawā (dawāyāt)* a container for *kuḥl*-powder (4.20I)

—— *dāya (dāyāt)* a pulley placed over a well (3.5)

ذ

ذ ر ب *dhārūb, dharb (dhawārīb)* a defect (4.18)

—— *adhrab (adhārīb)* something foul, filthy (3.8)

—— *dhirib* accustomed (4.20C)

ذ ر ى *dharā (yidhrī)* to shield (3.9, 4.2, 4.20G)
ذ ع ر ب *dha'rūb (dha'ārīb)* a defect (3.8)
ذ ل ق *dhalag (yidhlag)* to drip (3.2)
—— *dhallag* to cut (2.8)
ذ ل ل *dhalūl (dhalāyil)* a riding camel (1.7, 6.3, 6.14)
ذ م ل *dhumīla* a slow camel trot (1.7)
ذ ن ب *dhanab fās* a worthless person (lit. tail end of a hoe) (2.7)
ذ ه ن *dhihin (yidhhin)* to understand (6.6)
د و ب *dhōb* unadulterated (poison, medicine) (4.20C)
—— *dhāyib* sharp (2.8)
ذ و د *dhōd (dhīdān)* a small herd of camels (1.10, 6.7)

ر

ر ء س *rās* freshly brewed coffee (2.12, 4.19)
—— *rās al-jarīma* the scene of the crime (2.2)
ر ء ى *warrā* to show (3.9, 4.4, 6.1)
—— *rāy* mediation (1.7)
ر ب ب *rabāba (rabāb)* a one-string violin (6.13)
—— *bi-rubbin* for example (3.9)
ر ب ع *rabba'* to graze on spring pasture (2.5, 6.15); to have all four limbs bound (a horse) (7.6); to be replete with spring pasture (7.8)
—— *raba', rab' (rubū')* a defined group, friends (1.5, 1.8, 1.15, 2.2, 2.8, 2.12, 3.4, 3.5, 4.1, 4.15, 4.20H, 6.1, 6.2, 6.4, 6.16, 8.3)
—— *rab'a, rub'a (rab'āt)* a defined group, friends (1.8, 6.13); the guest section of a tent (1.10, 5.5, 5.7)
—— *ribā'ī (ribā')* a four-year-old horse (in its prime) (4.20B)
—— *marbū'* square-built, stocky (8.3)
—— *murabba'* binoculars (6.16)
ر ت ق *ratīg* thick, full (1.10)
ر ث ع *ratha' (yirtha')* to limp (4.20H)
ر ج د *rijid (rujūd)* cluster, group (6.13)
ر ج ل *marjala* self-respect as a man (6.15)
ر ج م *rājam* to grow in the form of a cairn (6.15)
—— *rijm (rujūm)* a cairn (6.15)
ر ح ل *rahūla (rahāyil)* a pack-camel (2.12); a riding-camel (6.16)
ر خ ى *arkhā* to emit (a moan) (4.20B)
—— *markhī, murakhkhī* hanging (i.e. *markhiyyit al-gilāda:* a woman (lit. of the hanging necklace) (4.1); loosened, slack (6.4, 6.11)
ر د ء *radā (yirdā) fī* to behave badly towards (1.4)
ر د ف *ridf* the riding of two persons on a camel (7.10)
ر ز ع *raza' (yirza')* to compose light rhymes (5.3)
ر ز ى *raziyya (razāyā)* something of little value (1.1, 3.11, 8.2)
ر ع ى *ra'ā (yir'ā, yir'ī), ra''ā* to see, look (1.2, 1.8, 2.6, 4.2, 4.4)
—— *ra'ā ba-sh-shōf* to glance, scan (1.2)

—— *ir'ā* behold! (3.8, 4.4)
—— *mirta'a* pasture (6.6)
ر ف ض *rafiḍ, rāfiḍ* gentle, humble (4.19)
ر ف ل *muraffil, rifāl* beltless (6.2, 7.7)
ر ق ب *ragaba, ragēba (ragāb)* a saddle between two hills or mountains (7.8)
—— *mirgib (marāgib), mirgāb (marāgīb)* mountain-peak, look-out (1.4, 3.8, 6.10)
ر ق د *ragad (yurgud)* to brood (on eggs) (2.6)
ر ق ق *ragīg (ragārīg)* a bought slave (2.8)
ر ك ب *rikāb* riding camels (5.7)
ر ك ك *markūk* murky, cloudy (water), hazy (*jaww markūk*: troubled times) (6.4)
ر م ث *ramath (yirmath)* to neglect (3.9)
ر م ر م *tiramram* to scout, 'sniff around' (4:20H)
—— *ramārīm* pickings of odds and ends (6.3)
ر م ل *rumla* widowhood (5.9)
ر م ه ن *ramhan (yiramhin)* to stop moving, acting (4.7)
ر ه ب *rihāba (rihāb)* a cloud (4.10)
—— *rīḥa* reputation (lit. smell) (4.8)
—— *mirwāḥ (marāwīḥ)* a swift horse (5.13)
ر و د *rīd* social desirability (3.6)
ر و ز *rawwaz* to balk, shy, sit down (6.9)
ر و م *rām (yirūm)* to suckle a kid as much as it wants (goat) (4.9)
ر و ى *rawiyān* sated with liquid, drink; no longer thirsty (4.13)
ر ى ب *rāyab* to perceive, see (6.10, 7.7)
ر ى ت *rēt!, yā rēt!* how I wish; would that it were so! (1.8, 4.15, 4.20D, 4.20G, 4.20I)
ر ى ش *rīsha (rīsh)* an army stripe (lit. a feather) (1.15)
ر ى ض *rayyaḍ* to remain (7.6)
ر ى ع *rī' (rī'ān)* a narrow winding canyon (1.1); the elevated margin of a mountain-rimmed wadi (4.17)

ز

ز ب د *zubēdī (zubēdiyyāt)* a coffee-spot (6.14)
ز ب ر *zābir* protruding (2.10)
ز ب ن *aztaban* to seek refuge with . . . (2.8)
—— *mazbūn* concealed (2.3)
ز ب ن ق *zibnāg (zabānīg)* a bud (1.10)
ز ج ر *zajar* a push (1.10)
ز ح ر *zaḥar* distress (6.9)
—— *zaḥīr* a deep-voiced call (4.20B)
ز ح ن *zaḥan* trouble (5.13)
ز ر ف *zaraf (yuzruf)* to falsify (4.1)

—— *zarf (azraf)* a sin, error (4.11);—*(zurūf)* a bullet (4.3)

ز ر ف ل *zarfal (yizarfil)* to start quickly (7.10)

ز ر ق *azrag (zurg)* black (4.20H, 6.15, 7.3)

ز ر و ع *zarwa' (yizarwa')* to run fearfully, quickly (2.4, 2.5, 4.18)

ز ع ب *za'āb* meagre, poor, little (crop) (7.6)

ز ق ح *zagaḥ (yizgaḥ)* to throw something down (1.9)

ز ق ف *zagaf (yizgaf)* to throw (6.2)

ز ق م *zagm (zugūm)* the protrusion of a mountain ridge, a mountain top (6.18)

ز ل ط *zulēyiṭ (zilṭān)* a newborn goat-kid (up to 3 months) (4.12)

ز ل ل *zall (yizill)* to roast (coffee) (4.17)

—— *zalāl* mood, temperament (3.1)

ز ل م *zalama (zilām)* a friend (2.5)

ز م ت *zumētān* a donkey (4.17)

ز م ل *zaml, zimāla (zamūl, zaml)* a male, usually pack, camel (1.15, 6.1, 6.9, 6.10, 6.15, 7.3)

—— *zaml* pedigree (of a camel) (3.8, 6.13)

ز ن د *zind (zunūd)* the instep of the foot, topside (4.15)

ز ه ب *zihāb* provisions (5.1); ammunition (6.14)

ز ه ر *zahar* renown (4.15); luck (6.9)

ز و د *zād* food (2.12)

ز و ز ى *zōzā (yizōzā)* to strut, pace (camel) (2.10)

ز و ع *aza'* to urge a mount (7.7)

ز و ل *zōl, ziwāl (zīlān)* a shadow, image (5.11, 6.1)

—— *azwal* most despicable, loathed (6.6)

ز و م *zōm (zōmāt)* a pile (of grain) (2.4)

ز ى ح *zāḥ (yizīḥ)* to get rid of, discard (3.11)

ز ى م *zām (yizīm)* to sigh (6.3)

س

س ء ل *is'ā* a conversation (lit. questioning) (2.9)

—— *mānī masālī* I don't care! (6.11)

س ب ب *sabab (asbāb)* fate, destiny (4.10, 5.10, 6.13)

س ب ت *sabit, sibt* the underside of the foot (4.4)

س ب ع *saba' (subū')* a stout-hearted person, stalwart (lit. lion) (1.5, 1.6, 2.7, 3.8, 3.11, 5.10, 7.10)

س ج د *sajjad* to calm (someone down) (6.12)

س ج ع *sajī'* brave (5.1, 7.7)

س ح و *saḥwān* flowing rapidly (2.3)

—— *siḥāwī (siḥāwiyya)* a broad, slightly sloping stretch of desert (6.8)

س د د *sadd (yisidd)* to avenge a misdeed (5.6)

—— *astadd* to seek revenge (5.6)

—— *saddān (sadād)* a sufficient person, one who does what's required (4.5, 4.15); one who helps people in need (2.10)

س ر ب *misrāb (masārīb)* path, track (3.8)
س ر ح *sarạḥ (yisraḥ)* to go to, or be at, pasture (1.2)
—— *sirāḥa (masārīḥ)* the going to, or being at, pasture (1.2, 4.7)
س ر د *insarad* to come one after another (4.8)
—— *sard (surūd)* single-file in a line (4.8)
—— *sarda (sard)* a thin, but strong, non-pregnant mare (horse) (4.16)
س ر س ب *sirsāb (sarāsīb)* single file (1.15)
س ر غ *surgh* hand-made reins of goat-hair and sheeps-wool (5.1)
س ف س ف *safsaf b . . .* to flutter (4.15)
س ف ف *safīfa (safāyif)* a saddle tassel (2.2, 2.12)
س ف ل *sāfal b . . .* to hold someone in contempt (2.3)
س ف ه *safīh (suffāh)* slanderer (3.7)
س ق ط *sagīṭ* the clang of a sword (4.20H)
—— *musaggiṭ* sharp (a sword) (4.20H)
س ق م *sagīm (sagāyim)* a rival, legal contestant (6.14)
س ك ب *sakkab* to glide forward (6.5)
س ك ك *sakk (yisikk)* to send (4.17); to turn sharply while riding (1.2, 3.3)
س ل ل *asall* to slip through, walk between (6.17)
—— *sulāla (salāyil)* a thoroughbred mare (horse) (5.13)
—— *silīl* the clang of a sword (5.13)
س ل م *salīmī* a type of sword (slightly bent and of good metal) (6.3)
س م ح ق *simḥāg (samāḥīg)* crown of the head (camel) (1.10)
س م ر *mismār (masāmīr)* a bullet (lit. a nail) (6.9)
—— *samār* black goats (1.9)
—— *sāmir* night-time dances (5.3)
س م ط *sammaṭ* to tie a pack on a saddle (1.10)
س م ن *samn* clarified butter (1.10, 2.12, 6.7)
س م ل ن *simlān* the balance, remainder (2.7)
س م ى *sammā* to utter (6.15)
س ن ب ك *sanbūk (sanābīk)* a long, narrow boat (6.4)
س ن د *sandī (sunūd, sanādī)* incline, ascent of mountain (2.10, 4.5)
س ن م *sināma (sinām)* a camel hump (4.4, 4.20H, 6.16)
س ن ى *sanā (sawānī)* a flame, fire (3.4, 4.9, 7.9)
س ه ج *mishāj* puffed (4.20C)
س و ر *sawāyir* the end of the spring pasture season (6.15)
س و س *sāyis (sawāyis)* expert (especially in training or raising animals) (4.9)
س و ط *sawṭ (sīṭān)* a strip (of belly-flesh, flab) (5.3)
س و ق *sāg (yisūg)* to pay a bride-price (4.20A)
—— *sawāg* livestock on sale (5.9)
—— *ʿalā sāg* one by one (3.2)
—— *sūg (sawag)* a city (lit. a market) (4.5)
س و م *sawīm (sawāyim)* a bargainer, purchaser (4.20E)
س و ى *sawwā* to make, do (2.7, 2.12)

—— *sawā (sawāyā)* the doing, a deed (2.7, 4.4); handwork (6.4)

س ى ر *misyār, masyār (masāyīr)* a journey (3.4)

س ى ل *siyāla (siyāl)* an Acacia raddiana tree (6.11)

س ى م *sīm* magic, hypnosis (6.3)

ش

ش ء م *shūm* bad (6.15, 7.9)

ش ب ب *shabbāba (shabbāb)* a shepherd's flute (4.10)

ش ب ر *shibriyya (shabārī)* a dagger (7.6)

ش ب ر ق *shibrāg* dark red (3.2)

ش ب ك *shābik an-nāb* with clenched canine teeth (1.12)

ش ح ى *mashḥā (mashāḥī)* journey, road (1.15, 2.5, 3.3, 3.9, 7.1, 7.7)

ش خ ت ر *shakhtūra (shakhātīr)* a jet of water (1.3; 7.10); top of high mountain (4.5)

ش د د *shadd (yishidd)* to saddle (4.15); to do something forcibly (*shadd al-ghalāṭ* to argue forcibly for the right to butcher an animal for the camp's guest) (3.3)

—— *shadād (ashidda)* camel riding-saddle (2.9, 2.12, 4.10, 4.20H, 7.10)

ش د ى *shadā (yishdī)* to resemble (4.20B, 5.6)

ش ذ ب *mashdhūb* lofty and exposed (a peak) (1.14)

ش ذ ر *shidhra* the tip of a sword (4.19)

ش ر ب *sharrab* to fill a vessel with liquid (5.1)

—— *shārib adh-dhilla* one accustomed to behaving vilely (4.17)

ش ر ح *sharḥa* longing (4.20I)

ش ر د *sharrad* to carry something off (2.5)

ش ر ش ح *sharshūḥ (sharāshīḥ)* a small herd (1.10)

ش ر ف *sharīfa* a flat platter on which meat is served (1.5)

ش ط ب *shaṭṭab* to overflow, to be finished (coffee being brewed) (4.19)

ش ع ب *sha'ab (yish'ab)* to cleave into two (1.12)

—— *shi'b (shi'bān)* small wadi (3.8)

—— *mish'āb (mashā'ib)* a forked riding stick (1.2)

ش ع ر *sha'r* goat hair (5.10)

ش ع ل ب *sha'lāba (sha'ālīb)* a flame (4.10)

ش ف ى *shafā (yishfī)* to satisfy (3.9, 5.1); to like (5.13)

ش ق ر *ashgar, shagra (shugr)* bronze-coloured, golden (coffee-pots) (1.6, 6.7); tawny (camel) (1.10, 2.6, 4.15, 5.1, 6.15); sorrel (horse) (5.12)

—— *shagāra* lightness of colour (people) (2.6)

ش ق ق *shigg (shugūg)* guest-tent; guest section of a tent (1.8, 3.6)

ش ك ح *ashkaḥ* light brown (2.12)

ش ل ت ح *shaltūḥ (shalātīḥ)* a tattered garment (1.2)

ش ل ق *mishlāg (mashālīg)* a band of camel-riders (6.7)

ش ل ل *shalīl (shalāyil)* a tapping, rapping sound (6.3)

—— *shilla (shilāl)* a group, troop (4.6, 4.17)

ش ل و ح *mushalwaḥ* rolled up (a sleeve) (2.1)

ش م ر خ *shamrūkha (shamārīkh)* a date-palm stamen (4.10)

ش م م *shimām* directly, straightaway (6.15)

ش ن ت ى *shintiyān* a type of short, pliable sword (1.6)

ش ن ش ن *shanshūn* dried out, stiff (2.1)

shinlāsh worthless (from *shī innahu lā shī*) (5.4)

ش ه ب *mishhabb* greyish-white (4.20B)

ش ه ل ل *shihlāl (shahālīl)* a strong jet of water (1.14)

ش و ر *mishwār (mashāwīr)* an excursion, mission, trip (6.9, 6.15)

ش و ش ح *shawshaḥ (yishawshaḥ)* to wave in the air, brandish (1.2, 4.20A)

ش و ف *shāf (yishūf)* to see (4.16, 4.17, 4.20A, 4.20I, 5.11, 7.12)

—— *shōf* a sight, vision (1.6, 2.12, 3.6, 7.7); seeing ability (6.16)

—— *shīfa (shīfāt)* benefit, good, use (lit. something seen) (1.5)

ش و ل *yishawwil* to raise its tail (horse, camel) (1.10)

—— *shāyla (shawlā)* an immediately post-natal camel-mare (lit. high-tailed) (5.1)

—— *mishwāl (mashāwīl)* a high-tailed horse (4.20G)

ش و ن *shūna (āt)* a pile, warehouse (7.12)

ش ى ب *shēb* white or grey hair (1.1, 4.2, 4.20E); an old man (4.8); old age (3.8)

—— *shāyiba* an old, white camel-mare (6.9)

ش ى ح *shīḥ* wormwood (Artemisia herba-alba) (1.2)

ش ى خ *shākh (yishīkh)* to appoint a chief (6.5)

ش ى ع *shayya'* to send (1.12)

ش ى ك *shīk* barbed-wire (2.5)

ش ى ل *shāl (yishīl)* to pack off (1.9); to knock someone off a horse (5.11)

—— *shēl* packing off (2.2)

ش ى م *shīma* bravery (2.2)

—— *shōmit ar-rās* self-esteem (4.19)

ش ى ن *shēn* bad, evil (4.15, 7.9, 7.12); ugly (1.15, 2.4)

ص

ص ح ح *ṣaḥḥ l . . .* to be able to . . . (7.3)

ص ح ص ح *imṣaḥṣaḥ* shiny (1.10)

ص د ر *maṣdar (maṣādir, maṣādīr)* a well (2.1)

ص ر ر *ṣurr (aṣrār)* binds for a camel's teats (6.18, 7.6)

ص ر ك *ṣarak (yiṣrik)* to gnash, scrape (teeth) (4.10, 6.16)

—— *ṣarīk* a gnashing sound (6.15)

ص ر م *ṣarām* last of the grain in the field (3.10)

—— *ṣarīma (ṣarāyim)* a two-rope bridle for training camels (2.2, 2.9)

ص ع ب *aṣṭa'ab* to be held firmly (2.10)

—— *maṣ'ab (maṣā'ib)* a tough person (4.20H)

ص ف ح *ṣafḥa (ṣafāḥ)* a side (4.4, 4.7)
ص ف ى *ṣaffiy* a bouncer, doorman (3.1)
ص ق ل *taṣaggal* to move about uneasily, to refuse food (6.18)
—— *ṣigīl* a scraping sound (1.3)
ص ل ب *ṣalīb* hard, uncompromising (3.8)
—— *ṣalība (ṣalāyib)* a heap (1.4)
—— *miṣlāb (maṣālīb)* cross-beams of a camel saddle (4.18)
ص ل ف ح *muṣalfaḥ* layered with fat (4.20H)
ص ل ى *ṣālā* to be near fire (4.9)
—— *ṣalā* the glow of a fire (5.1)
ص م ل *ṣamīl (ṣamāmīl)* a water-bag (2.3, 4.20H)
—— *ṣamīla (ṣamāyil)* gain, benefit (1.7, 1.13)
ص م م *ṣumm, ṣamīm* hard, firm, solid (ground, hoofs) (4.20B, 5.6, 6.3); *ṣumm al-ḥawāfir* horses (lit. solid of hoof) (4.20B)
ص ن ق ر *ṣangūr (ṣanāgīr)* a bird of prey (lit. a beak) (5.12, 7.10)
ص ن ن *muṣannī* a stinking one (originally a rutting camel that exudes a liquid, called *ṣunānī*, from the rear of the neck)
ص د د *ṣahad (yiṣhad)* to overburn (e.g. coffee-beans) (3.3); to burn, scorch (4.19)
ص و ب *ṣawb* towards, in the direction of (6.8)
ص و ر *ṣawwar* to create, form (3.10, 5.1)
ص و ن *minṣān* well attended (6.18)
ص ى د *ṣād (yiṣīd)* to afflict (2.5); to blemish, blight (2.12)
ص ى ن *ṣīn, ṣīniyya* a tray (2.9, 3.2, 3.6)

ض

ض ء ن *ḍān* small cattle (goats and sheep) (1.4, 3.8)
ض ب ب *ḍabb (yiḍibb)* to hold close and tight (4.11)
ض ب ح *ḍabīḥ (ḍabāyiḥ)* a loud noise (4.3)
ض د د *ḍidd (iḍdād)* an opponent, enemy (5.13)
ض ر م *ḍaram (ḍurmān)* a very worthy person (4.17)
ض ع ف *ḍaʿīf (ḍaʿāfīn, duʿāf)* a child (1.8)
ض ل ع *ḍilūʿ* pale (2.1)
ض و ى *ḍawā (yiḍwī)* to return from pasture in the evening (6.6); to return repeatedly (6.18)
ض ى ق *ḍīg (ḍīgāt)* a courtroom dock (4.4); confinement, ill luck (4.4, 7.3)

ط

ط ب ب *ṭabb (yiṭubb)* to come to a place, visit a place (6.7); to touch (6.18)
—— *maṭabb* a place (2.6)
ط ب خ *ṭabkha* coffee-beans (3.4)
ط ب ع *ṭabbaʿ* to break a camel for riding (2.10)
—— *ṭabāʿ* training (2.10, 3.7)
ط ب ق *ṭabbag* to shoe a horse (4.20B)

—— *ṭabāga (ṭabāg)* an area with narrow passages between limestone hills (6.7, 6.17)
ط ر ء *ṭarā (yiṭrā)* to tell (6.18, 7.7)
—— *taṭarrā* to recall, to mention (6.11)
—— *ṭiryā* a mention (2.7, 7.2)
ط ر ح *ṭarraḥ [ba-ẓ-ẓill]* to extend itself (a shadow) (4.17)
—— *ṭarḥ* a bunch (of dates) (4.10)
ط ر د *ṭarad (yuṭrud)* to hunt, fish (6.5)
—— *ṭārid ar-ribḥ* a merchant (lit. a pursuer of profit) (3.6)
—— *ṭārid al-hawā* a traveller (lit. one who chases the wind) (3.2)
—— *maṭrād* a form of interrogation torture in Egyptian prisons, whereby a prisoner, reportedly, is hung upside down and given 25 lashes on the feet (6.1).
ط ر ر *ṭarr (yiṭurr)* to guide or lead an animal (2.7)
ط ر ش *ṭarsh (ṭurūsh)* a number of pasturing camels (5.7)
ط ر ط ر *ṭarṭūr (ṭarāṭīr)* a pointed head-dress (2.8)
ط ر ق *ṭarrag* to direct an animal (towards . . .) (6.15)
—— *ṭarg* pounding (6.1)
—— *ṭirāgī, ṭurgī (ṭurgiyya)* a walker (6.13)
ط س س *ṭāsūs (ṭawāsīs)* a thoughtless person (6.6)
ط ش ش *ṭashsh (yiṭushsh)* to shake out, air (3.3)
ط ف ق *maṭfūg* distracted (3.2)
ط ق ق *ṭagg (yiṭugg)* to knock (4.7)
—— *ṭagga (ṭagāg, ṭaggāt)* handiwork (2.9)
ط ل ب *ṭalāba (ṭalāyib)* a trial, session (6.9)
ط ل ع *ṭalʿa (āt)* a steep and narrow wadi, an ascent (3.8, 6.10)
ط ل ق *ṭallag* to swear to divorce one's wife unless a condition (unrelated to the wife) is fulfilled (1.4, 2.10, 5.1)
ط ل ل *ṭall (yiṭill)* to climb a peak (1.14, 4.17); to raise (2.7)
ط م ن *ṭaman (yiṭman)* to be secure (Class. *yitma'an*) (3.3)
ط ن ب *ṭānab* to ask someone's aid or protection (originally by touching his tent-rope: *ṭanb*) (1.7)
—— *ṭanb (aṭnāb)* a tent-rope (3.7)
—— *ṭanīb (ṭanāyib)* one who receives protection from another (3.7, 3.9, 4.16, 6.7, 8.4); neighbour (1.9)
ط ن ط ر *ṭanṭūr (ṭanāṭīr)* a heap, protrusion, hump (6.9)
ط ن ى *taṭanna* to be flexible, pliable (1.6)
—— *ṭanā (ṭaniyyāt)* a child (7.3)
ط ه ر *maṭhūr (maṭāhīr)* a circumcised boy (4.3)
ط و ط ح *ittawṭaḥ (yittawṭaḥ)* to swing back and forth, sway (1.2)
—— *muṭawṭiḥ* in the act of shooting (6.16)
ط و ع *ṭāʿ (yiṭīʿ)* to heed, take one's word (6.6)
ط و ق *ṭōga (āt)* a group (6.13)
ط ى ب *ṭayyab* to mollify (5.4)

—— *ṭayyib, ṭāyib* still active, alive (5.10)
—— *'alā kēf mā ṭāb* as good as can be (6.13)
ط ى ح *ṭāḥ (yiṭīḥ)* to go down to, visit (4.5); to fall (4.20D, 6.4, 7.2)
—— *ṭawwaḥ* to cast something down (5.12)
—— *ṭayḥ* falling (2.2)

ظ

ظ ر ب *ẓarab (yiẓrab)* to stick, cling (7.7)
—— *ẓarūba (ẓarāyib)* a stud camel (2.7, 4.3, 7.10)
ظ ل م *ẓalma, ẓulm* injustice (2:2)
—— *ẓalīm* old, aged (6.14)
—— *aẓlūm (azālīm)* a black ostrich (6.3)

ع

ع ب ط *'abaṭ (yi'biṭ)* to hold under the armpit (4.20D)
ع ت ق *'utgiyya (āt)* an old hen (4.5)
ع ث ر *'athira ('awāthir)* a defect (5.6, 6.9)
ع ج ب *a'jab* to please, amaze (1.9, 4.9, 5.11)
ع ج ج *'ajj* dust
ع ج ر *'ujra ('ijār)* a low hill (1.3, 6.2)
ع ج ز *'ajūz ('ajāyiz)* an old woman (2.6, 8.4)
ع د د *'add* the counting of generations to determine the pedigree of a camel (2.9)
—— *'idd ('udūd)* a perennial well (2.4, 2.7, 4.10, 4.19, 5.11, 7.11); a storage box (*kasr 'idd* = brand new) (4.3).
ع د ل *'adīl ('adalā)* a counterweight (1.3, 4.2)
—— *a'dawdal (yi'dawdal)* to get fat and sway (a camel) (2.5)
—— *'adīla, mu'addila* a Martini rifle, a Martini-Henry breech-load rifle (6.2, 6.13, 7.12)
ع د م *'adām* nothingness (3.10); an Ephedra bush (4.4)
ع د و *'idwa ('idāw)* an elevated stretch along a wadi bed (1.13)
—— *'addā 'an* to distance something from someone (4.16, 4.19)
ع ذ ى *'idhī ('idhiyyāt)* a remote area (4.9)
ع ر د *'arad (yu'rud)* to compel by force (4.1)
ع ر ض *'urḍī ('arāḍī)* a troop of soldiers (from Turkish) (5.1)
ع ر ف *ta'rīfa (ta'rīf)* an Egyptian coin of little value (1.5)
ع ر ق *'irg ('urūg)* a spear (4.20H)
—— *'urūg* character, disposition (8.4)
ع ز ب *mu'azzib (ma'āzīb)* a host (1.4)
—— *mu'azziba (ma'āzīb)* a lone woman (6.8, 6.10)
ع ز ل *'azl* act of selection (1.9)
ع س ف *'asīf* thin (4.20I)
ع س م *'asām* sand dust in the air (6.16)
ع س ى *'asā* how? (preface to a question) (6.14)

ع ش ب *'ishib (a'shāb)* an annual plant (1.9, 2.4, 2.5)
ع ش ر *mu'ashshar (ma'āshīr)* a pregnant camel-mare (4.20B, 5.6, 6.9)
ع ص ب *'iṣāba ('iṣāyib)* a black cloth worn wrapped around a married woman's forehead to hold her hair together (5.10)
—— *'aṣīb ('asaba)* the root of a horse's tail (1.10)
ع ص ر *al-'aṣr* sometimes, at times (1.4)
ع ص ى *'āṣī ('āṣiyyāt)* a wild animal, game (6.2)
ع ط ى *mu'aṭṭā* (a saddle) held together by cross-beams (*'awāṭī*, sing. *'āṭiya*) (6.4)
ع ف ر *'afīr ('ufarā)* dry land (4.15)
ع ف ق *'afīg* goat-cheese (4.9)
ع ق ب *'aggab* to beget (1.7, 1.13, 2.3, 2.7); to handle, take care of (7.11)
—— *'agāb ('awāgib)* an outcome (5.2); an end (5.13, 6.5, 6.14)
ع ق د *'āgid* happy, satisfied (7.9)
ع ق ر *'agar (ya'gir)* to hamstring (4.17)
ع ق ر ق *'agrūg ('agārīg)* sterile (person) (2.8)
ع ق ل *'ugla* a wadi having one pool after another (5.9)
ع ك ش *'akāsh, 'akash ('ukūsh)* land covered with rocks and thorny plants (4.4)
ع ك ل *'akal ('uklān)* a mongrel dog (1.3)
ع ل ب *mu'alba* the nape of a camel's neck (2.8)
ع ل ق *ma'lūg (ma'ālīg)* saddlebags (2.8); the innards of a slaughtered animal (3.2)
ع ل م *'ilm ('ulūm)* judicial information (2.8); unfounded information, a lie, rumour (6.15)
—— *'alām(ak)* what's the matter; what's bothering you? (7.11)
ع م ر *'umr, mā 'umr, lā 'umr* never (2.7, 2.10, 4.8, 4.15, 4.18, 7.8)
ع م ل *ma'āmīl* utensils for making and serving coffee or tea (2.12)
ع ن د *'annad* to weave the dividing curtain of a tent (7.8)
—— *ma'nad (ma'ānid)* the dividing curtain of a tent (1.10)
ع ن ى *ma'nā (ma'ānī)* an interest, concern (3.9)
ع و د *'awdān, 'awdēn* on occasion (3.4); then, later, afterwards (7.10)
—— *'awda (āt)* an older camel-mare (2.7, 4.16); a horse (5.9)
ع و ق *'āg (yi'īg)* to be disappointed (1.10)
ع و ل *'āyil ('ayāl)* a small child (4.12)
ع ى ب *'āb (yi'īb)* to expose someone to shame (4.16); to be considered shameful (6.10); to do something shameful (6.10, 6.13)
—— *'ayb ('uyūb)* a breach of convention, a shameful deed (4.17, 6.10)
—— *'āyib* a camel that bites its master (5.3)
ع ى ر *'ayra* the choicest camel-mares (2.12, 4.15, 6.11)
ع ى ف *'āf (yi'īf)* to reject (6.1)
ع ى ق *'ayyag* to emerge (a tooth) (4.18)
ع ى ى *'ayyā* to resist (5.9); to refuse (4.4, 4.11, 4.12, 7.1)
—— *'ayā* fat in the hump of a camel (4.18)

غ

غ ب ر *ghubr* difficult, tormenting (6.16)

غ ب ط *ghabīṭ (ghibṭān)* a camel-saddle (6.4)

غ ب ن *ghabīn* sad (1.2)

غ ب ى *ghabā (yighbī)* to conceal (2.2)

غ ث ب ر *ghathbar* dregs (2.10)

غ د ر *ghadīr (ghudrān)* a rain-pool (2.11, 4.10)

غ د ى *ghadā b . . . (yighdī)* to flee, leave (4.16, 6.6, 6.10, 6.17)

غ ر ر *ghurra (ghurār)* a girl given in marriage (without bride-price) in partial payment for blood-price [lit., 'a blazoned one'] (5.4)

غ ر ز *gharīz* thick (rain, forest) (4.9)

غ ز ز *ghazz (yighuzz)* to fly a flag, to raise high (2.8, 2.10)

—— *ghuzz* a sovereign state (orig. Oġuz mamlūks in the Ayyūbid Sultanate) (5.9)

غ ز م *ghazīm* a sharp sound (2.2)

غ ص ب *ghaṣība (ghaṣīb)* an animal slaughtered by hand (3.7)

غ ض ض *ghaḍḍ (yighuḍḍ) al-bukā 'alā* to shed tears for . . . (4.16)

غ ض ى *ghaḍḍā* to divert someone from a course (2.9)

—— *ghaḍā* the Haloxylon persicum bush (3.2)

غ ط ر *mughaṭṭar* elegant (5.6)

غ ل ب *ghulb* difficulty, oppression, distress (6.8, 6.12)

غ ل س *ghils, ighlās* pretension (1.6)

غ ل ط *taghālaṭ* to argue for the right to feed a camp's guest (2.2)

—— *ghalāṭ* the arguing for the right to feed a camp's guest (2.2, 3.3)

غ ل ق *ghalga (ghulūg)* the tip of a teat (4.20B)

غ ل ي *ghalyūn (ghalāyīn)* a long smoking-pipe (4.20H)

غ م س *ghammas* to dip bread into a bowl and take hold of part of the food (the main bedouin manner of eating) (5.6)

غ م ق *ghamīg* deep, profound (1.10, 4.9)

غ و ج *ghawj, ghōj (ghījān)* a broad camel (4.3, 5.3); a swift horse (5.6)

غ و د *ghād, min ghād* off in the distance (5.3, 6.2)

غ و ش *ghōsh* thin bracelets generally worn by peasant women (7.8)

غ ى ب *ghāba (ghāb)* a powder pouch (4.10)

غ ى ر *ghēr* must! (1.15, 5.1)

—— *ghayyār (ghayyārīn)* one who 'steals' a goat or sheep to feed a guest (1.9)

غ ى ن *ghēn* clouds (1.11, 7.12)

ف

ف ء د *fāyid (fuwwād)* camel merchant (5.1)

ف ت ت *fatt* a soaked cereal of crumbled bread (1.10)

ف ج ج *fajj (fujūj)* an open space (1.10, 5.1)

ف ح ج *tafāḥaj* to walk in large steps with legs apart (4.3)

ف ح ف ح *faḥfaḥa (āt)* a slushy sound (1.4)

ف د د *fadd (yifidd)* to push aside (4.20E)
ف د ن *mafdūn* terrible (7.11)
ف ر ز *farīz* discerning, understanding, distinguishing (7.3)
ف ر ع ن *far'ūnī (fará'īn)* an Egyptian (lit. a Pharaonic) (4.5)
ف ر ق *furg* split (4.12)
—— *farīg (furgān)* a camp, encampment (1.4, 1.10, 3.8, 6.7, 6.18)
ف ر ك *farrak* to make something swerve (5.11)
ف ش ر *fashshār (fashshārīn)* a boaster (4.9)
ف ض ض *faḍḍ* to stop an activity, relieve one of an activity (4.12, 4.20H, 5.10, 6.6)
ف ض ح *faḍaḥ (yifḍaḥ)* to penetrate, pass through (3.2)
ف ض ى *fāḍiya* a non-pregnant woman (2.7)
ف ط ر *fāṭr (fuṭr)* a mature, camel-mare (often used as a disguise-word for hashish) (2.4, 2.5, 4.18, 4.20B)
ف ك ر *fakkar* to regard, look at (7.7)
—— *tafkīr* regarding, looking, observation (6.9)
ف ل ء *maflā (mafālī)* pasture, pastureland (2.6, 4.20B, 5.1, 5.3, 7.7)
ف ل ق *filāg (fulug)* an overworked and ill camel (6.7)
ف ل ل *filla* a detached house (from English 'villa') (4.6)
ف ن ى ر *funyār (fanānīr, fanāyīr)* a 'luxe' gas or kerosene lantern (5.1, 7.10)
ف و ت *fāt (yifūt)* to pass (1.9, 2.4, 6.13, 6.18, 7.10); to concede (5.1); to leave behind (1.5, 6.12)
fī there is, are (*passim*)
ف ى ح *fīḥa (fīḥ)* a sturdy camel-mare (with full udders) (1.2, 1.11)

ق

ق ب ب *gabb (gubūb)* the stomach area of a horse (1.10); broad and strong (camel) (2.2, 2.10, 5.7)
ق ب ل *gabīla (gabāyil)* group (6.2); tribal confederation (7.12)
—— *gubaylān* just now, very recently (4.7)
ق ب ى *gabā (gabāya)* a simple camel blanket (6.15)
ق د ح *gadaḥ (gidāḥ)* a bowl for milking camels (1.11, 2.11)
ق د ر *migdār* honour (1.9, 6.18); fate (pl. *magādīr*) (6.5)
ق د س *gādūs* one who brings water on an ass (6.6)
ق د م *migdim (magādim, magādīm)* the front-centre tent-pole (3.3); the front pommel of a saddle (4.3, 6.3)
ق د ى *gadā (yigdī)* to steer, direct (2.6)
ق ذ ر *gadhr* a vile person (6.6)
ق ذ ر ب *tagadhrab* to draw near to something (2.5)
ق ر ب *girba (girab)* a water-bag (6.1, 6.3)
ق ر ب س *garbūs (garābīs)* the front pommel of a horse's saddle (4.20D)

ق ر د د *gardūd (garādīd)* the top of a mountain range (6.18)
ق ر ر *garārī* official (chief) (7.6)

ق ر ط *garaṭ (yugruṭ)* to fling, throw (1.9, 4.16, 6.1)
—— *guraytalla* a little bit (4.6)
ق ر ط ع *gurṭāʿ (garāṭīʿ)* a draught (of drink), gulp (1.1)
ق ر ق ر *girgār* a laugh, laughter (1.9)
ق ر ق ض *gargaḍ (yigargaḍ)* to chomp, bite (2.3)
ق ر م ل *garmala (garāmīl)* a decorated braid (6.12)
ق ر ن *magran al-ʿalābī* the top of one's back (3.9)
ق ز ى *gazzā* to suffice (3.10)
ق س ى *gāsā* to be hard on someone or something (7.12)
ق ش ر *gishra (āt)* a loose woman (lit. a peel) (6.10)
ق ش ش *gashsh* provisions (2.7); a camel saddle (pl. *gushūsh*) (6.1)
ق ش ط *gashaṭ (yugshuṭ)* to tighten (a strap) (6.4)
—— *tagashshaṭ* to be in anticipation (have sleeves rolled up) (4.8)
—— *mugashshaṭ* rolled up (e.g a sleeve) (4.7)
ق ش ع *gashshaʿ* to walk with difficulty, to plod, stagger (6.15)
ق ش ل *gashal* worthless (5.11)
ق ص ر *gaṣr (guṣūr)* a stone dwelling or storehouse (2.11, 7.7)
—— *gāṣir (gāṣrīn)* a helpless, destitute person (4.2)
ق ص م *gaṣam (yugṣum), gaṣṣam* to crush, break (4.15, 4.18, 6.16)
ق ض ى *gaḍā maṣlakha* to look after one's own interests (3.9)
ق ط ر *gaṭīra (gaṭāyir)* a sailing-vessel in the Gulf of Suez (2.5)
ق ط ع *gaṭaʿ (yigṭaʿ)* to pass through, cross (4.4, 6.7)
ق ط م *mugaṭṭam* crushed, broken (7.8)
ق ط ن *gaṭīna (āt)* a piece of cotton used to soak up the last dregs of water in the well (2.4)
ق ط ى *gaṭāh (giṭī)* the croup of a horse, hinds of a camel (5.6)
ق ع د *magʿad (magāʿid)* the guest section of a tent; the guest-tent of an encampment (1.5, 2.9)
ق ف ف *gaff (yigiff)* to cower (5.11)
ق ف ى *agfā, tagāfa* to leave, go away, ride off, run off (1.11, 4.15, 4.19, 5.6, 6.9, 7.6); to follow (4.20F)
—— *tagaffā* to be chased (2.12); to be followed (4.20F)
—— *min gafā* behind, from behind (6.2)
—— *migfī (magāfī)* something fleeing (2.8)
ق ل ص *mugallaṣ* lacking, deficient (4.2)
ق ل ط *galaṭ (yiglaṭ)* to extend, hand over, serve (4.17)
ق ن ط ر *gunṭār (ganāṭīr)* a weight (300 lbs.) (4.1, 6.5)
ق ن ن *gann (yigann)* to do something well (2.12)
—— *gannan* to estimate (3.4)
—— *gann* law, order (2.12)
ق ن ى *gannā* to protect, remove from harm (2.12); to flow (2.12)
—— *ganā* lance (from reed or cane) (4.16, 5.11)
ق و د *gōd* livestock (2.9)
ق و ز *gōz (gīzān)* a hillock, mountain (2.4, 6.2, 6.18)

ق و ط ر *gōṭar (yigōṭar)* to go (1.15)

ق و ع *gāʿ (gīʿān)* a flat broad stretch of desert rimmed by high ground or mountains (2.5, 6.8, 6.13)

ق و ل *gōl, gōla (gōlāt)* a poem (4.14, 5.1, 6.13)

ق و م *gōm (gīmān)* a warring or raiding party (1.11); a group bent on revenge (often a blood feud) (6.15)

ق و ى *migwī (magāwī)* one who spends the night without having had dinner (6.14)

ق ى ظ *gayyaẓ* to come (the latter half of summer) (4.20C)

—— *gēẓ* the second half of summer (August–October) (1.15, 4.20C)

ق ى ف *gīfān* criticism (4.17)

ق ى ل *magīl (magāyil)* a place of rest (1.3); a midday rest (2.1)

ق ى ن *gīn* ankle of a horse (1.10)

ك

kidhī like this, that (Class. *ka-dhī*) (6.14 etc.)

ك ب ب *kabb (yikibb)* to get rid of, discard (3.11)

ك ب د *kibēdī (kibēdiyyāt)* a hawk (1.14)

ك ت ت *katt (yikatt)* to descend a wadi (1.9, 4.12, 8.4)

ك ر ب *karab (yukrub)* to tighten (2.2, 5.13)

ك ر ت م *kartūm (karātīm)* a mountain peak (rugged) (6.14)

ك ر ف *karaf (yukruf)* to sniff (1.10)

ك ر ك ش *karkūsh (karākīsh)* the lower part of a goat's breast bone, on which there is little meat (6.14)

ك ز ز *kazz (yikizz)* to spur on (1.14, 2.2, 5.1)

ك ز ى *kāzā* to be forceful (5.1)

ك س ح *kasḥān, kasīḥ* lazy, impotent (3.3)

ك س س *kuss (aksās)* pudenda (5.4)

ك ش خ ر *mukashkhirr* craggy, wizened (1.3)

ك ش ف *kashf al-asrār* slandering a host (lit. revealing the secrets) (3.4)

—— *kishāf* open ground (2.8)

ك ش ن *kashānī* kitchen work of peasant women (from *gīshān*: porcelain) (4.7)

ك ف ل *kafīl (kafalā)* warrantee, guarantor (2.8, 4.4, 6.14)

ك ل ع *kallāʿ* vile, evil, oppressive (7.9)

ك ن ن *kann (yikinn)* to act discreetly (3.3)

ك و د *kād* similar, equal to (4.1)

—— *mā kād* it is not difficult (2.10)

—— *kōd* perhaps, if by chance (1.9, 3.9, 6.13)

ك و ذ ب *kawdhab (yikawdhab)* to fib, to bluff (2.7)

ك و ر *kār (kiyār)* tendency (3.7); usage, being accustomed (4.20A); a calling, profession (5.6)

ك و س *minkās (manākīs)* a descent (1.6)

—— *kuwayyis* good (4.14)

ك و م *kōm (kawām)* a share (6.14); high (adj.) (6.15)
ك و ن *kawwan* to fight with (7.12)
—— *kāwan* to argue, fight with, scold (7.11)
—— *kawna, kōna, kawn, kōn (kawnāt, kōnāt)* battle, war (3.7, 5.12)
—— *mā kān* if only . . . (1.12)
ك ى ش *kīsh, kadīsh* a cross-breed (father mule, mother donkey) (4.3)
ك ى ف *kēf* coffee drink (as a stimulant) (2.12, 3.5)
ك ى ل *aktāl* to obtain large quantities (1.8)

ل

lē, lēsh why? (1.15, 1.15, etc.)
liʻād certainly (8.4)
limmā until (2.2, 6.14, 6.15); when (4.1 etc.)
lin if (1.10 etc.); behold! (1.12, 1.14)
ل ء م *lāyam* to catch (6.16)
ل ب د *tilbīd* stealth (4.1)
ل ب س *malbūs (malābīs)* a coat of mail (4.20C)
ل ب ن *laban* goat-milk (3.8); camel-milk (6.13)
ل ج ج *lajj (yilijj)* to resound (3.10, 4.1)
ل ح ط م *laḥṭūm (laḥāṭīm)* a narrow, rocky pass (6.3)
ل ح ظ *malḥaẓ ash-shawwāf* the sight of a rifle (5.11)
ل ح ق *laḥag (yilḥag)* to overtake (1.15, 2.8); to visit (3.8); to go along with, accompany (4.7)
—— *laḥīg* slenderness (1.10)
ل ح ى *liḥya (liḥā)* a man (lit. a beard) (4.15)
ل د ى *ladā (yildī)* to turn, enter (1.11)
ل ذ ذ *fī lidhīdh* in the midst of (2.8)
ل ذ ع *ladhdhaʻ* to prick (7.6, 7.7)
ل ز ز *lazz (yilizz)* to urge on an animal (1.10, 2.6); to get narrow (4.8); to narrow in on (7.6)
ل ز م *lāzim (lizām)* the court fee (also *ruzga*) in a bedouin trial (4.4)
—— *lāzim (lawāzim)* a social obligation, obligatory deed (2.2, 2.10, 4.5)
ل ط ح *laṭūḥ (laṭāyiḥ)* a judge ignorant of the law (2.7)
ل ط م *laṭam (yulṭum)* to strike, beat someone (8.4)
ل ط ى *lāṭā* around, surrounding (a shelter) (4.12)
ل ظ ظ *laẓẓ (yiliẓẓ)* to suck an udder (2.9)
ل ع ج *laʻaj (yilʻaj)* to flash (4.20C)
ل ف ى *lafā (yilfī) ʻalā* to visit, to stop off with, to come to (1.4, 1.6, 2.2, 2.8, 4.5, 4.15, 6.17, 6.18, 7.1, 7.7, 7.10)
ل ق ق *lagg (yilagg)* to lead, direct (6.1)
ل ق م *laggam* to pour a measured handful (*talgīma*) (3.2)
ل ق ى *lagā (yalgā)* to find (4.8, 6.17, 7.3)
—— *laggā* to go to, flee (4.2, 4.5, 5.2, 8.4); to steer, direct (6.18)

—— *malāgī (malāgiyyāt)* on the verge of calving (camel) (6.7); a junction of wadis (6.7, 8.4)

ل ك ز *lakaz (yilkiz)* to kick (a mount) with the heel (4.4)

—— *lakza (lakzāt)* a spur-prick (5.6)

ل ه ب *lahīb (lawāhīb)* the edge of a sword (4.16)

ل و ج *lāj (yilūj)* to sway (8.3)

ل و ى *liwiyya (lawāyā)* flag-pole (7.12)

ل ى ف *līf* the fibres of palm-fronds (5.10)

م

mīm (in the Negev 1948–63) the Military Administration (corruption of Heb. *memshal*: administration) (4.14)

م ح ل *maḥal (muḥūl)* drought (1.7, 1.8, 3.8)

م خ خ *mukhkh adh-dhahab* pure gold (4.20E)

م د د *madd (yimidd)* to hold something forward, to offer something by extending it (3.2, 4.19)

م ر ر *marīra (marāyir)* a man's head-ropes (band) (4.3, 6.15, 7.10)

م ر ح *maraḥ (yimriḥ), marraḥ* to spend the night (2.9, 4.9)

—— *marāḥ (marāyiḥ)* place of sleep, sleep (1.11)

م ر د *marad (yimrad)* to cohabitate with someone (orig. to ride) (4.8)

—— *mārid (murūd)* a horse (4.20D)

—— *amrad (mird)* a young man (lit. beardless) (4.16)

م ر ق *marag (yumrug)* to pass (1.10); to pass by (4.9)

م ز ن *mizna (mizn)* a raincloud (1.3, 4.15, 4.20D, 4.20F)

م ش ل ق *mashlag* to rip up (2.8)

م غ ر س *timaghras* to squirm out of (2.8)

م ك س *maks (amkās)* criticism, blame (4.19)

م ك ش *makīsh* refrained, shy (4.20I)

م ل ح *malḥa (malāḥ)* a smoke-blackened stone (3.3)

م ل ل *malla* the hot ashes of a campfire (4.6)

م ل ى *mallā* to bake bread in embers of a campfire (4.20A)

م ن *min* 'over and above' (2.5)

م و ت *al-mīta* and lastly . . . (4.7)

م ى ح *mayyāḥ* a drawer of water (4.20B)

م ى ل *mayyal* to deal unjustly (4.1)

م ى ى *miy, mā* water (2.8, 3.4, 4.20I, 5.3, 7.8, 7.12, 8.4)

ن

ن ج ب *manjūb (manājīb)* the rider of a swift camel (*najīb*) (1.14)

ن ج ر *nijr* see ج ر ن

ن ج ع *naja' (nujū')* section (of a tribe) (5.13)

ن ح ر *naḥr (yanḥar), tanaḥḥar* to ride towards to head in a direction (4.9, 4.20F)

ن ح ى *naḥā (yanḥā)* to direct, caution (3.8, 3.9, 6.8); to drive away, push away (1.10, 4.20B)

ن خ ط *nakhaṭ (yinkhaṭ)* to snort angrily (a horse) (5.11)

ن خ و *nakhā (yinkhā), astankhā* to call for aid (1.15, 3.9)

ن د ح *nadaḥ (yindaḥ)* to shake (4.20H)

ن د ر *tanaddar* to choose (2.7)

ن د ش *nādūsh* firm, tight (7.8)

ن د ى *nadiyān* moist, fat (from *nadā*, dew) (4.7)

ن ز ل *nazzal fī* to conscript (7.10)

ن س ف *mansaf (manāsif)* a platter of mutton and rice (2.12, 4.17)

ن س ن س *nisnās (nasānīs)* a legendary, elongated animal, or fleet bird (5.11)

ن ش ب *antashab* to get stuck, caught (4.6)

ن ش د *nashshad* to ask for (information about) (6.1, 6.7, 6.11)

—— *nāshad* to greet someone vociferously (3.6)

ن ش ل *nashshal* to draw water (4.9)

ن ش م *nishmī (nishāma)* a brave soul, person (1.11, 1.14, 4.5, 6.4, 6.18, 7.7)

ن ص ب *naṣība (naṣāyib)* a grave-stone (1.14)

ن ص ص *nuṣṣ (naṣāṣ)* a half (Class. *niṣf*) (6.3, 6.4, 6.12, 6.18, 7.6)

ن ض ى *naḍā, inḍī (naḍwa)* a swift camel (2.12, 4.15)

ن ط ط *naṭṭ (yinuṭṭ)* to jump, bound (3.8)

ن ظ ف *naẓīf* perfect (5.10)

ن ع ق *naʿīg* a shepherd's calling to the livestock to drink (4.9)

ن ف ر *nafar (yunfur)* to bray (a donkey) (1.2); to refuse to suckle (a she-goat) (4.9)

ن ف س *nafs ḥayy* an honest soul (1.6)

ن ف ض *nafaḍ (yunfuḍ) al-jēb* to admit to uncertainty (lit. to shake the collar) (3.8)

ن ف ل *nafīla* benefit (1.7)

—— *nāfila* something gratuitous, uncalled for (3.10)

ن ق د *nagd, nagad* the appraisal of perspective brides (6.12)

ن ق ل *nagīla* gossip (3.8)

ن ك س *nakas (yinkis)* to tilt something (7.8)

ن م ر *nimra* a government order (from English: number) (7.1)

ن د م *naham (yanham)* to yell at, scold (4.19)

ن و خ *manākh al-juzūm* testing place of resolve (6.1)

ن و ش *tanawwash* to start suddenly (6.14)

ن و م *nāyim rīḥ* useless (lit. still wind) (4.14)

ن و م س *nawmas (yinōmas)* to respect (2.10)

—— *nāmūs (nawāmīs)* decorum, proper behaviour, respect (6.6)

ن و و *naww* the winter-rain season introduced by the appearance of the Pleiades in the evening sky in November (6.15)

ن و ى *nāwā* to return to one's home (camel) (6.18)

ن ى ب — *nīb (niyāb), minwab (manāwīb)* a camel with canine teeth (6 years old) (3.8, 4.18)
ن ى ى — *nī, nay* rawness (2.12)

ه

ه ب ب — *habbit ar-rīḥ* good fortune (lit, a blowing wind) (7.12)
ه ب ش — *habsha* charcoal (4.12)
— *habūsh* rabble (7.8)
— *mihbāsh (mahābīsh)* a mortar for grinding coffee beans (6.14)
ه ب ى — *hibiyya (habāyā)* a stagnant pool (1.1)
ه ث ل — *hithl* dregs (5.5)
ه ج ر — *hajjar* to pace a mount (5.12)
— *hijār* the trotting gait of a horse (5.6); tethers, binds (3.7, 7.6)
ه ج ن — *hijīn (hijn)* a riding camel (4.4)
ه د د — *hadd (yihidd)* to attack (5.12)
— *hadd* a heap of stones from a broken mountain (6.18)
ه د ف — *ahdaf (hudf)* bent (5.12)
ه د ل ق — *hidlāg (hadālīg)* a bold attack (1.10)
ه د م — *hidm (hudūm)* paraphernalia of the saddle (6.1)
ه د ى — *hidiyya (hidāyā)* a vanguard of lancers (4.20D)
ه ذ ب — *hadība* a swift pace (4.18)
— *mihdhāb (mahādhīb)* a swift-pacing camel or horse (1.14)
ه ذ ل — *hidhīl* slow-moving (5.6)
ه ر ب س — *harbas (yiharbas)* to make dogs run off by saying *hirs* (1.3)
— *hirbās (harābīs)* a fleeing dog (5.11)
ه ر ج — *harj (hurūj, harjāt)* words, talk (2.2, 2.4, 3.7, 3.9, 3.10, 4.2, 4.5, 4.17, 4.19, 6.10, 6.14, 6.15, 7.6)
— *harjāt* conversation (2.2, 5.1)
— *harj al-gafā* backbiting (2.2)
ه ر د — *harad (yuhrud)* to descend (8.4)
ه ز ع — *imhazza'* fatty (1.10)
ه ش ل — *hashshāl* a passer-by (1.10)
ه ض ب — *haḍāb* hills, mountains (of limestone) (4.1, 7.12)
ه ف ى — *hafā (yihfā)* to be transient, move quickly (5.7, 5.12)
— *hāfī (hafāyā)* a vile, debased person (6.14, 7.10)
ه ق ى — *hāgī* (='ārif) to know, imagine (6.7)
— *hagwa* a thought (4.10)
ه ل ب — *halīb* pretty (3.8)
ه ل ب ج — *halbūj (hilbāj)* a 'good for nothing' (1.3)
ه ل ل — *hall (yihill)* to descend (7.6)
— *mahlūl (mahālīl)* a month (4.5); to last a month (7.7)
ه ل و س — *hilwās (halāwīs)* worries, concern (2.7); a stain (2.12)
— *hāmil (hamal)* a worthless person, fool (1.5, 2.10, 4.14, 5.10, 7.7)

ه م م *hamāyim* war materials (7.3)
ه ن ء *yā hanī* how fortunate! (1.2, 4.20D, 4.20E)
ه ن ب *hināba* a small wooden vessel containing up to a litre (6.13)
hāt! bring! (2.7, 4.4, 4.14, 6.16, 6.17)
ه و ج *hawj (hawāyij)* a round, volley (7.3)
ه و ج س *hawjasa (hawājīs)* a worrisome thought (6.6)
ه و ش *hawsh, hawsha (hawshāt)* a battle (3.9, 4.20H, 5.1)
ه و م *hām (hīmān)* a snake (6.1, 6.18)
ه و ى *hawā (yihwī)* to beat someone (2.6)
—— *hayya* a fight, row (4.7)
ه ى ء *hayā (yihyā)* to be suitable (7.5)
ه ى ت *hīt!* a word called to urge a camel to run (2.5)
ه ى ت ق *haytigān* a babbler, a worthless person (4.9)
ه ى ج *hēj (hījān)* a broad-framed camel (5.1)
ه ى ف *hāf (yihīf)* to be dry (4.11)
—— *hayf* thirst (3.5)
—— *hāyif* worthless, good for-nothing (6.5, 7.12)
ه ى ل *hayl* see ء ه ل

و

و ب ر *wabar* camel-hair (3.8)
و ب ش *wabsh* see ء ب ش
و ث ر *withr, maythūr (mawāthīr)* riding-saddle (2.3), saddle cushions, stuffing of the cushions, camel pack-saddle (4.19, 6.9)
و ج د *wajad (wujūd)* a pain (1.2, 1.11, 1.14, 4.4)
و ج ع *mawja' (mawājī')* a pain (1.1, 1.7, 2.2)
و ج ه *wijh* honour (lit. face) (2.8)
و ح ش *wahsh (wuhūsh)* a wild animal (1.3)
و ح ى *awhā* to feel, sense (6.11)
—— *wahiyya* a swift pace (4.15)
و د د *widd* to want (*widdī*: I want, *widdnā*: we want, etc.) (4.14)
و د ك *wadak* camel fat (7.5)
و د ى *waddā* see ء د ى
و د ى *wadiyya (wadāyā)* a date-palm (1.1)
و ر ى *warrā* see ر ء ى
و ر د *warīd (wurūd)* a battle (1.6); going to water the livestock (3.5, 4.7)
و ر ق *warag* paper money (1.15)
و ز ى *wāzā* to tire, impose upon, someone (3.9); to urge, incite (4.4)
و س ق *wasīg* plundered camels (2.8); camels taken by an enemy as security to force him to adjudicate a dispute (4.9)
و س م *wasm, wasīm (wusūm, awsām)* a camel-brand (2.2, 2.4); the period introduced by the nightfall appearance of the Pleiades in November (4.20C)

—— *wasmiyya* a rain that follows upon the nightfall appearance of the Pleiades in November (2.4)

و س ی *wasiyya* a bagatelle, something bought (7.10)

و ض ح *awḍaḥ (wuḍḥ)* a white camel (1.10)

—— *waḍḥā (wuḍayḥiyyāt)* a package of hashish wrapped in white oil-cloth (lit. a white camel-mare) (2.5)

—— *wuḍayḥī (wuḍayḥiyyāt)* a gazelle (4.20F)

و ق ع *wagīʿa (wagāyʿa)* carcass (7.7)

و ق ف *mawgaf (mawāgif)* wharf, docking for boats (4.8)

و ق م *wagam* approximately (4.1, 5.1, 5.13)

و ك د *wakād* see ء ك د

و ل س *wils* see ء ل س

و ل ف *walīf* see ء ل ف

و ل م *wilām* haste (6.16)

و ل ی *wiliyya (walāyā)* a woman, female (1.1, 7.10)

—— *wallā* to leave quickly, 'take off' (4.6; 4.20A)

—— *walā* Behold! (*walāh* Behold it . . .) (1.9); (*walānā* Behold we . . .) (8.4)

و م ی *awmā* to sway (like a poised snake) (6.1)

و ن ن *wann* see ء ن ن

و ن ی *wannā* see ء ن ی

و ه ت *wuhūt* tent cloth (3.8)

و ه م *mayhūm* a camel ill with a disease called *waham* (variously identified as intestinal worms or ague) (6.15, 6.16)

wāwī see ء و ی

و ی ق *wāyag* to come into sight suddenly (5.10, 5.12, 6.10)

—— *imwayyig* stretched, extended (1.10)

ی

yā either (7.4)

yāt which? (2.2)

yāmā often, how often! (2.2, 3.11, 6.5, 6.15)

ی د *īd (ayādī)* hand (1.4, 2.8, 3.15, 4.2, 4.10, 4.14, 6.2, 7.9, 7.11)

ی س ر *miyāsir (mayāsīr)* a camel-mare in heat (4.3)

ی ص ر *mayṣūra (mawāṣīr)* a metal pipe, gunbarrel (4.3)

ی م م *yamm* direction (1.10, 2.3); in the direction of, towards (1.11, 4.11, 4.13, 5.6, 6.7, 6.13, 6.15, 8.4)

—— *yammak* quickly, directly (2.3, 3.7)

ی و م *yōm* when (1.11, 7.9, 7.11)

—— *al-yawm!* Oh, were it so! (2.1, 5.13)

Bibliography

Abū-l-ʿAtāhiya, *Dīwān*, ed. Karam Bustānī (Beirut, 1964).

Abu-Lughod, Lila, *Veiled Sentiments: Honor and Poetry in a Bedouin Society* (Berkeley, 1986).

Alwaya, Semha, 'Formulas and Themes in Contemporary Bedouin Oral Poetry', *Journal of Arabic Literature*, 8 (1977).

Antonius, George, *The Arab Awakening* (New York, 1964).

Arberry, A. J., *Arabic Poetry: A Primer for Students* (Cambridge, 1965).

—— *The Seven Odes* (London, 1957)

ʿĀrif, ʿĀrif al-, *al-Qaḍāʾ bayn al-Badū* (Jerusalem, 1933).

—— *Taʾrīkh Biʾr al-Sabʿ wa-Qabāʾilihā* (Jerusalem, 1934).

Aṭrash, Shiblī al-, *Dīwān Shiblī al-Aṭrash al-Kabīr* (Damascus, n.d.).

Ayalon, David, 'Aspects of the Mamluk Phenomenon, Part 2', *Der Islam*, 54/1 (1977).

ʿAzzāwī, ʿAbbās al-, *ʿAshāʾir al-ʿIrāq* (4 vols.; Baghdad, 1937).

Bailey, Clinton, 'The Narrative Context of the Bedouin Qasida-poem', *Folklore Research Center Studies*, 3, ed. I. Ben-Ami (Jerusalem, 1972).

—— 'Bedouin Star-lore in Sinai and the Negev', *Bulletin of the School of Oriental and African Studies*, 37/3 (1974).

—— 'Bedouin Weddings in Sinai and the Negev', *Folklore Research Center Studies, 4. Studies in Wedding Customs*, ed. I. Ben-Ami (Jerusalem, 1974).

—— 'The Bedouin Concept of 'ADL as Justice', *Muslim World*, 66/2 (1976).

—— 'The Negev in the Nineteenth Century: Reconstructing History from Bedouin Oral Traditions', *Asian and African Studies*, 14/1 (1980).

—— 'Bedouin Religious Practices in Sinai and the Negev', *Anthropos*, 72/1, 2 (1982).

—— 'Bedouin Place-names in Sinai', *Palestine Exploration Quarterly*, 116/1, 2 (1984).

—— 'Dating the Arrival of the Bedouin Tribes in Sinai and the Negev', *Journal of the Social and Economic History of the Orient*, 28/1 (1985).

—— and Avinoam Danin, 'Desert Plants in Bedouin Life', in C. Bailey (ed.), *Notes on the Bedouins 5. Aspects of Bedouin Culture and Folklore in Sinai and the Negev* (Midrashat Sde-Boker, 1975, in Hebrew).

—— 'Bedouin Plant Utilization in Sinai and the Negev', *Economic Botany*, 35/2 (1981).

—— and Raphael Peled, *Shivtei ha-Beduim bi-Sinai* (A Survey of the Bedouin Tribes in Sinai; Tel Aviv, Israel Ministry of Defence, internal, 1975).

—— and Avshalom Shmueli, 'The Settlement of the Sinaitic 'Ayāydah in the Suez Canal Zone', *Palestine Exploration Quarterly*, 109/1 (1977).

Bilādī, 'Atīq Bin Ghayth al-, *Ṭarā'if w-Amthāl Sha'biyya min al-Jazīra al-'Arabiyya* (Beirut, 1975).

Blackman, Winifred, *The Fellahin of Upper Egypt* (London, 1927).

Blanc, Haim, 'The Arabic Dialect of the Negev Bedouins', *Proceedings of the Israel Academy of Sciences and Humanities*, 4/7 (1970).

Blunt, Anne, *Bedouin Tribes of the Euphrates* (New York, 1879).

Burckhardt, J. L., *Notes on the Bedouins and Wahabys* (2 vols.; London, 1831; repr. 1967).

Burton, Richard, *Pilgrimage to al-Madinah and Meccah* (2 vols.; London, 1855; repr. 1893).

Cagni, Luigi, *The Poem of Erra* (Malibu, 1977).

Canaan, Tewfik, *Muhammedan Saints and Sanctuaries in Palestine* (London, 1927).

Connelly, Bridget, *Arab Folk Epic and Identity* (Berkeley, 1986).

Dawney, G. P., 'Turkish Campaigns III: The Sinai Campaign, 1916–17', *Encyclopaedia Britannica* (12th edn., 1922).

Dickson, H. R. P., *The Arab of the Desert* (London, 1949).

—— *Kuwait and her Neighbours* (London, 1956).

Doughty, Charles M., *Travels in Arabia Deserta* (2 vols.; London, 1888; repr. 1937).

Ebeid R. Y. and M. J. L. Young, 'A List of the Apellations of the Prophet Muhammad', *Muslim World*, 66/4 (1976).

Encyclopaedia of Islam, ''Arūḍ', 'Djabrīl', 'Djanāba'.

Gevirtz, Stanley, *Patterns in the Early Poetry of Israel* (Chicago, 1963).

Gibb, H. A. R., *Arabic Literature: An Introduction* (Oxford, 1926; repr. 1963).

Goldziher, Ignaz, 'Über die Vorgeschichte der Higā'-Poesie', in *Abhandlung zur Arabischen Philologie*, Part 1 (Leyden, 1896).

Grunebaum, G. E. von, *Islam: Essays in the Nature and Growth of a Cultural Tradition* (London, 1961).

Gubser, Peter, *Politics and Change in al-Karak, Jordan* (London, 1973).

Guillaume, A., 'Abū'l-'Atāhiya'. *New Encyclopaedia of Islam*, i. 107–8.

—— *The Life of Muḥammad* (Oxford, 1955).

Heyd, Uriel, *Ottoman Documents on Palestine, 1552–1615* (Oxford, 1960).

Ibn Hishām, *al-Sīra al-Nabawiyya* (4 vols.; Beirut, 1971).

Ingham, Bruce, *Bedouin of Northern Arabia: Traditions of the Āl-Ḍhafīr* (London, 1986).

Jarvis, C. S., *Yesterday and To-day in Sinai* (London, 1931).

Jaussen, Antonin, *Coutumes des arabes au pays de Moab* (Paris, 1907; repr. 1948).

Jennings-Bramley, W. F., 'Bedouin of the Sinaitic Peninsula', *Palestine Exploration Fund Quarterly* (1905–1914).

Kaḥḥāla, 'Umr Riḍā, *Mu'jam Qabā'il al-'Arab* (4 vols.; Damascus, 1949).

Kammālī, Shafīq al-, *al-Shi'r 'inda-l-Badū* (Baghdad, 1964).

Klein, F. A., *The Religion of Islam* (New Delhi, 1906; repr. 1978).

Lane, E. W., *Arabic–English Lexicon* (London, 1863; new edn., 1984).

—— *The Manners and Customs of the Modern Egyptians* (London, 1836; new edn., 1954).

Lawrence, T. E., *Seven Pillars of Wisdom* (New York, 1937).

Lord, Albert B., *The Singer of Tales* (Cambridge, Mass., 1960).

Marx, Emanuel, *Bedouin of the Negev* (Manchester, 1967).

Merrill, Selah, *East of the Jordan* (New York, 1881).

Monroe, James, 'Oral Composition in Pre-Islamic Poetry: The Problem of Authenticity', *Journal of Arabic Literature*, 3 (1972).

The Mufaḍḍalīyāt: An Anthology of Ancient Arabian Odes, ed. and trans. C. J. Lyall, ii (Oxford, 1918).

Muhsim, H. V., 'Enumerating the Bedouin of Palestine', *Scripta Hierosolymitana* , 3. *Studies in Social Studies* (Jerusalem, 1955).

Murray, G. W., *Sons of Ishmael: A Study of the Egyptian Bedouin* (London, 1935).

Musil, Alois, *Arabia Petraea* (3 vols.; Wien, 1908).

—— *The Northern Hegaz* (New York, 1926).

—— *Arabia Deserta* (New York, 1927).

—— *The Middle Euphrates* (New York, 1927).

—— *The Manners and Customs of the Rwala Bedouins* (New York, 1928).

—— *Northern Negd* (New York, 1928).

Nawawī, Yaḥyā Bin S͟haraf al-Dīn al-, *al-Araba'īn al-Nawawiyya* (Cairo edn., 1979).

Nicholson, R. A., *A Literary History of the Arabs* (Cambridge, 1907; repr. 1966).

Oppenheim, Max von, *Die Beduinen* (4 vols.; Leipzig and Wiesbaden, 1949–68).

Palmer, E. H., *Desert of the Exodus* (London, 1872).

Peake, Frederick, *History and Tribes of Jordan* (Miami, 1958).

Philby, H. St. John, *The Land of Midian* (London, 1957).

Piamenta, Moshe, *Islam in Everyday Arabic Speech* (Leiden, 1979).

Pirie-Gordon, H., 'Turkish Campaigns IV: The Palestine Campaign', *Encyclopaedia Britannica* (12th edn., 1922).

Ringgren, Helmer, *Studies in Arabian Fatalism* (Uppsala, 1955).

Schwarzbaum, Haim, *The Mishle Shu'alim (Fox Fables) of Rabbi Berechiah ha-Nakdan* (Tel Aviv, 1979).

Serjeant, R. B., *South Arabian Poetry*, 1. *Prose and Poetry from Hadramawt* (London, 1951).

S͟huqayr, Na'ūm, *Ta'rīk͟h Sīnā' wa-l-'Arab* (Cairo, 1916).

Sīrat Banī Hilāl al-Kubrā (Cairo edn., 1963).

Socin, Albert, *Diwan aus Centralarabien*, (Leipzig, 1900–1).

Sowayan, Saad Abdullah, *Nabati Poetry: The Oral Poetry of Arabia* (Berkeley, 1985).

Spoer, H. H., 'Five Poems by Nimr ibn 'Adwān', *Journal of the American Oriental Society*, 43 (1923).

Thesiger, Wilfred, *Arabian Sands* (London, 1959; paperback, 1964).

Wavell, A. P., 'Operations in Palestine', *Encyclopaedia Britannica* (12th edn., 1922).

Wensinck, A. J., *et al.*, *Concordance de la tradition musulmane* (Leiden, 1936–69).

Wright, W., *A Grammar of the Arabic Language* (2 vols.; Cambridge, 1964).

Zūzanī, al-Ḥusayn ibn Aḥmad al-, *S̲h̲arḥ al-Mu'allaqāt al-Sab'* (Beirut, 1972).

Zwettler, Michael, *The Oral Tradition of Classical Arabic Literature* (Columbus, Ohio, 1978).

Index of Subjects

animals, allusions to:
bees 265
birds 284, 307, 334, 339
boars 36
bustards 89, 410
camels, *see* camels
cats 95 n. 19, 256
cattle egrets 52 n. 5
cranes 52, 129
crows 89, 202
dogs 45, 103, 315, 318
donkeys 193, 358
eagles 65, 257, 284
foxes 112, 311, 356
frogs 152
gazelles 98, 213, 244, 250, 344, 361
geese (wild) 209
grouse 209
hares 311, 339
hawks 33, 65, 106, 257, 265, 273, 292, 334, 358, 370, 377
hens 181
horses, *see* horses
hyenas 26, 36
ibex 192, 300, 306, 322
jackals 262, 311, 414
jerboa mice 26
kites 80
lions 36, 40, 93, 257 n. 8, 277, 323, 370, 413
ostriches 88, 105, 152, 237, 262, 292, 298, 338, 410, 411, 414
owls 334
oxen 306
panthers 46–7, 257
pigeons 234, 269, 277, 334
roosters 191–3
scorpions 60 n. 3, 130 n. 2
snakes 60, 214, 262, 315, 339, 377
vultures 80
wolves 27, 36, 78, 93, 95 n. 19, 112, 142, 143, 172, 181, 192, 219, 257 n. 8, 258, 262, 273, 285, 311, 323, 330, 334, 339, 384, 408
worms 61, 156, 315, 422
Arabia:
and bedouin of Sinai and the Negev 1, 3, 181, 208–10, 225, 226
poems from 13, 28, 30, 32, 50, 63, 75, 88, 97, 104, 128, 130, 132, 134, 136, 138, 141, 146, 151, 198, 201, 215, 219, 222, 230, 234, 236, 237, 241, 244, 246, 250, 355
see also Saudi Arabia
al-ʿĀrif, ʿĀrif 12, 14, 107 n. 20, 123

bedouin of Sinai and the Negev:
modernization of 6–7
numbers 4, 6
Bible, bedouin life reflected in:
Abraham 130 n. 1, 204, 407
Amos 413
Balaam 413, 416
Balak 416
David and Goliath 418
Deborah, Song of 414
genres of bedouin poetry 418
Lot 130 n. 1
material culture, biblical 407
Miriam 414
Moses 414, 423
Passover, Feast of 26 n. 4
Potiphar's wife 198
Proverbs, Book of 422–4
roles of bedouin poetry 416
Song of Songs 410
style of bedouin poetry 420
Tabernacles, Feast of 25 n. 3
themes of bedouin poetry 413
trees and bushes, biblical 407
see also parallelism
bidaʿ poems 8–9, 383–4, 387–8, 424–5
examples of 35, 46, 67, 183, 185, 188, 194, 200, 276, 355, 372
blacks, attitudes to 31, 100, 329, 330, 359
see also slaves

camels:
breeds: ʿAyāda 92 n. 5; Masāʿīd 92 n. 5, 302; Nubian 280; Sharārāt 88 n. 2, 209, 257, 394
colours 54, 58, 88, 116, 117, 130 n. 4, 209, 219, 257, 280, 292, 330, 363, 369
defects and diseases 86, 98, 308 n. 5, 330, 336 n. 1, 338
distinctive features 69, 99, 105, 116, 143, 200, 234, 261, 300, 312, 323, 334, 358 n. 10, 369
feed and feeding 54 n. 15, 195 n. 1, 234, 338

camels (*cont.*):
  fully-grown 34 n. 10, 141 n. 2, 142 n. 7, 220, 301 n. 5, 322
  gift for poets 115–18
  homing instinct 339
  imagery for: courage 293; cowardice 313; disloyalty 293; hashish 84–5, 86–7, 330–1; helplessness 89, 334; justice 31 n. 5, 172; loyalty 293; 313; pride 92, 313, speed 258, 283; women 308–9, 318
  meat of 220
  milk of 139 n. 11, 144, 220
  non-bearing mares, importance of 27, 102, 219, 273, 344, 356, 410
  packing 26 n. 9, 89, 234, 312, 313, 338
  payment for fines with 91
  pedigree: criteria for 98, 102 n. 4, 209, 257, 323 n. 4; importance of 174, 365; qualities 192, 302, 393
  pride in 143, 240
  raiding for 30, 50, 54, 63–5, 99, 240–1, 246, 288, 323, 362
  riding 178, 220 n. 4, 241, 361
  riding gear 99, 102, 117, 118, 174, 199, 235, 257, 262, 292, 300, 323
  rutting 164, 223 n. 8, 262
  sounds 234, 298 n. 6, 334 n. 1
  stud 174
  training of 106, 298 n. 6
  in warfare 247
chiefs:
  activities of 189, 357, 358, 370, 409–10
  attitudes to 42–3, 99–100, 142–3, 180, 203–6, 269, 293, 303, 361–2
children, attitudes to 46–8, 60–1, 89, 139, 148, 303 n. 7, 326–7, 351, 359
Christians:
  attitudes to 92 n. 1, 106 n. 6, 306 n. 2
  pilgrims to Mt Sinai 4, 5, 348, 350
coffee 52–3, 113, 239, 308, 336
  brewed freshly for honourable guests 133, 222–3
  proper preparation of 103, 117, 128–9, 130, 132–3, 136, 370, 395
  proper serving of 132–3, 134 n. 3, 223
coffee-pots 39, 52, 102, 117 n. 8, 129, 136, 257, 308, 317, 327, 362, 395
conflict:
  commensality and 92 n. 1
  force necessary in 95, 149, 408
  must consider consequences of 158
  resolution of 92, 248–9

dance 8, 277, 383–4
death:
  acceptance of 318
  angel of 238
  blessings for deceased 35–6
  burial 62, 65 n. 10, 156
  concepts of 62, 63–6; *see also* fatalism, expressions of
  disdain for 158, 247, 277, 408–9, 420
  drinking blood of slain enemy 116
  God determines time of 64, 138, 149
diction in poems, elevated 390–2
Doughty, Charles M. 33 nn. 2, 3, 52, 106 n. 6, 107 n. 15, 335 n. 4
dress, men's 30, 46, 57, 65, 100, 184, 190, 192, 243, 246, 258, 265, 277, 281, 283, 284, 293, 300, 311, 327, 332, 358, 361, 362, 369
drought 36, 42–3, 144
dry spittle (as sign of anguish and fear) 52, 57, 99, 177, 222, 244, 410

economic life:
  agriculture 1, 3, 45 n. 5, 83, 85 n. 2, 112, 116, 258, 270, 337 n. 3, 357–9
  fishing 302
  livestock raising 1, 28–9, 42, 46, 67–8, 139, 143–4, 147, 177 n. 1, 191–3, 331 n. 11, 334, 381
Egypt 6, 280, 288, 374–7
  bedouin attitudes to 38–41, 43 n. 2, 102 n. 4, 116 nn. 2, 3, 175 n. 3, 181, 185–7, 296 n. 1, 309, 324, 327, 337, 367, 368–71, 374–7
  customs of 94 n. 17, 100, 143, 293 nn. 8, 11, 296, 369 n. 5
  see also governments, peasants
emotions, bedouin attitudes to 18–24, 24–71, 120–1
Erra, Akkadian Poem of, 406–7

fatalism, expressions of 60–1, 62, 63–6, 277, 303, 365 n. 2, 408
fate, depictions of 26, 60, 62, 139, 149, 205, 292–3, 303, 409
  proverbs on 33 n. 4, 62 n. 2, 65 n. 7
flyting (*hijā'*) in bedouin poems 167, 176, 212, 215, 219, 222, 418–19
food, bedouin attitudes to:
  bread 45, 230, 268, 270, 362, 406–7
  camel meat 220, 356
  cheese 192
  clarified butter 53, 117, 308, 395
  coffee *see* coffee
  dates 220
  manner of eating 34 n. 9, 53 n. 7
  meat 25, 34 n. 9, 53, 92, 117, 139, 186, 215–16, 231, 265, 273, 331, 345, 362
  purchase of 229
  tea 117
formulas in bedouin poetry 393–400

gasīda-poem; *see* types of bedouin poems
Gaysiyya (peasants of the Hebron Hills) 261
genres of poetry 418–23
Gibb, H. A. R. 427

God:
bestows aid and blessings 171, 298, 339, 367, 375
brings rain 208, 258, 375
brings victory 347, 375, 376, 377
can harm 246, 293, 320, 331, 373
created the world 339, 369
dead return to 62, 65, 137 n. 7
decides fates 64, 138, 149
differentiates between man and beast 131 n. 6
forms people out of nothing 152
gives generously 189
heals people 339
is omnipotent 60, 64, 138, 149, 177, 236, 293, 317
poems dedicated to 118
protects reputations 313, 339 n. 6
receives penance 64
remembrance of name repels devil 118 n. 3, 135 n. 6, 152, 155, 231, 344, 349
sustains people 131, 133, 159, 323
warns people against evil 159
Goldziher, Ignaz 416
gossip, evil of 262, 272–3
government and authority:
attitudes to 3, 14, 38–40, 42–3, 104–8, 142–3, 154, 156, 166, 201, 203, 208, 281, 306, 344, 357–9, 367
expressions of deference to 38–40, 105–8, 116–18, 347, 370, 374–7
see also chiefs
governments, activity in Sinai and the Negev of 6, 42–3, 203–6, 288, 293, 295, 341–80
Great Britain 3, 11 n. 11, 14, 106 n. 6, 116, 117, 341–59, 367

ḥadīth, allusions to 154 n. 2, 155 nn. 2, 7, 8, 156 nn. 10, 11, 15, 157 nn. 19, 20, 22, 158 n. 32, 159 n. 34, 160 nn. 41, 42
hereditary qualities 36, 39, 69, 93, 169, 220
hijā', *see* flyting
honour 19–23, 226
'blackening' of 329, 330
component of one's security 19, 22–3, 125–7, 166–7
indicated by one's reception as a guest 133, 239
indicated by women's inviolability 26 n. 8, 68, 305–6, 365
symbolized by the beard 36
symbolized by the face 99, 223
see also shelter: tents
horses:
breeds: Kaḥīla 54; 'Ubayyāt 277
colours 234, 247
features 54 n. 14, 138 n. 1, 246, 268–9
feed 54 n. 15
hobbling 138, 358
as imagery for: age 327; courage 94; determination 168, 195; virility 265
prowess 234
in raids 246
riding methods 269
shod 94, 234
a source of power 139
training 89 n. 5
in warfare 83, 107, 116, 213, 237, 247, 258, 269, 275, 280–1, 284, 415–16
hospitality 1, 34, 130–1, 132–3
a bearable duty 148
camping near roads 53 n. 11
coffee, a symbol of 113
as a component of power 126
deference to guests 130, 132–3, 139 n. 9, 148, 222–3, 315, 412
dropping everything for a guest 134
fighting to sup a guest in the camp 79, 131
forcing guest to stay 34, 106, 231–2
given indiscriminately 186 n. 2
greeting guests cheerfully 103
'guests of God' 139
poor hospitality 44–5, 192
pouring clarified butter 53 n. 8, 117, 308
pouring suet 34, 345, 346
poverty impairs 89
publicizing hospitality received 36 n. 5, 135, 417
receiving guests at any hour 269
rejection of 92
rising to greet guests 130, 137
rules of 32–4, 44 n. 4, 53, 102–3, 132, 215–17, 232, 265, 412
serving guests from right to left 132, 338
slaughtering for a guest 36, 79 n. 11, 265, 273 n. 6, 338, 345, 356, 412
staying at home to receive guests 142, 216, 220 n. 10
stealing another's goat for a guest 47 n. 4
humour, bedouin:
defiance of convention and authority 165–6, 172, 194, 200, 201, 203, 208
lampoons against breaches of convention 164, 185, 188, 191, 263, 355–6
self-ridicule 166, 176, 180, 183, 372
hunting 172, 303, 339, 361

Ibn Rashīd dynasty 107, 219–21
imagery in bedouin poetry 392–3, 409–13
beneficence, images of: a lion 36; moisture 46 n. 2; a wall 265, 365; a well 93, 181, 280, 303 n. 8
derogation, images of: dry 46 n. 2, 376; a mud puddle 107, 303; short-armed 107; a slouch 36, 277; the tail end of a hoe 92
see also animals, camels, fate, horses, law, secrecy

imprisonment, bedouin attitudes to 24–7, 57–8, 183–4, 290, 291–3, 302, 315, 317, 320, 324, 339, 370, 401–2, 404
Iraq, bedouin of 226–7
Israel:
attitudes to 165, 203–6, 361–3, 364–5, 367–8, 372–3, 374–7
in the Negev 6, 111–12, 191, 203–6, 341–3, 361, 364–5
in Sinai 6, 35, 164, 188–90, 341–3, 367, 372–3, 374–7
Israelis alluded to 168, 367, 203, 204, 364–5, 384

Jarvis, C. S. 3, 11 n. 11
Jennings-Bramley, W. E. 3, 11 n. 11
Jews, attitudes to 181, 209
Jordan (also Transjordan) 1, 2, 5, 6, 38–40, 104–6, 115–18, 181, 227, 283, 369, 377, 401, 403

kinship:
betrayal of 24–7, 290, 299–300, 314–15, 323
maternal kin 36 n. 8, 39 n. 7, 142, 159 nn. 39, 40, 272 n. 1, 281 n. 9
responsibilities of 1, 36 n. 8, 53 n. 10, 92, 126, 147
solidarity 143, 147, 159 n. 39, 160, n. 41, 222–3, 313, 334–5, 393, 408, 420

law, bedouin 1, 5, 61, 94, 121
appeals 177
defining claims 327 n. 1
guarantees 178 n. 4
judges 5, 61, 91, 93, 95, 155, 177 n. 3, 181, 326
justice, image of 31 n. 5, 78 n. 1, 155, 172 n. 1, 393
oaths 131 n. 6, 322
ordeal by fire 181 n. 3, 324
reconciliation 248–9
regarding guests 47 n. 4, 79 n. 11
regarding homicide 77–80, 263–4
regarding women 75, 80n. 18, 93 nn. 8, 10, 11, 152, n. 3, 177, 327, 381
trials 91, 93, 177, 327
truces 97–100
vengeance 80 n. 19
witnesses 80, 327 n. 1
see also proverbs
Lawrence, T. E. 28, 44 n. 2, 115 n. 1, 350, 355
Lord, Albert, *see* Parry–Lord theory
luck, expressions of 33, 39, 177, 236, 376

Mamluks 275 n. 1
marriage 39, 63, 64, 75, 89, 226, 228, 233, 244–5, 315, 323, 330, 339
bride price 196, 230, 263 n. 1, 321
choice of bride 63 n. 1, 320 n. 2
choice of husband 89 n. 6, 220
divorce 34, 106, 226, 244–5, 248 n. 47, 256, 318, 407
elopement 91, 93, 214 n. 7
ḥinna, role of 118 n. 12
of interest 63, 263
of orphan girl 351 n. 20
qualities of wife 138, 147–8
related wives 75 n. 3, 148 n. 7, 305
to women of good stock 39, 142
to women of inferior tribe 272
medicine, bedouin:
cauterization 177, 320
concepts regarding health and illness 60 n. 2, 68 n. 1, 75, 79, 118 n. 12
liver: as source of anger 79, 181; as source of power 60 n. 2, 68 n. 1, 75, 223, 292
sucking poison from bites and stings 60
veterinary medicine 86, 308 n. 5, 331 n. 8, 336 n. 1, 338 n. 2, 457
memory, the role of, in composing poems 15, 400–5
metre, irregular 15, 387–90, 398–9
migration 1, 42, 46–8, 88–9, 426
Mishna 122, 408
monorhyme 17, 68, 424–5
Mu'allaqa 409, 411, 428
Muḥammad, the Prophet 52, 58 n. 8, 103, 114 n. 17, 157, 160, 178, 375 n. 1, 395
intercession requested 139, 349
pilgrimage made to tomb of 103 n. 11, 139
preached peace among men 178
music 50, 63, 169 n. 3, 195 n. 3, 261 n. 1, 263–4, 323 n. 5, 382–7
Musil, Alois 12, 14, 33, 50, 98 n. 2, 123, 395

Nicholson, R. A. 427

Palestinian political cause 40 n. 9, 203, 204–5, 361–3, 375 n. 2, 376
Palmer, E. H. 11 n. 11, 82 n. 1, 344
panegyric poems 38, 104, 115, 166, 168, 171, 174, 346, 374
mock panegyric 188, 203, 208
parallelism 57 n. 5, 423–4
repetitive parallelism, examples of 57, 69, 93, 139, 213–14, 234, 236–7, 247, 284
Parker, A. C. 3, 347 n. 5, 358 n. 5
Parry, Milman, *see* Parry–Lord theory
Parry–Lord theory 393–400, 404
peasants, bedouin attitudes to 26, 43, 270, 281 n. 9, 362, 366 n. 8; *see also* Egypt, Gaysiyya
plants and trees, desert:
acacia 112 n. 4, 200 n. 1, 318, 407
anabasis 86 n. 2
artemisia 25 n. 3, 29
atriplex 86 n. 2
ephedra 177 n. 2
genista 25 n. 2, 200 n. 1, 407
hammada 86 n. 2

lawsonia 117 n. 9
pistacia 53 n. 7, 112 n. 4
salsola 86 n. 2
scorzonera 99 n. 6
suaeda 86 n. 2
tamarix 53 n. 7, 86, 200 n. 1, 407
verbascum 31 n. 2
poetic licence 15, 390
pre-Islamic poetry 406–29
pride in bedouin lineage, expressions of 39–40, 102, 169, 270, 370–1
proverbs:
agriculture 381
camels 144 n. 13
children 39 n. 7, 303 n. 7
confederal privilege 255 n. 3
conflict 149 n. 10
convention 315 n. 3
death 62 n. 2
decorum 135 n. 5
disappointment 158 n. 31
fate, *see* fate
food and conflict 92 n. 1
friendship 76 n. 5, 92, 157 n. 25
government and authority 20, 154, 165
hereditary qualities 36 n. 7, 39 n. 7, 122, 249 n. 52, 315 n. 3
honour 93 n. 9, 305, 420
hospitality 33 n. 3, 79 n. 11, 132 n. 2, 133 n. 4
imprisonment 302 n. 5
imprudence 301 n. 6
injustice 80 n. 18, 331 n. 10
kinship responsibility 53 n. 10, 159 nn. 39, 40, 160 n. 41
land ownership 363 n. 10
law 79 n. 11, 93 n. 8, 152 n. 3, 248 nn. 49, 50, 51, 380
leadership 154
luck 33 n. 5
lying 356 n. 4
neighbours 122, 269 n. 3, 381, 408
patience 68 n. 3, 158 n. 27, 236 n. 26
poetry 425–6
purchases 158 n. 28
reconciliation 249 nn. 48–51
religion 381–2, 420
reputation 305
self-reliance 147 n. 1, 159 n. 34
stubbornness 320 n. 3
success 243 n. 38
vengeance 80 n. 18, 331 n. 10
vicissitudes of life 25, 94 n. 17, 158 n. 33, 243 n. 40, 404
war 92, 285 n. 3
women 93, 147 n. 4, 156 n. 12, 296 n. 2, 305, 381

Qur'ān 68 n. 3, 108 n. 22, 138 n. 2, 152 nn. 3, 6, 153, n. 1, 154, 155 nn. 4, 5, 156 nn. 9, 10, 13, 17, 157 nn. 21–4, 26, 158 nn. 27, 32, 33, 159 nn. 35–7, 278 n. 6, 303 n. 11, 349 n. 3

recitation of poetry 8. 122–4
religious attitudes and practices 1
ablution 184, 193
asceticism 107, 151–2, 153–60, 420–2
bad luck 236
belief in paradise 210 n. 5
blessings 139 n. 9, 171, 232 n. 15, 233 n. 18, 243 n. 37, 313 n. 3, 344, 347
devil 178, 205 n. 3, 231 n. 14, 296, 349
evil eye 169 n. 2, 178 n. 7, 239 n. 34, 349, 385
expiation 113
Gabriel, angel 139
holiday observance 24–6, 168, 317
holy tombs 46–7, 113, 266, 385–6
jihād 205, 348, 355, 367
Judgment Day 94, 139, 152, 159
magic 22, 118
pilgrimage, the *ḥajj* 3, 113, 139, 342, 344
Pillars of Islam 141 n. 3, 157 n. 19
praying and fasting 141, 157, 181 n. 6, 184
see also God; Muḥammad; Qur'ān
repartee, poems of 167, 176, 183, 212, 215, 219, 222, 225, 246
reputation:
based on lineage 280, 281 n. 8
based on respect for convention 147 n. 4, 164–6
based on virtues 93, 217 n. 3
image of face for 99, 223
importance of 36 n. 7, 125–6, 216–17, 257, 315, 323
importance of posthumous 36, 278 n. 6
importance of secrecy for 222–3, 313
role of women's behaviour in 139, 366
role of poetry 416–18
conveys social values 120–7, 419–23
as means of communication 72–4
entertains 164–7, 225–52
expresses attitudes to political events 203–6, 341–80
expresses emotions 18–24
in war and conflict 77–80, 82–3, 91–5, 97–100, 102–3, 253–87
romance and sex 63–6, 67–9, 75, 77–80, 88–9, 91–5, 139, 142, 164–5, 186–7, 190, 193, 194–6, 198–9, 200, 201–2, 212–14, 235, 241–2, 244, 250–1, 263–4, 269, 273, 290, 305–6, 310–11, 313, 319–20, 323, 319, 382–3, 410, 428

St Catherine's Monastery 5–6, 186
Saudi Arabia
bedouin attitudes to 181, 104–8, 208–10
cut off relations with Egypt 377
Ikhwān movement 106 n. 7, 201–2, 216

Saudi Arabia (*cont.*):
  rebellions against 104–8
  see also Arabia
sea craft 86–7, 300, 302, 330, 344–5
secrecy, importance of 26 n. 7, 139, 156, 223 n. 6, 359
  imagery of tent for, *see under* shelter: tents
security, pervasive concern with 19–23, 89, 125–7, 165, 305
shelter:
  houses 112 n. 2, 362
  shrub booths 112, 362
  tent camps 79, 131, 283, 338, 363
  tents: as image of tribal unity 409–10; as source of prestige 52, 138, 244, 257, 265, 272; as symbol of honour 26 n. 8, 192, 305–6, 323, 365 n. 6; as true bedouin shelter 52 n. 4, 239; parts of 52 n. 4, 135 n. 5; *see also* secrecy
Shuqayr, Na'ūm 12, 14, 346
slaves 30–1, 50, 106, 167, 212–14, 215–17, 232, 303, 346
  see also blacks
smuggling 6, 26 n. 9, 36, 38, 84–5, 86–7, 288–90, 297–8, 329–32, 354, 368–71, 373
  attitudes to 302 n. 6, 323 n. 9, 337 n. 3
  imagery for, in poetry 19, 69, 178 n. 8
  routes in Sinai and the Negev 288, 299, 302, 329, 401
social attitudes:
  convention, respect for 36 n. 6, 147 n. 4, 164, 223 n. 8, 315 n. 3
  decorum 31, 53 n. 12, 131 n. 7, 135 n. 5, 137, 142, 192
  friendship 53 n. 12, 88, 94, 127, 143, 160, 320, 413
  generosity 53 n. 8, 133, 135, 264–5, 412
  gossip 142 n. 9, 149, 419
  greed 164
  mercifulness 105, 157, 339
  moderation 158
  neighbourliness 148, 269, 381
  patience 68, 157, 236
  prudence 142, 147, 165
  self-respect 142, 165–6, 217, 223, 336–7
  self-sufficiency 89 n. 7, 126, 135, 143, 147 n. 1, 156, 159, 172, 327, 420
  wards, the protection of 133, 139, 167, 209, 212–14, 220, 265, 308 n. 4, 412, 419–20
  wealth and poverty 35, 133, 143, 147, 156, 158, 287, 362
  see also hospitality, proverbs, women
social organizations:
  blood-revenge groups 1, 53 n. 10, 147 n. 3, 148 n. 7, 305, 334–5, 370 n. 6
  confederations 1, 4, 253 n. 1, 254, 255 n. 3, 315 n. 5
  see also chiefs
Socin, Albert 122, 123
Sowayan, S. A. 16, 397
stars 292, 303
  Antares 322
  Pleiades 85, 237, 323, 331, 381, 401, 407
stress in poetry, unnatural 15, 382–7

themes in poetry, traditional 413–16
Tkatch 428
Turkey (also Ottoman Empire) 114 n. 6, 340–56
types of bedouin poems:
  bida' see *bida'* poems
  gaṣīda 9–10, 389–90, 424–5, 427
  ḥidā 382
  ḥijēnī 63–6, 201–2, 215–17, 354–6, 389
  imwēlī 385–6, 388
  marbūa' 153–60, 203–6, 250–1, 264–6, 348–51

vengeance 1, 20, 30–1, 40, 77–80, 91, 97–8, 269, 327, 330, 331
versions, poems with differing 11, 75, 82, 97, 104, 122–4, 138, 141, 146, 198, 212, 222, 228–9, 256, 273, 275, 283, 344, 346

War of Abū Sirḥān (1813–16) 253, 260, 270, 279
War of 'Awda and 'Āmr (1842–64) 253, 280 n. 5
War of Basūs, the pre-Islamic 281 n. 7, 408
War of Zāri' al-Huzayyil (1875–87) 14, 253–87, 341, 406, 427
War of 1948 (Arab-Israeli) 6, 110–14, 117 n. 7
War of 1956 (Arab-Israeli) 367
War of 1967 (Arab-Israeli) 188, 375, 377 n. 12
War of 1973 (Arab-Israeli) 39 n. 5, 375
warfare 39, 40, 54, 248, 288, 348–51
  attacks 285 n. 3
  attitudes to 149, 169, 410
  bells worn in 284
  blood of enemy drunk 116
  coats of mail worn in 237
  depicted as a well 39 n. 3, 135
  is fated 149
  fighters depicted as yellow-fanged beasts 257
  is harsh 169, 334, 367, 410
  on horseback 237, 247
  role of poetry in 416–18
weapons:
  daggers 31
  mitrailleuse 350
  rifles 138, 223, 258, 280, 318, 323, 327, 365, 367; flintlock 196; Martini 296; Mauser 25, 69, 175
  spears 57, 83, 214, 247, 262, 264, 266, 280, 356
  swords 40, 99, 149, 223, 237, 247, 265, 277, 283, 287, 415; as image for bravery 258
women:
  beauty, signs of 26, 89, 195–6, 199, 202, 250–1, 265, 277, 309, 318, 320, 384, 410

cause friction with in-laws 147 n. 4
characteristics: enviousness 226, 239; fickleness 156, 295–6; sexuality 198–9, 226; weakness of character 25, 27 n. 12, 298
consideration for 63, 158
determine children's qualities 39 n. 7, 69 n. 4, 281
domestic roles of 138, 164, 186 n. 5, 192 n. 4, 203
dress 26, 29, 75, 185–7, 195, 212, 273, 277, 296 n. 1, 311, 320, 366
fates depicted as 60 n. 1
importance of good reputation 139, 366
influenced by parental home 138 n. 2, 142 n. 7
misconduct 24–7, 80 n. 8, 93, 139 n. 7, 199 n. 1, 296, 315, 320
orphaned 351
peasant women 164, 185–7, 227, 362
poetesses 28, 63, 225–52, 261, 263–4; less restrained than men in expression 23, 382
protection of 165, 167, 250 n. 3, 265
referred to in poems in the masculine 64 n. 2, 68 n. 2, 92 n. 2
sing at festivities 169 n. 3, 261 n. 1, 263–4, 382
social outlook of 126–7, 147, 156
social status 1, 187 n. 7, 219–21, 345 n. 6, 359 n. 14
tattooed 26, 195
violation of 26 nn. 7, 8, 91–5, 165, 428; laws regarding 93, 381
widowhood 275
wives, treatment of 147 n. 4, 156, 158
see also marriage, proverbs, romance

Index of Arabic Names and Tribal Groups

'Abd al-'Azīz Ibn Sa'ūd, king of Saudi Arabia 104–8, 166, 201, 208–10, 403, 426
'Abd al-Ḥakīm 'Āmr, Egyptian minister of war 370
'Abd al-Qays ibn Khufaf, pre-Islamic poet 419, 420
'Abda ibn aṭ-Ṭabīb, pre-Islamic poet 419, 420
'Abdallāh Ḥimēd 'Awwād, reciter 141
'Abdallāh ibn al-Ḥusēn al-Hāshimī, king of Jordan 40 n. 13, 104 n. 1, 115–18, 369 n. 2, 403
'Abēdallāh Salām 'Awda, chief of the 'Alēgāt Zmēliyyīn and reciter 97
Abū-l-'Atāhiya, 8th-c. poet 156 nn. 14, 18, 420–2
Abū Hurēra 113, 351
Abū Khubēza aṣ-Ṣāni', poet of the Tiyaha Gderat 10, 284
Abū Zēd al-Hilālī, medieval legendary hero 8, 132 n. 2, 225, 258 n. 9, 394
Abū Zuwayyid, poet of the Rawala 219–21
'Adwān tribal confederation (Jordan) 2, 227
'Agēl tribe (Arabia) 44, 350
'Agēlī tribe (Sinai) 5, 102, 174, 176
see also Ṣabāḥ Ṣāliḥ al-Ghānim
Aḥaywāt tribal confederation (Sinai) 5, 77–80, 292, 297, 401
Aḥmad Abū Ṭugēga, chief of the Ḥuwēṭāt Tihāma 105
'Algēgāt tribal confederation (Sinai) 5, 183, 299
see also 'Aṭiyya Miz'ān 'Awwād
'Alī Sulēmān al-'Aṭāwna, chief of the Tiyāhā Nutūsh 279–81, 416
'Aliyyān Imṭer, poet of the Aḥaywāt Ṣafāyḥa 8, 396
'Alqama ibn 'Abāda, pre-Islamic poet 415, 426
'Amārāt division of the 'Anēza (Iraq) 226
'Āmir ibn aṭ-Ṭufayl, pre-Islamic poet 417
Amīra 'Abdallāh Swēlim 305, 310, 314
'Ammār 'Abdallāh Sālim 146
'Amr ibn al-Ahtam, 7th-c. poet 407, 420
'Amr Muḥammad aṣ-Ṣani', reciter 10, 97, 219, 283
'Āmr Salīm al-'Aṭāwna 253, 280
'Anēz Sālim Swēlim al-'Urḍī (also 'Anez abū Sālim), poet of the Tarābīn Ḥasāblah 9, 14, 86, 91, 120–1, 168, 208, 227, 288–340, 367, 374, 388, 391, 395, 396, 399, 400, 401, 402, 403, 404
poems composed by 24, 77, 91, 115, 127, 168, 208, 291, 297, 302, 307, 312, 314, 317, 319, 326, 329, 334, 337, 367, 374
'Anēza tribal confederation (Arabia, Syria, Iraq) 33, 50–2, 88 n. 1, 219, 226
see also 'Amārāt; Fugara; Ibn Hadhdhāl; Rawala
'Anēzān Sālim Swēlim al-'Urḍī, reciter 277, 326
'Antar ibn Shaddād, pre-Islamic poet 226
Anwar al-Sādāt, president of Egypt 166, 168–9, 205, 374–7, 403, 409
'Ārif Abū Rubē'a 11 n. 11
al-Aswad ibn Ya'fūr, pre-Islamic poet 410
'Aṭāwna tribe (Negev) 113, 253, 280
see also Mūsā Ḥasan al-'Aṭāwna; Tiyāhā; War of Zāri' al-Huzayyil
'Aṭiyya Miz'ān 'Awwād, poet of the 'Alēgāt Zmēliyyīn 9, 183, 299, 317, 388, 417
poems composed by 188, 299, 372
'Awda Abū Mu'ammar, chief of the 'Azāzma Mas'ūdiyyīn 203–5
'Awda Abū Tāyah, chief of the Ḥuwēṭat Ibn Jāzī 28
'Awda al-'Aṭāwna 280 n. 3
'Awda Huwēshil Sālim, reciter 138
'Awda Ijmēa' al-Ajrab, poet of the Muzēna Sakhāna 171
poem composed by 35
'Awda Imsallam Abū Ṣbēḥ, reciter 138, 268
'Awda Ṣāliḥ Imbārak, reciter 7, 8, 32, 291, 297, 307, 312, 317, 329, 334
'Awda Sālim 'Alī, reciter 104
'Awda Salīm al-'Aṭāwna, a chief of the Tiyāhā 'Aṭāwna 253, 280 n. 3
'Awda Sulēmān 'Aliyyān, reciter 28, 146
'Ayāyda tribal confederation (Sinai) 5, 92, 181 n. 3, 354
'Āyd 'Abēd Muḥammad 26 n. 7, 305, 319, 338
'Ayyād 'Awwād Ibn 'Adēsān, poet of the 'Azāzma Mas'ūdiyyīn 10, 123
poem composed by 361
'Azāzma tribal confederation (Negev) 5, 10, 123, 132 n. 2, 191–3, 203–6, 255, 256, 274, 281, 286, 361–3, 364–6

Badāra tribe (Sinai) 5
Banī 'Aṭiyya tribal confederation (Arabia) 2, 82–3

Banī Hilāl tribal confederation (Arabia) 5, 8, 132, 225, 258, 262, 286, 395
Banī Ṣakhr tribal confederation (Jordan) 2
Banī Shahr tribe (Arabia) 39 n. 6
Banī 'Ugba tribal confederation (Negev) 5, 212–14, 256, 272; (Arabia) 358
see also al-'Ugbī
Banī Wāṣil tribe (Sinai) 5
Bashāma, pre-Islamic poet 410
Bayyāḍiyyīn tribal confederation (Sinai) 5, 102, 107
Begūm tribal confederation (Arabia) 40, 377
Bilī tribal confederation (Sinai) 2, 5; (Arabia) 33 n. 2, 104–8, 122, 222, 355, 403

Dahshān Muḥammad Abū Sitta 255
Dawāghra tribal confederation (Sinai) 5, 213 n. 3, 228
Ḍayfallāh Imfarrij Imsā'id 305

Faraj Sa'īd al-Farārja 305
Faraj Sulēmān, poet of the Rumēlāt Busūm 8, 401
poems composed by 346, 357
al-Farazdaq, 7th-c. poet 407, 419
Fayṣal Sulṭān Āl Duwīsh, paramount chief of the Imṭēr 106
Fihayd al-Huzayyil, chief of the Tiyāhā Ḥukūk 255, 268–9
Fihayd Salīm Fihayd Ibn Jāzī 77–80
Frēḥ Farḥān Ḥusēn Abū Middēn, chief of the Ḥanājra Abū Middēn 357–8
Frēḥ Ibn Ṭallāg 284
Frēj as-Sākhin 385
Fu'ād Ṣāliḥ Ismā'īl 290, 367
Fugara tribe (Arabia) 33
Fuhaymān Ibn Rifāda 222–3

Gāsim Ibn 'Aṭiyya (al-'Aṭāwna) 280

Ḥājj Ḥimēdān 317
Ḥamāda tribe (Sinai) 5
Ḥamd al-'Arādī, poet of the Tarābīn Ḥasāblah 8
Ḥamd Sulēmān Salām Abū Nadā, reciter 24
Ḥamdān abū Salāma Abū Mas'ūd, poet of the Muzēna Darārma 8, 9, 124, 132, 146, 151, 289 n. 2, 388, 400, 410
poems composed by 67, 180, 194, 322
Ḥāmid Ibn Rifāda, chief of the Arabian Bilī 104–8
Ḥammād Khalīl Salmān Abū Rubē'a, chief of the Zullām Abū Rubēa' 204–5
Ḥammād Muḥammad Ḥamdān aṣ-Ṣūfī 5, 255, 256, 257, 263–6, 274, 285, 399
Ḥanājra tribal confederation (Negev) 5, 82, 261, 262, 285, 357
Ḥarba Ḥusēn Abū Sitta 263, 264, 265, 399
al-Ḥarīrī, 12th-c. poet 422
al-Ḥarith ibn Jabala, king of ancient Ghassān 415, 426
Ḥasāblah tribe (Sinai) 289–90
see also 'Anēz Sālim Swēlim al-'Urḍī; Tarābīn
Ḥasan 'Alī al-'Aṭāwna, chief of the Tiyāhā Nutūsh 11 n. 11, 280 n. 3
al-Ḥasan ibn Ṭalāl al-Hāshimī, crown prince of Jordan 369
Ḥassān Ibn Thābit, early Islamic poet 113
Ḥassān ibn Tubba', semi-legendary pre-Islamic ruler 300 n. 3
Ḥassān Jawwān, poet of the Arabian Ḥuwēṭāt, poem composed by 104
Ḥimēd Ibn Kuraydim 77
Ḥimēd Slēm Imbārak 385
Hitēm tribes 359 n. 14
Ḥusēn Abū Sitta 263, 264–5, 276–7, 280
al-Ḥusēn ibn 'Alī al-Hāshimī, Sharif of Mecca 28, 106, 355–6
al-Ḥusēn ibn Ṭalāl al-Hāshimī, king of Jordan 38–40, 169, 203, 205, 369, 377
Ḥusēn Saliī Ḥasan, reciter 354
Ḥusnī Mubārak, president of Egypt 38, 39
Ḥuwēṭāt tribal confederation:
Sinai 2, 5, 79, 344
Arabia 3, 28, 97–100, 105, 134, 181 n. 3, 215, 345
Huzayyil tribe (Negev) 82–3, 110–14, 254–5
see also War of Zārī' al-Huzayyil, Tiyāhā

Ibn Busēs, chief of the Banī 'Aṭiyya 82–3
Ibn Hadhdhāl tribe (Iraq) 8, 226–7
see also Jidēa' Ibn Hadhdhāl
'Īd Ahamad Naṣīr aṭ-Ṭulēlī, chief of the Ṣawālḥa Garārsha 171
'Īd Ḥammād Mas'ad, reciter 134, 136, 141
'Īd Ibn Rabī'a 362 n. 4
'Īd Imfarrij Imsā'id, poet of the Tarābīn Ḥasāblah 10, 30
poems composed by 60, 62, 200, 295
'Īd Isbēḥ Sālim al-Imṭērāt, reciter 10, 30, 222
'Īd Muṣliḥ Ḥamd Ibn 'Āmr, a chief of the Tiyāhā Ṣgērāt 91–5, 292–3
'Īd Sālim Ḥimēdī al-A'sam, reciter 10, 225, 283
'Īd Swēlim 'Awwād Ibn Rabī'a, chief of the 'Azāzma Zaraba 362
'Imrū al-Qays, pre-Islamic poet 428
Imsallam Ṣāliḥ al-'Urḍī 334
Imsallam Sālim Abū Nīfa, reciter 11 n. 11, 198
Imṭēr (*also* Muṭēr) tribal confederation (Arabia) 2, 106, 202, 213
Irgayya (wife of Jidēa' Ibn Hadhdhāl) 8, 225–52, 400
'Ishēsh 'Anēz Sālim al-'Urḍī 121, 326
'Iṣmet Inönu, prime minister of Turkey 350 n. 14

Jabāliyya tribal confederation (Sinai) 6, 186
see also Tu'ēmī Mūsā ad-Dagūnī

Jabr al-'Aṭāwna 280
Jaddūa' Salmān 'Alī al-Huzayyil, chief of the Tiyāhā al-Huzayyil 269 n. 9
Jahālīn tribal confederation (Judaean Desert) 94, 359
Jamāl 'Abd al-Nāṣir, president of Egypt 349, 351
Jamāl Pasha, governor of Syria 349, 351
Jarīr, 7th-c. poet 407, 419
Jassās, pre-Islamic legendary hero 80 n. 18, 281
Jāzī Imsallam Ḥamd al-'Arādī, poet of the Tarābīn Ḥasāblah 9, 84–5, 306 n. 1, 402
 poem composed by 42
Jidēa' Ibn Hadhdhāl, semi-legendary chief of the 'Anēza 'Amārāt 8, 11, 13, 14, 27, 225–52, 400, 406, 415
Jubārāt tribal confederation (Negev) 5, 256, 279–80
Juhayna tribal confederation (Arabia) 2, 222
Jum'a Ḥammād Ibn Jahāma 40 n. 9
Jum'a 'Īd Dakhīlallāh al-Farārja, poet of the Tarābīn Ḥasāblah 10, 302, 307, 401, 405, 407
 poems composed by 84, 86, 305, 310, 338
Jum'a Sālim Ibn Kuraydim, chief of the Aḥaywāt Karādma 77–8

Khālid 'Abd al-'Azīz Ibn Sa'ūd, king of Saudi Arabia 309
al-Khansā, pre-Islamic poetess 413, 427
Khidāsh ibn Zuhayr, pre-Islamic poet 414
Khlēf al-Ḥantashī, chief of the Fed'ān Ḥanātīsh 226, 227, 241–9, 400
Khlēf Imgēbil al-Hirsh, reciter 138, 164
Klayb (Klēb) ibn Rabī'a, pre-Islamic legendary hero 80 n. 18, 281 n. 7

Lāfī Faraj Sulēmān, poet of the Rumēlāt Busūm 8, 346, 357
 poem composed by 110

Ma'āza tribal confederation (Egypt) 329, 331
Maḥmūd Muḥammad Abū Badr, reciter 50
Majālī tribe (Jordan) 83
Malālḥa tribal confederation (Sinai) 5, 113
Masā'īd tribal confederation:
 Sinai 5, 91–5, 113, 302
 Arabia 97–100, 212–14
 see also camels, law: judges
Muḥammad Abū 'Alī ash-Shawā 269 n. 9
Muḥammad Abū Ṭugēga, chief of the Ḥuwēṭāt at-Tihāma 97–100, 345
Muḥammad Luwēmī Ṣabāḥ Abū Nadā, reciter 8
Muḥammad al-Qāḍī 123
Muḥammad Ṣādiq, Egyptian minister of war 375
Muḥammad Salāma 'Aliyyān al-Guṣayyir 292, 293
Muḥammad aṣ-Ṣūfī 255, 256
Muḥammad Ṭalāl Ibn Rashīd, Amir of Hā'il 219–21
al-Mukhabbal, pre-Islamic poet 410
Mūsā Ḥasan 'Alī al-'Aṭāwna, reciter and chief of the Tiyāhā Nutūsh 10–11, 12, 50, 54, 82, 104, 141, 148, 212, 222, 225, 228, 229, 256, 260, 261, 263, 264, 268, 269, 274, 275, 279, 280 n. 3, 283
Mūsā Sfērān, chief of the Muzēna Darārma 180
Muṣliḥ Mabrūk Imbārak, reciter 75, 141
Muṣliḥ Sālim Sulēmān Ibn 'Āmr, poet and a chief of the Tiyāhā Ṣgērāt 8, 10–11, 12, 44, 50, 63, 75, 104, 138, 141 n. 1, 146, 153, 201, 215, 256, 264, 275, 283, 285, 344, 346, 348, 355, 426
 poem composed by 153
Muṣṭafā Zabn al-'Ugbī, poet of the Tiyāhā Banī 'Ugba 10, 256, 416
 poems composed by 256, 272
al-Muthaqqib, pre-Islamic poet 419
Muzēna tribal confederation (Sinai) 5, 69, 385
 see also Ḥamdān abū Salāma Abū Mas'ūd
Muzzarid, pre-Islamic poet 417

Nabhān al-Ḥanjūrī 285
Nabhān aṣ-Ṣāni' 284
Naṣṣār Abū 'Uwēlī 257
Nāyif ibn 'Abdallāh al-Hāshimī 116
Nimr al-'Adwān, poet and paramount chief of the 'Adwān 227
Nimr Wākid al-Wuḥaydī 272–3
Nūrī Hazzā' Ibn Sha'lān, chief of the 'Anēza Rawala 219–21

Qābūs, sultan of Oman 38
Quḍā'a, pre-Islamic tribal group 137

Rabīa' Abū Ḥarbī, reciter 115, 334
Rabīa' az-Zmēlī, poet of the 'Alēgāt Zmēliyyīn 8
 poem composed by 171
Rāḍī Swēlim 'Atayyig, reciter 11, n. 11, 104, 115, 168
Rākān ibn Falāḥ Ibn Hithlēn, chief of the Arabian 'Ajmān 401
Rashād Hāshim 295
Ra'ūf Pasha, an Ottoman governor 285
Rawala tribe (Syria) 2, 123, 219
Rumēlāt tribal confederation (Sinai) 110–14, 270, n. 11, 346, 357–8

Ṣabāḥ Ṣāliḥ al-Ghānim, poet of the 'Agēlī 9, 88, 307, 394, 401, 413
 poems composed by 57, 102, 174, 176, 368
Sa'd abū Sālim az-Zmēlī, poet of the 'Alēgāt Zmēliyyīn 183–4
Ṣagr Abū Sitta, warrior 255, 263
Sa'īd al-Gdērī, poet of the Tiyāhā Gdērāt 283–4

Sa'īdiyyīn tribal confederation (Negev, Jordan) 2, 132 n. 2
Salāma Abū Amīra al-Mas'ūdī, judge 91–5
Salāma Abū Isbēt, reciter 225
Salāma Abū Swērih, poet of the Suwārka 416
poem composed by 279
Salāma Ḥimēd 'Īd al-Ashgar, reciter 105, n. 2, 222, 225
Salāma Ibn Sa'īd 363
Salāma Imsallam Sulēmān Ibn Sa'īd, chief of the 'Azāzma Mas'ūdiyyīn 361, 362
Ṣāliḥ Imbārak 'Īd, reciter and chief of the Muzēna Shaẓāẓna 8, 130, 181, 222, 225
Sālim Abū Furthēn al-Wajj, poet of the Ẓullām Janābīb 10
poem composed by 384
Sālim Farāj, chief of the Rumēlāt 'Ajālīn 358
Sālim Muḥammad Salāma Ibn 'Āmr, reciter 291
Sālim Muḥammad Sālim al-'Ugbī, reciter 10, 212, 256, 272
Sālim Salīm al-'Aṭāwna, a chief of the Tiyāhā Nutūsh 280 n. 3
Sālim Sulēmān Ibn 'Āmr 11 n. 11
Sālim Swēlim al-Wajj, reciter 198
Salīm Abū Ḥasan al-Mas'ūdī, judge 91–5
Salīm al-'Aṭāwna 280 n. 3
Salīm 'Īd Sālim Ibn Jāzī, reciter 117, 300 n. 3
Salīm Maḥmūd Abū Yamānī 168
Salmān 'Alī 'Azzām al-Huzayyil, chief of the Tiyāhā Ḥukūk 82–3, 253, 269–70
Salmān 'Alī Salmān al-Huzayyil, chief of the Tiyāha Huzayyil 110–14, 427
al-Samaw'āl ibn 'Adīya, pre-Islamic poet 427
Sa'ūd 'Abd al-'Azīz Ibn Sa'ūd, king of Saudi Arabia 367
Ṣawālḥa tribal confederation (Sinai: 'Awārma, Garārsha, Awlād Sa'īd) 5, 9
Shammar tribal confederation (Arabia) 2, 50–2
Sharārāt tribal confederation (Arabia) 88, 209, 228, 240, 242–3, 257, 394, 395
Shawāma tribe (Arabia) 33
Shiblī al-Aṭrash, a Syrian Druze poet 8, 350
Silmī Dakhīlallāh al-Jibrī, poet of the Ḥuwēṭāt 9
Sulēmān Abū Sitta, warrior 9
Sulēmān 'Aliyyān Sulēmān al-Guṣayyir, paramount chief of the Aḥaywāt Shawāfīn 77–80
Sulēmān 'Aṭaywī Imsallam 276 n. 1
Sulēmān 'Aṭiyya 'Abū Ras' 94 n. 13
Sulēmān 'Awwād Ibn 'Adēsān, poet of the 'Azāzma Mas'ūdiyyīn 10, 361
poems composed by 191, 201, 364
Sulēmān ad-Dilaydim al-Ma'āzī 329
Sulēmān Ḥamd al-'Arādī, reciter 42, 141
Sulēmān Ibn 'Āmr 11 n. 11
Sulēmān Ibn Rifāda, chief of the Arabian Bilī 222–3, 355 n. 1
Sulēmān Ibn Ṭallāg, warrior 276, 277, 280, 283
Sulēmān 'Īd Dakhīlallāh, reciter 128, 138
Sulēmān 'Īd Sālim Ibn Jāzī, chief of the Tarābīn Ḥasāblah xii
Sulēmān Ma'yūf, paramount chief of the Rumēlāt 346, 357
Sulēmān Salīm Muḥaysin Ibn Sarīa', chief of the Tarābīn Sarāy'a 7–8, 35–6, 291, 295, 305, 307, 317, 337, 399, 402
Sulēmān Sālim Salīm al-'Aṭāwna 185, 269 n. 9, 270, n. 10, 280, n. 3
Sulēmān az-Zēt, poet of the Ṣawālḥa Garārsha 9
Suwārka tribal confederation (Sinai) 5, 279
Suwayd, pre-Islamic poet 412
Swēlim Abū 'Argūb, poet of the 'Azāzma Farāḥīn 10
poems composed by 264, 285
Swēlim Abū Haddāf, poet of the Tarābīn 10
poems composed by 261, 268
Swēlim Sālim 'Alī, reciter 385
Swēlim Sulēmān 'Īd Abū Biliyya xii
Swēlim Zāyid al-Gunbēzt 94 n. 13

Ṭalāl ibn 'Abdallāh al-Hashimī, crown prince of Jordan 116
Tarābīn tribal confederation (Sinai, Negev) 3–5, 38, 40 n. 8, 77–80, 82, 84, 86, 91–5, 113, 132 n. 2, 253–87, 288–340, 357, 377 n. 15
see also 'Anēz Sālim Swēlim al-'Urdī
Ṭarafa, pre-Islamic poet 411
Ṭawara group of confederations (Sinai) 5
Tiyāhā tribal confederation (Sinai, Negev) 5, 82, 91–5, 113, 253–87
see also Mūsā Ḥasan al-'Aṭāwna; Muṣliḥ Sālim Sulēmān Ibn 'Āmr
Ṭu'ēmī Mūsā ad-Dagūnī, poet of the Jabāliyya Awlād-Jundi 9, 338
poems composed by 46, 185

'Ugbī tribe, *see* Banī 'Ugba

Wuḥaydāt tribe (Negev) 212, 256, 272–3
ah-Wuḥaydī, chief of the Wuḥaydāt 212

Zaghāba tribe (Arabia), *see* Banī Hilāl
Zāri' al-Huzayyil, military leader of the Huzayyil 14, 255, 256
az-Zirbāwī 363
Zuhayr ibn Abī Sālma, pre-Islamic poet 409, 410
Ẓullām tribal confederation (Negev) 10, 204, 384